日本生物武器作战调查资料

〔日〕近藤昭二　王　选／主编

第五册

社会科学文献出版社
SOCIAL SCIENCES ACADEMIC PRESS (CHINA)

目　录

7.3 The Report of “Q”

资料出处：Technical Library, Fort Dugway Proving Grounds, Utah, US.

内容点评：本资料为日军细菌部队人员向美国提供的人体实验解剖报告“Q”报告，即“鼠疫”报告。“Q”报告是三篇报告中篇幅最大的，共收入 57 名鼠疫患者的人体解剖报告，经研究，为 1940 年 6 月日军 731 部队鼠疫跳蚤攻击农安等地引发当地鼠疫流行，农安感染死亡者 39 人，“新京”（长春）18 人，其中 7 人为当时居住在“新京”的日本人。

报告前言中所称“1943”年农安地区鼠疫流行的年份有误，应为 1940 年。

UNCLASSIFIED
The Report of „Q"
DUGWAY PROVING GROUND TECHNICAL LIBRARY
Reviewed By
Date
Regraded Unclassified, by authority of
by C.V. Hill, on 6 May 60
UNCLASSIFIED

CONTENT.

CONFIDENTIAL UNCLASSIFIED

56-FDTS-197

Foreword.

1943. (25th. Sept.--7th- Nov), I have investigated plague-epidemies in two regions (Shinkyo-City and Noan-Prefecture in Manchuria). Noan-Prefecture was contaminated frequently with repeated plague-epidemies every year, but on the contary, Shinkyo-City has not been contaminated with plague-epidemies.

1943. Jun. occured suddenly plague-epidemies in Noan-region by some means.

These epidemies spreaded to the neighbouring districts gradually, and at last invaded to Shinkyo-City by means of communications about the middle of Sept., and caused explosive epidemies among the towns peoples, who had not sufficient herd-immunities of plague disease, and all I8 patients had died several days after infection.

Dr. Takahashi and others had carried out epidemiological and bacteriological investigations. Those reports, printed in Japanese were presented to U. S. Army already Jul. I948.

I and others had investigated patho-anatomically all cases, who had died in these two regions between 29th. Sept. and 5th. Nov..

I will insert these results in following capitals.

56-FDTS-197

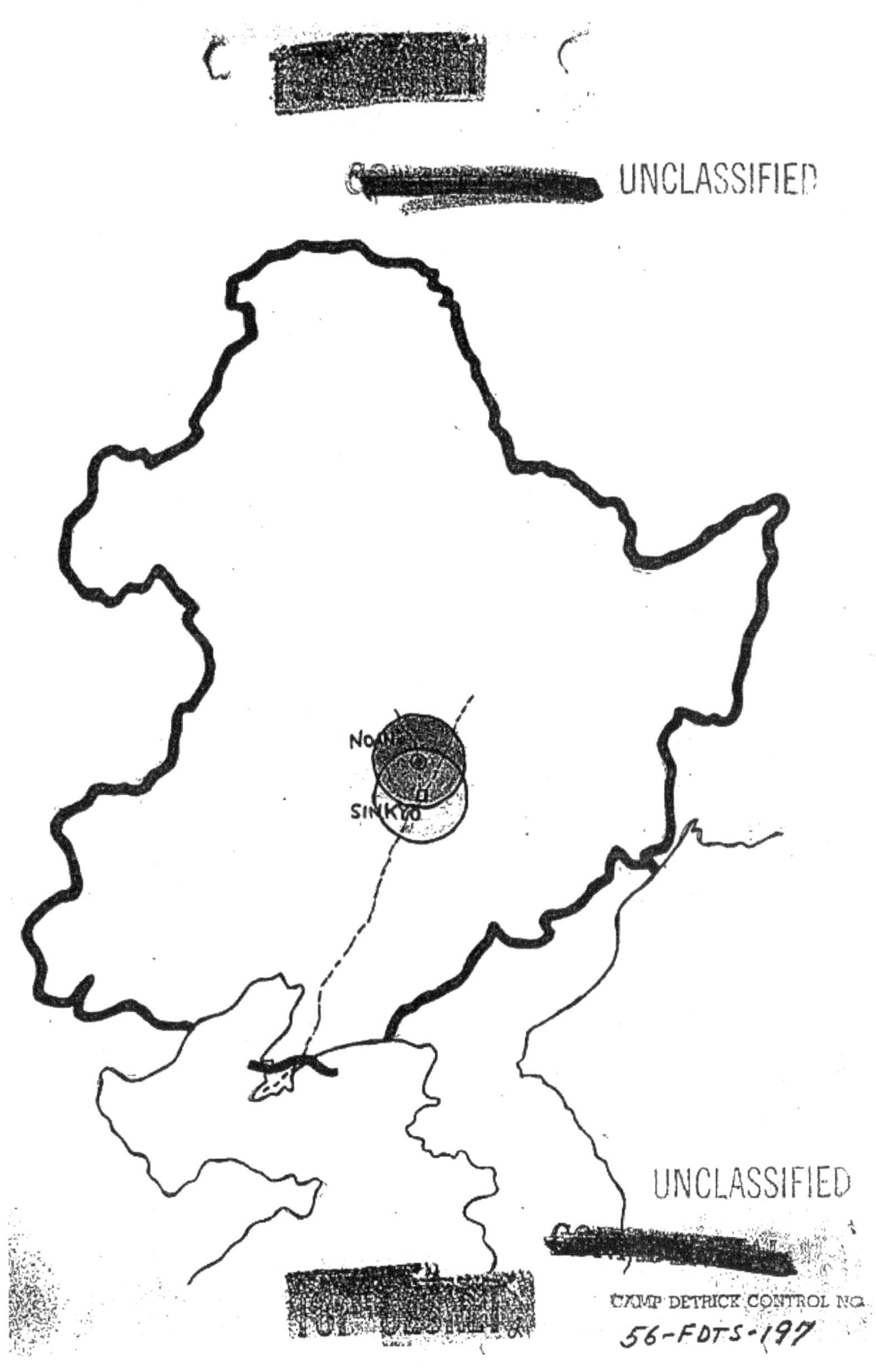
UNCLASSIFIED
NOAN
SINKYO
UNCLASSIFIED
CAMP DETRICK CONTROL NO.
56-FDTS-197

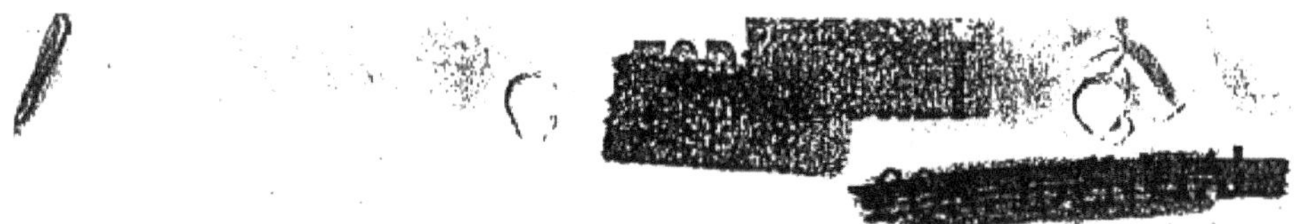

Brief out-line of all investigated cases. (1)

No.	Name.	years.	sex.	days of course.	Disease form.	Entrance port.
N-1.	K C	8	♀		C	
2.	M O	34	♀		C	
3.	C L	35	♀		G	r-axillaris
4.	E C	6	♂		C	r-axillaris
5.	E L	50	♂		G	l-inguinal
6.	H L	3	♀		C	
7.	S C	3	♂		S	
8.	K L	72	♀		S	r-submaxillaris
9.	F L	18	♀		S	
10.	C Z	51	♀		S	r-inguinal
11.	K K	40	♂		G	r-inguinal
12.	S K	12	♀		S	
14.	K O	35	♂		G	r-inguinal
15.	S L	30	♀		S	
16.	K T	8	♀		G	r-inguinal
17.	H C	28	♀		S	
18.	Z K	51	♂	3	G	r-inguinal
19.	S C	31	♂	2	G	r-inguinal
20.	K K	32	♀		G	l-axillaris
21.	K R	33	♂		G(C)	r-inguinal
23.	D C	63	♀	3	S	
24.	K C	3			G	r-inguinal
26.	S D	52			G	r-inguinal

3

UNCLASSIFIED

27.	N K	78	♂	5	L(S)	
29.	E M	31	♀	4	G	r-inguinal
30.	K C	6	♀		G	r-axillaris
31.	S C	8	♀		S	l-axillaris
32.	S R	62	♀		S	
33.	K L	22	♀		G(C)	r-inguinal
34.	H K	10	♂		G	r-inguinal
35.	K T	36	♂	5	G	l-axillaris
36.	K K	48	♀		G	r-supraclavicu- laris r-axillaris
38.	S S	12	♀	3	G	r-calf of leg
40.	G S	53	♀	3	G	r-inguinal
42.	F M	28	♂		G	r-inguinal
44.	U S	6	♂		G	l-axillaris
46.	K L	63	♂		C(G)	l-axillaris
47.	S S	30	♀		G	r-axillaris
49.	G S	60	♂		S	r-submaxillaris

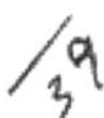

UNCLASSIFIED

UNCLASSIFIED

Brief out-line of all investigated cases. (2) CONFIDENTIAL

No.	Name.	years.	sex.	days of course.	Disease form .	Entrance port.
S--I.	K F	8	♀	8	G	l-inguinal
S- 2.	T T	8	♀	5	G-S	r-submaxillaris
S- 3.	S K	25	♂	5	G	r-inguinal
S- 4.	M M	23	♂	5	G	l-axillaris
S- 5.	M Y	21	♂	3	G	r-inguinal
S- 6.	F T	12	♀	6	G-S	r-axillaris
S- 8.	T L	10	♂	3	S	
S- 9.	G S	56	♂	6	L	
S- 10.	K K	45	♀	?	S	
S- 11.	H C	55	♂	18	G	r-inguinal
S- 12.	T F	27	♂	3	G	l-inguinal
S- 14.	T N	37	♂	4	C	Phlegmon
S- 15.	U S	18	♂	?	G	l-inguinal
S- 19.	Y T	58	♀	12	S	
S- 22.	M T	3	♀	21	G	l-submaxillaris
S- 26.	H K	31	♂	7	C	Phlegmon
S- 28.	F S	44	♂	2	G	r-inguinal
S- 38.	Y O	33	♂	7	S	

CONFIDENTIAL

UNCLASSIFIED

UNCLASSIFIED 

The classification of type of disease-form.

	S-district	N-district	Total cases
Glandular Plague	11 cases *	22 cases	33 cases
inguinal	7	13	20
axillaris	2	9	11
submaxillaris	2	0	2
Cutaneous Plague	2	5	7
Septicaemic Plague	4	12	16
Lung Plague (primary)	1 **	0	1

Note. *. 2 cases of them, in septicaemic course.

**. Infected during the nursing of patients.

UNCLASSIFIED

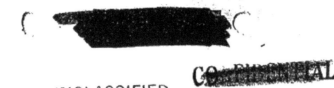

CONFIDENTIAL

UNCLASSIFIED

N. 1.

Years and sex.	48. ♀
Days of course.	
Entrance port.	Abdominal region. Cutaneous tissues of Septicemic.
~~Type~~ of disease.	

Heart.	Moderate degeneration and atrophy. Slight congestion and some bacterial masses in capillaries.
Aorta.	Considerable congestion of perivascular tissues.

Tonsil.	Submucous congestion and some bacterial masses in capillaries.
Pharynx.	Intense congestion.
Bronchus.	
Epiglottis.	Considerable congestion and edema.
Lung.	Bronchiolitis catarrhalis gravis. Multiple lobular pneumonia in gray hepatisation.
Pleura.	Plecuritis sero-fibrino-fibrosa partialis dextra. Remarkable congestion and some bacterial disseminat~~ie~~tion in pleural tissues.

Liver.	Hepatitis serosa II-III, with some leucocytes and ~~som~~ some bacterial masses in capillaries and. Multiple miliary necropis.

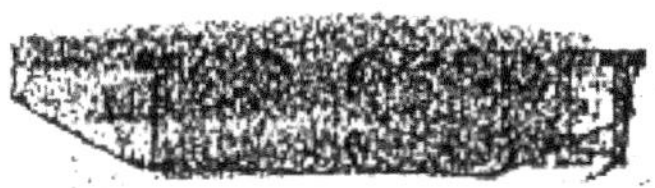

7

UNCLASSIFIED

Stomach.	Rather atrophic.
Small-Intestine.	Almost normal.
Large intestine.	Almost normal. Rather atrophic glandular cells.
Kidney.	Slight Glomerulo-nephrosis with slight polar edema.
	Nephrosis I (at some places III).

Spleen.	Angio-folliculitis exsudativa
	Fasciculitis exsudativa.

Pancreas.	Intense congestion and some parenchymatous degeneration in cortical tissues and some bacterial masses in capillaries.
Thyreoid.	Moderate follicular collapse.
Pituitary B.	--
Ovary.	--

Lymph-nodes	Dymphadenitis haemorrhagica totalis (r. Axillar).

Skin.	Phlegmons with some cutaneous ulcer (diameter 7.0 cm) at abdomianl region.

UNCLASSIFIED

8

2.

Years and sex.	34. ♀ UNCLASSIFIED CONFIDENTIAL
Days of course.	?
Entrance-port.	Cutaneous tissues.
Type-of disease.	Cutaneous plague and hemorrhagic diathesis.

Heart.	Some degeneration and atrophia. Considerable congestion and some hemorrhages. Slight dilatation of r. and l. ventricle.
Aorta.	Almost normal. Slight congestion of periadventtial tissues.

Tonsil.	Considerable congestion and edema. Some bacterial masses in capillaries.
Pharynx.	Considerable congestion (some bacterial masses in capillaries) and diffuse leucocytes dissemination.
Epiglotis.	No remarkable changes, macroscopically.
Bronchus.	Considerable congestion and some bacterial masses in capillaries.

Lung.	Diffuse Alveolitis. Edema pulmonum inflammatorium.

UNCLASSIFIED CONFIDENTIAL

TOP SECRET

Pleura.	Pleuritis fibrosa (r).

9

UNCLASSIFIED

Liver. Hepatitis serosa I-II, with multiple diffuse hemorrhage es.

Some histiocytes incapillaries.

Stomach. No remarkable changes.

Small-Intestiue. Consid. catarrh.

Large-Intestine. Colitis catarrhalis in medium degree.

Intense congestion, some round cell accumulation in submucous tissues.

Intense congestion and some hemorrhages in subserous tissues.

Kindney. Slight Glomerulo-nephrosis with slight polar changes.

Nephrosis I-

Spleen. Angio-Folliculitis haemorrhagico-exsudativa.

with slight proli-Ferative tendency, with some bionecrosis (plague Knot), with slight leukocytes emigration.

Spleno-Fasciculitis exsudativa, with severe leukocytes dissemination and myeloic metaplasia

----

Pancreas. Slight parenchymatous degeneration.

Supra-renal. Intense degeneration. Honeycombed degeneration of cortical cells.

Intense congestion in all layers of cortical tissues and some hemorrhages in Z. reticularis.

Some bacterial masses in coritical capillaries.

10 UNCLASSIFIED

Edematous swelling of v.centralis-walls.

Thyreoid. Slight hyperplasia of follicular epitheliums.

Some round cell accumulation.

Pituitary B. Slight congestion and slight dissiociation of cell arrangements. Some parenchymatous degeneration.

Uterus. No remarkable changes.

Lymph-node.

Axillaris (r). L. haemorrhagico-purulenta.

Inguinal (r). L. haemorrhagico-purulenta with plenty leucocytes and some bacterial masses in follicular tissues.

Mesenterial. Catarrh and slight congestion.

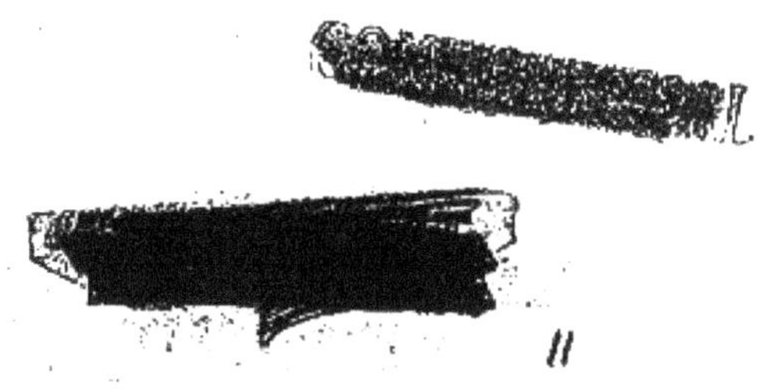

11

3.

Years and sex.	35 ♀
Days of course.	?
Entrance-port.	r-Axillaris.
Type of disease.	G.

Heart.	Parenchyatous degeneration and some subepicardial hemorrhages.
Aorta.	Almost normal.

Tonsil.	No remarkable changes.
Pharynx.	No remarkable changes.
Epiglotis.	Considerable congestion and edema. Some leucocytes and some bacterial disseminations.
Bronchus.	Intense congestion and multiple miliary necrosis with plenty leucocytes and bacterial accumulations. Some hemorrhages.

Lung.	Considerable diffuse "Alveolitis and Edema pulmonum inflammatorium with some pulmonal congestion. (right, superior and inferior, and left, inferior). Multiple lobular pneumoria in gray hepatisation right, median and left, superior). Bronchiolitis catarrhalis acuta in medium degree. Peribronchiolitis with some bacterial dissemination (right, median and left, inferior).

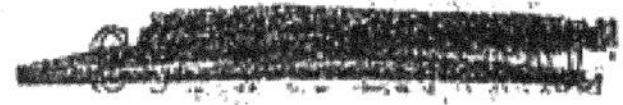

12

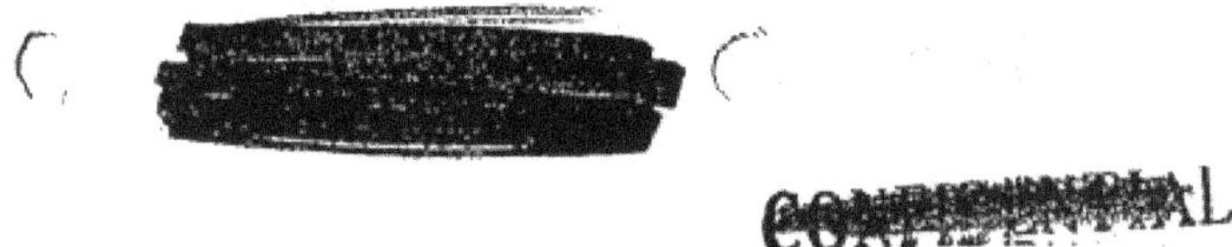

Pleura. Pleuritis fibrino-purulenta(right, superior).

Liver. Hepatitis serosa III, with some hemorrhages in central acinuses. Plenty leucocytes incapillaries.

Stomach. No remarkable changes.

Small-Intestine. Light catarrh and slith hyperplaia of germinative centres of lymphatic nodulus with some follicular congestion and some bacterial dissemination.

Large-Intestine. Colitis catarrhalis in medium degree.
considerable congestion and slight round cell infiltrate in submucous tissues.
Slight hyperplasia of lymphatic nodulus with some follicular congestion.

Kidney. Slight glomerulo-nephrosis with slight polar changes.
Nephrosis I with some round cell infiltration.
Nephritis subacuta at some places, with some hyalinous glomerular loops, some round cell infiltration, slight hyperplasia of connective tissues and some hyaline cylinders in ubular spaces.

Spleen. Angio-Folliculitis exsudativa
Spleno-Fasciculitis exsudativa
with slight leucocytes dissemination

Pancreas. Slight parenchymatous degeneration.

13

CONFIDENTIAL

Supra-renal.	Atrophia. Slight round cell infiltration in cortical tissues. some hemorrhages in cortical tissues.
Thyreoid.	No remarkable changes.
Pituitary B.	Missed.
Uterus.	Consid. congestion slight edema. Some hemorrhages.
Skin.	No remarkable changes, any where.

Lymphnodulus.

Axillaris (r).	L. haemorrhagica.
Mesenterial.	L. acuta with considerable congestion in follicular tissues.
Peribronchial.	L. acuta with considerable congestion and some bacterial dissemination.

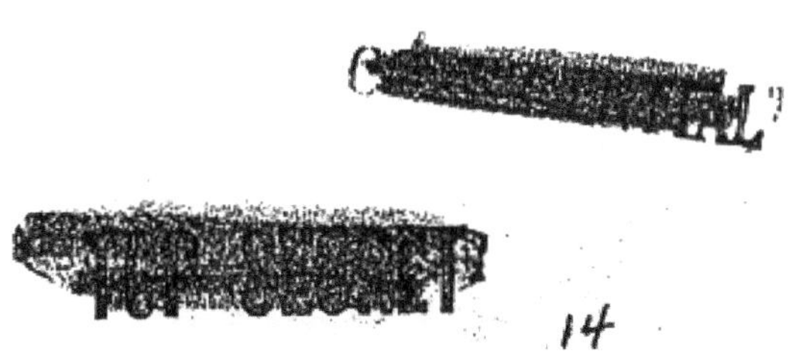

14

4.

Years and sex.	6. ♂
Days of course.	?
Entrance-port.	r-arm.
Type of disease.	Cutaneous plague.

Heart. Considerable congestion and some hemorrhages. Some perivasular granulom with so me round cell accumul. Slight dilatation of r. and l. vehtricle.

Aorta. No remarkable chan ges.

Tonsil.

Pharynx. Acute catarrh. Considerable congestion slight hyperplasia of lymphatic nodulus with so me increased reticulum cells.

Epiglotis. Intense congestion and intense edema. Some leucocytes-dissemination.

Bronchus. Slight congestion and no remarkable changes.

Lung. Slight diffuse Alveolitis and Edema pulmonum inflammatorium in so me lobular areas. Multiple miliary leucocytic pneumonia (right, median). Bronchiolitis catarrhalis in medium degree (left, inferion).

15

CONFIDENTIAL

Pleura. No ~~r~~remarkable change.

Liver. Hepatitis serosa II with multiple miliary necrosis.
Plenty leucocytes in capillaries.

Stomach. Slight catarrh.

Small-Intestine. Slight cataarh.

Large-Intestine. Slight congestion.

Liver. Hepatitis serosa II with multiple miliary necrosis.
Plenty leucocytes in capillaries.

Stomach. Slight catarrh.

Small-Intestne. Slight catarrh.

Large-Intestine. Slight congestion.

Kidney. Slight Glomerulo-nephrosis with some polar changes.
At some places Glmmerulo-nephrosis bionecroticans
(bionecrotic swelling of glomerular loops).
Nephrsois I (or III at some placees).

Spleen. Angio-Folliculitis exsudativa
Spleno-Fasciculitis exsudativa
with slight leucocytes dissemination and slight
myeloic-metaplaia

Pancreas. Missedm

Supra-renal. In outlysis.

Thyreoid. Intense follicular collapse.

CONFIDENTIAL

16

Pituitary B.   Missed.

Testicles.   Atrophia testis.

Skin.   Cutaneuus plague (phlegmons), r-arm.

Lymph-node.

Axillaris (r).   L. hemorrhagico-purulenta with serrere hemorrhages, plenty leucocytes and partial necrosis.

Peribronchial.   Slight catarrh with some leucocytes and cousid. Congestion in follicular tissues.

Deocoecal.   Slight catarrh and considerable congestion.

Mesenterial.   Slight catarrh and considerable congestion.

Retroperitoneal.   Intense congestion, necrotic ruins of follicular capillary walls and intense perivascular bemorrhages, exudation and leucocytes-dissemination.

Inguinal.   Catarrh and considerable congestion.

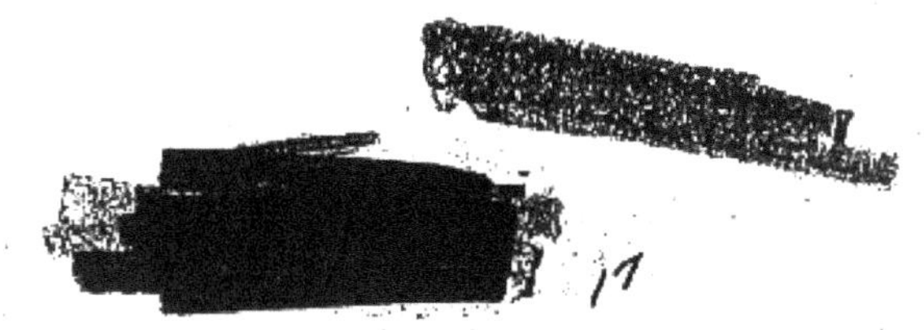

CONFIDENTIAL

5.

Years and sex.	50. ♂
Days of course.	?
Entrance-port.	l-Inguinalis.
Type of disease.	G.

Heart.	Some degeneration. Some hemorrhages in interstitium and in epicardial tissues. Dilatation of conus-portion of r. ventricle.
Aorta.	Almost normal.

Tonsil.	No remarkable changes.
Pharynx.	considerable congestion, intense hyperplasia of lymphatic nodulus with slight follicular congestion, hemorrhages, and some seollen reticumulum cells and a few bacterial masses.
Epiglotis.	slight congestion, macroscopically,
Bronchus.	intense congestion (some bacterial masses in capill) and multiple miliary necrois with plenty leucocytes and plenty bacterial accumulation.

Lung.	Multiple lobular (rather lebar) preumonia in gray hepatisation. Peribronchiolitis catarrhalis with bacterial dissemi-nation and edematous swelling.

CONFIDENTIAL

18

CONFIDENTIAL

	(Acinous, productive tuberculosis in the right, inferio -lobe).
Pleura.	Pleuritis fibrinofibrosa (right, inferio and median. left, superior).
Liver.	Hepatitis aerosa II.
Stomach.	Considerable congestion and multiple partial hemeo-rrhages in mucous tissues. Ingense degeneration of mucous epitheliums.
Small-Intestine.	consid. catarrh
Large-Intestine.	Slight catarrh and slight congestion. slight hyperpla-sia of lymphatic nodulus with slight follicular congest.

~~Kind~~

Kidney.	Glomerulo-nephrosis bionecroticans with slight polar changes. Nephrosis I (or III at some places). Some petechyn in pyelum.

Spleen.	Angio-Folliculitis haemorrhagico-exsudativa Spleno-Fasciculitis exsudativa

----

Pancreas.	Slight parenchymatous degeneration.
Supra-renal.	Atrophia, dissociation and some degeneration of cortical cal cells. Iultiple hemorrhages in Z. fasciculata and Z. reticul-aris.

CONFIDENTIAL

19

	Bionecrotic ruins of cortic[illegible]places.
Thyroid.	Intoxications-thyreoid with some degenerative changes of follicular epitheliums and some congestion.
Pituitary body.	missed.
Testicles.	Atrophia testis.

Brain.	Not investigated.
Skin.	No remarkable changes.
Lymph-node.	

Inguinal. L. Necraticans totalis.

Peribronchial. L. haemorrhagico-necraticans with some bacterial masses, some hemorrhages and partial necrosis.

Retroperitoneal. Intense congestion and some hemorrhages.

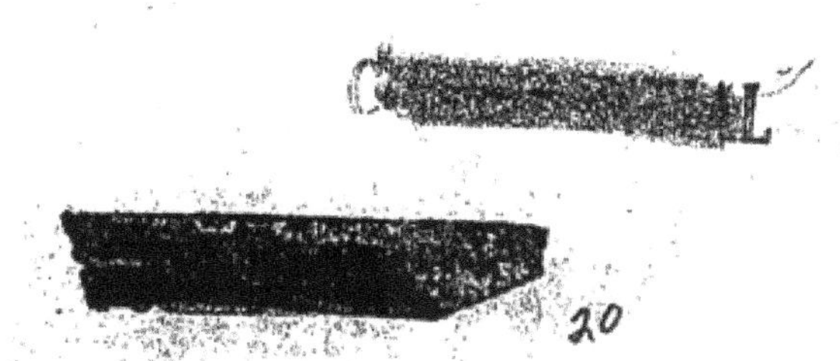

6.

CONFIDENTIAL

Years and sex.	3. ♀
Days of course.	?
Entrance-port.	Diffuse phlogmons (r. and l. thinghs).
Type of disease.	Cutaneous plague. Sepsis:

Heart.	Intense atrophia and some degeneration. Slight dilatation of r. ventricle.
Aorta.	Considerable congestion of periadventitial tissues.

Tonsil.	No remarkable changes.
Pharynx.	No remarkable changes.
Epiglotis.	No remarkable changes.
bronchus.	No remarkable changes.

Lung.	(right)	Multiple acino-lobular pneumonia with numerous leucocytes-dissemination or in gray hepatisation. Bronchislitis catarrhalis in severe degree.
	(left)	Slight diffuse Alveolitis. Stasis et edema pulmonum in medium dggree.

Plerua. No remarkable changes.

Liver. intense fatty degeneration all over the liver tissues with multiple miliary necrosis.

Stomach. Slight catarrh.

Small-Intestime. Almost normal.

Large-Intestine. Almost normal.

Kidney. Slight Glomerulo-nephrosis with slight polar changes. Nephrosis I (or III at some places) with some interstitial edema.

Spleen. missed.

Pancreas. Missed.

Supra-renal.

thyreid.

Pituitary Body.

Testicle.

Skin. No remarkable changes, any where.

Lymph-node.

Sepsis. Without any sighificant changes of lymph-nods.

Mesenterial. Sinus-catarrh

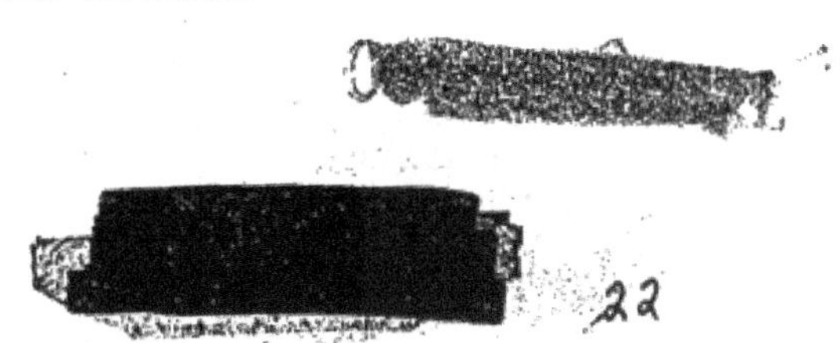

22

CONFIDENTIAL

7.

Years and sex.	3. ♂
Days of course.	?
Entrance-port.	Edematous swelling of reface.
	Congestion of rebreast.
Type of disease.	Sepsis.

Heart.	Consdierable degeneration and some bacterial masses in capillaries.
Aorts.	Thin aorta.

Tonsil	Tonsillitis acuta with sonsiderable congestion.
Pharynx.	Acute catarrh. Intesne congestion and some bacterial masses in capillaries.
	Hyperplasia of lymphatic nodulus with some miliary necrosis (bacterial accumulation) and some swollen reticulum cells.
Epiglotis.	Slight congestion, macroscopically.
Bronchus.	Intesne congestion and intense edema.
	Some perivascular bacterial accumulations.

Lungs	Diffuse Alveolitis.
	Edema pulmonum inflammatorium.
	in some lobular areas.

CONFIDENTIAL

Pleura.	Pleuritis exsudativa. (right and left)

23

Liver.	Hepatiits serosa
Stomach.	Slight catarrh.
	Remarkable hyperplasia of lymphatic nodulus with some bacterial accumulation and some edematous swelling.
	Intesne congestion and slight hemorrhages in mucous tissues.
	Intense congestion and intense edema and some round cell, infiltration in submucous tissues.
Small-Intest.	Slight Catarrh.
Large-Intest.	Slight catarrh.

Kidney.	Glemerulo-nephrosis bionecroticans with slight polar changes.
	Nephrosis I (or III at some places). , with miliary necrotic portion of some tubular epitheliums.
	(Tubulus-stueck controtus I.)

Spleen.	Angio-Folliculitis exsudativa
	Spleno-Fasciculitis exsudativa
	with severe leuco dissemination and slight myeloic-metaplasia

----

Pancreas.	Slight parenchymatous degeneration.
Supra-renal.	Missed.
Thyreoid.	Intense follicular collapse-
Pituitary B.	Missed.
Testivles.	Atrophia testis.

24

Skin. Edematous swelling with some congestion (r-face).

Some congestion (r-breast).

Lymph-node.

Inguinal. L. haemorrhagica. Intense congestion.

diffuse hemorrhages and some bacterial dissemination.

Mesenterial. L. haemorrhagica with diffuse hemorrhages and

diffuse bacterial dissemination.

Ceruicalis (1). Catarrh and considerable congestion.

25

CONFIDENTIAL

8.

Years and dex. 72. ♀

Days of course. ?

Entracne port. R-submaxilaris.

Type of disease. Sepsis.

Heart. Some, basophilic degneration.

Aorta. Considerable atherosclerosis.

Tonsil. Tonsillitis acuata purulenta.

Pharynx. Considezble congestion, macroscopically.

Epiglotis. Some congestion, macroscopically.

Bronchus. Intense congestion and intense edema. Some perivascular bacterial accumulations.

Lung. (right, inferior).

Multiple lobular pneumonia in gray hepatisation.

Bronchiolitis catarrhalis acuta gravis and

Peribronchiolitis with some bacterial accumulation.

(ritght superior and left)

No particular changes.

CONFIDENTIAL

Pleura. Pleuritis fibrino-fibrosa duplex totalis.

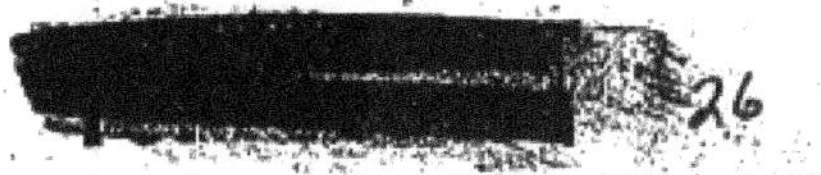

26

Liver.   Repatitis serosa I, with multiple submiliary necrosis.
Intense fatty degeneration.

Stomach.   No remarkable changes.

Small-Intestne. Slight catarrh.

Large. Intestine. Slight congestion.

Kidney.   Considerable Glomerulo-nephrois with considerable polar changes. Some hyalinous glomerular loops.
Nephrosis I, with some perivascular cirrhotic changes at some places considerable edem . slight hyperplasia of connective tissues and some degener ative changes of tubular epitheliums).

Spleen.   Angio-Folliculitis exsudativa
Spleno-Fasciculitis exsudativa
with severe leukocytes dissemination and slight myeloic metaplaia.

Panereas.   Slight parenchymatous degeneration.

Supra-renal.   Considerable cloudy swellihg of cortical cells-
Edmema of central veins-walls and some bacterial masses in capillaries.

Thyreoid.   In activated state, with intense congestion.
Struma colloides diffusa proliferativa.

Pituitary B.

Testicle.   Atrophia testis

27

CONFIDENTIAL

Skin.　　No remarkable congetion, any where.

slight congestion (r-Submaxillaris).

Lymph-node.

Submaxillaris. (r)	L. haemorrhagico-purulenta with diffuse bacterial dissemination.
Submaxillaris. (l)	L. acuta with intense congestion and edema.
Peribronclrial.	L. haemorrhagica with diffuse hemorrhages some bacterial disseminat, and bioncrotic smelling of fallicular tissues.
Retroperitonel.	Intense congestion, multiple hemorrhages and some bacterial dissemination.

CONFIDENTIAL

9.

Years and sex. 18. ♀

Days of course. ?

Entracne port. ?

Type of disease. Sepsis-

Heabt.

Aorta. Slight congestion of periadventitial tissues.

Tonsil. No remarkable hanges, macroscopically.

Pharynx. No remarkble changes, macroscàpically.

Epiglotis. No remarkable changes, macroscopically.

Bronchus. Slight congestion and no remarkable changes.

Lung. No remarkable changes.

Slight diffuse Alveolitis.

Pleura. No remarkable changes.

29

CONFIDENTIAL

Liver. Hepatitis serosa I, and slight or intense fatty degenerat.

Stomach. No remarkable changes.

Small-Intestine. Slight catarrh and considerable congestion, (some eleucocytes incapillaries).

Large-Ingestne. Considerable catarrh and considerble congestion. in sunmucous tissues.

Kidney. Slight Glomerulo-nephrosis with conciderable polar changes.
Nephrosis I.

Spleen. Angio-Folliculitis exsudativa
with slight proliferative tendency
Spleno-Fasciculitis exsudativa
with slight leucocytes dissemination

Pancreas. Slight degeneration of parenchymatous cells.

CONFIDENTIAL

Skin. Edematous swelling and congestion (1-breast. near mam a).

80

CONFIDENTIAL

Lymph-node.

Inguinal. (1)	L. haemorrhagico-purulenta totalis, with consid. congestion, some hemorrhages and diffuse bacterial dissemination.
Mesenterial.	L. catarrhalis.

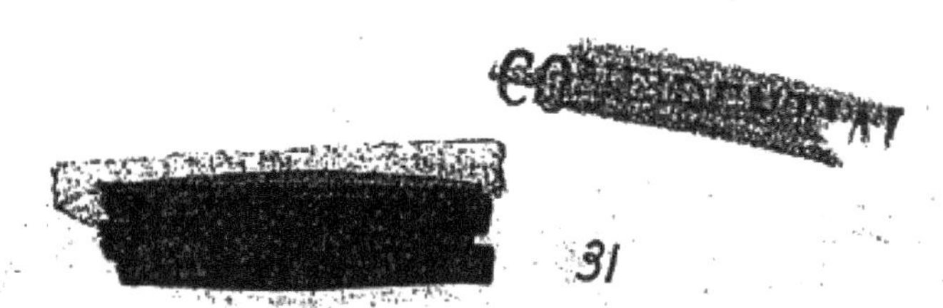

CONFIDENTIAL

IO.

YEArs and sex.	51. ♀
Days of course.	?
Entrance-port.	?
Type of disease.	Sepais.

Heart.	Some degeneration and some congestion (some bacterial masses in capillaries).
Aorta.	Almost normal with slight congestion some eucocytes in capillaries) of periadventitial tiuses.

Tonsil.	tonsillitis acuta, with intra and perifollicular congestion and some bacterieal masses in capillaries.
Pharynx.	Slight congestion, macroscopically.
Epiglotis.	Intesne congestion (some bacterial masses in capill) and intesne edema in submucous tissues.
Bronchus.	Intense congestion, multiple miliary necroisis with plenty bacterial accumulation.

Lung.	Multiple lobular (rather lobar) pneumonia in gray hepatisation (right, inferior). Some acinous leucocytic pneumonia and Edema et stasis pulmonum.

CONFIDENTIAL

Pleura.	Some congestion, some bacterial masses in capillaries and some hemorrhagic places. 32

CONFIDENTIAL

	Pleuritis fibrosa partialis dextra with Pleui-ties ~~and some~~ fibrosa obsoleta totalissinistra.
Liver.	Hepatitis serosa III, with multiple miliray necrosis (exsudative form). Plenty leucocytes in capillaries and intense fatty degeneration.
Stomach.	Slight catarrh.
Small-Intestine.	Slight catarrh and considerable congetion in submucous tissues.
Large-Intestine.	S.ight congestion.

Kidney.	Considerable Glomerulo.-nephrosis with some polar changes. Nephrosis I.

Spleen.	Angio-Folliculitis exsudativa with slight proliferative tendency Spleno-Fasciculitis exsudativa with severe leukocytes dissemination and slight myeloic-metaplasia

----

Pancreas.	Sligh parenchymatous degeneration.
Supra-renal.	Considerable degeneration of cortical cells. Inteane congestion in Z.reticuluris.
Thyreoid.	Slight congestion and atrophic folliculary epitheliums.
Pituitary Body.	Missed.
Tisticles.	Atrophia testis.

"CONFIDENTIAL"

33

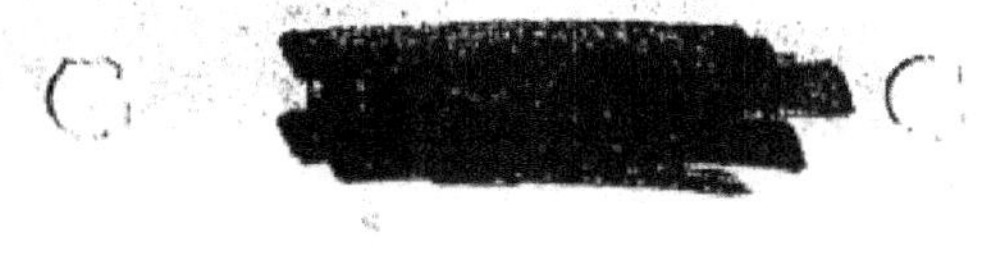

Skin. no remrkable congestion or swelling, any where.

Lymph-node.

Sulumaxillaris. (r)	L. haemorrhagica, with consid. congestion multiple hemorrhages and diffuse bacterial dissemination.
Submaxillaris.	L. haemorrhagica with the some changes.
Peribronchial.	L. hamorrhagico-purulenta with remarkable congestion and plenty of bact. dissemin.
Peribronchial.	L. haemorrbagico-purulenta totalis with the same changes.
Mesenterial.	Catarrh.

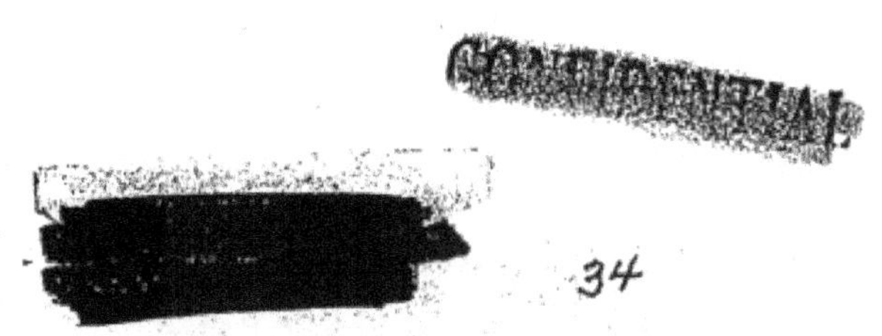

34

CONFIDENTIAL

II.

Years and sex.	40. ♂
Days of course.	?
Entrnace-port.	r-Inguinalis.
Type of disease.	G.

Heart.	Considerable degeneration. Slight dilatation of r. and l. ventricles.
Arota.	Almost normal. some fattyplaces.

Tonsil.	Considerable submucous congestion.
Pharynx.	Considerable congestion and some round cell accumulat.
Epiglotis.	Intense congestion and some hemorrhages. Some leucocytes in capillaries.
Bronchus.	Slight congestion and slight hemorrhages.

Lung.	Multiple lobular or acino-lobular pneumonia (right lung. Edema pulmonum inflammatorium (right, inferior and left superior). (left, inferior). Multiple lobular (rather lobar) pneumonia. Bronchiolitis catarrhalis acuta and Peribronchiolitis with some leucocytes-dissemination and fibrin-separation.
Pleura.	Pleuritis sero-fibrinosa. Pleuritis fibrino-haemorrhagica.

CONFIDENTIAL

35

Liver. Hepatitis serosa I-II, with multiple miliary necrosis in exudative form).

Stomach. considerable congestion and partia hemorrhages and slight edema in mucous tissues.

small-Intestine. Considerable catarrh considerable hyperplasia of lymphatic nodulus with some peri and inta follicular congestion.

Considerable congestion in submucoustissues.

Large-Intestine. No remarkable changes

Kidney. Slight glomerule-nephrosis with slight polar changes.

Nephrosis I.

Spleen. Angio-Folliculitis haemorrhagico-exsudativa.

Spleno-Fasciculitis exsudativa.

with slight leukocytes dissemination, and myeloic-metaplasia.

Pancresas. Slight parenchymatous deenertion.

Supra-renal. Considerale degeneration of cortical and medullary cells.

Slight round cell accumulation in medullary tissues.

Thyreoid. In inactivatated state. Atrophic follicular cells.

Pituitary Body. Missed.

Testicles. Atrophia testis.

36

CONFIDENTIAL

Skin. Edmatous swelling and some congestion (scrotum).

Lymph-node.

Inguinal. Intense pericapsulitis.

L. haemorrhagico-necroticuns totalis.

Retroperitoneal. L. haemorrhagico-sero-purulenta totalis.

Intense pericapsulitis.

Peribronchial. L. purulenta with some bacteeial dissemin

and plenty of leucocytes.

Mesenterial. Catarrh, intense congestion multiple hemorrhages and

leucocytes- dissemination.

CONFIDENTIAL

37

12.

Years and sex.	12. ♀
Day ~~eod~~ of course.	?
Entrance-port.	?
Type of disease.	Sepsis. hemorrhagic diathesis.

Heart.	Considerable degeneration and considerable congestion. (Some bacterial masses in capillaries). Slight dilatation of r-ventricle.
Aorata.	Almost normal.

Tonsil.	Tonsillitis acuta, with some, submucous congestion, submiliary ulcers. Submucous congestion and some bacterial masses in capillaries. Slight swelling of lymphatic nodulus with multipple milliary necrosis due to bacterial accumulation) and intense perifollicular congestion.
Pharynx.	Considerable congestion.
Epiglotis.	Considerable congestion andsome wandering cells disseminat.
Bronchus.	Intense congestion some bacterial masses in capillaries) and some wandering cells infiltration.

Lung.	Bronchiolitis catarrhalis acuta gravis.
	Diffuse Alveolitis with some bacterial dissemination at some places.
Pleura.	Pleuritis fibrine-fibrosa totalis dextra.
Oesophagus.	Some submucous hemorrhages.
Liver.	Repatitis serosa I-II with some leucocytes capillaries.
	Intense fatty degeneration.
	Multiple miliary necrosis.
	Some lymphocytes-accumulation in Glisson's capsule.
Stomach.	Slight congestion and sonsiderable edema in mucous tissues. Considerable congestion in submucous tissues.
Small-Intestine.	Enteririts catarrhalis with considerable hyperplasia of lymphatic nodulus.
	Considerable perivascular round cell accumulation in submucous tissues.
Large-Intestine.	Slight catarrh.
	Considerable congestion in submucous tissues.
	considerable hyperplasia of lymphatic nodulus with intense follicular congestion and sme miliary hemorrhages.
	Considerable congestion, some miliary hemorrhages in subserous tissues.

Kidney.	Glomerulo-nephrois bionecroticans with some polar changes.
	Nephrosis I (or III at some places) with some hyaline cy[illegible] spaces.

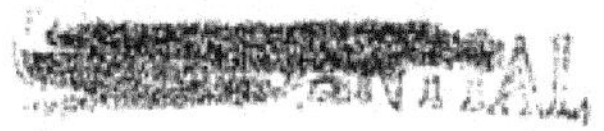

Spleen.	Angio-Folliculitis exsudativa, with slight leukocytes emigration, with polar edema and milliary necrosis (sperma like necrosis). Spleno Fasciculitis exsudativa, with severe leukocytes dissemination and slight myeloic metaplasia, with some milliary necrosis.

Pancreas.	Slight parenchymatous degeneration.
Supra-renal.	Epinephritis serosa II. considerable hemorrhagesin Z. fasciculata and Z. reticularis.

CONFIDENTIAL

	Come round cell accumulation in cortical tissues and some bacterial masses in cortical capillaries.	
Thyreoid.	Follicular collapse and some congestion.	
Pituitary Body.	missed.	
Testicles.	Atrophia testis.	

Skin.	No remarkable congestion or swelling, any where.	

Lymphnodulue.	Submaxillaris (1).	L. haemorrhagico-purulenta totalis.
	Perihronchial.	L. catarrhalis acuta with consider. consider. congestion, some bacterial dissemin and.remarhable increase of reticulum cells.
	Mesenterial.	L. catarrhalis acuta with considerable congest. and slight hemorrhages.
	Inguinal.	Catarrh with some bacterial masses in capillarico.

I4.

Years and sex.	35. ♂
Days of course.	?
Entrance part.	r-Inguinalis.
Type of disease.	G.

Heabt.	Consideable degeneration and considerable congestion (Come bacterial masses in capillaries). Hypertophia and dilatation of r. and l. ventricles.
Aorata.	Some fatty palces. Slight engestion of periadventitial tissues (with some bacterial masses in capillaries).

Tonsil.	No remarkable changes.
Pharynx.	Considerable congestion (some bacterial masses in capillaries). Diffuse hemorrhages in intermuscular tissues.
Epiglotis.	Considerable congestion and some wandering cells infiltration (some ducocytes, some lymphocyes and some histiocytes).
Bronchus.	Consid-rable congest on and some, hemorrhages.

Lung.	Multiple lobular (rather lobar) pneumonia in gray hepatisation (in all lobes). Bronchiolitis catarrhalis gravis. (especially in the left lung).

Pleura. Partial subpleural hemorrhages

Liver. Hepatitis serosa I-II, with somebacterial masses in capillaries and diffuse infense fatty degeneration. Some lymphocytes in Glisson' scapsule.

Stomach. Slight congestion in mucous tissues.

Small-Intestine. Almost normal.

Large-Intestine. Atrophic glandular cells.

Kidney. Considerable Glomerulo-nophrozis with slight polar changes.
Nephrosis I.
Some. petechyns in pyelum.

Spleen. Angio-Folliculitis haemarrhagico-exsudativa
with polar edema
Spleno-Fasciculitis exsudativa
with slight leukocytes dissemination and slight myeloic-metaplasia

----

Pancreas. Some parenchymatous degeneration.
Vacuolar degeneration of island-cells.
Catarrh of efferent ducts.

Supra-renal. Epinephritis II-III (partially).
Intense hemorrhages in Z.reticularis.

43

	Intense degeneration of central veins walls.
Thyreoid.	slight hyperplasia of follicular epitheliums and considerable congestion.
Pituitary B.	Missed.
Testicles.	Atrophia testis.

Skin.	No remarkable edematous swelling or congestion, any where.

Lymph-node.

Inguinal (r)	L. haemorrhagico-necraticans totalis.
Mesenterial	L. catarrhalis acuta with consid congestion, Some bact dissemin and luonecrotic surelling of reticulum fibres.
Peribroncbial	Catarrh and intense congestion in follicular tissues.
Peribronchial. (Bifulcatio)	L. haemorrhagica totalis.

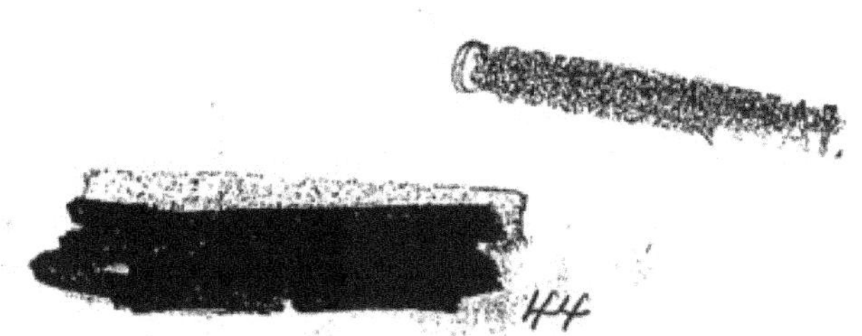

15.

Years and sex. 30. ♀

Days of course. ?

Entrance-part. ?

Type of disease. Sepsis.

Heart. Considerable degeneration. Considerable congestion and some, bacterial masses in capillaries.

Aorta. Almost normal. some fatty places.

Some hemorrhages in r-vorhof. auricles.

Tonsil. No remarkable changes.

Pharynx. No remarkable changes.

Epiglotis. No remarkable changes.

Bronchus. No remarkable changes.

Lung. (right, superior). Multiple acinous exudative pneumonia.

(right, inferior). Multiple lobular (rather lobar) pneumonia.

Bronchiolitis catarrhalis gravis.

Peribronchiolitis.

(left, superior). Diffuse Alveolitis and Edema pulmonum inflammatorium in some acino-lobular areas.

Bronchiolitis catarrhalis and Peribronchiolitis.

(left, in ferior) Lobar hemorrhagic pneumonia.

Bronchiolitis catarrhalis gravis and

Peribronchiolitis.

45

CONFIDENTIAL

Pleura.　　Pleuritis sero-fibrinosa sinistra.

Liver.　　Hepatitis serosa I, with some leucocytes in capillaries. Intense fatty degeneration. Some lymphocytes accumulation in Glisson's capsule.

Slight catarrh.

Small-Intestine. Slight catarrh and slight hyperplasia of lymphatic nodulus (slight follicular congestion).

Large-Intestine. Slight catarnh-

Kidney.　　Slight Glomerulo-nephrosis with slight polar changes. Nephrosis L.

Spleen.　　Angio-Folliculitis haemorrhagico-exsudativa
Spleno-Fasciculitis exsudativa
with severe leukocytes dissemination and slight myeloic-metaplasia.

Pancreass.　　No remarkable changes with slight parenchym tous degeneration.

Supra-renal. Liffuse intense hemorrhages in Z. reticularis and Z. fasciculata.

Intense degeneration or ruining processes of cortical cells.

Some bacterial masses in cortical capillaries.

Intense edematous swelling of central veins walls.

Thyreoid.　　Follicular collapse with considerable congestion.

CONFIDENTIAL

46

Pituitary Body. missed.

Testicles. Atrophia testis

Skin. No remarkable congestion or swelling, any where.

Lymph-node.

Peribronchial. L. acuta with multiple. localised hemo-rrhages and some bact dissemination.

Peribronchial. L. haemorrhagico-purulenta with some bacterial dissemination.

Inguinal (r) L. haemorrhagico-purulenta.

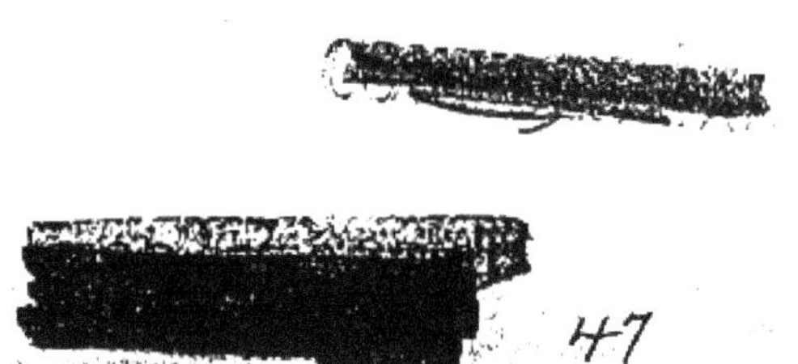

47

16.

Years and sex.	8. ♀
Days of course.	?
Entrance port.	r-Inguinalis.
Type of disease.	G.

Heart.	Considerable congestion (some leucocytes and some bacterial masses incapillaries) and some degeneration. Some petechia in epicardial tissues. Slight dilatation of l-ventricles.
Aorta.	Almost normal.

Tonsil.	Tonsilltis acuta with considerable edema, congestion and some swelling of follicular tissues,
Pharynx.	Acute catarrh, with intense congestion (some bacilus embolus). some hemorrhages and slight hyperplasia of lymphatic nodulus with some swollen reticulum cells.
Epiglotis.	Intense congestion and some round cell accumulation.
Bronchus.	Considerable congestion.

Lung.	Diffuse Alveolitis and Edema pulmonum inflammatorium. Bronchiolitis catarrhalis.

48

	Remarkable hemorrhage in some acino-lobular areas. (right, superior.)
Pleura.	Pleuritis fibrino-fibrosa (right, inferior, left, superior).
Liver.	Hepatitis serosa I-II, with some leucocytes in capillaries and some intense fatty degeneration. Diffuse hemorrhages and some lymphocytes in Glisson's capauel.
Stomach.	No remarkable changes.
Small-Intestine.	Considerable congestion in submucous tissues.
Large-Intestine.	Atriphic glandular cells.

Kidney.	Slight Glomerulo-nephrosis with considerable polar changes es. Nephrosis I.

Spleen.	Misses.

Pnaacnreas.	Slight parenchyatous degeneration.
Supra-renal.	Intesne atrophia. Considerable degeneration of cortical cells. considerable congestion in Z. reticularis and in Z. fasciculata (partially).
Thyreoid.	With some degeneration of follicular epitheliums

49

CONFIDENTIAL

and considerable congestion (Intoxication-thyreoid).

Struma coloides non-proliferativa.

Pituitary Body.

Testicles. Atrophia testis.

Skin. No remarkable swelling or congestion, any where.

Lymph-node.

Axillaris. L. haemorrhagica acuta. Intense congestion.

Inguinal. L. haemorrhagica acuta with intense congestion.

Mesenterial. L. haemorrhagica with intense congestion.

Mesenterial. L. acuta with intense congestion and edema.
(radix)

Peribronchial. L. acuta with consid. congestion.

CONFIDENTIAL

50

n 17.

Years and sex. 28. ♀

Days of course. ?

Entrance-port. ?

Type of disease. Sepsis.

Heart. Considerable degeneration. Intense congestion (with some bacterial masses in capilh ries).
Some petechias in epicardial tissues.
Slight dilatation of r-ventricle.

Aorta. Almost normal.

Tonsil Tonsillits acuta.

Pharynx.

Epiglotis. Considerable congestion, some leucocytes-dissemination and reactive hyperplasia of lymphaic nodulus with some swollen reticulum cells.

Bronchus. Intense congestion, bacterial masses and some leucocytes dissemination insubmucous tissues.
Multiple miliary necrosis and multiple miliary hemorrhagic places.

Lung. Lobar or multiple lobular pneumonia in gray hepatisation.
Bronchiolitis catarrhalis acuta gravis and Peribronchiolitis with bacterial dissemination

51

and edema. CONFIDENTIAL

	Diffuse Alveolitis with remarkable in flamma-tory edema. (left, inferior)
Pleura.	Pleuritis fibrino-purulenta duplex.

Liver.	Hepatitis serosa II-III, with diffuse hemorrhages in acinuses.
	Some diffuse hemorrhages in Glisson's capsule.
Stomach.	No remarkable changes.
Smmm-Intestine.	Slight catarrh and considerable congetion.
Large-Intestine.	Atrophic glandular cells and slgith congestion.

Kidney.	Slight Glomerulo-nephrosis with slight polar changes.
	Nephrosis I.

Spleen.	Angio-Folliculitis exsudativa with some bio-necrosis, with polar edema and polar milliary bio-necrosis.
	Spleno-Fasciculitis exsudativa. with some bio-necrosis and with slight leu-kocytes dissemination.

--------------------- CONFIDENTIAL

Pancreas.	Slight parenchymstous degenertion.
Supra-renal.	Diffce congestion in Z. reticularis and Z. fasciculata.

52

Multiple diffuse or localised hemorrhages in medullary tissues.

Some bacterial masses in cortical capillaries.

Interse degeneration of central veins walls. and some localised he morrhages.

Thyreoid. Activated state and considerable congestion. Struma coloides proliferative.

Pituitary B.

Testicles. Atrophia testis.

Skin. No remarkable congestion and swelling, any where.

Lymph-node.

Ingnunal (l). L. acuta with intense congestion.

Inguinal (r). L. acuta with intense congestion.

Mesenterial. L. acuta with intense congestion.

Lung-hilus. Intense pericapsulitis with haemorrhagico exudative changes and L - haemorrhagico (totalis) and necroticans (partial)

Peribronchial. Catarrh, intense congestion and slight hemorrhages.

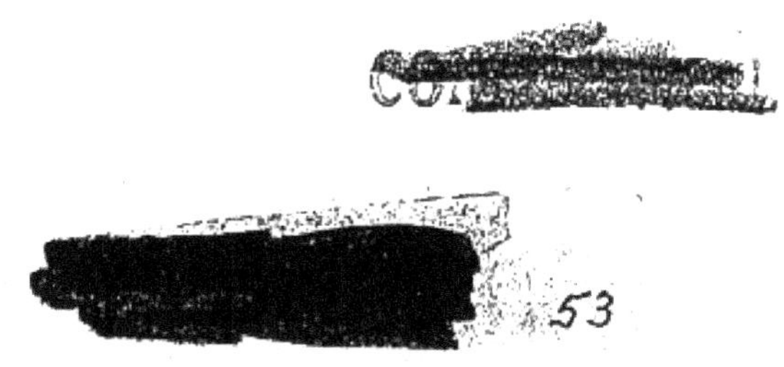

53

18

Years and sex. 51. ♂

Days of course. 3 days.

Entrance-port. r-Inguinalis.

Type of diseas. G.

Heart. Degeneration. Intense congestion ans sme hemorrhages. Slight dilation of r. and l ventricle.

Aorta. Almost normal. Slight congestion of periadnetitial tissues, And some diffues hemorrhages.

Tonsil. No remarkbale changes.

Pharynx. No remarkble changes.

Epiglottis No. remarkable changes.

Bronchus. No remarlable changes.

Lung(r) Slight emphyema.

(l) slight brochiolits.

No changes else.

Pleura. No remarkagle changes.

Liver. Hepatitis serosa I, with plenty of leucocytes in capillaries. Diffues slight hemorrhages in Glissons's capsule.

Stomach. Considerable congewtion in subnocous tissues.

Small-Intestine Consid. catarrh. Condiderable congestion and some licalised hemorrhages in G submoucous tissues.

Duodenao part. Slight congdstion and some leucoc tes and some bacterial masses in capillaries,

Large-Intestine Slight catarrh. Consideravle congestion and some miliary hemorrhages in subnucous tisses.

54

Kidney	Glomerulo-nephrosis bionecroticans with some polar changes. Nephrosis I.

CONFIDENTIAL

Spleen	Angio-folliculitis exsudativa with polar edema and polar some miliary bio-necrosis .
	Spleno-fasciculitis exsudativa with slight leucocytes dissemination, with some miliary bio-necrosis.

Pancreas.	Slight parenchymatousdegeneration.
Supra-renal.	Intense degeneration of cortical cells.
	Considerable congestion)some bacterial masses in capillaries) and some round cell accumulation in Z. reticularis and Z. fasciculata.
	Some bacterial masses in cortical capillaries.
Thyreoid.	Activated stasis with slight congestion.
Testicles.	Atrophia testis,

Skin.	Diffuse phlegnons right lower abdom.
	right high.

Lymph-node.

Inguinal(r)	L. haemorrhagico-necroticans totalis.
Retroperitoneal	L.haemorrhagico- necroticans totalis.
Retroperitoneal	Intense Pericapsulitis and intermuscular abscesses.

CONFIDENTIAL

55

19.

Years and sex.	31. ♂
Days of course.	2 days.
Entrance -port.	L-Inguinalis.
Tyoe of disease.	G.

--------------- -----------

Heart.	Cloudy ro cauolar degeneration. Slight dilation of r ventricle.
Aorta.	Almost normal.

Tosil.	No remarkablr changes.
Pharynx.	Very slight congestion and no remarkable changes.
Epiglottis.	No remarkable changes.
Bronchus.	Intense congestion, slight hemorrhagew and some leucocytes and some bacterila dissemination in submucous tissues.

Lung(right)	Multiple lobular (ratherlobar) pneumonia in gray hepatisation. Endobronchiolisits and Peribronchiolitis with congestion and bacterial accumulation.
(left)	Diffuse intense Alveolitis. Edema pulmonum inflammation with localised hemorrhagic places.
Pleura.	Pleuritis fibrino-purulenta with considerable congestion, considerable hemorrhages and plenty of bacterial masses in subpleural tissues.

56

CONFIDENTIAL

Liver.	Hepatitis serosa I-II.
Stomach.	Gastritis catarrhalis hypertrophicans.
Small-Intestine	Considerable congestion.
Large-Intestine.	Considerablc catahhh and consid. congstion in submucous tissues.

Kidney.	Slight Glomerulo-nephrosis with slight polar changes.
	Nephrosis I with slight round cell infiltration.

Spleen.	Angio-folliculits exsudativa.
	Spleno-fasiculitis exsudativa, with slight leucocytes dissemination.

Pamcrea.	No remarkable dhanges, slight pare chymatous degeneration.
Supra_remal.	Considerable degeneration of cortical tissues.
	Considerable congestion(in all layers) of cortical and medullary tissues. Some hemorrhages in cortical tissues.
	Intense degenerqtion of central veins walls.
Thyreoid.	Slight activated state, slight congestion.
Testicles.	Atrophia testis.

Skin.	No remarkable congestion and swelling, and where.

Lymph-node.

CONFIDENTIAL

Axillaris(r)	L. haemorrhagico-pulrlenta totalis.
Peribronchial.	L- haemorrhagico-purulenta with some bacterial dissemination, some [illegible] some leucocytes accumulation.

57

Inguinal(1)	L. haemorrhagica totalis.
Mesenterial	L. acuta with considerable congdstion and slight perivascular hemorrhages.

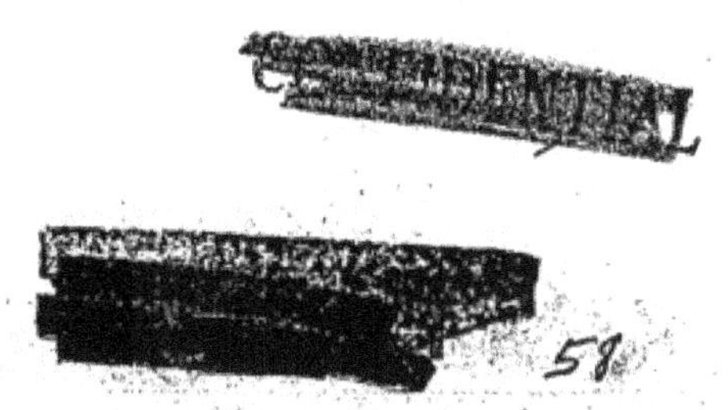

20. CONFIDENTIAL

Years and sex.	32. ♀
Days of course	?
Entrance-port.	1-Axillaris.
Type of disease.	G. Atonic diathesis.

Heart.	Degeneration, drop-heart.
Aorta.	Almost normal. Suspender-like aorta.

Tonsil.	Catahhh and submucous congestion. Slight hyperpl.sia of lymphatic nodulus with bionecrotic swelling of teticulum cells.
Pharynx.	Acute catarrh with intense congestion and slight perifollicular hemorrhages. Some leucocytes and bacterial dissemiantion in submucous tisses. Slight hyperpl.sia of lymphatic nodulus with swollen reticulum cells.
Epiglottis.	Considerable congestion, macroscopically.
Bronchus.	Considerable congestion.

Lung.

(right, superior).	Multiple lobular pneumonia in gray hepatisation. Bronchiolits catarrhalis and Peribronchiolitis with bacterial dissemiantion.

(right,inferior and left, superior and inferior)

Slight diffuse Alveolitis.

Edema pulumonum inflammatorium(in high degree, especially, in the left lung).

Pleura.	Pleutitis [illegible]talis dextra.

CONFIDENTIAL

59

CONFIDENTIAL

Liver.	Hepatitis serosa I,with multiplw miliary mecrosis. (in rather productive form.)
	Some histiocytes in capillaries.
Stomach.	No remarkable changes.
Small-Intestine.	No- remarkable changes.
Large-Intestine.	No remarkable changes.

Kidney.	Slight Glomerulo-nephrosis (glomeruli with some degenerqtive changes), with some polar chagnes.. Nephrosis 1, with conspicuous congestion and some hemorrhages in cortical tissues.
	Some hemorrhagic fnfarcts.

Spleen.	Angio-folliculitis haemorrhagico-exsudativa. With polar hemorrhages.
	Spleno-fasciculitis exsudativa with slight leukocytes dissemination.

Pancrea.	Slight parenchymatous degeneration.
Supra-renal.	Epinephritis II, with intense congestion and intensse hemorrhages in Z.reticulatis and Z. fasciculata.
	Some bacillus in cortical capillaries.
Thyreoid.	Follicular collapse.
Ovary.	-
Uterus.	Submucous congestion and some perivascular round cell infiltration.
Pituitary B.	-

CONFIDENTIAL

60

CONFIDENTIAL

Skin.	No remarkable congestion and swelling, any where.
Lymph-node.	
Axillaris(r).	Intense pericapsulitis with intense congestion and consid. hemorrhages.
	L.exsuativo-haemorrhagica with intense congestion and consideragle hemorrhages.
Inguinal(l)	Catarrh and considerable congestion.
Mesenterial	Catarrh and considerable congestion.

CONFIDENTIAL

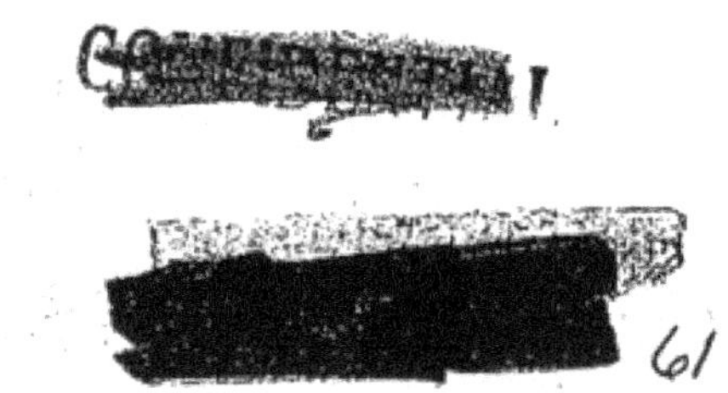

61

21.

Years and sex.	33 ♂
Days of course	?
Entrance-port	r-Inguinalis.
Type of disease.	G. Hemorrhagic diathesis.

Heart.	Considerable congestion(some bacterial masses in capillaries) and some hemorrhages in epicardial tissues. Hypertrophia and dilation of r. and l. ventricles.
Aorta.	Considerable congestion(some leucocytes in capillaries) and considerable congestion of periadventitial tissues.

Tonsil.	Tonsillitis acuta with intense congestion and odema. Some bacillus in epitheliums.
Pharynx.	Slight congestion, macroscopically.
Epiglottis.	Slight congestion, macroscopically.
Brochus.	Considerable congsetion.

Lung.	Slight diffuse Alveolitis. Brochiolitis catarrhalis levis. Edema pulmonum inflammatorium(especially in right, inferior and left, inferior lobes).
Pleura.	Considerable subpleural congestion and hemorrhages.

62

CONFIDENTIAL

Liver	Hepatitis serosa I-II. With some hemorrhages in in central zone of acinuses. Some leucocytes in capillaries.
Stomach.	Considerable congestion(some bacterial masses in capill.) and considerable edema in mucous tissues.
Small-Intestine	Rather atrophie glandular cells, some hemorrhages in submucous tissues.
Large-Intestine	Considerable congestion and slight hyperplasia of lymphnodulus with some follicular congestion. Some hemorrhages in subserous tissues.

Kidney.

Spleen. Angio-folliculitis haemorrhagico-exsudativa with polar ede,a amd polar miliary necrosis(sperma-like necrosis),wotj slight leucocytes emigration. Spleno-fasciculitis exsudativa. with severe leucocytes dissemiantion, with some miliary necrosis(sperma-like necrosis).

Bamcreas-	Slight degeneration. Vacuolar degeneration of islanf cells.
Supra-remal.	Epinephritis II-III(partially). Some. hemorrhages in Z. reticularis and Z. fasciculata.
Thyreoids.	In actifated state. Consideragle congestion.

CONFIDENTIAL

63

Pittuitary Body.

Testicles. Atrophia testis.

Skin. Diffuse phlegnons and diffse hemorrhages.
r-Inguinal parts and r-thigh.

Lymph-node.

Inguinal(r) L- haemorrhagico-èxsuativa totalis with some bact. dissemiantion.

Perobronchial L- haemorrhagico-exsudative with some bacterial masses.

Perobronchial L- acuta with considerable congestion and intense pericapsulitis with severe congestion and some bact. dissemination.

Retroperitoneal. L- haemorrhagico- totals with intense pericapsilitis with diffuse hemorrhages.

Cervicalis(r). Catarrh and congestion.

Axillaris(r). Catarrh and congestion.

64

CONFIDENTIAL

23.

Years and sex. 63. ♀

Days of course. 3 days.

Entrance-ports. ?

Type of disease. Sepsis.

Heart. Considerable congestion.(Some leucocytes ih capillaries). Slight fibrosis aroud blodd-vessels.

Aorta. Considerable congestion of periafventitial tissues.

Tonsil. Tosillitisacuta.

Considerable congestion and ede,a. Some leucocytes-diss-emination.

Pharynx. Considerable congestion and some hemorrhages.

Epiglottis. Intense congestion.

Bronchus. Considerable congewtion.

Lung Considerable congestion andedema of alveolar walls.

Very slight catarrhalic bronchiolitis.

No remarkable inflammatory changes.

Pleura. Pleuritis fibrino-purulenta dextra.

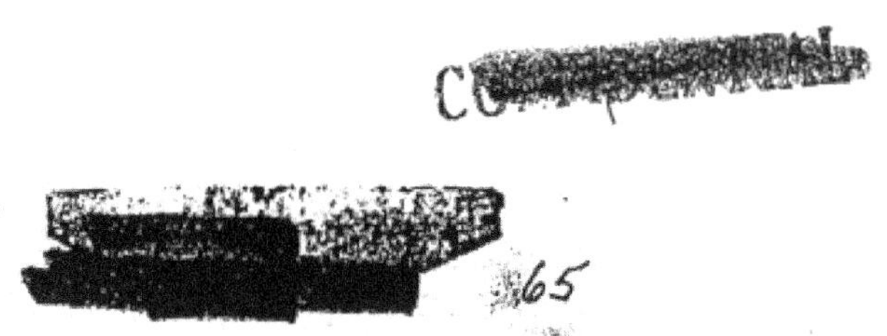

CONFIDENTIAL

Liver. Hepatitis serosa I,with some multiple miliary necrosis. Some leucocytes and histiocytes in capillaries.

Stomach. Slight eatahhr.

Small-Intestine Almost normal.

Large-Intestine Condiderable catarrh.

Kideny. Slight Glomerulo-nephrosis with slight polar changes. Nephrosis. I.

Spleen. Perisplenitis fibrosa.
Angio-folliculitis haemorrhagico-exsudativa.
With polar edema and polar miliary bionecrosis.
Spleno-fascuculitis exsudativa. with severe leucocytes dissemination and a slight myeloic metaplasia, with some miliary bionecrosis.

Pancreas. Considerable degeneration of parenchymatous cells.

Supra-renal. Many degenreated cerical cells.
Consideravle congewtion and some hemorrhages in Z. reticularis and Z. fasciculata.

Thyreoids. Slight congestion and some round cell infiltration.
Some degenerctive dhanges of follicular epitheliums.
Struma collides nodosa macrofollicularis.

Pituitary Body. Slight congestion(some leucocutes in capillaries). and some cloudy swelling of parenchymatous cells.

Ovary. -

CONFIDENTIAL

-66

skin.　　No remarkable congestion and swelling, any whrer.

Lymph-node.

Peribronchial L. catarrahlis levis.

Mesenterial　No remarkable changes.

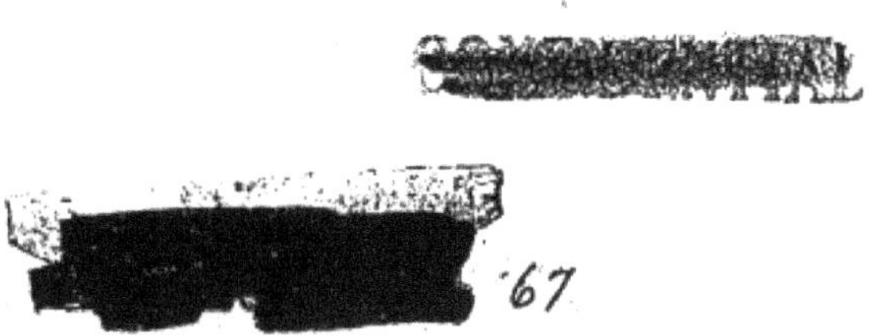

67

24.

Years and sex. 3 ↑

Days of course. ?

Entrance_port. r-Inguinalis.

Type of disease. G.

Heart. Considerabel degeneration2and some hemorrhagies.
Some bacterial masses in capillaries.
Slight dilatation of r-vnetricles.

Aorta. Considerable atherosclerosis.
Considerable congestion of periadventitial tissues.

Tonsil. Slight congestion,macroscopically.

Pharynx. Catrrh and consideragle congestion and catarrhl

Epiglottis. No remarkable changes.

Brochus. Intense congestion add roudn cell infiltration.

Lung. Diffuse Alveolitis.
Edema pulumonum inflammatorium with hemorrhagic reaction.

Pleura . No remarkable changes.

Liver. Hepatitis serosa I, with intense fatty degeneration and some leucocutes in capiilaries.

Stomach, No remarkable changes, macroscopically.

Smaohl.Intestine No remarkabel changes.

Large-Intestine No remarabke chagges.

Kideny. Glomerulo-nephrosis bionecroticans and slight polar

changes. Nephrosis I.

Spleen. Angio.folliculitis haemorrhagico-exsudativa,with polar edema.

Spleno-fasculitid exsuativa, with leucocytes dissemination and slight myeloic metaplasia.

Pancrea. Slight parenchmatous degenration and no remarkablre changes else.

Supra-renal. Considerable edema and some degeneration of cortical cells.

Thyreoid. Follicular collapse.

Pituitary. B. Misse.

Testicles. Atrophia testis.

Skin. No remarkable congestion and swelling, any whree.

Lymph-node.

Inguinal(r) L.purulenta grqvis totalis.

Mesenterial L. acuta withconsiderqvle congestion.

Peribroncial L. acuta with considerable congewtion.

69

26.

Years and sex.	52 ♀
Days of course	4 days.
Entrance-port.	r-Ingiunalis.
Type pf diseaze.	G.

Heart. Some bacterial masses in capillaries and no remarkable changes. Slight dilatation of r. and l ventricles.

Aorta. No remarkable changes.

Tonsil. No remarkable changes.

Pharynx. No remarkagle changes.

Epiglotis. Slightcongestion.

Brochuns. I ntense congstion.

Lung Slight diffuse Alve litis with slight bacyerial emigrqtion in alveolar walls and with slight congestion of alveolar walls.

Pleura. Pleuritis fibrino-fibrosa dextra.

Liver Hepatitis serosa I. with some net-necrosis like chamges. Some leucocytes in capillaries.

Stomach. Gastriris catarrhalis hypertrophicans.

Small-Intestine Almost normal.

Large-Ingestine Catarrh.

Kidney. Considerable Glomerulo-nephrosis wihh some polar chantes, Nephrosis I.

Spleen.	Angio-folliculitis haemorrhagico-exduativa with slight proliferqtive tendency)reticulum cell). With polar hemorrhate, Spleno-fascuculitis exsudativa with slight leucocytes dissemiantion.

Pancrea.	Slight parenchymatous degenerqtion.
Supre-renalis I	Intense degener-tion of cortical cells. Considerable congesrion in Z. reticularis and Z. fascuculata. Some localised hemorrhages in Z, reticularis.And mulitple round cell accumulation in Z. reticularis. Some bacter al masses in capillaries.
Thyreoid.	Slight degnerqtion of follicular epitheliums. Slight leucocytes-emigrqtion. Struma colloides macrofollicularis diffusa,withsome lymphatic nodulus.
Pititqry B.	Considerable congestion and some bacterila masses in capillaries and subendotheliar edema. Cloudy vacuolar degeneration of rqther atrophie glandualr cells.

71

Skin.   No remarkable changes. (Swelling and congestion).

Lymph-node.

Inguinal(1).   L. haemorrhaiga totalis.

Inguinal(1)   L. haemorrhaigca totalis.

Retroperitoneal   L. haemorrhaigoc.necrotican totalis and intense pericapsulitis with diffues hemorrhages.

Peribronchial.   L. haemorrhaigoco-purulenta et necroticans partialos , with plentu of bacterial dissemination.

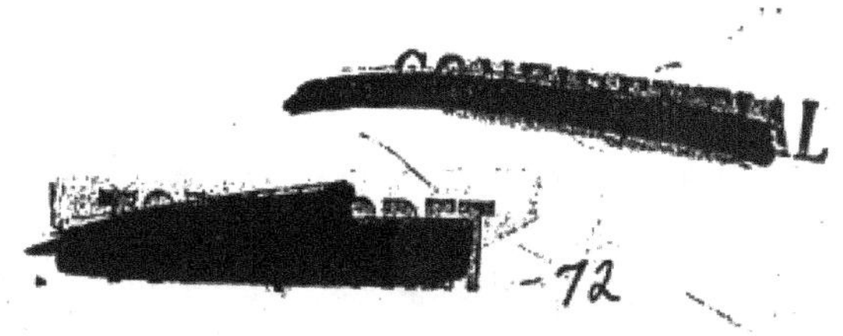

27.

Years and sex. 78. ♂

Days of course. 5 days.

Entranceport. ?

Type of disease, Sepsis(main pathological changes exsist in lung).

Heart. Some basophilic degrneration.

Aorta. Slight atherosclerosis.

Tonsil- No remarkable changes.

Pharynx. Slight congestion and some round cell infiltration.

Epiglottis. Slight congestion and some round cell finriltration.

Bronchus. Considerable congestion.

Lung. Lobular pneumonia in obstructive stage(right, superior). Bronchiolitis catarrhalis in medium degree(right , superior).

Pleura. No remarkable changes.

Liver. Annala cei rrhosis with mulitiple miliary necrosis in rather productive form.

Stomacj. Slight edema in mucous tissues.

Small-Intestine. Considerable congestion in submocous tissues.

Large_Intesine. Considerable congestion in submucous tissues.

Kidney. Considerable Glomerulo-nephrosis with slight polar changes. Nephrosis I. (or iii at same places), with some round cell infiltraiton in cortical tissues some edema in medullary tissues.

73

Spleen. Angio-folliculitis haemorrhagico.exsudativa with slight proliferqtive tendency.
Spleno-fasciculitis exsudativa with slight proliferative tendency(sinus endothel).

Pamcreas- No remarkable changes.

Supra_renal. Epinephritis II-III(partically).
Multiple honeycommbed degeneration with intense hemorrhages in Z. reticularis. Some round cell infiltration in Z. fasciculata.

Thyreoid. Missed.

Pituitaur B. Missed.

Testicles. Atrophia testis.

Skin No remarkable congestion or swelling, any where.

Lymph-nods.

Peribronchial L. haemorrhagica totalis.

Mesenter al L. acuta with considerable congestion.

74

TOP SECRET

29.

Years and sex.	31. ♀
Days of course.	4 days.
Entrance-part.	r-Inguinalis.
Type of disease.	G.

Heart.	Considerable congestion and some bacterial masses in capillaries. Intense degeneratioj, esp. at perivascular portions.
Aorta.	Almost normal.

Tonsil.	No remarkable changes.
Pharynx.	No remarkable changese.
Epiglottis.	No remarkable changes.
Bronchus.	Considerqble congestion and no remarkable changes.

Lung.	Mulitp.e lobular pneumonia in obsyructive stage. Bronchiolitis catarrhalis in medium degree(right, inferior and left, inferior).
Pleura.	Pleuritis fibrino-purulenta partialis dextra. (right, superior).
Liver.	Hepatitis serosa II-I.,with muliple miliary necrosis. Intense fatty degeneration and some leucocytes in capillaries.
Stomach.	Slight congestion in mucous tissues.
Small-Intestine	Consideragle datarrh and slight congsetion(some bacterial masses in capillaries). Slight hyperplssia of lymphatic nodulus with some swollen reticulum cells.
Large-Intestine.	Almost normal.

751

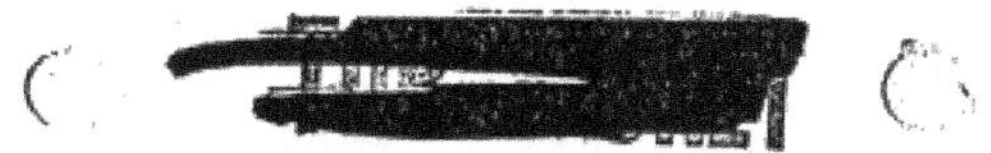

Kid ney. Considerable Glomerulo-nephrosis with some polar changes. Nephrosis. I.

Spleen. Angio-folliculitis haemorrhagico-exsudativa with polar plasma cell reaction.

Spleno-fasciculitis exsuadativa with slight leuco-cytes dissemiantion with slight proliferative tendency.

Pancreas. Considerable degeneration and consid. congestion (some bacterial masses im capillaries).

Supra-renal. Considerqvle degenration of cortical cells. Considerable congdtion and some diffuse hemo-rrhages in Z. reticu laris. Some bacterial masses in cortical capillaries. Some vacuolar degenerqtion of cortical c3lls.

Thyreoid. Intoxication-thyreoid with some degenerated folli-culär epithelium and some congdstion.

Pituitary B. Considerable congestion and some endotheliar edema. Cloudy swelling of parwnchymatous cells.

Ovary.

Skin. No remarkable congestion or swelling, anu whree.

Lymp-node.

Inguinal(r). Lymphonodulus post extripatio.

Cervicalsi Catarrh and congsetion.
Peribronchial Catarrh and slight congestion.

76

30.

Years and sex.	6. ♀
Days of course.	?
Entrance-port.	r-Axillaris.
Type of disease.	G.

Heart. Considerable degeneration and slight congesion.

Aorta. Almost normal.

Tosil.

Pharynx. Catarrh and intense submucouscongestion and slight hemorrhages.

Swelling of lymphaticnoduluswith some swellne reticulum. Cells and a few bacterial masses in germiative centres.

Bronchus. Considergble congestion.

Lung. Slight diffuse Alveolitis with lsight inflammatory edema in some acinous areas.

Pleura. Pleuritis fibros(r. inferior and superio, l, suerior).

Liver. Hepatitis serosa I.

Stomach. Slight congestion in mucoustissues.

Small-Intest. Enteritiw floocularis.

Large-Intest. Almost normal.

Kidney. Glomerulo-nephrosis bionecroticans with slight polar changes. Nephrosis. (or III at some places).

77

Spleen. Angio-folliculits haemorrhagico-exsudativa. Spleno-fasciculitis exsudativa with slight proliferative tendency, with slight leucocytes dissemination and slight myeloic metaplasia.

Pancreas. No remarkable changes, slight parenchmatous degeneration.

Supra-renal. Epinephritis II. Intense degeneration of nervous cells om ,edullary tissues.

Thyreoid. In inactivated stage. Atrophic follicular cells.

Pititaru B. Misse.

Ovary.

Skin. Intense congestion and edema(r,breast, large).

Lymph-node

Axillaris(r) L.haemorrhagico-necroticans totalis.

Axillaris(l) L. acuta with intense congestion and swelling.

Inguinal(r). L. acuts with intense congestion.

Inguinal(r) L. acuta qith intense congestion.

Mesenterial. Intense pericapsulitis with some hemorrhages.
L. acuta with intense congestion.

Peribronchial. L. haemorrhagioc-necroticans.

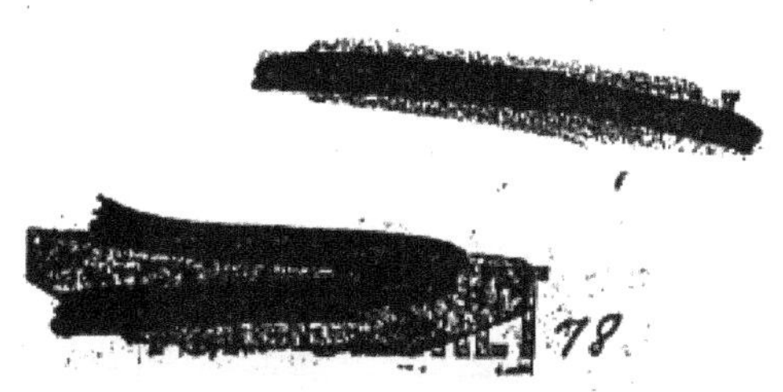

(■■■■■■T (

31.

Years and sex. 8. ♀

Days of course. ?

Entrance-port. 1-Axillaris.

Type of disease. Sepsis. Main pathological changes in lung.

Heart. Considerable degeneration sna some hemorrhages.

Aorta. Almost normal.

Tonsil. Tonsillits acuta, with intense congestion and slight hemorrhages, a few leucocutes, a few lymphocutes and a few histiocytes in submucoustissues.
A few bacterial dissemination in submucous tisses.

Pharynx. Intense congestion, slighthemorrhages and some round cell dissemination in submucous tissues.
Some bacterial masses in capillaties.

Epigolttis. Intense congestion, slight hemorrhages nad some round cell dissemination in submucous tissues.
Intense edema.

Bronchus. Considerable congestion adn somebacterial masses in capillaries.

Lung. Multiple lobular pneumonia in gray hepatisation.
Small vavern-formation in ritht inferior and left inferior lobes.
Bronchiolitis cataffhalis gravis.
Peribronchiolitis bionecroticans.(rightm iflferior).

■■■■■■■■ 79

Edema pulmonum inflammatorium(right, superior).

Pleura. Pleuritis fibrino-purulenta.(left,superior and inferior. right, inferior.).

Liver.

Stomach. Almost normal.

Small-Intestine. Slight hyperplasia of lymphatic nodulus.

Large-Intestine. Almost normal, atrophic glandular cells.

Kidney. Considerable Glomerulo-nephrosis with some polar changes.

Nephrosis I.

Some petechias in pyelum.

Spleen. Angiofolliculitis haemorrhagico-exsudativa with slight proliferative tendency.

Spleno-fascuculitis exsudativa with leucocytes dissmenation,with slight proliferative tendency.

Pancreas. No remarkable changes and slighr parnechymatous degeneration.

Supra-renal. Many degenerated cortical cells.

Intense congestion and some hemorrhages in subcapsular, cortical and medullary tissues.

Thyreoids. In degenerated state, with some degenerative changes of follicular epitheliums and some congestion.

Intense atrophic follicular cells.

80

Pituitary B.   Slight congestion and some parenchymatous degeneration.

Ovary.   No remarkable changes.

Skin.   No remarkable congestion and swelling, any where.

Lymph.node.

Axillaris(l). L. haemorrhagico-necroticanstotalis.

Mesenterial. Some congestion.

Inguinal   Considerable congestion in follicult tissues.

Peribronchial L.haemorrhagico-necroticans partialis.

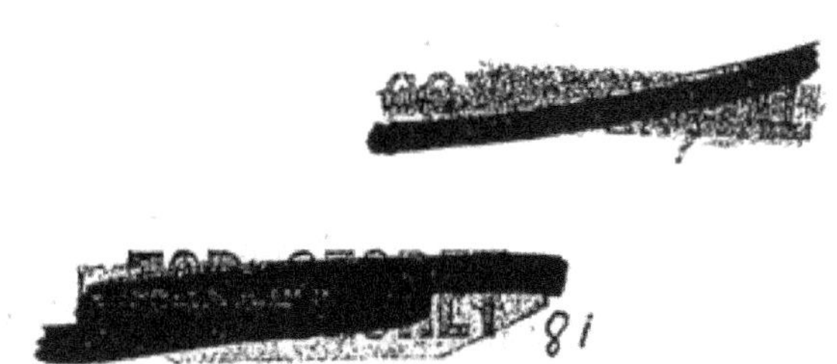

81

32.

Years and sex. 62. ♀

Daysof course 6 days.

Entranceport. ?

Type of disease. Sepsis.

Hearts. Intense degeneration. Intense congestion and some bacterial masses in capillaires.

Slight dilatation of r. ventricle.

Aorta. Intense atherosclelosis.

Tonsil. Tosillitis hemorrhagica acuta.

Pharynx. No remarkable changes.

Epiglottis. No remarkable changes.

Bronchus. No remarkable changes.

Lung. Lobar pneumonia in gray hepatisation(right, median and inferior).

Bronchiolitiw catarrhalis.

Edema et stasis pulmonum.

Pleura. Pleuritis fibrino-fibrosa(right,inferior).

Liver. Hepatitis serosa I, with intense fatty degeneration and some leucocytes in capillaries.

Stomach. Considerable dongestion and some leucocytes in capillaries. in submucous tissues.

Small-Intensine. Consideravle congestion and some leucocytes and Some bacterial masses in capillaries.

Larfe-Intestine. Considerable catarrh and considerable congestion.

82

((

Kidney. Glomerulo-nephrosis bionecroticans with some polar changes.
Nephrosis I. (or IIIat some places).

Spleen Missed.

Pancreas No remarkable changes and slight parenchymatous degeneration.

Supra-renal. Epinephriris serosa II(or III at some places).
Some hemorrhages in Z. reticlaris and some bacterial masses in cortical capillarics.

Thyreoid. In inactivated state. Struma colloides macrofollicularis.

Pituitary B. Missed.

Ovary.

Skin. No remarkable congestion or swelling ,any where.

Lymph-node.

Inguinal. (sepsis) L.acuta with consid. congestion and scattered bacterial disseminations.

Peribronchial Catarrh and intense follicular congestion.

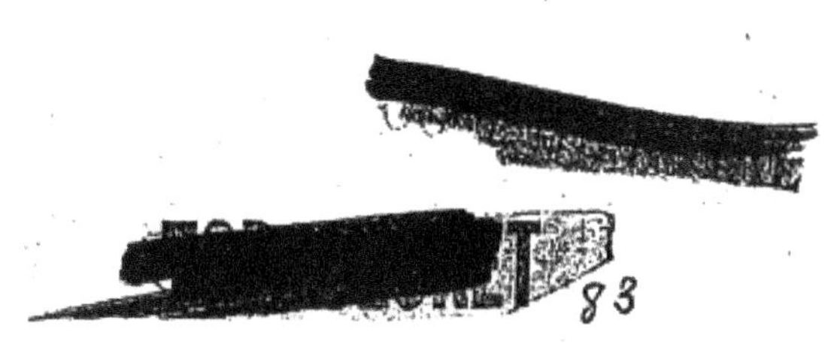

83

33.

Years and sex.	22. ♀
Days of course.	?
Entrance-port.	r-Inguinalis.
Type of disease.	G.

Heart. Intense degeneration.

Aorta. Suspender-like aorta.

Tonsil. Considerable congestion and edema in submucous tissues. Slight swelling of follicular tissues.

Pharynx. No remarkable changes.

Epiglottis. No remarkable changes.

Bronchus. Intense congestion and some round cell accumulation.

Lung. Slight pulmonal congestion(right, superio and inferio). Brochiolitis catarrhlis(right, inferior). No particular changes in left lung.

Pleura. Pleuritis fibrino-fibrosa patialis(right ,superior),

Liver. Hepatitis serosa II,with some leucocytesin capillaries. Intense fatty degeneration and some net-necrosis like changes.

Stomach. Considerable congestion and some localised hemorrhages in mucous tissues.

Small-Intestine. Consideravlw congestion.

Large-Intestine. Considerable catarrh.Considerable congestion and some

84

Liver. Hepatitis serosa II,wotj some leucocytes in capillaries.

Large-Intestine. Consideragle catarrh. Considerable congestion and some edematous swelling in mucous tisses.
Intense congestion and some diffuse hemorrhages in subserous tissues.

Kidney. Glomerulo-nephrosis bionecroticans, with some polar changes.
Nephrosis I (or IIIat some places),with conspicuous hyaline droplets degeneration of sme tubulat epi- theliums.

Spleen. Peri-splenitis fibrosa.
Angio-folliculitis haemorrhagico-exsudativa.
Spleno-fasciculitis exsudativa with leucocytes dissemination.

Pancrea. Slight parenchymatous degenerqtion and no remarkable changes.

Supra-real. Some degenerqtive changes of cortical cells and some round cell accumulation in cortical tissues.

Thyreoid. Considerable congestion and some degenerative changes of follicular epitheliums. Some round cell infiltration.
Struma parenchymatosa levis.

Uterus. Considerable congestion and some perivascular round cell accumulation.

Ovary.

85

Skin. Congestion and swelling(r-Inguinal parts).

Lymph-node.

Inguinal(r).	L.haemorrhagicoexsudativeo-purulenta totalis.
	Intense pericapsulitis with diffuse hemorrhages.
	Intense cutaneous edema and hyperemia.
Retroperitoneal	L. haemorrhagico-necroticans totalis.
	Intense pericapsulitis wth diffuse hemorrhages.
Peribrochial.	L. acuta with considerable congetion and partial hemorrhages.
Mesenterial.	L. acuta with consid. congestion and multiple hemorrhages.

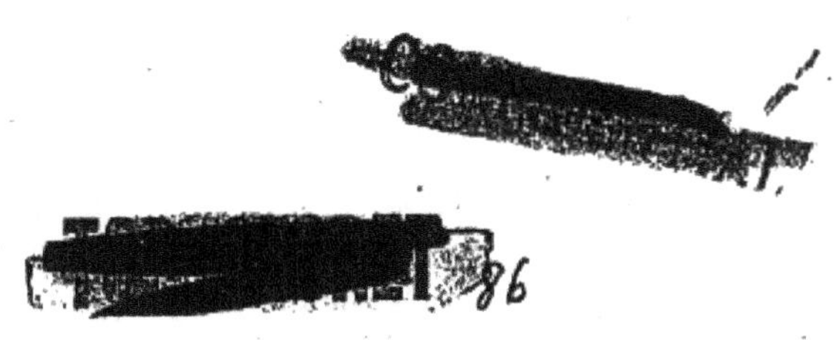

86

([redacted] (

34.

Years and sex. 10. ♂

Days of course. ?

Entrance-port. r-Inguinalis.

Type of disease. G.

Heart. Some myecytes aroud blood-vessels.
Some hemorrh gic places in epicardial tissues.
Slight parenchymatousdegeneration .

Aorta. No remarkable changes.

Tonsil No remarkable chagnes.

Pharynx. No remarkable changese.

Epiglottis. No remarkable changes.

Bronchus. No remarkagle changes, macroscopically.

Lung. Diffuse Alveolitis with acinous leucocytic pneumonia.
Bronchiolitis aatarrhalis levis.
Stasis et edema pulmonum levis(left,inferior).

Pleura. Pleuritis fibrino-fibrosa sinistra.
Some subpleural hemorrhage.

Liver.

Stomach. Almost normal.

Small-Intestine. Slight congestion and slight perivascular round cell accumulation in submucous tissues.

Laege-Intestine. Considerable [redacted] slight hyperplasia of

87

lymphatic nodulus with some swollen reticulum cells, some follicular congestion and slight hemorrhages.

Kidney. Slight Glomerulo-nephrosis with some polar changes. Nephrosis I.

Spleen. Plague-knots.

Pancreas. Slight degeneretion of parenchymatous cells.

Supra-renal. Epinephritis II,with some hemorrhages in Z.reticulatis and intense roud cell accumulation in medullary tissues.

Thyreoid. Degerated state with some degenerative chagme s of follicular epitheliums,

Struma parenchymatosa levis.

Pituitary B. Considerable congestion and some leucocytes in capillaries.

Intense edmatous swelling of subendotheliar tissues.

Slight parnnchymatous degeneretion.

Testicle. Atrophia testis

Thymus. Persistences.

Skin. No remarkable congew tion and swelling ,any where.

Lymph-node.

Axillaris(r). L.haemorrhaigco-necroticans totalis.

Submaxillaris L.acuta haemorrhagica with [illegible] congestion adn leucocytes accumul.

88

Inguinal. Consideragle congestion in follicular tissues.

Mesenterial Considerqvle congestion.

Peribronchial Catarrh and follicular congestion.

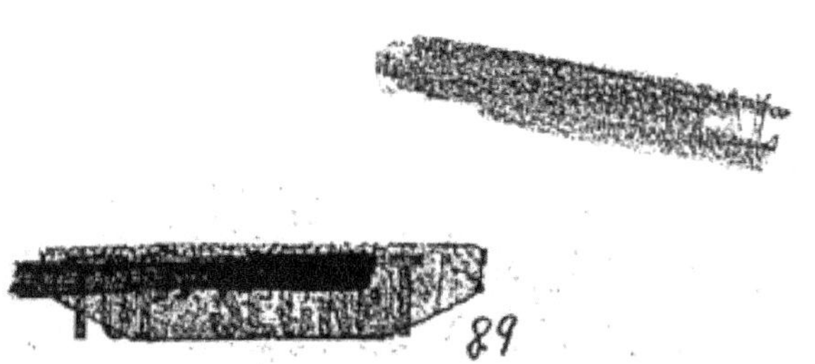

89

TOP SECRET

35.

Years and sex.	36. ♂
Days of course.	5 days.
Entrance-port.	1-Axillaris.
Typer of disease.	G.

CONFIDENTIAL

Heart.	Considerable congestion and some leucocytes in capillaries. Some mesenchymal reaction.
Aorta.	Almost noraml.

Tonsil.	No remarkable changes.
Pharynx.	Slight congestion.
Epitlogotis.	Intense congestion and round cell disseminations.
Bronchus.	Intense congestion, some bacterial accumualtion and plenty leucocytes disseminations.

Lung. Multiple lobular (rather lobar) pneumonia in gray hepatisation. (right, superior and left, inferior).

Bronchiolitis catarrhalis

in medium degree. (left, inferior)

in severe degree. (right, superior)

Peribronchiolitis with leucocytes-dissemination and bacterial accumulation. (left, inferior).

Stasis et edema pulmonum. (right, inferior and left, superior).

CONFIDENTIAL

TOP SECRET

90

Pleura.	Pleuritis fibrino-fibrosa partialis. (left, superior. right inferior.) Pleuritis fibrino-purulenta. (right, inferior.)
Liver.	Hepatitis serosa I-II, with some lymphocytes and some histiocytes in capillaries. Some edematous swelling in glisson's capsules-
Stomach.	Slight catarrh.
Small-Intestinen.	No remarkable changes.
Earge-intestine.	No remarkable cahanges.

Kidney.	Slight Glomerulo-nephrosis with some polarch-anges. Nephrosis I.

Spleen.	Angio-Folliculitis haemorrhagico-exsudativa with polar hemorrhage and polar plasma cell reaction, with slight proliferative tendency Spleno-Fasciculitis exsudativa with slight leukocytes dissemination with some plasma cell reaction.

Pancreas.	Slight parenchymatous degeneration and no remarkable changes.
Supra-renal.	Considerable degeneration of cortical cells. Intense congestion and some hemorrhages in Z. reticularis.
Thyreoid.	Degenerated state (with some degenerative changes of follicular epitheliums) and some congestion.

91

Struma colloides diffusa. 

Pituitary Body. Considerable congestion and some leucocytes in capillaries.

Some cloudy swelling of parenchymatous cells.

Testicls.

Brains. Clight congestion of meningen....

Skin. No remarkable congestion or swelling, any where.

Lymph--node.

Axillaris (1). L. haemorrhagico-necroticans totalis.

Peribronclual. Intense pericupsulits with some leucocytes and bacterial dissemination.

L. haemorrhagica with multiple hemorrhages, consid. congestion and edema.

Mesenterial. L. acuta with considerable congestion.

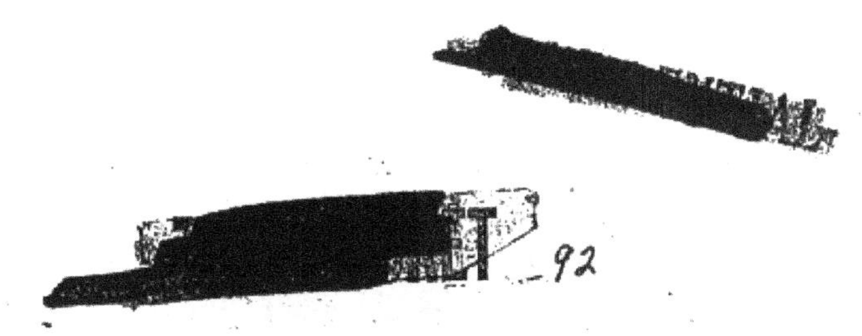

92

36.

Years and sex.	48. ♀
Days of course.	?
Entrance-port.	r-Supraclavicular and r-Axillar parts.
Type of disease.	G.

Heart.	Some hemorrhages in interstitium and epicardial tissues. Some degeneration.
Aorta.	Almost normal.

Tonsil.	Slight congestion.
Pharynx.	Slight congestion. ressecus piriformis- considerable congestion and edema. Slight hyperplasia of lymphatic nodulus with some swollen reticulum cells, some bacterial dissemination and(some leucocytes) in germinative centres.
Epiglotis.	Considerable congestion and intense edema. Some leucocytes -disseminations.
Bronchus.	Intense congestion and some slight hemorrhages- Plenty bacterial disseminations.

Lung.	Multiple acino-lobular pneumonia and Edema et stasis pulmonum all over the pulmonal tissues. (right, superior). Edema pulmonum inflammatorium, stasis,

93

(TOP SECRET (

inferior). (left, superior and inferior).
Multiple acino-lobular pneumonia in gray hepat-
tisation.
Bronchiolitis catarrhalis and Peribronchiolitis with some bacterial dissemination.

Pleura. Pleuritis fibrino-fibrosa partialis, dextra.

Liver. Hepatitis sersa II with some lymphocytes and histiocytes in capillaries.
Slight edema in Glisson$ capsule.

Stomach. Gastritis catarrhalis.

Small-Intestine. Slight hyperplasia of lymphatic nodulus.

Large-ntestine. Slight catarrh and considerable congestion.

Kidney, Slight Glomerulo-nephrosis with some polar changes.
Nephrosis I.

Spleen. Angio-Folliculitis exsudativa
with polar edema and hemorrage
Spleno-Fasciculitis exsudativa
with slight leukocytes dissemination.

Pancreas. Slight parenchymatous degeneration.

Supra-renal. Epinephritis serosa II or III (at some places).
Diffuse hemorrhages in Z. reticularis and Z. fasciculata.

194

Pituitary Body. Considerable congestion and some leucocytes in capillaries.

Remarkable subendotheliar edema.

Some cloudy swelling of parenchyma cells.

Ovary.

Follopia tube. Catarrhalic inflamation with hemorrhagic-serous masses in tube.

Slight congestion, slight hemorrhages and some round cell infiltration in submucous tissues.

Skin. Congestion at supra-clavicular portions.

Brain. Slight congestion of meningen.

Lymph-node.

Supra-clavinular. L. necroticans totalis.

Intraclarrinular L. necroticans totalis.

Axillatis (r). L. necroticans totalis.

Peribronchial. L. haemorrhagico-necroticans partialis.

95

38.

Years and sex. 12. ♀

Days of course. 3 days.

Entrance-port. r-calf of leg.

Type of diseass. Cutaneous plague.

Heart. Slight degeneration and some hemorrhages in epicardial tissues.

Aorta. No remarkable changes.

Tonsil. Tonsillitis catarrhalis levis.

Pharynx. No remarkable changes.

Epiglotis. No remarkable changes.

Bronchus. No remarkable changes.

Bronchus. No remarkable changes.

Lung. Slight pulmonal congestion.

No remarkable changes else.

Pleura. Pleuritis fibrosa obsoleta (left, superior).

Pleuritis exsudativa dextra.

396

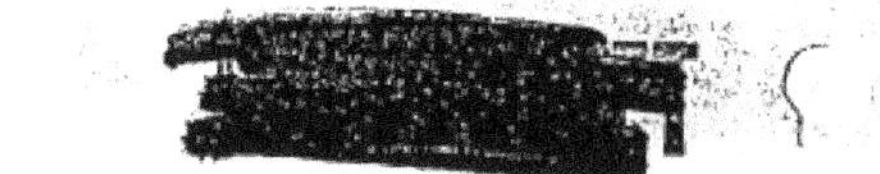

Liver. Hepatitis serosa II, with some leucocytes and some histiocytes in capillaries. Pseudo-biliary tracts.

Stomach. Gastritis catarrhalis hypertrophicans.

Small-Intestine. Thin walls. Considerable congestion and intense hyperplasia of lymphatic nodulus with very slight follicular congestion (congenital hyperplasia).

Large. Intestine. Conside rable congestion and some localised heomrrhages, Considerable edema and some round cell infiltration in submucous tissues.

Kidney. Glomerulo-nephrosis bionecroticans with slight polar changes. Nephrosis I, with some peterphias in pyelums.

Spleen. Angio-Folliculitis exsudativa
with polar edema, with slight proliferative tendency.
Spleno Fasciculitis.
with severe leickocytes dissemination

Pancreas. Slight parenchymatous degeneration.

Supra-renal. Many degenerated cortical cells. considerable congestion and multiple hemorrhages in Z. fasciculata and subcapsular tissues.

Thyreoid. In inactivated state with atrophic follicular cells. Some lymphocytes-accumulations.

Pituitary Body. Intense congestion and some bacterial masses in

capillaries.

Slight parenchyatous degeneration.

Submiliary hemorrhages in anterior lobe.

Ovary.

Skin. Phlegmons at r-calf of leg.

Pus in r. knee-joit cavity.

Lymphnode. Inguinal (r). L. (hamorrhagico)-seropurulenta with intense congestion, plenty of leucocytes emigration and remarkable exudation.

Retro-peritoneal. Intense pericapsultis with diffuse hemorrhages.

L. haemorrhagico-necroticans with flaky, bacterial dissemination.

Mesenterial. L. acuta haemorrhagica partialis.

Peribronchilaris. Intense congestion in follicular tissues.

40.

Years and sex.	53. ♀
Days of course.	3 days.
Entrance-port.	r-Inguinalis.
Type of disease.	Cutaneous plague.

Heart.	Atrophic. Some degeneration. Localised intense edematous swelling of blood-vessels walls.
Aorta.	Intense Atheroscerosis. Intense congestion some leucocytes in capillaries and slight localised hemorrhages of periadventitial tissues.

Tonsil.	Catarrhal and considerable submucous congestion.
Pharynx.	Slight congestion.
Epiglotis.	No remarkable changes.
Bronchus.	No remarkable changes.

Lung.	Bronchiolitis catarrhalis and Multiple lobular pneumonia in obstructive stage. (right, superior). Diffuse Alveolitis with slight inflammatory edema. (right, inferior and left, superior and inferior).

Pleura. Pleuritis fibrino-hemorrhagica, with massive Subpleural bacterial accum ulation.

Liver. Hepatitis serosa I-II, with some histiocytes in capillaries.

Stomach. Considerbale catarrh.

Small-Intestine. Considerable catarrh.

Large-Intestine. Slight congestion.

Kidney. Considerable Glomerulo-nepahrosis with slight polar changes.

Nephrosis I. some petechias in pyelums.

Spleen. Angio-Folliculitis haemorrhagico-exsudativa.

with polar edema and polar hemorrhage,

with slight proliferative tendency

Spleno-Fasciculitis exsudativa.

with slight leukocytes dissemination and slight myeloic metaplasia

----

Pnaoreas. Slight parenchymatous deeneration.

Supr r-renal. Epinephritis serosa II with intense edema in cortical tissues and some hemorrhages in Z. reticularis.

Multiple round cell accumulation in Z. reticularis.

Hyaline droplets- degeneration in medullary tissues.

Thyroeid,

Pituitary Body. Intense congestion and intense edema-

Some degenerative changes of parenchymatous...

Slight hemorrhages in anterior CONFIDENTIAL

Ovary.

Brain. Considerable congestion of meningen.

Skin. Ulcersat r- breast. finder top large.

Diffuse phlegmons at r- breast.

Lymph-node.

Inguinal (r). L. haemorrhagico-sero-purulents totalis.

Phlegmons of adjacent outaneous tissues.

Retro-peritoneal. L. haemorrhagico-purulenta and

intense pericapsulitis.

with diffuse hemorrhages totalis.

Axillaris (l). L. haemorrhagica acuta with consid,

congestion and some partial hemorrhages.

Axillaris (r). L. haemorrhagica acuta with consid

congestion and some partial hemorrhages.

Peribronchial. L. haemorrhagico-·purulenta with consid.

congestion, partial hemorrhages and plenty bacterial dis-

semunation.

Mesenterial. L. acuta with considerable congestion, edema

and some leucocytes-dissemination.

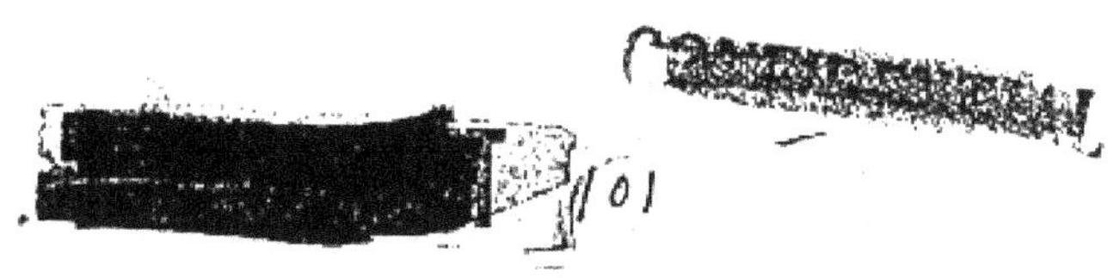

42.

CONFIDENTIAL

Years and sex.	28. ♂
Days of course.	?
Entrance-port.	r-Inguinalis-
Type of disease.	G.

Heart.	Considerable degeneration and some hemorrhages in inters interstitium. Slight dilatation of r. ventricle. Some petechias at epicardial tissues and pericardial tissues.
Aorta.	Thin, suspender like aorta.

Tonsil.	Fonsillitis hemorrhagico-necroticans.
Pharynx.	Considerable congestion, macroscopically.
Epiglotis.	Considerable congestion.
Brouchus.	Considerable congestion.

Lung. (right)	Multiple lobular (rather lobar) pneumonia. Bronchiolitis catarrhalis and Peribronchiolitis with massive bacterial dissemination.
(left)	Diffuse Alveolitis with Edema pulmonum inflammatorium all over the pulmonal tissues.

102

Pleura. Pleuritis fibrino-fibrosa partialis (1).

Liver. Hepatitis serosa I-II, with considerable histiocytes in capillaries.

Stomach. Slight congestion.

Small-Intestine. Considerable catarrha and slight hyperplasia of lymphatic nodulus with some follicular congestion.

Lagge-Intestine. Considerable congestion. Slight hyperplasia of lymphatic nodulus with intense follicular congestion. Intense congestion of subseous tissuses.

Kidnys. Considerable Glomerulo-nephrosis with slight polar changes.
Nephrosis I. Some petechyids in pyelum.

Spleen. Angio-Folliculitis haemerrhagico-exsudativa with polar hemorrhage, with slight proliferative tendency, with polar plasma cell reaction
Spleno-Fasciculitis exsudativa with proliferative tendency, with some plasma cell reaction.

Pancreas. Slight parenchymatous degeneration.

Supra-renal. Epinephritis II, with honeycombed degeneration in Z. fasciculata and multiple localised hemorrhages in Z. reticulatis and Z. fasciculata.
Some round cell accumulation in cortical tissues.

Pituitary Body. Intense congestion and edema.

103

Intense subcapsular hemorrhages and some slight hemorrhages in anterior lobe.
Considerable degeneration of pa renchymatous cells.
Considerable congestion and slight hemorrhages in posterioc lobe.

Thyreoid.

Testicles. Atrophia testis.

Skin. No remarkable congestion or swelling, any where.

Lymph-node. Inguinal. past operation, phlegmons of adjacent cutaneous tissues.
Retro. peritoneal. L. haemorrhagico-necroticans totalis and intense pericapsulitis with diffuse hemorrhages.
Mesenterial. Considerable congestion.
Submaxillaris. L. haemorrhagico-necroticans totalis.

104

((

44.

Years and sex. 6. ♂

Days of course. ?

Entrance-ports. 1-Axillaris.

Type of disease. G-

CONFIDENTIAL

Heart. Atrophic. Slight dilatation of r. vnetricles. Some parenchymatous degeneration.

Aorta. No remarkable changes.

Tosnil. Slight congestion, macroscopically.

Pharynx. Acute catarrh. Considerable congestion and some bacterial dissemination in submucous tissues. Slight hyperplasia of gemminative centres with some Swollen reticulum cells.

Epiglotis. Slight congestion, macroscopically.

Bronchus.

Lung. Diffuse Alveolitis with Edema pulmonum inflammatorium all over the pulmonal tissues. Bronchiolitis catarrhalis. Peribronchiolitis with slight edema and bacterial dissemination. (left lung)

Pleura.	Bleuritis exsudativa (l)- CONFIDENTIAL
	Pleuritis with some subpleural bemorrhages (r)-
Liver.	Hepatitis serosa I-II, with multiple miliary knots, (in proliferative form). Some histiocytes in capi- llar-
Stomach.	some submucous hemorrhages in submucous tissues. Thin walls.
Small-Intestine.	Almost normal.
Large-Netestine.	Almost normal.

Kidney.	Glomerulo-nephrosis bionecroticans, with some polar changes.
	Nephrosis I.

Spleen.	Angio-Folliculitis haemarrhagico-exsudativa
	spleno-Fasciculitis exsudativa with leukocytes dissemination and slight myeloic-metaplasia

----

Pancrens.	Slight parenchymatous degeneration.
Supra-renal.	Considerable congestion and some degeneration of cortical cells. No remarkable changes. else.
Thyroeid.	Follicular collapss.
Pituitary B.	Considerable congestion and some leucocytes in capillaries.
	Subendotheliar edema. Some cloudy degeneration of parenchymatous-cells.

CONFIDENTIAL

106

Ovary.

Skin. No remarkable congestion and swelling, any where.

Lymph-node.

Axillaris (r). L. haemorrhugico-necroticans partialis.

Inguinal (l). L. catarrhalis acuta with consid. Congestion.

Inguinal ((r). With the same changes.

Mesenterial. L. acuta catarrhalis et haemorrhagica with some hemorrhages, some leucocytes and bacterial dissemination and edematous smelling.

107

46.

Years and sex.	63. ♂
Days of course.	?
Entrance-port.	r-breast- r- Axillaris.
Type of disease.	cutaneous plague.

Heart. Slight degeneration. Slight dilatation of r. ventricle.

Aorta. No remarkable changes.

Tonsil. Slight congestion.

Pharynx.

Epiglotis. No remarkable changes.

Bronchus.

Lung. Edema pulmonum inflammatorium in severe degree. Multiple lobular (rather lobar) pneumonia. (left, inferior).

Pleura. Pleuritis fibrino-fibrosa (right, sup rior).

1.08

Liver. Hepatitis sersoa I, with multiple submiliary necrosis. Considerable histiocytes incapillaries.

Stomach. Almost normal.

Small-Intestine. Almost normal.

Large. Intestine. Rather atrophic glandular cells. Slight hyperplasia of lymphatic nodulus.

Kidney.

Spleen. Angio-Folliculitis exsudativa with diffuse Bionecrosis

Spleno-Fasciculitis necroticans diffuse necrosis and bionecrosis

----

Inyreoid. Degenerted state with some degenerative changes of follicular epithliums. Slight congestion.

Testicles. Atrophia testis.

Skin. Slight congestion and swelling of eye-lid. Erytherm and edematous swelling of r- breast.

Lymph-node.

Edema and intense congestion of cutaneous tissues.

109

Axillaris (r). L. haemorrhagico-purulents in medium degree, with consid. congestion and localised hemorrhages and some leucocytes. dissemination.

Peribronclial. L. (haemorrhagico) - necroticans totalis.

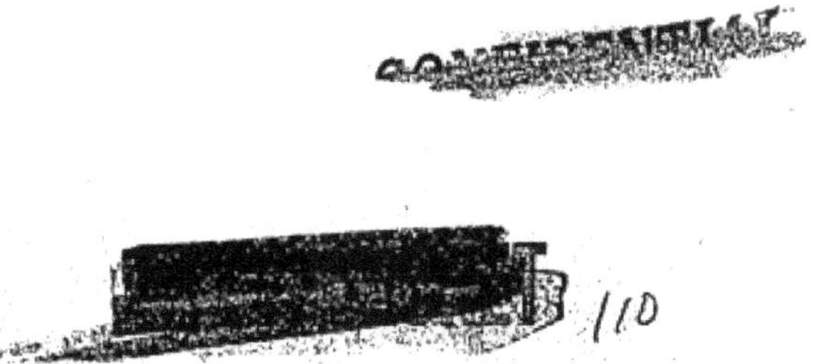

((

47.

Years and sex. 30. ♀

Days of course. ?

Entrance-port. r-Axillaris.

Type of disease. G.

Jeart- Some degeneration and some hemorrhages in interstitiums.

Slight dilatation of f. and l. ventricles.

Aorta. No remarkable changes.

Tonsil. Tonsillitis acuta, with intense congestion and some multiple miliary necrosis (due to bacterial accumulation) in germinative centres.

Pharynx. considerable congestion.

Epiglotis. Slight congestion and some wandering cells (some of them, leucocytes). -accumulatons.

Lung. (right, superior) Edema pulmonum gravis with bacterial dessemination.

Bronchiolitis catarrhalis and Peribronchiolitis.

(right, inferior). Edema pulmonum gravis with bacterial dissemination.

Slight hyperplasia of alveolar epithelium.

(left, superior). Slight pulmonal congestion.

Bronchiolitis catarrhalis in medium degree.

111

(left, inferior). Slight diffuse Alveolitis with slight hyperplasia of alveolar epithelium.

Pleura. Pleuritis fibrinosa partialis with multiple subpleural hemorrhage.

Liver. Hepatitis serosa II-III, with multiple submiliary necrosis (in exudative form). Intanse fatty degeneration and some histiocytes in capillaries.

Stomach. Almost normal.

Small-Intestine. Slight catarhr and slight congestion.

Large-Intestine. No remarkable changes.

Kidney. Slight glomerulo-nephrosis with slight polar changes. Nephrosis I, with intense vacuolar degneration of tubular epitheliums.

Spleen. Angio-Folliculitis haemorrhagico-exsudativa with proliferative tendency (Reticulum cell).
Spleno-Fasciculitis exsudativa with slight leukocytes dissemination.

Pancreas. Slight parenchymatous degeneration.

Supra-renal. Epinephritis II with hoenycombed degeneration of cortical cells. Some lacterial masses in cortical capillar ies. Some leucocytes-accumulation in cortical capillaries.

Thyreoid. Slight degeneration of follicular epitheliums.

112

Pituitary Body. Slight congestion and edema. Some degeneration of parenchymatous cells-
Considerable congestion and slight hemorrhages in anterior lobe.

Brain. Considerable congestion of meningen.

Skin. No remarkable congestion or swelling, any where.

Lymph-node.

Axillaris (r). L. haemorrhagico-necroticans totalis.

Axillaris (l). L. haemorrhagico-necroticans totalis.

Cerricalis. L. haemor rhagico-necroticans totalis.

Mesenterial. L. catarrhalis acuta with consid, congestion.

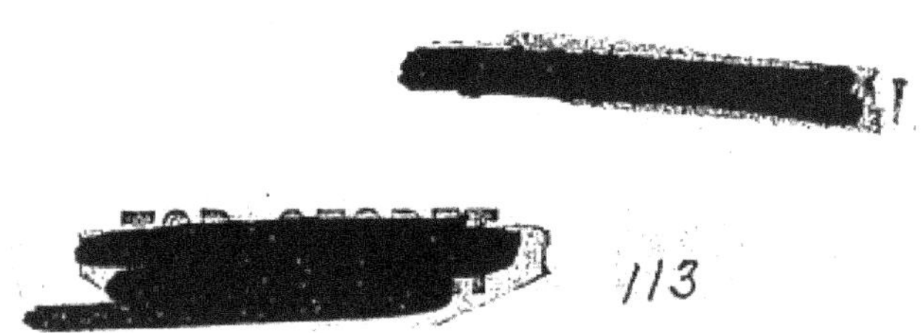

113

49.

Years and sex. 60. ♂

Days of course. ?

Entrance-port. r-Submaxillaris.

Type of disease. Sepsis. Main pathological changes in lung.

Heart. Remarkable hypertrophia and dilatation of r. and l. ventricles. (ca. 3 of normal).
Intense degeneration and considerable congestion.

Aorta. Slight atherosclelosis and slight congestion of peri-adventitial tissues.

Tonsil

Pharynx. Considerable congestion.

Epiglotis. Intense congestion, and Edema.

Bronchus. Considerable congestion.

Lung. (right, superior). Edema pulmonum gragis.

(right, inferior). Stasis pulmonum levis.
Bronchiolitis catarrhalis levis.

(left, superior). Lobar pneumonia in gray hepatisation
Bronchiolitis catarrhalis and Peribronchiolitis with bacterial accumulation.

(left, inferior). Diffuse Alveolitis
Acinous leucocytic pneumonia.
Edema pulmonum all over the pulmonal tissues.

Pleura. Pleuritis fibrinosa (left, superior).

CONFIDENTIAL

-114

Liver. Hepatits serosa.

Stomach. considerable congestion in submucous tissues.

Small-Intestine. Almost normal.

Large-Intestine. Almost normal.

Kiddey. Considerable Glomerulo-nephrosis with slight polar changes.
Nephrosis I.

Spleen. Angio-Folliculitis haemorrhagico-exsudativa
with slight proliferative tendency (Reticulum cell).
Spleno-Fasciculitis exsudativa
with slight leukocytes dissemination.

Pancreas. Slight parenchymatous degeneration.

Supra-renal. Epinephritis III, with diffuse intense hemorrhages in
Z. reticularis and some round cell acculumlation in
Z. reticularis.
Intense parenchyamtous degeneration of cortic l cells.
Anisonuclei of medullary cells.

Tyhreoid. Struma parechymatosa.
Some degenerative changes of follicular pepitheliums
and some congestion.

Pituitary Body. Intense congestion and submiliary loclalised hemorrhages.

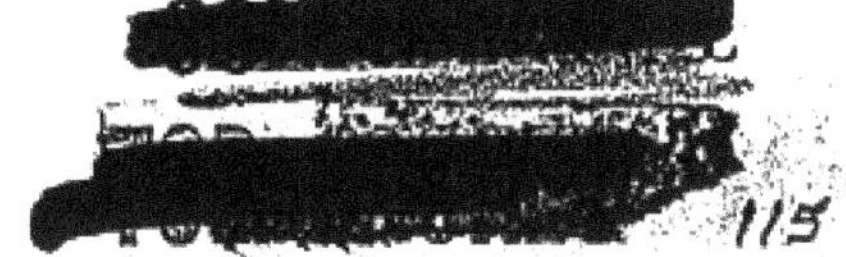

115

Intense andenodotheliar edema.
Intense cloudy swelling of payenchymatous cells-
considerable congestion, partial hemorrhages and
some round cell infiltration in posterir lobe.

Skin. Edematous swelling of eye-lid.

Lymph-node.

Ceruicalis. L. haemorrhagica partialis with intense congestion and partial hemorrhages.

Peribronehial. L. haemorrhagica pabtialis with intense congestion, some localised bemorrhages, serous exudation and some leucocytes and bacterial dixsemination.

116

S. I.

years and sex. 8, ♀

---

days of course. 8 days.

Entrance-port. l-inguinal.

Type of disease G.

Heart. Considerable degeneration. Slight hemorrhages.

Aorta. No remarkable changes.

Tonsil. No remarkable changes.

Pharynx. No remarkable changes.

Epiglottis. No remarkable changes.

Bronchus. No remarkable changes.

---------------- Bronchiolitis catarrhalis levis.

Lung. (right.) Slight pulmonal edema with some bacterial accumulation at some places.

(left.) Slight pulmonal congestion with some bacterial emigration at some places.

Liver. Hepatitis serosa II. Net-necrosis like changes in acinuses and multiple submiliary necrosis. Plenty leucocytes in capillaries.

Stomach. No remarkable changes.

Small-Intestine. No remarkable changes.

Large-Intestine. Atrophic glandular cells, Slight hyperplasia of lymphatic nodulus.

117

Kindney. Considerable Glomerulo-nephrosis with considerable polar changes. Nephrosis I.

Spleen. Angio- Follicultis exsudativa
with polar edema and miliary necrosis (sperma like necrosis).
Spleno- Fascicultis exsudativa.
with severe leukocytes dissemination and slight myeloic-metaplasia.
with some miliary necrosis (rather exsudative form).

Pancreas. Slight degeneration of parenchym cells.

Supra-renal. Intense degeneration of parenchym cells.
Considerable congestion and some round cell infilt.

Thyreoid. Missed.

Pituitary Body.

Ovary.

Lymph-node. Peribronchial. L. catarrhalis with conisderable congestion.
Mesenterial. Normal.

L. ..... (The Abbreviation of "Lymphoadenitis."
The same applies to those that follow.)

118

S. 2.

Years and sex.	8. ♀
Days of course.	5 days.
Entrance-port.	r-Submaxillaris.
Type of disease.	G S.

Heart.	Slight degeneration.
Aorta.	Almost normal. Slight congestion of periadventitial tissues.

Tonsil.	Tonsillitis haemorrhagico-purulenta.
Pharynx.	Intense congestion and intense edema. Considerable hyperplasia of lymphatic nods with intense follicular congestion and some swollen reticulum cells and some bacterial accumulation.
Epiglottis.	No remarkable changes.
Bronchus.	Considerable congestion in submucous tissues.

Lung.	Slight diffuse Alveolitis with leucocytes-dissemination. Hyperplasia of alveolar epithelium. Stasis et edema pulmonum levis. (right, superior).
Pleura.	Pleuritis fibrino-fibrosa interlobaris (right, inferior and left, inferior).

Liver.	
Small-Intestine.	Considerable catarrh. Consid. congestion and edema

119

in mucous tissues.

Slight hyperplasia of lymphatic nodulus with intense follicular congestion, some hemorrhages and some bacterial dissemination in follicular tissues.

Considerable congestion and some perivascular bacterial accumulation, some histiocytes in submucous tissues.

Large-Intestine. Catarrh, consid. congestion and slight hyperplasia of lymphatic nodulus.

Kidney. Slight Glomerulo-nephrosis with some polar changes. Nephrosis I (or III at some places) with some bacillus embolus.

Spleen. Angio-Folliculitis haemorrhagico-exsudativa with slight proliferative tendency, Spleno-Fasciculitis exsudativa with leukocytes dissemination.

Pancreas. Slight degeneration of parenchym cells).

Supra-renal. Intense degeneration of cortical cells. Intense congestion and some hemorrhages in cortical tissues.

Thyreoid. Intoxication-Thyreoid with consid. congestion, slight desquamation of follicular epitheliums, some degenerative changes of follcicular epithe-

20

([redacted] (

liums.

Pitiuitary Body. Missed.

Ovary.

Brain.

Skin. No remarkable changes.

---- --------

Lymph-node.

Inguinal (r). L. haemorrhagica with intense congestion and some localised hemorrhages.

Inguinal (l). With the same changes.

Mesenterial. With the same changes.

Peribronchial. L. Haemorrhagica with intense congestion and diffuse hemorrhages.

Cervicalis. L. haemorrhagica with intense congestion and diffuse hemorrhages.

Axillaris (r). The same changes.

121

S. 3.

Year and sex. 25. ♂

Days of course. 5 days.

Entrance-port. r-Inguinal.

Type of disease. G.

Heart. Intense degeneration.

Aorta. Normal.

Tonsil. Tonsillitis hemorrhagica acuta.

Pharynx. Submucous congestion.

Epiglottis. consid. congestion and edema. some leucocytes dissemin. Some bacterial dissemin. in submucous tissues.

Bronchus. Intense congestion, Multiple miliary necrosis with plenty leucocytes and massive bacterial accumulation. Some hemorrhages in submucous tissues.

Lung. Diffuse Alveolitis and Edema pulmonum inflammatorium. Multiple lobular pneumonia in gray hepatisation (right).

Pleura. Pleuritis fibrinosa dextra.

Liver. Hepatitis serosa III-IV, with multiple miliary hemorrhages and diffuse large necrosis (hemorrhagic-exsudative). Intense edema at Glisson's capsule.

Stomach. Slight catarrh.

. 122

Small-Intestine.	Atrophic glandular cells.
Large-Intestine.	Considerable submucous congestion.
Kidney.	Considerable Glomerulo-nephrosis with some polar changes. Nephrosis I (or II at some places.)

Spleen.	Angio-Folliculitis exsudativa, with slight proliferative tendency. Spleno-Fasciculitis exsudativa, with severe leukocytes dissemination and slight myeloic-metaplasia.

Pancreas.	
Supra-renal.	
Thyreoid.	In inactivated state (slight hyperplasia of follicular epitheliums).
Pituitary Body.	Misse
Testicle.	Atrophia testis.

Skin.	No remarkable changes.

Lymph-node.	Inguinal (r). L. haemorrhagica-sero-purulenta totalis. Retro-peritoneal. Intense periadenitis with diffuse hemorrhages and flaky barcterial dissemination. Mesenterial. L. catarrhalis with consid. congestion.

123

Peribronchial. L. haemorrhagico-necroticans totalis.

Peribronchial. L. haemorrhagico-necroticans totalis.
(Bifulcation)

Cernicalis (1). L. haemorrhagico-necroticans partialis.

124

S. 4.

Years and sex.	23. ♂
Bays of course.	5 days.
Entrance-port.	1-Axillaris.
Type of disease.	G.

Heart.	Considerable degeneration. Consid. congestion (some leucocytes in capillaries) and some slight hemorrhages.
Aorta.	No remarkable changes, slight atheromatosis.

Tonsil.	Tonsillitis necroticans.
Pharynx.	Catarrh. Consid. congestion and slight submiliary hemorrhages in follicular tissues. Perifollciular bacterial accumulation.
Epiglotis.	Intense congestion and edema, some leucocytes-disseminat.
Bronchus.	Slight congestion and no remarkable changes.

Lung.	Diffuse Alveolitis. Edema pulmonum inflammatorium with the desquamation of alveolar epithelium. Bronchiolitis catarrhalis and Peribronchiolitis with congestion and edematous swelling.
Pleura.	No remarkable changes.

125

CONFIDENTIAL

Liver.	Hepatitis serosa III with multiple miliary necorsis (in exudative form). Intense fatty degeneration and some or plenty leucocytes in capillaries. consid. edema in Glisson's capsule.
Stomach.	Slight congestion.
Small-Intestine.	Consid. catarrh, Slight hyperplasia of lymphatic nodulus with some follcicular congestion.
Duodenalparts.	Almost normal.
Large-Intetine.	Slight catarrh and some round cell infiltration in submucous tissues.

Kidney.	Consid. Glomerulo-nephrosis with intense polar changes. Nephrosis I.

Spleen.	Angio-Folliculitis exsudativa, with slight leukocytes emigration. with polar edema and miliary necrosis (sperma like necrosis. Spleno-Fasciculitis excudativa. with slight lenkocytes dissemination, with some miliary bionecrosis.

Pancreas.	Some degeneration of parenchym cells. Vacuolar degeneration of island-cells.
Supra-renal.	Consid. congestion, consid. leucocytes and mono-

CONFIDENTIAL

126

cytes accumulation at in capillaries of pericap-
sular and subcapsular portions.
Edema in cortical tissues.
Honeycombed degeneration or consid. degneration of
medullary cells.
Some bacterial masses in medullary capillaries.

Thyreoids. In inactivated state.

Testicle. Atrophia testis.

Pituitary Body. Missed.

Skin. No remarkable changes.

Lymph-node.

Cervicalis. L. haemorrhagico-exsudativa totalis.

Axillaris (1). L. haemorrhagico-exsudativa totalis.

Perihronchial. L. haemorrhagico-purulenta with intense
Congestion, edema, some leucocytes and
bacterial dissemination.
Intense pericapsulitis with diffuse hemorrhages and flaky bacterial dissemination.

Peribronchial. (bifurcation) L. haemorrhagico-purulenta with intense
congestion, diffuse hemorrhages, flaky
bacterial dissemination and some leucocytes.
Intense periadenitis with intense congestion
and diffuse hemorrhages.

127

S. 5.

Years and sex.	21. ♂
Days of course.	3 days.
Entrance-port.	r-inguinalis.
Type of disease.	G. Hemorrhagic diathesis.

Heart.	Atrophia (fusca) cordis. Edema in interstitium. Slight dilatation of r. ventricle.
Aorta.	No remarkable changes.

Tonsil.	Tonsillitis haemorrhagico-purulenta acuta.
Pharynx.	Consd. congestion and intense hyperplasia of lymphatic nodulus with slight follicular congestion, slight hemorrhages, some swollen reticulum cells and a few bacillus-dissemination in follicular tissues.
Bronchus.	Intense congestion (some bac.-embolus). Multiple miliary necrosis with plenty leucocytes and plenty bacillus-accumulation.
Epiglottis.	

Lung.	Slight diffuse Alveolitis. Edema pulmonum inflammatorium in medium degree. Bronchiolitis catarrhalis acuta. Peribronchiolitis with edematous swelling. (right).
Pleura.	No remarkable changes.

128

( (

Liver.	Hepatitis serosa II, intense fatty degeneration and some leucocytes in capillaries.
Stomach.	Consid. congestion in mucous and submucous tissues.
Small-intest.	Almost normal.
Large-Intest.	Slight catarrh. Consid. congestion and edema. Some round cell infiltration in submucous tissues.

Spleen.	Angio-Folliculitis hemorrhagico-exsudativa with polar edema and miliary necrosis (sperma like necrosis). Spleno-Fasciculitis exsudativa with severe leukocytes dissemination and slight myeloic-metaplasia, with some miliary necrosis.

Kidney.	Consid. Glomerulo-nephrosis with some polar changes. Nephrosis I and at some places Nephritis interstitialis, with some round cell accumulat., edema and some increased connective tissues.

Pancreas.	Considerable parenchymatous degeneration.
Supra-renal.	Consid. degeneration of cortical cells. Consid. congestion and some hemorrhages in Z. reticulars.
Thyreoids.	In activated state, with intense congestion. Struma parenchymatosa levis.
Pituitary Body.	

129

Testicles. Atrophia testis.

Brain.

Skin. No remarkable changes.

Lymph-node.

Inguinal (1). L. haemorrhagico-necroticans tetalis with intense pericapsulitis (diffuse hemorrhages).

Retro-peritoneal. Intense pericapsulitis with diffuse hemorrhages. L. haemorrhagico-necroticans totalis.

Mesenterial. L. haemorrhagico-purulenta partialis with considerable congestion, some localised haemorrhages, same leucocytes and some bacterial dissemination.

Peribronchial. Slight pericapsulitis with L. haemorrhagica partialis with intense congestion and some leucocytes dissemination.

Cerhicalis. Catarrh and follicular congestion.

130

S. 6.

Years and sex. 12. ♀

Days of course. 6 days.

Entrance-port. r-Inguinal.

Type of disease. G.

Heart. Considerable degeneration.

Aorta. Almost normal.

Tonsil. Tonsillits necroticans.

Pharynx. No remarkable changes.

Epiglottis. No remarkable changes.

Bronchus. No remarkable changes.

Lung. Slight diffuse Alveolitis with slight pulmonal congestion and pulmonal edema, accompanied with some bacterial dissemination at some places.

Pleura. Pleuritis sero-fibrinosa dextra.

Liver. Diffuse intense fatty degeneration all over the acinuses.

Stomach. Gastritis catarrhalis.

Duodenal part. Almost normal.

Somall-Intest. Considerable catarrh.

Slight congestion and slight hyperplasia of lymphatic nodulus, with follicular congestion and some increased cloudy reticulum cells.

- 131

Large-Intest. Catarrh.

Spleen. Angio-Folliculitis exsudativa

Spleno-Fasciculitis exsudativa

with slight leukocytes dissemination and slight myeloic-metaplasia.

Kidney. Slight Glomerulo-nephrosis with some polar changes.

Nephrosis I.

Pancreas.

Supra-renal.

Thyreoids. Follicular collapse. Considerable congestion and some lymphocytes in capillaries.

Ovary. Congestion and some bacillus-embolus.

Thymus. Perstistence. Congestion and some increased reticulum cells.

Brain. No remarkable changes.

Skin. No remarkable changes, any where.

Lymph-node.

Axillaris (r). L. haemorrhagica with intense congestion and diffuse hemorrhages.

Slight pericapusulitis with some congestion.

132

Submaxillaris.	L. haemorrhagico-necroticans totalis and intense pericapsulitis with diffuse hemorrhages.
Peribronchial.	L. haemorrhagico-necroticans partialis.
Mesenterial.	L. haemorrhagico-necroticans with some leucocytes dissemination, some bacterial accumulation and some miliary necrosis.
Cerbucalis.	L. haemarrhagico-necroticans.

133

S. 8.

Years and sex.	10. ♂
Days of course.	3 days.
Entrance-port.	?
Type of disease.	Septicaemia. Hemorrhagic diathesis.

Heart.	Intense degenertion. Intense cardial callosity at some places. Some bacillus-embolus.
Aorta.	Almost normal.

Tonsil.	Tonsillitis septicae. Consid. congestion and some bac-embolus.
Pharynx.	No remarkable changes.
Epiglottis.	No remarkable changes.
Bronchus.	Intense congestion, some bacillus and leucocytes dissemination in submucous tissues.

Lung. (right, superior)	Lobar pneumonia in gray hepatisation. Bronchiolitis catarrhalis levis.
(right, inferior)	Multiple acino-lobular pneumonia with Edema pulmonum inflammatorium in severe degree.
(left, superior)	Multiple lobular (rather lobar) pneumonia in gray hepatisation. Bronchiolitis catarrhalis acuta.
(left, inferior)	Multiple acino-lobular pneumonia with hemorrhagic changes. Stasis[illegible]

134

	Bronchiolitis catarrhalis acuta.
Pleura.	Pleuritis sero-haemorrhagica.

Liver.	Hepatitis serosa II- III, with multiple miliary necrosis (some histiocytes-accumulation).
Stomach.	Slight catarrh.
Small-Intestine.	Considerable catarrh. Slight hyperplasia of lymphatic nodulus with some increased reticulum cells.
Large-Intestine.	Almost normal.

Kidney.	Considerable Glomerulo-nephrosis with some polar changes. Nephrosis I.
....	Angio-Folliculitis haemorrhagico-exsudativa, with slight proliferative tendency.
Spleen.	Spleno-Fasciculitis exsudativa. with leukocytes dissemination.

Pnacreas.	
Supra-renal.	Atrophic supra-renal. Some degeneration of cortical cells. Consid. congestion and intense hyperplasia of capillary endothel cells. Intense hyaline droplets formation in medullary cells. Some bacillus in medullary capillaries and some

135

~~Leucocytes~~	~~some~~ leucocytes at pericapillary portions.
Thyreoids.	Follicular collapse.
Testicels.	Atrophia testis III.
Pituitary B.	

Skin.	Nor remarkable changes any where.

Lymph-node.

Axillaris (r).	Intense pericapsulitis with some leucocytes dissimin. L. catarrhalis acuta with some congestion and some bacterial dissemination.
Suhmaxillaris. (r. l.)	L. haemorrhagico-necroticans partialis with some leucocytes dissemination.
Inguinal (r. l.)	L. acuta with consid, congestion and some hemorrhages.
Mesenterial.	Considerable congestion and slight catarrh.
Peribronchial.	L. haemorrhagico- necroticans partialis.

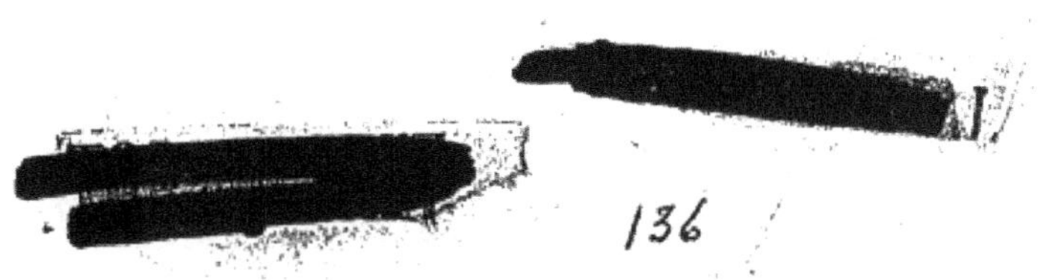

136

S. 9.

Years and sex.	56. ♂	
Days of course.	6 days.	
Entrance-port	Lung.	
Type of disease.	Primary lung plague.	slight hemorrhagic diathesis.

Heart.	Intense degenertion, Atrophia fusca.
Aorta.	Almost normal.

Tonsil.	No remarkable changes.
Pharynx.	No remarkable changes.
Epiglottis.	No remarkable changes.
Bronchus.	Intense congestion, some bacillus and some leucocytes dissemination in submucous tissues.

Lung. (right)	Slight diffuse Alveolitis.
	Stasis et edema pulmonum levis.
(left.)	Multiple acino-lobular pneumonia.
	Bronchiolitis catarrhalis acuta.

Pleura.	Pleuritis fibrino-fibrosa duplex.

Liver.	Hepatitis serosa III with multiple miliary necrosis (exudative-hemorrhagic form). Plenty leucocytes and some [illegible]ies.

137

Gallbladder.	Sub mucous congestion.
Spleen	Angio-Folliculitis haemorrhagico-exsudativa with slight proliferative tendency Spleno-Fasciculitis exsudativa with severe leukocytes dissemination. with slight proliferative tendency.
Stomach.	Gastritis catarrhalis.
Small-Intest.	Consid. catarrh.
Large-Intestine.	Consid. catarrh. Slight hyperplasia of lymphatic nodulus with some follicular congestion.
Kidney.	Considerable Glomerulo-nephrises with some polar changes. Nephrosis I.
Prostata.	Considerable hypertrophia.
Pancreas.	Some parenchymatous degeneration and consid. congestion.
Supra-renal.	Consid. cloudy degeneration and some honeycombed degeneration of cortical cells. Atrophia fusca. Bionecrotic miliary places in Z. fasculata. Consid. congestion and some increased capillary endothel cells. Hyaline-droplets formation in medullary cells. Some bacillus in cortical capillaries.

138

Thyreoid. In statical state.

Pituitary Bldy.

Testcles.

Skin. No remarkable changes any where.

Lymph-node.

Peribronchial. L. acuta with considerable congestion, some leucocytes and some bacterial dåsse-mination.

Mesenterial. Almost mormal.

139

S. IO.

Years and sex,	45 ♀
Days of course.	?
Entrance-Port.	Sepsis.
Type of disease.	Sepsis (Main pathological changes in lung). Hemorrhagic diathesis.

Heart.	Slight degeneration.
Aorta.	Almost normal. Slight congestion of p riadventitial tissues.

Tonsil.	No remarkable changes.
Pharynx.	Considerable congestion, slight edema and some bacterial dissemination,
Epigolotis.	No remarkable changes.
Bronchus.	Intense congestion and considerable round cell accumulat. in submucous tissues.
Lung.	Multiple lobular pneumonia with intense exudative-leucocytic-hemorrhagic changes. Bronchiolitis catarrhalis acuta gravis. Peribronchiolitis with bacterial dissemination.
Pleura.	Remarkable pleural congestion

140

Liver.	Hepatitis serosa III, with multiple miliary necrosis
~~Lober.~~	(hemorrhagic-exsudative form).
Galle-bladder	Plenty leucocytes and some bacillus in capillaries.
	Submucous congestion.
Stomach.	Gastritis catarrhalis.
Small-Intesti.	No remarkable changes, macroscopically.
Large-Intestire.	No remarkable changes, macroscopically.

Kidney. Considerable Glomerulo-nephrosis with sme polar changes. Nephrosis with intense congestion in coritcal tissues and scattered some hemorrhages in cortical tissues.

Spleen. Angio-Folliculitis exsudativa
with slight proliferative tendency
Spleno-Fasciculitis exsudativa
with severe leukocytes dissemination and slight mueloic-metaplasia, with slight proliferative tendency.

Pnacreas. Slighthparenchymatous degeneration and consid. congestion.

Supra-renal. Epinephritis II.
Consid. congestion and some hemorrhages in Z. reticularis and Z. fasciculata and some round cell accumulation in cortical tissues. Some bacillus in cortical capillaries.

141

Thyreoid.	In degenerative form (some degenerative changes of follicular epitheiums).
	Struma parenchymatosa levis.
Pituitary B.	Missed.
Testicles.	Atropha testis.

Brains.

Skin.		No remarkable changes, any where.
Lymph-node.		
	Axillaris (r).	L. purulenta with plenty leucocytes.
	Axillaris (l).	L. purulenta with plenty leucocytes.
	Peribronchial.	L. L. necroticans totalis with flaky bact-dissemin:
		Intense peri-capsulitis with flaky bact-dissemin.
	Inguinal (r).	L. purulenta with intense congestion and some leueocytes and some bact. dissemination.
	Inguinal (l).	With the same changes.
	Mesenterial.	L. catarrhalis with considerable congestion.

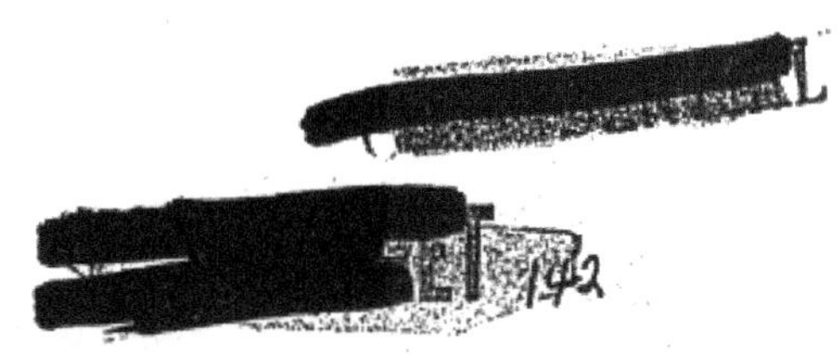

S. II.

Years and sex.	55. ♂
Days of course.	18 days.
Entrance-port.	r-Inguinalis.
Type of disease.	G. Hemorrhagic diathesis.

Heart.	
Aorta.	Almost normal.

Tonsil.	Tonsillitis acuta with intense congestion, edematous swelling and some bact-dissemination in follicular tissues.
Pharynx.	Considerable congestion and some bacillus in capilaries.
Epiglotis.	No remarkable, changes, macroscopiclly.
Bronchus.	No remarkable changes.
Lung.	Diffuse Alveolitis and Edema pulmonum inflammatorium Remarkable Anthracosis.
Pleura.	Pleurtis fibrosa sinistra- Remarkable Anthracosis.

143

Liver.

Stomach. Intense congestion and multiple diffuse hemorrhages in mucous tissues and intense perivascular hemorrhages in submucous tissues.

Small-Intestine. Considerable catarrh.
Considerable congestion and slight hemorrhages in mucous tissues. Considerable congestion in submucous tissues

Duodenal part. Consid. congestion and localised hemorrhages in mucous tissues.

Large-Intestine. Almost normal.

Spleen. Angio-Folliculitis naemorrhagico-exsudativa, with polar edema and miliary necrosis
Spleno-Fasciculibe exsudation with slight leukocytes dissemination and myeloio-metar-plasia with some miliary necrosis.

Pancreas. Degeneration of parenchymatous cells and some swelling of island-cells.

Supra-renal. Multiple localised or rather diffuse hemorrhages in all layers of supra- renal.
Some bacterial dissmination and bionecrotic swellinge of adjacent cortical cells.
Some round cell accumulation in cortical and medullary tissues.

144

Thyreoid. Follicular collapse. Intense congestion and some bacterial masses incapillaries.

Pituitary B. Missed.

Testicles. Atrophia testis. No remarkable changes.

Sking. Tongue. Submucous submiliary hemorrhages and intense edema. Some bacterial accumulation in hemorrhagic part.

Skin. No remarkable chan ges, any where.

Lymph-node.

Inguinal (r). L. haemerrhagica totalis and necroticans partial.

Retro-Pertitoneal. With the same changes with intense pericapsulitis (diffuse hemorrhages).

Mesenterial. L. acuta with intense congestion, some leucocytes and some bact-dissemination.

Axillaris (r). L. haemorrhagico-purulenta with intense congestion, diffuse hemorrhages and edema.

Peribronchial. L. haemorrhagica with intense congestion and diffuse hemorrhages.

145

S. I2.

Years and sex. 27. ♂

Days of Course. 3 days.

Entrance -port. 1-Inguinal.

Type of disease. G.

Heart. Intense degenertion, Considerable congestion and some bacillus in capillaries. Hemorrhages in subepicardial tissues. Slight dilation of r-ventricle.

Aorta. Almost normal.

Tonsil. Catarrh. Intense congestion. Slight swollen lymph atic apparats with some bacillus in follicular tissues.

Pharynx.

Epiglotis. Slight congestion and slight edema.

Bronchs. considerabl congestion, slight edema and slight hemorrhages. Some bacillus in capillaries.

Lung.

(right.) Multiple lobular pneumonia in gray hepatisation.
Bronchiolitis catarrhalis gravis.
Peribronchiolitis with intense edema and congestion.

(left.) Diffuse Alveolitis and
Edema pulmonum inflammatorium.

146

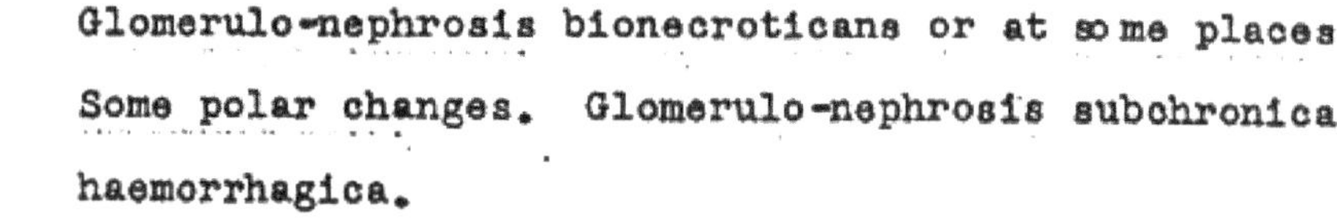

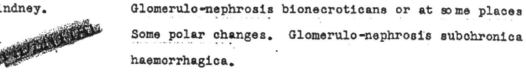

Pleura.	Pleuritis fibrosa totalis dextra.
Kindney.	Glomerulo-nephrosis bionecroticans or at some places Some polar changes. Glomerulo-nephrosis subchronica haemorrhagica.

Liver.	Hepatitis serosa II-III, with consid. bacillus in capillaries.
Stomach.	Intense congestion (bacillus-embolus) and intense localised hemorrhages in mucous tissues. Considerable congestion in submucous tissues.
Small-Intestine.	Considerable catarrh. Considerable congestion (some bac-embolus) in mucous and submucous tissues. Slight hyperplasia of germinative centres of lymph-nods.
Large-Intesine.	Catarrh. Considerable congestion (some leucocytes, and bacillus in capilries). Slight hyperplasia of lymph-nods.

Spleen.	Angio-Folliculitis exsudativa. with polar edema and polar miliary necrosis (Spelma like necrosis). Spleno-Fasciculitis exsudativa with severe leukocytes dissemination with some miliary necrosis cspelma like necrosis)

Pancreas.	Missed,
Supra-renal.	Missed.

1447

Thyreoid.	Slight congedtion and slight degeneration of follicular cells. Struma colloides diffusa.
Testicle.	Atrophia testis.
Skin.	Phlegmon (r-buttocks) with intense Lymphangitis.

Lymph-nods.

Inguinal (1).	L. haemorrhagico-purulenta tetalis and intense periadenitis.
Inguinal (r).	L. haemorrhagico-purulenta totalis.
Mesenterial.	L. haemorrhagica with intense congestion and diffuse hemorrhages.
Peribronchial.	L. haemorrhagica.

S. I4.

Years and sex.	37. ♂
Days of course.	4 days.
Entrance -port.	Cutaneous plague.
Type of disease.	Cutaneos plage.

Heart.	Considerable degeneration.
Aorta.	Almost normal.

Tonsil.	No remarkable changes, macroscopically.
Pharynx.	Submucous congestion and some leucocytes dissemination.
Epiglotis.	No remarkable changes.
Bronchus.	Slight congestion and slight edema, (No remarkable changes).
Lung.	Emphysema bullosum levis. Submiliary leucocytic pneumonic places.
Pleura.	Pleuritis fibrino-fibrosa sinistra.
Liver.	Annular liver-cirrhosis. Multiple miliary necrosis with 2 type, a) hemorrhagic- exsudative and b) rather proliferative form.

([redacted] (

	Some leucocytes in Glisson's capsule.
Stomach.	Considerable congestion (many leucocytes in capillaries) in mucous and submucous tissues.
Small-Intestine.	Considerable congestion (some leucocytes capillaries) in submueous tissues.
Large-Intestine.	No remarkable changes, macroscopically.

Kidney.	Considerable Glmoerulo-nephrosis with slight polar change Nephrosis I with some hemorrhages in medullary tissues and some hyaline cylinders in tublar spaces.
Prostata.	Intense congestion and some hemorrhagic-necrtotic places. Some bacillus in capillaries.

Spllen.	Angio-Folliculitis with polar edema Spleno-Fascicultis exsudativa with slight leukocytes dissemination.

Pnacreas.	Slight parenchymatous degeneration).
Supra-renal.	Considerable degeneration or vacuolar degeneration in cortical tissues. Considerable congestion in all layers and some hemorrhages in Z. reticularis and some round cell accumulation in Z. reticularis.
Thyreoid.	Intense follicular collapse.
Testicle.	Atrophia testis.

Skin. Diffuse phlegmons and muscle-abscesses (l and r arm).

Lymph-node.

Axillaris (l). L. haemorrhagica with cousid congestion and diffuse hemorrhages and some leucocytes-dissemination.

Intense pericapsulitis.

Axillaris (r). With the same changes.

Mesenterial. L. haemorrhagica partialis with intense congest. and diffus hemorrhages.

Perihronchial. L. haemorrhagica partialis.

S. I5.

Years and sex.	18. ♂
Days of course.	?
Entrance-port.	l-Inguinalis.
Type of disease.	G.

Heart.	No remarkable changes.
Aorta.	No remarkable changes.

Tonsil.	Tonsillitis auuta catarrhalis. with intense follicular congestion, plenty bacilus-accumulate, and some submiliary necrosis.
Pharynx.	No remarkable changes, macroscopically,
Bronchus.	Considerable congestion in submucous tissues.

Lung.	Stasis et edema pulmonum inflammatorium. Diffuse Alveolitis. (left)
Liver.	Hepatitis serosa II, with multiple miliary necrosis (exudative form). Plenty leucocytes in capillaries. Some edema and some lymphocytes in Glisson's capsule.
Stomach.	Considerable congestion in submucous tissues.
Small-Intestine.	Considerable catarrh, considerable congestion and remarkable hyperplaisa of lymph-nodulus. Bionecrotic swelling of germinative centres with some leucocytes and some bacillus in follicular tissues.

Large-Intestine. Catarrh.

Kidney. Considerable Glmoerulo-nephrosis with some polar changes.
Nephrosis I.

Spleen. Angio-Folliculitis haemorrhagico-exsudativa with slight leukocytees emigration.
Spleno-Fasciculitis exsudativa with severe leukocytes dissemination and slight myeloic-metaplasia, with some plasma cell reaction.

Pancreas.

Supra-renal. Epinephritis II. Some hemorrhages and some round cell accumulation in Z. reticularis. Considerable hyperplasia of capillary endothel cells.

Thyreoid. Supermiliary hemorrhagic necrosis with plenty bacterial and leucocytes dissemination.
Struma parenchymatosa levis.
Acute hemorrhagic inglammation of para-thyreoid deal lymph-nods.

Pituitary Body. Missesd.

Testicles. No remarkable changes.

Skin. No remarkable changes, any where.

153

Lymph-nods.

Inguinal (1). L. haemorrhagico-purulenta totalis and intense pericapsulitis.

Retro-peritoneal. with the same changes and intense pericapsulitis.

Mesenterial. L. purulenta with diffuse leucocytes-disseminat.

Peribronchial. L. catarrhalis leuis with considerable congest. and some leucocytes-dissemination.

Parathyreiodeal. L. haemorrhagico-necroticans graris.

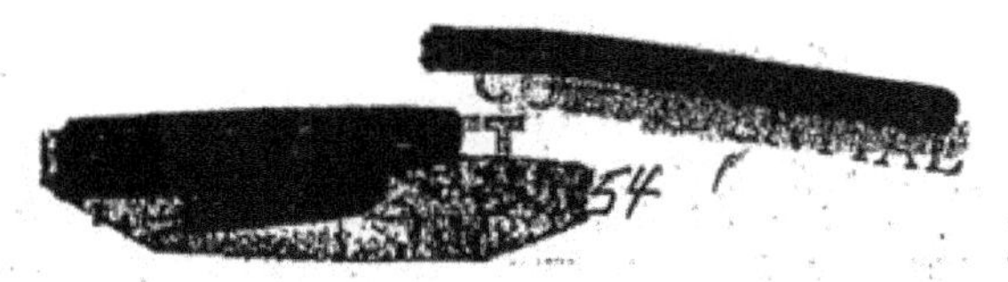

S. I9.

Years and sex.	58. ♀ .
Days of course.	12 days.
Entrance-port.	?
Type of disease.	Sepsis-----lung-plague.

Heart.	Slight dilatation of reventricle.
	Slight degeneration and some myocytes.
Aorta.	Almost normal. Remarkable Atherosclerosis.

Tonsil.	No remarkable changes.
Epiglotis.	No remarkable changes, macroscopically.
Bronchus.	Bronchitis chronica with considerable congestion.

Lung.	Diffuse Alveolitis.
	No remarkable changes else.

Pleura.	Pleruitis fibrosa dextra.
	Considerable pleural congestion and some bacillus
	in capill[illegible]

155

Liver. Hepatitis serosa III.

ßtomach. Almost normal.

Small-Intestine. Atrophic glandular cells Some round cells in submucous tissues.

Targe-Intestine. Almost normal.

Kidney. Glomerulo-nephrosis bionecroticans with some polar changes. Nephrosis I (or III at someplaces).

Spleen. Angio-Follicultis exsudativa
with slight proliferative tendency, with polar edema and polar plasma cell reaction
Spleno-Fasciculitis exsudativa
with leukocytes dissemination, with slight proliferative tendency, with some plasma-cell reaction

----

Pancreas. Slight degeneration.

Supra-renal.

Thyreoid. In inactivited state. Follicular atrophy some fibrosis.

Pituirary Body.

Ovary.

Skin. No remarkable changes.

156

Lymph-nods.

Mesenterial. L. catarrhalis with consid-congestion and considerable hemorrhages.

Inguinal (l). L. catarrhalis with considerable congestion.

Inguinal (r). L. haemorrhagico-purulenta with intense perifocal exudation.

Peribronchial. Catarrh and fallicular congestion with some bacterial dissemination.

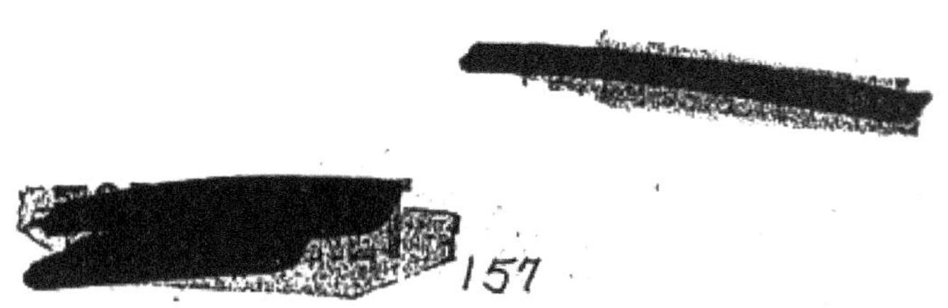

157

S. 22.

Year and sex. 3. ♀

Days of course. 21 days.

Entrance-port. 1-Submaxillaris.

Type of disease. Chrochin course. G.

Heart. Intense degeneration with some mesenchymal reaction. Histicocytes-accumulation around blood-vessels and some bacillus in capillaries. Some eosinophilic cells in interstitium.

Aorta. No remarkable changes.

Tonsil.

Pharynx. Acute catarrh. consid. congestion and slight hemorrhages.
Slight edema slight hyperplasia of lymphatic nodulus with some increased reticulum cells.
Catarrh. Slight hyperplasia of lymphatic nodulus with some congestion, rather more or less remarkable hyperplasia of histiocytes and some lymphocytes in submucous tissues.

Epiglotis. Slight congestion and slight hyperplasia of connective tissues.

Bronchus. Slight congestion and slight hyprplasia of connective tissues.

158

81 22.

Lung. (right) Lobular pneumonia in gray hepatisation. CONFIDENTIAL
Slight proliferative reaction of alveolar epithelium.

Lung. (right)	Lobular pneumonia in gray hepatisation. Slight proliferative reaction of alveolar epithelium.
(left)	Diffuse Alveolitis and Multiple acinous Pneumonia.
Pleura.	Pleuritis haemorrhagico-exsudativa dextra.

Liver.	Chronic course. Intense hyperplasia of histiocytes or Kupffer's cells. Multiple miliary knots with many Kupffeer's cells.
Stomach.	Edema in mucous tissues and hyaline swelling of capillary-walls. Slight hyperplasia of histiocytes in mucous tissues.
Small-Intestine.	Catarrh. Considerable congestion and considerable hyperplaisa of histiocytes and fibrolasts in mcous tissues. Hyperplasia of lymphatic nodulus with swollen germinative centres. Some increased reticulum cells, some lymphocytes and a few leucocytes in germinative centres. Considerable congestion and some hyperplasia of capilary walls. Slight congestion and slight round cell infiltration in submucous tissues.

159

Large-Intestine.. Catarrh. Hyaline swelling of capillary walls. Slight hyperplasia of lymph-nodula with some increased reticulum cells.

Kidney. Slight Glomerulo-nephrosis with some polar changes. Nephrosis I with intense round cell accumulation (some many histiocytes and some leucoytes).

Spleen. Angio-Folliculitis exsudativa
with slight proliferative tendency
Spleno-Fasciculitis exsudativa
with slight proliferative tendancy,
with slight leukocytes dissemination and slight
myeloic metaplasia

Pnacreas. Considerable degeneration and considerable congestion. Some bacillus in capilaries.

Supra-renal. Intense Histiocytes-accumulation. Considerable parench-ym degeneration and some cell groups of hypertrophic crtical cells.
Considerable congestion and some hemorrhages in Z. reticularis.
Intense hyperplasia of capillary endothel cells.

Thyreoid. Almost normal, considerable congestion.

Pituitary Body.

Ovary.

Skin.

160

Lymph-nods.

Submaxillaris (l).	L. catarrhalis with inflammatory reticuloendotheliose (intense hyperplaisa of reticulumcells.
Submaxillaris (r).	With the same changes.
	Muscular abscees in r. Submaxillar portion.
Mesenterial.	Considerable congestion, slight hemorrhages and consid hyperplasia of reticulum cells.
Peribronchial.	L. catarrhalis with hyperplasia of reticulum cells.
Inguinal (r. l.)	Sinus-reticulosis.
Axillaris (r. l.)	Sinus - reticulasis.

161

S. 26.

Years and sex. 31 ♂

Days of corusse 7 days.

Entrance-port. r-

Type of disease. Cutaneous plague.

Heart. Slight degeneration.

Aorta. Slight congestion of periadventital tissues.

Tonsil No remarkable changes.

Pharynx. No remarkable changes.

Epiglotis. No remarkable changes.

Bronchus. Slight congestion and no remarkable changes.

Lung. Diffuse Alveolitis and

Edema pulmonum inflammatorium.

Pleura. No remarkable changes.

Liver. Hepatitis serosa III, with wultiple miliary necrosis (in exudative forma). Some bacillus in capillarires.

Stomach. Gastritis catarrhalis in medium degree.

Small-Intestine. Consid. catarrha and consdi. congestion.

Large-Intestine. Considerable congestion and some round cell infiltration in mucous tissues.

Kidney. Some Glomerulo-nephrosis with some polar changes.
Bacillus in glomerular loops.
Nephrosis I.

Spleen. Angio-Folliculitis exsudativa
with slight proliferative tendency, with polar edema
Spleno- Fasciculitis exsudativa

Pancreas. Considerable degemeration of parenchym cells.

Supra-renal. Considerable degeneration of cortical cells.
Some localised hemorrhages in Z.reticularis.

Thyreoid. In inactivitated state. Rather anemic.

Pituitary Body. Missed.

Testicles. Atrophia testis.

Skin. Diffuse phlegmons

Lymph-node.

Phlegmon at I- femoral portion.

Femoral and L. haemorrhagico-necro-purulenta totalis with
Inguinal (1) diffuse hemorrhages, diffuse necrosis and diffuse bacterial dissemination.

Petro-peritoneal. With the same changes and intense peri-capsular congestion and hemorrhages.

163

S. 28.

Years and sex.	44 ~~33~~. ♂
Days of course	7 days.
Entrance-port.	?
Type of disease.	Sepsis hemorrhagic diathesies.

Heart.	Atrophia. Considerable congestion (some leucocytes in capillaries) and some hemorrhages.
Aorta.	Almost normal.

Tonsil.	No remarkable changes.
Pharynx.	No remarkable changes.
Epiglotis.	No remarkable changes, macroscopically.
Bronchus.	No remarkable, changes, macroscopically.

Lung.	Slight diffuse Alveolitis and Edema pulmonum inflammatorium in eme lobular areas.
Pleura.	No remarkable changes.

Liver. Hepatitis serosa, with multiple miliary necrosis.

Stomach. Slight catarrh.

Small-Intestine. Almost normal.

Large-Intestine. Almost normal.

Kidney. Considerable Glomrulo-nephrosis with some polar changes.

Nephrosis I.

Spleen. Angio-Folliculitis haemorrhagico-exsudativa

with polar edema and polar milliary necrosis

Spleno-Fasciculitis exsudativa

with leukocytes dissemination and slight myeloic-metaplasia

with some milliary Bionecrosis.

Pancreas. Slight parenchymatous degeneration.

Supra-renal. Intense congestion and some multiple miliary hemorrhages in cortical tissues and some diffuse hemorrhages in Z. reticularis.

Intense cloudy swelling of cortcal cells.

Thyreoid.

Pirtuitary Body. Intense congestion (some leucocytes in capillaries).

Subendotheliar edema and intense cloudy degeneration of parenchymatous cells.

Testicles. Atrophia testis

165

Skin. No remarkable changes, any where.

Lymph-node.

Inguinal. (r)	L. haemorrhagica totalis and intense
Femoral (r)	Pericapsulitis with diffuse hemorrhages.
Resenterial.	With the same changes.
Mesenterial.	Pericapsulitis with some leucocytes and somewhat diffuse hemorrhages.
	L. acuta with intense congestion and edema.
Peribronchial.	L. acuta with intense congestion (some bact in capillares) and some leucocytes dissemin.
	Considerable catarrhalic changes.

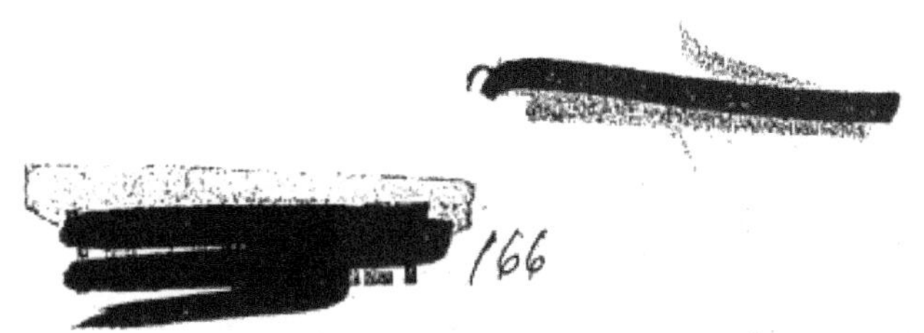

166

S. 38.

Years and sex.	53. ♂
Days of course.	?
Entrance-port.	Abdominal cutaneous tissues----Sepsis.
Type of sieese.	Sepsis.

Heart.	Some degeneration and strophia. Slight congestion and some bacterial masses in capillaries.
Aorta.	Considerable congestion (some leucocytes in capillaries) of peri-adventitial tissues.

Tonsil.	Considerable submucous congestion (some bacillus in capillaries) and edema.
Pharynx.	Intense congestion and intense edema with consid. hyperplasia of lymphatic nodulus intense follicular congestion and some swollen reticulum cells and some bacterial accumulation).
Epiglotis.	Intense congestion and edema. Slight hemorrhages and some leucocytes accumultion in submucous tissues.
Bronchus.	Intense congestion and some bacillus in capillaries.

Lung. (right)	Multiple lobular (rather lobar) pneumonia in gray hepatisation.
(left)	Multiple acino-lobular pneumonia.

167

Pleura. Remarkable congestion and leucocytes-dissemination
Pleuritis sero-fibrinosa partialis dextr CONFIDENTIAL

Liver. Hepatitis a rosa II-III., with some multiple miliary necrosis. Some leucocytes and some bacillus in capillaries.

Stomach. Rather atrophic glandular cells, no remarkable changes.

Small-Intestine. Almost normal.

Large-Intestine. Almost normal. Rather atrophic glandular cells.

Kidney. Slight Glmmerulo-nephrosis with slight polar changes.
Nephrosis I (or III at some places).

Spleen. Angio-Folliculitis haemorrhagico-exsudativa
with slight proliferative tendency
with some necrosis and slight or severe leukocytes emigration
Spleno-Fasciculitis exsudativa
with slight proliferative tendeney and leukocytes dissemination

----

Pancreas. Inteane congestion and some parenchymatous degenerà.

Supra-renal. Epinephritis III.
Some bacterial masses in capillaries and some round cell accumulation in cortical tissues.

Thyreoid. Slight follicular changes. Collapse.

Pituitary Body. Missed.

168

Ovary.

Skin. Vlcer (7.0 cm. diameter) at abdominal cutaneous tissues, and phlegmonous infiltration in neighboring tissues.

Lymph-nods.

Lymph-node.

Lung-hilus. L. acuta purulenta with considerable. congestion and some bacterial dissemination Condiderable pericapsulitis with some leucocytes-dissemination.

Peribronchial. L. haemorrhagica with intense congestion and some hemorrhages and some leucocytes-dissemination. pericapsulitis with some congestion and some leucocy-tes dissemination.

Mesenterial. Catarrh and fallicular congestion.

169

Heart

HEART.

(A) Microscopical Investigation.

N-1. Atrophia and parenchymatous degeneration, slight congestion and some bacterial masses in capillarios. Edema.

N-2. Atrophia and parenchymatous degeneration, considerable congestion and some hemorrhages in interstitial and epicardial tissues. Some bacterial masses in capillaries and slight fibrosis.

N-3. Parenchymatous degeneration.

N-4. Considerable congestion and some hemorrhages in interstitium and epicardium. Perivascular round-cell-accumulation as glanurom, accompanied with some leucocytes. Muscular fibres around them fall into necrobiosis.

N-5. Parenchymatous degenration and some hemorrhages in interstitium and epicardium.

N-6. Atrophia cordis gravis.

N-7. Parenchymatous degeneration, and considerable congestion, (with some bacterial masses in capillaries), accompanied with some myocytes around small vessels.

N-8. Basophilic degeneration.

N-10. Parenchymatous degeneration, considerable congestion with some bacterial masses and some leucocytes as capillaries contents.

N-11. Parenchymatous degeneration and some myocytes around small vessels.

N-12. Parenchymatous degeneration, considerable congestion with some bacterial masse as capillaries contents, and some interstitial edema.

N-14. considerable congestion with some bacterial masses as contenst, and some hemorrhages in interstitium and epicardium. CONFIDENTIAL

N-15. Considerable congestion with some bacterial masses and some leucocytes as capillarie-contents.

N-16. Considerable congestion with some bacterial masses and some leucocytes as contents, accompanied with slight mesenchymal reactions.

N-17. Parenchymatous degeneration and severe venous congestion with some bacterial masses as capillaries contents.

N-18. Parenchymatous degeneration and severe venous congestion, accompanied with some hemorrhages in interstitium.

N-19. Cloudy swelling and vacuolar degeneration, accomapanied with some myocytes around small vessels.

N-20. Parenchymatous degeneration.

N-21. Considerable venous congestion with some bacterial masses as capillaries contents, accompanied with some hemorrhages in interstitium.

N-23. Considerable congestion and slight fibrosis around small vessels.

N-24. Hemorrhages in epicardium and some myocytes in endocardium. Some bacterial masses as capillaries contents.

N-26. Some bacterial masses in capillaries and no remarkable changes else.

N-27. Basophilic degeneration and some myocytes in interstitium.

172

N-29. Considerable congestion and some bacterial masses in capillaries contesnts. Severe parenchymatous degeneration at perivascular portions (Small vessels with some bacteria).

N-32. Hemorrhages in interstitium and epicardium. Some myocytes around small vessels.

N-33. Severe parenchymatous degeneration.

N-34. Some myocytes around small vessels.

N-35. Considerable congestion with some bacterial masses in capillaries-accompanied with slight mesenchymal reaction.

N-36. Some hemorrhages in epicardium and myocardium.

N-38. Slight parenchymatous degeneration.

N-40. Atrophia and some parenchymatous degeneration. Localised severe edematous swelling of blood-vessel-walls and at some places with localised callosity.

N-42. Some hemorrhages in interstitium and some myocytes around small vessels.

N-44. Atrophia and parenchymatous degeneration.

N-47. Some hemorrhages in interstitium.

N-49. Considerable parenchymatous degeneration and considerable congestion. Some hemorrhages in interstitium.

S-1. Considerable congestion and slight hemorrhages in interstitium. Some myelocytes in capillaries.

173

S-2. Some myocytes around small vessels.

S-3. Severe parenchymatous degeneration.

S-4. Considerable parenchymatous degeneration and considerable congestion with some monocytes and some leucocytes in capillaries, accompanied with some hemorrhages in interstitium and epicardium.

S-5. Atrophia and edema.

S-6. Considerable congestion and some lymphocytes and monocytes in capillaries.

S-8. Severe parenchymatous degeneration. Remarkable cardiac callosity, due to some anamnestic diseases with lime-deposition.

S-9. Severe parenchymatous degeneration.

S-10. Slight parenchymatous degeneration.

S-12. Parenchymatous degeneration, considerable congestion and some bacterial masses in capillaries.

S-14. Slight parenchymatous degeneration.

S-15. No remarkable changes.

S-16. Some myocytes in epicardium.

S-22. Stronger endocardial reactions and stronger mesenchymal reactions in myocardium. Considerable accumulation of histiocytes around small blood-vessels and some infiltration of eosinophilic cells in endocardium and interstitium. Some bacterial masses in capillaries.

S-26. Slight parenchymatous degeneration.

S-28. Slight parenchymatous degeneration and some bacterial masses in capillaries.

174

S-35. Atrophia and parenchymatous degeneration. Considerable congestion with some bacterial masses in capillaries and some hemorrhages in interstitium.

K-1. Parenchymatous degeneration and slight hemorrhages in interstitium and epicardium.

K-2. Parenchymatous degeneration and some edematous swelling of blood-vessel-walls.

175

(B) S U M M A R Y.

a) Endocardium:

Generally slight edema and no clear changes else.

In one case (No. s-22), stronger endocard-reaction(mesenchymal reation) with eosinophilic leucocytes.

b) Myocardium:

Severe atrophia and severe cloudy swelling in all cases.

with glassy muascular fibres.	in 9	cases.
with vacuolar degeneration.	in 26	cases.
with basophilic degeneration.	in 2	cases.

Considerable edema,	in all	cases.
in severe degree.	in 5	cases.

Diapedic hemorrhages.	in 35 cases and
in severe degree	in 5 cases of them.

Venous congestion in all cases.

with some leucocytes as contents	in 30 cases.
with some bacterial masses as cont.	in 22 cases.
with some myelocytes	in 1 cases.

Leucocytes-lymphocytes infiltration.

in slight degree. in 8 cases.

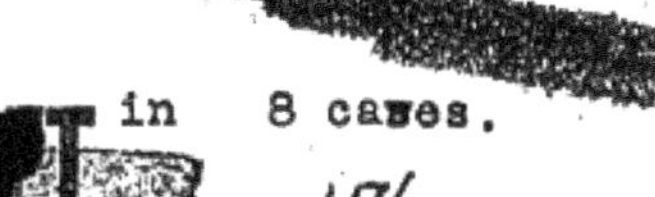

176

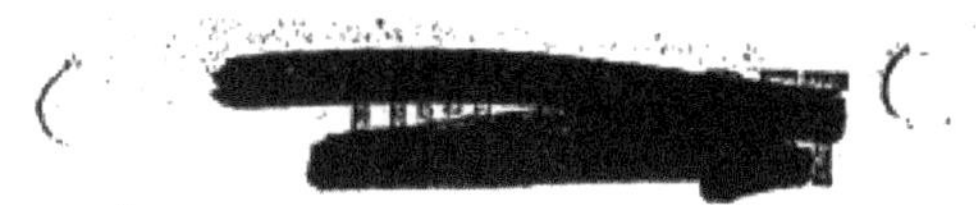

in severe degree. in 2 cases.

Edematous swelling of blood-vessel-walls. in all cases.

in slight degree. in 48 cases.

In severe degree, with some exudative-regressive changes. in 2 cases.

Perivascular edema. in all cases.

Mesenchymal reaction are not so remarkable in all Cases, except 2 cases.

In 1 case with 22 days course, intense mesenchymal reaction with small nodulus formation around small vessels and capillaries.

In 1 case, some mesenchymal reactions with granulom-formation (accompanied with eosinophilic leucocytes) around small blood vessels and capillaries. Bionecrotic changes of muscular fibres around granulom.

with cardiac callosity. in 4 cases.

(due to other factors).

(c) Epicardium :

Generally slight edema and considerable congestion in all cases.

with in severe degree in 7 cases.

with lymphocytes and leucocytes-infiltration in 15 cases.

177

HEART

			N 1	N 2	N 3	N 4	N 5	N 6	N 7	N 8	N 10	N 11	N 12	N 14	N 15	N 16	N 17	N 18	N 19	N 20
Parenchyma of Myocardium	Fragmentation		+++	—	÷	—	∸	—	—	—	(++)	—	—	—	—	—	—	÷	—	++
	Brown Pigment		++	—	+	∸	÷	—	—	++	+	++	+	+	+	—	+	++	∸	++
	Atrophia		++	(+++)	+	++	+	+++	++	÷	+	∸	+	(+)	+	+	+	(+)	÷	++
	Hypertrophia		∸	—	∸	—	—	—	—	∸	÷	÷	—	÷	—	—	∸	∸	—	—
	Disappearance of Striations		++	(+++)	++	+	++	(++)	(+++)	+	++	++	+	÷	+	+	++	++	++	++
	Cloudy Swelling		++	++	++	++	++	(++)	++	++	++	++	++	+	++	(++)	++	(+++)	++	++
	Vacuolar Degeneration		∸	(+)	(∸)	∸	—	—	—	—	∸	—	—	∸	—	—	÷	—	(++)	—
	Hyaline Degeneration		—	—	—	—	—	—	—	—	—	—	—	—	—	—	—	(∸)	∸	—
	Waxy Necrosis		—	—	—	—	—	—	—	—	—	—	—	—	—	—	—	—	—	—
	Changes of Nuclei	Pyknosis	÷	+	÷	+	+	÷	∸	∸	∸	∸	∸	∸	∸	+	+	∸	÷	∸
		Swelling	∸	—	∸	∸	∸	—	∸	∸	÷	∸	—	∸	∸	—	÷	—	∸	∸
		Karyolysis	÷	÷	∸	+	÷	∸	÷	÷	+	÷	∸	∸	∸	∸	∸	+	÷	÷
		Disappearance	∸	∸	∸	÷	÷	÷	÷	÷	+	÷	∸	∸	—	—	∸	÷	÷	÷
Interstitium of Myocardium	Edema		++	(+)	÷	÷	+	÷	+	+	+	(+)	(++)	÷	÷	÷	+	÷	÷	++
	Hemorrhage		—	+	∸	++	+	—	—	—	÷	÷	÷	÷	+	÷	∸	+	∸	÷
	Contents of Blood Vessels	Erythrocytes	÷	++	+	++	÷	++	÷	÷	++	+	+	++	++	++	+++	+++	+	+
		Leucocytes	+	÷	+	—	—	—	∸	÷	(+)	—	—	÷	+++	(++)	÷	++	—	—
		Lymphocytes	+	÷	∸	∸	—	—	∸	∸	—	—	—	∸	÷	∸	—	—	—	∸
		Monocytes	∸	—	—	—	—	—	÷	÷	∸	—	—	—	∸	—	—	—	∸	—
	Infiltration of Leucocytes		∸	∸	—	++	—	—	∸	∸	∸	—	—	—	÷	÷	∸	∸	—	—
	Infiltration of Lymphocytes		—	∸	∸	(+++)	—	∸	∸	—	÷	—	—	—	—	—	∸	∸	—	∸
	Proliferation of Histiocytes		÷	∸	∸	÷	÷	∸	∸	∸	∸	∸	—	∸	∸	∸	∸	÷	∸	∸
	Changes of Vessel walls	Thickening	—	—	—	—	—	—	—	—	—	+	—	—	—	—	÷	—	—	—
		Edema	÷	—	÷	∸	∸	—	∸	(+)	÷	∸	∸	∸	÷	—	∸	÷	∸	÷
		Adventitial Cells	∸	÷	÷	(+)	—	÷	÷	∸	—	—	∸	—	—	(+)	÷	—	—	∸
	Perivascular Edema		++	—	+	+	÷	÷	÷	÷	+	÷	+	÷	+	÷	(++)	+	÷	+
Endocard.	Edema		++	÷	+	|	|	+	∸	+	∸	÷	|	÷	|	∸	÷	∸	|	÷
	Infiltration	Erythrocytes	—	—	—	|	|	—	—	—	—	—	|	—	|	—	—	—	|	—
		Leucocytes	—	—	—	|	|	—	—	—	—	—	|	—	|	—	—	—	|	—
		Lymphocytes	—	∸	∸	|	|	—	∸	—	—	—	|	—	|	∸	—	—	|	—
	Proliferation of Mesenchym Cells		∸	∸	∸	|	|	—	÷	÷	—	—	|	—	|	(÷)	—	—	|	—
Epicardium	Edema		÷	++	÷	÷	÷	+	+	+	÷	÷	++	+	+	÷	+	|	÷	+
	Congestion		+	++	++	++	÷	÷	÷	—	++	+	—	++	++	++	++	|	+	+
	Infiltration	Erythrocytes	÷	++	—	+	++	—	—	—	—	÷	—	÷	÷	∸	÷	|	(÷)	—
		Leucocytes	—	+	—	÷	∸	—	—	—	∸	∸	∸	—	∸	—	—	|	—	—
		Lymphocytes	∸	÷	+	+	—	÷	∸	÷	÷	—	+	∸	∸	÷	÷	|	∸	+
		Histiocytes	∸	÷	∸	∸	∸	+	∸	∸	÷	÷	÷	÷	—	÷	∸	|	∸	+

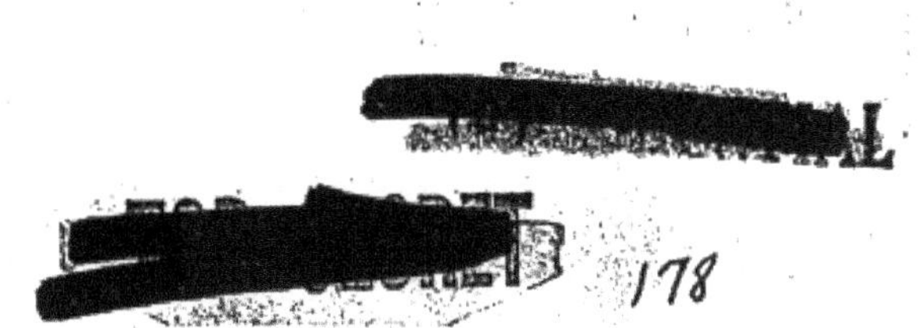

178

HEART

			N 21	N 23	N 24	N 26	N 27	N 29	N 30	N 32	N 33	N 34	N 35	N 36	N 38	N 40	N 42	N 44	N 46	N 47
Parenchyma of Myocardium	Fragmentation		−	−	+	−	−	+	÷	+	−	−	÷	÷	÷	−	÷	−		÷
	Brown Pigment		(+)	++	÷	+	+++	÷	−	(++)	−	÷	÷	+++	+	++	÷	−		(÷)
	Atrophia		÷	÷	+	÷	÷	(+++)	(++)	+	+	+	÷	+	+	÷	+	++		++
	Hypertrophia		−	−	÷	−	−	−	−	−	−	−	−	−	−	−	−	−		−
	Disappearance of Striations		+	+	+	+÷	++	++	(++÷)	++	++	+	+	+	+	+	+	++		+
	Cloudy Swelling		+	++÷	+÷	+÷	++	++	(+++÷)	+÷	++	+	+÷	+	+	+	+	++÷	S	+÷
	Vacuolar Degeneration		−	−	−	−	÷	÷	÷	−	÷	÷	÷	÷	−	÷	−	÷	E	−
	Hyaline Degeneration		−	−	−	−	−	−	÷	−	÷	−	−	−	−	−	−	−	G	−
	Waxy Necrosis		−	−	−	−	−	−	−	−	−	−	−	−	−	−	−	−	N	−
	Changes of Nuclei	Pyknosis	÷	÷	÷	÷	÷	+	(+)	÷	÷	÷	÷	÷	÷	÷	÷	÷	A	÷
		Swelling	÷	÷	÷	÷	÷	÷	÷	÷	÷	÷	÷	−	÷	−	÷	÷	H	−
		Karyolysis	÷	÷	÷	÷	÷	÷	(+)	÷	÷	÷	÷	÷	÷	÷	÷	÷	C	÷
		Disappearance	÷	÷	÷	÷	÷	÷	(+)	÷	÷	÷	÷	÷	−	÷	÷	÷		÷
Interstitium of Myocardium	Edema		÷	÷	+	÷	÷	+	+	÷	+	+	÷	+	+	÷	÷	÷	L	+
	Hemorrhage		++	+	−	÷	−	÷	−	(++)	÷	÷	÷	+	−	−	+	÷	A	+÷
	Contents of Blood Vessels	Erythrocytes	++	++	+	+	+	+	++	+÷	++	++	++	+	+	++	++	÷	T	+
		Leucocytes	++	+	÷	++	−	−	÷	++	÷	÷	+	÷	+	−	−	−	R	÷
		Lymphocytes	÷	÷	−	+	−	÷	÷	÷	÷	÷	÷	÷	÷	−	÷	−	O	÷
		Monocytes	÷	÷	−	÷	−	−	÷	÷	÷	÷	÷	÷	÷	−	÷	−	M	−
	Infiltration of Leucocytes		÷	÷	−	−	−	−	−	(÷)	÷	−	−	−	−	−	−	−	T	−
	Infiltration of Lymphocytes		÷	÷	−	−	−	−	−	(÷)	−	−	÷	−	÷	−	÷	−	S	−
	Proliferation of Histiocytes		÷	÷	÷	÷	÷	−	÷	÷	−	−	÷	÷	−	−	÷	÷	O	÷
	Changes of Vessel Walls	Thickening	−	−	−	−	÷	−	−	−	−	−	−	−	−	−	−	−	P	−
		Edema	÷	÷	−	÷	÷	÷	÷	÷	−	÷	÷	÷	÷	(+)	÷	−		÷
		Adventitial Cells	−	÷	÷	÷	÷	(÷)	+	−	−	−	(+)	÷	÷	−	÷	−	E	−
	Perivascular Edema		+	÷	÷	÷	÷	÷	+	÷	+	÷	÷	÷	÷	+÷	÷	+	S	+
Endocard.	Edema		÷	÷	÷	÷	÷	(+)	÷	÷	÷	÷	+	÷	+	÷	÷	+	N	÷
	Infiltration	Erythrocytes	−	−	−	−	−	−	−	−	−	−	−	−	−	−	−	−	E	−
		Leucocytes	−	−	−	−	−	−	−	−	−	−	−	−	−	−	−	÷	T	−
		Lymphocytes	−	−	−	−	−	−	−	−	−	÷	÷	−	−	−	−	÷	N	−
	Proliferation of Mesenchym Cells		−	−	÷	−	−	÷	−	−	−	(+)	÷	(÷)	−	(÷)	(÷)	÷	I	−
Epicardium	Edema		+	÷	+	÷	÷	|	+	÷	÷	÷	÷	÷	+	÷	÷	+		÷
	Congestion		+	++	++	+	++	|	+	++	+	++	++	++	|	+	÷	+		++
	Infiltration	Erythrocytes	+	÷	+	−	−	|	÷	+	−	÷	÷	++	|	−	÷	+		+
		Leucocytes	÷	−	−	−	−	|	−	÷	−	−	÷	+	|	−	−	÷		−
		Lymphocytes	÷	÷	÷	÷	+	|	÷	(+)	÷	÷	÷	+	|	(÷)	÷	÷		+
		Histiocytes	÷	÷	÷	÷	+	|	÷	÷	÷	÷	+	÷	|	(÷)	÷	+		÷

179

HEART

			S 1	S 2	S 3	S 4	S 5	S 6	S 8	S 9	S 10	S 12	S 14	S 15	S 19	S 22	S 26	S 28	S 35	K 1	K 2
Parenchyma of Myocardium	Fragmentation		—	—	++	÷	∸	—	÷	÷	÷	—	—	—	—	—	—	÷	—	—	÷
	Brown Pigment		+	—	∸	—	∸	—	+÷	+÷	+÷	+	+	÷	÷	—	÷	(+÷)	—	++÷	∸
	Atrophia		÷	+	+	+÷	(++)	÷	+÷	++÷	+	÷	++	÷	÷	+÷	÷	÷	++÷	÷	(++)
	Hypertrophia		—	—	∸	—	—	—	—	—	—	—	—	—	—	—	—	—	—	—	—
	Disappearance of Striations		+	+÷	++÷	++÷	+	÷	+++	+++	+÷	+÷	+÷	++÷	+	+	+	+	+÷	++	++
	Cloudy Swelling		+	+÷	++÷	++÷	+	÷	+++	+++	+÷	++	+÷	++÷	+	+÷	+	+	+÷	++	++÷
	Vacuolar Degeneration		—	÷	+	÷	÷	—	+÷	+	—	—	—	∸	—	∸	—	∸	—	—	∸
	Hyaline Degeneration		—	—	∸	—	—	—	+	+	—	—	—	—	—	—	—	—	—	—	—
	Waxy Necrosis		—	—	—	—	—	—	—	—	—	—	—	—	—	—	—	—	—	—	—
	Changes of Nuclei	Pyknosis	—	∸	÷	+	∸	—	÷	∸	—	∸	÷	∸	∸	∸	∸	∸	÷	∸	÷
		Swelling	÷	∸	÷	∸	÷	—	÷	∸	—	∸	—	÷	∸	∸	∸	∸	—	∸	—
		Karyolysis	÷	÷	+	÷	∸	∸	++	+÷	÷	÷	+	+	÷	÷	÷	÷	÷	+	+
		Disappearance	∸	∸	+	÷	—	—	+	+	∸	∸	÷	∸	∸	∸	∸	∸	—	∸	÷
Interstitium of Myocardium	Edema		÷	÷	+	+÷	++	÷	(++÷)	+	+÷	÷	+	÷	(+)	÷	+	÷	+	÷	+
	Hemorrhage		+	∸	—	+	—	(÷)	÷	—	—	—	÷	∸	—	—	+	÷	(+)	+	+
	Contents of Blood vessels	Erythrocytes	+	++	+	+	+	+	÷	+	+	++	+	÷	÷	÷	++	÷	+	++	÷
		Leucocytes	++	÷	—	+	∸	÷	—	÷	∸	÷	—	∸	—	—	—	—	∸	—	—
		Lymphocytes	∸	—	∸	÷	—	÷	÷	—	∸	∸	—	∸	—	—	—	—	—	∸	—
		Monocytes	∸	∸	—	∸	∸	—	÷	∸	∸	∸	—	∸	—	—	—	∸	—	∸	—
	Infiltration of Leucocytes		∸	—	—	÷	—	—	—	—	—	—	—	∸	—	+	—	—	—	—	—
	Infiltration of Lymphocytes		—	∸	∸	∸	∸	÷	—	—	∸	—	—	∸	∸	∸	∸	—	—	∸	÷
	Proliferation of Histiocytes		÷	∸	∸	∸	∸	∸	(÷)	∸	∸	∸	—	∸	∸	+++	∸	∸	∸	∸	÷
	Changes of Vessel Walls	Thickening	—	—	—	—	—	—	∸	—	—	—	—	—	—	—	—	—	—	—	—
		Edema	∸	∸	∸	+	∸	∸	—	∸	∸	∸	∸	÷	∸	∸	∸	÷	∸	∸	÷
		Adventitial Cells	—	÷	÷	∸	∸	+	(÷)	(÷)	÷	—	—	÷	—	++	—	—	—	∸	—
	Perivascular Edema		+	÷	+	+÷	++	÷	÷	÷	+	÷	+	+	+	÷	+	÷	÷	+	+
Endocard.	Edema		÷	÷	÷	|	+	÷	÷	∸	÷	÷	+	|	|	÷	+	|	÷	÷	+
	Infiltration	Erythrocytes	—	—	—	|	—	—	—	—	—	—	—	|	|	—	—	|	—	—	—
		Leucocytes	—	—	—	|	—	—	—	—	—	—	—	|	|	+	—	|	—	—	—
		Lymphocytes	—	—	—	|	—	—	—	—	∸	—	—	|	|	∸	—	|	—	—	—
	Proliferation of Mesenchym Cells		—	—	—	|	—	—	(÷)	—	∸	—	—	|	|	+++	—	|	—	∸	—
Epicardium	Edema		+	+	÷	+	+	÷	÷	+	+	÷	÷	÷	+	÷	—	|	+	÷	÷
	Congestion		+	+	+	++	++	++	+	+	+÷	+	+	+	÷	÷	+	|	++	÷	+÷
	Infiltration	Erythrocytes	—	—	—	∸	—	+	—	—	—	—	∸	÷	—	+	÷	|	—	÷	÷
		Leucocytes	∸	—	—	—	—	—	—	—	—	—	—	—	—	÷	—	|	—	—	—
		Lymphocytes	÷	∸	∸	+	∸	+	∸	∸	∸	∸	∸	∸	—	÷	∸	|	+	—	—
		Histiocytes	÷	∸	∸	÷	(∸)	+÷	∸	∸	÷	÷	÷	∸	∸	++	÷	|	÷	∸	∸

Congestion and some pericapillary bleeding.

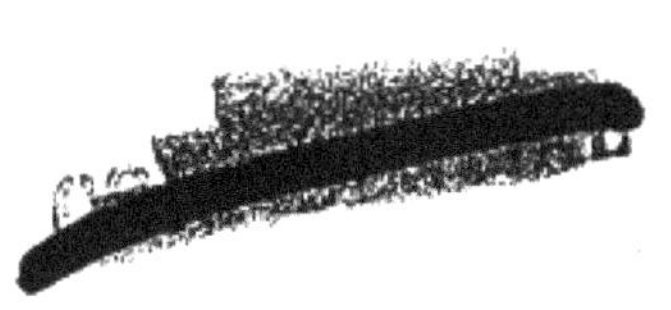

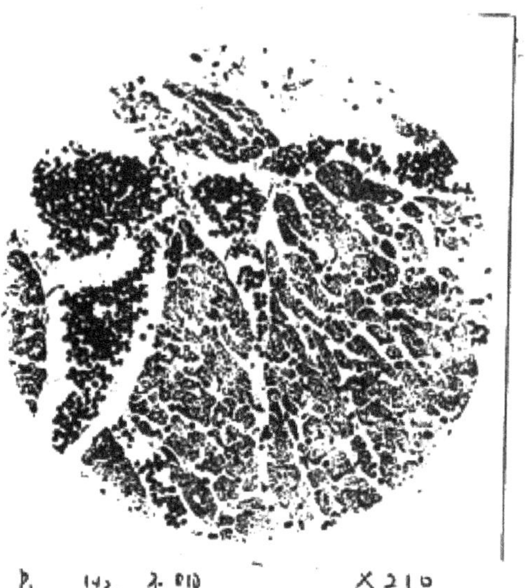

P. 142. 7.010 X210

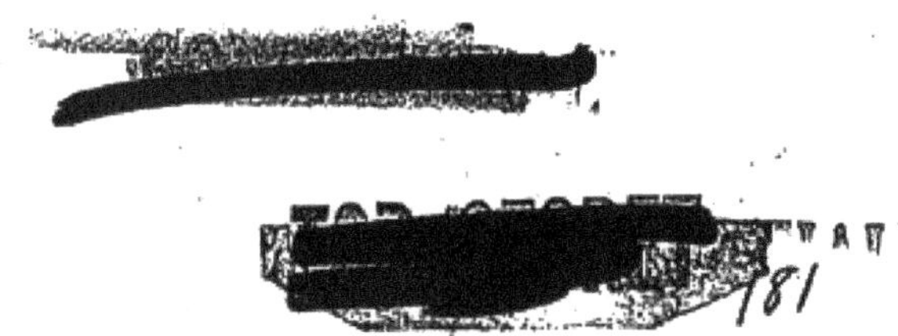

Mesenchymal reaction with some wandering cells.

Endocard-reaction(mesenchymal reaction) in severe degree.

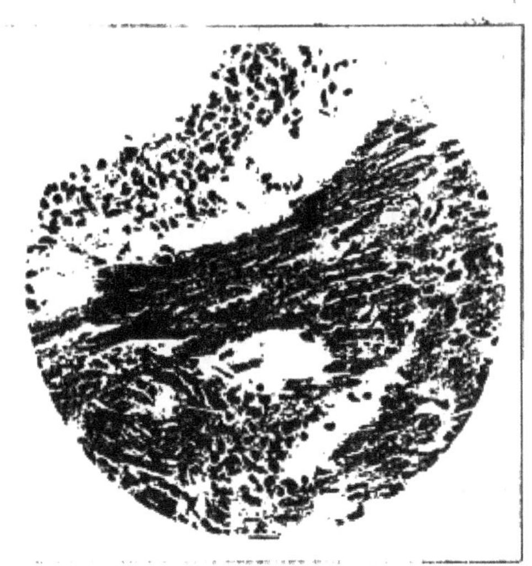

182

Degeneratio myocardii gravis.

Rheumatoid-knot at perivascular portion.

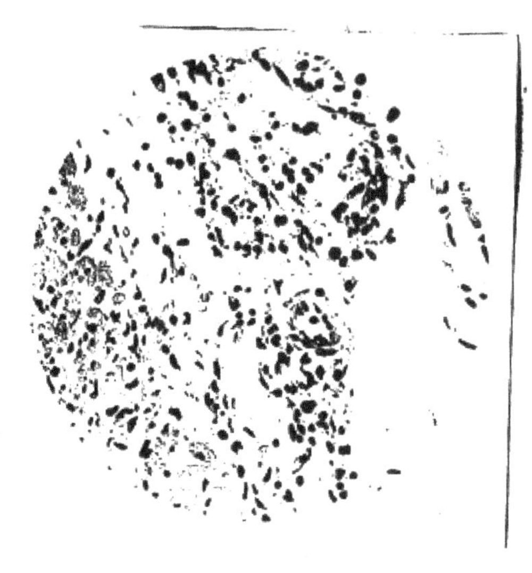

183

Lung

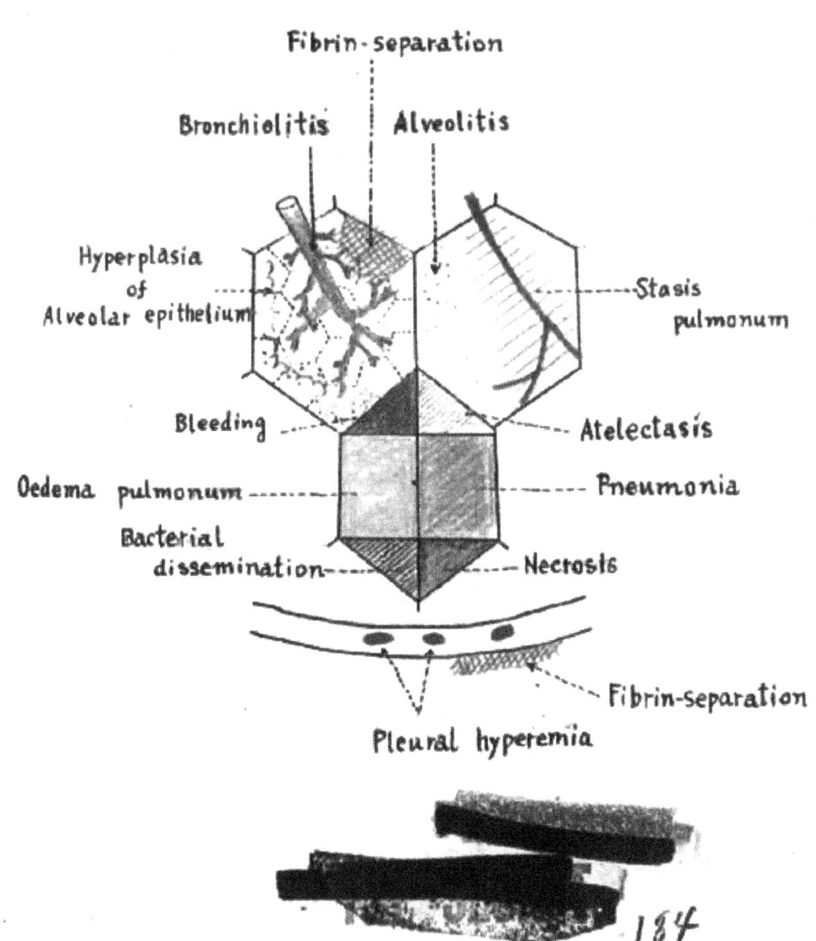
Fibrin-separation
Bronchiolitis
Alveolitis
Hyperplasia of Alveolar epithelium
Stasis pulmonum
Bleeding
Atelectasis
Oedema pulmonum
Pneumonia
Bacterial dissemination
Necrosis
Fibrin-separation
Pleural hyperemia
184

(A) Microssop. Investigation.

1. 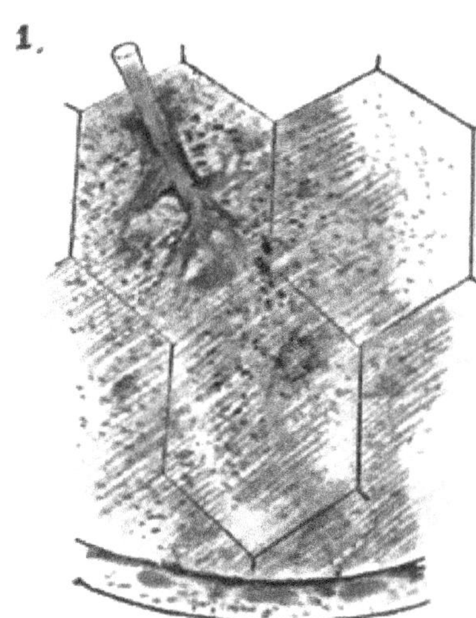

I. Lobar pneumonia, exudative-hemorrhagic.

. Lobar pnemonia with numerous leucocytes, massive serous exudates, some erythrocytes and some desquamated alveolar epitheliums all over the pulmonal tissues, with some bacterial accumulation at some places.

. Fibrinous and edematous swelling of alveolar walls.

. Considerable edematous swelling, considerable congestion and some bacterial dissemination in pleural tissues and some bacterial accumulation in subpleural tissues.

. Considerable anthracosis of pulmonal and pleural tissues.

3. 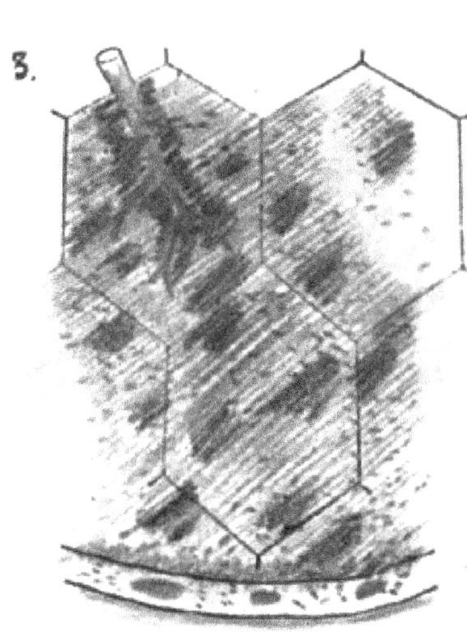

2. (missed.)

3. left, superior.

. Lobar pneumonia with numerous leucocytes, massive serous exsudates, some desquamated alveolar epitheliums, and some bacterial dissemination at some places all over the pulmonal tissues.

. Edematous and fibrinous swelling of alveolar walls.

185

. Intense edematous swelling of inter-lobular connective tissues and some bacterial accumulation at the perivascular tissues.

. Bronchitis catarrhalis with massive mucous masse:

. Pleuritis exsudativa with some bacterial and leucocytic dissemination in the pleural tissues with some serous masses on the pleural surfaces.

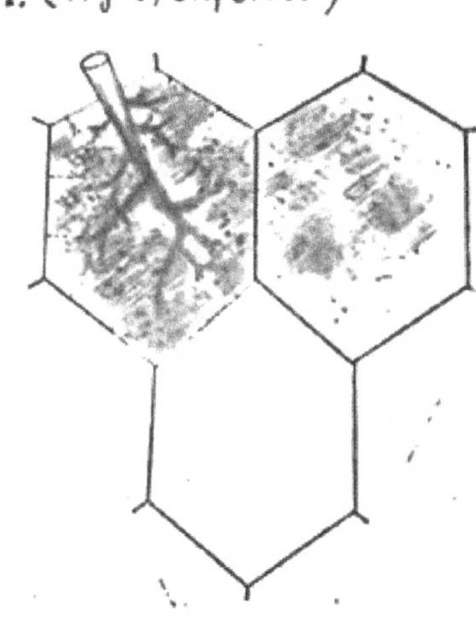

4.(right, superior.)

. Bronchitis and Bronchiolitis catarrhalis.

. Slight Alveoliitis with slight edematous swelling and moderate congestion of alveolar walls, and following changes :

. Some acinous areas with inflammatory edema, some desquamáted alveolar epighelíums, slight leucocytes-dissemination and slight hemorrhages.

——— multiple acinous pneumonic changes.

. Considerable congestion in the inter-lobular connective tissues.

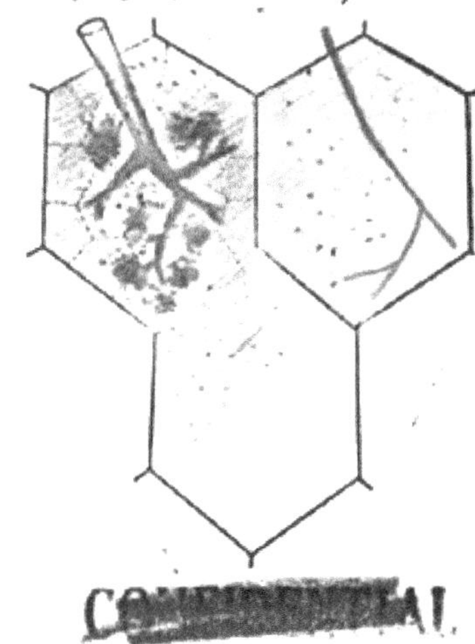

4.(right, median.)

. Bronchitis and Bronchiolitis catarrhalis.

. Considerable congestion and slight swelling of alveolar walls (slight Alveolitis) and atelectasis.

. At some acinous or miliary areas with some leucocytes-dissemination.

Without any remarkable perifocal changes. ---

186

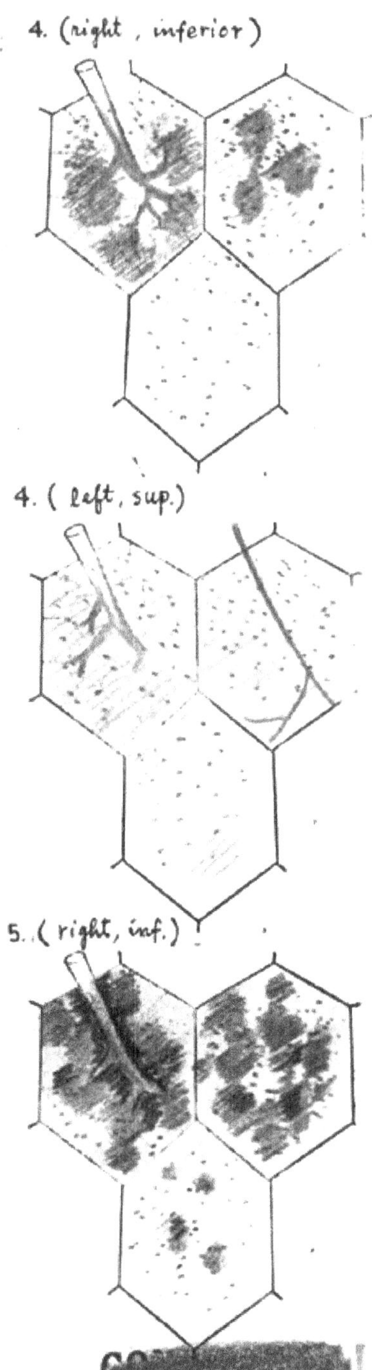

multiple miliary leucocytic pneumonia.

4.(right, inferior.)

. Bronchitis catarrhalis.

. Some acinous or acinous-lobular areas with massive serous exudates, some desquamated alveolar epitheliums slight leucocytes-dissemination, and slight hemorrhages. --multiple acinous,exudative pneumonic changes.

. Diffuse edematous swelling and some congestion of alveolar walls (slight diffuse Alveolitis).

4.(left, superior.)

. Diffuse Alveolitis with some edematous swelling, some congestion and some leucocytes-emigration in alveolar walls.

. At some lobular areas with some inflammatory edema and some slight desquamted alveolar epighelíums. ---- Stasis et edema pulmonum.

. Considerable congestion and some edematous swelling in interlobular connective tissues.

4.(left, inferior.)

. With the same changes, as above mentioned.

5.(right, inferior.)

. Remarkable inflammatory edema all over the pulmonal tissues with massive serous exudats, some leucocytes-dissemination (at some places with

187

CONFIDENTIAL

multiple acinous or acino-miliary pneumonic changes with numerous leucocytes-emigrations), some desquamated alveolar epitheliums, slight hemorrhages and massive bacterial accumulation at some places.

5. (left.)

. Peribronchiolar tissues with some bacterial accumulation and considerable edematous swelling.

. Hyalinous degneration of muscle-fibres of bronchial walls.

5. (left.)

. Lobar pneumonia with numerous leucocytes and bacterial dissemination all over the pulmonal tissues with some desquamated alveolar epitheliums and some serous exudates.

. Peribronchitis with remarkable edematous swelling, fibrin- separation and some hyalinous degeneration of muscle-fibres of bronchial walls.

6. (right.)

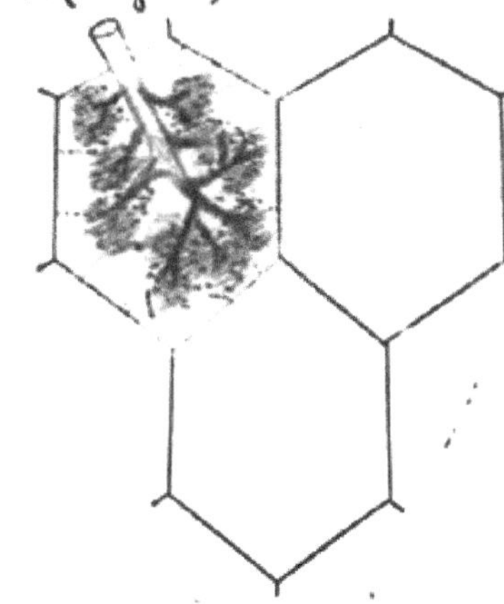

6. (right.) (mainly at the intercary portion of lung).

. Acinous-lobular leucocytic pneumonia with numerous leucocytes-dissemination and some edematous exsudates. These pneumonic areas are bounded more or less sharply without any remarkable perifocal changes.

. Bronchus without any slignificant changes and bronchiolus with severe catarrh (massive mucous secretion).

188

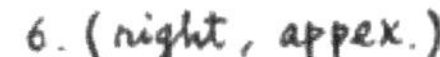

6.(right, appex.)

. Slight diffuse Alveolitis with considerable edematous swelling, considerable congestion and some leucocytes-accumulation in alveolar walls.

. These Alveolitis spread at some acino-lobular areas into the pneumonic changes with some inflammatory edema, some leucocytes-emigration and some desquamated alveolar epitheliums.

. Considerable congestion and slight edematous swelling of interlobular connective tissues.

7. (left.)

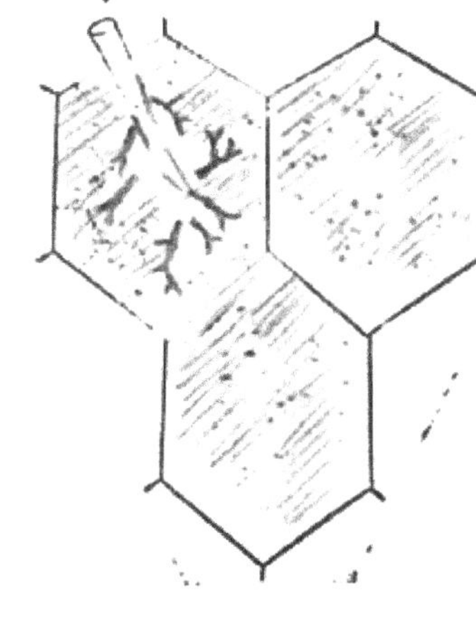

7.(left.)

. Slight diffuse Alveolitis with considerable

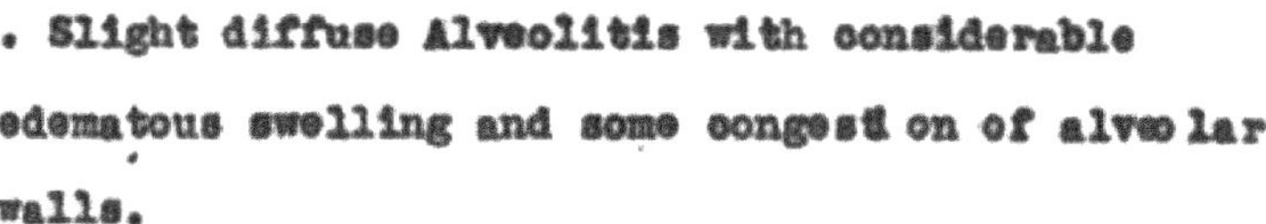

edematous swelling and some congestion of alveolar walls.

. In some acino-lobular areas with some inflammatory edema, slight leucocytes-emigrations, some desquamated alveolar epitheliums and slight leakage of erythrocytes in alveoli.

8.(right and left.)

. No particular changes.

9. (missed).

10. (right, sup.)

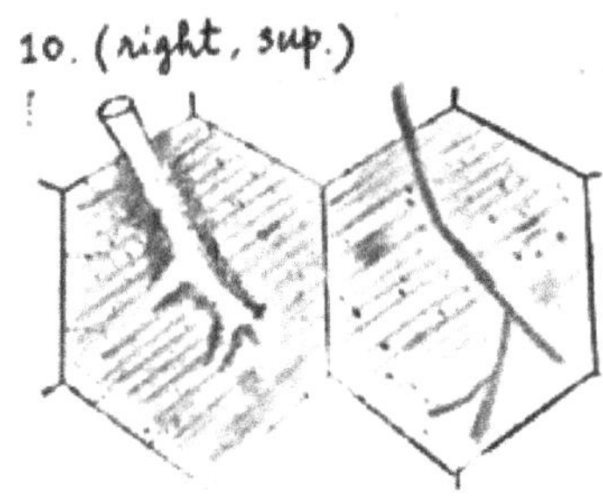

10.(right, superior.)

. Edema (inflammatory edema) and stasis pulmonum, with considerable congestion, considerable edematous swelling of alveolar walls and considerable

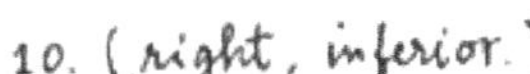

serous exsudat and slight leucocytes-emigration all over the pulmonal tissues.

. Slight congestion and slight edematous swelling of interlobular connective tissues.

10. (right, inferior.)

. Lobar pneumonia in the gray hepatisation, with numerous leucocytes, some serous exsudates, at some places slight hemorrhages or at some places some bacterial accumulation, all over the pulmonal tissues.

. Intense fibrinous swelling of alveolar walls.

. Some bacterial accumulation at perivascular portions.

10. (left, superior.)

. Edema pulmonum levis.

10. (left, inferior.)

. Edema pulmonum levis.

11. (right, superior.)

. Multiple (hematogenous) lobular pneumonia with numerous leucocytes, some desquamated alveolar epigheliums and some serous exsudates.

. Interlobular connective tissues with intense edematous swelling, some fibrinous separative masses and some leucocytes emigration, especially at perivascular portions.

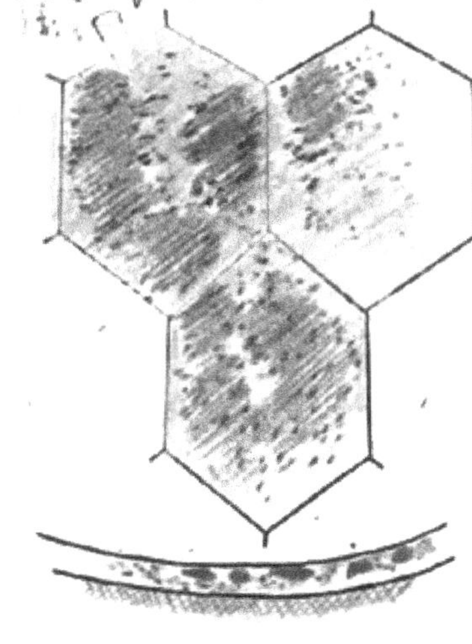

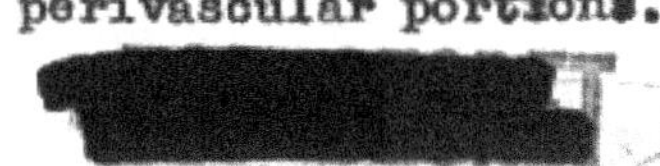

190

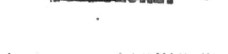

• Considerable congestion and some edematous swelling of the pleural tissues with some sero-fibrinous masses on the pleural surfaces.

• Considerable congestion, some edematous swelling and some leucocytes-emigration in pleural tissues with some sero-fibrinous masses on the pleural surfaces. -- Pleuritis fibrino-exsudativa.

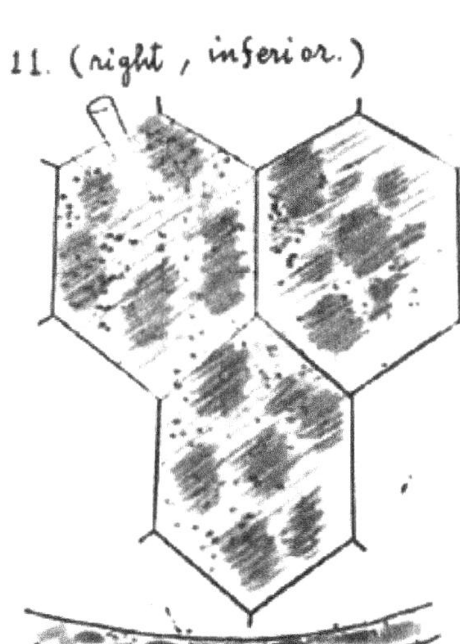

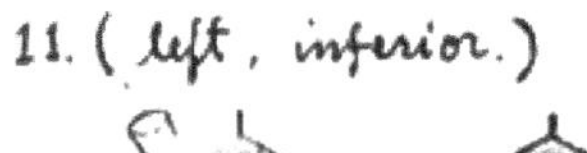

11. (right, inferior.)

• Diffuse Alveolitis with following changes :

• Multifocal acino-lobular pneumonia with some leucocytes-emigration and considerable serous exudation.

• And intense inflammatory edema all over the pulmonal tissues with massive serous exudates.

• Intense edematous swelling of inter-lobular connective tissues.

• Pleuritis fibrino-haemorrhagica with considerable congestion, some edematous swelling, some leucocytes-emigration in pleural tissues and some sero-fibrinous masses on the pleural surfaces.

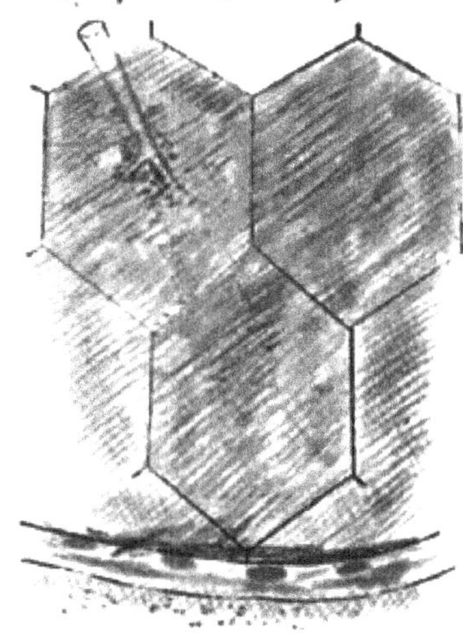

11. (left, inferior.)

• Lobar pneumonia with remarkable leucocytes-emigration and remarkable separation of fibrinous masses all over the pulmonal tissues.

• Intense fibrinous and hyalinous and hyalinous swelling [illegible] with considerable

191

12.

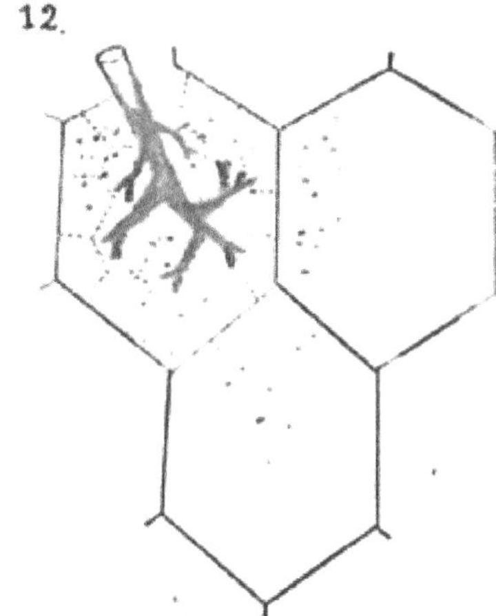

edematous swelling, some congestion and some separated fibrinous amsses. CONFIDENTIAL

. Intense edematous swelling, some leucocytes dissemination and some fibrinous separation at peribronchial, perivascular and inter-lobular connective tissues.

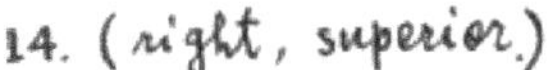

14. (right, superior.)

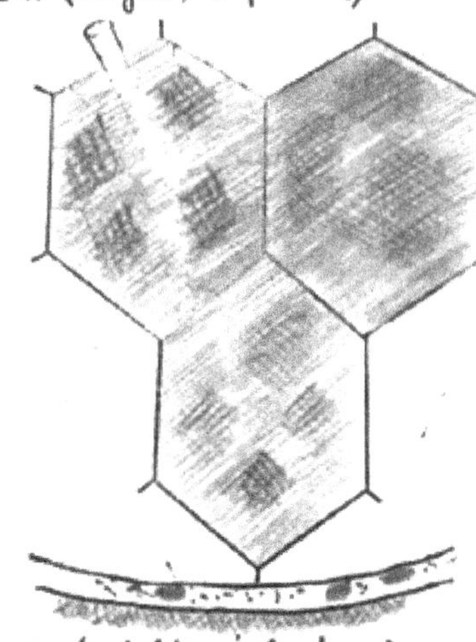

12.

. Bronchiolitis catarrhalis with considerable edematous swelling of alveolar walls with slight congestion and slight desquamation of alveolar epitheliums.

14. (right, superior.)

. Lobar pneumonia with numerous leucocytes and massive fibrinous masses all over the pulmonal tissues.

. Intense fibrinous swelling of alveolar walls.

. At the other hand, slight tendency of proliferative reaction with some histiocytes-increase in the inter-lobular and pleural connective tissues.

14. (right, inferior.)

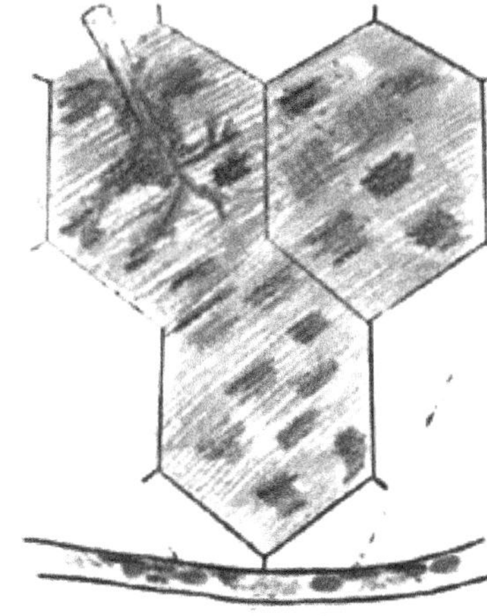

14.(right, inferior.)

. Lobar pneumonia with the same changes all over the pulmonal tissues.

. Pleuritis fibrino-haemorrhagica with considerable congestion, some edematous swelling and some sero-fibrinous masses on the pleural surfaces.

192

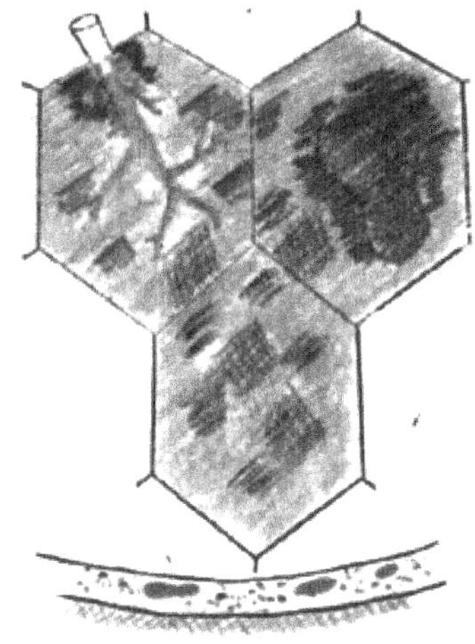

14.(left, superior.)

. Lobar pneumonia with numerous leucocytes, some fibrinous masses all over the pulmonal tissues and, at some places, with remarkable hemorrhages.

. Intense fibrinous swelling of alveolar walls, accompanied at the other hand with some increase of alveolar epitheliums.

. Lobar pneumonia fall into structureless, necrotic changes at some places.

. Bronchilolitis catarrhalis gravis with massive leucocytes and some mucous masses as contents.

. Peribronchiolitis gravis with remarkable fibrinous-hemorrhagic changes.

. Pleuritis fibrino-haemorrhagica with considerable congestion, remarkable edema, separation of some fibrinous masses, some leucocytes-emigration in pleural tissues and some serous masses on the pleural tissues and some serous masses on the pleural surface.

. Remarkable edematous and fibrinous swelling of inter-lobular connective tissues.

14.(left, inferior.)

. Lobar pneumonia with the same changes, as above mentioned and furthermore some bacterial dissemination.

193

15.(right, inferior.)

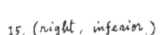

. Lobar pneumonia with numerous leucocytes and some fibrinous masses all over the pulmonal tissues.

. Intense fibrinous swelling of alveolar walls.

. Some remarkable bacterial accumulation at the peribronchiolar tissues and some pertial hemorrhages at some perivascular tissues.

. Considerable congestion and some partial hemorrhages in interlobular connective tissues.

. Bronchitis and Bronchiolitis catarrhalis gravis with numerous hemorrhagic masses, massive mucous or serous masses, some leucocytes and some desquamated epitheliums.

. Peribronchial tissues with remarkable edematous swelling, some bacterial dissemination and some leucocytes-emigration.

. Intense congestion and some intense partial hemorrhages in interlobular connective tissues.

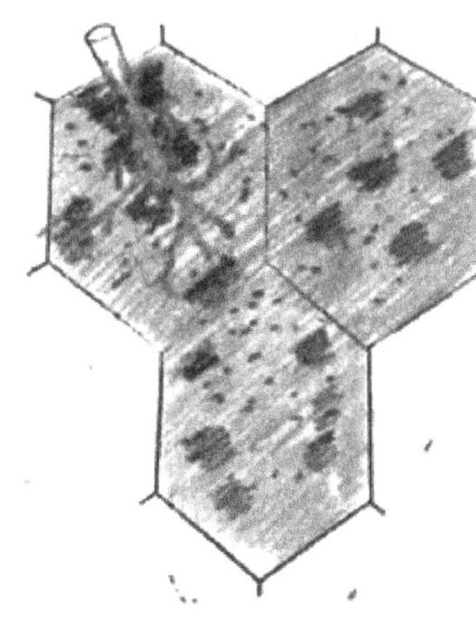

15.(left, superior.)

. Diffuse slight Alveolitis with considerable edematous swelling, and some congestion of alveolar walls and some following changes :

. Here and there are multifocal acino-lobular areas with intense exudative changes (considerable inflammatory edema, some leakage of

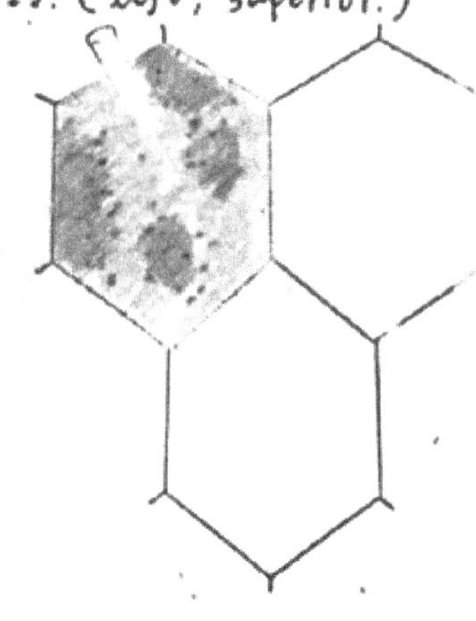

194

of erythrocytes and a few of leucocytes in alveoli).

15. (left, inferior.)

15. (left, inferior.)

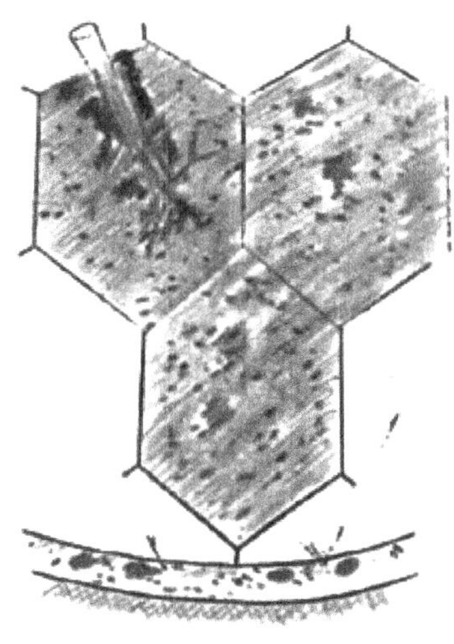

. Lobar pneumonia with numerous leucocytes and some hemorrhages all over the pulmonal tissues. Intense fibrinous and hyalinous swelling of alveolar walls.

. Considerable congestion and some edematous swelling of interlobular connective tissues and some bacterial accumulation at peribronchial tissues.

. Bronchitis catarrhalis gravis with massive serous or mucous masses, some leucocytes, some desquamated epithelia and intense Peribronchitis with intense edematous swelling, considerable bacterial-accumulation and some congestion.

. Remarkable congestion and some remarkable partial hemorrhages in interlobular connective tissues.

. Pleural tissues with remarkable congestion, remarkable edematous swelling, some bacterial dissemination and some fibrinous masses.

. Some bacterial accumulation at subpleural tissues and some sero-fibrinous masses on the pleural surface.

. Some anthracosis in the pulmonal and pleural

1195

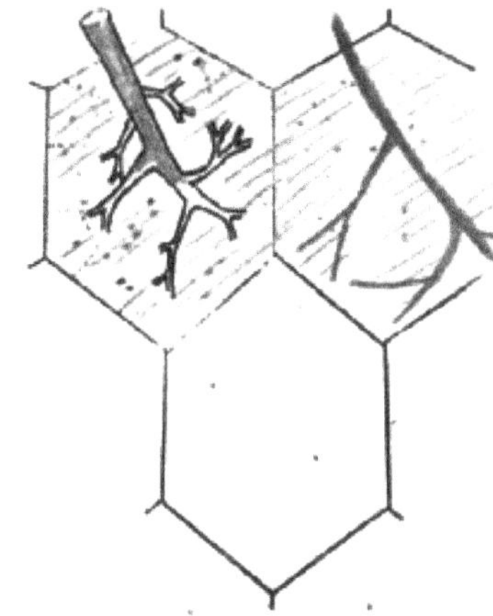

tissues.

16. (left, inferior.)

. Diffuse Alveolitis with considerable congestion, some edematous swelling and some leucocytes and lymphocytes-emigration in. alveolar walls.

. Some serous masses in alveoli--Stasis et edema pulmonum levis.

. Bronchitis catarrhalis with some mucous masses. Bronchiolus terminalis without any significant changes.

. Considerable congestion and slight edematous swelling of intelobular tissues.

18. (right and left.)

. Slight emphysema and no remarkable changes else.

17.

17.

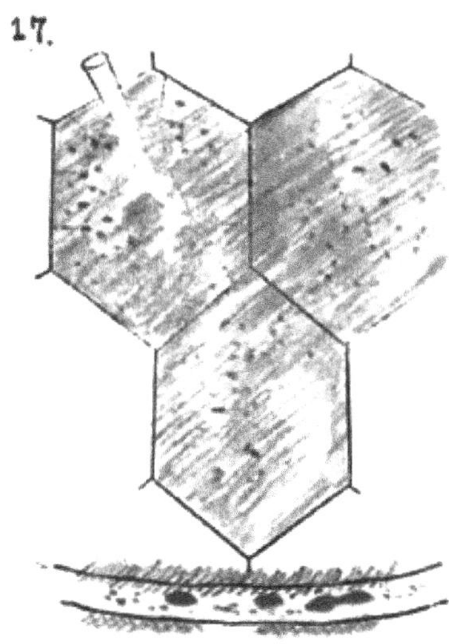

. Lobar pneumonia with some (not numerous) leucocytes -emigration, massive inflammatory sevous masses, some desquamated alveolar epithelia and some erythrocytes-leakage in alveoli all over the pulmonal tissues.

. Accompanied with some bacterial dissemination.

. Intense fibrinous or hyalinous swelling of alveolar walls at some places.

. Bronchitis catarrhalis with massive serous masses

196

and peribronchial tissues with considerable edematous with considerable edematous swelling and some bacterial accumulation.

. Considerable edematous swelling and some congestion of pleural tissues with some bacterial accumulation in subpleural tissues.

19. (right, superior)

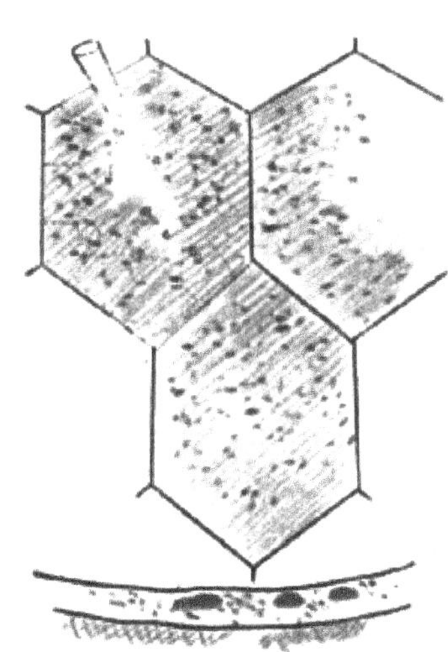

19. (right, superior.)

. Lobar pneumonia with some leucocytes-dissemination, massive serous masses, some desquamated alveolar epitheliums and some erythrocytes-leakages in alveoli all over the pulmonal tissues.

. Intense fibrinous swelling, some congestion and some edematous swelling of alveolar walls.

. Considerable edematous swelling of inter-lobular tissues and edematous degeneration of muscle-fibres of bronchial walls.

. Bronchitis catarrhalis with some serous or mucous masses as contents.

. Pleuritis fibrino-haemorrhagica with considerable congestion, some edematous swelling, some leucocytes -emigration and some bacterial accumulation in pleural tissues with some fibrinous masses on the pleural surfaces.

197

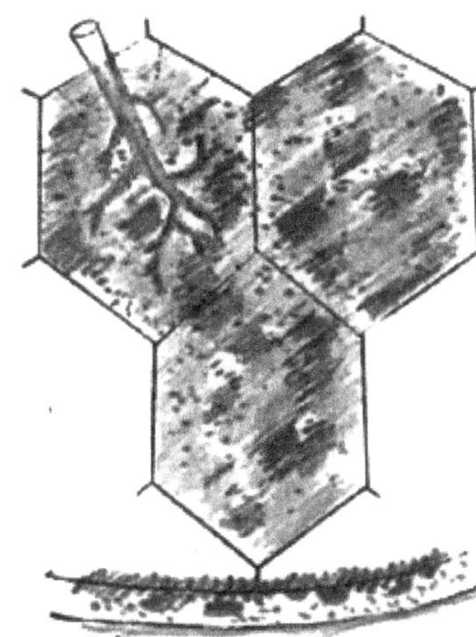

19. (right, inferior.)

19.
(right, inferirior.)

. Lobar pneumonia with some leucocytes-emigration, massive serous masses and some erythrocytes-leackages in alveoli of multiple lobular areas of pulmonal tissues.

. Accompanied with some bacterial dissemination.

. Bronchitis catarrhalis with some mucous masses.

. Peribronchial tissues with some edematous swelling and some bacterial accumulation.

. Pleuritis haemorrhagica with remarkable congestion, some diffuse hemorrhages and some leucocytes--dissemination in plerual tissues with some sero-fibrinous masses on the pleural surfaces.

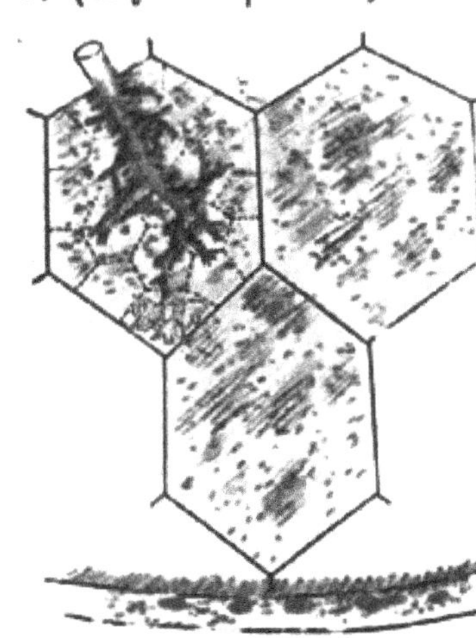

19. (left, superior.)

19.(left, superior.)

. Diffuse intense Alveolitis with considerable edematous swelling, congestion and some bacterial dissemination (at some places) in alveolar walls.

. Intense inflammatory edema, some erythrocytes-leakages, some leucocytes-dissemination and afew of bacterial accumulation (at some places) in alveoli all over the pulmonal tissues.

. Bronchitis and Bronchiolitis catarrhalis with some mucous masses as contents and Peribronchiolitis with some bacterial accumulation and some

198

edematous swelling and conge[illegible]

. Considerable congestion, some partial hemorrhages and some leucocytes-dissem ination in pleural tissues and some bacterial accumulation in subpleural tissues.

. Considerable congestion, some partial intense hemorrhages and considerable edematous swelling of interlobular tissues.

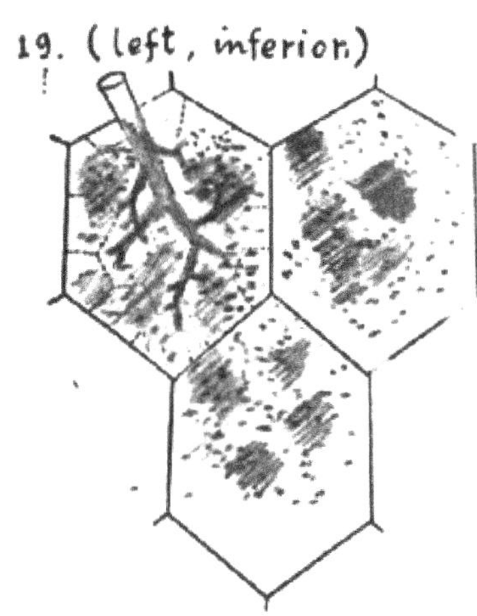

19. (left, inferior.)

. Diffuse Alveolitis with considerable congestion, some edematous swelling and some leucocytes-dissemination in alveolar walls and following changes :

. At some places (multiple acino-lobular areas) with considerable inflammatory edema, some erythrocytes--leakages, some leucocytes-dissemination and some desquamated alveolar epithelia in alveoli.

--- Acino-lobular pneumonia.

. Bronchitis catarrhalis with some mucous masses and some decayed masses as contents.

. Intense congestion and some edematous swelling of interlobular tissues.

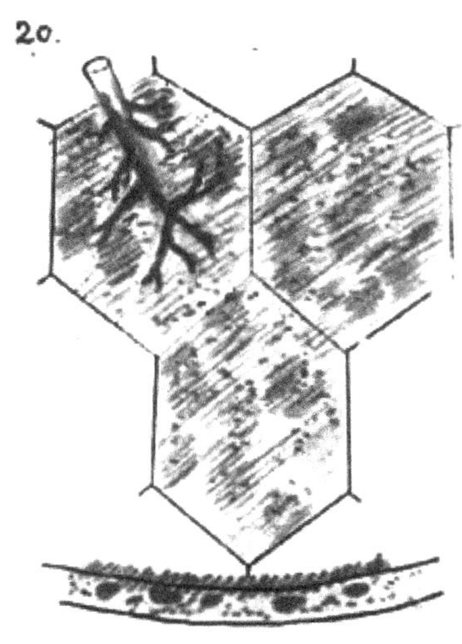

20.

. Diffuse intense Alveolitis with intense leucocytes-emigration, some congestion and some edematous swelling of alveolar walls.

199

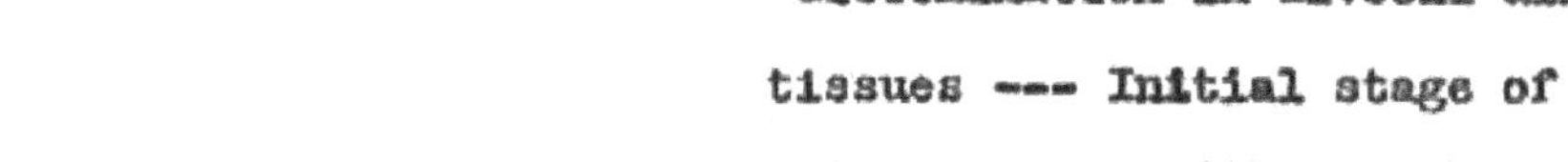

• Intense inflammatory edema with some leucocytes' -dissemination in alveoli all over the pulmonal tissues --- Initial stage of lobar pneumonia.

• Accompanied with some bacterial accumulation at some places.

21. (right, superior.)

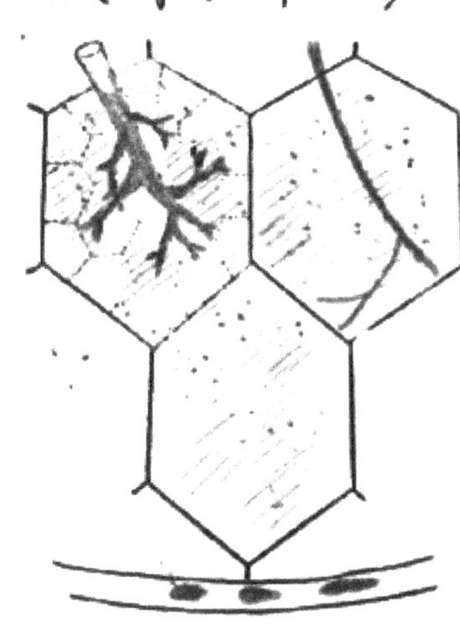

• Bronchitis catarrhalis with massive serous masses some leucocytes and some desquamated epitheliums as contents. Peribronchial tissues with considerabl edematous swelling.

• Considerable congestion and considerable edematou swelling of pleural tissues.

21. (right, superior.)

• Slight diffuse Alveolitis with considerable cong-estion and some edematous swelling of alveolar walls.

• Considerable congestion of inter-lobular connecti-ve tissues.

21. (right, inferior.)

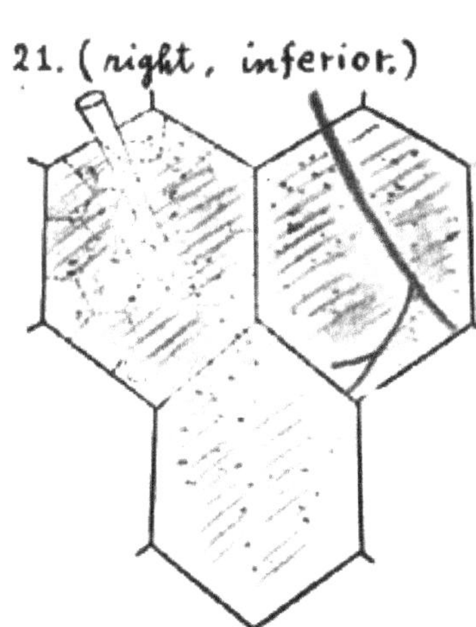

• Bronchitis and Bronchiolitis catarrhalis with som mucous masses .

• Intense congestion and some edematous swelling of pleural tissues.

21. (right, inferior.)

• Slight diffuse Alveolitis with considerable congestion, considerable edematous swelling and some separated fibrinous masses and a few of leucocytes-emigration in alveolar walls.

21. (left, superior.)

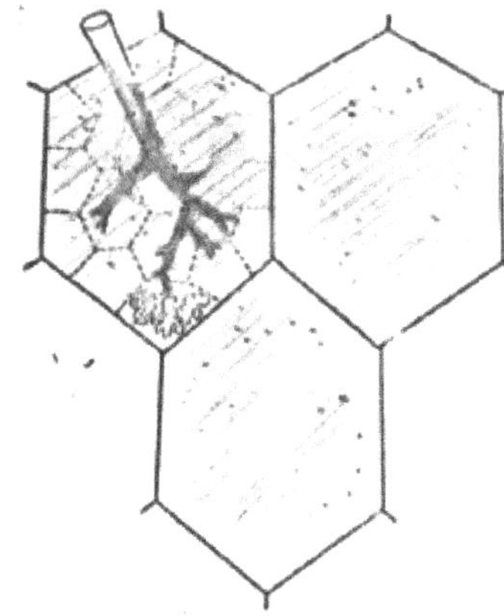

• Some inflammatory edema, some desquamated alveolar epithelia in alveoli scattered all over the pulmonal tissues.

---Edema pulmonum levis.

• Slight edematous swelling of pleural tissues.

21. (left, superior.)

• Slight diffuse alveolitis with considerable congestion, slight edematous swelling of alveolar walls and

21. (left, inferior.)

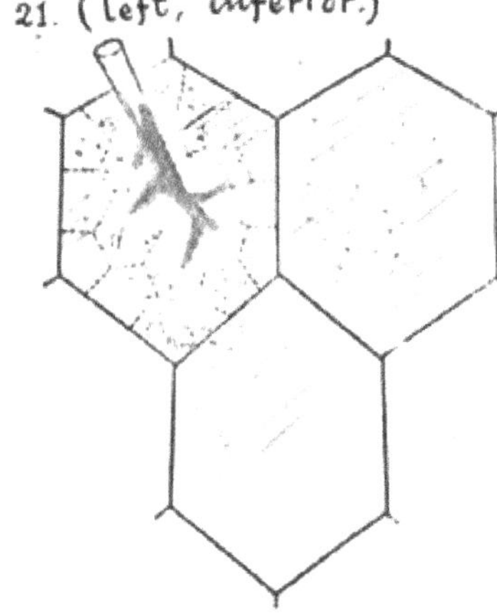

• Some inflammatory edema all over the pulmonal tissues-Edema pulmonum levis.

• Bronchitis catarrhalis levis with some mucous masses and some hemorrhagic masses as contents.

21. (left, inferior.)

• Slight congestion, slight edematous swelling, a few of leucocytes-dissemination in alveolar walls and some desquamated alveolar epithelia.

• Bronchitis catarrhalis levis with some mucous masses as contents.

23, (right, superior.)

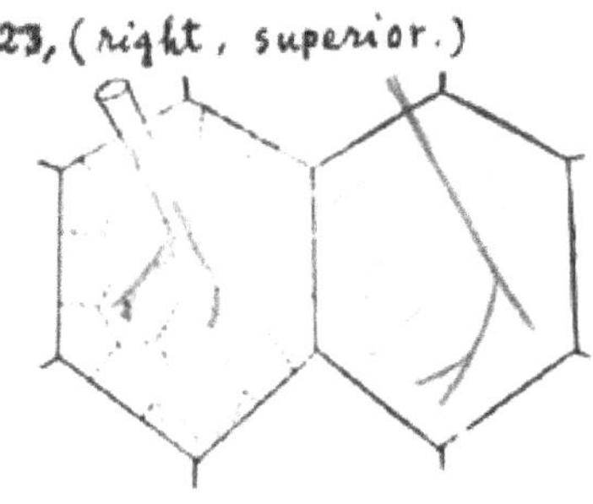

23. (right, superior.)

• Considerable congestion and some edematous swelling of alveolar walls.

201

. Very slight Bronchitis catarrhalis.

. No remarkable changes else.

23.(left, superior.)

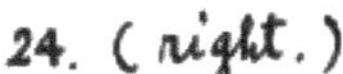

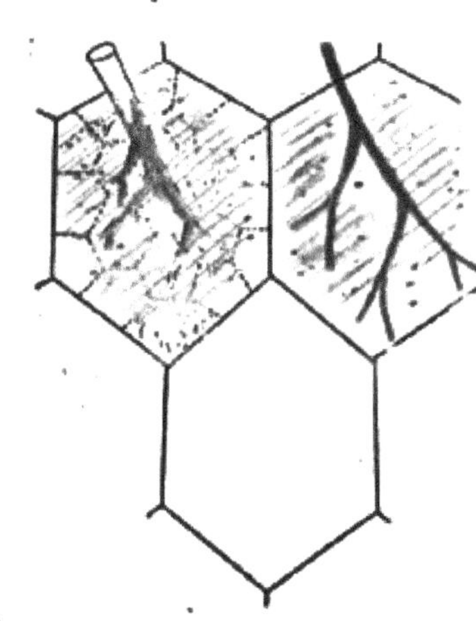

. With thr same changes as above mentioned.

24.(right.)

.Diffuse considerable Alveolitis with some congestion, some leucocytes-dissemination and some edematous swelling of alveolar walls and following changes:

. Considerable inflammatory edema, some erythrocytes-leakages in alveoli scattered all over the pulmonal tissues.

. Considerable congestion and some edematous swelling of interlobular connective tissues.

24.(left.)

. With the same changes and

. Considerable congestion of pleural tissues.

26.

. Diffuse exudative-leucocytic lobar pneumonia with intense massive serous ingflammatory exudates, some leucocytes-dissemination and some erythrocytes -leakage in alveoli all over the pulmonal tissues.

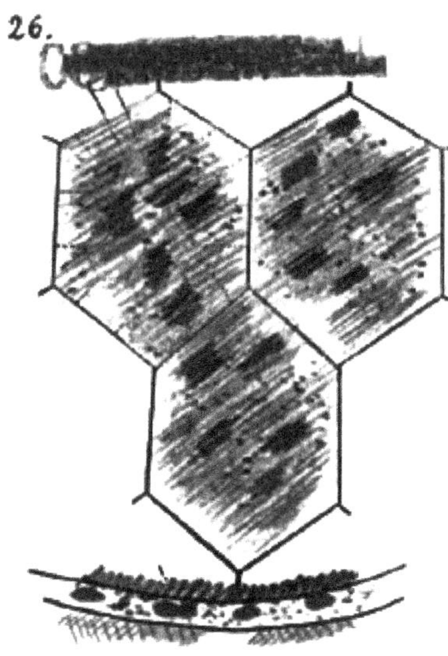

---Lobar pneumonia in the beginning stage.

• Bronchitis catarrhalis with massive serous and mucous masses and some desquamated epithelia as contents.

• Remarkable edematous swelling of interlobular connective tissues.

• Some bacterial accumulation and some edematous swelling of peri-bronchial tissues.

• Considerable edematous swelling, and some congestion of pleural tissues with some fibrinous masses of the pleural surfaces. --- Pleuritis fibrino-exsudativa.

• Some bacterial dissemination in subpleural tissues and

• Some bacterial dissemination all over the pulmonal tissues.

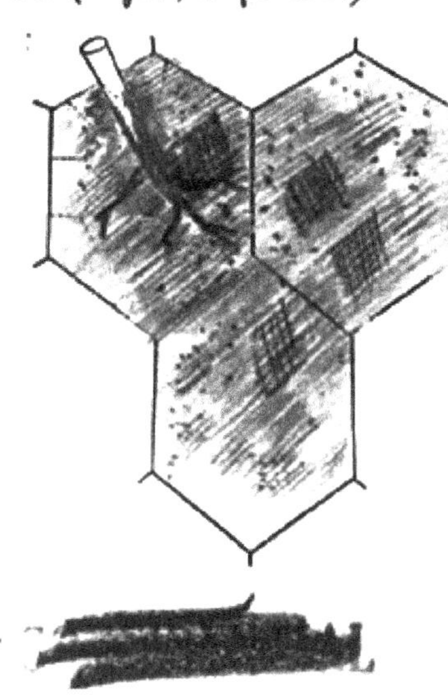

29. (right, superior.)

• Lobar pneumonia with remarkable leucocytes-dissemination, massive serous exudates, some desquamated alveolar epithelia and some separated fibrinous masses in alveoli all over the pulmonal tissues.

• Intense fibrinous swelling of alveolar walls.

• Intense edema and some separated fibrinous masses in interlobular connective tissues.

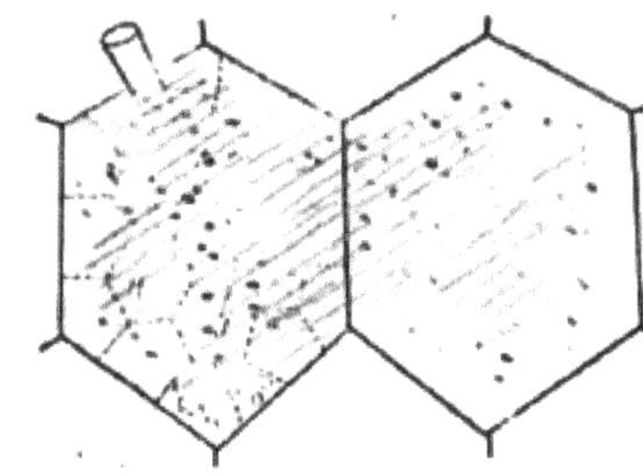

30. (right, superior.)

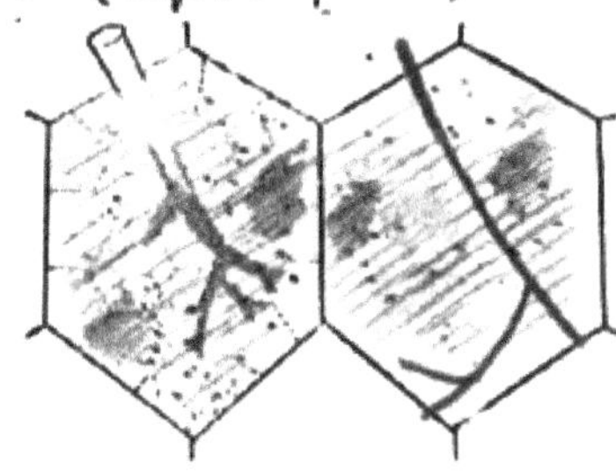

30. (left, superior.)

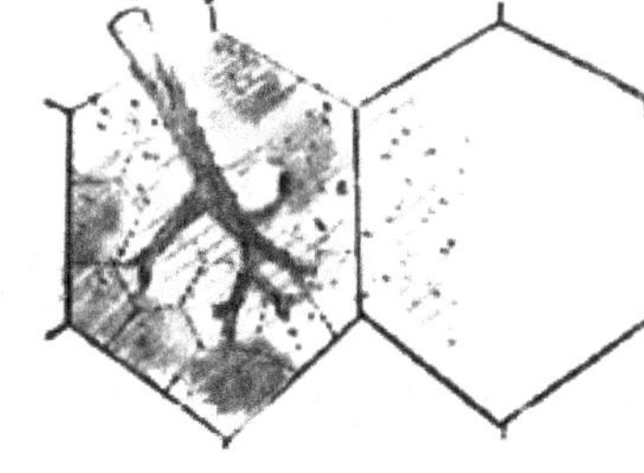

30. (left, inferior.)

29.(left, inferior.)

• With the same changes as above mentioned.

30.(right, superior.)

• Very slight diffuse Alveolitis with some edematous swelling and some slight congestion of alveolar walls.

• Slight exudative changes in some acinous areas.

30.(left, superior.)

• Slight diffuse Alveolitis with edematous swelling and some emigrated wandering cells in alveolar walls

• With some exudative changes in some acinous areas.

• Considerable congestion and slight edematous swelling of interlobular connective tissues.

30.(left, inferior.)

• Diffuse slight Alveolitis with considerable edematous swelling and some emigrated wandering cells in alveolar walls.

• Some exudative changes in some acinous areas with some serous exudates.

• Edematous swelling of peribronchial tissues.

31.(right,superior.)

Bronchiolitis catarrhalis gravis (with massive desquamated epitheliums, serous exudates

204

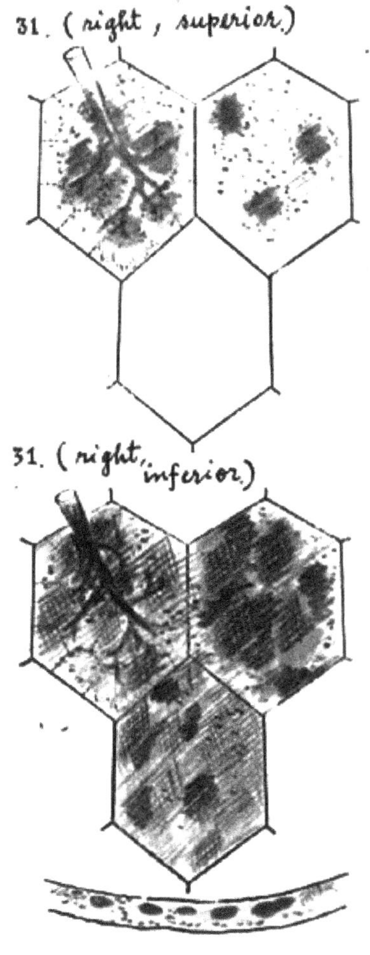

and some leucocytes) and cons[illegible] Peribronchiolitis, with some congestion.

. Some acinous exudative-catarrhalic places with some wandering cells, some desquamated epitheliums and massive serous exsudates.

. In other general tissues there is intense inflammatory edema.

31.(right inferior.)

. Bronchioligis catarrhalis gravis with massive desquamated epitheliums, some wandering cells and some serous exudates. At some bronchioli, bionecrotic swelling of bronchiolar walls (Bronchiolitis bionecroticans.)

. Lobular pneumonia in gray hepatisation, with massive leucocytes, desquamated epitheliums and some fibrinous masses.

. Considerable edematous swelling and some congestion in pleura.

31.(left, inferior.)

. Endobronchiolitis catarrhalis gravis, with massive desquamated epitheliums, some cellular fragments, some wandering cells and some serous exudates. At some places, intense necrotic swelling or ruins of alveolar walls and some bacterial accumulation.

205

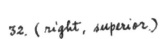

. Some lobular pneumonia in gray hepatisation, with massive leucocytes, some desquamated epitheliums, some cellular fragemnats and some serous inflammatory fluids.

. Intense edema of peribronchiolar or perivascular tissues.

32. (right, superior.)

32. (right, superior.)

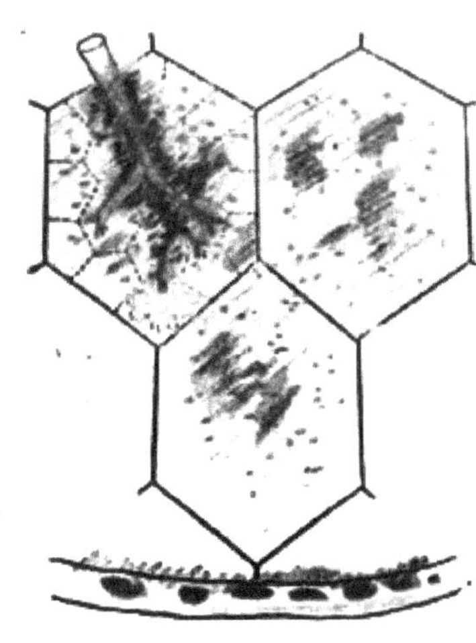

. Bronchiolitis catarrhalis gravis with massive desquamated bronchiolar epitheliums and serous fluids.

. Peribronchiolitis with remarkable congestion and plenty of bacterial accumulation.

. Remarkable edematous swelling of alveolar walls (slight diffuse Alveolitis) with considerable inflammatory edema all over the investigated areas (massive exudates, some desquamated epitheliums, some leucocytes and at some places remarkable bacterial disseminations).

. Thickening (with remaekable anthracosis) and considerable congestion and edema of pleural tissues.

32. (right inferior.)

. Bronchiolitis catarrhalis gravis with massive serous exudates and massive desquamated epitheliums.

. Diffus[illegible]y edema all over the

206

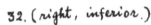

32. (right, inferior.)

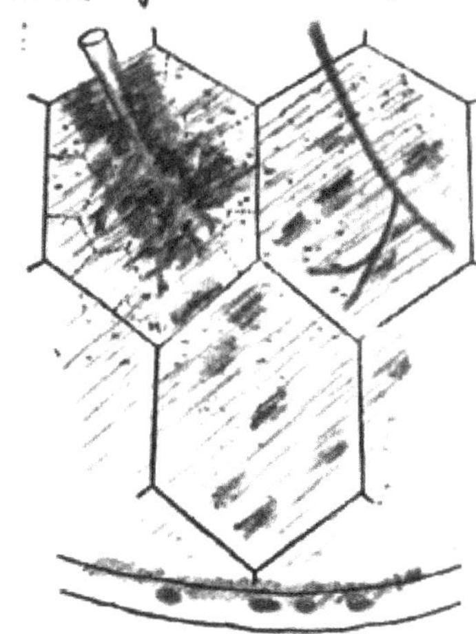

pulmonal tissues with massive exudative fluids, plenty of bacterial dissemination, some leucocytes -emigration and some desquamated alveolar epitheliums.

. Intense swelling of alveolar walls with remarkable bacterial accumulation and swollen alveolar epitheliums. (diffuse Alveolitis).

. At some places, caused some pneumonic places with more or less remarkable leucocytes-emigration in acinous-lobular areas.

: intense bacterial accumulation in subpleural and peribronchiolar tissues.

. Edematous swelling and sweous exudation of pleural tissues (Pleuritis exsudativa).

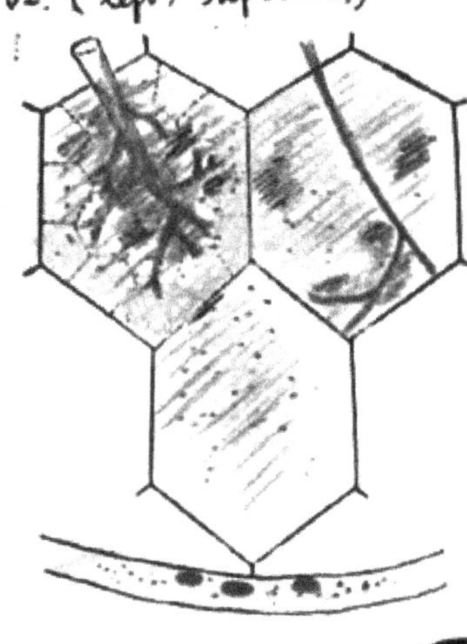

32.(left, superior.)

. Bronchiolitis catarrhalis in medium degree, with edematous swelling and some bacterial accumulation at peribronchiolar tissues.

. Slight diffuse Alveolitis with edematous swelling and considerable congestion of alveolar walls.

. Scattered inflammatory edema in some alveoli, with some serous fluids, some desquamated epitheliums, some leucocytes-emigration and at some places some bacterial accumulation.

107

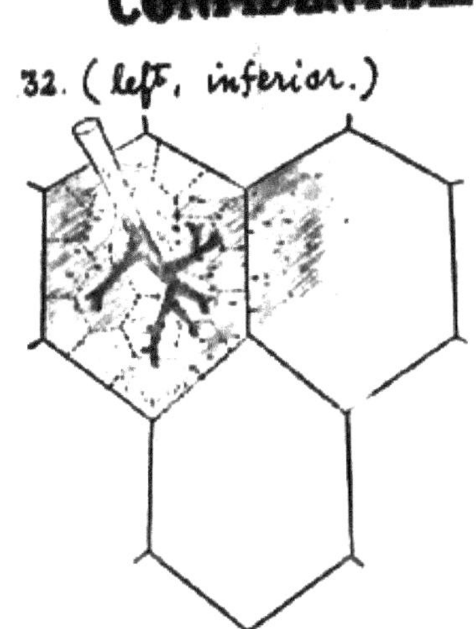

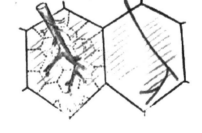

. Compensatoric alveoli, at some places.

. Slight or considerable congesition and edema, with remarkable anthracosis of pleural-tissues and some subpleural bacterial accumulation.

32.(left, inferior.)

. Bronchiolitis catarrhalis in slight degree.

. Edematous swelling of alveolar walls with scattered edema in some atelectatic alveoli.

. some compensatoric emphysematous alveoli.

33.(right, superior.)

. No particular changes. Somewhat emphysematous at some places and somewhat atelectatic at some places.

. Slight alveolar congestion.

33. (right, inferior.)

33.(right inferior.)

. Endobronchiolitis catarrhalis in medium degree, with massive serous exudates and some desquamative epithel. cells.

. Slight pulmonal congestion and some edematous swelling of alveolar walls.

. No remarkable changes else.

33.(left, superior.)

. No remarkable changes.

208

. Rather emphysematous, and slight edema of peribronchiolar and perivascular tissues.

33.(left, inferior.)

. No particular changes and very slight edematous swelling of alveolar walls.

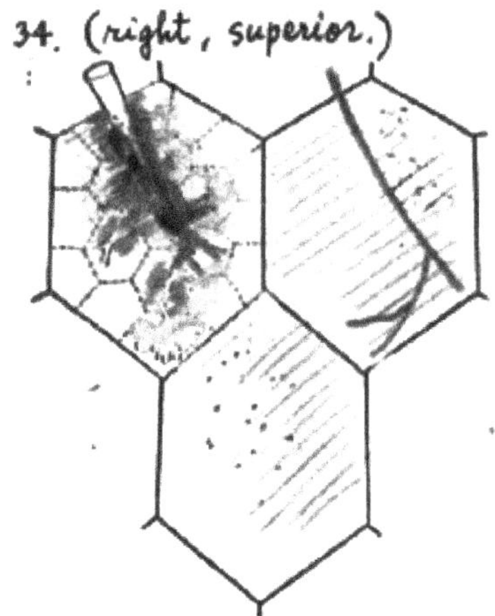

34.(right, superior.)

. Endobronchiolitis catarrhalis levis, with slight serous exudation and some Peribronchiolitis with considerable congestion.

. Diffuse Alveolitis with considerable alveolar congestion and some wandering cell-emigration in alveolar walls.

34.(right, inferior.)

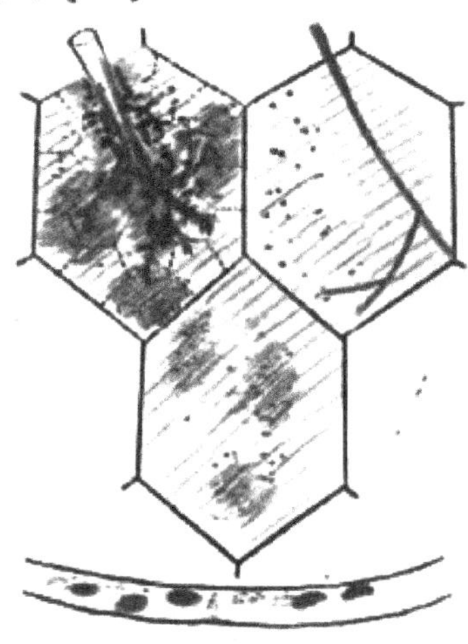

. Endobronchiolitis catarrhalis and intense Peribronchiolitis with intense congestion, some leucocytes -emigration and some increased histiocytes and small-round-cells.

. Diffuse considerable Alveolitis and considerable alveolar congestion.

. At some places, these Alveolitis proceed to form some acinous leucocytic pneumonic places.

. Intense congestion, some edematous swelling and some round-cell-dissemination in pleural tissues.

209

34. (left, superior.)

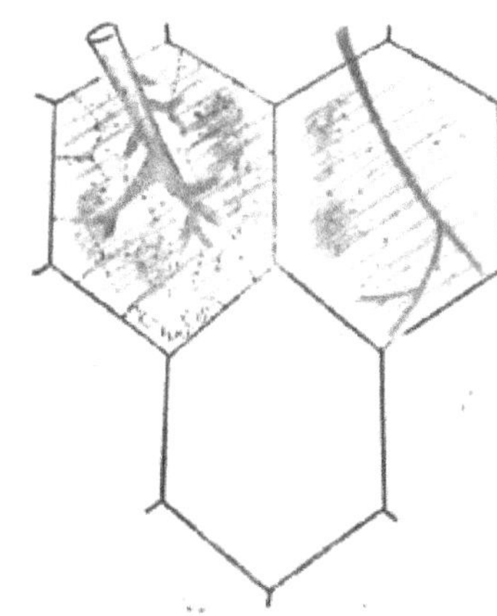

34. (left, superior.)

. Bronchiolitis catarrhalis in medium degree, with massice catarrhalic masses.

. Stasis et edema pulmonum levis. Slight diffuse alveolitis.

. Leucocytic accumulation in some acinous places.

34. (left inferior.)

. Stasis pulmonum and edematous swelling of alveolar walls.

. Some pleural congestion.

35. (right, superior.)

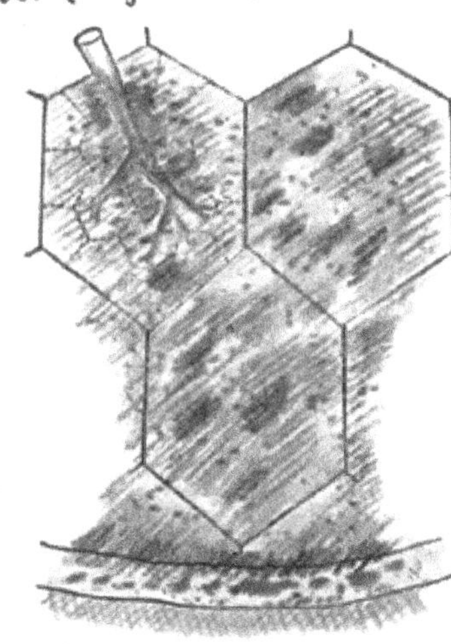

35. (right superior.)

. Lober pneumonia. Pneumonic changes all over the investigated areas with plenty of leucocytes, serous fluids, some erythrocytes and some bacterial dissemination.

. Intense edematous swelling of alveolar walls.

. Intense edematous and fibrinous swelling of interlobular connective tissues.

. Bronchiolitis catarrhalis with massive serous fluids and some desquamated epitheliums.

. Pleuritis fibrino-hemorrhagica.

35. (left, inferior.)

. Lobar pneumonia, with the same changes as above mentioned.

. Intense infiltration with numerous leucocytes,

210

some round-cell-accumulation and edema at peribronchiolar and perivascular tissues.

• Some bacterial accumulation at some peribronchiolar tissues.

• Pleuritis fibrinoua.

36.(left.)

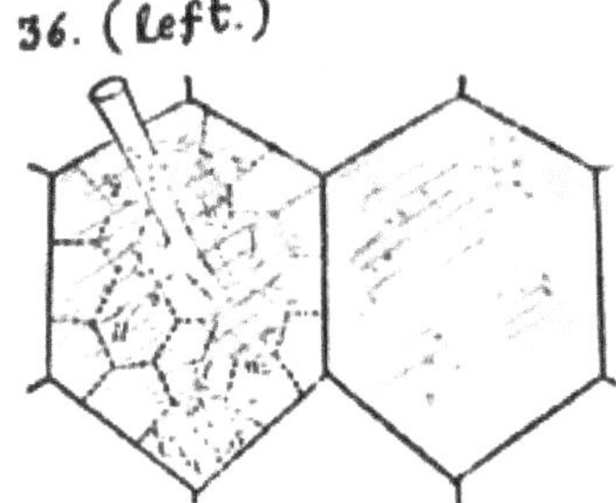

• Emphysema at some places., and Edema pulmonum levis at some places.

• Slight edematous swelling and some leucocytes -accumulation in alveolar walls.

38.

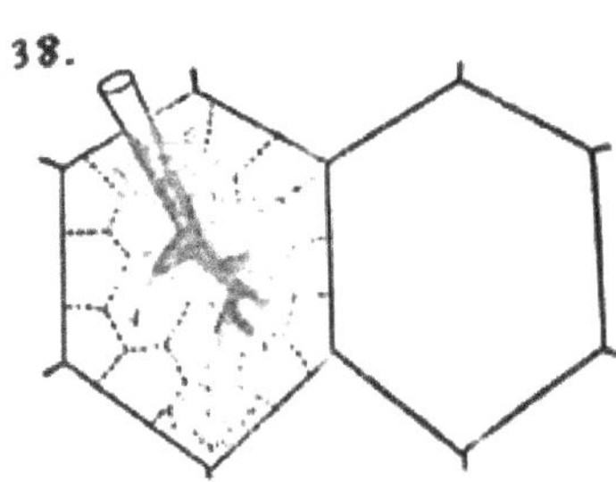

• No particular changes and slight catarrhalic Bronchiolitis.

• Slight edematous swelling of peribronchiolar and perivascular tissues.

40.(right, superior.)

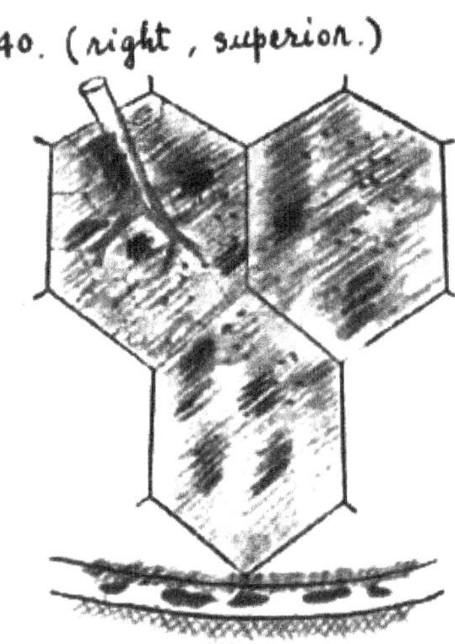

• Multifocal lobular pneumonia with remarkable inflammatory edema, considerable leucocytes-dissemination, some bacterial masses and some desquamated epitheliums.

• Intense edematous or fibrinous swelling of alveolar walls.

• Bronchiolitis catarrhalis levis with slight serous fluids.

• Pleuritis sero-fibrinosa with some subpleural congestion.

211

42.

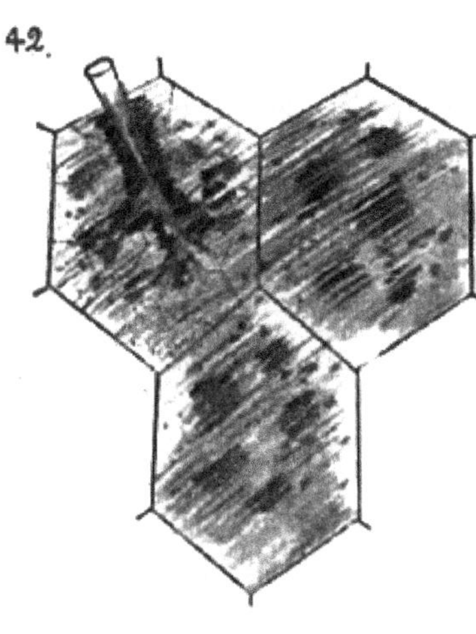

• Lobar pnuemonia. Pneumonic changes all over the investigated areas, with massive exudates, considerable leucocytes-emigration, some desquamted epitheliums and some diffuse bacterial dissemination.

• Edematous or fibrinous swelling of alveolar walls.

• Remarkable edematous swelling, some leucocytes--emigration and massive bacterial dissemination at peribronchiolar and perivascular tissues.

44. (right.)

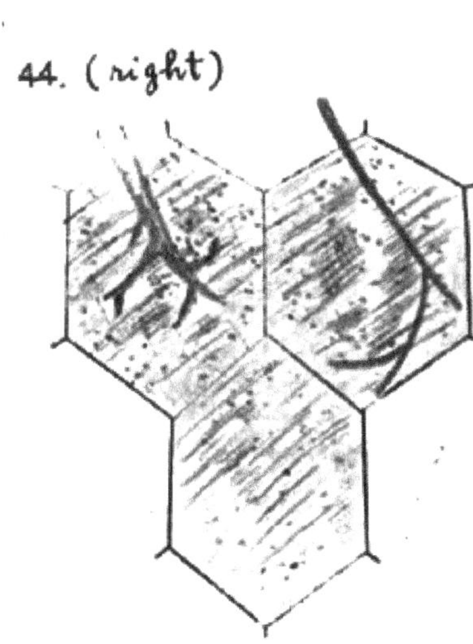

• Diffuse slight Alveolitis with intense edematous swelling and considerable congestion of alveolar walls and

• Remarkable inflammatory edema all over the plumonal tissues, with considerable serous fluids, some desquamated alveolar epitheliums, separation of some fibrinous masses, a little of erythrocytes and some bacterial dissemination.

• Considerable congestion of interlobular connective tissues.

• Bronchiolitis catarrhalis in slight degree.

• Slight edematous swelling and congestion of pleural tissues.

212

44.(left.)

. With the same changes, as avobe mentioned.

. Diffuse Alveolitis with considerable edematous swelling of alveolar walls with some inflammatory edema, all over the pulmonal tissues.

. Bronchiolitis catarrhalis with some desquamated epitheliums, some bacterial masses and the others.

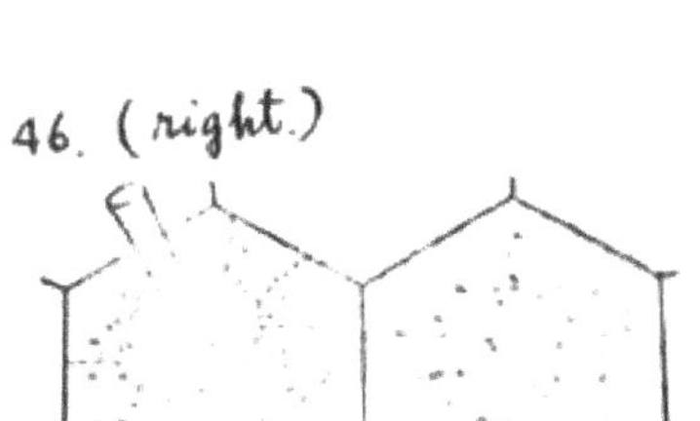

46.(right.)

. Edema pulmonum gravis with extraordinary remarkable edema all over the investigated area.

. Intense edematous swelling of alveolar walls.

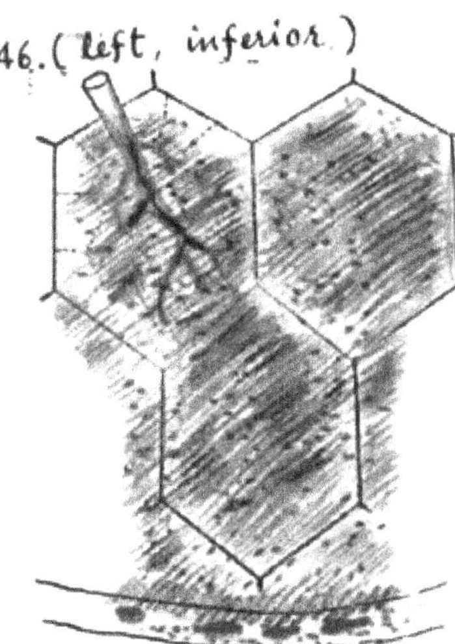

46.(left, inferior.)

. Lobar pneumonia. Pneumonic changes all over the investigated area, with massive serous fluids, more or less remarkable leucocytes-emigration, some bacterial dissemination, some erythrocytes and some desquamated alveolar epitheliums.

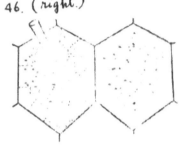

. At some places it is accompanied with remarkable inflammatory edema and intense edematous or fibrinous swelling of alveolar walls.

. Some subpleural bacterial accumulation.

47. (right. sup.) Edema et stasis pulmonum with the remarkable edematous swelling of alveolar walls and some serous fluids in alveoli all over the investigated areas.

213

of alveolar walls at some places and no particular changes in the other general tissues.

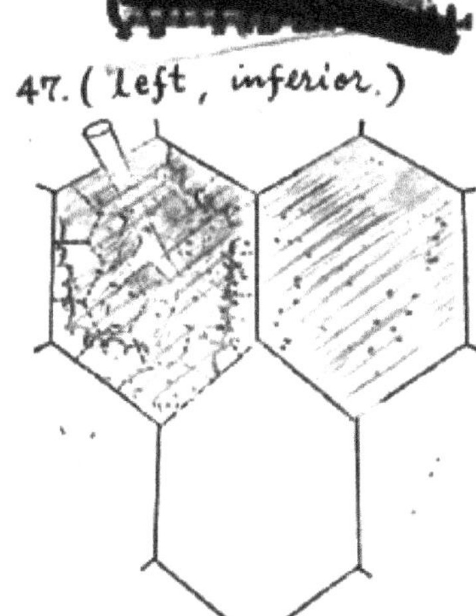

47. (left, inferior.)

Slight but diffuse Alveolitis with considerable swelling or roughness and slight congestion of alveolar walls. More or less considerable hyperplasia of alveolar epitheliums (without leucocytes-emigration).

• At some places with considerable edema and some desquamated epithelial cells to cause somewhat atelectatic places (with some desquamated epitheliums).

• Considerable roughness and congestion of pleural tissues.

49.

(right, inferior.)

• Slight congestion of alveolar walls and slight Bronchitis catarrhalis.

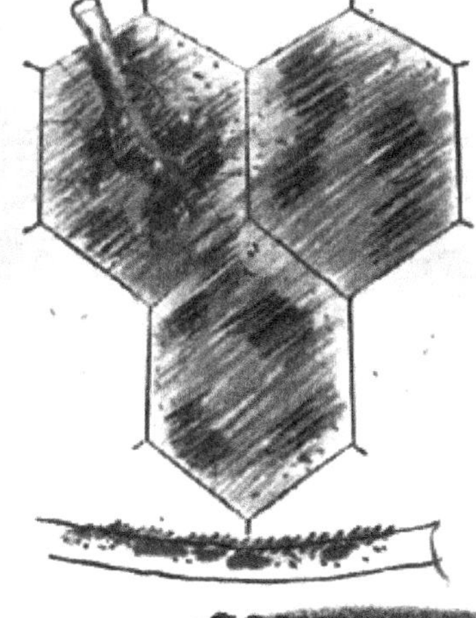

49.(left, superior.)

• Lobar pneumonia with numerous leucocytes, some desquamated alveolar epithelia, all over the pulmonal tissues.

• Intense fibrinous swelling of alveolar walls.

• Bronchitis catarrhalis with massive serous masses, some desquamated epithelia and some leucocytes as bronchial contensts.

214

. Some bacterial accumulation (especially at peribronchial tissues)
and bacterial dissemination in pulmonal tissues.
. Remarkable congestion, some intense hemorrhages and some leucocytes-dissemination in pleural tissues with some sero-fibrinous masses on the pleural surface. --- Pleuritis fibrino-hemorrhagica.

49. (left, inferior.)

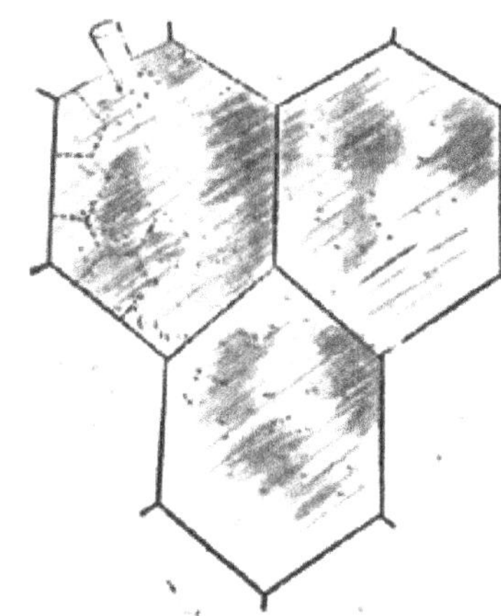

49.(left, inferior.)
. Diffuse Alveolitis with considerable congestion and some leucocytes-emigration in alveolar walls and
. Considerable inflammatory edema in alveoli, scattered all over the pulmonal tissues and some following changes;
. At some acinous areas, pneumonic changes with some leucocytes-emigration.

49. (right, superior.)

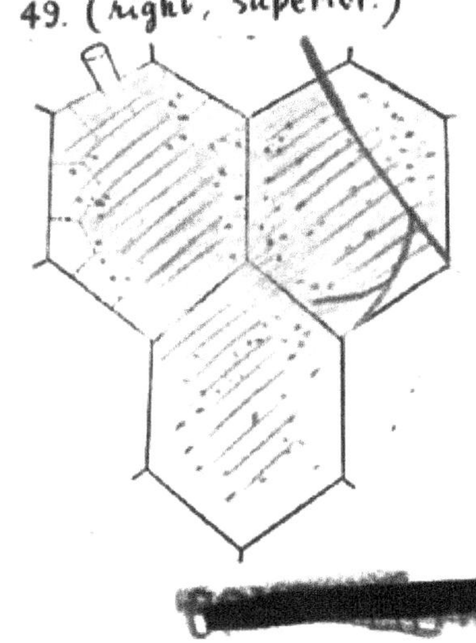

49.(right, superior.)
. Edema pulmonum with massive serous exudates in alveoli all over the pulmonal tissues.
. Considerable congestion and slight edematous swelling of alveolar walls with some erythrocytes -leakages in alveoli.
. Considerable anthracosis of pleural tissues.

215

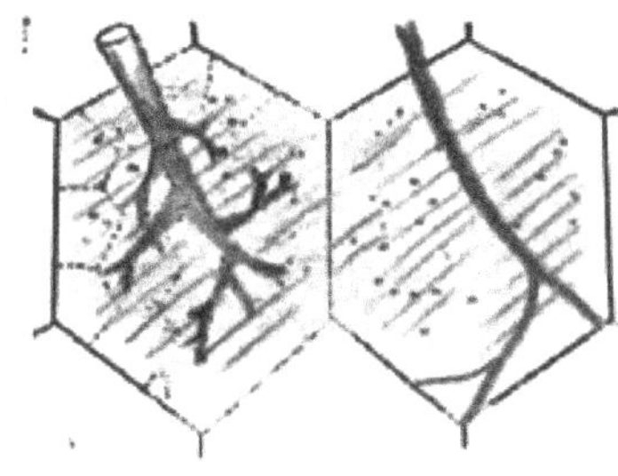

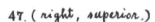

• Bronchiolitis catarrhalis with some catarrhalic masses and some desquamated epitheliums.

• Peribronchiolar tissues with considerable edemaotus swelling.

• Some bacterial accumulation in the alveolar capillaries.

• Intense edematous roughness of pleural tissues.

47. (right, inferior.)

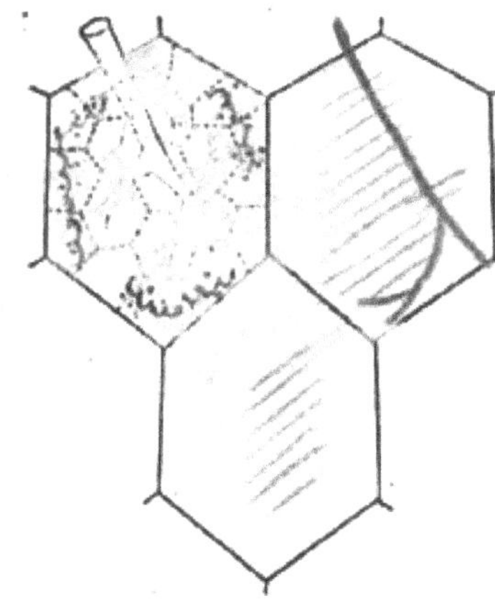

47. (right, inferior.)

• Edema pulmonum with massive serous fluid and some desquamated epitheliums all over the investigated areas.

• Considerable roughness, considerable congestion of alveolar walls with slight hyperplasia of alveolar epitheliums. Cuboidal hyperplasia of alveolar epitheliums, esp. at the intercalary portions.

• A few bacterial accumulation in alveolar capillaries.

• Considerable congestion of interlobular connective tissues.

• Slight congestion of pleural tissues with considerable anthracosis.

47. (left, superior.)

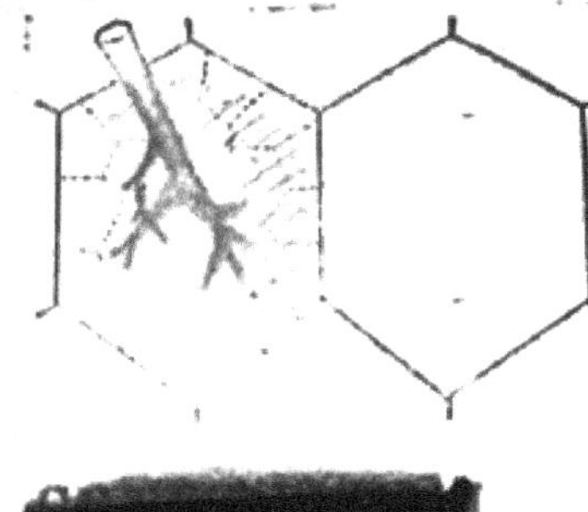

47. (~~ri~~ left, superior.)

Bronchiolitis catarrhalis in medium degree with considerable desquamation of alveolar epitheliums.

• Considerable edematous swelling and considerable congestion

216

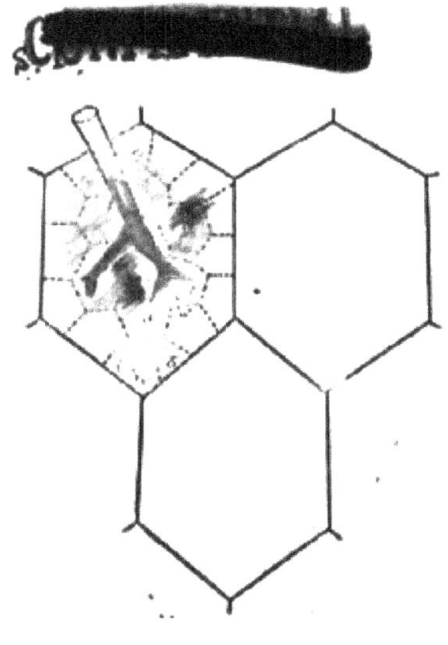

S.I.

. Slight edema with considerable swelling of alveolar walls (with some swollen alvelar epitheliums). At some places, some bacterial accumulation.

. Bronchiliolitis catarrhalis in slight degree.

S.2.(right, superior.)

. Slight, diffuse Alveolitis with considerable swelling, some cellular infiltration (some leucocytes and some lymphocytes), with slightly increased alveolar epitheliums. -

. Considerable congestion of alveolar walls and some serous fluids in some alveoli. Stasis at edema pulmonum levis.

S.2. (right, superior.)

. Edematous swelling of interlobular connective tissues.

S.2. (right, inferior.)

. With the same changes, as above mantioned,

. slightly hyperplasied lymph-nodulus at peri-bronchiolar portions.

S.2.(left, superior.)

. With the same changes, as above mentioned.

S.2.(left, inferior.)

. With the same changes, as above mentioned.

211

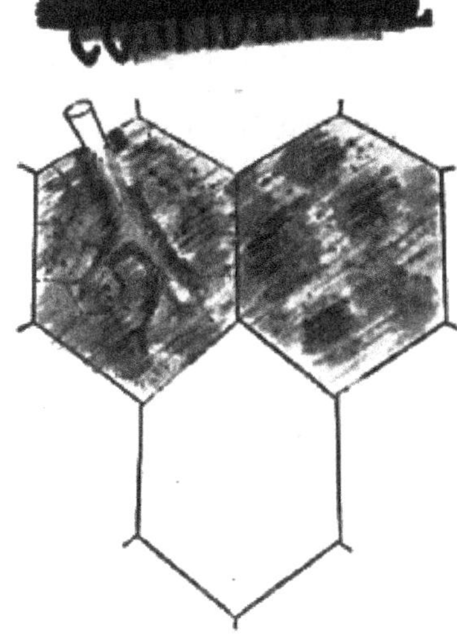

S-3.

. Hematogenous lobular pneumonia. Lobular pneumonic places with numerous bacterial dissemination, considerable leucocytes-emigration, massive edematous exudates, some erythrocytes and some desquamated epitheliums.

. In the neighbouring tissues, with intense inflammatory edema, intense edematous and fibrinous swelling of alveolar walls, with some bacterial accumulation in alveolar capillaries and some swollen alveolar epitheliums.

. In alveoli, considerable serous exudates, some desquamated epitheliums and some leucocytes. --- Diffuse Alveolitis and inflammatory edema.

S.4.

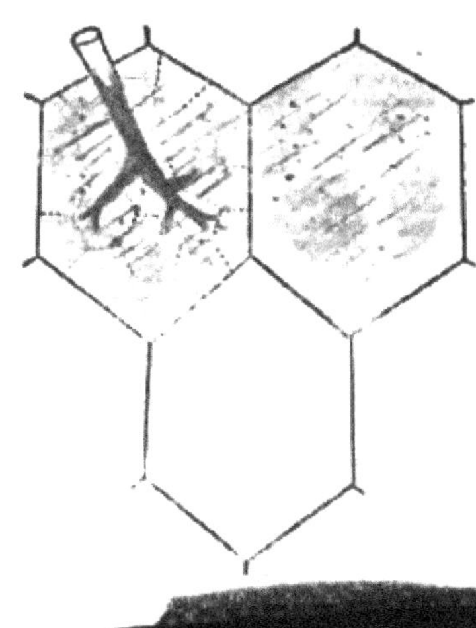

. Diffuse Alveolitis and considerable inflammatory edema.

Considerable edematous swelling and some congestion and slightly increased alveolar epitheliums at alveolar walls.

. In alveoli, some edema (serous fluid) and some desquamated epitheliums (some of them, heart -disease-cells).

. Bronchiolitis catarrhalis in medium degree with some serous fluids and some desquamated

218

epitheliums.

. Edematous swelling of peribronchiolar and

perivascular tissues and slight roughness of pleural tissues with some subpleural congestion.

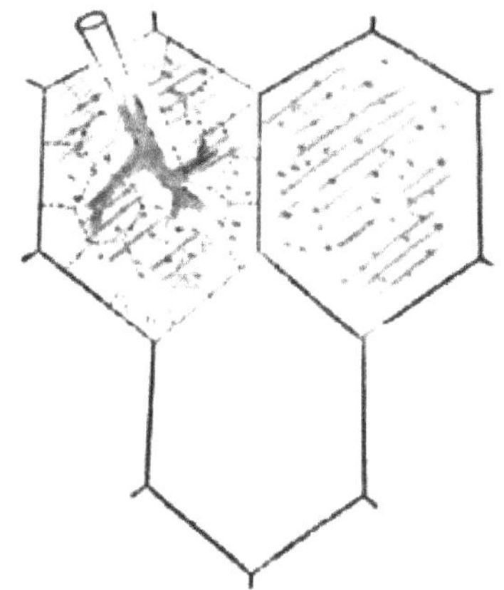

S.5.

. Slight diffuse Alveolitis with more or less remarkable inflammatory edema.

. Considerable swelling, considerable congestion, some swollen alveolar epitheliums of alveolar walls and more or less remarkable inflammatory edema in alveoli, all over the investigated area.

. Bronchiolitis catarrhalis in slight degree, at some places in medium degree, with some serous fluids and some desquamated epitheliums.

. Considerable roughness and slight congestion of pleural tissues.

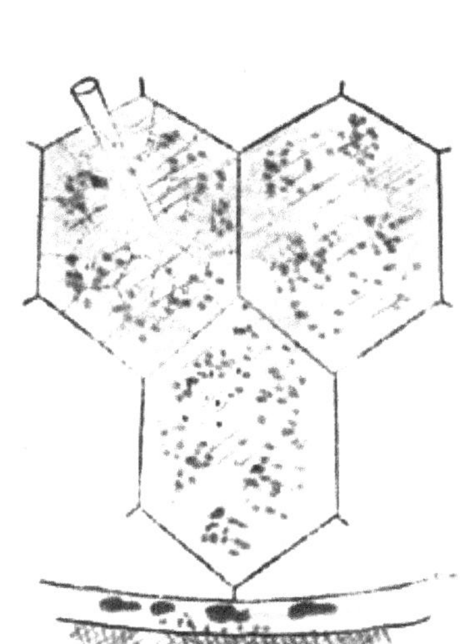

S-6.(left, inferior.)

. Considerable diffuse Alveolitis with remarkable edematous swelling, intense congestion, some leucocytes and some lymphocytes-disseminations and some bacterial disseminations at alvolar walls.

219

S.8. (right, superior.)

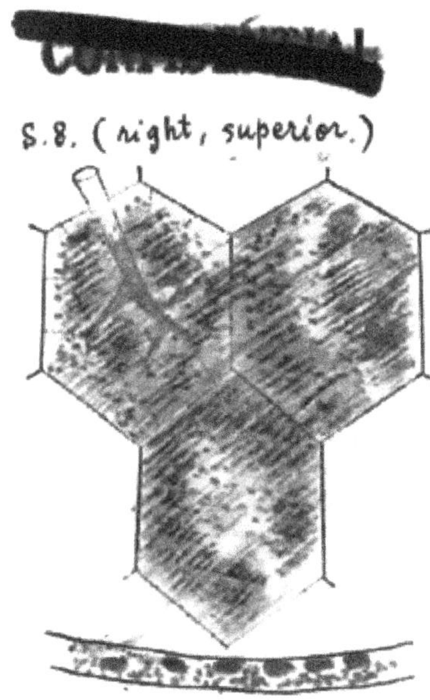

. Considerable inflammatory edema and some hemorrhages all over the pulmonal tissues.

. Pleuritis sero-fibrinosa with some fibrinous masses on the pleural surfaces.

S-8. (right, superior.)~~and inferior.)~~

. Lobar pneumonia with massive serous exsudation, numerous leucocytes, massive bacterial accumulation, some erythrecytes and some desquamated epithelial cells all over the pulmonal tissues.

. Slight Bronchiolitis catarrhalis with some desquamated epithelial cells.

. Pleuritis hemorrhagico-exsudativa with some edematous swelling, intense congestion and somewhat thickning accompanied with some subpleural bacterial disseminations.

S.8. ~~left, superior.~~ (right, inferior.)

. Lobar pneumonia with the same changes, as above mentioned.

S.8. (left, superior.)

. Bronchiolitis catarrhalis with massive desquamated epitheliums.

. Some lobular areas with hemorrhagic pneumonic changes and

S.8. (left, superior.)

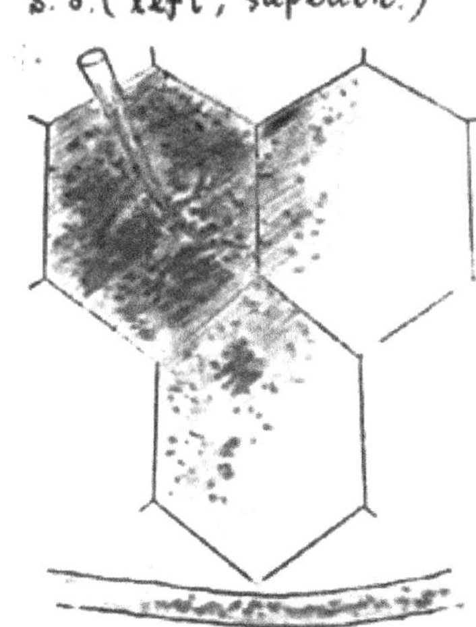

220

Some lobular areas with some leucocytes and some bacterial disseminations (leucocytic pneumonia).

. Considerable congestion and some edematous swelling of pleural tissues.

S. 9. (right, superior.)

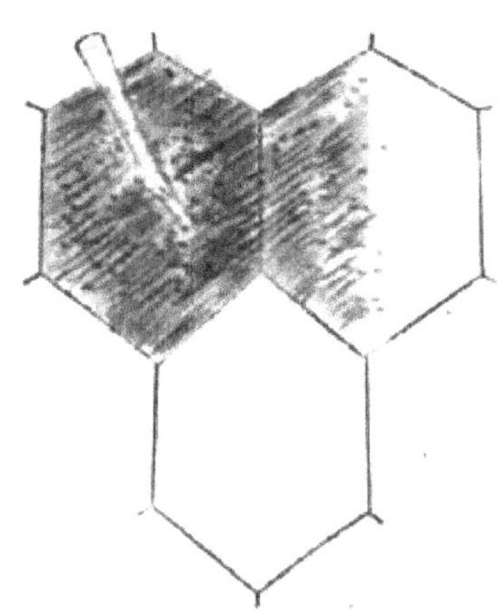

. Lobular pneumonia with numerous bacterial masses, numerous leucocytes, some erythrocytes and some fibrinous separations in some lobular areas.

. Fibrinous swelling and some congestion of alveolar walls.

9. (right, inferior.)

. Lobular pneumonia with the same changes as above mentioned.

. Compensatoric emphysema at perifocal pulmonal tissues.

S. 10.

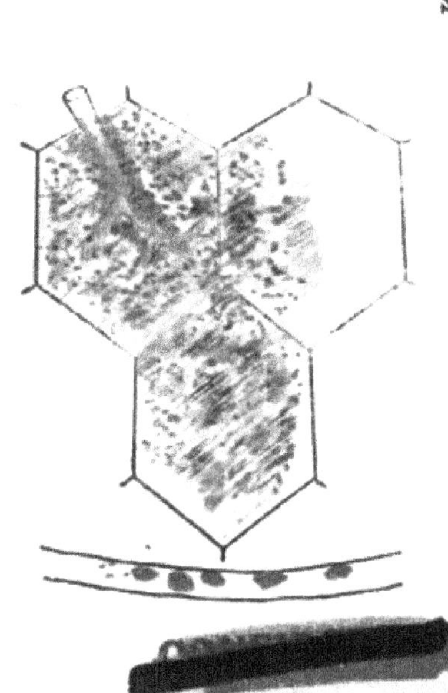

. Lobar sero-hemorrhagic pneumonia with massive serous inflammatory edematous exudation, some erythrocytes, some desquamated epitheliums and a few of leucocytes all over the pulmonal tissues.

. Fibrinous swelling and some considerable congestion of alveolar walls.

. Massive bacterial accumulation at perivascular portions.

. Bronchiolitis catarrhalis with some serous

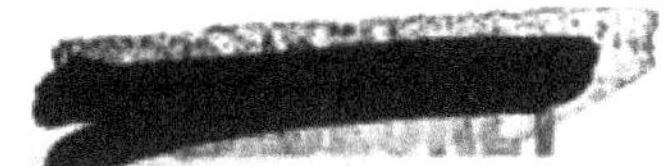

221

masses.

. Considerable congestion and some edematous swelling of pleural tissues.

S.12.

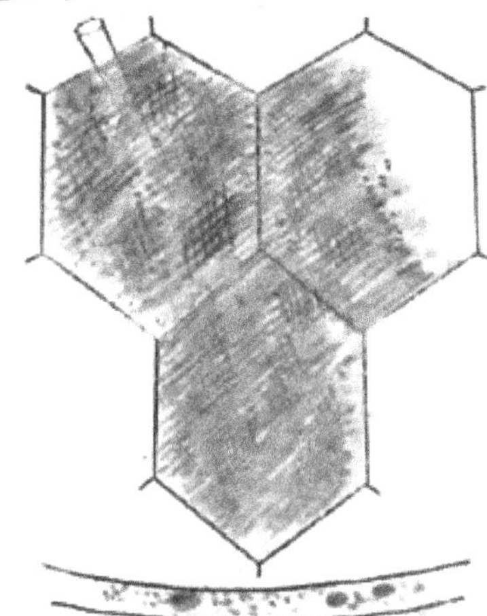

S.12.

Lobar pneumonia in gray hepatisation, with numerous leucocytes, some desquamated epitheliums and some fibrinous masses all over the pulmonal tissues.

. Fibrionous swelling of alveolar walls.

. Bronchiolitis catarrhalis which has plenty of leucocytes and some serous masses as contents.

. Peribronchiolitis with remarkable edematous swelling and some congestion.

. Considerable congestion and some edematous swelling of pleural tissues with some serous exudations.

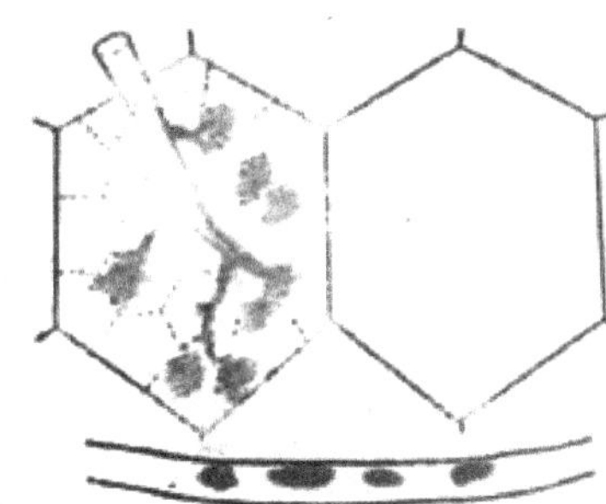

S.14. (right.)

. Generally with emphysematous pulmonal tissues.

. Some submiliary pneumonic places, especially at the intercalary portions of lung. Leucocytic pneumonia without any reactive perifocal changes.

. Considerable congestion in pleral tissues.

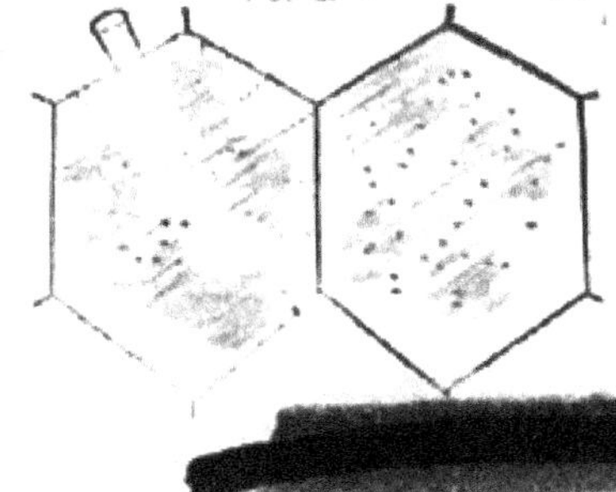

S.11. (right.)

. Diffuse Alveolitis with edematous swelling, some congestion and some leucocytes dissemination at

222

alveolar walls.

. Considerable inflammatory edema, some desquamated epitheliums and a few leucocytes in alveoli. Edema pulmonum.

. Remarkable Anthracosis of pulmonal and pleural tissues.

S. 11. (left.)

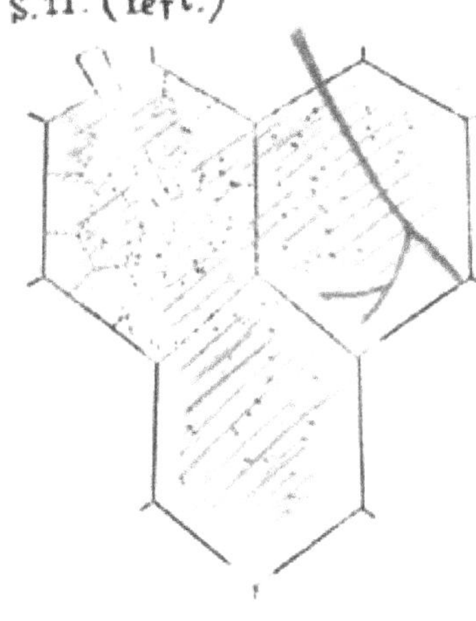

. Diffuse slight Alveolitis with considerable edematous swelling, considerable congestion and some leucocytes-dissemination in alveolar walls.

. Remarkable inflammatory edema all over the pulmonal tissues, with some desquamated epitheliums.

. Bronchiolitis carrhalis with massive serous exudats.

S. 15. (right.)

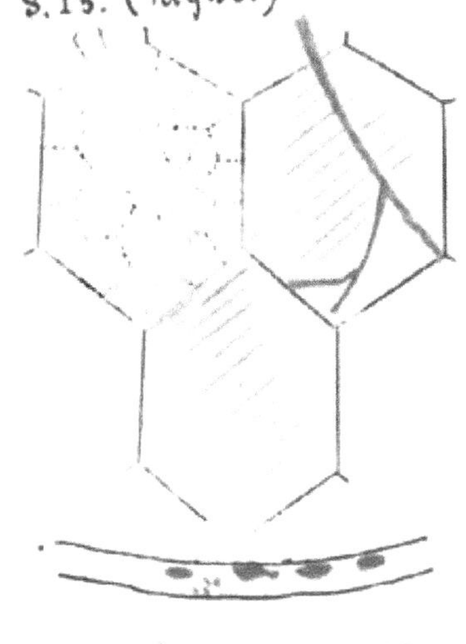

. Considerable edematous swelling, some congestion and a few leucocytes-accumulation in alveolar walls and slight inflammatory edema in alveoli.

. Considerable edematous swelling and some congestion in pleural tissues.

S. 15. (left.)

. Diffuse Alveolitis with intense edematous swelling. considerable congestion and some

223

CONFIDENTIAL

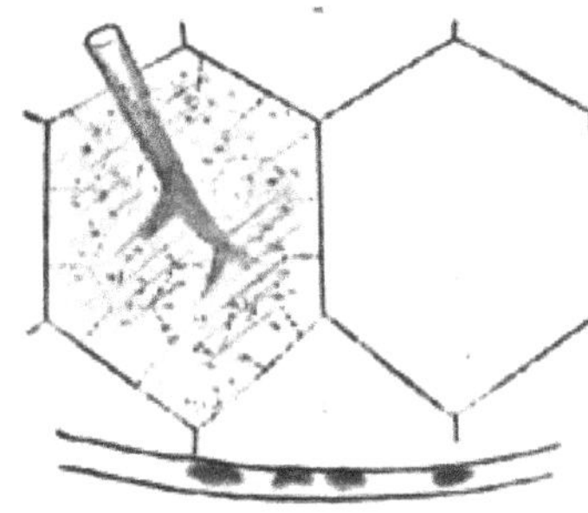

leucocytes-dissemination in alveolar walls.

. Some inflammatory edema in some alveoli = Edema pulmonum levis.

. Bronchiolitis catarrhalis with some desquamated epithelial cells.

. Considerable congestion of pleural tissues.

S.19.

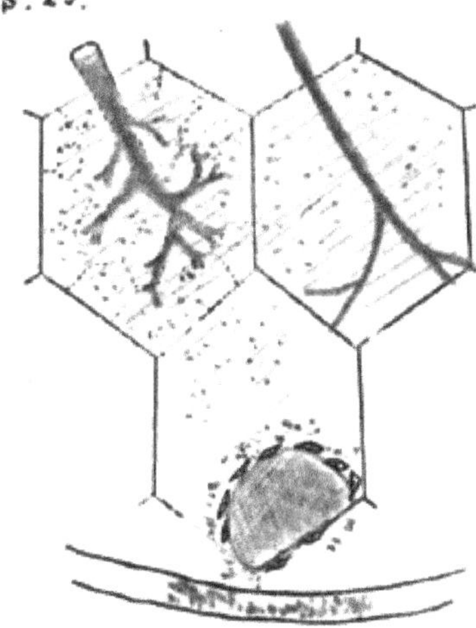

. Slight diffuse Alveoltis with considerable congestion and some edematous swelling of alveolar walls and some desquamated alveolar epithelia.

. Considerable congestion of interlobular connective tissues.

. With one sugar-corn large primary seat of tuberculous affection :

The most part of the seatr fall into caseous necrotic masses and bounded with thick walls of increased connective tissues. Without any significant perifocal reactions.

S.22.

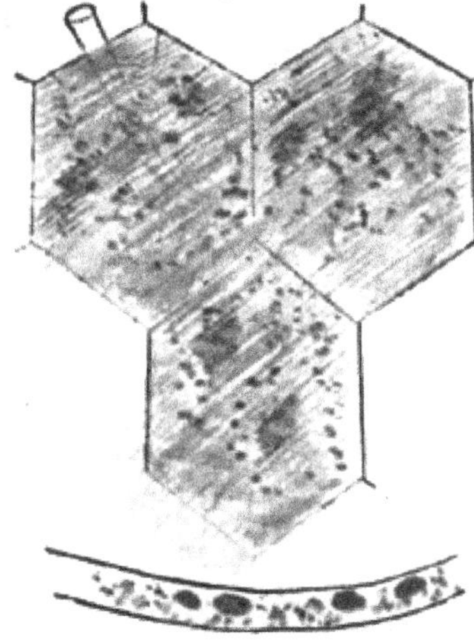

. Lobar pneumonia with numerous leucocytes-dissemination and some desquamated alveolar epithelia, some separated fibrinous masses and some serous masses in alveoli all over the pulmonal tissues. At some places of them, considerable hemorrhages.

. Considerable congestion, some leucocytes-emigration and some increased alveolar epithelia at

224

alveolar walls.

. Remarkable fibrinous and edematous swelling of interlobular connective tissues.

. Bronchitis catarrhalis with some mucous masses, some erythrocytes and some desquamated epithelia and some leucocyte as bronchial contents.

. Remarkable congestion, some hemorrhages, some edematous swelling and some leucocytes-dissemination in pleural tissues.

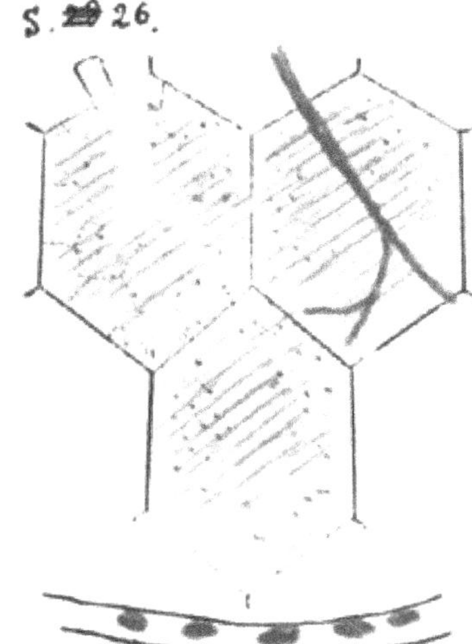

S.26.

. Diffuse Alveolitis with considerable edematous swelling and some congestion in alveolar walls.

. Considerable inflammatory edema and some desquamated epitheliums (some of them, heart-disease-cells) in lobular areas.

. Considerable congestion in inter-lobular connective tissues.

. Considerable congestion of pleural tissues.

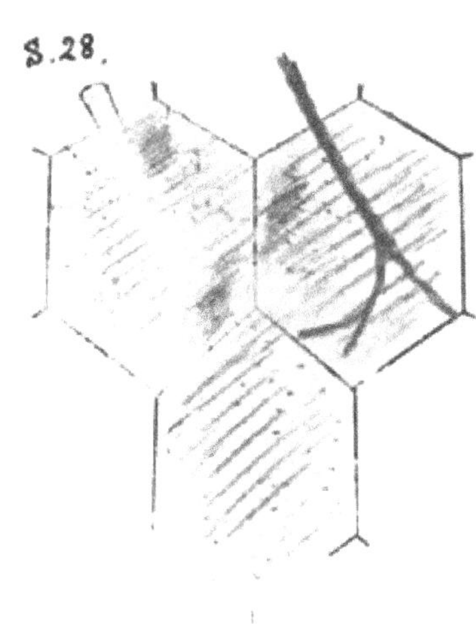

S.28.

. Slight Alveolitis with considerable congestion and edematous swelling of alveolar walls.

. In some lobular or acinous areas, some considerable serous exudation, Edema et stasis pulmonum.

225

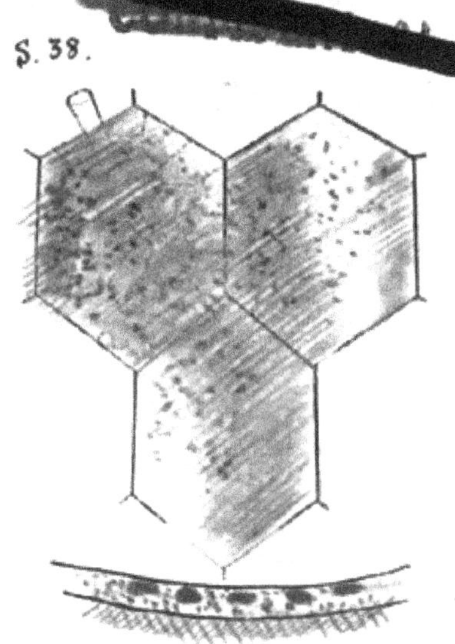

S. 38.

. Lobar pneumonia in gray hepatisation, with neumerous leucocytes, some desquamated epitheliums, some erythrocytes (partial hemorrhages) and some serous exudation all over the pulmonal tissues.

. Fibrinous, edematous swelling and some leucocytes-dissemination in alveolar walls.

. Remarkable congestion, some edematous swelling and some wendering-cells-dissemination in pleural tissues.

226

(B) S U M M A R Y.

(I)

The bird's- eye view of all investigated cases.

1. right. — Multiple lobular pneumonia in gray hepatisation. Pleuritis sero-fibrino-fibrosa paritialis. Remarkable congestion and some bacterial dissemination in pleural tissues.
Bronchitis catarrhalis acuta gravis.

left. — Multiple lobular pneumonia in gray hepatisation. Remarkable congestion and some bacterial dissemination in pleural tissues.
Bronchitis catarrhalis gravis.

---

2. right. — Diffuse Alveolitis and Edema pulmonum inflammatorium.
Pleuritis fibrino-fibrosa.

left. — Diffuse sligth Alveolitis and Edema pulmonum inflammtorium in slight degree.
Pleuritis fibrino-fibrosa.

---

3. right, superior. — Considerable diffuse Alveolitis and Edema pulmonum inflammatorium with some pulmonal congestion.
Bronchitis catahalis acuta in medium degree.
Pleuritis fibrino-purulenta gircumscripta.

right, median. — Multiple lobular pneumonia in gray hepatisation.
Brohchitis catarrhalis in medium degree.
Peribronchitis with some bacterial dissemination.

right, inferior. — Considerable diffuse Alveolitis and Stais et edema pulmonum inflammatorium.
Bronchitis catarrhalis in medium degree.

left, superior. — Multiple lobular pneumonia in gray hepatisation, with exudative-leucocytic-hemorrhagic reaction.
Bronchitis catarrhalis in medium degree.
Pleuritis exsudativa with some bacterial and some leucocytes dissemination in plenral tissues.

left, inferior. — Considerable diffuse Alvleolitis and Stasis et edema pulmonum in medium degree.
Bronchitis catarrhalis in medium degree.
Peribronchitis with some bacterial dissemination.
Pleuritis fibroinosa zircumscripta.

4.	right, superior.	Slight diffuse Alveolitis and Edema pulmonum inflammatorium in some acino-lobular areas.
	right, inferior.	Slight diffuse Alveolitis and Some leucocytes-dissemination in some acinous areas, accompaneid with some bacterial dissemination.
	right, median.	Slight diffuse Alveolitis and Some leueocytes-dissemination in some acinous areas. Multiple miliary leucocytic pneumonia.
	left, superior.	Slight diffuse Alveolitis and Edema pulmonum inflammatorium in some lobular areas.
	left, inferior.	Slight diffuse Alveolitis and Edema pulmonum inflammatorium in some lobular areas. Bronchitis catarrhalis in medium degree.
5.	right, superior.	Multiple lobular (rather lobar) pneumonia in gray hepatisation. Multiple acinous pneumonia and Edema pulmonum inflammatorium in severe degree. Peribronchitis catarrhalis with some bacterial dissemination.
	right, inferior.	Acino-productive tuberculosis, without remarkable reactive changes. Pleuritis fibrino-fibrosa.
	left, superior.	Multiple lobular (rather lobar) pneumonia, in gray hepatisation. Peribronchitis catarrhalis with some bacterial dissemination and some edematous swelling.
	left, inferior.	Multiple lobular (rather lobar) pneumonia, in gray hepatisation. Peribroonhitis with somebacterial dissemination and some edematous swelling.
6.	right, superior.	Multiple acino-lobular pneumonia with numerous leucocytes-dissemination. Bronchiolitis catarrhalis in severe degree.
	right, inferior.	Multiple acino-lobular pneumonia in gray hepatisation. Bronchiolitis catarrhalis in severe degree.
	right, apex.	Slight diffuse Alveolitis and Edema pulmonum inflammatorium with some leucocytes-dissemination in some acino-lobular areas.

228

	left, superior.	Slight diffuse Alveolitis and Stasis et edema pulmonum in medium degree.
	left, inferior.	Diffuse Alveolitis with Stasis et edema pulmonum in medium degree.
7.	right.	Slight diffuse Alveolitis and Edema pulmonum in some lobular areas. Pleuritis fibrino-fibrosa.
	left.	Diffuse Alveolitis and Edema pulmonum inflammatorium with some leucocytes-dissemination and ~~pb~~ some acinolobular areas.
8.	right, superior.	No particular changes and Pleuritis fibrino-fibrosa.
	right, inferior.	Multiple lobular pneumonia in gray hepatisation. Bronchitis catarrhalis acuta gravis and Peribronchitis with some bacterial accumulation. Plerutis fibrino-fibrosa totalis.
	left.	Very slight diffuse Alveolitis and No particular changes else.
9.	right.	No remarkable, changes. Slight diffuse Alveolitis.
	left.	No remarkable changes. Slight diffuse Alveolitis.
10.	right, superior.	Edema et stasis pulmonum with some leucocytes-dissemination.
	right, inferior.	Multiple lobular (rather lobar) pneumonia in gray hepatisation.
	left, superior.	Some acinous leucocytic pneumonia and Edema et stasis pulmonum. Pleuritis fibrino-fibrosa.
	left, inferior.	Some acinous leucocytic pneumonia and Edema et stasis pulmonum. Pleuritis fibrino-fibaosa.
11.	right, superior.	Multiple lobular pneumonia and Pleuritis sero-fibrinosa

229

		Some acino-miliary productive tuberculosis.
	right, inferior.	Diffuse Alveolitis and Multiple acino-lobular pneumonia. Edema pulmonum inflammatorium all over the pulmonal tissues. Pleuritis fibrino-haemorrhagica.
	right, median.	Diffuse Alveolitis and Multiple lobular pneumonia.
	left, superior.	Diffuse Alveolitis and Edema pulmonum in some lobular areas. Compensatoric emphysematic places.
	left, inferior.	Multiple, lobular (rather lobar) pneumonia. Bronchitis catarrhalis acuta and Peribronchitis with some leucocytes-dissemination and some fibrinous separation. Pleuritis fibrinosa with some pleural congestion.
12.	right.	Bronchitis catarrhalis acuta gravis. Slight diffuse Alveolitis with some bacterial dissemination and some leucocytes at some places.
	left.	Bronchitis catarrhalis acuta gravis and Diffuse Alvelitis with some bacterial dissemination at some places.
14.	right, superor.	Multiple lobular (rather lobar) pneumonia in gray hepatisation. Slight proliferation of histiocytes in interlobular connective tissues. Pleuritis fibrino-fibrosa partialis.
	right, inferior.	Multiple lobular (rather lobar) pneumonia. Pleuritis fibrino-haemorrhagica.
	left, superior.	Multiple lobular (rather lobar) pneumonia. Bronchitis catarrhalis gravis. Pleuritis fibrino-haemorrhagica.
	left, inferior.	Multiple lobular pneumonia (rather lobar). Bronchitis catarrhalis gravis. Pleuritis fibrino-haemorrhagica.

230

15.	right, superior.	Multiple acinous exudative pneumonia.
	right, inferior.	Multiple lobular (rather lobar) pneumonia and Bronchitis catarrhalis gravis. Peribronchitis with remarkable bacterial accumulation.
	left, superior.	Diffuse Alveolitis and Edema pulmonum inflammatorium in some acino-lobular areas. Bronchitis catarhalis and Peribronchitis with edematous swelling.
16.	right, superior.	Diffuse Alveolitis and Edema pulmonum inflammatorium all over the pulmonal tissues. Remarkable hemorrhages in some acino-lobular areas. Bronchitis catarrhalis in severe degree. Pleuritis fibrinosa partialis.
	right, inferior.	Slight diffuse Alveolitis and Edema pulmonum inflammatorium leivs. Bronchitis catarrhalis and Pleuritis fibrino-fibrosa.
	left, superior.	Diffuse Alveolitis and Edema pulmonum inflammatorium levis. Bronchitis catarrhalis.
	left, inferior.	Dkffuse Alveolitis. Edema pulmonum levis. Bronchitis catarrhalis.
17.	right, superior.	Multiple lobular pneumonia in somewhat gray hepatisation. Bronchitis catarrhalis acuta in severe degree and Peribronchitis with some edema and some bacterial dissemination.
	right, median.	Lobar pneumonia in grey hepatisation.
	right, inferior.	Multiple lobular (rather lobar) pneumonia in gray hepatisation. Bronchitis catarrhalis acuta in severe degree and Peribronchitis with some bacterial accumulation.
	left, superior.	Lobar pneumonia in gray hepatisation. Bronchitis catarrhalis acuta in severe degree.
	left, inferior.	Diffuse Alveolitis with remarkable infàlmmatory edema all over the pulmonal tissues.

231

((

18.	right.	Slight emphysema and no remarkable changes else.
	left.	Slight Bronchitis and no remarkable changes else. 61
19.	right, superior.	Multiple lobular (rather lobar) pneumonia. Bronchitis catarrhalis in medium degree. Pleuritis haemorrhagico-fibrinousa.
	right, inferior.	Multiple lobular (rather lobar) pneumonia in grady hepatisation. Bronchitis and Pribronchitis with some congestion and some bacterial accumulation. Pleuritis haemorrhagico-fibrinosa.
	left, superior.	Diffuse intense Alveolitis. Edema pulmonum inflammatorium all over the pulmonal tissues. Some congestion, some localised hemorrhages and some leucocytes-dissemination in pleural tissues.
	left, inferior.	Diffuse Alveolitis and Edema pulmonum inflammtorium with some hemorrhages and some leucocytes-emigration in some acino-lobular areas. Bronchitis catarrhalis in medium degree.
20.	right, superior.	Multiple lobular pneumonia in gray hepatisation. Bronchitis catarrhalis and Peribronchitis with some bacterial dissemination. Pleuritis fibrino-fibrosa partialis.
	right, inferior.	Slight fiffuse Alveolitis with Edema pulmonum inflammatorium levis.
	left, superior.	Slight diffuse Alveolitis. Edema pulmonum inflammatorium all over the pulmonal tissues. Pleuritis fibrino-fibrosa partialis.
	left, inferior.	Slight diffuse Alveolitis. Bronchitis catarrhalis in slight degree. Edema pulmonum inflammatorium all over the pulmonal tissues, with some bacterial dissemination.

232

21.	right, superior.	Slight diffuse Alveolitis. Edema pulmonum levis. Bronchitis catarrhalis in slight degree. Intense pleural congestion.
	right, inferior.	Slight diffuse Alveolitis. Edema pulmonum inflammatorium with some desquamated alveolar epitheliums, all over the pulmonal tissues.
	left, superior.	Slight diffuse Alveolitis. Edema pulmonum inflammatorium, all over the pulmonal tissues. Pleuritis fibrino-fibrosa partialis.
	left, inferior.	Slight diffuse Alveolitis. Bronchitis catarrhalis levis.
23.	right, superior.	Considerable congestion and edema of alveolar walls. Very slight Bronchitis catarrhalis. No significant inflammtory changes. Pleuritis fibrino-fibrosa partialis. Primary seat of tuberculous affection.
	right, inferior.	Slight congestion of alveolar walls. No significant inflammtory changes.
	left, superior.	Slight congestion of alveolar walls. No significant inflammtory changes.
	left, inferior.	Slight congestion of alveolar walls. No significant inflammtory changes.
24.	right.	Diffuse Alveolitis and Edema pulmonum inflammatorium with some hemorrhages all over the pulmonal tissues.
	left.	Diffuse Alveolitis and Edema pulmonum inflammatorium with some hemorrhagic reaction. Pleuritis fibrionsa partialis.
26.	right.	Diffuse slight Alveolitis with slight bacterial emigration in alveolar walls. Pleuritis fibrino-fibrosa totalis (right, inf).
	left.	Slight diffuse Alveolitis with Slight congestion of alveolar walls.

233

([redacted] (

Pleuritis fibrino-fibrosa partialis (left, superior) with some acinous productive tuberculosis.

---

27. right, superior. Some lobular pneumonia in obstructive stage. Edema pulmonum inflammatorium with intense edema and some intense congestion of alveolar walls.
Bronchitis catarrhalis in medium degree.

right, inferior. Diffuse Alveolitis with some edema and stasis of pulmonal tissues.

left, superior. Diffuse Alveolitis with considerable pulmonal congestion and some inflammatory edema.

left, inferior. Diffuse slight Alveolitis with considerable pulmonal congestion and some inflammtory edema.

---

29. right, superior. Multiple lobular pneumonia in obstruction-stage.
Pleuritis fibrino-fibrosa.

right, inferior. Multiple lobular (rather lobar) pneumonia in obstruction-stage.
Bronchitis catarrhalis in medium degree and Peribrocnhitis with some bacterial dissemination.
Pleuritis fibrino-exsudativa.

left, superior. Multiple lobular penumonia.

left, inferior. Multiple lobular (rather lobar) pneumonia in obstruction-stage with some inflammatory edema, some leucocytes-emigration and some hemorrhages.
Bronchitis catarrhalis in medium degree.

---

30. right, superior. Slight diffuse Alveolitis with slight inflammatory edema in some acinous places.
Pleuritis fibrino-fibrosa partialis.

right, inferior. Slight diffuse Alveolitis with slight inflammatory edema in some acinous areas.

left, superior. Slight diffuse Alveolitis with slight inflammatory edema in some acinous ateas.

left, inferior. Slight diffuse Alveolitis with Slight inflammatory edema in some acinous areas.

234

31.	right, superior.	Bronchitis catarrhalis gravis and Peribronchitis with some edematous swelling. Edema pulmonum inflammatorium with some wandering cells-emigration in some acinous areas.
	right, inferior.	Bronchitis catarrhalis gravis and Peribronchitis binnecroticans. Multiple lobular pneumonia in grey hepatisation with some small cavern-formation.
	left, superior.	Multiple lobular pneumonia in grey hepatisation.
	left, inferior.	Multiple lobular pneumonia in grey hepatisation, with sme caverns formation. Endobronchitis catarrhalis in intense severe degree and Peribronchitis with intense edema.

32.	right, superior.	Intense congestion and edema of alveolar walls and considerable inflammatory edema.
	right, inferior and median.	Lobar pneumonia in gray hepatisation. Bronchitis cataerrhalis in medium degree. Pleuritis fibrino-fibrosa partials.
	left, superior.	Intense congestion of alveolar walls and some inflammtory edema.
	left, inferior.	Intense congestion of alveolar walls and some inflammatory edema. Bronchitis catarrhalis in medium degree.

33.	right, supperior.	No significant changes. Slight congestion of alveolar walls. Pleuritis fibrino-fibrosa partialis.
	right, inferior.	Bronchitis catarrhalis in medium degree. Slight puulonal congestion.
	left, superior.	No particular changes.
	left, inferior.	No particular changes.

34.	right, superior.	Diffuse Alveolitis and Some acinous leucocytic pneumonia. Endobronchitis catarrhalis levis. Pleuritis fibrino-fibrosa totalis.

235

	right, inferior.	Diffuse Alveolitis with Some acinous leucocytic pneumonia. Intense congestion, edematous swelling and some round-cells-dissemination in pleural tissues. Pleuritis fibrino-fibrosa totalis.
	left, superiar.	Slight diffuse Alveolitis with some acinous leucocytic pneumonic areas. Bronchitis catarrhalis in medium degree.
	left, inferior.	Stasis et edema pulmonum levis. Bronchitis catarrhalis levis. Some pleural congestion.
35.	right, superior.	Multiple lobular (rather lobar) pneumonia in gray hepatisation. Bronchitis catarrhalis in severe degree. Pleuritis fibrino-haemorrhagica.
	right, inferior.	Edema et stasis pulmonum.
	left, superior.	Edema et stais pulmonum.
	left, inferior.	Multiple lobular (rather lobar) pneumonia in gray hepatisation. Bronchitis catarrhalis in medium degree and Peribronchitis with some leucocytes-dissemination and some bacterial accumlation. Pleuritis fibrinosa et fibrino-fibrosa.
36.	right, superior.	Multiple acinou-lobular pneumonia. Edema et stasis pulmonum all over the pulmonal tissues.
	right, inferior.	Edema pulmonum inflammatorium in severe degree, with some leucocytes-dissemination all over the pulmonal tidsues. Bronchitis and Peribronchitis with some bacterial dissemination in peribronchial and pleural tissues.
	left, superior.	Multiple acino-locbular pneumonia in gray hepatisation. Bronchitis and Peribronchitis. Some bacterial accumulation in subpleural tissues.

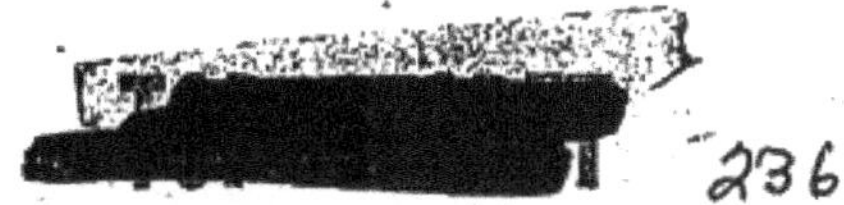

236

38.	right.	Slight pulmonal congestion and no remarkable changes else.
	left.	Slight pulmonal congestion and no remarkable changes else. Pleuritis fibrosa (left, supe rior).
40.	right, superior.	Multiple lobular pneumonia in obstructivestage. Pleuritis fibrino-exsudativa. Bronchitis catarrhalis.
	right, inferior.	Diffuse Alveolitis.
	left, superior.	Diffuse Alveolitis with some slight inflammatory edema.
	left, inferior.	Diffuse Alveolitis with some slight diffuse inflammatory edema.
42.	right.	Multiple lobular (rather lobar) pneumonia. Bronchitis and Peribronchitis with massive bacterial dssemination.
	left.	Diffuse Alveolitis with Edema pulmonum inflammatorium in medium degree, all over the pulmonal tissues.
44.	right.	Diffuse Alveolitis with Edema pulmonum inflammatorium all over the pulmonal tissues. Bronchitis catarrhalis in medium degree.
	left.	Diffuse Alveolitis with Edema puulmonum inflammatorium a l over the pulmonal tissues. Bronchitis catarrhalis and Peribronchitis with slight edema and some bacterial dissemination.
46.	right.	Edema pulmonum inflammatorium in severe degree.
	left, superior.	Edema pulmonum inflammatorium in severe degree.
	left, inferior.	Multiple, lobular (rather lobar) pnuemonia. Edema pulmonum inflammtorium in severe degree, all over the pulmonal tissues. Some subpleural bacterial accumulation.
47.	right, superor.	Edema pulmonum in severe degree all over the pulmonal tissues, with some bacterial dissemination.

237

Bronchitis and Peribronchitis with considerable congestion and edema.
Pleuritis fibrosa partialis.

	right, inferior.	Edema pulmonum in severe degree all over the pulmonal tissues, with some bacterial masses in alveolar walls. Slight hyperplasia of alveolar epitheliums at the intercalary portion of lung, as slight proliferative changes. Slight pleural congestion.
	left, superior.	Slight pulmonal congestion. Bronchitis catarhalis in medium degree.
	left, inferior.	Slight diffuse Alveolitis with some hyperplasia of alveolar epithelium. Considerable pleural edema.
49.	right, superior.	Edema pulmonum in severe degree, all over the pulmonal tissues.
	right, inferior.	Slight pulmonal congestion. Slight Bronchitis catarhalis.
	left, superior.	Lobar pneumonia in gray hepatisation. Bronchitis catarrhalis and Peribronchitis with some bacterial accumulation. Pleuritis fibrino-haemorrhagica.
	left, inferior.	Diffuse Alveolitis with some leucocytes-emigration. Some leucocytic pneumonia in some acinous areas. Edema pulmonum in medium degree, all over the pulmonal tissues. Pleuritis fibrino-fibrosa duplex.
S-1.	right.	Slight pulmonal edema with some bacterial accumulation at some places. Bronchitis catarrhalis in slight degree.
	left.	Slight pulmonal congestion with some bacterial emigration at some places.
S-2.	right, superior.	Slight diffuse Alveolitis with some leucocytes-dissemination and some increased alveolar epithelium. Stasis et edema pulmonum levis. Pleuritis fibrino-fibrosa interlobaris.

238

	right, inferior.	Slight diffuse Alveolitis with some leucocytes-dissemination and some increased alveolar epithelium.
	left, superior.	Slight diffuse Alveolitis with some leucocytes-dissemination and some increased alveolar epithelium.
	left, inferior.	Slight diuffuse Alveolitis with some leucocytes dissemination. Pleuritis fibrino-fibrosa interlobaris.
S-3.	right.	Diffuse Alveolitis and Edema pulmonum inflammatorium with some leucocytes-dissemination. Pleuritis fibrinosa. Multuple lobular pneumonia in gray hepatisation.
	left.	Diffuse Alveolitis and Edema pulmonum inflammatorium in medium degree.
S-4.	right.	Diffuse Alveolitis with Edema pulmonum inflammatorium, with some desquamated alveolar epitheliums. Bronchitis catarrhalis acuta and Peribronchitis with some edematous swelling. Some pleural edema and some subpleural congestion.
	left.	Diffuse Alveolitis with Edema pulmonum inflammatorium, with some desquamated alveolar epitheliums. Bronchitis catarrhalis and Peribronchitis with some congestion and some edema.
S-5.	right.	Slight diffuse Alveolitis and Edema pulmonum inflammatorium in medium degree. Bronchitis catarrhalis and Peribronchitis with some edematous swelling.
	left.	Slight diffuse Alveolitis and Edema pulmonum inflammatorium in medium degree. Bronchitis catarrhalis acuta in slight degree. Some pleural congestion. No particular changes else.
S-6.	right, superior.	Slight Alveolitis with slight congestion and pulmonal edema, accompanied with some bacterial dissemination at some places.
	righh, inferior.	Slight diffuse Alveolitis with some congestion

239

		and pulmonal edema, accompanied with some bacterial dissemination at some places. Pleuritis sero-fibrinosa.
	left, superior.	Slight diffuse Alveolitis with some pulmonal congestion and edema, accompanied with some bacterial dissemination at some places.
	left, inferior.	Slight diffuse Alveolitis with some pulmonal congestion and edema, accompanied with some bacterial dissemination at some places.

S-8.	right, superior.	Lobar pneumonia in gray hepatisation. Slight Bronchitis catarrhalis. Pleuritis sero-haemorrhagica. Some subpleural and pulmonal bacterial dissemination.
	right, inferior.	Multiple acino-lobular pnuemonia, with Edema pulmonum inflammatorium in severe degree. Pleuritis sero-haemorrhagica. Some subpleural bacterial dissemination.
	left, superior.	Multiple lobular (rather lobar) pneumonia in gray hepatisation. Bronchitis catarrhalis acuta in medium degree. Bacterial dissemination in pulmonal and subpleural tisseues. Pleuritis sero-haemorrhagica.
	left, inferior.	Multiple acino-lobular pneumonia with leucocytic and hemorrhagic changes. Remarkable pulmonal congestion and edema. Bronchitis catarrhalis acuta in medium degree. Pleuritis sero-fibrinosa.

S-9.	right, superior.	Slight diffuse Alveolitis with slight pulmonal congestion and edema.
	right, inferior.	Slight diffuse alveolitis with slight pulmonal congestion and edema.
	left, superior.	Multiple acino-lobular pneumonia and Bronchitis catarrhalis acuta in medium degree.
	left, inferior.	Multiple acino-lobular pneumonia and

240

		Bronchitis catarrhalis acuta in medium degree. Primary plague-lung-pneumonia.
		Pleuritis fibrino-fibrosa duplex.
S-10.	right, superior.	Multiple lobular pneumonia with intense exudative-leucocytic-hemorrhagic changes. Bronchitis catarrhalis acuta in severe degree. Peribronchitis with some bacterial dissemination.
	right, inferior.	Multiple lobular pneumonia with intense exudative-leucocytic-hemorrhagic changes. Bronchitis catarrhalis acuta in severe degree. Peribrocnhitis with some bacterial dissemination.
	left, superior.	Multiple lobular pneumonia with intense exudative-leucocytic-hemorrhagic changes. Bronchitis catarrhalis in severe degree and Peribronchitis with some bacterial dissemination.
	left, inferior.	Multiple lobular pneumonia with intense exudative-leucocytic-hemorrhagic changes. Bronchitis catarrhalis acuta in severe degree. Peribronchitis with some bacterial dissemination. Remarkable pleural congestion (right and left).
S-11.	right, superior and inferior.	Diffuse Alveolitis and Edema pulmonum inflammatorium all over the pulmonal tissues. Remarkable Anthracosis of pulmonal and pleural tissues.
	left, superior and inferior.	Diffuse Alveolitis and Considerable pulmonal congestion and edema. Remarkable pulmonal and pleural Anthracosis.
S-12.	right, superior. and inferior.	Multiple lobular pneumonia in gray hepatisation. Pleuritis exsudativa. Bronchitis catarrhalis in severe degree and Penibronchitis with intense edema and congestion.
	left, superior and inferior.	Diffuse Alveolitis and Edema pulmonum inflammatorium. Some pleural congestion.
S-14.	right.	Emphysema bullosum levis. Some submiliary leucocytic pneumonic places.

CONFIDENTIAL

241

		Considerable congestion of pleural tissues.
	left.	Emphysema bullosum levis. Some submiliary leucocytic pneumonic places. Pleuritis fibrino-fibrosa (left, apex).
S-15.	right.	Statis et edema pulmonum. Congestion and edema of plural tissues.
	left.	Diffuse Alveolitis with Edema pulmonum inflammatorium levis. Congestion of plerual tissues.
S-19.	right.	Diffuse Slight Alveolitis. Primary seat of tuberculous affection. Pleuritis fibrino-fibrosa.
	left.	Diffuse Alveolitis and Some leucocytic-exudative changes in some acinous areas.
S-22.	right.	Some lobular pneumonia in gray hepatisation. Pleuritis exsudativo-haemorrhagica. Slight proliferative reaction of alveolar epitheliums at the other hand.
	left.	Diffuse Alveolitis and Multiple acinous pneumonic places with some leucocytes-emigration.
S-26.	right.	Diffuse Alveolitis and Edema pulmonum inflammatorium. Considerable congestion of pleural tissues.
	left.	Diffuse Alveolitis and Edema pulmonum inflammatorium. Considerable congestion of pleural tissues.
S-28.	right.	Slight diffuse Alveolitis and Edema pulmonum inflammatorium in some lobular areas. Pleuritis inter-lobaris.
	left.	Slight diffuse Alveolitis and Edema pulmonum inflammatorium in some lobular areas.
S-38.	right.	Multiple lobular (rather lobar) pneumonia in gray hepatisation. Pleuritis sero-fibrinosa with intense congestion

242

	and some leucocytes-dissemination in pleural tissues.
left.	Multiple acino-lobular pneumonia. Remarkable congestion and some leucocytes-dissemination in plerual tissues.

CONFIDENTIAL

843

SUMMARY.

A) Primary lung-plague in I case, which was infected during the nursing of the patient. I case.

S-9.

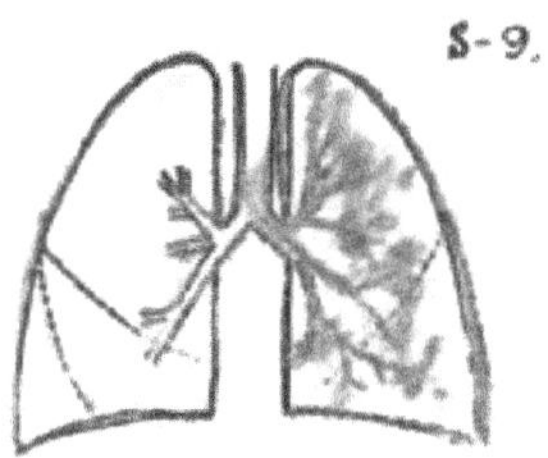

244

B) Metastatic changes in pulmonal tissues.

(I) Metastatic changes in form "diffuse Alveolitis".

a) Diffuse Alveolitis, without any remarkable changes 12 cases.

CONFIDENTIAL

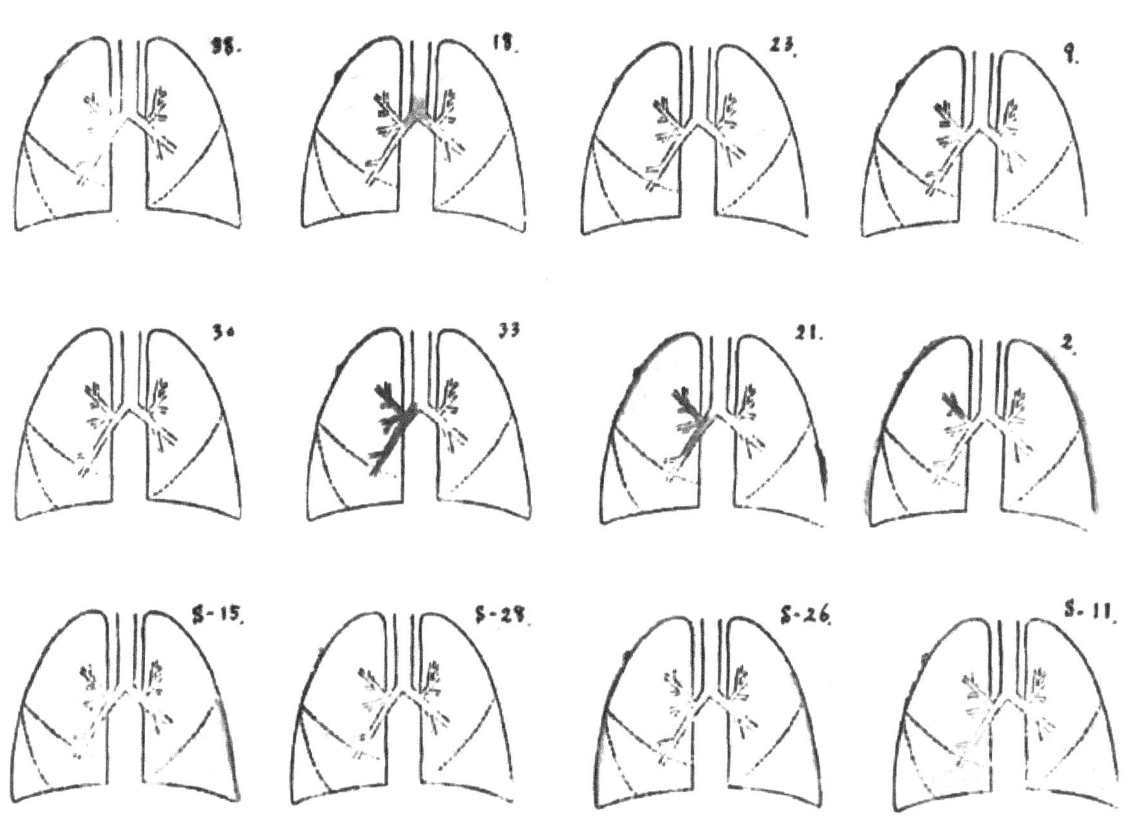

245

b) Diffuse Alveolitis, accompanied with Bronchitis. 3 cases.

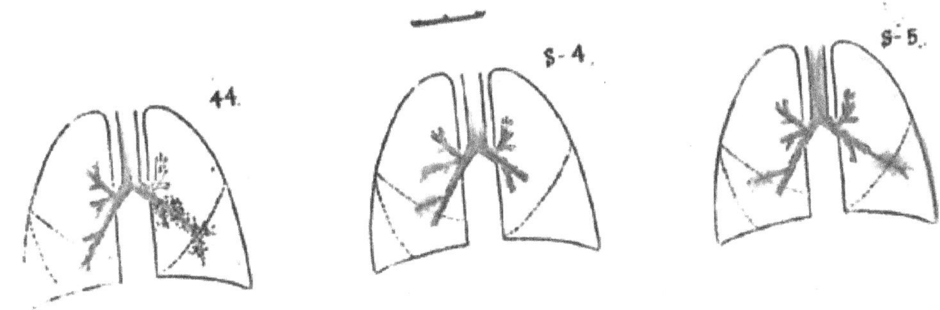

c) Diffuse Alveolitis, accompanied with some leucocytes dissemination all over the pulmonal tissues. 2 cases.

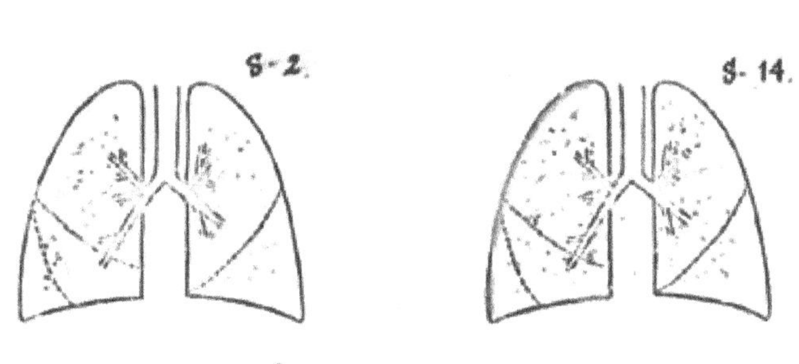

d) Diffuse Alveolitis with disseminated hemorrhages in pulmonal tissues. 2 cases.

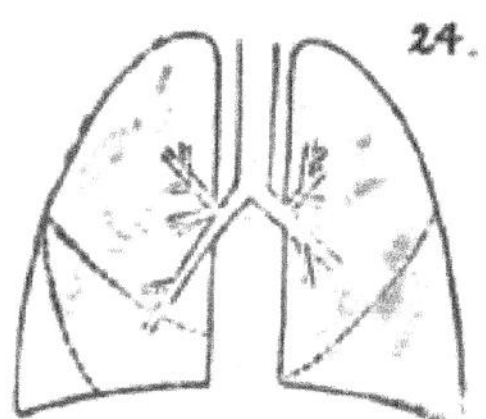

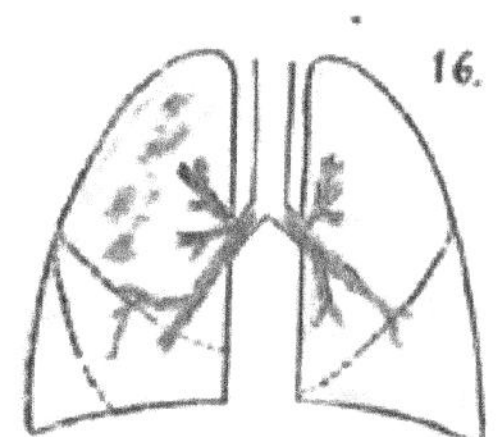

e) Diffuse Alveolitis with bacterial dissemination. 5 cases

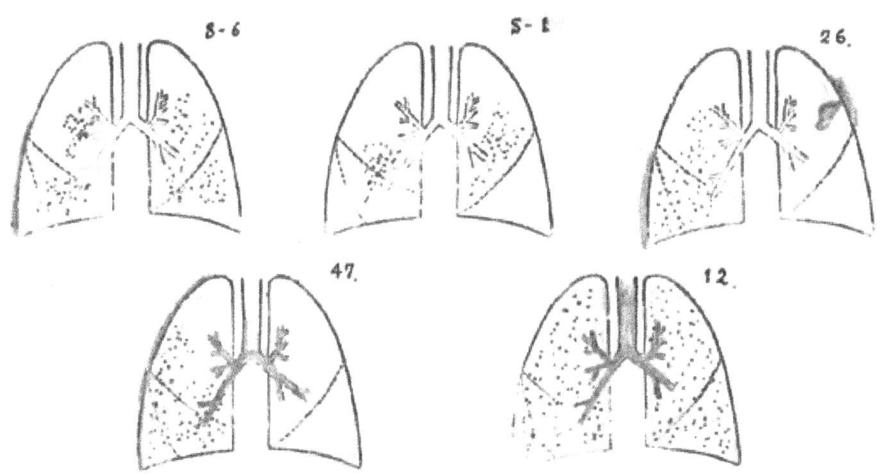

2) Metastatic changes in form " acinous pneumonia ".

3 cases.

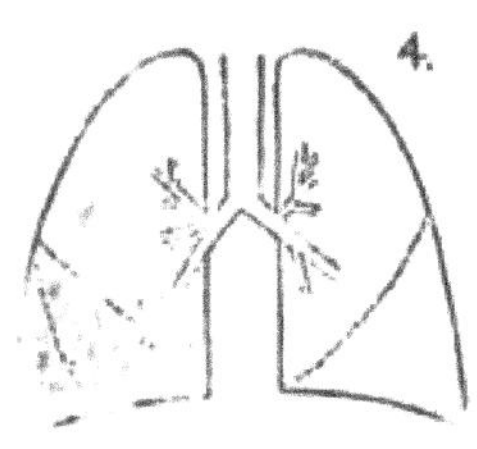

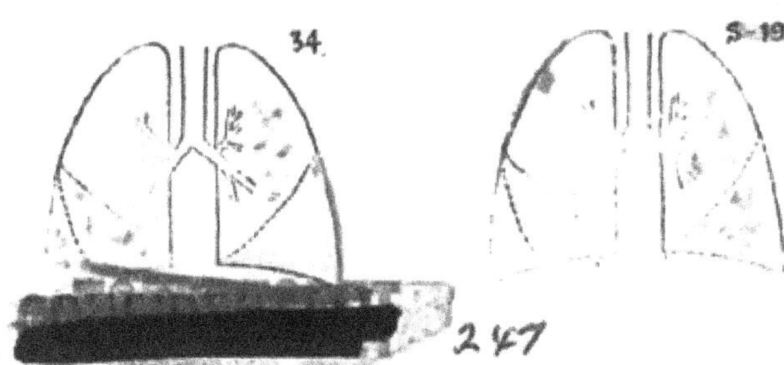

247

3) Metastatic changes in form " lobular pneumonia ". 

7 % cases.

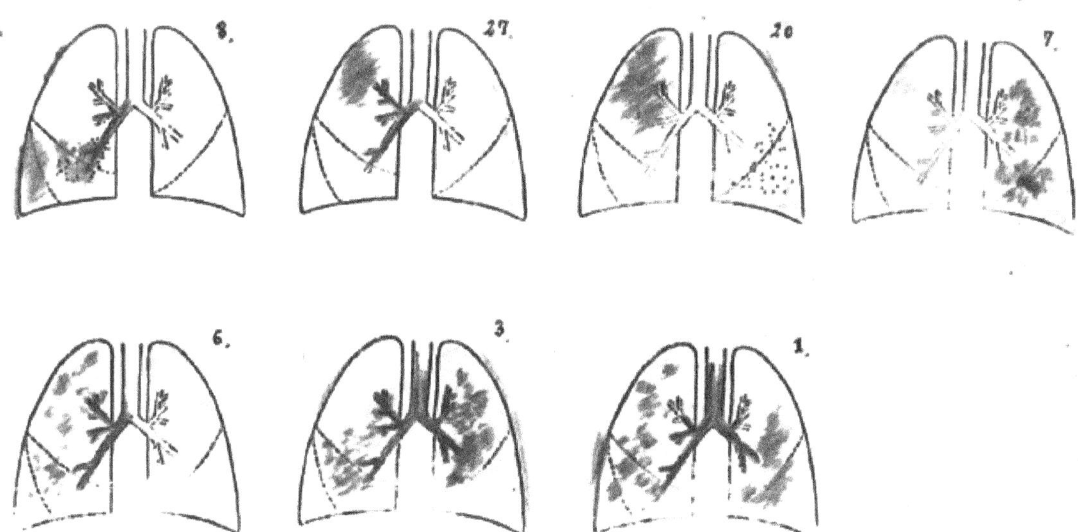

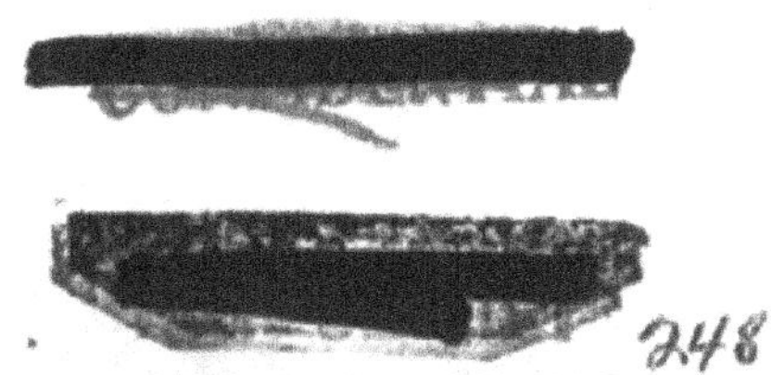

4) Metastatic changes in form "multiple lobular pneumonia (rather lobar pneumonia)".

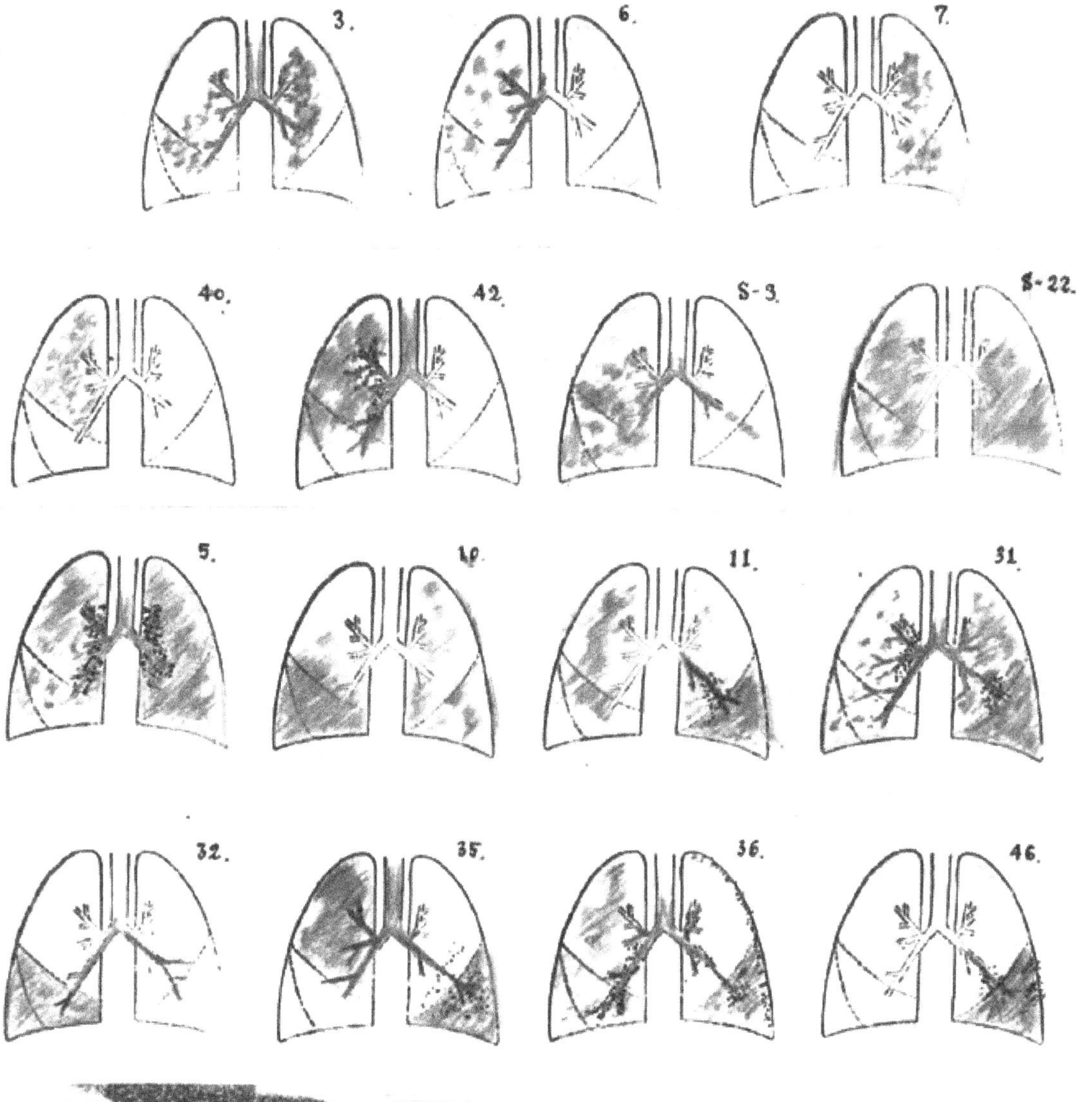

3. 6. 7.

40. 42. S-3. S-22.

5. 10. 11. 31.

32. 35. 36. 46.

249

49.　S-10　S-12　S-38

14.　15.　17.　19.

29.　S-8

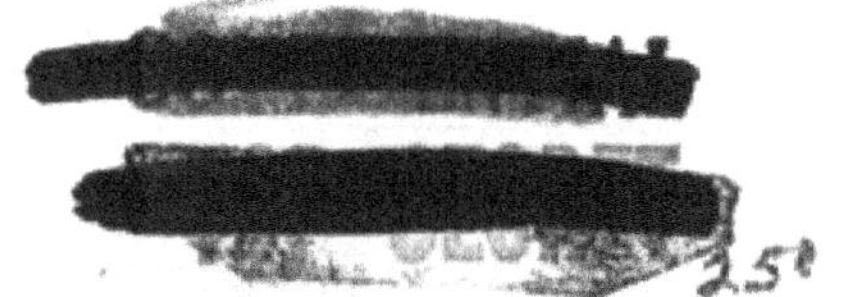

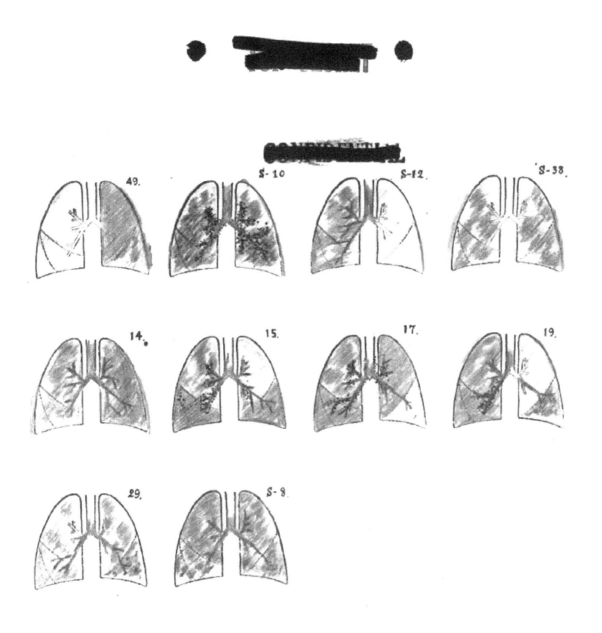

LUNG

			N 1	N 3	N 4 r.s	〃 r.m	〃 r.i	〃 l.	N 5 r.	〃 l.	N 6	〃 s	N 7	N 8	N 10 r.s	〃 r.i	〃 l.s	〃 l.i	N 11 r.s	〃 r.i	〃 l.i	N 12	N 14 r.s	〃 r.i
Alveoli		Emphysema	−	−	÷	÷	−	−	−	−	÷	−	÷	−	÷	−	÷	−	÷	−	−	−	−	−
Alveoli		Atelectasis	−	−	÷	+:	÷	÷	−	÷	÷	÷	÷	÷	−	−	÷	÷	÷	−	−	÷	−	−
Alveoli	Alveolar Spaces	Edema	+	++	÷	÷	÷	+	++	++	÷	+	+	−	++	++	+	+	+	+++	−	÷	+	÷
Alveoli	Alveolar Spaces	Fibrin	÷	÷	÷	÷	÷	−	−	÷	÷	−	−	−	−	÷	−	−	÷	÷	÷	−	++	÷
Alveoli	Alveolar Spaces	Erythrocytes	+++	÷	÷	÷	÷	÷	÷	÷	÷	(+)	÷	−	÷	+:	−	−	−	÷	+	−	(+)	÷
Alveoli	Alveolar Spaces	Leucocytes	++	+++	÷	÷	÷	÷	+:	++:	+	÷	÷	−	÷	+++	(÷)	−	++:	++	+++	−	++	+:
Alveoli	Alveolar Spaces	Lymphocytes	÷	÷	÷	−	÷	−	÷	−	−	÷	÷	−	−	−	−	−	÷	÷	÷	−	−	−
Alveoli	Alveolar Spaces	Desquamated Epithelial Cells	+	+:	+	÷	÷	÷	+	÷	+++	÷	+	−	÷	÷	(÷)	(÷)	÷	÷	+	÷	+	÷
Alveoli	Alveolar Spaces	Heart Desease Cells	−	÷	÷	÷	÷	−	−	−	−	÷	÷	−	−	−	(÷)	(÷)	÷	÷	−	÷	−	−
Alveoli	Alveolar Spaces	Colonies of Bacterium	+	+++	−	−	−	÷	++	+++	−	−	÷	−	+	++++	+	++	+	÷	+	−	(+)	+
Alveoli	Alveolar Walls	Congestion of Capillaries	−	÷	+:	+:	+	++	+	+	(+)	+++	+	÷	+	÷	÷	÷	+	+	÷	+	÷	+
Alveoli	Alveolar Walls	Swelling of Walls	÷	÷	+	÷	÷	+	÷	÷	÷	+:	÷	÷	÷	÷	+	+:	+	+	÷	+	÷	÷
Alveoli	Alveolar Walls	Thickening of Walls	−	−	−	−	−	−	−	−	−	÷	÷	−	−	−	−	−	−	−	−	−	−	−
Alveoli	Alveolar Walls	Hyperplasia of Wall Cells	−	−	(÷)	−	÷	−	−	−	÷	÷	÷	−	−	−	−	÷	÷	−	−	÷	÷	−
Alveoli	Alveolar Walls	Leucocytes in Capillaries	−	÷	÷	÷	÷	÷	÷	÷	÷	÷	÷	÷	+	−	÷	÷	+	÷	÷	÷	÷	÷
Alveoli	Alveolar Walls	Lymphocytes in Capillaries	−	−	÷	÷	÷	÷	÷	−	−	+	÷	−	−	−	−	÷	−	−	−	÷	−	−
Alveoli	Alveolar Walls	Colonies of Bacterium	÷	++	−	−	−	+	+	+	−	−	−	−	÷	+++	÷	÷	−	÷	÷	(+)	(÷)	÷
Bronchioli	Contents	Desquamated Epithelial Cells	+	÷	+:	+:	+:	(+++)	÷	++	(+++)	÷	++	(÷)	−	+	÷	−	(÷)	÷	÷	+:	(+)	÷
Bronchioli	Contents	Mucus	−	−	++	++	++	(+++)	+	−	÷	÷	÷	−	−	−	÷	−	(÷)	−	÷	÷	(+)	−
Bronchioli	Contents	Fibrin	÷	−	−	−	−	−	÷	÷	−	−	−	−	−	+	÷	−	(÷)	÷	+	−	+	−
Bronchioli	Contents	Erythrocytes	÷	(÷)	−	−	−	−	÷	÷	−	−	−	−	−	+	÷	−	−	÷	÷	÷	÷	−
Bronchioli	Contents	Leucocytes	+	(+)	−	−	−	−	+:	+	÷	−	−	−	−	++	÷	−	(÷)	+++	+:	−	+	−
Bronchioli	Contents	Lymphocytes	÷	−	−	−	−	−	÷	−	−	−	−	−	−	−	−	−	−	÷	÷	÷	÷	−
Bronchioli	Contents	Colonies of Bacterium	÷	(+)	−	−	−	÷	+	÷	−	−	−	−	−	++++	÷	−	−	÷	−	+	−	−
Bronchioli	Peribronchial Tissues	Congestion	−	++	+	÷	÷	+++	+	++	+	÷	+	÷	+:	÷	÷	−	−	+:	÷	(+++)	+:	++
Bronchioli	Peribronchial Tissues	Edema	++	+	÷	÷	÷	+	÷	+++	÷	−	÷	−	+	|	÷	÷	(+++)	+	+++	÷	÷	+
Bronchioli	Peribronchial Tissues	Erythrocytes	÷	÷	−	−	−	−	÷	+	−	−	−	−	÷	++	−	−	−	÷	÷	−	−	÷
Bronchioli	Peribronchial Tissues	Leucocytes	++	++:	÷	÷	÷	÷	÷	÷	÷	÷	−	−	÷	÷	÷	−	÷	÷	+++	−	(+)	++
Bronchioli	Peribronchial Tissues	Lymphocytes	÷	÷	÷	÷	÷	÷	÷	÷	÷	÷	÷	−	÷	+	−	−	−	÷	÷	÷	÷	−
Bronchioli	Peribronchial Tissues	Histiocytes	−	÷	÷	÷	÷	÷	−	÷	+	÷	÷	−	÷	−	÷	−	−	÷	÷	÷	÷	÷
Bronchioli	Peribronchial Tissues	Colonies of Bacterium	÷	++	−	−	−	−	+	+++	−	−	−	−	(++)	++++	÷	÷	−	÷	−	−	(+)	÷
Blood Vessels	Contents	Erythrocytes	++	++:	++	+	++:	+++	+++:	+++	++	+++:	++	÷	+:	+	+++:	++:	++	++:	÷	+:	÷	(÷)
Blood Vessels	Contents	Leucocytes	÷	÷	(+)	+	÷	÷	÷	−	÷	(+)	÷	+	÷	÷	÷	÷	÷	÷	÷	÷	÷	−
Blood Vessels	Contents	Lymphocytes	−	−	÷	÷	÷	−	−	−	÷	(÷)	÷	÷	÷	−	−	−	−	−	−	÷	÷	−
Blood Vessels	Contents	Monocytes	−	−	÷	÷	÷	−	−	−	÷	(÷)	÷	÷	÷	−	−	−	−	−	−	÷	−	−
Blood Vessels	Contents	Colonies of Bacterium	−	−	−	(+)	−	−	−	−	−	−	−	−	−	−	−	−	−	÷	−	−	−	−
Blood Vessels	Perivascular Tissues	Edema	÷	+:	+	+	+	+	+	+	÷	÷	÷	+	÷	+	÷	÷	+:	+	+++	+	+:	+
Blood Vessels	Perivascular Tissues	Hemorrhage	−	÷	−	−	−	−	÷	÷	−	−	(+++)	−	−	÷	−	÷	−	−	÷	−	−	÷
Blood Vessels	Perivascular Tissues	Infiltration: Leucocytes	÷	−	−	−	−	−	÷	−	−	−	−	−	−	÷	−	−	(++)	−	++	−	÷	÷
Blood Vessels	Perivascular Tissues	Infiltration: Lymphocytes	−	−	÷	−	−	−	−	−	−	−	−	−	−	−	−	−	÷	−	−	−	−	−
Blood Vessels	Perivascular Tissues	Proliferation of Histiocytic Cells	−	÷	÷	÷	−	÷	−	−	−	−	÷	−	÷	−	−	−	÷	−	+	−	÷	÷
Blood Vessels	Perivascular Tissues	Colonies of Bacterium	(+)	+	−	−	−	−	÷	÷	−	−	−	−	−	+++	−	−	−	−	(+)	−	−	(÷)
Pleura		Fibrin - Separation	−	−	−	−	−	−	|	|	−	−	−	−	−	+	|	|	+	+	++	−	+	+
Pleura		Thickening	−	−	−	−	−	−	|	|	÷	−	−	÷	−	−	|	|	÷	÷	÷	−	÷	÷
Pleura		Congestion	+++	++	++	−	÷	−	|	|	÷	÷	÷	÷	++:	++	|	|	++	++	++:	÷	++	++
Pleura		Edema	++:	(++)	÷	÷	÷	÷	|	|	−	−	÷	÷	÷	+	|	|	+	+	++	÷	+	÷
Pleura		Hemorrhage	+	÷	−	−	−	−	|	|	−	−	−	−	÷	++	|	|	÷	÷	++	−	÷	÷
Pleura	Infiltration	Leucocytes	÷	++	−	−	−	−	|	|	−	−	−	−	−	++	|	|	++	÷	+++	÷	÷	+
Pleura	Infiltration	Lymphocytes	−	÷	−	−	−	−	|	|	−	−	−	−	÷	÷	|	|	−	−	−	÷	−	−
Pleura		Proliferation of Histiocytic Cells	−	÷	−	−	−	−	|	|	−	−	−	−	÷	−	|	|	−	÷	÷	−	+	÷
Pleura		Colonies of Bacterium	++	+++	−	−	−	−	|	|	−	−	−	−	−	++++	|	|	+	−	+	−	(+)	+

251

LUNG

		N 14 l.s	〃 l.i	N 15 r.s	〃 r.i	〃 l.s	〃 l.i	N 16 r.s	〃 r.i	〃 l.i	N 17	N 18	N 19 r.s	〃 r.i	〃 l.s	〃 l.i	N 20	N 21 r.s	〃 r.i	〃 l.s	〃 l.i	N 23 r.s	〃 l.s
Alveoli	Emphysema	−	−	+±	−	+	−	−	−	−	−	+	−	−	−	−	−	−	−	−	±	−	+±
Alveoli	Atelectasis	−	−	±	−	±	−	−	−	±	±	±	−	−	−	±	−	±	±	±	(+)	±	±
Alveoli, Alveolar Spaces	Edema	(+)	±	+	++	+	±	++	+	±	++	−	±	++	++±	+	++±	−	+	±	(±)	(±)	±
Alveoli, Alveolar Spaces	Fibrin	++	+	±	+	−	+±	−	−	−	−	−	±	−	−	−	−	−	−	−	−	−	−
Alveoli, Alveolar Spaces	Erythrocytes	(±)	±	(±)	+	±	+±	+	±	±	±	−	±	±	±	±	±	−	−	−	−	(±)	−
Alveoli, Alveolar Spaces	Leucocytes	++	++	+	++	(+)	++	−	−	±	+±	−	+±	+	±	+	++	−	−	−	−	−	−
Alveoli, Alveolar Spaces	Lymphocytes	±	±	±	±	−	−	−	±	±	−	−	±	±	±	±	±	−	−	−	−	−	−
Alveoli, Alveolar Spaces	Desquamated Epithelial Cells	+±	±	±	±	±	±	±	±	±	+	−	±	+	+	±	+±	(±)	(+)	±	±	−	−
Alveoli, Alveolar Spaces	Heart Desease Cells	−	−	−	−	±	−	−	±	±	±	−	−	±	±	±	±	(±)	±	(±)	±	−	−
Alveoli, Alveolar Spaces	Colonies of Bacterium	±	++	++	+	+	+	±	−	−	+	−	+	++	+++	+	+	−	−	−	−	−	−
Alveoli, Alveolar Walls	Congestion of Capillaries	±	+	±	+±	+	+±	+	+±	++	+	−	+	+	+	+	±	±	±	+	±	+	+
Alveoli, Alveolar Walls	Swelling of Walls	+	±	+	±	+	±	±	+	±	±	−	±	±	−	±	+	±	±	±	±	+	++
Alveoli, Alveolar Walls	Thickening of Walls	±	−	−	−	−	−	−	−	−	−	−	−	−	−	−	−	−	−	−	−	−	−
Alveoli, Alveolar Walls	Hyperplasia of Wall Cells	(+)	−	−	−	−	−	−	±	±	−	−	−	−	−	−	±	−	−	−	−	−	−
Alveoli, Alveolar Walls	Leucocytes in Capillaries	±	±	±	±	±	±	±	±	+	±	(±)	±	±	±	±	±	±	±	−	±	±	(±)
Alveoli, Alveolar Walls	Lymphocytes in Capillaries	±	±	−	−	±	−	±	±	±	−	−	−	−	−	−	±	−	−	−	−	±	−
Alveoli, Alveolar Walls	Colonies of Bacterium	−	±	−	−	±	+	±	−	−	−	−	−	−	−	±	±	−	−	−	−	−	−
Bronchioli, Contents	Desquamated Epithelial Cells	(+++)	+	++±	++	±	++	+	±	(+)	++	±	+	+	+±	(+±)	+±	++	±	(+)	±	±	+
Bronchioli, Contents	Mucus	+±	−	−	−	−	−	+±	±	(++)	−	±	−	±	++	±	±	+	−	−	±	±	±
Bronchioli, Contents	Fibrin	+±	±	−	+	±	+	−	±	(±)	−	−	±	−	±	−	(±)	−	−	−	−	−	−
Bronchioli, Contents	Erythrocytes	+	±	±	+	(+)	±	±	±	−	±	−	±	±	±	±	±	−	−	±	−	−	−
Bronchioli, Contents	Leucocytes	+±	±	±	+±	(+)	++	±	−	−	+±	−	±	±	±	±	±	−	−	−	−	−	−
Bronchioli, Contents	Lymphocytes	−	±	−	−	±	−	−	−	−	±	−	−	−	−	−	±	−	−	−	−	−	−
Bronchioli, Contents	Colonies of Bacterium	−	−	−	+	+	+	+	±	(±)	++	−	±	+	++	+	±	−	−	−	−	−	−
Bronchioli, Peribronchial Tissues	Congestion	(+++)	±	+	++	±	+++	++	+±	±	++	±	±	++	+	++	+±	++	−	+	−	±	+
Bronchioli, Peribronchial Tissues	Edema	(+)	±	±	+	±	+±	+	±	±	+	±	+±	±	±	±	±	+	±	+	+	±	±
Bronchioli, Peribronchial Tissues	Erythrocytes	(+)	−	−	±	−	+	±	−	−	±	−	±	−	±	±	±	−	−	−	−	−	−
Bronchioli, Peribronchial Tissues	Leucocytes	+±	+	−	±	±	+	−	±	−	±	−	±	±	−	(±)	±	−	−	−	±	−	−
Bronchioli, Peribronchial Tissues	Lymphocytes	+	±	±	±	±	+	+	±	±	±	−	±	±	±	±	±	±	±	−	±	−	±
Bronchioli, Peribronchial Tissues	Histiocytes	+±	−	−	±	±	±	±	±	±	−	−	±	±	−	±	−	±	±	−	±	−	−
Bronchioli, Peribronchial Tissues	Colonies of Bacterium	(+++)	±	+	++	−	++	−	−	−	+±	−	±	±	+	−	±	−	−	−	−	−	−
Blood Vessels, Contents	Erythrocytes	±	±	±	+++±	++	++	++	++	+++	+±	±	±	+++	+±	++	+±	++	+±	+±	++	++	++
Blood Vessels, Contents	Leucocytes	±	±	+	±	±	±	−	±	±	±	±	−	−	−	±	±	±	−	±	±	±	−
Blood Vessels, Contents	Lymphocytes	−	−	±	±	−	−	−	±	±	±	−	−	−	−	−	−	−	−	−	−	−	−
Blood Vessels, Contents	Monocytes	−	−	±	±	−	−	−	−	±	±	−	−	−	−	−	±	−	−	−	−	−	−
Blood Vessels, Contents	Colonies of Bacterium	−	−	−	−	−	−	−	−	−	−	−	−	−	−	±	−	−	−	−	−	−	−
Blood Vessels, Perivascular Tissues	Edema	+	+	±	+	±	+	+±	±	±	+	±	+	±	±	±	+	±	+±	±	±	±	±
Blood Vessels, Perivascular Tissues	Hemorrhage	(+±)	−	−	+	−	(+)	(±)	−	−	−	−	±	−	±	−	−	−	−	−	−	−	−
Blood Vessels, Perivascular Tissues	Infiltration: Leucocytes	±	±	−	±	−	±	−	−	−	−	−	±	−	−	−	−	−	−	−	−	−	−
Blood Vessels, Perivascular Tissues	Infiltration: Lymphocytes	−	−	−	−	−	−	−	−	−	−	−	−	−	−	−	−	−	±	−	−	−	−
Blood Vessels, Perivascular Tissues	Proliferation of Histiocytic Cells	+	±	−	−	−	−	−	±	−	−	−	±	±	−	−	±	±	±	−	−	−	−
Blood Vessels, Perivascular Tissues	Colonies of Bacterium	−	±	−	+	−	+	−	−	−	±	−	−	±	±	−	±	−	−	−	−	−	−
Pleura	Fibrin-Separation	+	+	−	|	−	±	−	−	−	±	−	±	−	−	−	−	−	−	|	|	−	|
Pleura	Thickening	±	−	−	|	−	−	−	+	−	−	−	−	−	−	−	−	−	−	|	|	−	|
Pleura	Congestion	++	++	−	|	±	+++	±	+	±	++	±	++±	++±	++	±	++	++	+	|	|	±	|
Pleura	Edema	+	±	±	|	±	+++	±	+±	±	±	±	+	±	±	±	±	±	+	|	|	±	|
Pleura	Hemorrhage	±	±	−	|	−	±	−	±	−	±	−	+	+±	±	−	±	−	−	|	|	−	|
Pleura	Infiltration: Leucocytes	±	±	−	|	−	±	−	−	−	±	−	±	±	−	−	−	−	−	|	|	−	|
Pleura	Infiltration: Lymphocytes	±	−	−	|	−	±	−	−	−	±	−	−	−	−	−	−	−	−	|	|	−	|
Pleura	Proliferation of Histiocytic Cells	+	±	−	|	−	±	−	±	−	±	−	±	±	−	−	−	±	±	|	|	−	|
Pleura	Colonies of Bacterium	−	−	−	|	−	±	−	−	−	+	−	+	+	+	−	+	−	−	|	|	−	|

252

LUNG

			N 24 r	〃 l	N 26	N 29 r	〃 l	N 30 r	〃 l.s	〃 l.i	N 31 r.s	〃 r.i	〃 l.i	N 32 r.s	〃 r.i	〃 l.s	〃 l.i	N 33 r.s	〃 r.i	〃 l.s	〃 l.i	N 34 r.s	〃 r.i	〃 l.s
Alveoli		Emphysema	−	−	−	−	−	∸	−	÷	++	−	∸	÷	−	+:	+	+	÷	÷	÷	−	−	−
		Atelectasis	−	−	−	−	−	−	−	∸	÷	−	−	−	−	÷	÷	÷	∸	−	÷	−	÷	∸
	Alveolar Spaces	Edema	÷	÷	+++	+	+	(÷)	÷	(+)	+:	÷	++	+	+++	+:	∸	−	∸	−	−	÷	(÷)	(+)
		Fibrin	−	−	−	+	+	(÷)	−	−	∸	++	++	−	−	−	−	−	−	−	−	−	−	−
		Erythrocytes	÷	÷	+	÷	÷	−	−	(÷)	÷	+	+:	÷	−	÷	−	(∸)	−	−	−	∸	(÷)	−
		Leucocytes	∸	∸	+++	++	++	(÷)	∸	(+)	÷	++:	(++)	(+)	+	(÷)	−	−	−	−	−	(+)	(++)	(++)
		Lymphocytes	−	∸	−	−	−	−	−	(÷)	−	−	−	−	−	−	−	−	−	−	−	−	−	(÷)
		Desquamated Epithelial Cells	(+)	÷	++	+	++	(+)	∸	(++)	+:	++	+	(+)	÷	÷	÷	−	−	−	−	÷	(++)	(+)
		Heart Desease Cells	∸	−	−	−	−	∸	−	(÷)	÷	−	−	−	−	−	∸	−	−	−	−	∸	−	−
		Colonies of Bacterium	÷	−	+++	+	−	−	−	(÷)	−	÷	−	÷	+	∸	−	−	−	−	−	−	−	−
	Alveolar Walls	Congestion of Capillaries	+:	++	+	÷	÷	+	+:	+	÷	(+)	÷	÷	÷	+:	÷	(+:)	(+)	∸	÷	+:	++	++
		Swelling of Walls	+	+	+	+	+	÷	+	+	÷	++	++	++	+	+	÷	∸	+	(÷)	÷	÷	+	÷
		Thickening of Walls	−	−	−	−	−	−	−	−	−	−	−	−	−	−	−	−	−	−	−	−	÷	(÷)
		Hyperplasia of Wall Cells	÷	÷	−	−	−	(÷)	÷	(÷)	÷	−	−	(÷)	−	÷	−	−	(∸)	−	−	÷	+	(÷)
		Leucocytes in Capillaries	+	÷	−	÷	÷	(+)	÷	÷	∸	÷	++	(+)	÷	÷	∸	∸	∸	−	(÷)	+	+:	+
		Lymphocytes in Capillaries	∸	÷	−	−	−	∸	∸	÷	−	−	−	−	−	∸	∸	∸	−	−	(÷)	÷	÷	÷
		Colonies of Bacterium	−	−	−	−	−	−	−	−	−	−	−	÷	÷	−	−	−	−	−	−	−	−	−
Bronchioli	Contents	Desquamated Epithelial Cells	+	÷	+:	|	++	(÷)	+	+++	++	++	+++	+++	+++	++	++	∸	++	∸	−	+:	+	+
		Mucus	÷	∸	−	|	++	−	−	+++	∸	−	−	∸	+	++	−	÷	++	∸	−	∸	÷	+
		Fibrin	−	−	−	|	÷	−	−	−	−	−	−	−	∸	−	−	−	−	−	−	−	−	−
		Erythrocytes	−	−	+	|	÷	−	−	∸	∸	−	÷	−	−	÷	−	÷	÷	−	−	−	−	−
		Leucocytes	−	−	+++	|	+	−	−	∸	++	+++	+++	−	++	+:	−	−	+	−	−	−	(+)	−
		Lymphocytes	−	−	∸	|	−	−	−	∸	∸	−	−	−	−	−	−	−	−	−	−	−	−	−
		Colonies of Bacterium	−	−	+	|	−	−	−	−	∸	(+++)	(++)	−	−	÷	−	−	−	−	−	−	−	−
	Peribronchial Tissues	Congestion	÷	÷	+:	|	++	÷	÷	+	++	++	++	+	÷	+	∸	+	+	+	÷	++:	+++	++
		Edema	∸	∸	++	|	+	∸	∸	+	∸	+	+:	++	++	÷	−	∸	÷	+	∸	(++)	+	∸
		Erythrocytes	(∸)	−	−	|	÷	−	−	−	÷	÷	+	÷	−	∸	−	−	−	−	−	∸	−	−
		Leucocytes	−	−	+	|	÷	−	−	−	∸	+	+	÷	++	∸	−	∸	∸	−	−	÷	+:	+
		Lymphocytes	÷	÷	+	|	÷	÷	∸	÷	∸	∸	+	+	÷	∸	−	∸	∸	−	∸	(++)	++	÷
		Histiocytes	÷	∸	÷	|	÷	∸	∸	∸	+	÷	+++	+++	+:	÷	∸	−	∸	−	∸	+:	++	÷
		Colonies of Bacterium	−	−	++	|	−	−	−	−	−	−	−	++	++++	÷	−	−	∸	−	−	−	−	−
Blood Vessels	Contents	Erythrocytes	+	+:	++	÷	++	++	++	+	+	÷	÷	+:	÷	+:	÷	(+)	−	++	++	++	+++	+++
		Leucocytes	∸	∸	−	−	∸	∸	∸	÷	−	−	∸	÷	(+++)	−	∸	(++)	++:	−	−	−	−	−
		Lymphocytes	−	÷	−	−	∸	−	÷	∸	−	−	−	∸	−	−	−	−	+	−	−	∸	∸	−
		Monocytes	−	−	−	−	−	−	−	−	−	−	−	÷	(+)	−	−	−	−	−	−	−	−	−
		Colonies of Bacterium	−	−	−	−	−	−	−	−	−	−	−	−	−	−	−	−	−	−	−	−	−	−
	Perivascular Tissues	Edema	+	÷	++	÷	+:	÷	÷	÷	+	+++	+++	+	(+)	+	÷	−	−	÷	÷	∸	∸	÷
		Hemorrhage	−	−	−	÷	÷	−	−	−	−	∸	∸	÷	−	(÷)	−	+	∸	−	−	−	−	−
		Infiltration Leucocytes	−	−	+	+	+	−	−	−	÷	∸	−	−	÷	∸	−	−	−	−	−	−	++	∸
		Infiltration Lymphocytes	−	−	−	−	−	−	−	−	−	−	−	−	−	∸	−	−	−	−	−	−	∸	−
		Proliferation of Histiocytic Cells	−	−	−	÷	+	−	−	−	∸	∸	∸	÷	÷	÷	∸	−	−	−	∸	−	++	−
		Colonies of Bacterium	−	−	÷	−	−	−	−	−	−	−	−	++	(++)	(++)	−	−	−	−	−	−	−	−
Pleura		Fibrin-Separation	|	−	+	|	|	|	−	|	−	−	−	−	+	−	−	−	−	|	|	÷	−	|
		Thickening	|	−	−	|	|	|	−	|	−	∸	−	÷	÷	−	−	+	÷	|	|	−	−	|
		Congestion	|	÷	+	|	|	|	+	|	−	+++	÷	+:	÷	+:	−	÷	÷	|	|	++	+++	|
		Edema	|	÷	÷	|	|	|	÷	|	÷	+:	÷	÷	+:	+	−	∸	−	|	|	∸	÷	|
		Hemorrhage	|	−	∸	|	|	|	−	|	−	−	−	∸	−	−	−	−	−	|	|	−	∸	|
		Infiltration Leucocytes	|	−	÷	|	|	|	−	|	−	−	−	−	+	−	−	−	−	|	|	−	+	|
		Infiltration Lymphocytes	|	−	∸	|	|	|	−	|	−	−	−	−	∸	÷	−	−	−	|	|	−	−	|
		Proliferation of Histiocytic Cells	|	∸	−	|	|	|	−	|	−	÷	−	÷	÷	÷	−	−	−	|	|	−	÷	|
		Colonies of Bacterium	|	−	+:	|	|	|	−	|	−	−	−	−	+++	÷	−	−	−	|	|	−	−	|

253

LUNG

			N 34 l.i	N 35 r.s	" l.i	N 36 r	" l	N 38	N 40	N 42	N 44 r	" l	N 46 r	" l	N 47 r.s	" r.l	" l.s	" l.i	N 49 r.s	" r.i	" l.s	" l.i	S 1	S 2 r.s	" r.i
Alveoli		Emphysema	−	−	−	−	⊹	÷	−	−	−	−	−	−	÷	−	÷	÷	÷	+	−	÷	−	−	÷
		Atelectasis	−	−	−	−	−	÷	−	−	−	÷	−	−	−	÷	÷	+	−	÷	−	÷	÷	+	÷
	Alveolar Spaces	Edema	−	+++	+++	+++	+	(÷)	++	+++	⊹	⊹	++++	+++	+	⊹	÷	(+)	⊹	÷	++	⊹	÷	÷	÷
		Fibrin	−	−	−	−	−	−	(÷)	−	÷	÷	−	÷	−	−	−	−	−	−	+	−	−	−	−
		Erythrocytes	−	(+++)	÷	÷	÷	−	÷	÷	+	⊹	÷	+	−	÷	÷	−	÷	−	+	÷	−	÷	−
		Leucocytes	−	++++	++++	(+)	÷	−	⊹	++	⊹	÷	|	+++	−	−	−	−	(÷)	−	+++	(+++)	−	−	−
		Lymphocytes	−	÷	÷	−	−	−	÷	÷	÷	÷	|	−	−	−	−	−	−	−	÷	−	−	−	=
		Desquamated Epithelial Cells	(÷)	++	⊹	(÷)	÷	−	++	⊹	+	÷	|	++	÷	(+++)	−	(⊹)	÷	−	++	(++)	÷	÷	÷
		Heart Desease Cells	−	−	−	−	÷	−	÷	−	−	÷	|	−	−	(+)	−	(+)	÷	−	−	÷	−	÷	÷
		Colonies of Bacterium	−	+++	++++	+	÷	−	++	+	+	÷	|	++	−	÷	−	−	÷	−	+++	÷	−	−	−
	Alveolar walls	Congestion of Capillaries	⊹	(+)	÷	+	+	÷	⊹	+	+	+	|	÷	⊹	⊹	+	+	+	÷	÷	÷	÷	++	⊹
		Swelling of walls	+	++	+	−	÷	÷	÷	÷	÷	+	|	++	+	+	÷	÷	÷	÷	+	÷	÷	+	+
		Thickening of walls	−	−	−	−	−	−	−	−	−	−	|	−	−	÷	−	−	−	−	−	−	−	÷	÷
		Hyperplasia of wall Cells	÷	−	−	−	−	−	−	−	−	÷	|	−	−	÷	−	÷	−	−	−	−	(÷)	÷	÷
		Leucocytes in Capillaries	÷	÷	÷	+	÷	÷	÷	÷	÷	÷	|	÷	÷	÷	−	÷	÷	÷	÷	++	÷	÷	÷
		Lymphocytes in Capillaries	÷	−	−	÷	÷	−	−	−	−	÷	|	−	÷	−	−	−	÷	−	−	÷	÷	÷	÷
		Colonies of Bacterium	−	+	−	÷	÷	(++)	−	−	÷	−	|	−	−	÷	−	−	−	−	−	−	−	−	−
Bronchioli	Contents	Desquamated Epithelial Cells	(+)	+++	+++	++	+	÷	(÷)	÷	(+++)	÷	|	+++	+⊹	÷	+++	÷	−	(+)	÷	÷	+	(÷)	(÷)
		Mucus	(÷)	|	|	−	−	−	(÷)	÷	÷	÷	|	|	++	÷	+	÷	÷	(++)	÷	−	÷	÷	÷
		Fibrin	−	(+++)	−	−	−	−	−	−	−	−	|	|	−	−	−	−	−	−	+⊹	−	−	−	−
		Erythrocytes	−	+	−	(÷)	−	−	(÷)	÷	−	÷	|	÷	−	−	−	−	−	−	÷	÷	−	(÷)	−
		Leucocytes	−	++	+++	(++)	−	−	(÷)	÷	−	(÷)	|	⊹	−	−	−	−	−	−	÷	÷	−	−	(÷)
		Lymphocytes	−	−	−	÷	−	−	−	−	−	−	|	−	−	−	−	−	−	−	−	−	−	−	−
		Colonies of Bacterium	−	+	+++	−	−	−	÷	−	−	−	|	+	−	−	−	−	−	−	+	−	−	−	−
	Peribronchial Tissues	Congestion	⊹	+	+	+++	+	+	+	+	++	+	|	++	+	+	+	÷	⊹	+	÷	÷	÷	+	÷
		Edema	÷	+	+	+++	+	⊹	÷	+	÷	÷	|	+	+	÷	÷	÷	÷	÷	÷	÷	÷	+	+
		Erythrocytes	÷	+	÷	÷	−	−	−	−	−	÷	|	|	÷	−	÷	−	−	−	÷	−	−	−	−
		Leucocytes	÷	+++	+++	÷	−	−	−	÷	−	−	|	|	−	−	−	−	−	−	+	÷	÷	−	−
		Lymphocytes	−	++	÷	÷	÷	÷	−	÷	÷	÷	|	|	÷	+	−	÷	−	−	÷	−	÷	÷	(+)
		Histiocytes	÷	÷	÷	÷	÷	−	−	÷	÷	÷	|	|	÷	÷	−	÷	÷	−	÷	÷	÷	−	÷
		Colonies of Bacterium	−	+++	+++	+++	+	−	−	++	+	−	|	+++	−	−	−	−	−	−	÷	−	−	−	−
Blood Vessels	Contents	Erythrocytes	++	(++)	−	+++	++	⊹	++	⊹	++	⊹	+++	++	++	+	+	++	++	++	÷	++	++	++	+⊹
		Leucocytes	÷	÷	−	÷	−	−	÷	÷	−	÷	−	−	−	−	−	÷	−	−	÷	÷	÷	÷	+
		Lymphocytes	−	÷	−	−	−	+	−	÷	−	−	−	−	−	−	−	−	−	−	−	−	÷	÷	÷
		Monocytes	−	÷	−	−	−	−	÷	−	−	÷	−	−	−	−	−	(+)	−	−	−	÷	−	−	−
		Colonies of Bacterium	−	−	−	−	(÷)	−	−	−	−	−	−	−	−	−	−	−	−	−	−	−	−	−	−
	Perivascular Tissues	Edema	÷	+	+	+++	÷	+	÷	⊹	÷	(++)	+	÷	÷	÷	÷	÷	÷	÷	+	÷	+	+	+
		Hemorrhage	−	÷	−	−	−	−	−	÷	−	−	−	−	−	−	−	−	−	−	÷	−	−	−	−
		Infiltration: Leucocytes	−	÷	+++	−	−	−	−	÷	−	−	−	−	−	−	−	−	−	−	÷	−	(÷)	−	−
		Infiltration: Lymphocytes	−	÷	−	−	−	−	−	÷	−	−	−	−	−	−	−	−	−	−	−	−	(÷)	−	−
		Proliferation of Histiocytic Cells	÷	÷	−	−	÷	−	÷	÷	÷	÷	−	−	−	÷	−	−	−	−	−	−	(÷)	−	−
		Colonies of Bacterium	−	−	+++	−	÷	−	−	+	÷	−	−	−	−	−	−	−	−	−	÷	−	−	−	−
Pleura		Fibrin-Separation	−	++	+	−	−	|	+	|	−	−	−	−	−	−	−	−	−	−	÷	−	÷	−	−
		Thickening	−	÷	−	−	−	|	−	|	−	−	−	−	−	−	−	−	−	−	÷	−	−	−	−
		Congestion	⊹	÷	÷	+++	++	|	⊹	|	⊹	+	+	++	÷	⊹	÷	++	+	÷	+	÷	÷	−	÷
		Edema	−	++	⊹	÷	÷	|	÷	|	÷	÷	÷	÷	++	÷	÷	÷	÷	÷	÷	÷	÷	÷	÷
		Hemorrhage	÷	+	−	÷	−	|	(+)	|	−	−	−	−	−	−	−	−	−	−	÷	−	−	−	−
		Infiltration: Leucocytes	−	+	++	−	−	|	÷	|	−	−	−	−	−	−	−	−	−	−	++	−	−	−	−
		Infiltration: Lymphocytes	−	÷	÷	÷	÷	|	÷	|	÷	−	−	−	−	−	−	−	−	−	÷	−	−	−	−
		Proliferation of Histiocytic Cells	−	+	÷	÷	÷	|	÷	|	÷	−	−	−	−	÷	−	÷	−	−	÷	−	−	−	−
		Colonies of Bacterium	−	+++	++	+	÷	|	++	|	−	÷	−	+++	−	−	−	−	−	−	+	−	−	−	−

LUNG

			S2 l.s	l.i	S3	S4	S5	S6	S8 r.s	r.i	l.s	S9 r.s	r.i	S10	S11 r	l	S12	S14	S15 r	l	S19	S22	S26	S28	S38
Alveoli		Emphysema	−	±	−	−	−	−	−	−	±	−	±	−	±	−	−	+±	−	−	±	−	−	−	−
		Atelectasis	±	±	±	−	±	±	−	−	±	−	±	−	+	−	−	±	−	±	±	−	−	−	−
	Alveolar Spaces	Edema	±	±	++	+±	+±	+	++±	++	±	±	±	++	+	+++	±	−	+	±	−	+	++	++	+
		Fibrin	−	−	±	±	−	−	−	±	−	±	±	±	−	−	+	−	−	−	−	+	−	−	±
		Erythrocytes	−	(±)	±	±	±	+	+	+	+±	+	+	+±	−	±	+	−	−	−	±	++	±	±	(+++)
		Leucocytes	−	±	+±	±	±	±	++	+++	(+)	++±	++±	±	−	±	++	(+++)	−	±	−	+++	±	−	+++
		Lymphocytes	−	−	±	±	±	±	−	±	−	±	±	−	−	−	−	−	−	−	−	−	−	−	−
		Desquamated Epithelial Cells	±	±	+±	++	±	+	+	+±	±	±	+	+±	(+)	(+)	+±	(+++)	±	+	±	+	++	±	+
		Heart Desease Cells	±	±	++	+±	±	±	±	±	±	−	−	+	±	±	±	−	−	+	±	−	++	−	−
		Colonies of Bacterium	−	−	+++	−	−	±	+++	++	±	+++	++	±	−	−	−	−	−	−	−	++	+	±	−
	Alveolar Walls	Congestion of Capillaries	++	+±	+	+	+	+	+	+±	(+)	+±	±	+	+	+	±	±	±	±	+±	+	+±	++	+
		Swelling of Walls	+	+	+	±	±	±	±	++	±	+	±	±	±	±	±	±	±	+	±	±	±	±	+
		Thickening of Walls	−	±	−	−	−	−	−	−	−	−	−	−	−	−	−	−	−	−	−	−	−	−	−
		Hyperplasia of Wall Cells	±	+	−	±	±	±	−	−	−	±	−	−	−	−	−	(±)	−	−	±	±	−	−	−
		Leucocytes in Capillaries	±	±	±	±	±	±	+	±	±	+	±	−	±	±	±	±	±	±	±	+	±	±	+
		Lymphocytes in Capillaries	±	±	−	±	±	±	±	−	±	−	−	−	±	−	−	−	−	−	−	−	±	±	−
		Colonies of Bacterium	−	−	+	−	−	±	−	−	−	+	−	±	−	−	−	−	−	−	−	−	±	−	±
Bronchioli	Contents	Desquamated Epithelial Cells	(±)	−	|	++	±	±	−	±	(++)	±	±	+	+	±	++	++	±	+±	++	++	±	+	++
		Mucus	(±)	±	|	++	±	±	−	+	±	+	+	+	−	±	−	±	−	++	++	++	±	±	+
		Fibrin	−	−	|	−	−	−	−	±	−	−	−	−	−	−	±	−	−	−	−	±	−	−	±
		Erythrocytes	(±)	(±)	|	−	±	−	±	±	(++)	−	±	±	−	−	±	−	−	±	−	±	−	−	±
		Leucocytes	−	−	|	−	−	−	±	++	−	±	±	±	−	−	++	+	−	±	−	++	−	−	+++
		Lymphocytes	−	−	|	−	−	−	−	±	−	−	−	−	−	−	−	−	−	−	−	−	−	−	−
		Colonies of Bacterium	−	−	|	−	−	−	−	++	−	+	±	−	−	−	−	−	−	−	−	−	−	−	−
	Peribronchial Tissues	Congestion	+	±	+	++	±	±	+	++	+	+	±	+	±	+	±	±	±	+++	++	++	+±	+	±
		Edema	+	+±	++	+	±	±	±	±	±	±	+	±	±	+	+	±	±	±	±	(+)	+	±	±
		Erythrocytes	−	−	−	−	−	−	±	+	−	−	±	±	−	−	±	−	−	−	±	±	−	−	+
		Leucocytes	−	±	±	−	−	−	+	++	−	++	±	±	±	−	−	±	−	±	±	±	−	−	+++
		Lymphocytes	(+)	(++)	±	±	±	±	−	±	±	±	−	−	±	−	−	±	−	−	±	±	−	±	−
		Histiocytes	−	±	±	±	±	±	±	±	±	±	±	±	±	±	±	±	±	±	±	++	±	±	±
		Colonies of Bacterium	−	−	+++	−	−	−	+	+++	−	+	−	++	−	−	−	−	−	−	−	−	−	−	+
Blood Vessels	Contents	Erythrocytes	++±	++	+	+++	+	++	++	++	+	±	±	+±	+±	++	±	++	++	++	++	±	+±	++±	±
		Leucocytes	±	±	±	±	±	+	±	±	±	±	±	−	−	−	−	(+)	±	−	±	±	±	±	−
		Lymphocytes	±	±	−	±	±	−	−	−	±	−	−	−	−	±	−	−	−	−	−	−	−	−	−
		Monocytes	−	−	−	−	−	−	−	−	−	−	−	−	−	±	−	−	±	−	−	−	−	−	−
		Colonies of Bacterium	−	−	−	−	−	−	−	−	−	−	−	−	−	−	−	−	−	−	−	−	−	−	−
	Perivascular Tissues	Edema	±	±	++	++	+±	++	±	+	±	±	±	±	±	(++)	+±	±	±	±	+	+	±	±	+
		Hemorrhage	−	−	−	−	−	−	−	±	−	±	−	±	−	−	±	−	−	−	±	−	−	−	±
		Infiltration: Leucocytes	−	−	±	−	−	−	±	+	−	±	−	±	−	−	−	−	−	−	−	(+)	−	−	+±
		Infiltration: Lymphocytes	−	−	−	−	−	−	−	−	−	−	−	−	−	−	−	−	−	−	−	−	−	−	−
		Proliferation of Histiocytic Cells	−	−	−	−	±	−	±	±	−	±	±	±	−	−	±	±	−	−	+	±	−	−	±
		Colonies of Bacterium	−	−	+++	−	−	−	−	+	−	−	−	(++)	−	−	−	−	−	−	−	−	−	−	−
Pleura		Fibrin-Separation	−	−	−	−	−	+	−	−	−	|	|	−	±	|	+	−	−	−	−	±	−	|	+
		Thickening	−	−	−	±	−	−	±	−	−	|	|	−	−	|	−	−	−	−	±	−	−	|	−
		Congestion	±	±	+++	+±	++	+	+++	++	±	|	|	+++	−	|	+	++	+±	++	±	++	+±	|	+++
		Edema	±	±	±	±	±	(+)	±	+	+	|	|	±	±	|	±	±	±	±	±	±	±	|	±
		Hemorrhage	−	−	−	−	±	−	++	±	±	|	|	±	−	|	±	−	−	−	++	±	±	|	±
		Infiltration: Leucocytes	−	−	−	−	−	−	+	−	−	|	|	±	−	|	±	−	−	−	−	+	−	|	+±
		Infiltration: Lymphocytes	−	−	−	−	−	±	−	−	−	|	|	−	−	|	±	−	−	−	±	−	−	|	−
		Proliferation of Histiocytic Cells	−	(±)	−	−	±	±	±	±	−	|	|	±	−	|	+	±	±	−	±	+±	−	|	+
		Colonies of Bacterium	−	−	±	−	−	[illegible]	[illegible]	[illegible]	[illegible]	[illegible]	[illegible]	[illegible]	[illegible]	|	−	−	−	−	−	±	−	|	−

255

Bronchiolitiw catarrhalis
grqvis and bacterial caccumulation
at peribronchiolar tissues.

N-32
(right superior)

(X80)

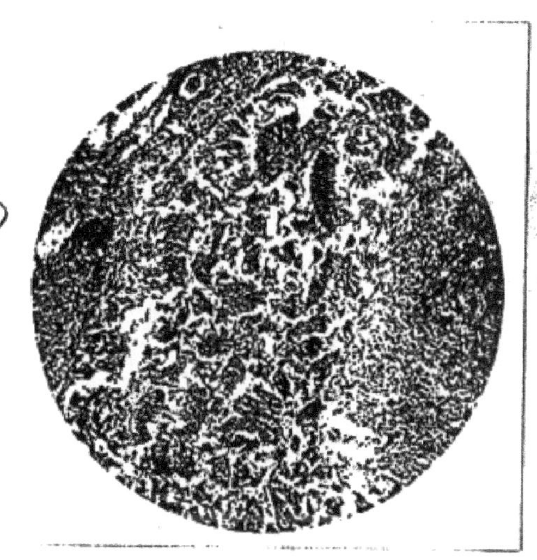

Peribronchiolitis and
acinous pneumonic changes.

N-34
(right inferior)

(×80)

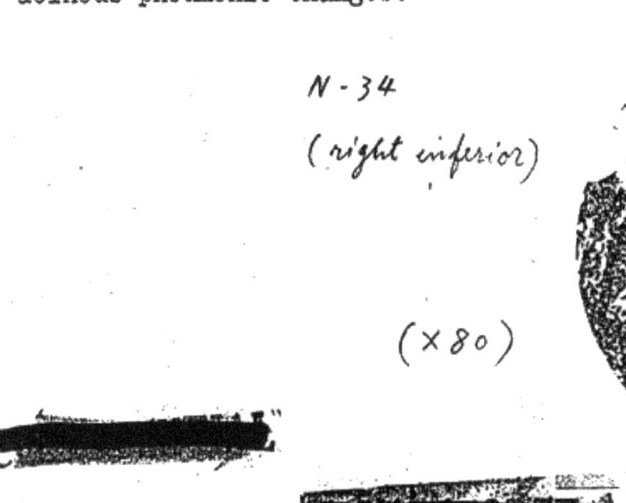

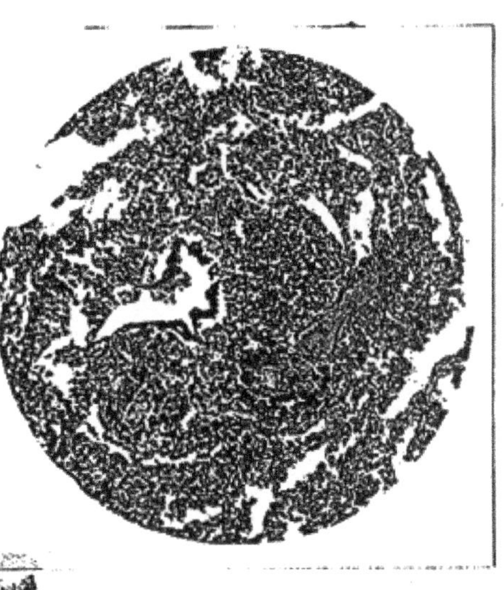

256

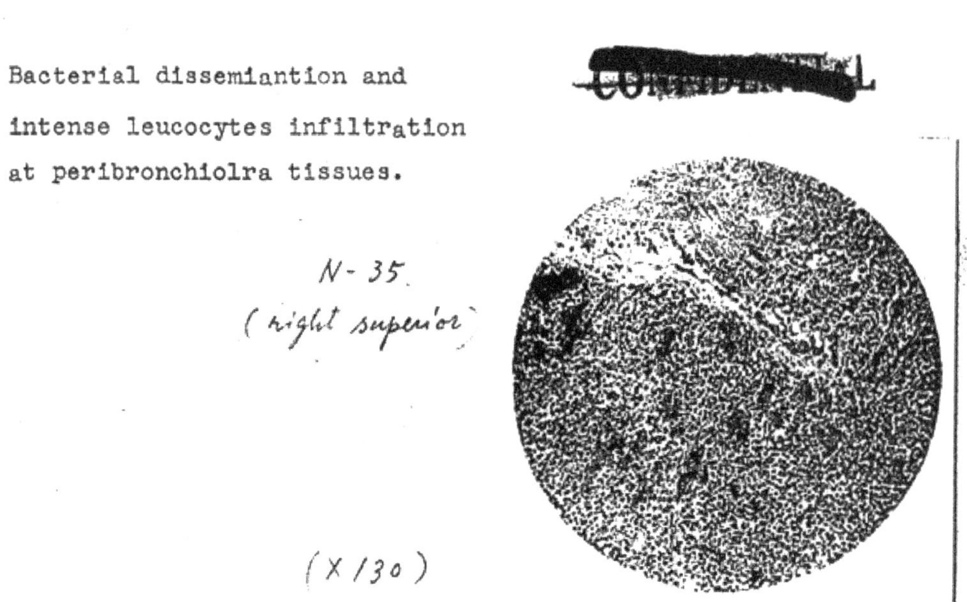

Bacterial dissemiantion and intense leucocytes infiltration at peribronchiolra tissues.

N-35
(right superior)

(X130)

Bionecrotic changes at peribronchiolar tissues, a ccompanied with some bacteroaö dissemination.

N-5

(X60)

257

Submiliary pneumonia at the intercalary portion of lung.

S-14. (right)

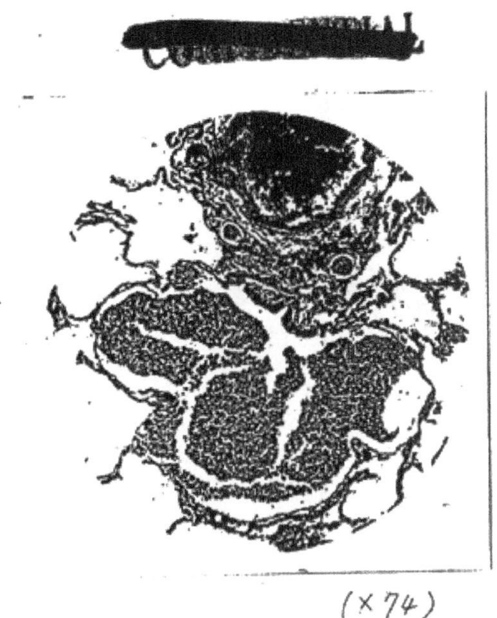

(×74)

Acino-lobular pneumonia.

N.-6 (right)

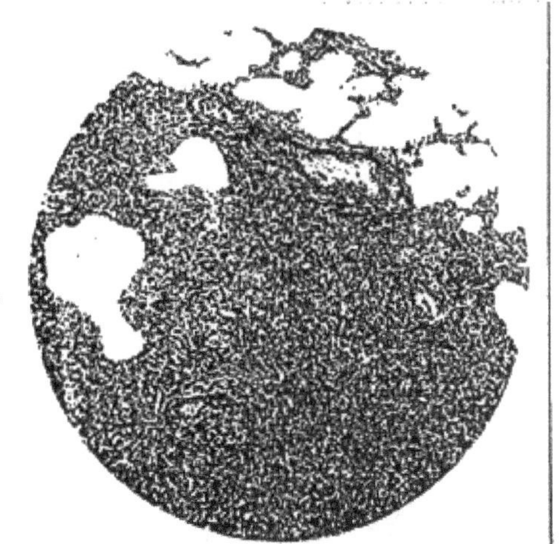

(×80)

258

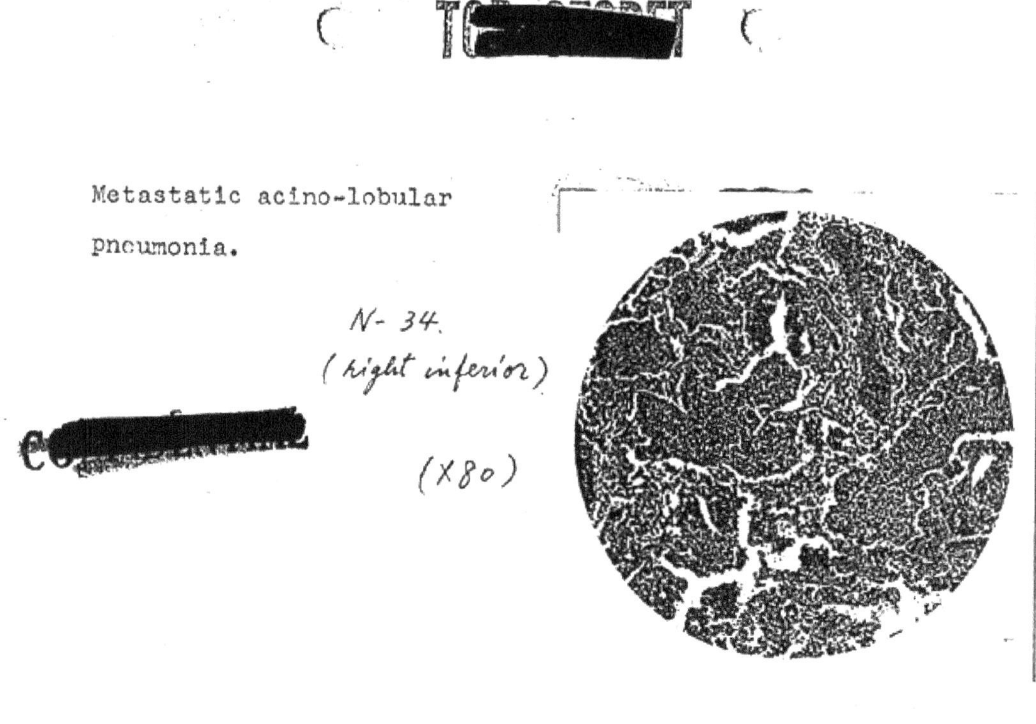

Metastatic acino-lobular pneumonia.

N-34.
(right inferior)

(×80)

Lobular pneumonia.

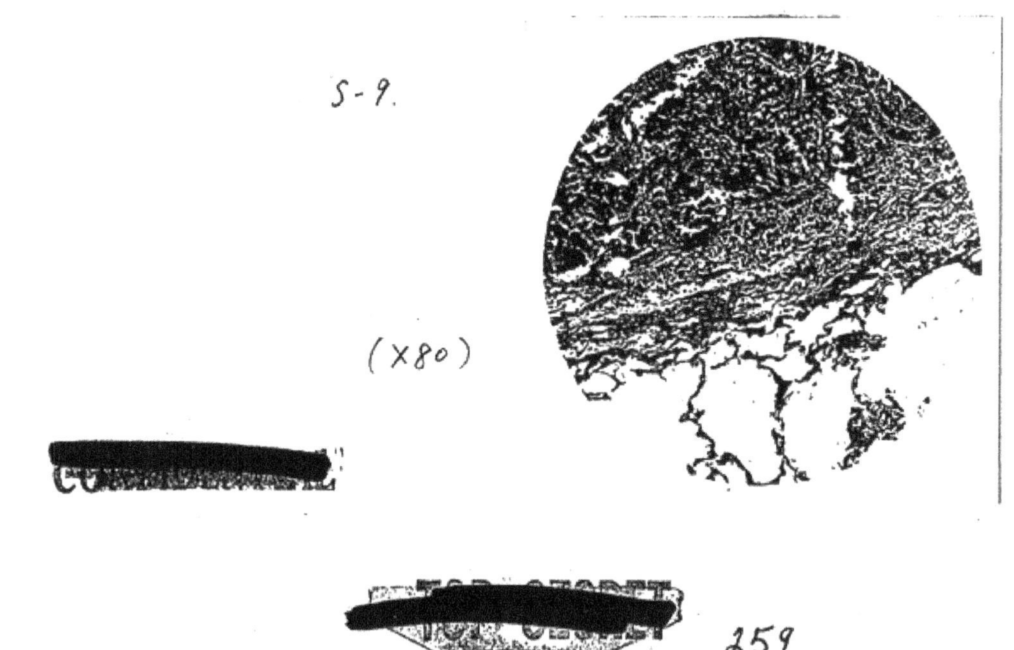

S-9.

(×80)

259

Lobar pneumonia.

Sero-hemorrhagic.

S-10

(×80)

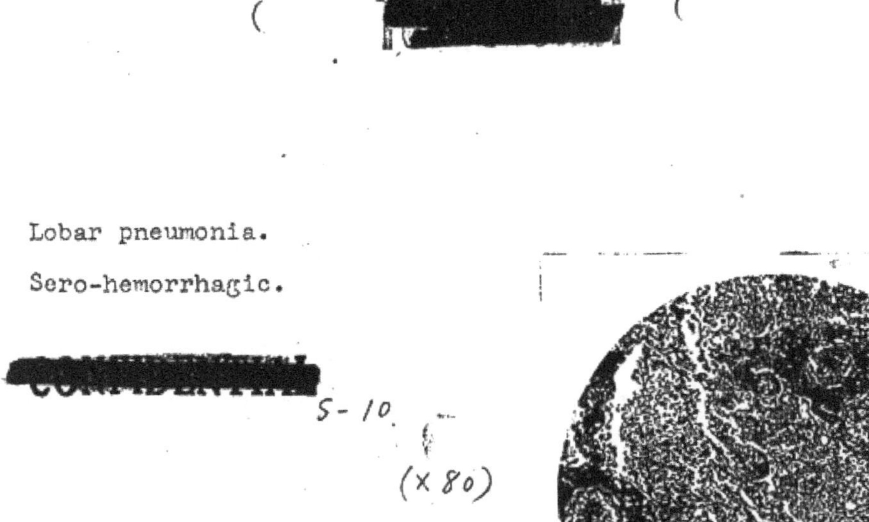

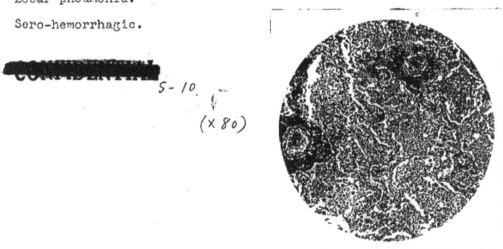

Lobar pneumonia, sero-leucocytic.

N-5 (left)

(×80)

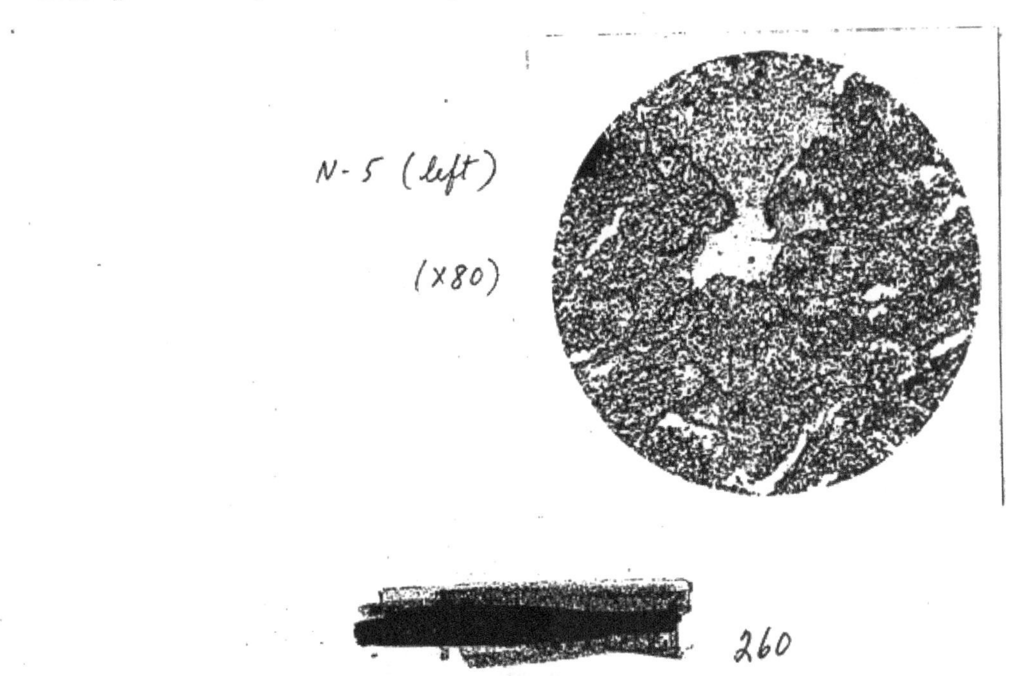

260

Lobar pneumonia.exudative-
hemorrhagic.

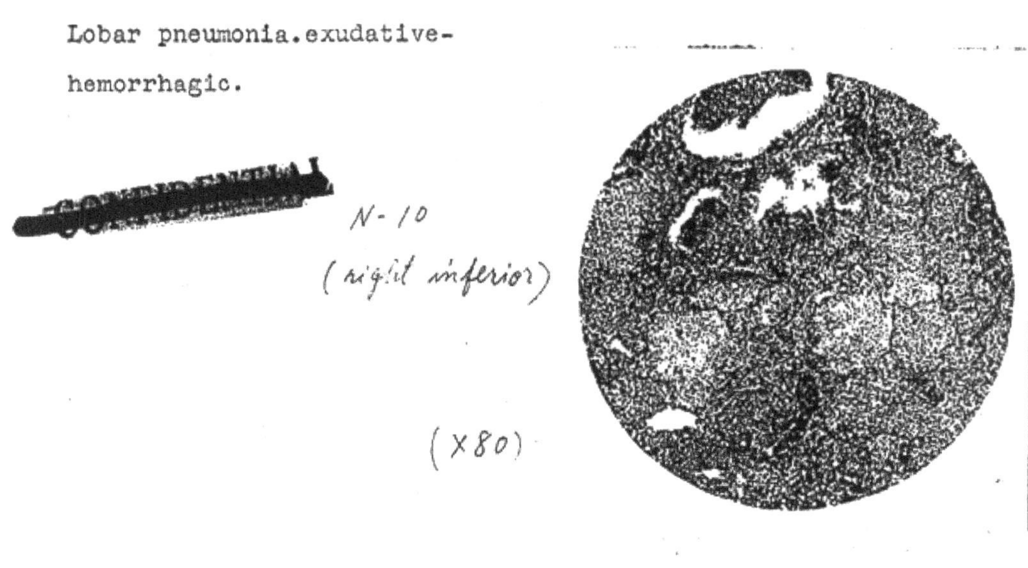

Lobar pneumonia.fibrinous-
hemorrhagic.

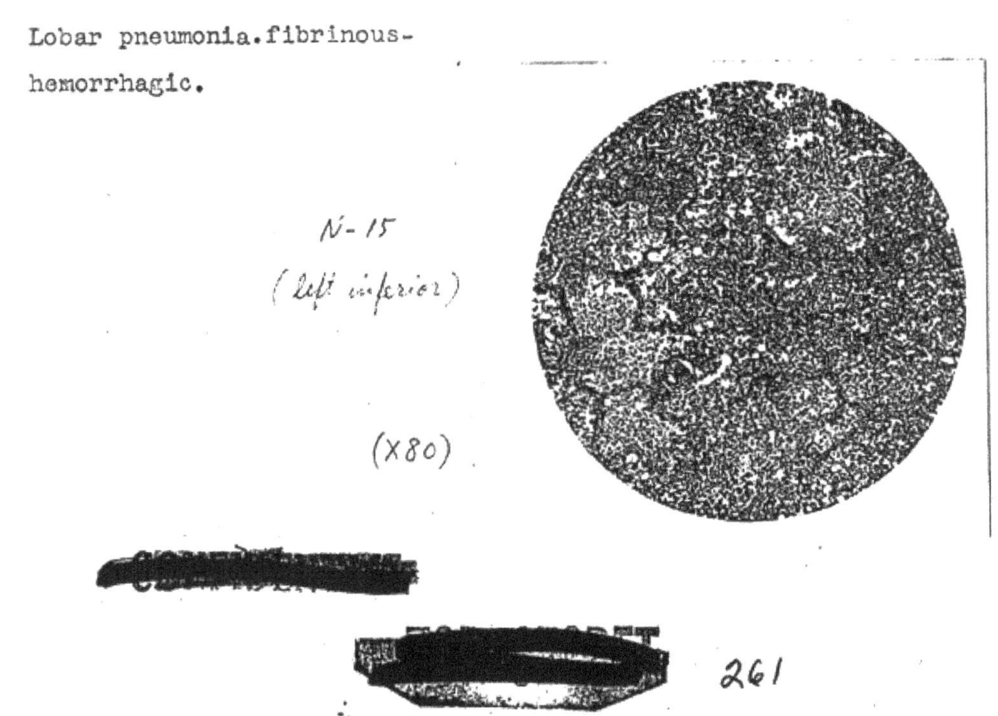

261

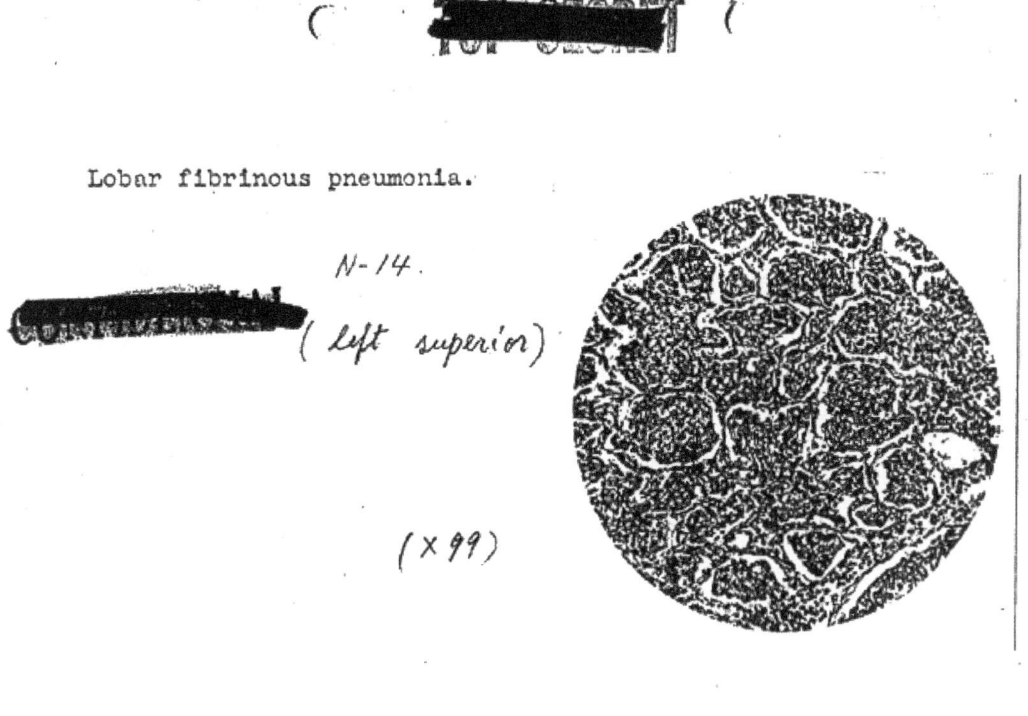

Lobar fibrinous pneumonia.

Lobar fibrinous pneumonia.

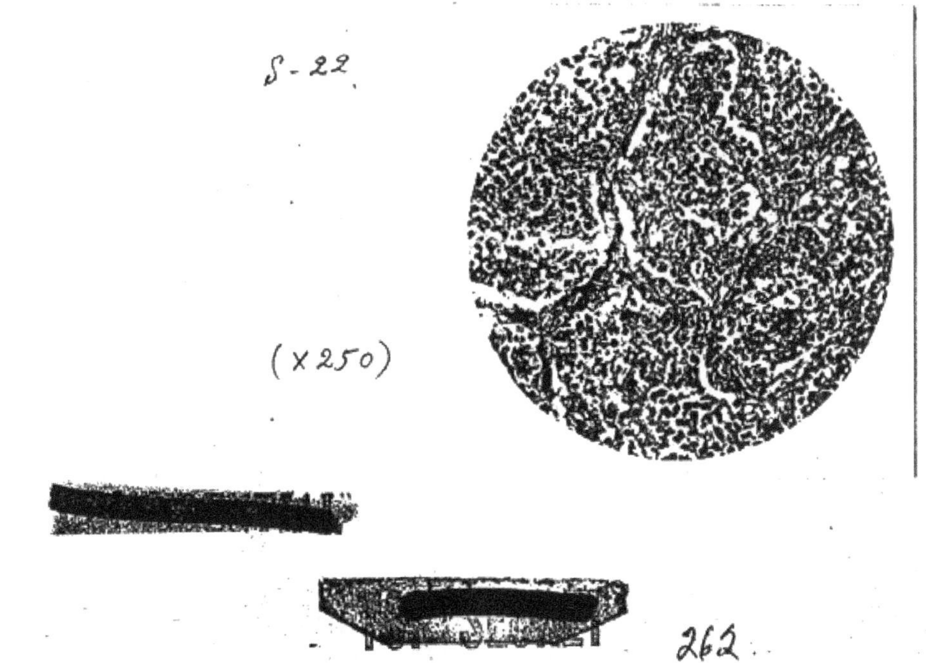

Lobar pneumonia,leucocytic - necrotic.

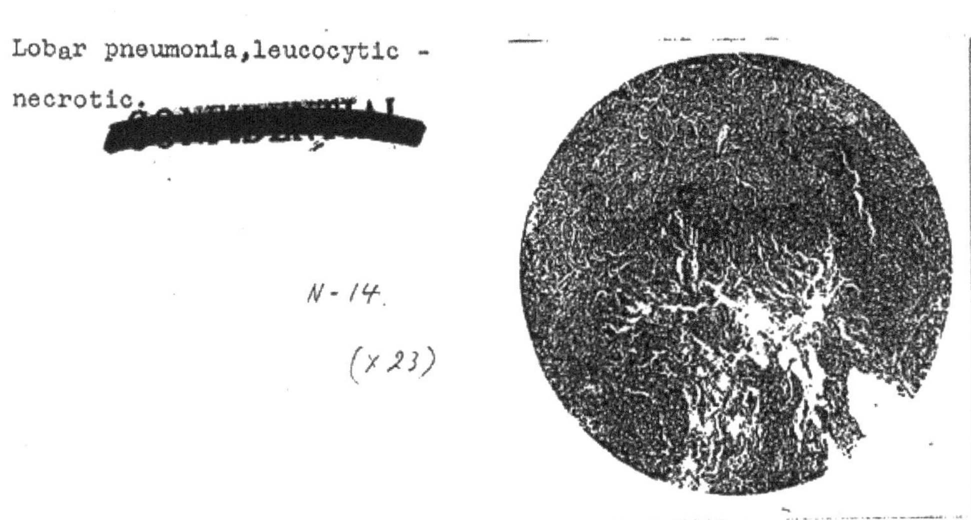

N-14.

(x23)

Pleuritis haemorrhagico-purulenta.

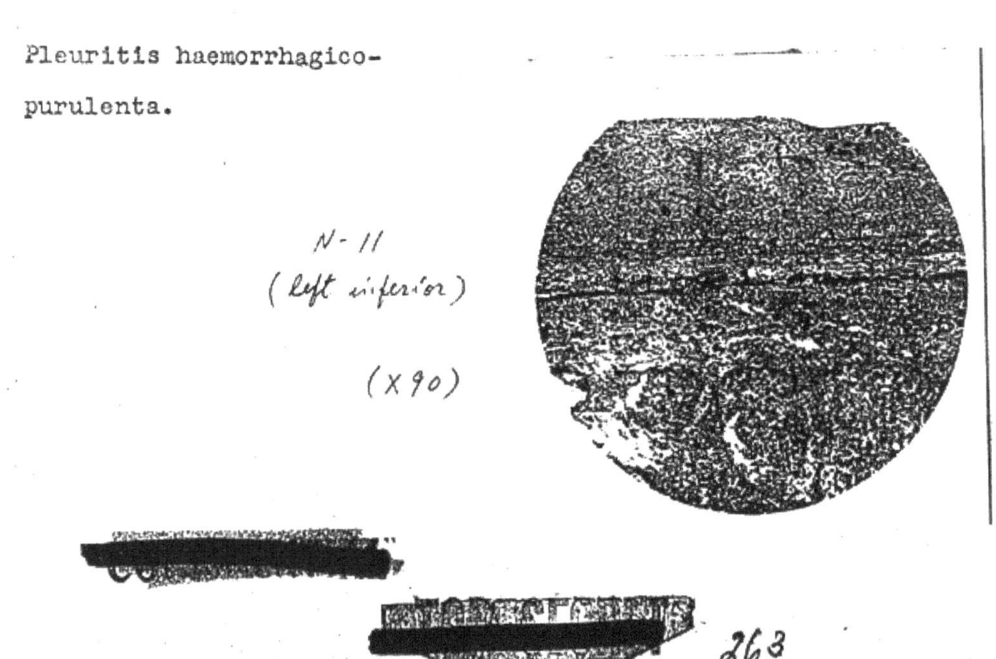

N-11

(left inferior)

(x90)

263

Tonsil

264

TONSIL.

(A) Microscop. Investigation.

3.

Edema and degeneration of mucous membrane with some lymphocytes-emigration in interepitheliar spaces and some desquamative changes (in crypts, some quantitiy of degenerated epitheliums, some leucocytes and various exudative fluids).

Lymphatic follicles in intense congestion and considerable edematous swelling and some of the fall into bionecrotic changes with many karyolytic masses in germinative centres.

In submucous tissues, intense edema, intense congestion and some leucocytes (and some plasma-cells)-emigration.

Many degenerated muscle fibres with considerable leucocytes-emigration and some diffuse hemorrhages in intermuscular tissues.

4.

Intense edema and degeneration of mucous membrane, accomapnied with some desquamative changes.

Some lymphatic follicles are destroyed with some bionecrotic changes of germinative centres (many karyolytic masses in germinative centres).

In submucous tissues, considerable congestion and some wandering cell dissemination (chiefly plasma-cells and some eosinophilic leucocytes).

Degeneration of muscle fibres with some round-cell-emigration among them.

II.

Intense edema and degeneration of mucous membrane with some leucocy-

265

tes and some erythrocytes- emigration in interepitheliar spaces. Just under the mucous membrane, some localised remarkable hemorrhages.
Follicles very in size and form and some of them are intensively demaged with edematous or hyalinous swelling and at some places some hemorrhages in germinative centres.
But one characteristic follicle with intense edematous swelling, due to remarkable accumulation of protein-masses in protoplasma (to form small or large granules in protoplasma). or furthermore bionecrotic changes of reticulum-cells and-fibres.
Considerable congestion of submucous and follicular capillaries, accompanied with intense round-cell-infiltration in submucous tissues.

I4.

Degeneration and edematous swelling of mucous membrane with some lymphocytes and some erythrocytes emigration in interepitheliar spaces and some desquamative changes (massive desquamated epitheliums, some fibrinous masses, some leucocytes and various serous fluids in crypts).
Follicular tissues with considerable edematous swelling and some follicular congestion, and germinative centres with edematous or hyalinous degeneration of reticulum-fibres and some slight hemorrhages.
Submucous tissues with considerable congestion (and remarkable hyperplasia of capillary endothelial cells). considerable edema

-266

and intense diffuse round-cell-infiltrations. 

I6.

Intense edematous swelling and multiple necrosis of mucous membrane with some desquamative changes (in crypts, a large quantity of degenerated epitheliums, fibrinous and bacterial masses and others). Lymphatic follicles vary in size and form.

Intense swelling of follicular tissues with indistinct borders, and accompanied with considerable follicular congestion (and considerable hyperplasia of capillary endothelial cells).

Edematous swelling of germinative centres, accompanied with slight hemorrages at some places and some epitheloid cells formation at some places.

Edematous swelling of germinative centres, accompanied with considerable congestion and some hemorrhages and at some places some epitheloid cells formations.

Submucous tissues with considerable congestion and some round-cells -accumulation, accompanied with some hemorhages in intermuscular tissues.

I9.

Intense edema or multiple diffuse necrosis of mucous membrane, with some lympheocytes and some erythrocytes-emigration in interepithelial spaces and remarkable desquamative changes (separation of some fibrinous masses, some leucocytes and some exudates in crypts). Edematous swelling of rather atrophic follicular tissues, with indistinct borders.

And also, edematous swelling of germinative centres with some leucocy-

tes or karyolytic masses-accumulations.

Edematous swelling (with indistinct borders) of follicular tissues, accompanied with intense follicular congestion (and some hyperplasia of capillary endothelial cells and separation of fibrinous masses to form some fibrinous thrombus).

Edematous swelling of germinative centres, accompanied with some leucocytes or some karyolytic masses-accumulations.

Submucous tissues with intense round-cell-dissemination and some hemorrhages.

20.

Intense edema of mucous membrane with some lymphocytes-and some erythrocytes-emigration in interepitheliar spaces and intense, desquamative changes (in crypts, a large quantity of degenerated epitheliums, some leucocytes some lymphocytes and some bacterial masses).

Lymphatic follicles fall into intense, diffuse necrosis with plenty of bacterial and leucocytes-disseminations.

Submucous tissues with intense congestion (some bacterial masses in capillaries) and intense round-cell-infiltrations.

Generally with more or less remarkable diffuse hemorrhages in submucous and intermuscular tissues.

Collapse of glandular tissues, with some congestion and some leucocytes-emigration in glandular tissues.

2I.

Intense edema and multiple diffuse necrosis of mucous membrane, with some bacterial dissemination in interepitheliar spaces and

268

some desquamative changes (massive bacteriaial masses in crypts), and some lymphocytes and some erythrocytes-emigration in interepitheliar spaces.
Edematous swelling (with indistinct borders) of follicular tissues and some edematous swelling of germinative centres.
Submucous tissues with considerable congestion (some bacterial masses in capillaries), intense diffuse hemorrhages and some round-cells -infiltrations.

28.

multiple necrotic changes of mucous membrane with intense desquamative changes (massive desquamated epithliums and massive bacterial masses in crypts) and intense edema and some hemorrhagic changes of mucous membranse, accompanied with intense hemorrhages in subepitheliar tissues.
Congestion and some perifocal hemorrhages.
Germinative centres are accomapnied with considerable swelling of reticulum-fibres, some leucocytes-emigration and some hemorrhages.
In submucous tissues; considerable congestion and some round-cell -dissemination (some of them, plasma-cells).

30.

Intense degeneration and edema of mucous membrane with some lymphocytes and some erythorocytes-emigration in interepitheliar spaces.
In submucous tissues: extraordinary intense capillary congestion (and some bacterial masses in capillaries) all over the submucous tissues.
Considerable swelling (and with indistinct borders) of follicular

269

tissues and some swelling of germinative centres with considerable swelling of reticulum-fibres, intense capillary congestion and at some places some hemorrhages.

More or less remarkable, diffuse hemorrhages also in intermuscular tissues.

32.

Remarkable degeneration and swelling of mucous mebrane with some lymphocytes and some erythrocytes in interepitheliar spaces, and at some places with remarkable necrosis of mucous epitheliums, accompanied with some desquamative changes (massive desquamated crypts).

Intense swelling (with indistinct borders) of follicular tissues and considdrable swelling of germinative centes with some swollen and some slight hemorrhages.

In submucous tissues: intense diffuse round-cell-dissemination and considerable hemorrhages.

Many waxy degenerated muscle-fibres and some leucocytes- emigration in intermuscular tissues.

33.

Multiple necrotic changes of mucous membrane with intense desquamtive chamges (many desquamated epitheliums, remarkable separation of fibrinous and bacterial masses in crypts).

Considerable swelling of follicular tissues with intense follicular congestion and intense hemorrhages in intra-and perifollicular tissues.

In submucous tissues: extraordinary remarkable capillary congestion and intense diffuse, blood-sea-like hemorrhages.

270

Some hemorrhages and edema also in intermuscular tissues.

34.

Intense degeneration and edema of mucous membrane, and at some places intene necrosis (with some superficial ulcers) with some intense desquamative changes (in crypts, a large quantity of fibrinous and bacterial masses).

Considerable swelling (with indistinct borders) of follicular tissues with some follicular congestion.

Considerable swelling of germinative centres with some swollen reticulum fibres, and some leucocytes- and some erythrocytes-emigrations.

Considerable congestion (and some leucocytes in capillaries and some intermuscular tissues) and some leucocytes-emigration, esp. at perivascular portions, in submucous tissues.

36.

Intense and diffuse edema or degeneration of mucous epitheliums, with intense emigration of leucocytes (and some plasma-cells) in interepitheliar spaces, accompanied with remarkable dissociation and some vacuolar degeneration of epitheliums.

Intense swelling of follicular tissues with remarkable leucocytes-emigration.

In submucous tissues, remarkable congestion (and some hyperplasia of capilary endothelial cells). considdrable edema and some leucocytes-emigrations.

In intermuscular tissues, considerable edema and some leucocytes-emigration.

In crypts, a large quantity of desquamated epitheliums, some leucocy-

271

tes and some fibrinous masses.

38.

Generally with intense, diffuse necrosis of mucous membrane with some bacterial dissemination and intense edematous swelling of mucous tissues with some erythrocytes-emigration in interepithelial spaces.

Considerable swelling of follicular tissues with intense bionecrotic changes of germinative centres (bionecrotic swelling of reticulumfibres with intense congestion, some bacterial masses in capillaries,

and some leucocytes-emigration in germinative centres).

In submucous tissues, intense congestion (with plenty of bacterial masses in capillaries and hyalnious degeneration of blood-vessel-walls).

Many waxy degenerated muscle-fibres and some intense edema and some leucocytes or bacterial dissemination in intermuscular tissues.

39.

Diffuse edema and degeneration of mucous membrane with some vacuolar degeneration of epitheliums.

Considerable swelling of follicular tissues (with indistinct borders) and intense swelling of germinative centres with intense congestion, some leucocytes-emigration and some swollen reticulum-fibres.

In submucous tissues, intense diffuse edema, remarkable stagnation of lymph and some plasma cell infiltration.

In intermuscular tissues, some leucocytes-emigrations.

40.

Intense edema and degeneration of mucous membrane with some lympho-

272

cytes and some erythrocytes-emigration in interepitheliar spaces.
In crypts, large quantity of desquamated epitheliums, plenty of erythrocytes, some fibrinous masses and some leucocytes.
Intense swelling of lymphatic follicles (with indistinct borders), with considerable follicular congestion and some hemorrhages.
Intense swelling of germinative centres with some swollen retiuclum-fibres.
In submucous tissues, remarkable capillary congestion, considerable edema and some plasma-cell-infiltrations.
In intermuscular tissues, intense congestion (and some bacterial masses in capillaries) and some hemorrhagic changes.

42.

Considerable swelling of mucous membrane with some erythrocytes-emigration in interepitheliar spaces.
In submucous tissues, extraordinary remarkable congestion (plenty of bacterial masses in capillaries) and multiple intense hemorrhages and flaky bacterial dissemination all over the submucous tissues (to cause diffuse necrotic ruins of submucous tissues).
In intermuscular tissues, also intense bacterial dissemination, intense congestion and some multiple intense hemorrhages.
Intense edematous swelling of follicular tissues (with indistinct borders) and considerable swelling of germinative centres with some swollen reticulum-fibres, some leucocytes-emigration (with plenty of nuclear fragments) and some hemorrhages.
Collapse of glandular tissues with some leucocytes-emigration in glands.

273

47.

Multiple intense necrosis of mucous membrane with some intense desquamative changes (in crypts, a large quantity of desquamated epitheliums, some fibrinous masses and some bacterial masses) and intense edematous swelling of mucous epitheliums.
Swelling of rather atrophic follicular tissues (with indistinct borders) and considerable swelling of germinative centres with some swollen reticulum-fibres.
In submucous tissues, some considerable congestion and some hemorrhages, accompanied with some plasma-cell-infiltrations.
Collapse of glandular tissues with some leucocytes- emigration in glands.

S-I.

Intense hemorrhagic-necrotic changes of submucous tissues with remarkable congestion (plenty of bacterial masses in capillaries). multiple hemorrhages and flaky bacterial dissemination all over the submucous tissues.
Intense edematous swelling and at some places, diffuse necrosis (with some superficial ulcers) of mucous membrane, due to some bacterial disseminations.
Intense swelling or complete necrotic ruins of follicular tissues, with plenty of bacterial disseminations.
In submucous tissues, intense congestion, multiple intense hemorrhages and diffuse bacterial dissemination all over the submucous tissues.
Many waxy degenerated muscle-fibres with remarkable fragmentation and intermuscular tissues with intense leucocytes-emigration, intense

274

edema and some hemorrhages.

S-2.

Diffuse intense bacterial dissemination and multiple intense hemorrhages all over the investigated areas.

Intense edema and degeneration of mucous membrane with intense leucocytes-emigration in interepitheliar spaces and at some places with intense diffuse necrosis (and some superficial ulcers) of mucous membrane, with some bacterial accumulation in interepitheliar spaces and intense desquamative changes (in crypts, a large quantity of degenerated epitheliums, some fibrinous masses and some bacterial masses).

Intense swelling or at some places complete necrosis of follicular tissues and germinative centres, due to flaky bacterial disseminations. Intense follicular congestion and some bacterial masses in capillaries.

In submucous tissues, intense congestion (some bacterial masses in capillaries) and multiple diffuse hemorrhages, and in intermuscular tissues, intense diffuse hemorrhagic-necrotic ruins of tissues, due to flaky bacterial dissemination and diffuse hemorrhages.

S-4.

Intense necrotic ruins of mucous membrane, due to intense bacterial disseminations.

In crypts, a large quantity of desquamated epitheliums, massive fibrinous and bacterial masses and various serous fluids.

In submucous tissues, intense congestion and some bacterial masses

275

in capillaries and some places with massive bacterial accumulation to form diffuse necrotic ruins of submucous tissues.
Considerable swelling of follicular tissues with considerable edema and some follicular congestion (some bacterial masses in capillaries) and considerable swelling of germinative centres.
In submucous tissues, remarkable stagnation of lymphs, accompanied with plenty of bacterial accumulations.
In intermuscular tissues, many waxy degenerated muscle-fibres and remarkable bacterial disseminations.

S-II.

Intense edema and degeneration of mucous membrane with some desquamative changes (in crypts, a little quantity of degenerated epitheliums, some fibrinous masses, and various secretoric fluids).
Considerable swelling of follicular tissues with intense follicular congestion and slight hemorrhages, and considerable swelling of germinative centres with considerable congestions.
In submucous tissues, intense congestion and some bacterial masses in capillaries.
Many waxy degenerated muscle-fibres and some edema and some round-cell-infiltration in intermuscular tissues.
Intense collapse of glandular tissues with some leucocytes-emigration and slight hemorrhages (with some capillary congestion).

276

The bird's-eye view of all investigated cases are as follows:

1. No remarkable changes.

2. Tonsillitis acuta with considerable congestion and some bacterial dissemination in follicular tissues.

3. Tonsillitis acuta with some congestion, some hemorrhages in follicular tissues and some leucocytes-dissemination in submucous tissues.

4. Tonsillitis necroticans in medium degree, with some bionecrotic changes in germinative centers and some leucocytes-dissemination in submucous tissues.

5. No remarkable changes.

6. No remarkable changes.

7. Tonsillitis acuta with considerable follicular congestion.

8. Tonsillitis acuta purulenta with some leucocytes-dissemination in follicular tissues.

9. No remarkable changes.

10. Tonsillitis acuta with inter- and intrafollicular congestion and some bacterial masses in follicular capillaries.

11. Tonsillitis haemorrhagica with considerable congestion, some remarkable hemorrhages and some bacterial dissemination in follicular tissues.

12. Tonsillitis haemorrhagico-necroticans with considerable congestion, multiple miliary necrosis and some bacterial dissemination in follicular tissues and intense perifollicular congestion.

13. Tonsillitis catarrhalis acuta with some follicular congestion, slight hemorrhages and some edema in follicular tissues and intense diffuse round cell infiltration in submucous tissues.

15. No remarkable changes.

16. Tonsillitis haemorrhagico-purulenta, with considerable congestion, some hemorrhages and edema in follicular tissues, multiple necrosis of mucous menbrane and some round cell infiltration in submucous tissues.

17. Tonsillitis acuta with some follicular congestion.

18. No remarkable changes.

277

19. Tonsillitis acuta with intense follicular congestion, some leucocytes-dissemination in germinative centres and some intense round cell dissemination in submucous tissues.

20. Tonsillitis necroticans with intense diffuse necrosis and plenty leucocytes-dissemination in follicular tissues and intense round cell dissemination in submucous tissues.

21. Tonsillitis catarrhalis acuta with intense follicular congestion and edema, multiple diffuse necrotis of mucous menbrane.

23. Tonsillitis acuta with considerable congestion, edema and some leucocytes-dissemination in follicular tissues.

24. Slight follicular congestion and no remarkable changes else.

26. NO remarkable changes.

27. No remarkable changes.

28. Tonsillitis hemorrhagica acuta in medium degree, with some follicular congestion, some leucocytes-dissemination in germinative centres, some congestion and some round cell dissemination in submucous tissues and multiple diffuse necrosis of mucous menbrane.

29. No remarkable changes.

30. Tonsillitis acuta hemorrhagica in slight degree, with intense congestion and slight paritail hemorrhages in follicular tissues, and intense congestion insubmucous tissues.

31. Tonsillitis acuta with intense congestion and slight hemorrhages in submucous tissues and slight edematous swelling of follicular tissues

32. Tonsillitis acuta with intense edematous swelling of follicular tissues, intense diffuse round cell dissemination in submucous tissues and intense degeneration (with intense necrotis at some places) of mucous epithelium.

278

33. Tonsillitis acuta hemorrhagica with
intense follicular congestion and intense hemorrhages, 1
intense hemorrhages in submucous tissues and
intense multiple hemorrhages in intermuscular tissues, multiple necrotic changes of mucous epitheliums.

34. Tonsillitis acuta with
some edematous swelling of follicular tissues,
slight hemorrhages and some leucocytes-dissemination in germinative centres and
some hemorrhages and some leucocytes-dissemination in submucous tissues.

35. No remarkable changes.

36. Tonsillitis acuta with
intense edema and some leucocytes dissemination in follicular tissues,
intense congestion and some leucocytes dissemination innsubmucous tissues and
intense diffuse degeneration of mucous membrane.

38. Tonsillitis acuta with
considerable edema and some bionecrotic changes in follicular tissues,
intense congestion in submucous tissues and
intense diffuse necrosis of mucous mebrane.

39. Tonsillitis acuta with
considerable edema in follicular tissues,
some remarkable congestion and some leucocytes-dissemination in follicular germinative centres,
some inflammtory chnges in submucous tissues, and
diffuse degeneration of mucous membrane.

40. Tonsillitis acuta hemorrhagica with
considerable congestion and slight hemorrhages in follicular tissues,
intense congestion in submucous tissues, and
intense congestion and some hemorrhages in intermuscsular tissues.

42. Fonsillitis hemorrhagico-necroticans with
intense congestion, multiple intense hemorrhages and flaky bacterial dissemination, in submucous tissues,
intense swelling and slight hemorrhages in follicular tissues and

-279

edematous swelling of mucous mebrane.

44. Tonsillitis acuta with slight follicular congestion.

46. Tonsilltis acuta with slight follciular congestion.

47. Tonsillitis acuta with
considerable swelling of follicular tissues,
considerable congestion and some hemorrhages in
submucous tissues.

49. No reamrkable changes.

S-I. Tonsillitis hemorrhagico-necroticans with
intense diffuse hemorrhagic, necrotic changes in
follicular tissues with flaky bacterial dissemination, intense congestion, multiple intense hemorrhages and intense bacterial dissemination in
submucous tissues.

S-2. Tonsillitis hemorrhagico-purulenta with
intense congestion, multiple intense hemorrhages
and remarkable bacterial dissemination in follicular
tissues, intense congestion, hemorrhages and
intense bacterial dissemination in submucous and
intermuscular tissues.

S-3. Tonsillitis acuta hemorrhagica.

S-4. Tonsillitis hemorrhagico-necroticans with
intense edema, congestion and some hemorrhages in
follicular tissues,
intense congestion, some hemorrhages and intense
bacterial dissemination in submuocus tissues in
submucous and intermuscular tissues.

S-5. Tonsillitis hemorrhagico-purulenta acuta.

S-6. Tonsillitis hemorrhagico-necroticans.

S-8. Tonsillitis septica with intense follicular congestion and some
bacterial embolus.

S-9. No remarkable changes.

S-10. No remarkable changes.

280

S-11. Tonsillitis acuta with
intense follicular congestion and some hemorrhages, intense congestion and some round cell dissemination in submucous tissues.

S-12. Tonsilltis acuta catarrhalis with
considerable congestion, some hemorrhages and some intense bacterial dissemination in follicular tisues.

S-14. No remarkable changes.

S-15. Tonsillitis hemorrhagico-necroticans partialis with,
intense congestion, some hemorrhages and intense bacterial dissemination in follicular tissues, accompanied with multiple miliary necrosis.

S-16. No remarkable changes.

S-19. No remarkable changes.

S-22. No remarkable changes.

S-26. No remarkable changes.

S-28. Nor remarkable changes.

S-38. Tonsillitis acuta catarrhalis with
considerale congestion (with some bacterial masses in capillaries) and edema in follicular tissues.

281

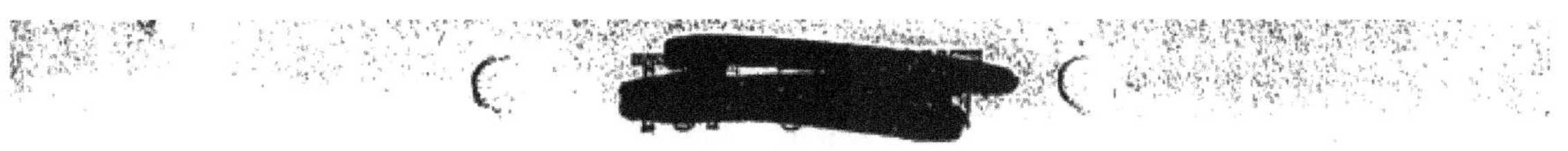

Bionecrotic changes at submucous tissues, accompanied with some bacterial dissemination.

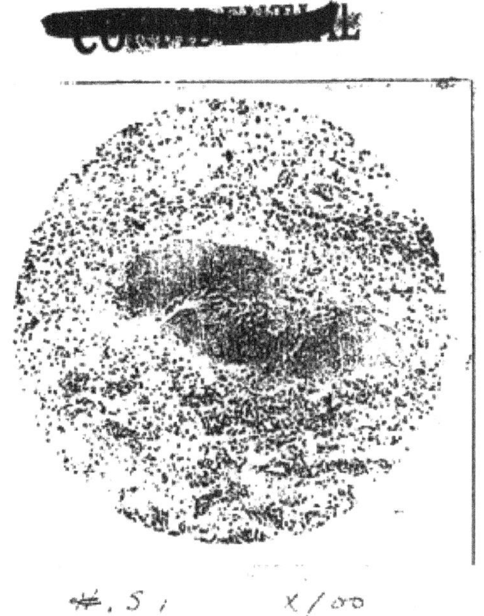

#.51　　x100

282

Intense congestion and remarkable perivascular bacterial accumulation, in submucous and mucous tissues.

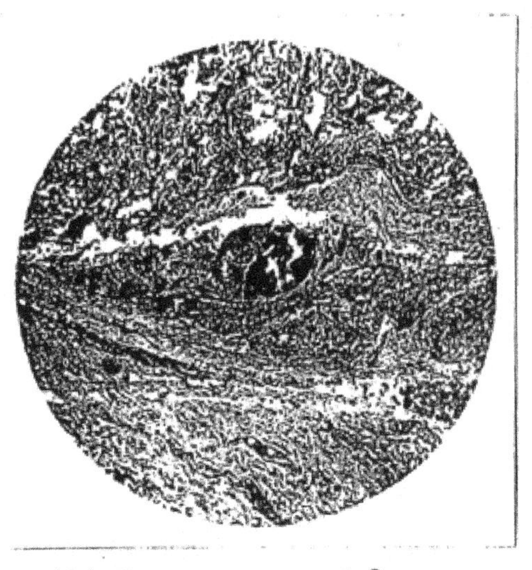

N 42 ×90

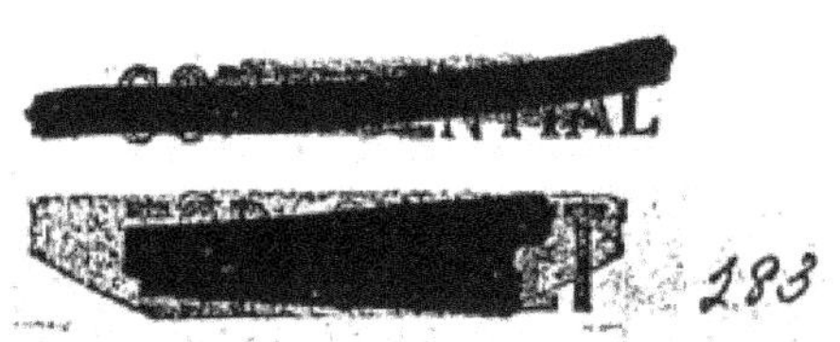

283

Tonsillitis supprativa,with many necrotic masses in crypts.

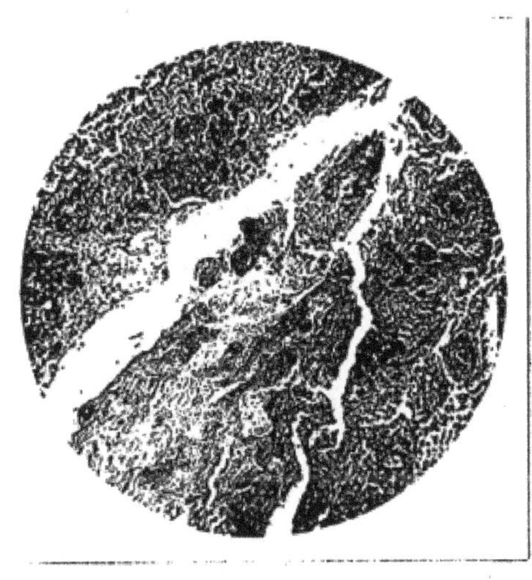

Tonsillitis supprqtiva acuta,with many necrotic masses in crypts.

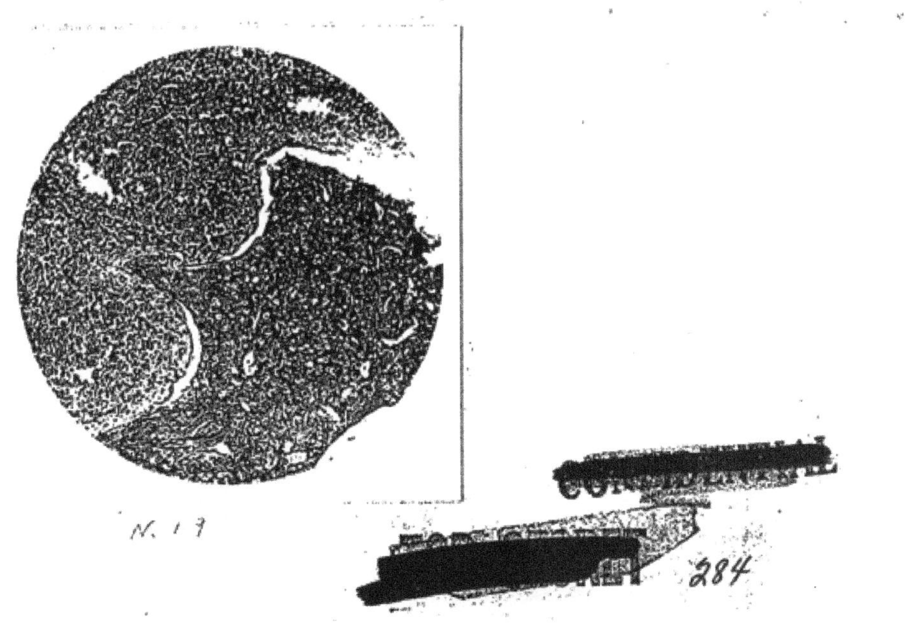

N. 17

284

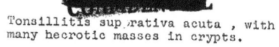

Tonsillitis sup rativa acuta , with many hecrotic masses in crypts.

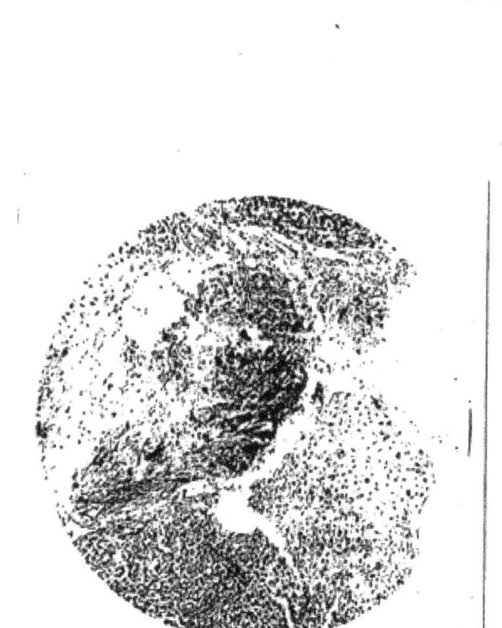

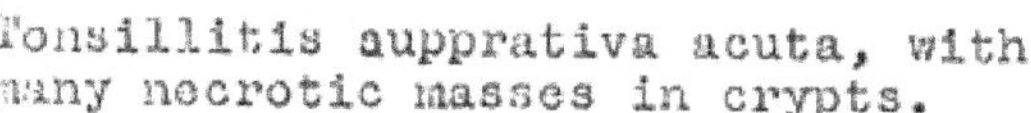

Tonsillitis supprativa acuta, with many necrotic masses in crypts.

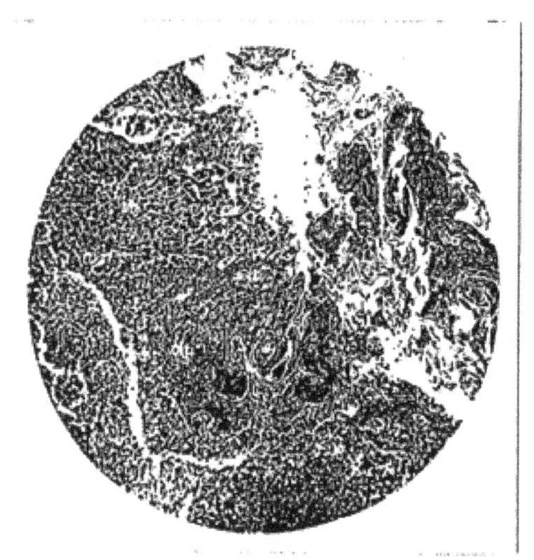

285

Necrotic chamges of epitheliums and many decayed masses in crypts.

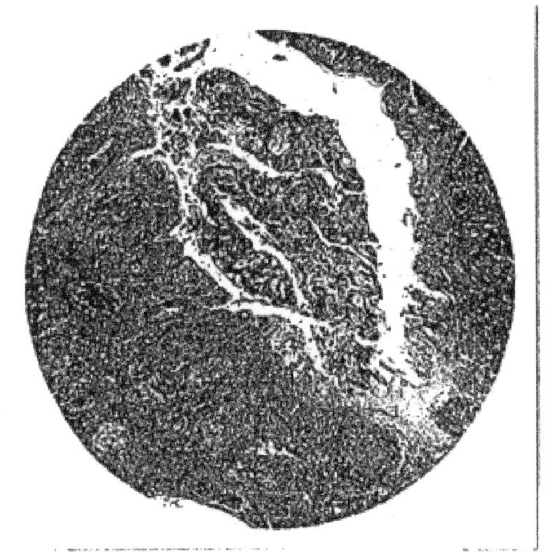

Necrotic changes of epitheliums.

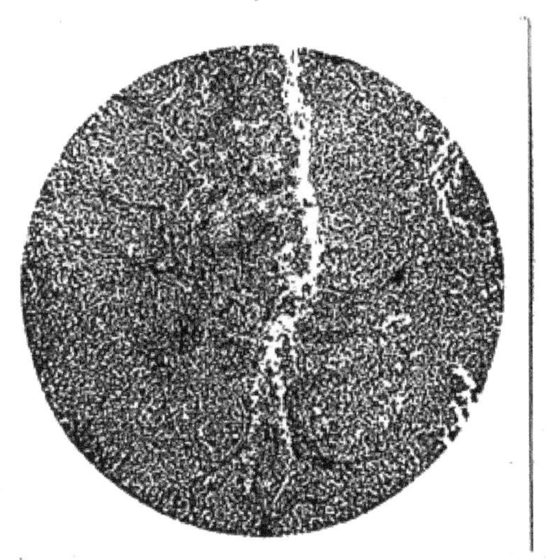

286

Intense submucous congestion.

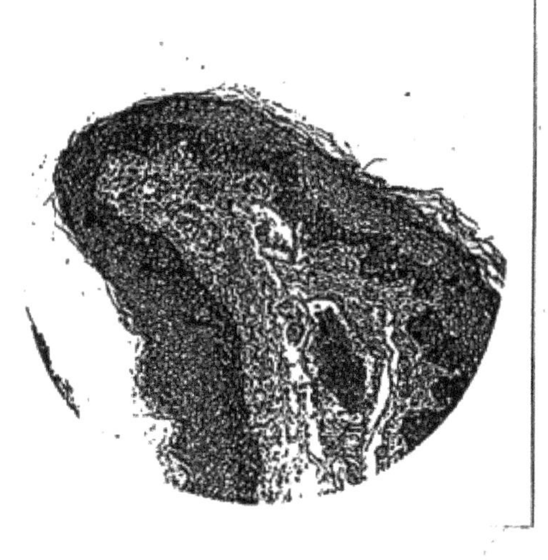

Intense submucous congestion, in high power.

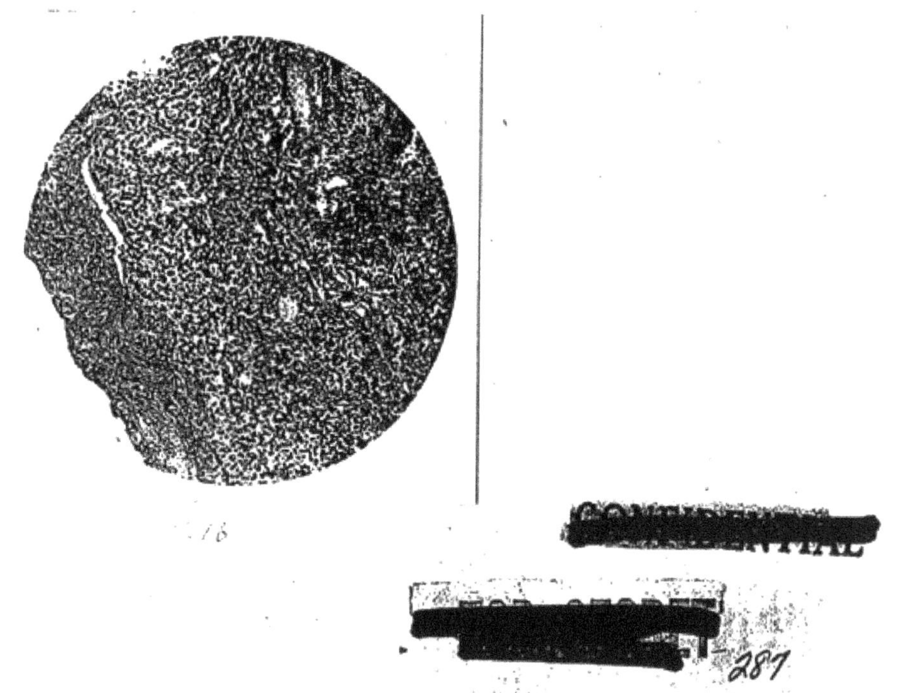

287

Intense congestion in subepitheliar layers. In high power.

Intense congestion in subepithelial layer. In high power.

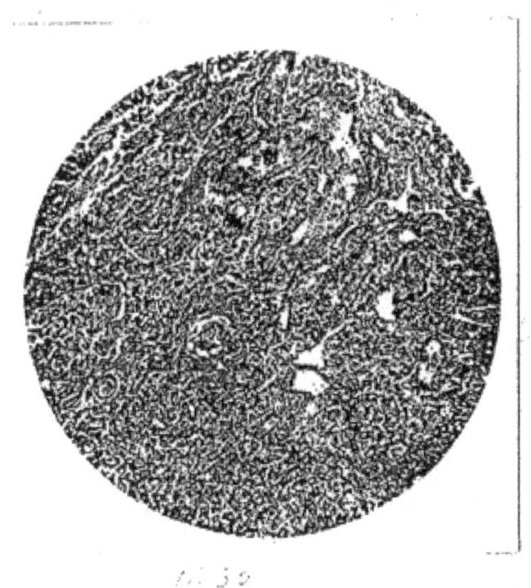

288

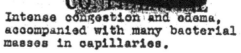

Intense congestion and edema, accompanied with many bacterial masses in capillaries.

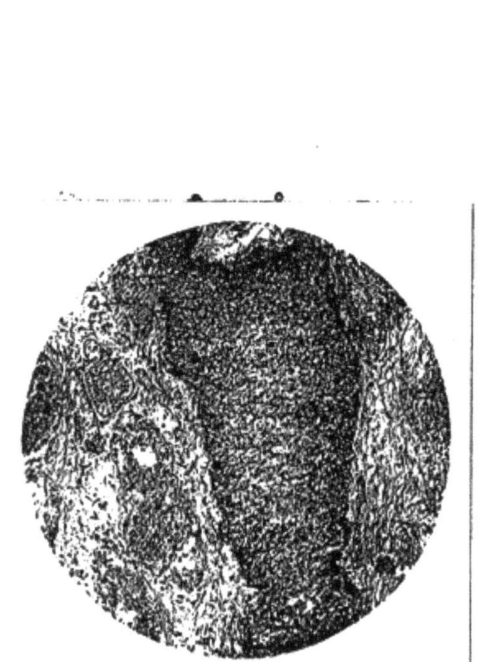

Bacterial thrombus, in high power.

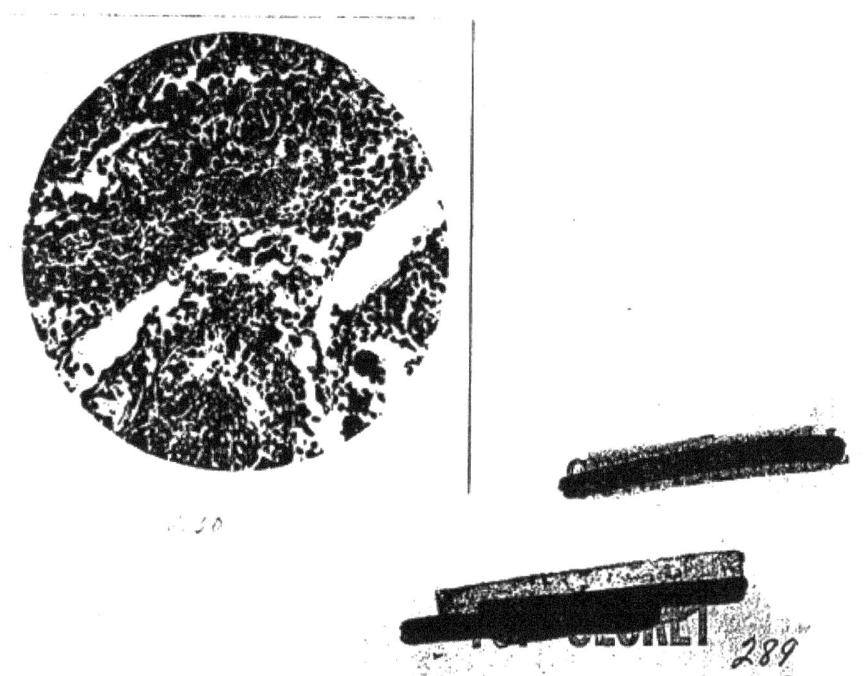

289

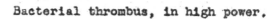

Intense perifolliicular congestion.

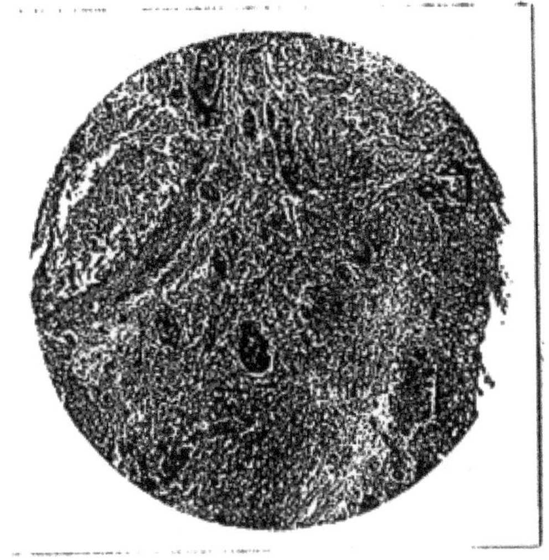

Intense perifolliicular congestion.

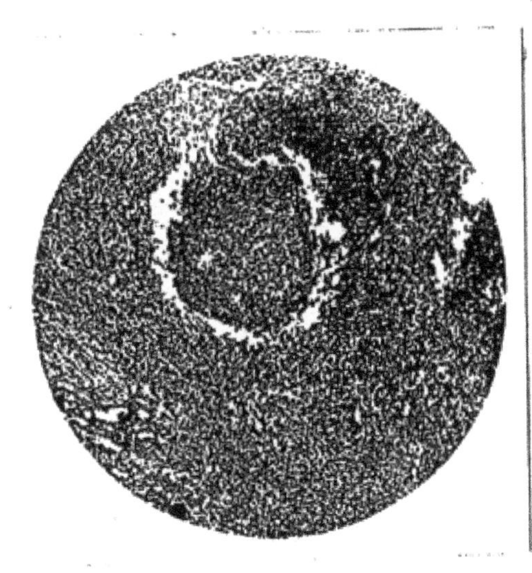

290

Leucocytes dissemination in inter_muscular tissues.

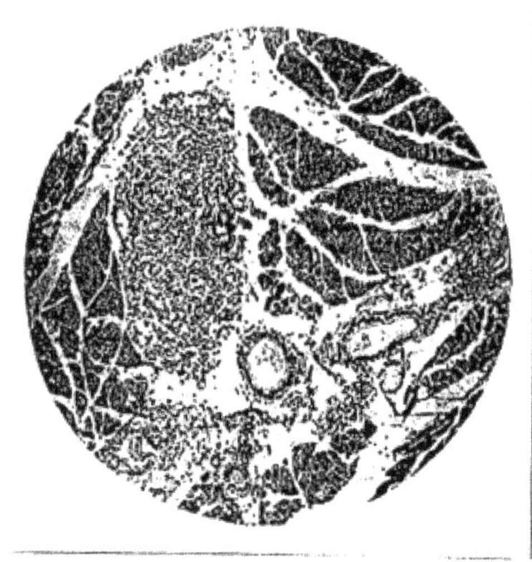

Leucocytes-dissemination in inter-musculer tissues.

291

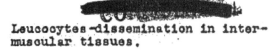

Leucocytes-dissemination in inter-muscular tissues.

Leucocytes-dissemination in inter-muscular tissues.

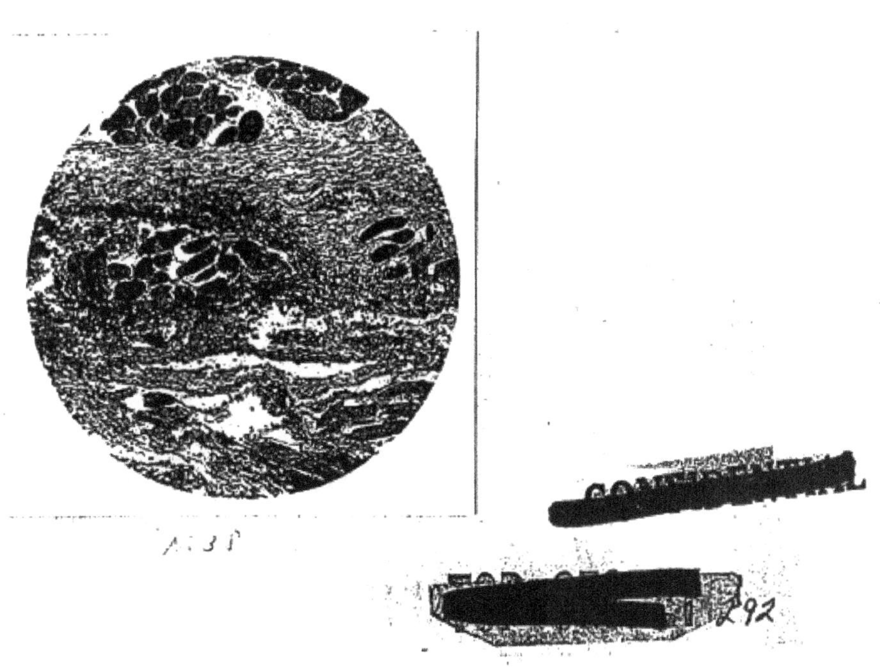

Diffuse hemorrhages in submucous tissues.

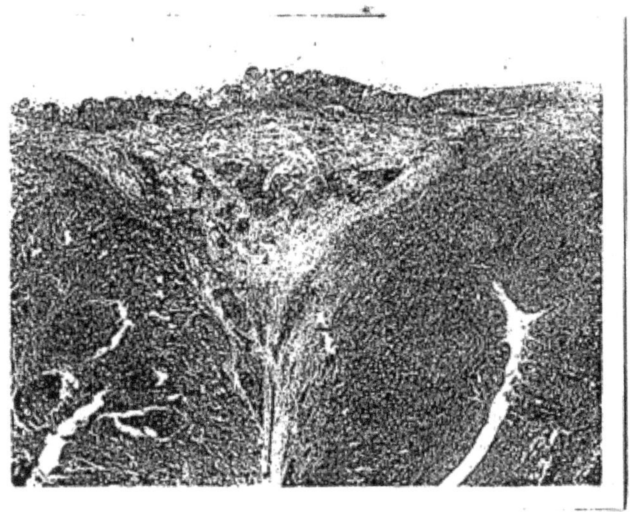

Bionecrotic changes of follicles.

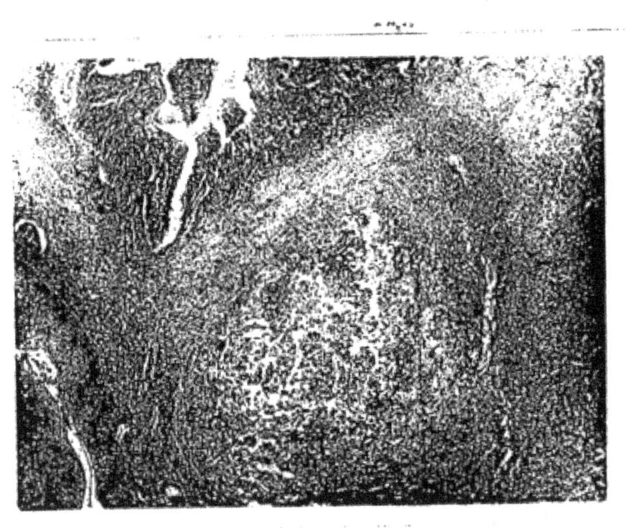

293

Intense necrotic changes of follicle, in high power.

X 120

Intense necrotic changes ōf follicle, in high power.

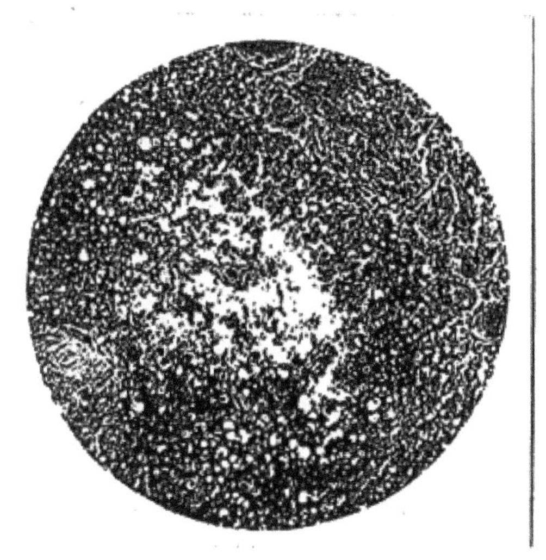

294

Necrotic changes of follicle.

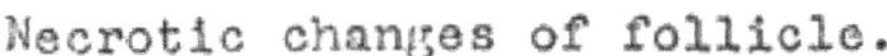

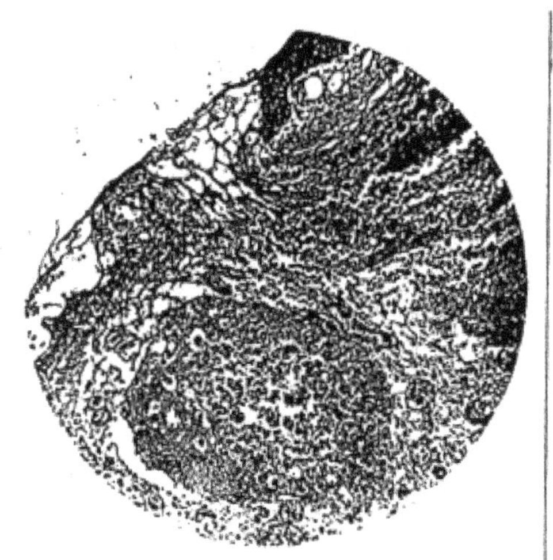

Intense necrotic changes of follicle.
~~In highn power~~.

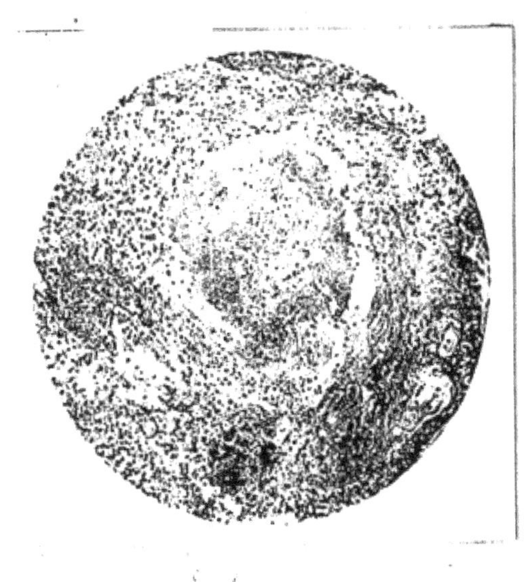

295

Diffuse hemorrhagic necrotic changes in submucous and follicular tissues.

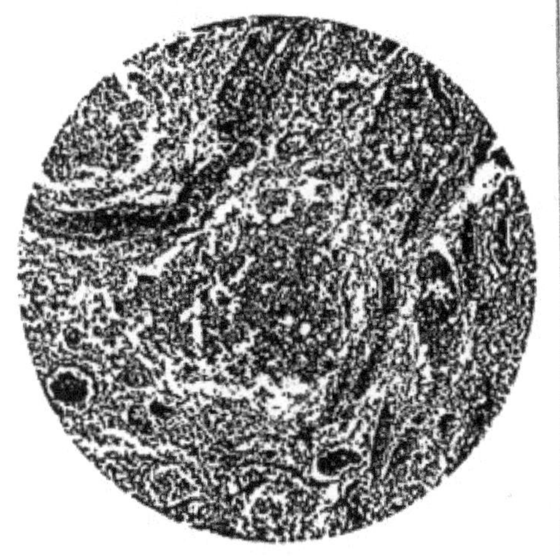

Diffuse necrotic changes ,in follicular tissues ,accompanied with bacterial dissemination.

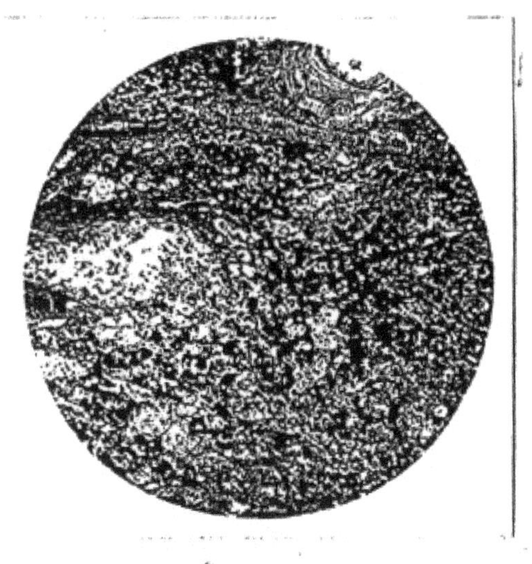

296

Bacterial thrombus, in high power.

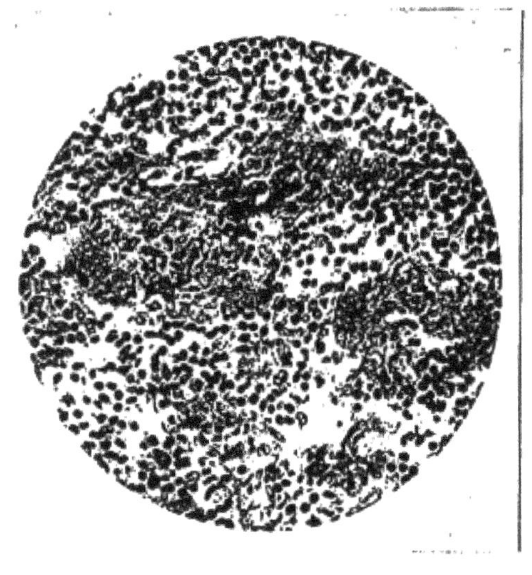

Bacterial thrombus , in high power.

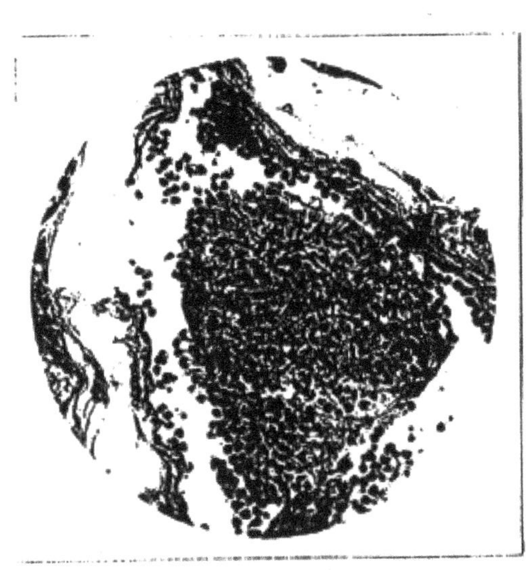

297

Pharynx
&
Bronchus

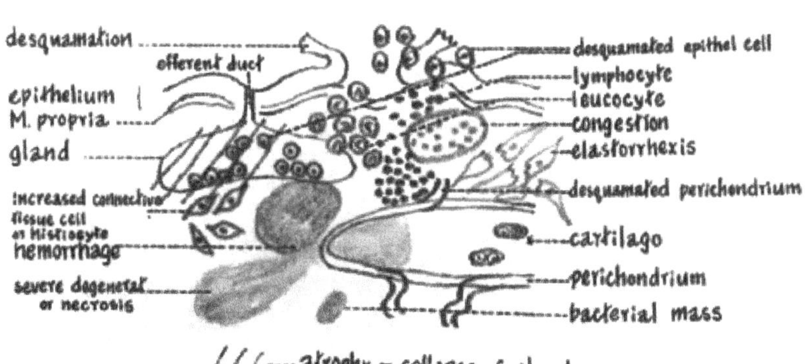
desquamation
efferent duct
epithelium
M. propria
gland
increased connective tissue cell or Histiocyte
hemorrhage
severe degenerat. or necrosis
desquamated epithel cell
lymphocyte
leucocyte
congestion
elastorrhexis
desquamated perichondrium
cartilago
perichondrium
bacterial mass
/// atrophy or collapse of gland

298

B R O N C H U S

(A) Microscopical Investigation

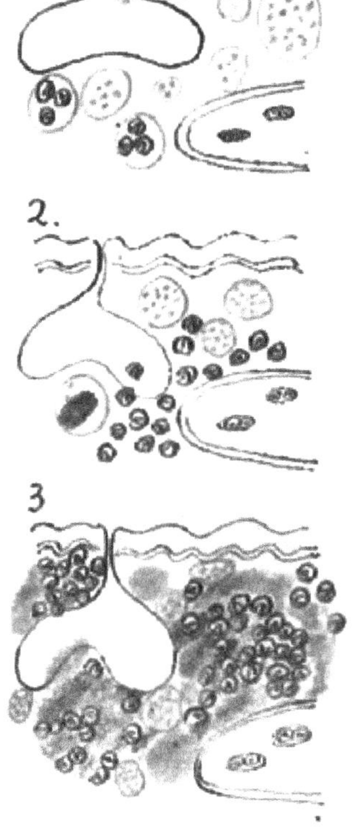

1. Epiglottis.

Considerable congestion and considerable edema-teus swelling in submucous tissues, with some leu-cocytes as capillary contents.

2. Pharynx. (esp. Recessus piriformis).

Considerable congestion (with some bacterial masses as capillary contents) and diffuse consider-able leucocytes-emigrations in submucous tissues.

3. Bronchus.

Remarkable congestion and considerable edematous swelling. At some places, plenty of leucocytes as capillary-contents and at some places, multiple supermiliary abscesses with plenty of leucocytes, massive bacterial and necrotic accumulations. With severe perifocal changes. (hemorrhages and leuco-cytes-emigrations).

And at some places, (in subepithelial or inter-glandular tissues), considerable leucocytes-infilt-rations with slight localised bleedings.

3. Epiglottis.

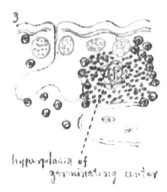

Considerable congestion and considerable, at some places remarkable, edemateus swelling in sub-mucous tissues with considerable leucocytes emig-rations, especially at peri-lymphonodular tissues. Slight hyperplasia of germinative centres with some, cloudy swollen reticulum cells and some leucocytes in considerably edematously swollen tissues.

3

hyperplasia of germinating center

299

4. Bronchus.

Slight congestion and no remarkable changes else.

4. Epiglottis.

Severe congestion (with some leucocytes-emigrations at perivascular parts) and severe serous exudation in submucous tissues.

5. Bronchus.

Remarkable congestion (with some bacterial masses as capillary contents) and considerable swelling in subepithelier, interglandular and inter-lymphonodular tissues. At some places of them, intense bacterial accumulations with plenty of leucocytes, massive bacterial and necrotic masses to form multiple supermiliary abscesses.

7. Bronchus.

Considerable congestion and edema in subepithelier, inter-glandular and inter-lymphonodular tissues.

9. Bronchu.

Slight congestion and slight edema in submucous tissues with slight round-cell-infiltrations.

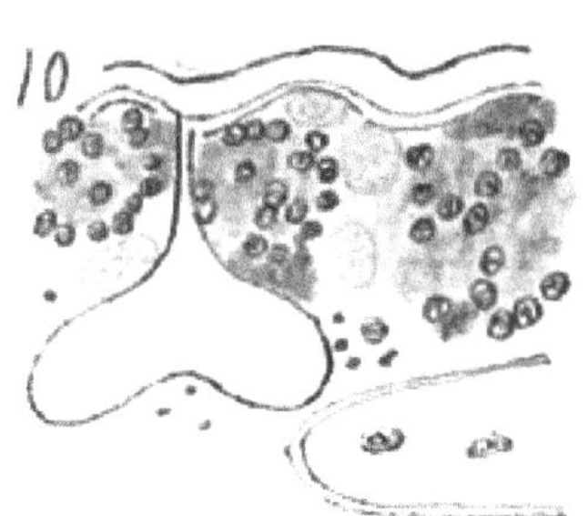

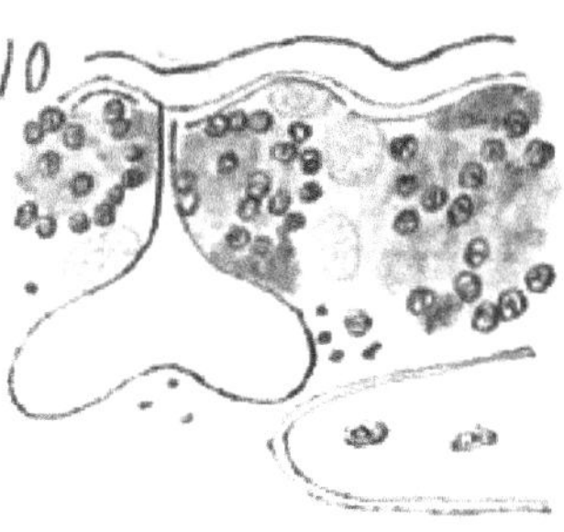

10. Bronchus.

Remarkable congestion (with plenty of bacterial masses as capillary contents) and severe edema in submucous tissues. At some places, esp. in subepithelial tissues, massive bacterial accumulation to form multiple miliary abscesses with plenty of leucocytes, necrotic masses and severe serous exudations.

10. Epiglottis.

Remarkable congestion and severe edematous swelling with severe diffuse bacterial and leucocytic emigrations, especially in subepitheliar and interglandular tissues with plenty of leucocytes.

11. Bronchus.

Considerable congestion and edematous swelling in subepitheliar, interglandular and inter-lymphonodular tissues with slight localised hemorrhages, remarkable edema and some leucocytic infiltrations.

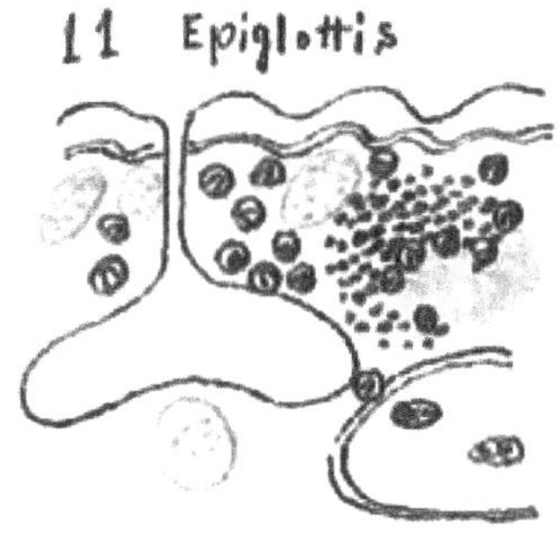

11. Epiglottis.

Remarkable congestion, considerable edema and some leucocytes-emigrations in submucous tissues. Intense congestion, edematous swelling, slight localised hemorrhages and plenty of leucocytes-accumulations in lymphonodular tissues.

11. Pharynx (esp. Recessus piriformis).

Considerable congestion and edema with some round-cells-infiltration.

12. Bronchus.

Remarkable congestion (with some bacterial masses as capillary contents) and considerable edematous swelling in subepitheliar and inter-glandular tissues with some wandering-cell-emigrations.

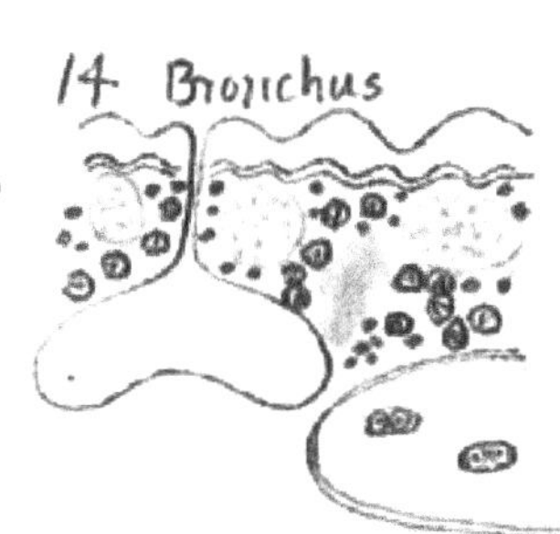

14. Bronchus.

Considerable congestion in subepitheliar and inter-glandular tissues with some slight hemorrhages and considerable edema in submucous tissues. Considerable round-cell (lymphocytes and some leu-

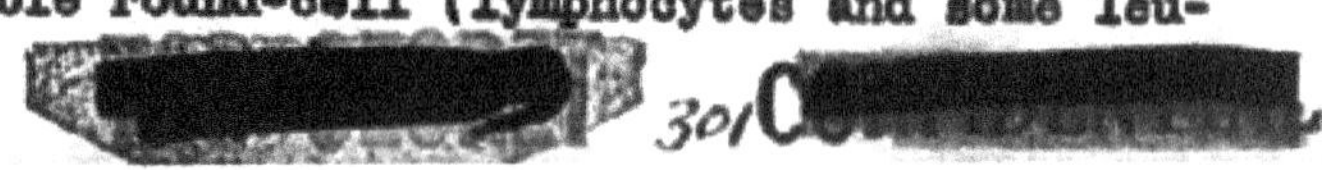
301

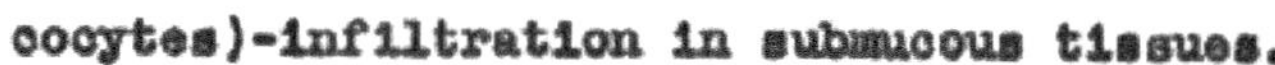

cocytes)-infiltration in submucous tissues.

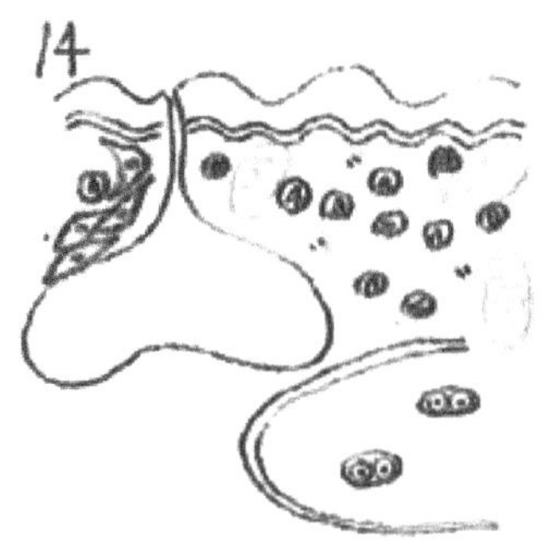

14. Epiglottis.

Considerable congestion and edema with some considerable round-cell-disseminations (some histiocytes and some leucocytes, some eosino-philic cells).

16. Bronchus.

Considerable congestion and slight edema in subepitheliar and interglandular tissues.

16. Pharynx and epiglottis.

Remarkable congestion and edema in subepitheliar and inter-glandular tissues with considerable round-cell-disseminations.

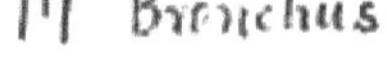

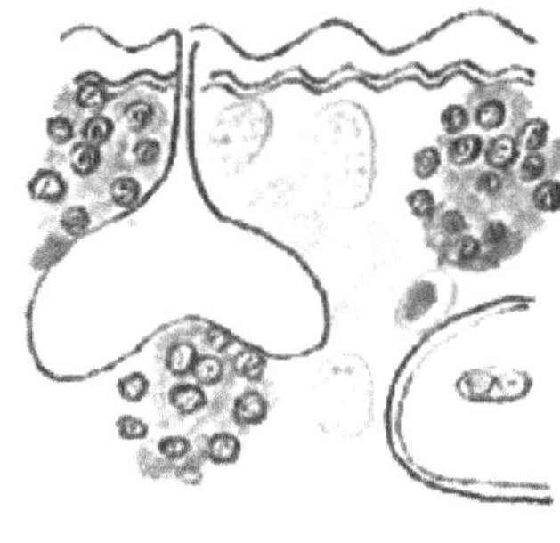

17. Bronchus.

Remarkable congestion (with some bacterial masses as capillary contents) and severe edematous swelling in subepitheliar, interglandular and inter-lymphonodular tissues with multiple miliary abscesses, due to massive bacterial, leucocytic and necrotic accumulations.

Multiple slight localised hemorrhages in submucous tissues.

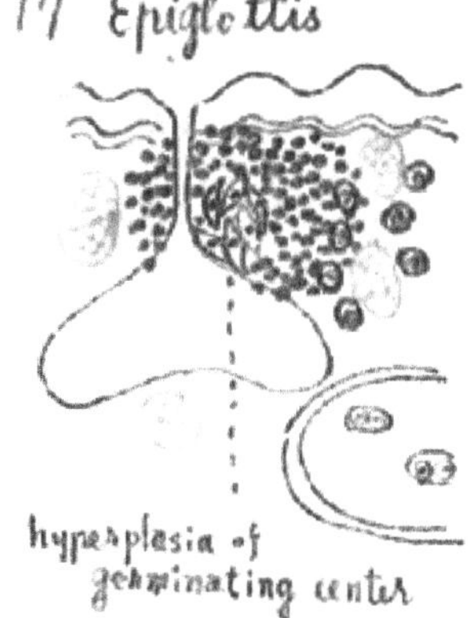

17. Epiglottis.

Considerable congestion and some leucocytes-infiltration in submucous tissues, especially in subepitheliar and inter-glandular tissues. Considerable hyperplasia of lymph-nodulus with considerable congestion, edematous swelling of reticulum-fibres and considerably increased reticulum cells in severe cloudy swelling and considerable hyperplasia of

germinating center.
~~ger,omatove comtres wotj sp,e omcreased retocüöi,~~
~~cells in severe cloudy swelling.~~

With some leucocytic infiltrations.

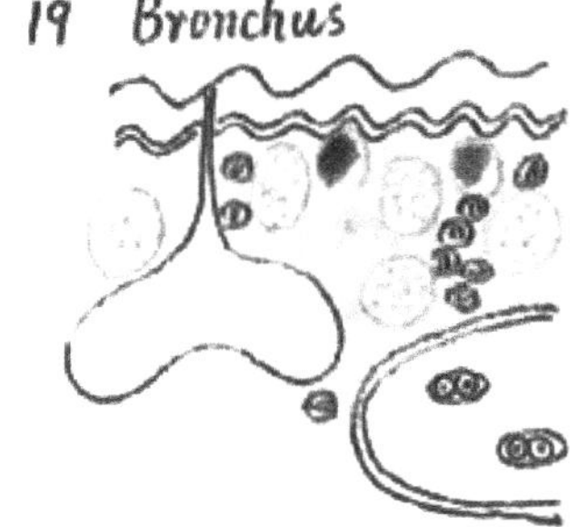

19. Bronchus.

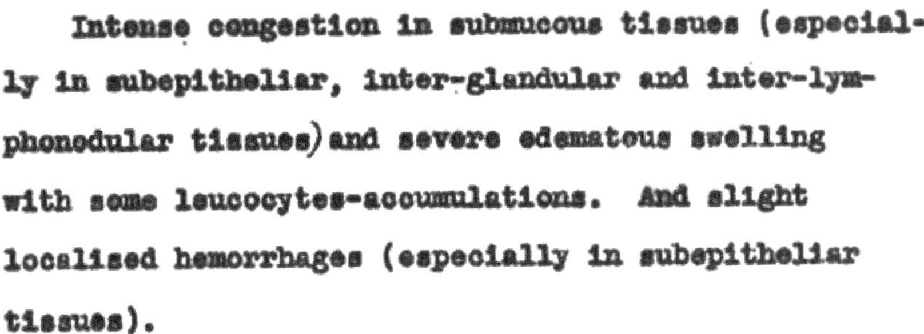

Intense congestion in submucous tissues (especially in subepitheliar, inter-glandular and inter-lymphonodular tissues) and severe edematous swelling with some leucocytes-accumulations. And slight localised hemorrhages (especially in subepitheliar tissues).

Remarkable bacterialaaccumulations in capillary-plexus in subepitheliar and inter-glandular tissues.

20. Bronchus.

Considerable congestion (esp. in subepitheliar and inter-glandular tissues) and remarkable edematous swelling in submuceus tissues with some round-cell-disseminations.

21. Bronchus.

Considerable congestion (esp. in subepitheliar and inter-glandular tissues) and some round-cell-infiltrations in submucous tissues.

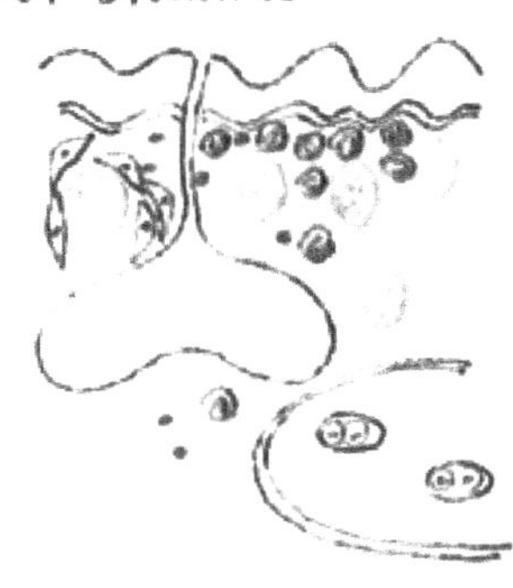

24. Bronchus.

Remarkable congestion, considerable edematous swelling and some round cell disseminations (some histiocytes, some lymphocytes and some leucocytes) in submucous tissues (esp. in subepitheliar and inter-glandular tissues).

26. Bronchus.

303

Intense congestion, slight edematous swelling and some wandering-cell-dissemination in submucous tissues (esp. in subepitheliar and inter-glandular tissues).

26. Epiglottis.

Slight congestion and no remarkable changes else.

27. Pharynx (especially Recessus piriformis).

Slight congestion and no remarkable changes else.

27. Epiglottis.

Slight congestion and slight round-cell-disseminations (some lymphocytes, some plasma-cells and some leucocytes).

29. Bronchus.

Considerable congestion, severe edematous swelling and some round-cell-dissemination in submucous tissues.

30. Bronchus.

Considerable congestion, slight edematous swelling and some round-cell-infiltrations.

31. Bronchus.

Considerable congestion, slight edematous swelling, some round-cell-disseminations, and considerable hyperplasia of lymph-nodulus.

33. Bronchus.

Remarkable congestion and slight edematous swelling in submucous tissues (esp. in subepitheliar and inter-glandular tissues) and some wandering-cell-

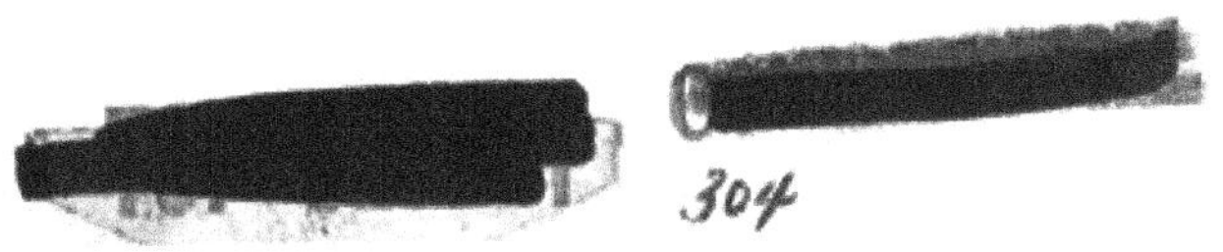

disseminations (some lymphocytes and leucocytes). Considerable hyperplasia of lymphatic nodulus ~~in slight degree.~~

35. Bronchus. 

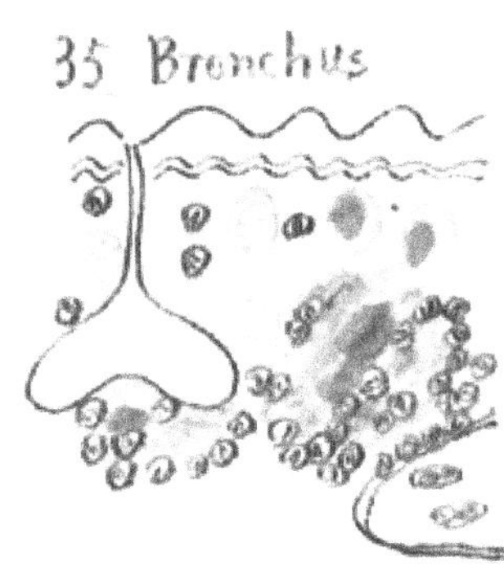

Remarkable congestion (some bacterial masses as capillar contents) and severe edematous swelling in submucous tissues (esp. in subephteliar, inter-glandular and inter-lymphonodular tissues).

At some places massive bacterial accumulations to form multiple miliary abscesses with massive bacterial disseminations, plenty of leucocytes-accumulations and severe necrotic ruins of tissues.

35. Epiglottis.

Remarkable congestion, considerable edematous and some round-cell-disseminations.

36. Epiglottis.

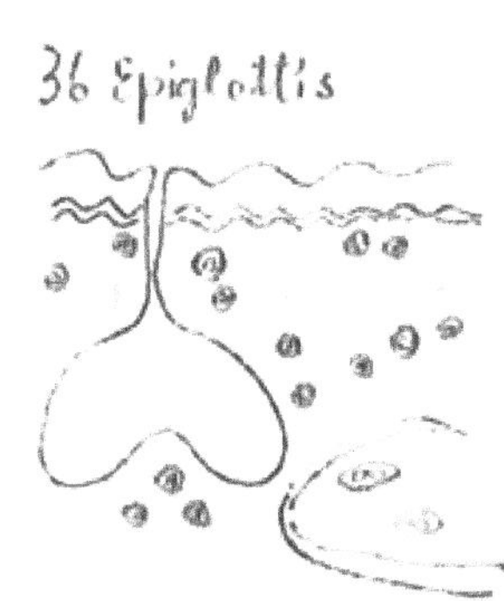

Considerable congestion and at some places (esp. at margin-portions of epiglottis), extremely severe serous exudations and considerable leucocytes-disseminations, accompanied with severe diffuse edematous swelling of submucous tissues.

42. Bronchus.

Considerable congestion and slight round-cell-disseminations.

46. Bronchus.

Slight congestion and very slight edematous swelling. No remarkable changes else.

46. Epiglottis.

Considerable congestion and slight edematous

swelling.

47. Bronchus

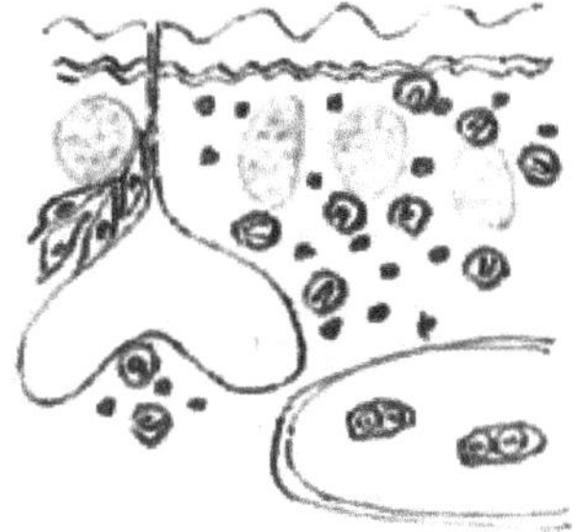

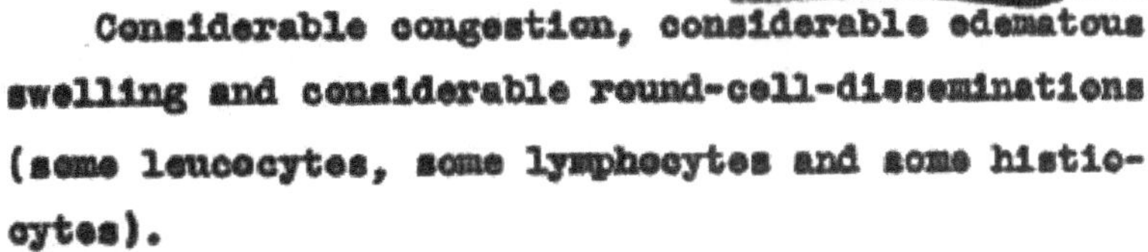

47. Bronchus.

Considerable congestion, considerable edematous swelling and considerable round-cell-disseminations (some leucocytes, some lymphocytes and some histiocytes).

49. Bronchus.

Considerable congestion, and edema in submucous tissues (esp. in subepitheliar and inter-glandular tissues).

49. Epiglottis.

Intense congestion, considerable edema and some round-cell-disseminations(mainly lymphocytes).

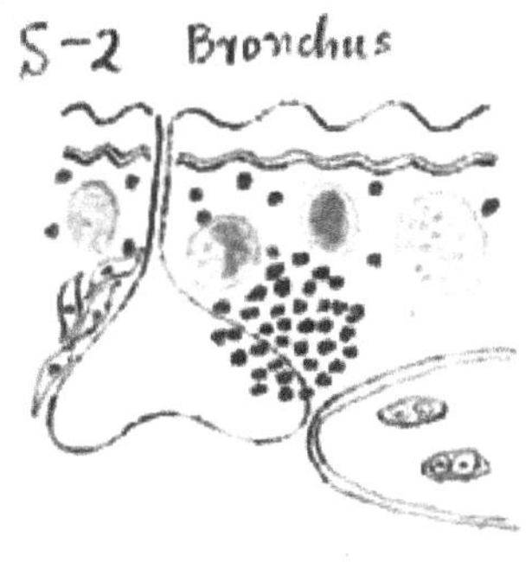

S-2. Bronchus.

Considerable congestion (with some bacterial masses as capillary contents), slight edematous swelling and some wandering-cell-dissemination (some histiocytes, some plasma-cells and lymphocytes), accompanied with slight hyperplasia of lymphatic nodulus.

S-3. Bronchus.

Remarkable congestion, severe edematous swelling and considerable disseminations of wandering cells (some leucocytes, lymphocytes and plasma-cells) in submucous tissues (esp. in subepitheliar, and inter-glandular tissues).

S-4. Bronchus.

306

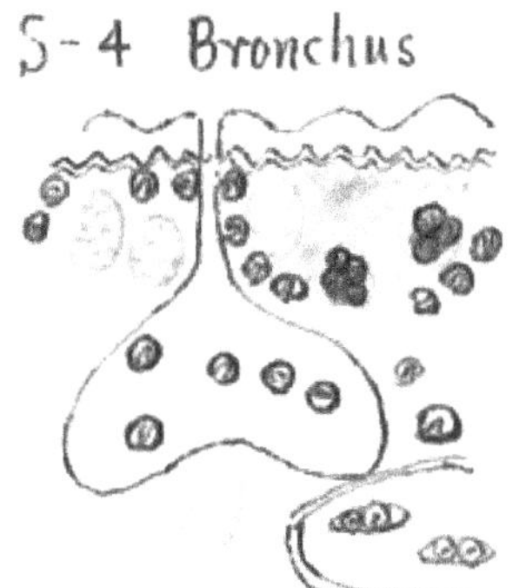

Intense congestion with some leucocytes as capillary contents). Remarkable hemorrhages in subepitheliar tissues, severe edematous swelling and considerable leucocytes disseminations in submucous tissues (esp. in subepitheliar and interglandular tissues).

S-5. Bronchus.

Considerable congestion (some leucocytes as capillary contents), considerable edema and at some places in subepitheliar tissues and some leucocytes-accumulations in submucous tissues (esp. in subepitheliar and inter-glandular tissues).

S-8. Bronchus.

Slight congestion and slight edema. No remarkable changes else.

S-9 Bronchus

S-9. Bronchus.

Remarkable congestion, severe edematous swelling and plenty of leucocytes accumulations in submucous tissues, esp. in subepitheliar and interglandular tissues.

Some leucocytes and some bacterial masses as capillary contents.

S-10 Bronchus

S-10. Bronchus.

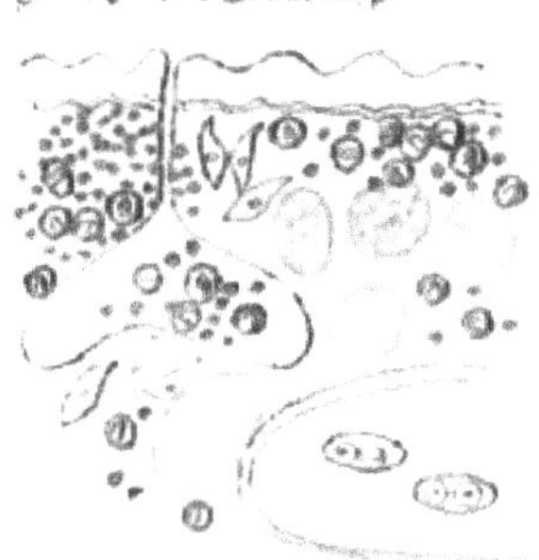

Remarkable congestion, severe edematous swelling and considerable round-cell-disseminations (some leucocytes, lymphocytes and histiocytes, accompanied with the concentrated accumulations at some places) in submucous tissues (esp. in subepitheliar, interglandular and inter-lymphonodular tissues).

S-12. Bronchus.

Considerable congestion, slight edema and slight accumulations of lymphocytes in glandular tissues: no remarkable changes else.

S-14. Bronchus.

Slight congestion and considerable edematous swelling in submucous tissues, especially in subepithelial, inter-glandular and inter-lymphonodular tissues. Slight increased lymphocytes in inter-glandular tissues.

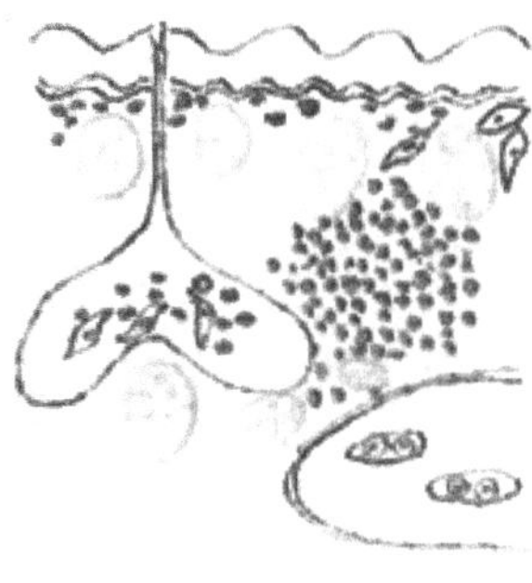

S-15. Bronchus.

Considerable congestion, edematous swelling and slight round-cell-dissemination in submucous tissues, esp. in subepithelial, inter-glandular and inter-lymphonodular tissues: considerable hyperplasia of lympbatic nodulus with severe edematous swelling and considerable congestion.

S-16. Bronchus.

Slight congestion, slight wandering-cell-disseminations and at some places slight accumulation of lymphocytes. No remarkable changes else.

S-22. Bronchus

S-22. Bronchus.

Slight congestion and slight lymphocytes-dissemination in submucous tissues, accompanied with slight hyperplasia of basal membrane of rather atrophic glandular cells and slight hyperplasia of connective tissues.

308

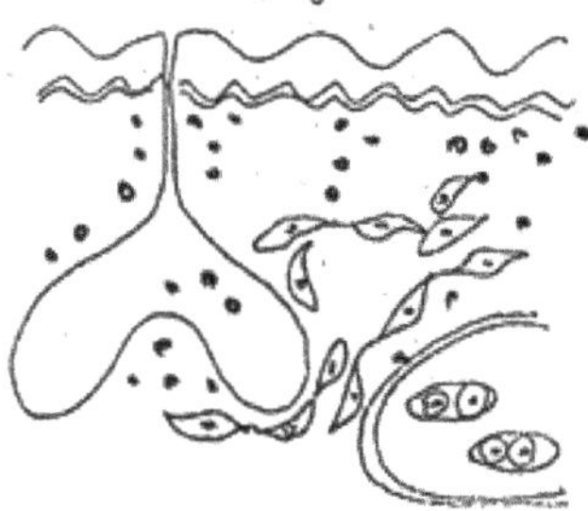

S-22. Epiglottis.

Slight congestion, no edematous swelling in rather cirrhotic submucous tissues and slight lymphocytes-disseminations.

S-26. Bronchus.

Slight congestion and no considerable changes else.

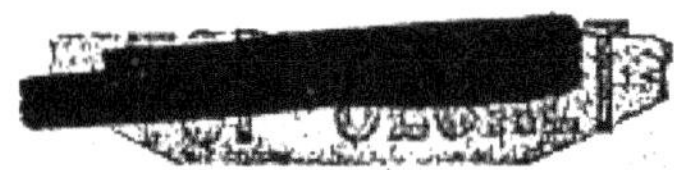

309

(B) S U M M A R Y

(I)

The bird's-eye view of all investigated cases.

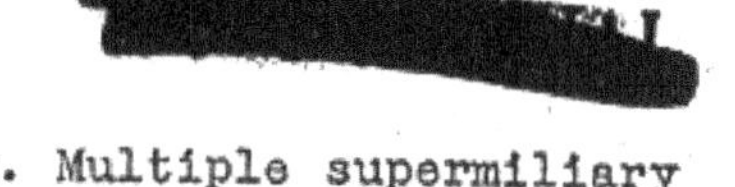

Bronchus :

3. Remarkable congestion and edematous swelling. Multiple supermiliary abscess(with plenty of leucocytes and bacterial masses) and peri-focal hemorrhagic and leucocytid infiltration.

4. No remarkable changes, except slight congestion,

5. Remarkable congestion and edematous swelling. Multiple supermiliary abscess(with plenty of leucocytes and bacterial masses).

7. Considerable congestion and edematous swelling.

9. Slight congstion,edema and round cell-infiltration.

10. Remarkable congestion and severe edema. Mulitple miliary abscesses. (with plenty of leucocytes and bacterial masses).

11. Considerable congestion, edematous swelling and leucocytes-emigration. Slight hemorrhages.

12. Remarkable congestion, edema and round cell-emigration.

14. Considerable congestion and slight hemorrhages. Considerable round cell-infiltration.

16. Considerable congestion and slight edema.

17. Remarkable congestion and edema. Multiple supermiliary abscesses (with plenty of leycocytes and bacterial masses and hemorrhages).

19. Intense congestion and edematous swelling with leucocytes-accumulation. Slight hemorrhages and much bacterial masses as subepithelial capillary-contents.

310

20.Remarkable congestion and edema. Round cell-infiltration.

21.Considerable congestion and round cell-infiltration.

24.Remarkable congestion and edema. Round cell-infiltration(which content also histiocytes).

26.Intense congestion and slight edema. Round cell-infiltration.

29.Consideragle dongestion and severe edematous swelling. Round cell-infiltration.

30.Considerabld congestion and slight edematous swelling. Round cell-infiltration.

31.Considerable congestion and slight edematous swelling. Round cell-infiltration. Considerable hyperplasia of lymphonodulus.

33.Remarkable congestion and slight edematous swelling. Round cell-infiltration.

35. Remarkable congestion and severe dedematous swelling. Multiple miliary abscesse.(with bacterial masses and plenty of leucocytes).

42.Considerable dongestion and slight round cell infiltration.

47.Considerable congestion adn edematous swelling. Round cell infiltration(which content also histiocytes).

49.Considerable congestion and edema. Round cell infiltration.

S-2 Considerabledongestion and bacterial masses as capillary contents. Slight edematous swelling and round cell infiltration.(which content also hisiocytes and plasma cells). Slight hyperplasia of lymphonodulus.

S-3.Remarkable congestion and edematous swelling. Round cell infiltration. (which content also plasma cells).

311

S-4. Intense congestion and severe edematous swelling. Remarkable hemorrhages in subepithelial tissues.
Considerable leucocytes infiltration.

S-5 Considerable dongestion and edema. Leucocytes infiltration.

S-8. No remarkable changes.

S-9. Remarkable congestion and severe edematous swelling. Considerable round cell infiltration.

S- 12 Considerable dongestion. Slight edema and lymphocytes accumulation.

S-14 Slight congestion and consideragle edematous swelling.
Slight lymphocytes infiltration.

S-15 Considerable congestion and edematous swelling. Considerable Hyperplasia of kymphonodulus.

S-26 Slight congestion.

S-22 Slight congestion and swelling of basal membrane.

S-s6 No remarkable changes.

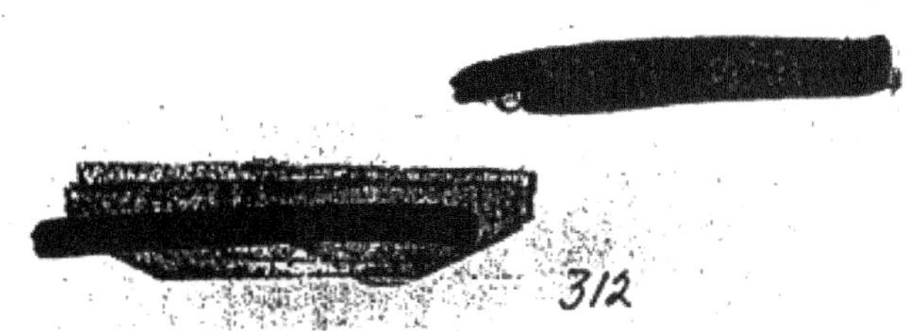

312

Epiglottis.

1. Considerable congestion and edematous swelling in subnucous tissues.

3. Considerable congestion and remarkable leucocytes-emigration at peri-lymphonodular tissues.
   Slight hyperplasia of germinal canter of lymphonodule.

4. Severe congestion and perivascular leucocytes and serous infiltration.

10. Remarkable congestion and severe edematous swelling with leucocytes emigration.

11. Remarkable congestion and edema in sugnucous tissues.
    Slight hemorrhages and leucocytes emigration in lymphonodular tissues.

14. Condåderable congestion and edema. Round cell infiltration.

16. Remarkable congestion and edema. Round cell infiltration.

17. Considerable congestion and leucocytes emigration.
    Hyperplssia of lymphonodulew with increased reticulum cells.

26. Slight congestion.

27. Slight congstiona and round cell infiltration.

35. Remarkable congestion and edema. Round cell infiltration.

36. Considerable ongestion and edema.Considerable leucocytes infiltratiom.

42. Slight congestion and slight edematous swelling.

S-22 Slight congestion and cerrhotic changes in subnucoustisses.

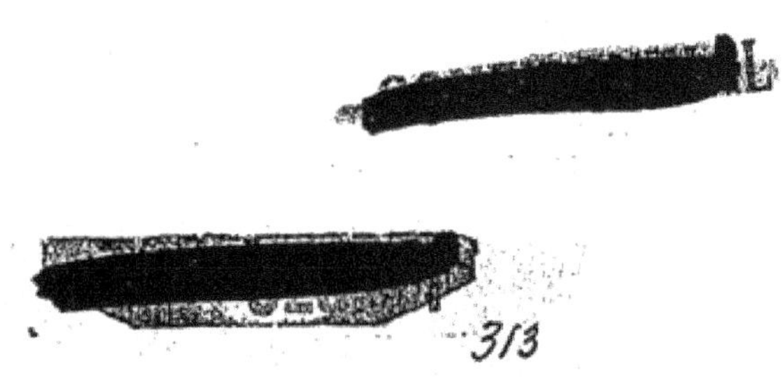

313

Pharynx: (esp. Recessus piriformis.)

2. Considerable congestion and diffuse leucocytes-emigration.
   Bacterial masses as capillary contents.

11. Considerable congestion and round cell infiltration.

16. Remarkable congestion and edema. Round cell infiltration.

27. Slight congestion.

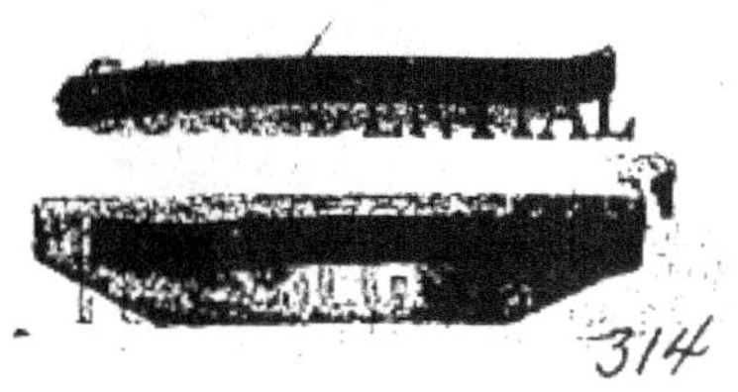

314

(2)

Generally, consideravle congestion and more or less edematous swelling and lymphocytes infiltration are recognised in all cases. Remarkable changes are leucocytic-hemorrhagic infiltration, round cell infiltration(especially, histiocytes and plasma cells), multiple super-miliary or miliary abscess(with plenty of leucocytes and bacterialm,asses) and hyperplssia of lymphonodules(with increased reticulum cells of germinal center).

According to these remarkable changes, all cases are divided as followed.

	Brochus (36 cases)	Epiglottis (14 cases)	Recessus piriformis (4 cases)
with leucocytic infilt.	8	5	1
with hemorrhagic infilt.	6	1	
with round cell infilt.	15	5	2
with abscess (Bronchitis purulenta)	5		
with hyperplasia of lymphonodulus	4	2	

Bacterial masses are sometimes recognised as capillary contents or in subnucous tissues, and reaction in form of leucocytic-hemorrhagic infiltration or hyperplasia of lymphonodulus to tend abscess- formation in bronchus 5 cases.

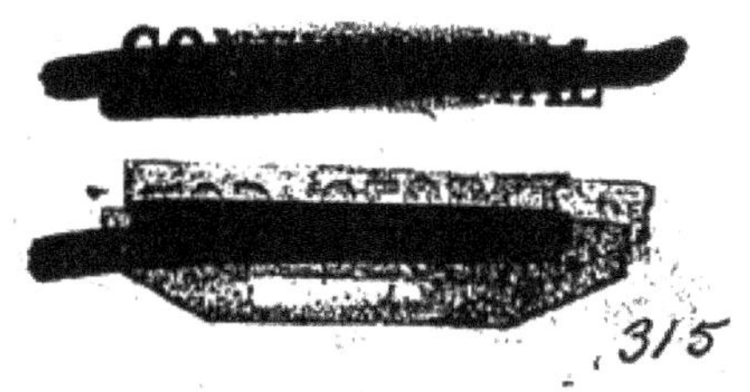

315

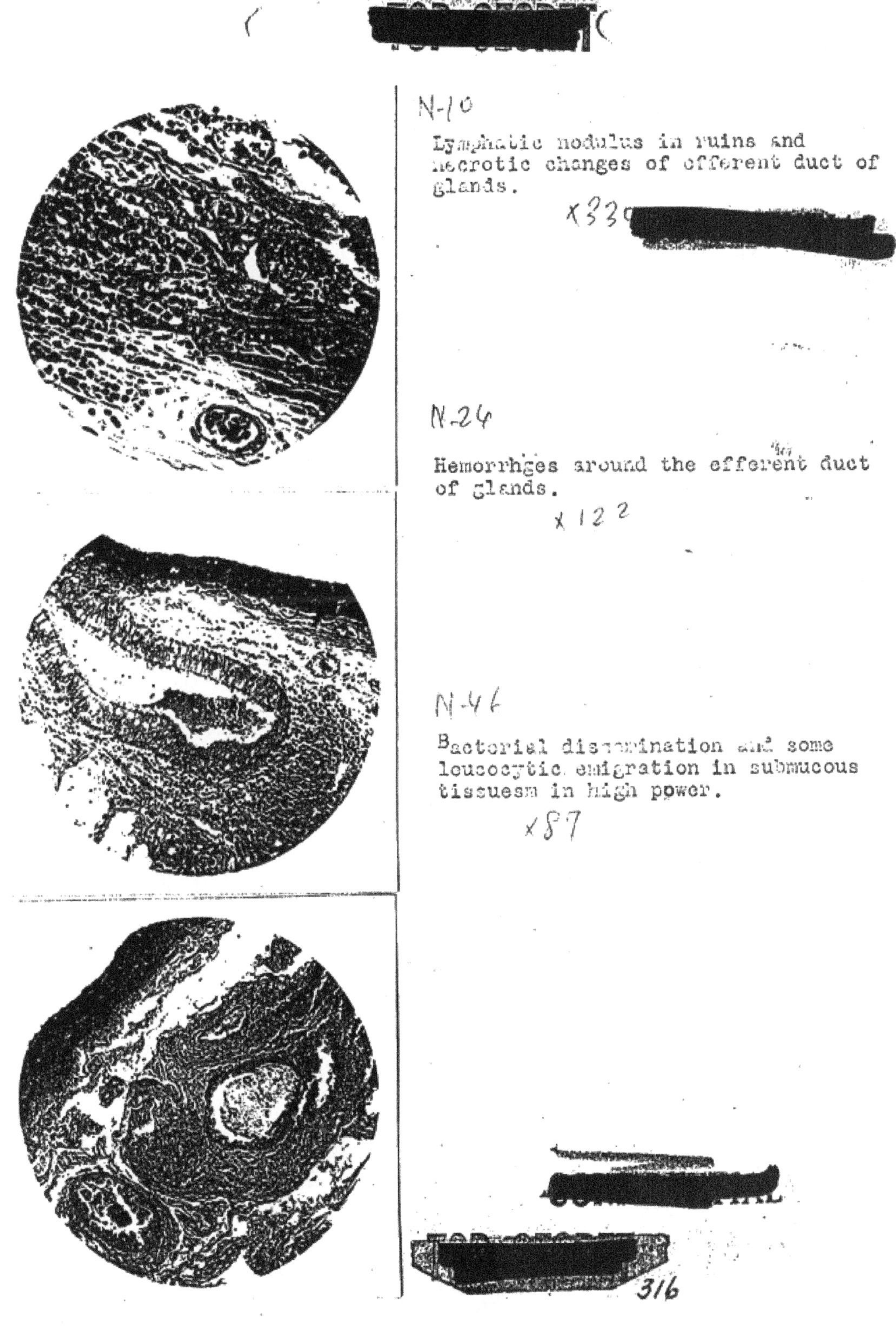

N-10

Lymphatic nodulus in ruins and necrotic changes of efferent duct of glands.

x33

N-24

Hemorrhges around the efferent duct of glands.

x122

N-46

Bacterial dissemination and some leucocytic emigration in submucous tissuesm in high power.

x87

316

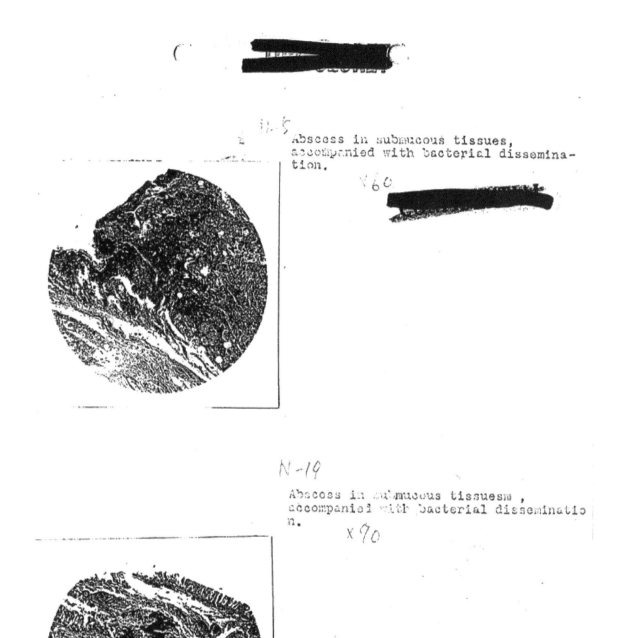

Abscess in submucous tissues, accompanied with bacterial dissemination.

x60

N-19

Abscess in submucous tissuesm , accompanied with bacterial disseminatio n.

x90

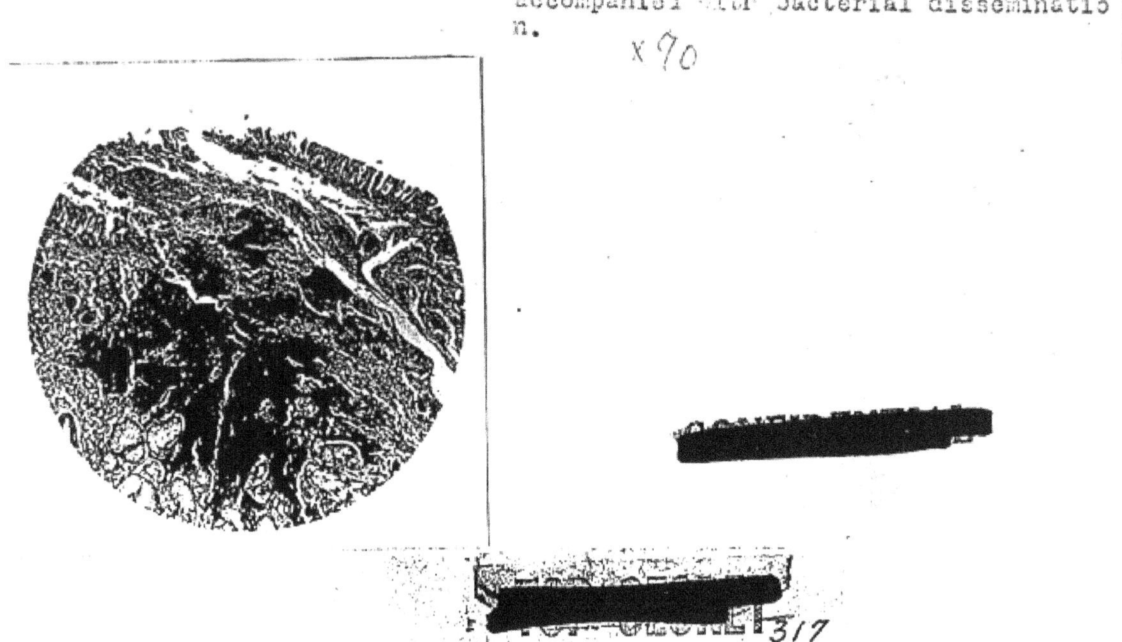

317

Hemorrhages in submucous tissues.

x 73

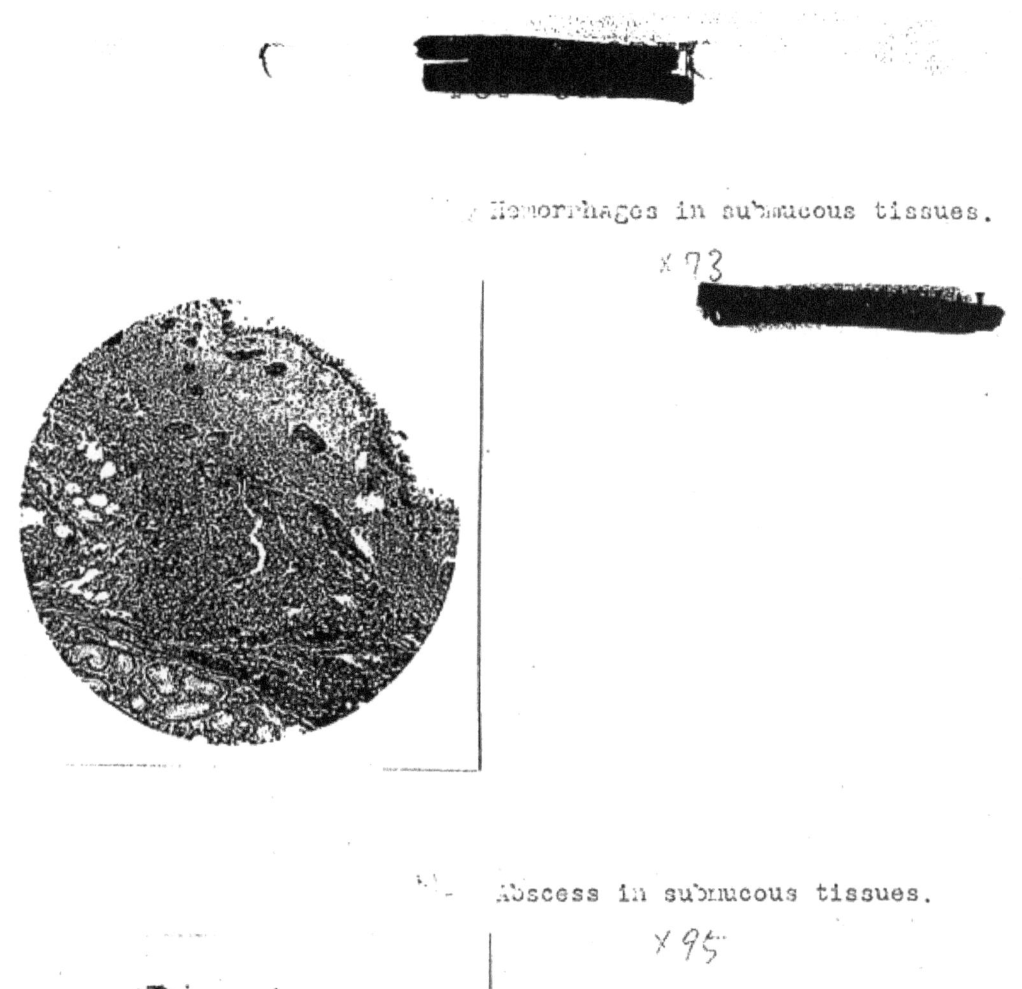

Abscess in submucous tissues.

x 95

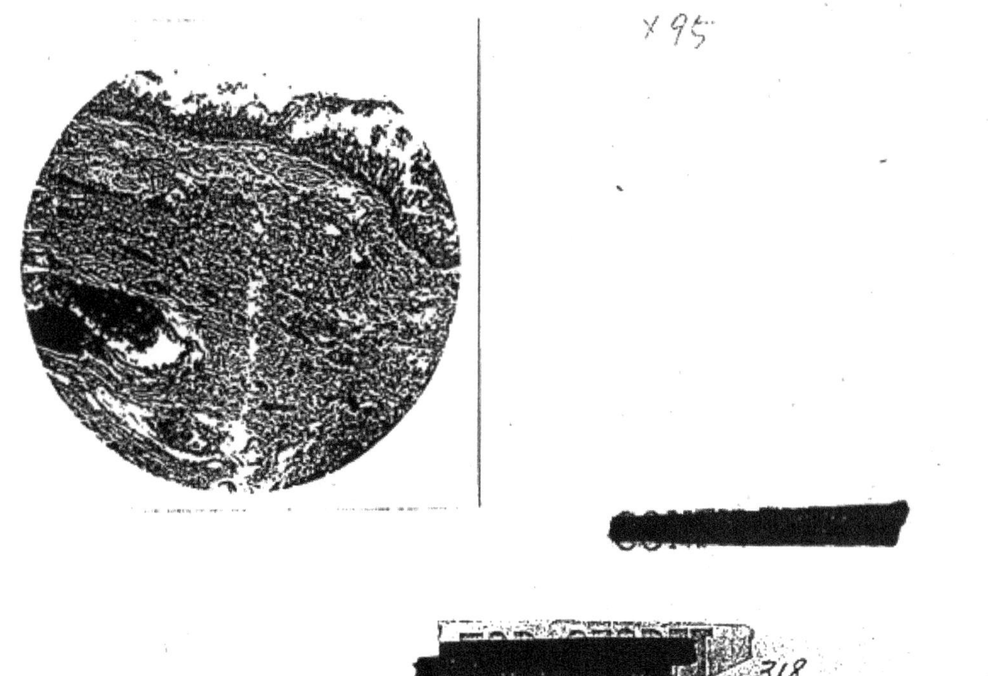

318

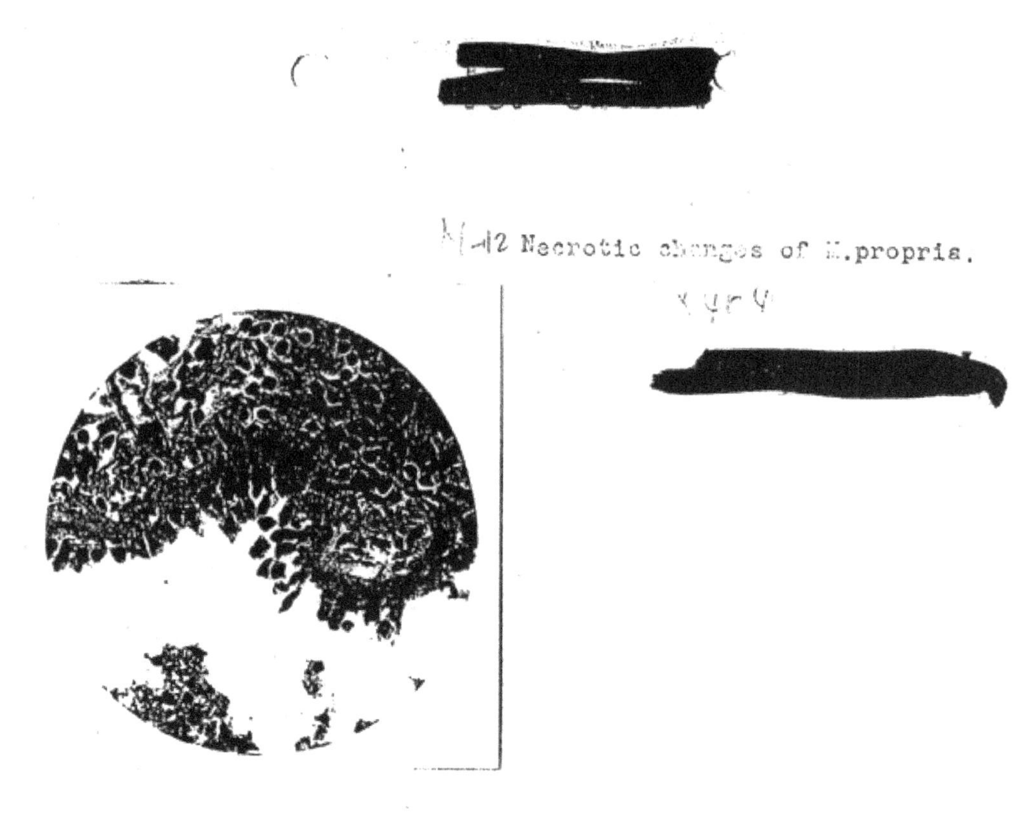

N-12 Necrotic changes of M.propria.

x484

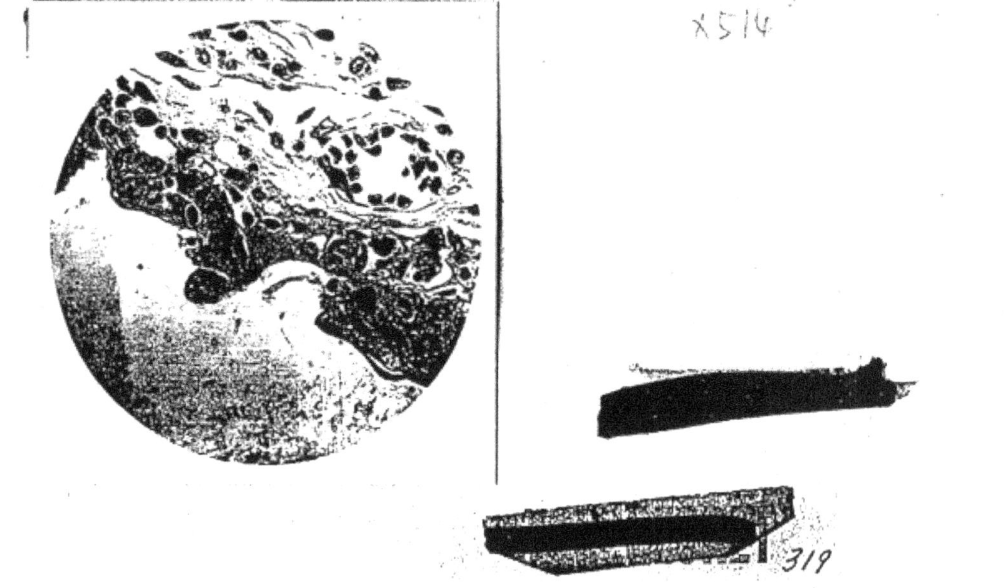

S-7 Necrotic changes of M.propria, accompanied with some bactrial dissemination.

x514

319

Catarrhal;ic changes and submucous hemorrhages.

X42.8

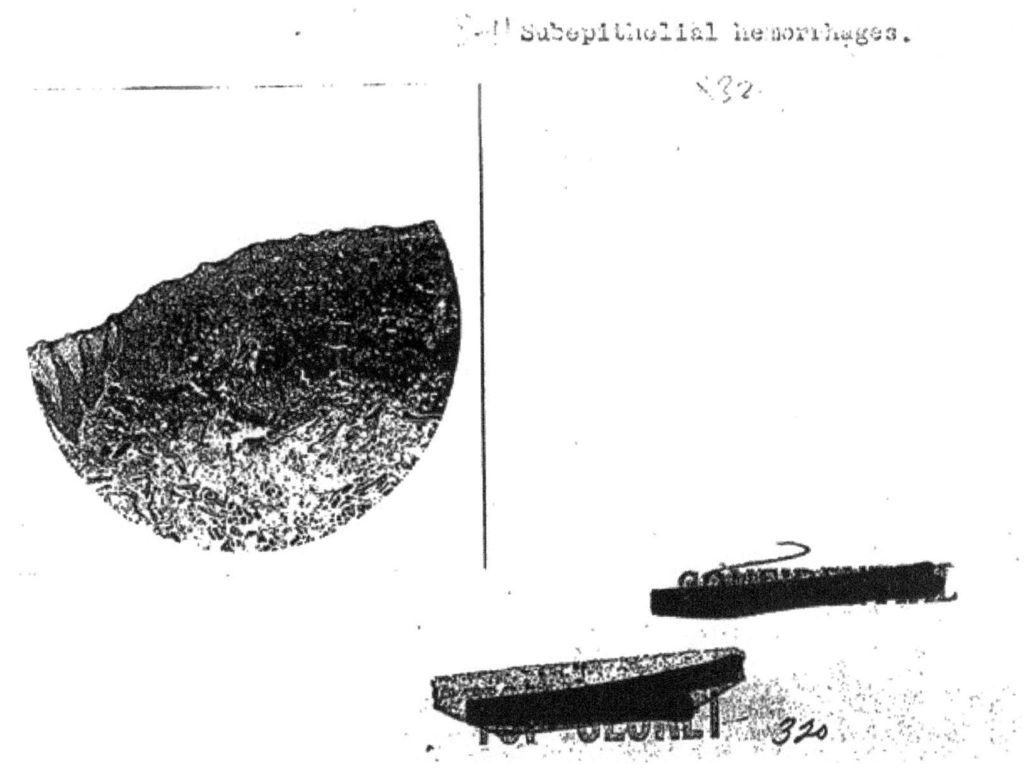

Subepithelial hemorrhages.

X32

320

5 Softning of cartilage and some hemorrhages.

x 32

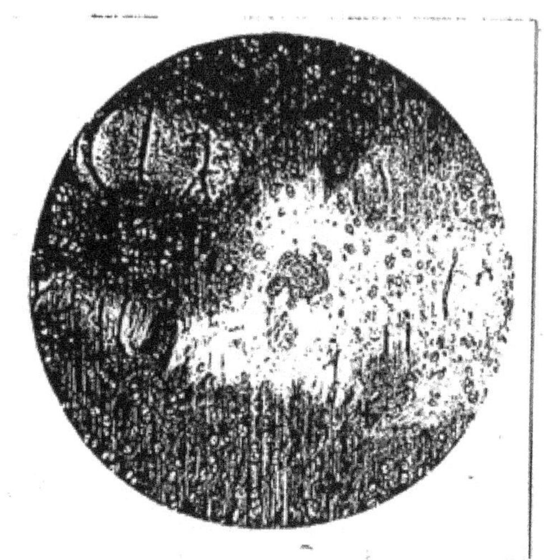

5-3 Elastorrhexis (edematous swelling) of submucous tissues.

x 130

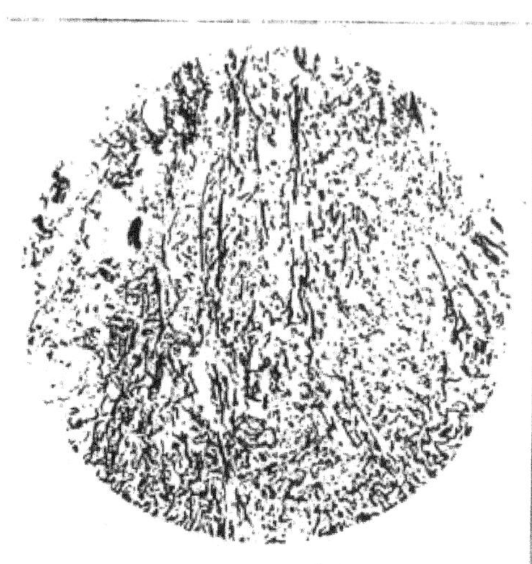

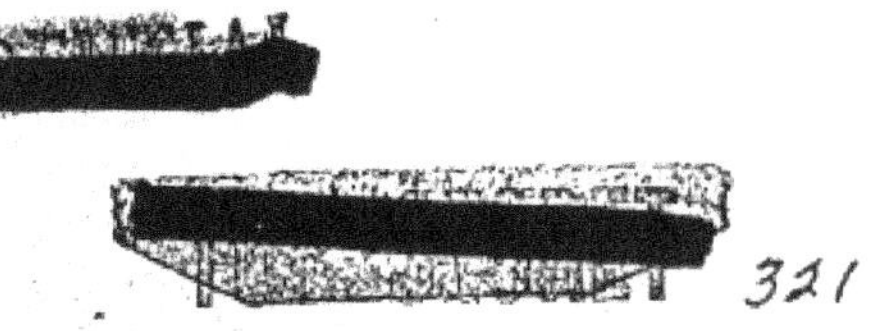

321

Liver

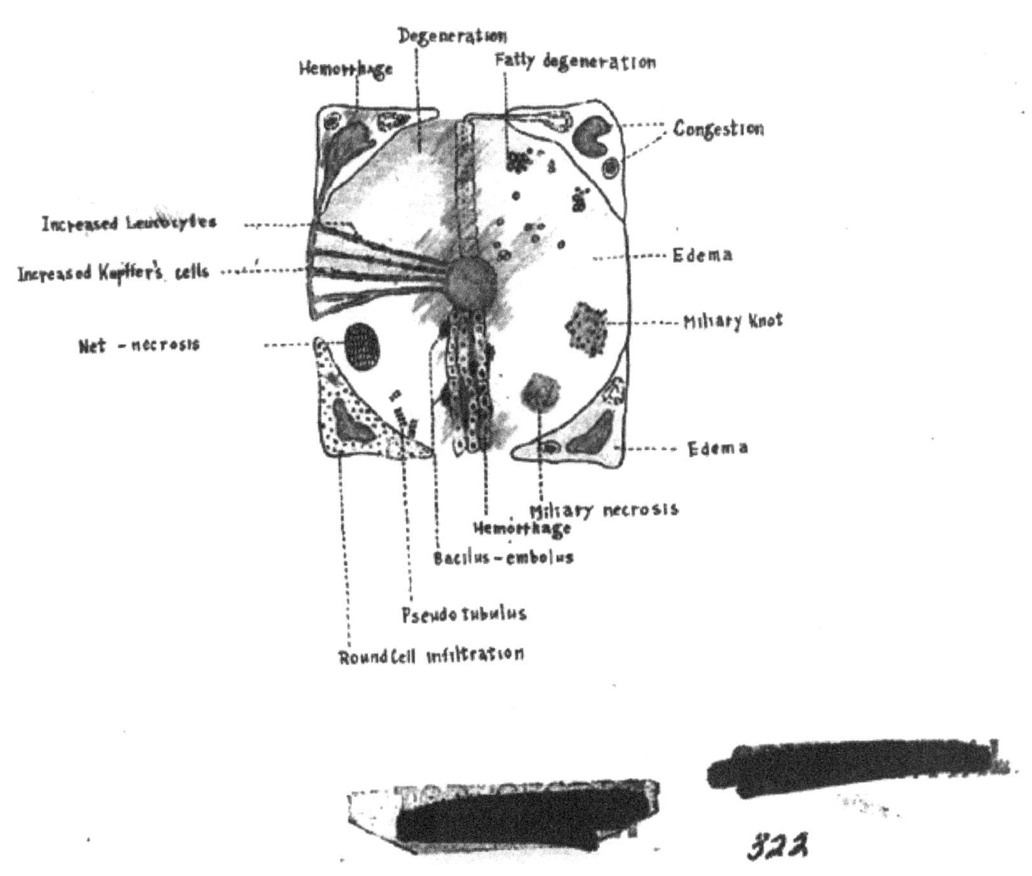
Degeneration
Hemorrhage
Fatty degeneration
Congestion
Increased Leucocytes
Increased Kupffer's cells
Edema
Miliary Knot
Net - necrosis
Edema
Miliary necrosis
Hemorrhage
Bacilus - embolus
Pseudo tubulus
Round Cell infiltration
322

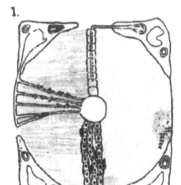

1.

L I V E R

(A) Microscopical Investigation.

1.

Hepatitis serosa II-III. ~~Severe congestion and~~ remarkable exsudation in Disse's spaces with many leukocytes and bacterial embolus in capillary-nets. Parenchymatous degeneration (cloudy swelling) caused by severe congestion and multiple miliary hemorrhagic knots, due to capillary-disturbances. And also there are pseudobiliary-tract in acinus.

2.

2.

Hepatitis serosa I-II. Remarkable exsudative-hemorrhagic changes in Disse's space and multiple diffuse hemorrhagic places in acinar size, due to capillary disturbance. Parenchymatous cells at haemorrhagic parts fall into completely necrosis ordiminishing autolytically. Parenchymatous cells of yet remained acinus fall also into severe cloudy swelling with remarkable brown-pigments atrophie. And increased Kupfer'cells.

3.

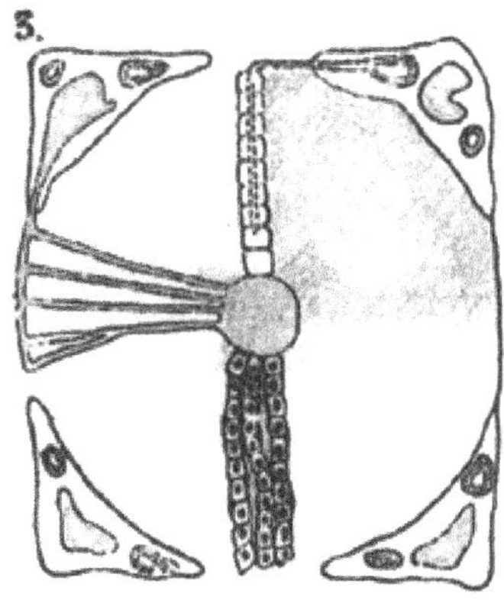

3.

Hepatitis serosa II. Severe congetion and slight hemorrhages in central zone of acinus.

323

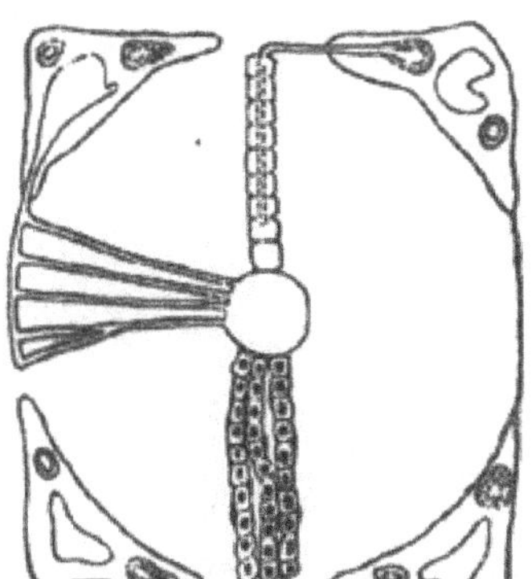

with plenty leucocytes as capillary contents. ~~Remarkable~~ Slight cloudy swelling, brown pigments atrophia and fatty degeneration of parenchmatous cells.

4.

Hepatitis serosa II with remarkable exsudative change in Disse's space and remarkable leucocyte-emigration (mainly eosinophilic leukocytes and some lymphocytes) in capillary-nets in acinus and in Glisson's capsule. Increased leucocytes raised at some place multiple miliary necrosis, which are formed in focal parts with necrotic masses and in perifocal parts with some reactions (mainly plenty eosinophilic leukocytes, some lymphocytes and slightly increased histiocytic cells). Parenchmatous cells in neighbouring tissues fall into totally bionecrosis.

4.

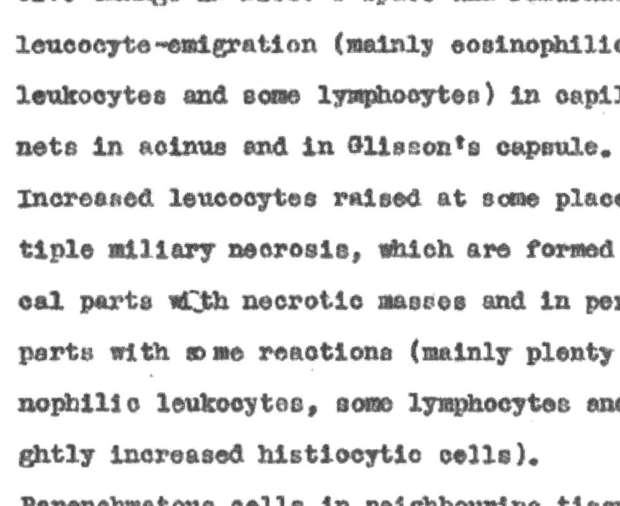

5.

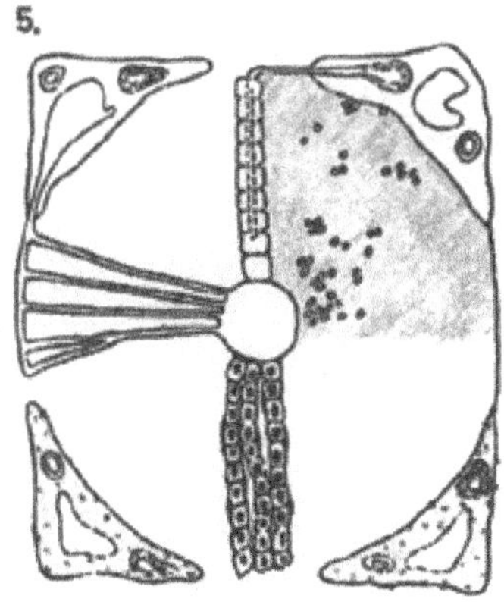

5.

Hepatitis serosa II. Slight congetion and exsudation in Disse's space with some lymphocytes as capillary contents. ~~Cloudy or~~ fatty degeneration of paronchmatous cells in medium degree.

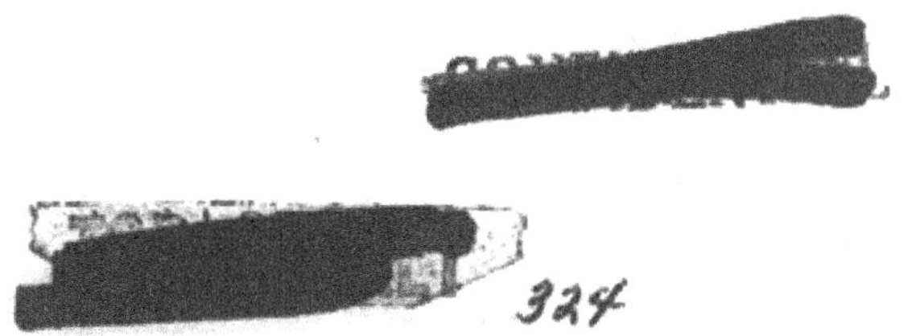

324

6.

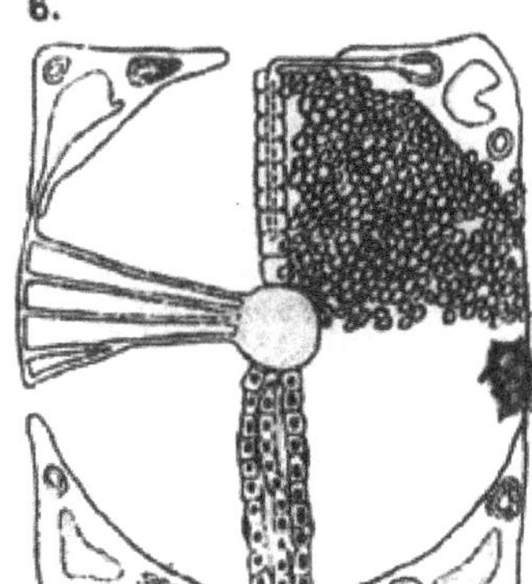

6.

Almost all parenchymatous cells fall into extremly severe fatty degeneration (appearance of grobe or fine vacuolar fatty substances all over liver-tissue -- severest fatty degeneration). Considerable exsudative reactions in Disse's space. And there are miliary knots with remarkable histiocytic cells.

7.

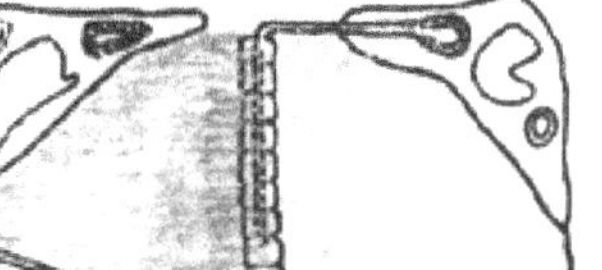

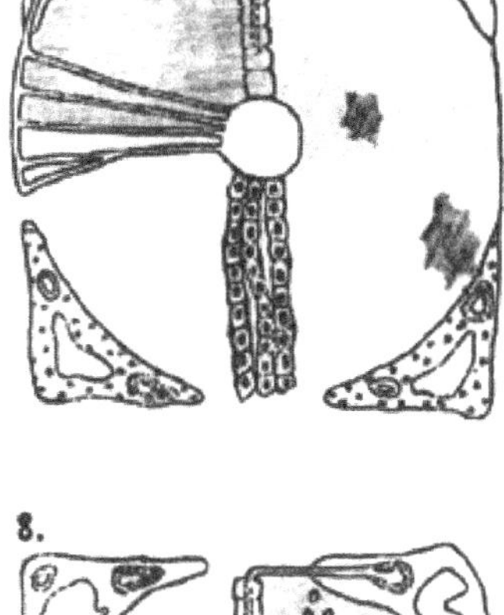

8.

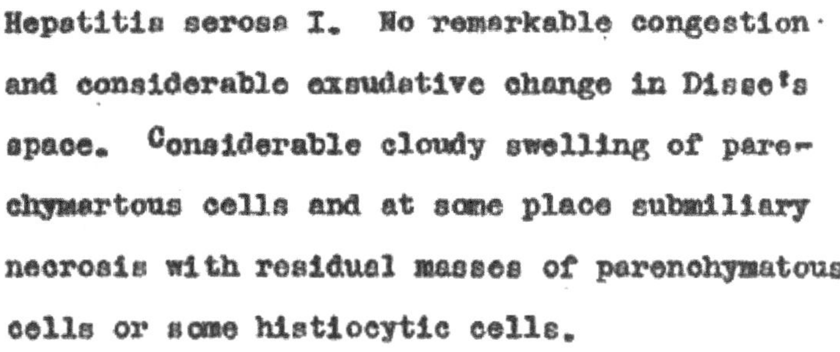

Hepatitis serosa I. No remarkable congestion and considerable exsudative change in Disse's space. Considerable cloudy swelling of parechymertous cells and at some place submiliary necrosis with residual masses of parenchymatous cells or some histiocytic cells.

Remarkable lymphocytes infiltration in Glisson's capsule.

8.

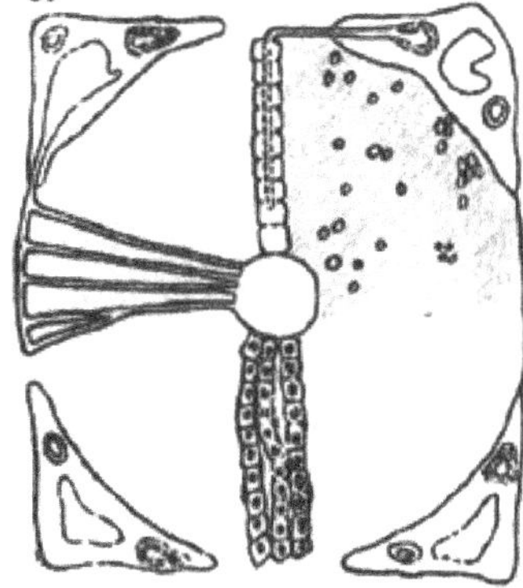

8.

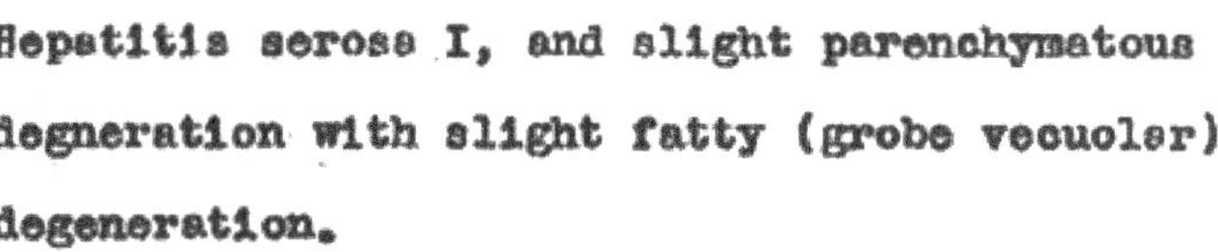

Hepatitis serosa I, and slight parenchymatous degneration with slight fatty (grobe vecuoler) degeneration.

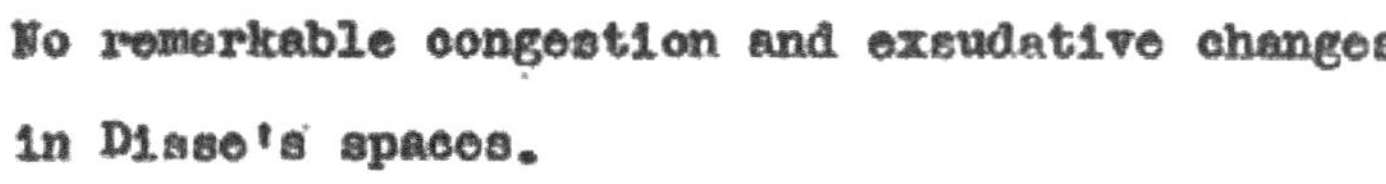

No remarkable congestion and exsudative changes in Disse's spaces.

Some postmortal change in this specimen.

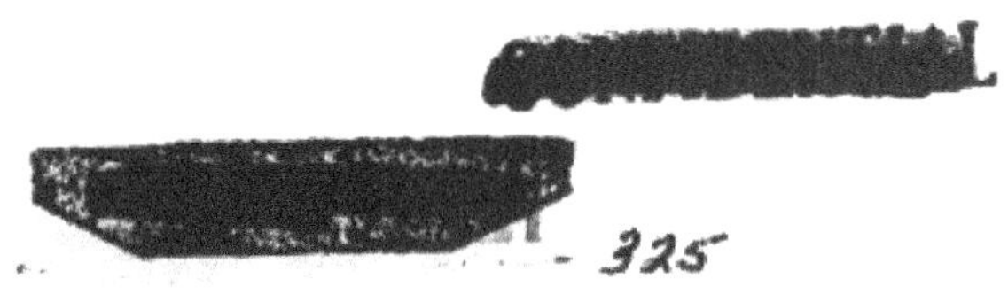

- 325

9.

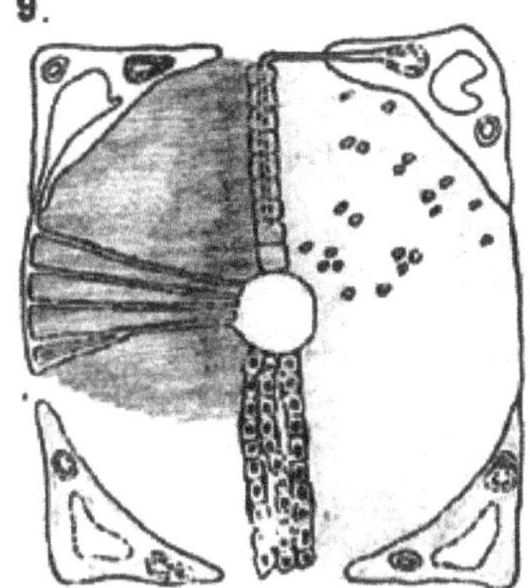

9.

Hepatitis serosa I and considerable parenchimatous degeneration with slight fatty degeneration. Remarkable exsudative charges in Disse's spaces.

CONFIDENTIAL

I0.

Hepatitis serosa III. Slight congestion and severe exsudative change in Disse's spaces. Increased leukocytes as capillary contents and considerable parenchmatous degeneration with slight fatty degeneration.

10.

Multiple supermiliary necrosis which are formed with residual masses of parenchymatous cells, and some wandering cells.

And some bacterial embolus.

II.

Hepatitis serosa I-II. Considerable congestion and somewhat increased Kupfer's cells as capillary contents to form at some places submiliary necrosis (central necrotic parts with slight perifocal cell reaction).

11.

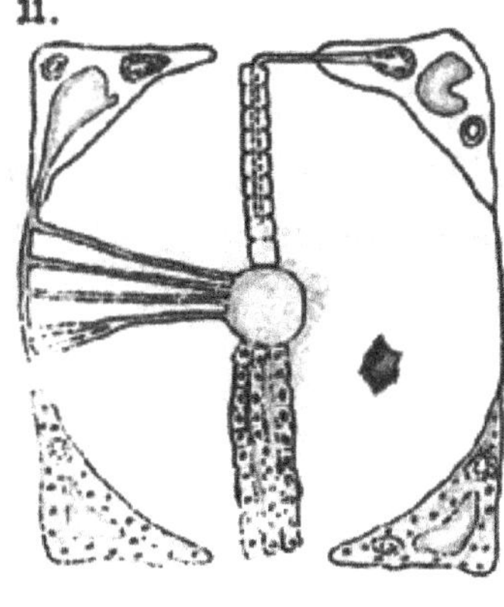

I2.

Hepatitis serosa I-II and multiple miliary necrosis.

CONFIDENTIAL

326

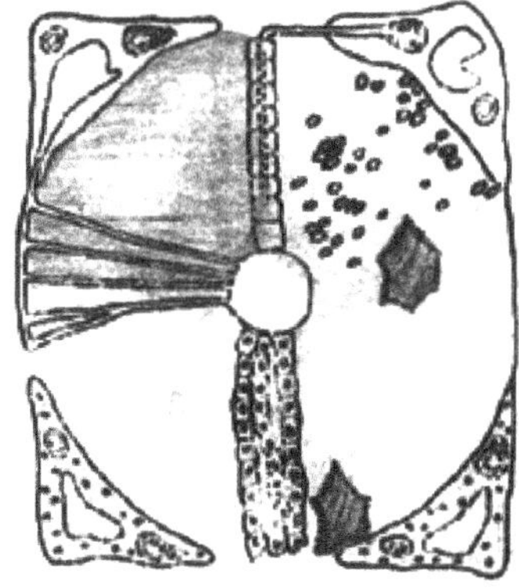

Considerable exsudative changes in Disse's spaces with some leukocytes (esp. eosinophilic leukocytes) and some lymphocytes as capillary contents. Formation of multiple miliary necrosis in peripheral zone of acinus, which are formed in focal parts with residual decayed masses of parenchymatous cells and in perifocal parts with slight exsudative changes (some leukocytes-accumulation and slightly increased histiocytes). Slight small round-cell-accumulation in subendothelial layers of central veins and considerable round cell infiltration at Glisson's capsule. Moderate cloudy swelling and fatty degeneration of parenchymatous cells.

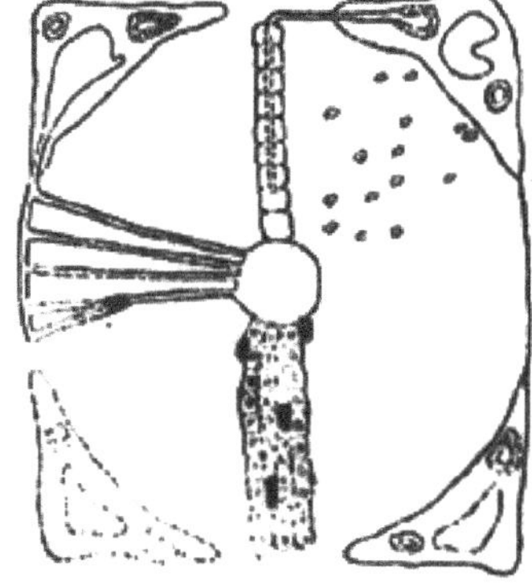

I4.

Hepatitis serosa I-II. Slight congestion and slight exsudative changes in Disse's spaces with some leukocytes as capillary contents. More or less cloudy swelling and slight fatty degeneration of parenchymacous cells. And also bacterial embolus in capillary-nets.

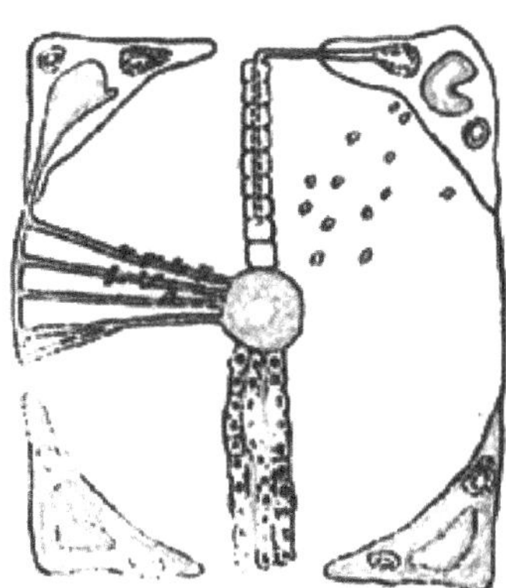

I5.

Hepatitis serose I. Remarkable congestion and some leukocytes as capillary contents. No remarkable exsudation in Disse's spaces.

CONFIDENTIAL

327

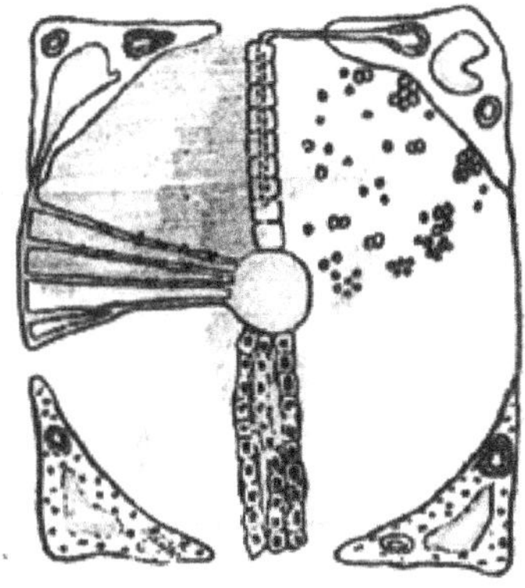

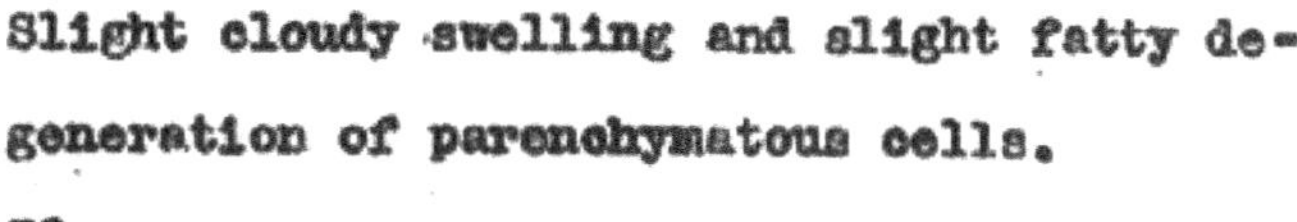

Slight cloudy swelling and slight fatty degeneration of parenchymatous cells.

I6.

Hepatitis serosa I-II.

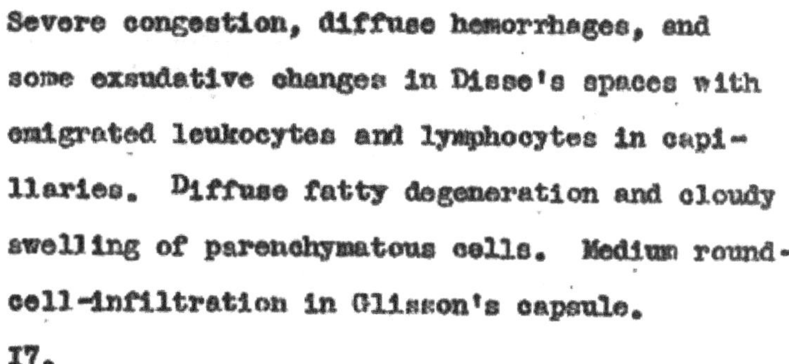

Severe congestion, diffuse hemorrhages, and some exsudative changes in Disse's spaces with emigrated leukocytes and lymphocytes in capillaries. Diffuse fatty degeneration and cloudy swelling of parenchymatous cells. Medium round-cell-infiltration in Glisson's capsule.

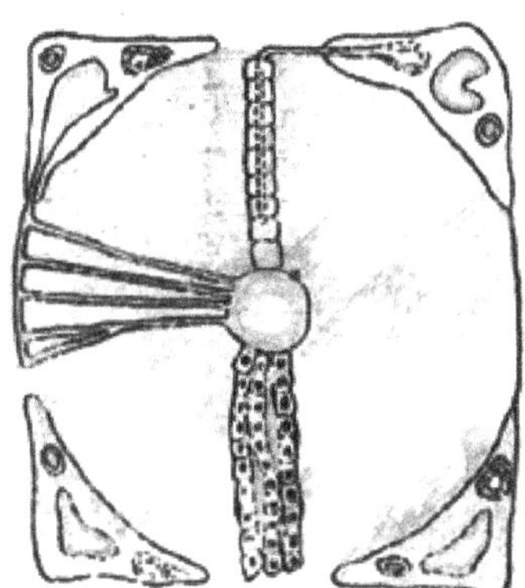

I7.

Hepatitis serosa II-III. Considerable parenchymatous degeneration, due to severe congestion and hemorrhage in acinus.

At some places (parenchyma or capsule), there are recognized hemorrhages in high degree.

I8.

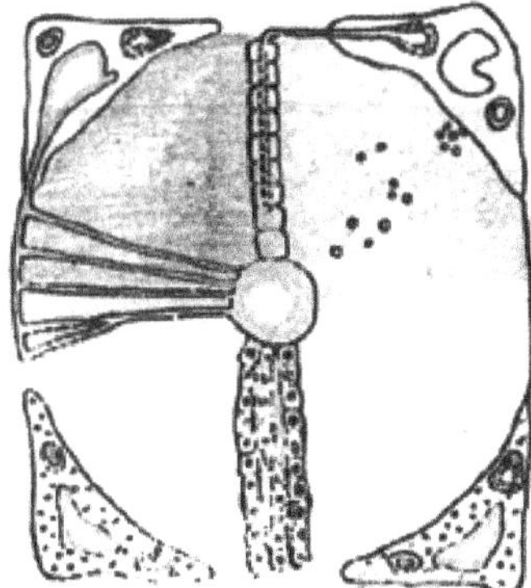

Hepatitis serosa I. Considerable congestion and exsudation in Disse's spaces with remarkable leukocytes as capillary contents.

Cloudy swelling and brown-pigmentation in remarkable degree.

Slight diffuse hemorrhages in Glisson's capsule.

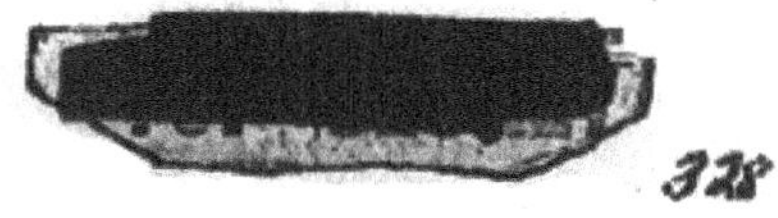

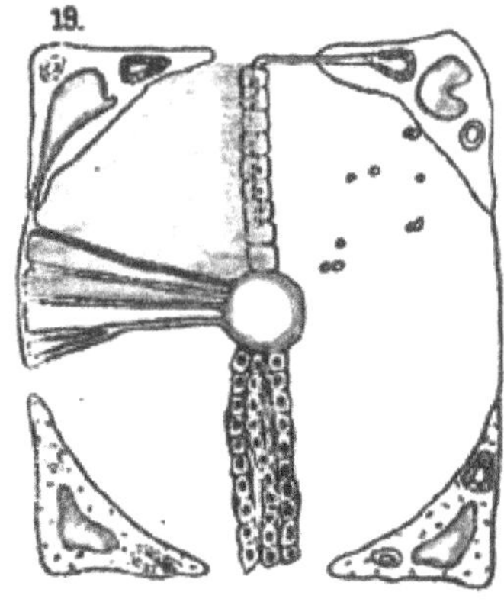

I9.

Hepatitis serosa I-II. Slight congestion and exsudation in Disse's spaces. And considerable parecbymatous degeneration.

20.

Hepatitis serosa I and multiple miliary necrosis in rather proliferative form.

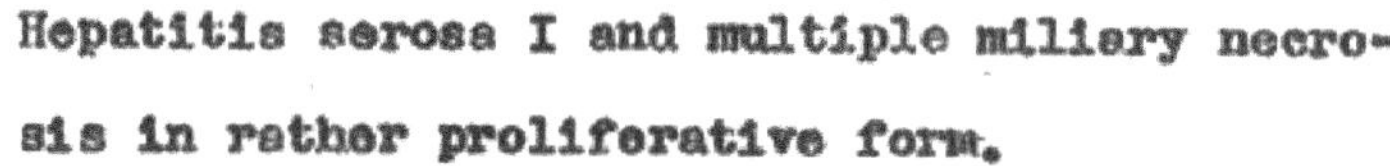

No remarkable congestion and exsudation in Disse's spaces. With slightly increased Kupffer's cells. Multiple miliary necrosis in rather proliferative form. (Miliary knots with central necrotic parts are bounded proliferatively with more or less considerably increased histiocytes-walls).

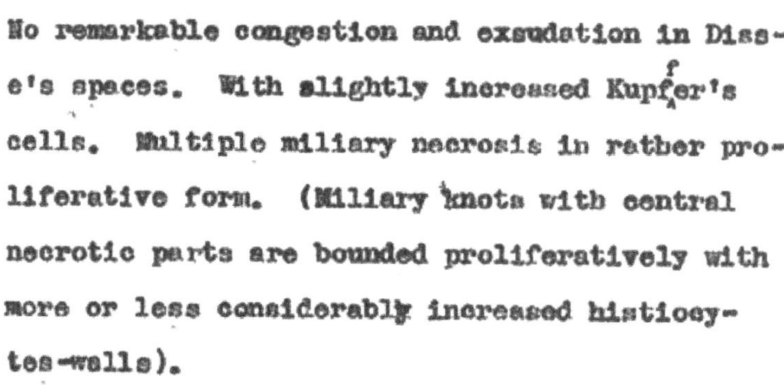

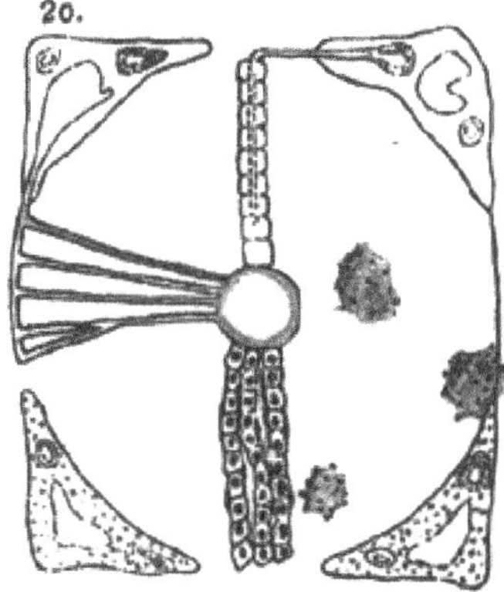

2I.

Hepatitis serosa I-II with slight congestion, (esp. considerably central hemorrhage) and considerable exsudation in Disse's spaces with some leukocytes as capillary contents.

23.

Hepatitis serosa I with slight congestion and exsudation in Disse's spaces with some leukocytes as capillary contents to form at some places miliary knots, constitued with leukocytes and decayed parenchymatous cells in focal

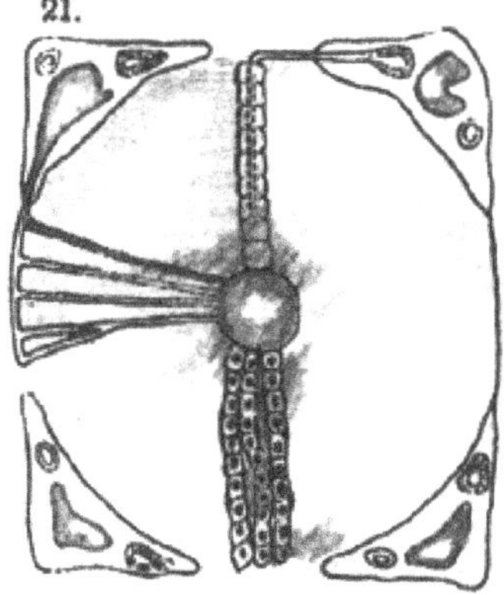

329

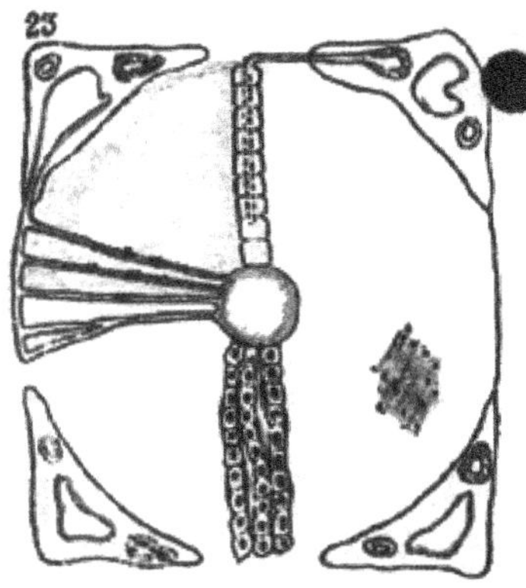

parts and slightly increased histiocytes in perifocal reactive zone. Considerable cloudy swelling of parenchymatous cells and slight edematous swelling of Glisson's capsule.

24.

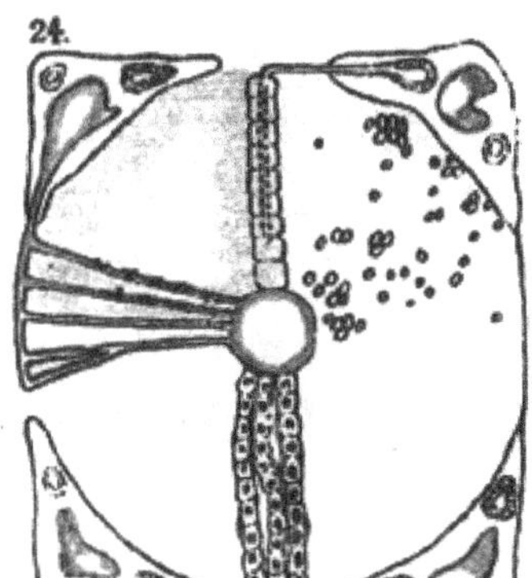

Hepatitis serosa I. Considerable fatty degeneration. And considerable congestion and exsudation. A little leukocytes in capillary-nets. Histiocytes not increased.

26.

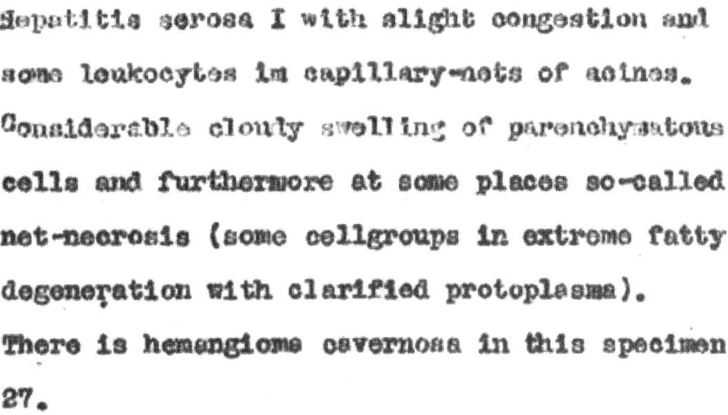

Hepatitis serosa I with slight congestion and some leukocytes in capillary-nets of acines. Considerable cloudy swelling of parenchymatous cells and furthermore at some places so-called net-necrosis (some cellgroups in extreme fatty degeneration with clarified protoplasma). There is hemangiome cavernosa in this specimen.

27.

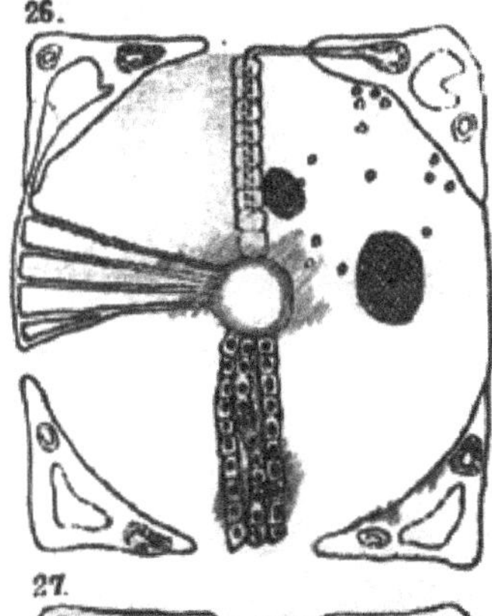

Initial stage of annular liver-cirrhosis with increased connective tissues and remarkable lymphocytes infiltration in Glisson's capsule. Millary knots, which are formed by considerable histiocytes, lymphocytes and residual masses, at some place. Slight cloudy swelling and very slight fatty dgeneration of parenchymatous cells.

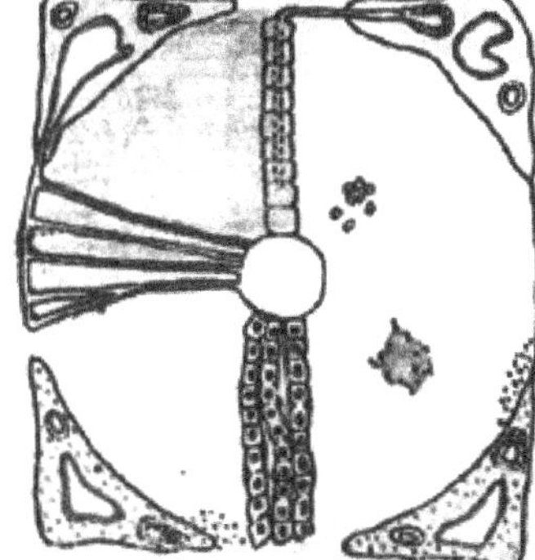

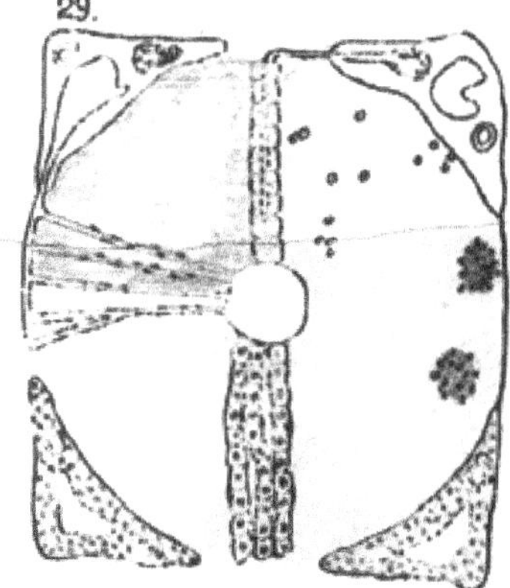

29.
Hepatitis serosa 1-11 with remarkable exsudative changes in Disse's spaces.
Some leukocytes and lymphocytes as capillary contents and slightly increased Kupffer's cells.
At some place, multiple miliary knots, constituted with some lymphocytes and some histiocytes accumulation.
Cloudy swelling and slight fatty degeneration of parenchym cells and lymphocyte infiltrations at Glisson's capsule.

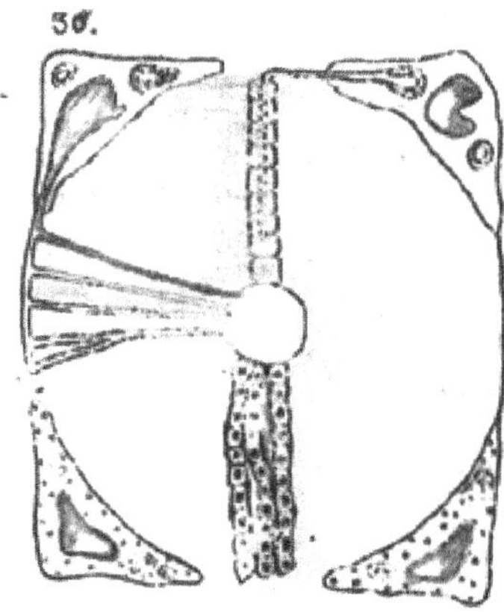

30.
Hepatitis serosa 1 with considerable exsudation in Disse's spaces and considerable congestion with a little lymphocytes as capillary contents.

31.
Hepatitis serosa 1. Considerable exsudative changes in Disse's spaces. No remarkable changes else.

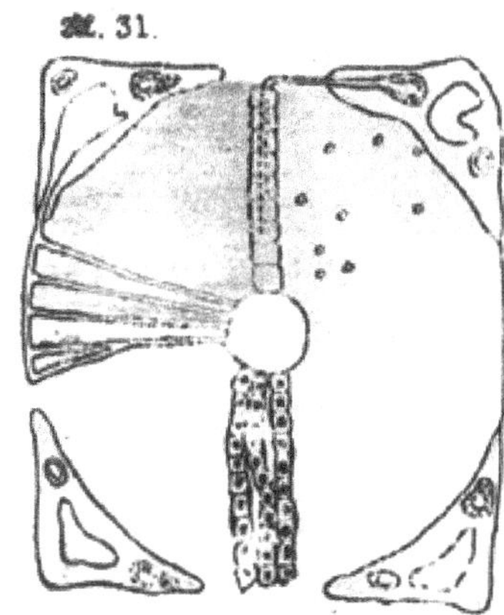

32.
Hepatitis serosa I. Considerable congestion and exsudation in Disse's spaces. Some leukocytes, a little lymphicytes and slightly increased histiocytes as capillary contents. Moderate cloudy

931

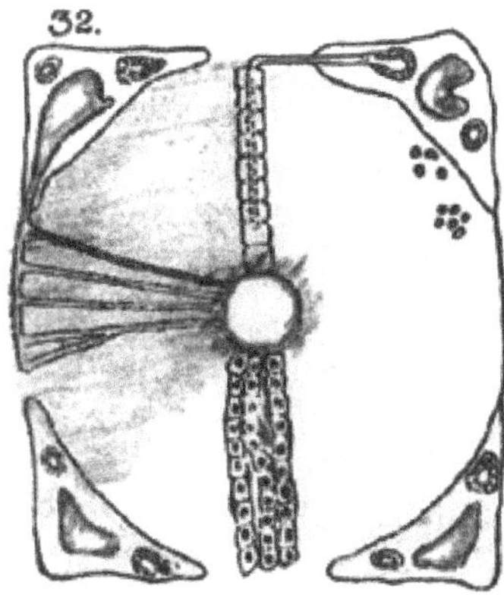

swelling of parenchymatous cells. Slight fatty degeneration.

Here and there are recognized necrosis around the central veins.

33.

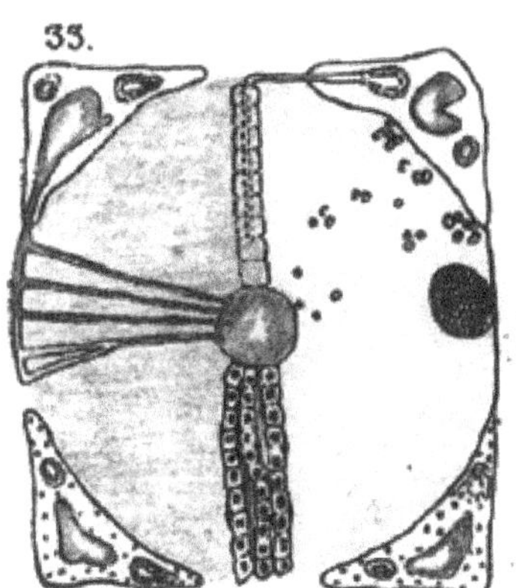

Hepatitis serosa II with considerable congestion. Some lymphocytes, a little leukocytes and a little histiocytes as capillary contents. Remarkable exsudation in Disse's spaces. Considerable fatty degeneration and furthermore net-necrosis of parenchymatous cells (some cells groupe fall into extremly severe fatty degeneration with more or less clarified protoplasms). Remarkable dissotiation of cell-arrangements.

34.

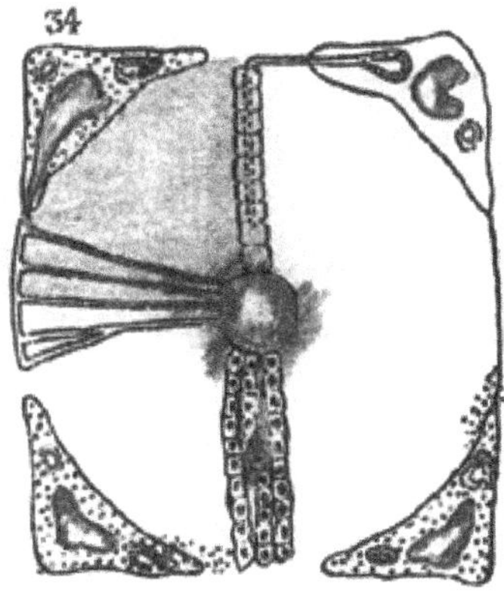

Hepatitis serosa I with remarkable congestion ~~and exsudative changes in Disse's spaces.~~ Some leukocytes, some lymphocytes as capillary-contents. And cloudy swelling are condiderably. Slight edematous swelling and severe lymphocytes (and some eosinophilic leukocytes) infiltration in Glisson's capsule.

332

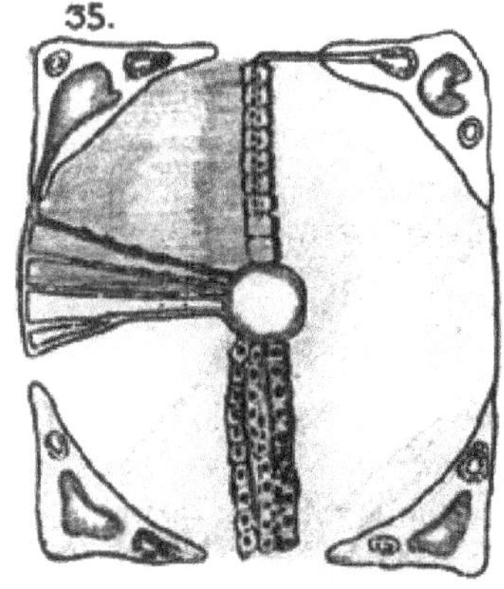

35.

Hepatitis serosa I-II with considerable congetion and severe exsudative changes in Disse's spaces. Some lymphocytes and considerably increased histiocytic cells. Considerable cloudy swelling of parenchymatous cells and edematous swelling in Glisson's capsule.

36.

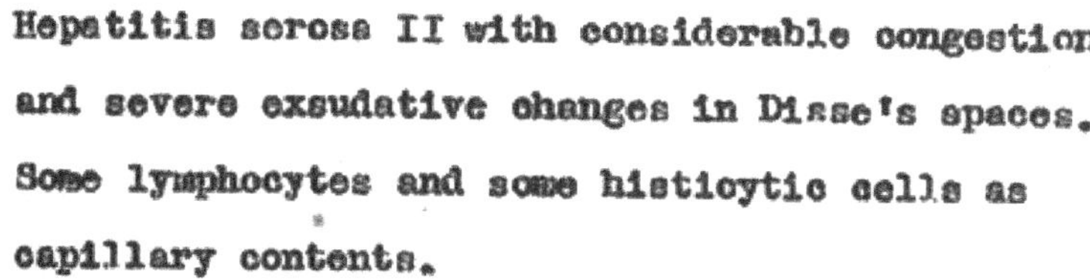

Hepatitis serosa II with considerable congestion and severe exsudative changes in Disse's spaces. Some lymphocytes and some histiocytic cells as capillary contents.

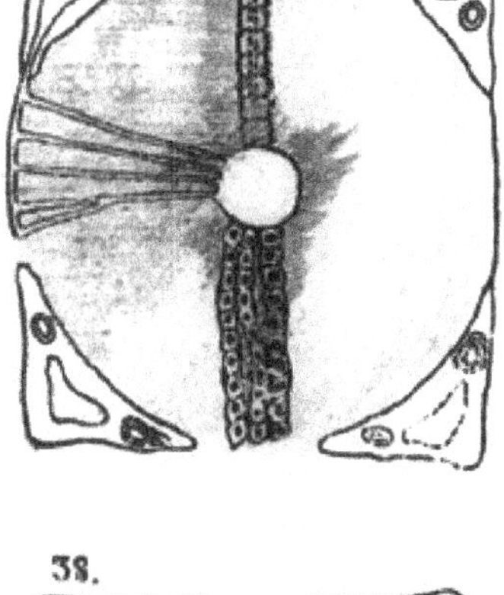

Moderate cloudy swelling with brown atrophia, and slight edematous swelling of Glisson's capsule.

38.

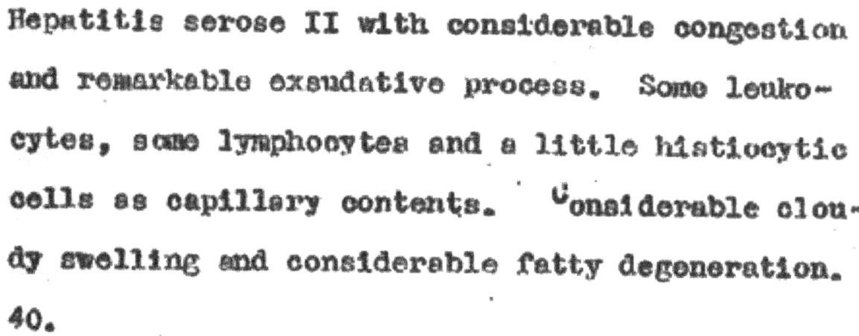

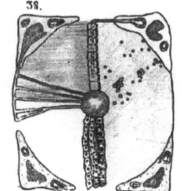

Hepatitis serose II with considerable congestion and remarkable exsudative process. Some leukocytes, some lymphocytes and a little histiocytic cells as capillary contents. Considerable cloudy swelling and considerable fatty degeneration.

40.

Hepatitis serosa I-II with considerable congestion and exsudative process. Some lymphocytes and a little histiocytic cells as capillary contents.

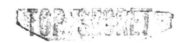

333

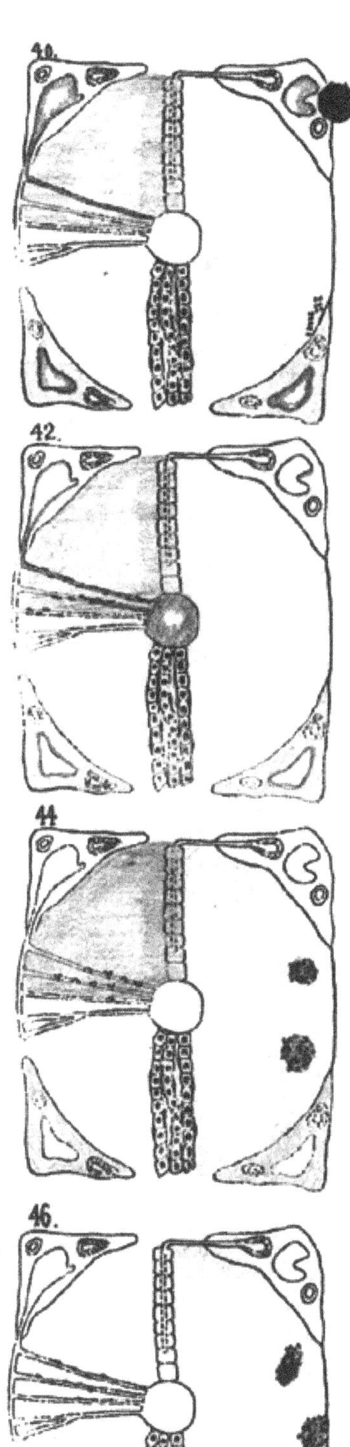

Considerable cloudy swelling of parenchymatous cells. Considerable congestion in Glisson-'s capsule. And there are recognized pseudo-biliary tract in peripheral zone of acinus.

42.

Hepatitis serosa I-II with considerable congestion ans sever exsudative reaction in Disse's spaces. Some lymphocytes and considerably increased Kupfer's cells. Considerable cloudy swelling of parenchymatous cells.

44.

Hepatitis serosa I-II with slight congestion and remarkable exsudative changes in Disse's spaces. Some lymphocytes, some leukocytes and a little histiocytic cells. These are more or less degenerative. At some place, multiple submiliary knots, constituted with some histiocytic cells in initial stage of miliary knots-formation.

46.

Hepatitis serosa I. Remarkable exsudative changes in Disse's spaces with considerably increased Kupfer's cells and some lymphocytes as capillary

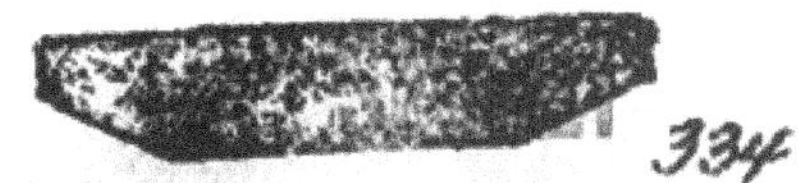

334

contents to form at some place multiple submiliary knots, which are formed mainly lymphocytes, some histicytes and some residual masses of decayed parenchymatous cells. Brown atrophia and slight fatty degeneration of parenchymatous cells. Some postmortal change in this specimen.

47.

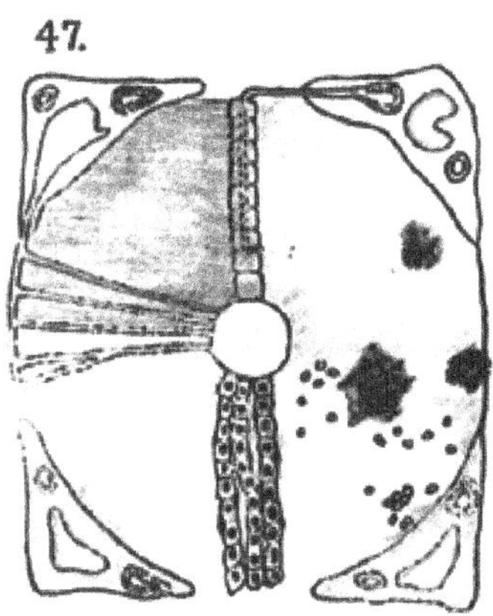

47.

Hepatitis serosa II-III. Considerable congestion and exudation in Disse's spaces with some lymphocytes and some histiocytic cells to form at some place submiliary knots in rather exsudative form. These knots are formed with some wandering cells accumlation and accompanied with severe degenerative process of neighbouring parnchymatous cells. Generally in liver-tissues, considerable cloudy swelling and slight fatty degeneration.

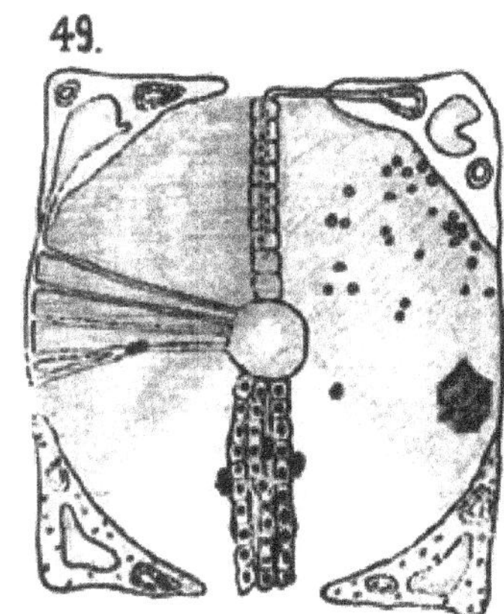

49.

49.

Hepatitis serosa I. Remarkable congestion and intense exsudative changes in Disse's spaces with slight fatty degeneration and cloudy swelling of parenchymatous cells.

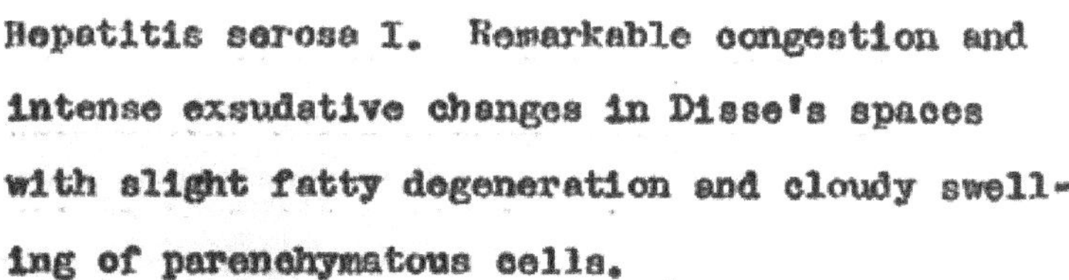

A millet-corn large abscess and multiple miliary necrosis with many bacterial accumulations, plenty leucocytes, some lymphocytes and some decayed masses of parenchymatous cells.

Intense localised fatty degeneration at subcap-

336

S-1.

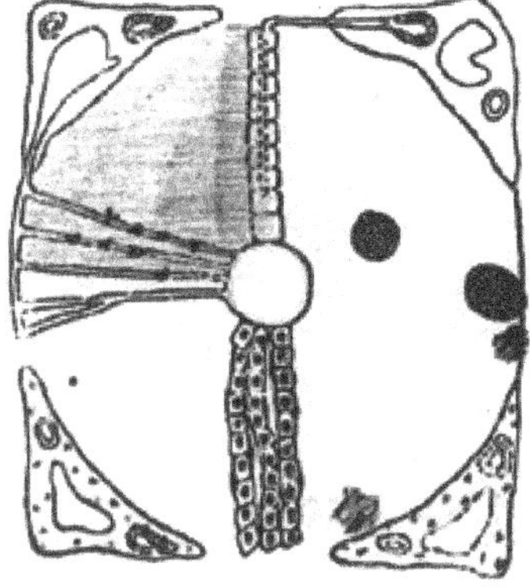

sular portions. Some eosinophilic leucocytes in capsule.

S-I.

Hepatitis serosa II. Remarkable exsudation and considerable congestion with plenty leucocytes as capillary contents.

Slight cloudy swelling of parenchymatous cells with multiple submiliary necrosis mainly in peripheral zone of acinus, which are formed with some residual masses of parenchymatous cells and round cell accumulation in capillary-nets. There are recognized net-necrosis in acinus.

S-2.

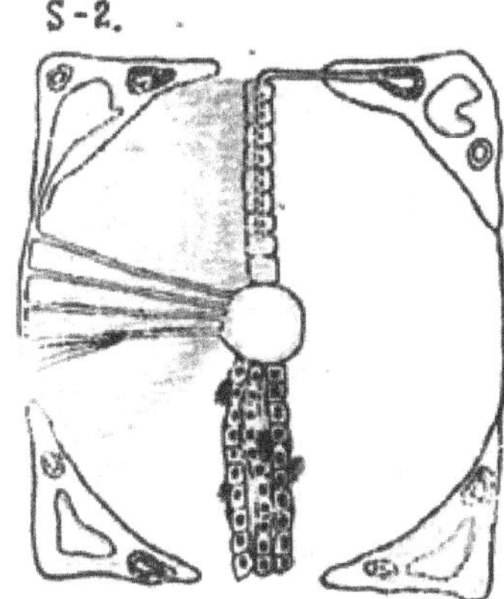

S-2.

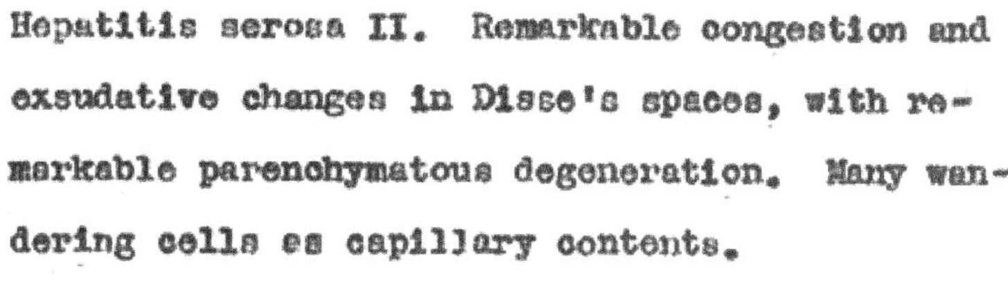

Hepatitis serosa II. Remarkable congestion and exsudative changes in Disse's spaces, with remarkable parenchymatous degeneration. Many wandering cells as capillary contents.

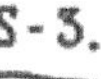

S-3.

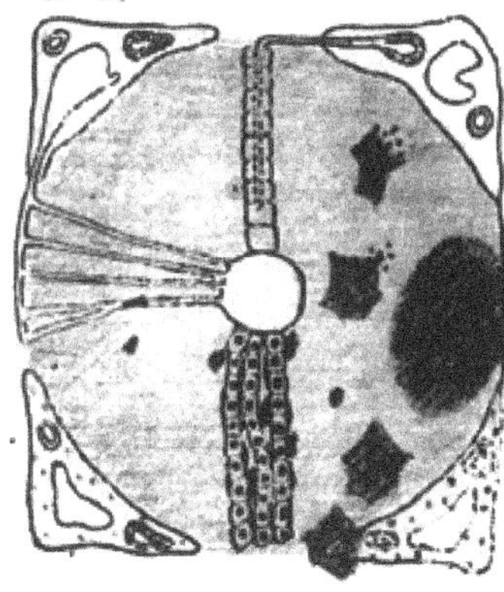

S-3.

Hepatitis serosa III-IIII. A little finger top large necrosis. Extremly large quantity of bacterial massec in pfortader veins and capillary nets in acinus. And necrotic ruins of blood vessels walls with extremly severe perivasculer

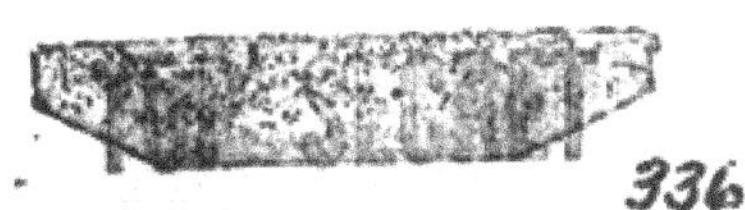

336

inflammatory reactions: severe odema, diffuse hemorrhage, some leukocytes emigation, bacterial accumulation in the neighbouring tissues and severe degeneration or necrotic ruins of parenchymatous cells. At the margin parts of necrosis exist considerable leukocytes infiltration in the severly exsudative tissues.

These inflammatory changes spread with more or less hemorrhagic-exsudative reactions and parenchymatous degenerations to the neighbouring tissues. At other hands, multiple miliary necrosis with residual masses or some lymphocytes and histiocytes.

In Glisson's capsule, exist remarkable edematous swelling and some wandering cells accumulations.

S-4.

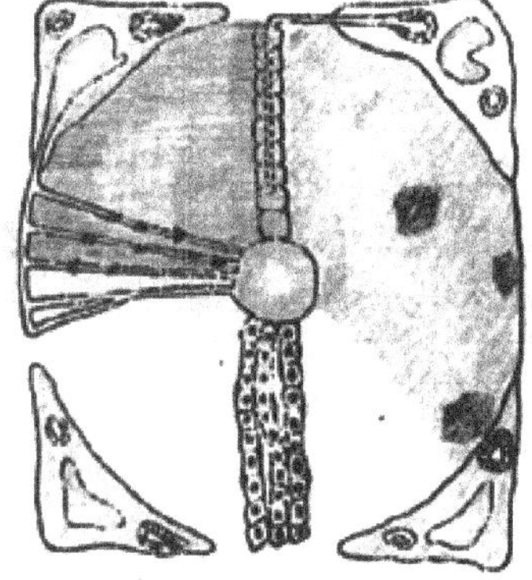

Hepatitis serosa III. Remarkable exsudation with plenty leukocytes (some of them eosinophilic cells), and a little lymphocytes as capillary contents. At some places, multiple supermiliary knots, which are formed with residual masses of parenchymatous cells, a little leukocytes and lymphocytes and some histiocytes. Considerable cloudy swelling of parenchymatous cells.

TOP SECRET 397

S-5.

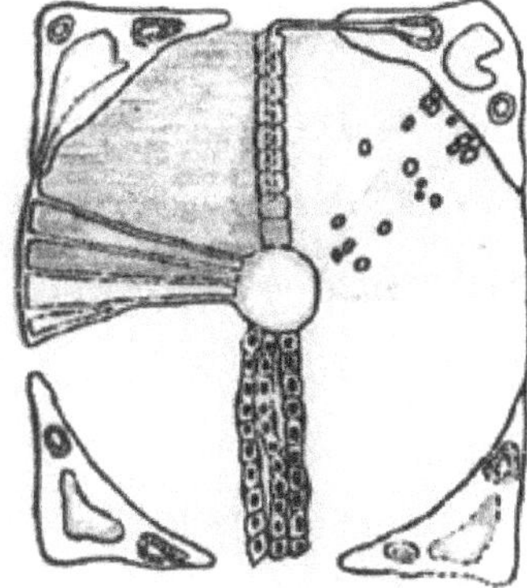

In Glisson's capsule, exist considerable congestion and considerable edematous swelling.

S-5.

Hepatitis serosa II. Considerable exsudation in Disse's spaces and considerable congestion with some leukocytes as capillary contents. Slight fatty degeneration and considerable cloudy swelling of parenchymatous cells with considerable brown pigments.

S-6.

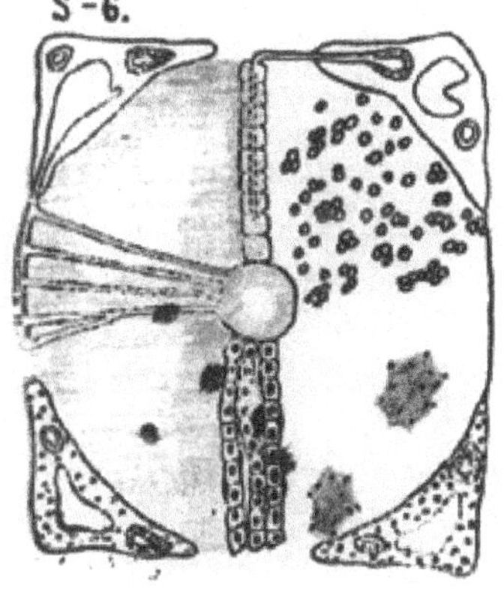

S-6.

Parenchymatous cells fall into extromly severe and diffuse fatty degeneration or structurlose necrotic masses. At some places, multiple miliary necrosis which are formed with histiocytic cells, bacteria-colonies and residual masses of parenchymatous cells.

S-8.

S-8.

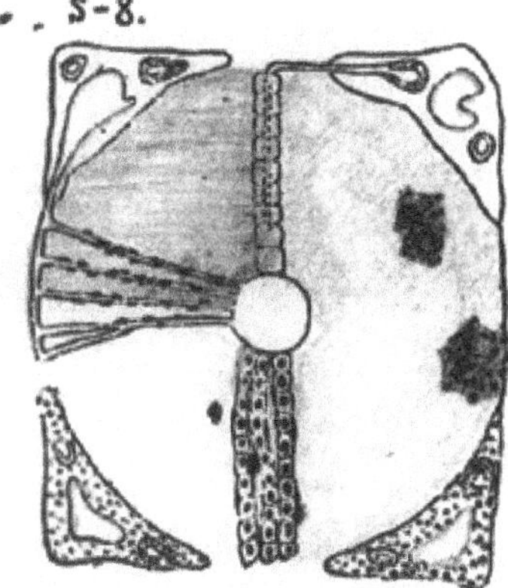

Hepatitis serosa II-III. Considerable congestion and ~~considerable~~ remarkable exsuative changes in Disse's spaces with more or less remarkable leukocytes emigration and bacterial accumulation as capillary contents and at other hands considerably increased histiocytic cells as slight proliferative changes. At some place, esp. at surrounding tissues of bacterial accumulation, exist multiple

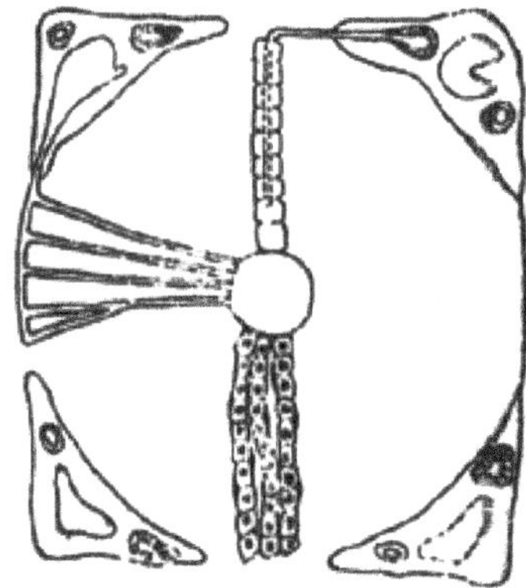

miliary or supermiliary necrosis (focal parts are formed with necrotic or residual masses of parenchymatuus cells and surrounded with some lymphocytes and slightly increased histiocytic cells as perifocal cell-reaction). Considerable cloudy swelling of parenchymatous cells with some brown pigments.

S-9.

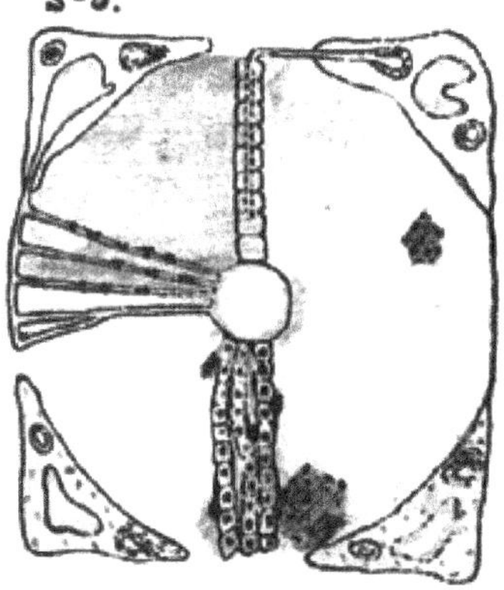

S-9.

Hepatitis serosa II-III. Multiple supermiliary or miliary necrosis with decayed masses of parenchymatous cells in focal parts and plenty wandering cells in perifocal parts.

Considerable cloudy swelling of parenchymatous cells with plenty brown-pigments.

Considerable congestion and exsudative changes in Disse's spaces, with some bacterial masses in capillary-nets.

S-lo.

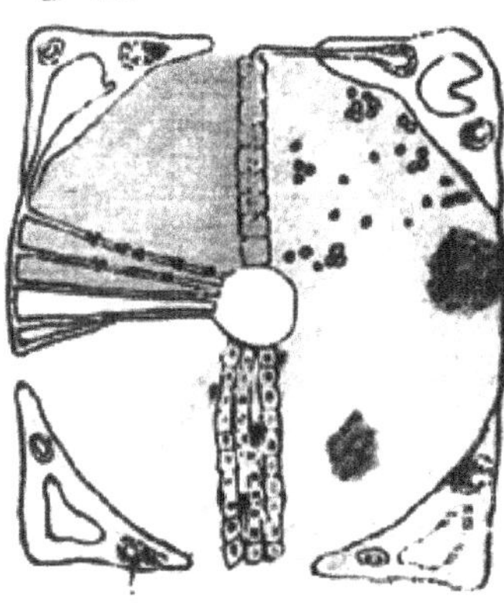

S-IO.

Hepatitis serosa III. Remarkable exsudation and considerable congestion with plenty leukocytes and bacterial accumulation as capillary contents. Bacterial masses in pfortader-veins or capillary-nets in acinus and multiple miliary or supermiliary necrosis in extremly exsudative form: some of them with remarkable hemorrhages and residual masses of decayed prenchymatous cells.

339

Considerable cloudy swelling and considerable fatty degeneration of parenchymatous cells and atrophia, due to extraordinary exsudative changes.

With some brown pigments.

S-11.

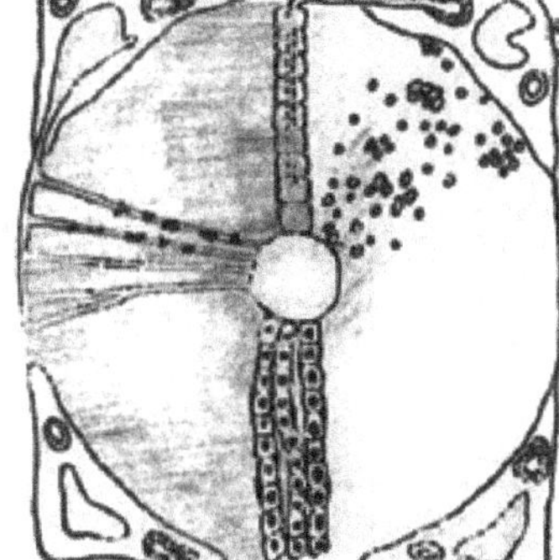

S-II.

Hepatitis serosa II-III. Remarkable congestion and remarkable exsudative changes in Disse's spaces.

At some places (mostly in central zone of acinuses), some hemorrhage and some parts of them fall into necrosis.

Generally intense parenchymatous degeneration with slight vacuolar degeneration.

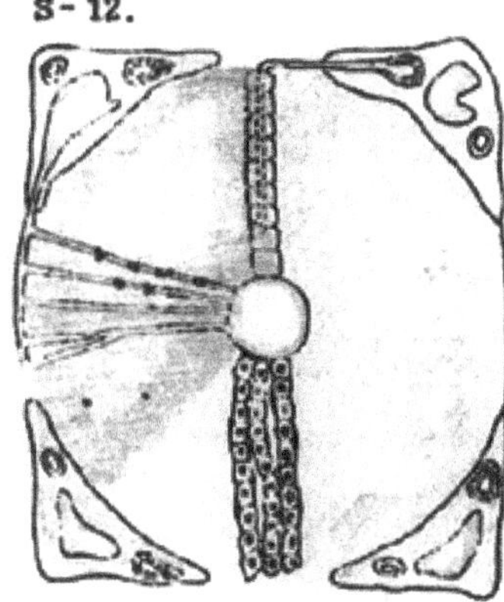

S-I2.

Hepatitis serosa II. ~~Severe~~ Considerable congestion and remarkable exsudative changes in Disse's spaces, with slight dissociation of cellular arrangements and considerable cloudy swelling of parenchymatous cells.

S-I4.

Initial places, multiple miliary necrosis: some of them rather in hemorrhagic form (slight fresh

340

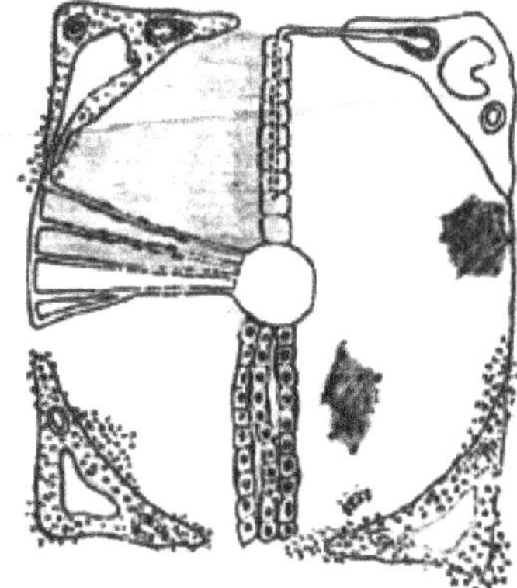

hemorrhages and considerably increased histiocytes) and some of them rather in proliferative form (remarkably increased histiocytes, some leucocytes and some residual masse of decayed parenchymatous cells).

Considerable cloudy swelling of parenchymatous cells and compensatoric hypertrophia, due to annular liver-cirrhosis.

Remarkable wandering cells (some of them, eosinophilic leucocytes) -infiltration in Glisson's capsule.

S-15.

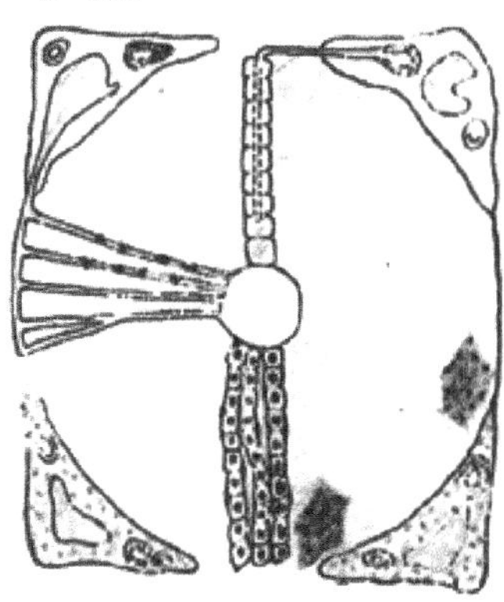

S-15.

Hepatitis serosa II. Remarkable congestion and remarkable exsudative changes in Disse's spaces with plenty leukocytes as capillary contents and formation of mutiple miliary necrosis in remarkable exsudative forms: some of them in fresh hemorrhages and some of them in remarkable exsudation with some leukocytes, some residual masses of decayed parenchymatous cells and some histiocytes. Remarkable lymphocytes infiltration and edematous swelling of Glisson's capsule.

341

S.-19.

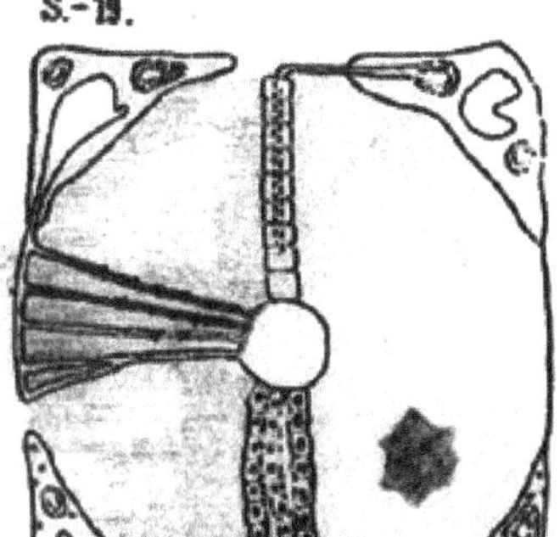

S-19.

Hepatitis serosa III-IV. Remarkable congestion and severe exsudative changes in Disse's spaces, with considerable dissociation and remarkable cloudy swelling of parenchymatous cells.

Multiple miliary necrosis, constituted with plenty decayed masses of parenchymatous cells.

S-22.

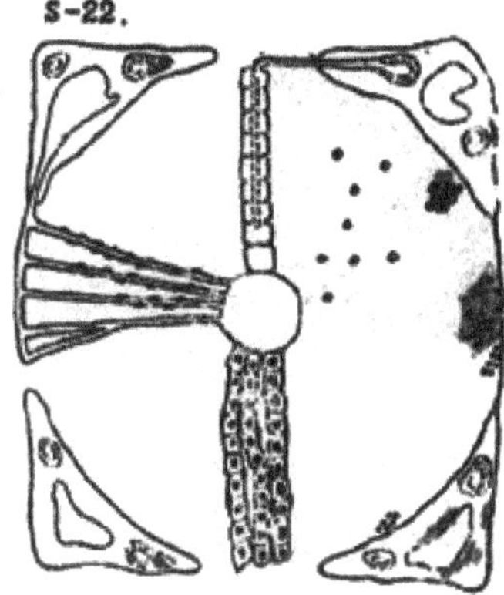

S-22.

Hepatitis serosa I, Slight congestion remarkable exsudative changes in Disse's spaces.

More or less remarkable increased Kupfer's cells, due to rather chronic (22 days) course. And than submiliary necrosis with histiocytic cells and decayed masses of prenchymatous cells.

Small slightly localised fatty degeneration of parenchymatous cells.

S-26.

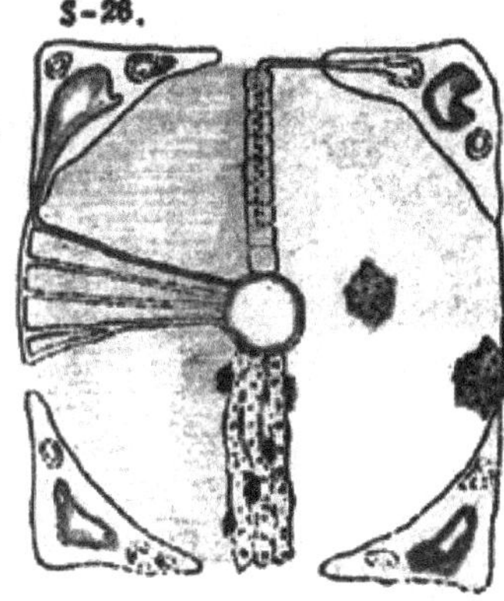

S-26.

Hepatitis serosa III. Considerable congestion and considerable exsudation in Disse's spaces with bacterial embolus in capillary-nets.

Remarkable cloudy swelling of parenchymatous cells, at some places, esp. at bacterial deposits, multiple miliary or submiliary necrosis, which are formed in focal parts with necrotic decayed masses of parenchymatous cells and bacterial accumlation and in perifocal parts with some leukocytes, slight hemorrhage and slightly increased histiocytic cells. Remarkable degenerative parenchymatous cells.

S-28.

Initial stage of annular-liver-cirrhosis and compensatoric hypertrophic parenchymatous cells, due to annular cirrhosis.

Remarkable congestion and exsudation in Disse's spaces with plenty leukocytes as capillary contents. These severe capillary disturbances caused at some places hemorrhagic knots (frosh hemorrhagic miliary necrosis(and at some places miliary knots in rather proliferative from (considerable histiocytes accumulation with a little lymphocytes at hemorrhagic places). Slight parenchymatous degeneration and slight fatty degeneration of parenchymatous cells.

S-28.

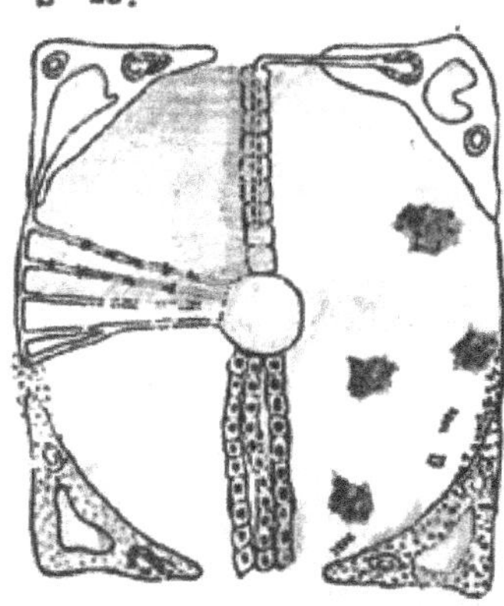

343

Considerable congestion, diffuse hemorrhages and considerable wandering cells infiltration in Glisson's capsule.

S-38.

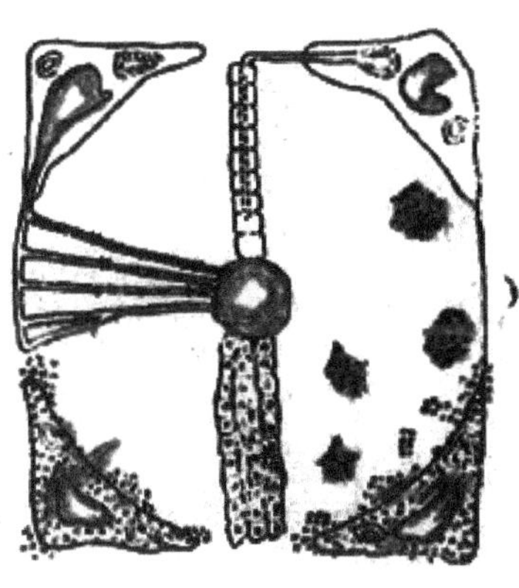

Hepatitis serosa III-IV. Considerable congestion and severe exsudative changes in Disse's spaces, with remarkable dissociation and cloudy swelling of parenchymatous cells.

Multiple miliary necrosis with plenty leucocytes, many histiocytes and some lymphocytes and some lymphocytes and some decayed mases of parenchymatous cells.

344

The bird-eye views of all investigated cases:

I.	II-III.	Some LK. Some bac.	M.M.N.	
2.	I-II.	Some bac.	Multiple diffuse hemorrhages.	
3.	III.	Plenty LK.	Hemorrhages in central zone.	
4.	II.	Plenty LK.	M.M.N.	
5.	II.			
6.	Severe fatty degeneration all over the acinuses.		M.M.N.	
8.	I.	Fatty degen.	M.SN.N.	Plenty Lm.
9.	I.	Slight fatty degen.		
IO.	III.	Plenty LK, Slight fatty degeneration.	M.M.N.	In exs. form.
II.	I-II.		M.SM.N. in exs. form.	

345

I2.	I-II.	Some LK.	Fatty degen.	M.M.N. Cell-accumulation in subendothelíar tissues of centrál veins.	Some Lm.
I4.	I-II.	Some LK. Some bac.	Slight fatty degeneration.		
I5.	I.	Some LK.	Diffuse fatty degeneration.		Some Lm.
I6.	I-II.	Some LK.	Diffues fatty Degeneration.	Diffuse hemorrhages.	Some Im.
I7.	II-III.			Diffuse hemorrhages	Diffuse hemorrhages.
I8.	I.	Plenty LK.			Slight diffuse hemorrhages.
I9.	I-II.				
20.	I.	Some hst.		M.M.N. in rather Prolif. form.	

346

2I.	I-II.	Some LK.		hemorrhages in central zone.
23.	I.	Some LK. Some hst.		M.M.N.
24.	I.	A few LK.	Fatty degen.	
26.	I.	Some LK.	Net-nectosis. Net-necrosis.	
27.	Annular cirrhosis.			M.M.N. in rather prolif.form.
29.	I-II.	Some LK. Some hst.	Slight fatty degeneration.	M.M.N. in Prolif-form.
30.	I.	A few Lm.		
3I.	I.			
32.	I.	Some LK. a few lm. Some hst.	Slight fatty degeneration.	

347

33.	II.	Some Lm. Some hst. A few LK.	Fatty degenerat. Net-Necrosis.	Net-Necro- sis	Edema
35.	I-II.	Some Lm. Consd. hst.			Edema
36.	II.	Some LK. Some Lm. A few hst.	Pseudo-Buliary- tracts.		
40.	I-II.	Some Lm. A few hst.			
42.	I-II.	Some Lm. Some LK. Some hst.			
44.	I-III.	Some Lm. Some LK. Some hst.		M.SM.N. in rather prolif. form.	
46.	I.	Corsd. hst.		M.SM.N.	
47.	II-III.	Some Lm. Some hst.	Fatty degen.	M.SM.N. in exs. form.	
49.	I.		Fatty degen.	M.M.N.	

348

I.	II.	Plenty LK.	Net-Necrotis	M.SM.N. Netlnecrosis.	
2.	II.	Some LK. Some Lm.			
3.	III-IV.			Diffuse, large Decrosis in intense exsudative form. M.M.N.	Intense edema.
4.	III.	Plenty LK.	Fatty degen.	M.M.N. in exs. form.	Congest. Edema.
5.	II.	Some L Plenty LK.	Fatty deger.		
6.	Diffuse flatty degeneration or structureless necrosis all over the acinuses.				
8.	II-III.	Plenty LK. Some bac. A few hst.		M.M.N.(with some hst).	
9.	II-III.	Some bact.		M.M.N.	

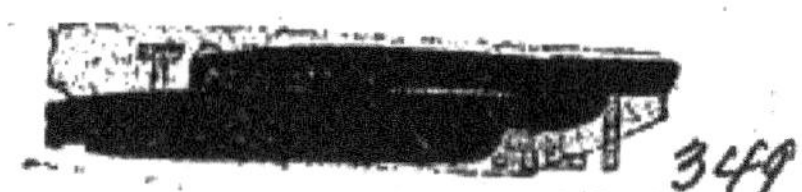
349

I0.	III.	Plenty LK. Some bac.		M.M.N.(ex-sud-hemorrhag. form).	
II.	II-III.			M.M.N.(ex-sud-hemorrhg. form).	
I2.	II.				
I4.	Annular Cirrhosis.			M.M.N. in 2 types. a) hemorrhag-exsudativ. b) rather prol.	Some LK.
I5. -----	III.	Plenty LK.		M.M.N. in intense exsudative form.	Edema Some Im.
I6.	III.				
I9.	III-IV.			M.M.N.	
22.	chronic course.	Remarkable hyperplasia of hst.	Localised fatty degene rated places.	M.M.N. in prolif. form.	

350

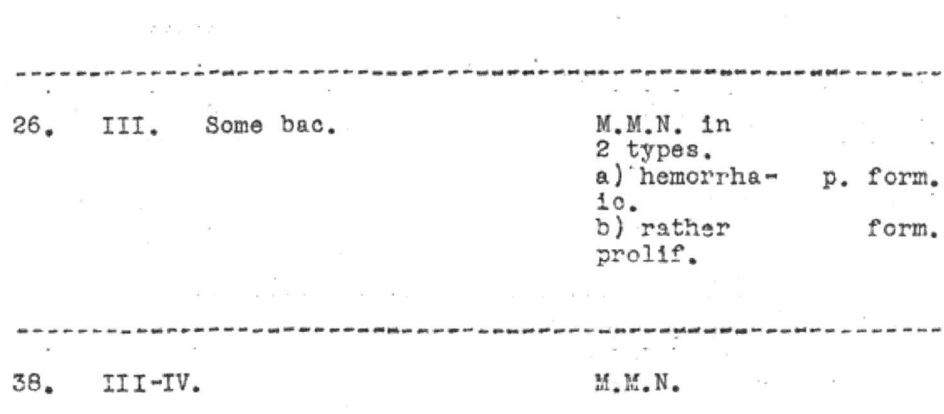

26.	III.	Some bac.	M.M.N. in 2 types. a) hemorrha- ic. b) rather prolif.	 p. form. form.
38.	III-IV.		M.M.N.	

351

Plague-infection caused at first more or less intense Hepatitis serosa.

Hepatitis serosa I.	I5 cases.
I - II.	II cases.
II.	II cases.
II - III.	6 cases.
III.	4 cases.
III - IV.	3 cases.
Diffuse intense degeneration all over the acinus es.	7 cases.

.) Some cases in acute stage, are accompanied with some or plenty leucocytes and some bacterial emigration in capillary nets of acinus. With the lapses of time, increases Histiocytes (or Kupfer's cells) gradually and in chronic course (22 days) caused some inflammatory reticulo-endotheiolose-like changes.

Appearance of some leucocytes in capillary nets	I7 cases.
Some bacterial masses.	II cases.
With some histiocytes.	2 cases.
With remarkably increased histiocytes.	I cases.

352

.) Generally caused plague-infection aome parenchymatous distubances: Some cases with intense fatty degenertion (appaesrance of grobe or fine vacuolar fatty substances all over the liver tissues) or some cases with so-called net-necrosis-like degeneration. These severe degenerative changes are recognized mainly in infantcases.

With intense fatty degeneration. 26 cases.
With intense fatty degeneration. cases.
With so -called net-necrosis-like changes. 3 cases.
With intenst, diffuse fatty degeneration (or structureless necosis) all over the liver tissues. I cases.

Sometimes caused multiple miliary or submiliary necoris:n some cases (in acute stage) with exsudative or exsudative-hemorrhagic form and some cases (in rather chrouic stage), with rather proliferative form.

Multiple miliary necrosis in intense hemorragic form. 6 cases.
Multiple miliary necrosis in intense exsudative form. 11 cases.

353

( (

Multiple miliary necrosis
in exsudative form. cases.
Multiple miliary necrosis
in rather proliferative form. 12 cases.

B). In Glisson's capsule:
Some cases are accompanied with some edema, hemorrhages and some round cell infiltration.

Edema in Glisson's capsule. 32 cases.
Hemorrhages in " 5 cases.
Round cell infiltration
(some of them, leucocytic). 34 cases.

354

LIVER

			N 1	N 2	N 3	N 4	N 5	N 6	N 7	N 8	N 9	N 10	N 11	N 12	N 14	N 15	N 16	N 17	N 18	N 19	N 20
Cell Cord	Irregular Arrangement		+	∸	∸	∸	∸	ǀ	∸	÷	+	(+:)	—	—	∸	÷	÷	∸	∸	∸	∸
	Dissociation		(+++)	(÷)	—	—	(÷)	ǀ	—	—	∸	(+)	—	(÷)	—	—	⊥	∸	—	—	∸
Parenchymal Cells	Clouding		(+++)	+	÷	÷	÷	ǀ	+	÷	+:	(+++)	÷	+	÷	÷	+	+	+	+	÷
	Atrophia		(+)	÷	∸	∸	∸	ǀ	∸	∸	+	(+++)	—	∸	—	÷	÷	÷	∸	—	∸
	Hypertrophia		∸	—	÷	—	÷	ǀ	—	∸	—	—	—	—	—	—	—	∸	∸	∸	+
	Fatty Degeneration	central	—	—	÷	—	+	+++	—	(+)	∸	÷	—	+	∸	∸	+	—	(∸)	(∸)	—
		intermediary	—	—	÷	—	÷	+++	—	÷	∸	÷	—	+	∸	∸	+	—	(÷)	(∸)	(∸)
		peripheral	(∸)	(∸)	∸	—	∸	+++	—	(+)	∸	÷	—	+	∸	∸	+	—	(÷)	(∸)	—
	Brown Pigment		+	+:	+	—	∸	ǀ	÷	—	—	(+)	+	(÷)	∸	+	—	+	++:	—	÷
Interstitium	V. centralis	Dilatation	(+)	+:	++	+	+	(+)	∸	+	+	÷	+	÷	÷	+	+	+	÷	÷	+
		Congestion	ǀ	÷	++:	÷	∸	++	∸	ǀ	ǀ	÷	++	÷	÷	+:	++	+:	+	+	+
	Capillaries	Dilatation	++	++:	+	+	÷	∸	(+)	+	(++)	++	÷	+	÷	+	+:	++	+	+	+
		Congestion	÷	÷	++	+	÷	(+)	∸	ǀ	÷	÷	+	÷	÷	+:	++:	+++	++	+	+
		Leucocytes	+:	∸	∸	+	∸	(∸)	(∸)	+	÷	++	∸	÷	÷	+	+	+	++	(∸)	—
		Lymphocytes	+	÷	÷	+	÷	÷	÷	÷	∸	÷	÷	÷	+	÷	+	÷	∸	∸	+
		Monocytes	÷	∸	∸	∸	∸	∸	∸	—	∸	÷	∸	÷	∸	∸	∸	∸	—	—	∸
	Edema		++	+:	+:	+:	+:	∸	+	+	++	++:	÷	+:	÷	∸	÷	+	(++)	÷	÷
	Hemorrhage		(÷)	÷	÷	(∸)	∸	—	(∸)	ǀ	ǀ	÷	(÷)	+	—	∸	+:	++:	∸	—	(∸)
	Kupffer's Cells	Proliferation	∸	+	÷	∸	∸	—	—	—	∸	—	—	÷	÷	—	—	—	—	—	+
		Swelling	+	÷	÷	∸	÷	÷	÷	÷	÷	∸	÷	∸	∸	—	—	∸	—	∸	÷
		Hemosiderin	—	∸	—	—	—	—	—	—	+	—	—	—	—	—	—	—	—	—	—
	Bacterium		++	—	—	—	—	—	—	—	—	+	—	—	+	—	+	—	÷	∸	—
	Congestion of V. hepatica		ǀ	+	++:	+	÷	++	ǀ	ǀ	ǀ	÷	+:	+	÷	++	++	+:	++	+	+
Glisson's Capsules	Production of Connective Tissue		—	—	—	∸	—	—	—	—	—	—	—	—	—	—	—	—	—	—	—
	Pseudobiliary Tracts		∸	∸	—	—	—	—	—	—	—	—	—	—	—	—	—	—	—	—	—
	Edema		÷	÷	÷	÷	+	∸	÷	÷	+	+	(+)	++	÷	+	÷	+	÷	∸	÷
	Hemorrhage		—	—	—	∸	∸	—	—	—	—	—	—	(÷)	—	—	∸	÷	∸	—	—
	Infiltration	Lymphocytes	÷	(+)	÷	(+++)	+	—	+:	÷	(÷)	+	+	+	∸	(÷)	++	∸	+	+	++
		Leucocytes	—	—	—	(+++)	∸	—	—	—	—	—	—	—	—	—	∸	—	+:	∸	—
	Proliferation	Histiocytes	—	—	—	÷	—	∸	∸	—	—	—	—	∸	—	—	∸	∸	∸	—	(++)
		Plasma Cells	—	—	—	—	—	—	—	—	—	—	—	—	—	—	—	—	—	—	—
	Congestion of A. hepatica		ǀ	÷	÷	∸	∸	∸	ǀ	ǀ	ǀ	∸	∸	∸	÷	÷	∸	+	+	∸	÷
	Congestion of V. pforte		ǀ	+:	++:	+	÷	++	ǀ	ǀ	ǀ	÷	+:	÷	÷	++	+:	+:	++	++	∸
Miliary Necrosis	Necrosis		—	—	—	++	—	∸	++	—	—	+	+	++	—	—	—	—	—	—	++
	Lymphocytes		—	—	—	+	—	∸	∸	—	—	∸	∸	∸	—	—	—	—	—	—	+:
	Leucocytes		—	—	—	—	—	∸	—	—	—	(∸)	—	(∸)	—	—	—	—	—	—	—
	Histiocytic Cells		—	—	—	+	—	++	∸	—	—	+	∸	÷	—	—	—	—	—	—	++
	Erythrocytes		—	—	—	(∸)	—	—	—	—	—	—	∸	+:	—	—	—	—	—	—	∸

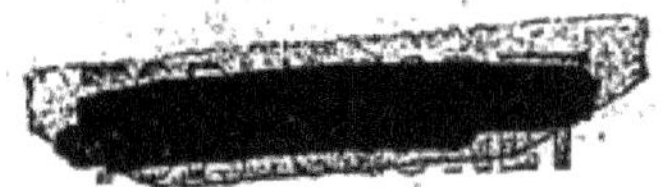

355

LIVER

			N 21	N 23	N 24	N 26	N 27	N 29	N 30	N 31	N 32	N 33	N 34	N 35	N 36	N 38	N 40	N 42	N 44	N 46	N 47
Cell Cord	Irregular Arrangement		(÷)	÷	÷	÷	+	+	+	÷	(÷)	+	÷	÷	++	÷	÷	÷	÷	÷	(+)
	Dissociation		(÷)	−	÷	−	÷	(+)	(÷)	−	(÷)	+	−	−	++÷	−	(÷)	(÷)	(÷)	(÷)	÷
Parenchymal Cells	Clouding		(+÷)	+	+	+	+	+	(+)	+	(+÷)	++	+	+	+÷	+	+	+	+	+	(+)
	Atrophia		(÷)	÷	÷	−	(+)	(+)	÷	÷	(÷)	(+÷)	−	÷	(++)	÷	÷	+	(+)	+	(+)
	Hypertrophia		÷	(÷)	−	−	−	−	−	−	−	−	−	−	−	−	÷	−	−	÷	÷
	Fatty Degeneration	Central	÷	(÷)	+	(÷)	÷	(÷)	−	(÷)	÷	÷	−	÷	(÷)	+	÷	−	−	÷	÷
		intermediary	−	(÷)	+	÷	−	(÷)	−	(÷)	−	÷	÷	÷	(÷)	(+)	÷	−	−	(÷)	÷
		peripheral	÷	(÷)	+	(÷)	−	(÷)	−	(÷)	(÷)	+	÷	÷	(÷)	÷	÷	−	−	(÷)	÷
	Brown Pigment		−	(÷)	−	+÷	÷	−	−	÷	÷	÷	(÷)	(÷)	++÷	(÷)	(+÷)	+	−	+	−
Interstitium	V. centralis	Dilatation	+	÷	÷	÷	(÷)	÷	÷	+	+	÷	÷	÷	÷	÷	÷	+	÷	+	÷
		Congestion	+÷	+	+	÷	÷	|	÷	|	+	+÷	++	+	+	++	÷	++	÷	|	÷
	Capillaries	Dilatation	(+÷)	++	+	(+)	(++)	+	+÷	÷	++	++	÷	+÷	(++)	+÷	÷	+	(+)	(++)	+
		Congestion	+	+÷	+	+	+	|	(+)	÷	+÷	+÷	(++)	(+)	(+)	+	+	+	(÷)	|	+
		Leucocytes	÷	(+)	+	+	(÷)	(÷)	(÷)	(÷)	+	÷	÷	÷	−	÷	÷	−	(+)	−	÷
		Lymphocytes	÷	÷	÷	÷	÷	+	÷	÷	÷	÷	+	÷	÷	÷	÷	÷	÷	÷	÷
		Monocytes	÷	÷	÷	÷	÷	÷	÷	÷	÷	÷	÷	−	+	÷	÷	÷	÷	÷	÷
	Edema		+	+	+	+	(÷)	++÷	(++)	+	(++)	(+÷)	÷	++÷	++÷	(++)	+÷	+++	(++)	++	+
	Hemorrhage		(+)	−	÷	(+)	÷	−	÷	·+·	|	÷	÷	÷	+	÷	÷	÷	÷	|	(÷)
	Kupffer's Cells	Proliferation	−	−	−	−	÷	÷	÷	−	(÷)	(÷)	÷	+	÷	(÷)	÷	+	−	+	−
		Swelling	÷	−	−	÷	÷	÷	÷	÷	÷	(÷)	−	÷	÷	÷	÷	+	÷	÷	÷
		Hemosiderin	(÷)	−	−	−	−	−	−	−	−	−	−	−	−	−	−	−	−	−	−
	Bacterium		−	−	−	−	−	−	÷	−	−	÷	−	−	−	−	−	−	−	÷	−
	Congestion of V. hepatica		++	+÷	+÷	÷	+	|	÷	+	|	++	++	++÷	÷	+++	+	+	÷	|	÷
Glisson's Capsules	Production of Connective Tissue		−	−	−	−	+	−	−	−	−	−	−	−	−	−	−	−	−	−	−
	Pseudobiliary Tracts		−	−	−	−	−	−	−	−	−	−	−	−	−	−	÷	÷	−	−	−
	Edema		+	+	÷	÷	++	(+)	÷	+	+	÷	÷	+÷	÷	+÷	+	+	+	(+)	+
	Hemorrhage		−	−	−	−	−	−	−	(÷)	·+·	·|·	÷	−	−	−	−	−	−	−	(÷)
	Infiltration	Lymphocytes	÷	÷	÷	÷	++	(+++)	+	÷	÷	+	++÷	÷	÷	(÷)	÷	÷	÷	÷	÷
		Leucocytes	−	−	(÷)	−	−	−	−	−	−	−	−	−	−	−	−	−	−	−	−
	Proliferation	Histiocytes	−	−	−	−	+÷	−	−	÷	÷	÷	+	−	÷	(+)	−	÷	−	÷	÷
		Plasma Cells	−	−	−	−	−	−	−	−	−	−	−	−	−	−	−	−	−	−	−
	Congestion of A. hepatica		÷	÷	÷	÷	÷	|	÷	÷	+	+	+	÷	÷	(+)	÷	÷	÷	|	+
	Congestion of V. pforte		++	+	+÷	÷	+	|	+÷	+	+	++	++	+÷	÷	+++	++	+	÷	|	+
Miliary Necrosis	Necrosis		−	++	−	−	−	÷	−	−	−	−	−	−	−	−	−	÷	+	+	+
	Lymphocytes		−	÷	−	−	−	+	−	−	−	−	−	−	−	−	−	−	−	÷	+
	Leucocytes		−	÷	−	−	−	−	−	−	−	−	−	−	−	−	−	−	−	−	−
	Histiocytic Cells		−	÷	−	−	−	+	−	−	−	−	−	−	−	−	−	−	+÷	÷	·+·
	Erythrocytes		−	−	−	−	−	−	−	−	−	−	−	−	−	−	−	−	(÷)	−	÷

356

LIVER

			N 49	S 1	S 2	S 3	S 4	S 5	S 6	S 8	S 9	S 10	S 11	S 12	S 14	S 15	S 19	S 22	S 26	S 28	S 38
Cell Cord	Irregular Arrangement		÷	÷	+	++	÷	÷	—	÷	(+)	+÷	÷	÷	+	+	+	÷	÷	(+)	+
	Dissociation		—	(÷)	(÷)	(++÷)	(÷)	—	—	÷	(÷)	+	(÷)	÷	—	(÷)	+÷	—	—	—	+÷
Parenchymal Cells	Clouding		+÷	÷	+÷	(+++)	+	+	++	+	(+)	+	—	—	—	÷	—	÷	++	÷	+÷
	Atrophia		÷	(+)	÷	(++÷)	÷	÷	÷	(+)	÷	(+÷)	(++)	(+)	÷	÷	(++÷)	÷	÷	(÷)	(+÷)
	Hypertrophia		—	—	—	—	—	—	—	—	—	—	—	—	—	—	—	—	—	+÷	—
	Fatty Degeneration	central	÷	(÷)	—	—	—	÷	++	—	—	÷	+	—	—	—	÷	(÷)	—	÷	÷
		intermediary	÷	(÷)	—	—	—	÷	++	(÷)	—	÷	+	—	—	—	÷	(÷)	—	÷	÷
		peripheral	+	(÷)	—	—	—	÷	++	—	(÷)	(+)	+	—	—	—	÷	(÷)	—	÷	÷
	Brown Pigment		÷	—	—	÷	÷	(+÷)	—	+÷	++	÷	+÷	÷	—	—	÷	—	(+)	—	÷
Interstitium	V. centralis	Dilatation	÷	÷	÷	—	÷	÷	—	+	÷	+	÷	+	—	÷	÷	÷	÷	÷	÷
		Congestion	+÷	+	+	+	+÷	+	(+÷)	÷	+	|	++÷	+÷	÷	÷	|	÷	+	+÷	+÷
	Capillaries	Dilatation	(+÷)	+÷	++	—	(+++)	(+÷)	÷	+÷	÷	++	÷	(+)	(÷)	(+++)	++÷	÷	(+)	(+)	+
		Congestion	(+÷)	+	++÷	|	+	+	(+)	(+)	+	|	+÷	+	+	(+÷)	+÷	÷	(+)	(+)	÷
		Leucocytes	÷	+	++	—	+÷	÷	÷	++	++	+÷	(+)	+	÷	+÷	+÷	—	÷	+÷	+
		Lymphocytes	÷	÷	+	|	÷	÷	÷	÷	÷	÷	÷	÷	÷	÷	+	÷	÷	÷	+
		Monocytes	÷	÷	÷	|	+	÷	÷	÷	÷	÷	÷	÷	÷	÷	÷	÷	÷	÷	÷
	Edema		+÷	++	++	+++	+÷	(+)	÷	++	++÷	++÷	++	++	÷	(+++)	++÷	+÷	(+)	+	++÷
	Hemorrhage		÷	—	÷	|	(÷)	—	(÷)	(+)	(+)	|	+	—	(÷)	÷	|	(÷)	—	÷	÷
	Kupffer's Cells	Proliferation	—	÷	—	÷	—	—	—	+÷	÷	÷	—	÷	+	—	÷	++	—	÷	÷
		Swelling	(÷)	÷	÷	÷	—	—	÷	+	+	÷	—	+	÷	÷	+	(++)	÷	÷	—
		Hemosiderin	—	—	—	—	—	—	—	—	÷	÷	—	—	+	—	÷	—	—	—	—
	Bacterium		++	÷	++	+++	—	—	+++	+	++	+	—	—	÷	—	—	—	+++	÷	—
	Congestion of V. hepatica		(++)	÷	+	|	+÷	++	+÷	+	+	|	++	+÷	+	+÷	|	÷	+	++	+÷
Glisson's Capsules	Production of Connective Tissue		—	—	—	—	—	—	—	—	—	—	—	—	+	÷	—	÷	—	+÷	—
	Pseudobiliary Tracts		—	—	—	—	—	—	÷	÷	—	—	—	—	÷	÷	—	÷	—	÷	—
	Edema		+÷	+	++	+÷	+÷	÷	÷	÷	+÷	++	++	+÷	÷	+	++	÷	+	÷	++
	Hemorrhage		÷	—	—	|	—	—	—	—	—	—	—	—	—	÷	|	÷	—	++	÷
	Infiltration	Lymphocytes	+	+	÷	÷	÷	÷	++	(+)	+	÷	÷	÷	+++	(++)	+	(÷)	(÷)	(+÷)	+
		Leucocytes	÷	—	—	—	—	—	(÷)	—	—	—	—	—	÷	(÷)	—	—	—	÷	—
	Proliferation	Histiocytes	÷	÷	—	÷	—	—	÷	+÷	÷	÷	÷	÷	+	÷	÷	÷	÷	++	—
		Plasma Cells	—	—	—	—	—	—	—	—	—	—	—	—	—	÷	—	—	—	—	—
	Congestion of A. hepatica		÷	÷	÷	|	÷	÷	÷	÷	+	|	—	—	÷	÷	|	÷	÷	÷	—
	Congestion of V. porte		(++)	÷	+	|	+÷	++	+÷	+	+÷	|	—	—	+	++÷	|	÷	+÷	++÷	+÷
Miliary Necrosis	Necrosis		+	+	—	++	++	—	+	++	++	++	—	—	++÷	÷	++	+	÷	+	+÷
	Lymphocytes		÷	+	—	+	÷	—	÷	—	÷	÷	—	—	÷	÷	÷	÷	(÷)	÷	÷
	Leucocytes		+	—	—	—	÷	—	÷	(÷)	÷	—	—	—	÷	÷	—	—	(÷)	—	+÷
	Histiocytic Cells		+÷	÷	—	+	÷	—	+	+÷	+÷	++	—	—	+	+	÷	+÷	++	÷	+
	Erythrocytes		—	—	—	÷	—	—	+	+	+	—	—	—	(÷)	÷	—	÷	(÷)	—	—

357

Hepatitis serosa I.

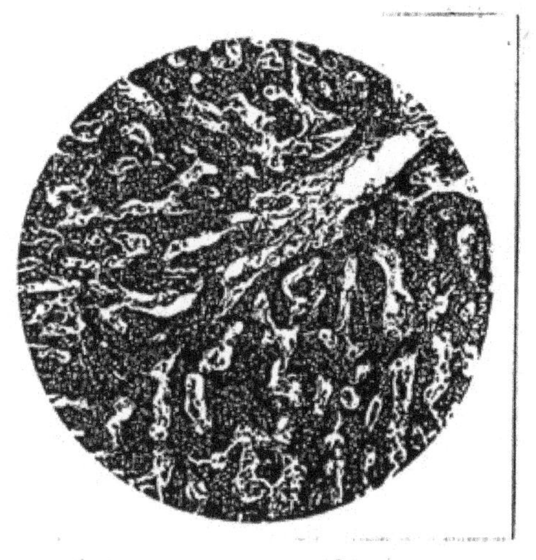

x 170

Hepatitis serosa II.

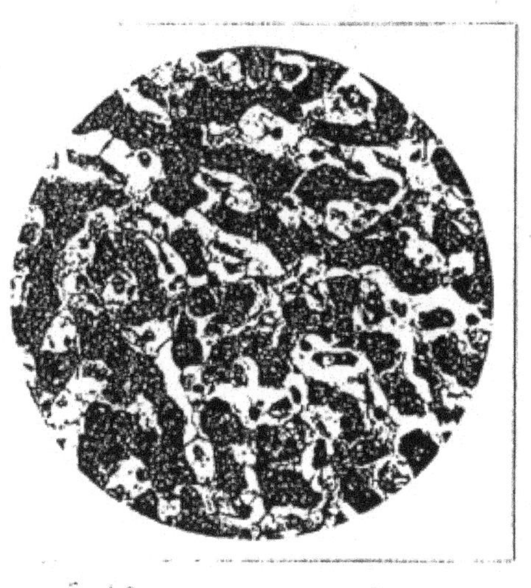

5-12　　x 280

358

Hepatitis serosa II-III.

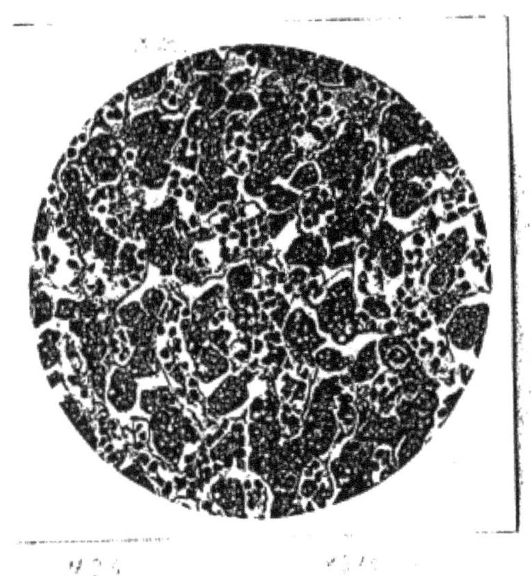

Diffuse hemorrhagic place.

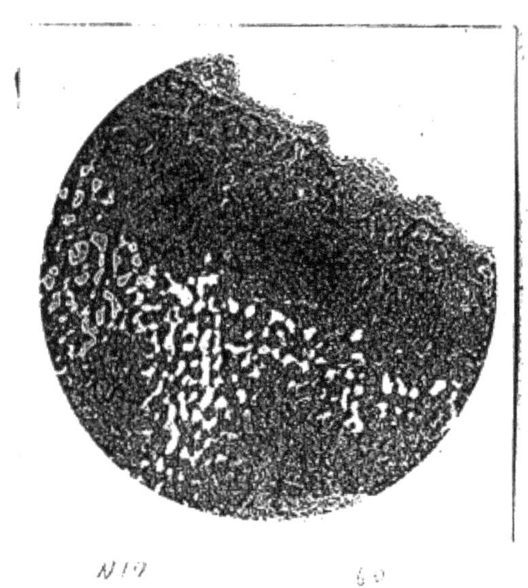

359

Intense fatty degeneration.

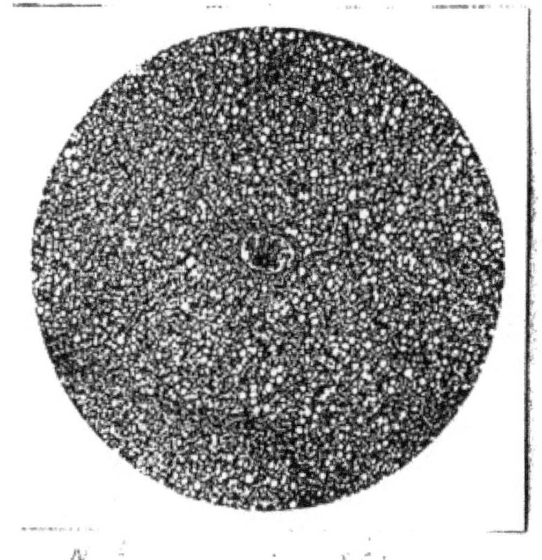

So-called net-like necrosis.

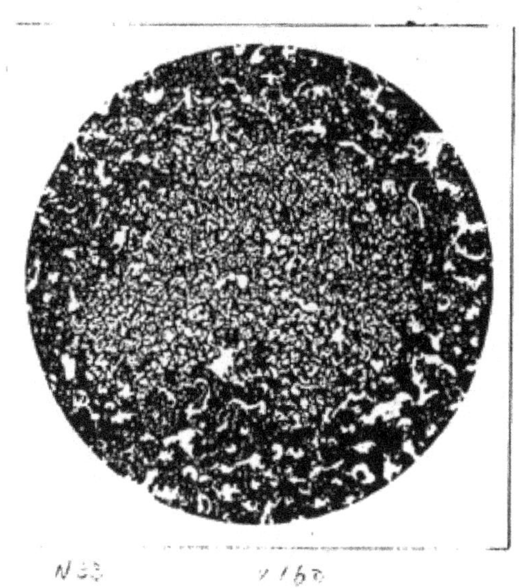

Millet corn large necrosis.

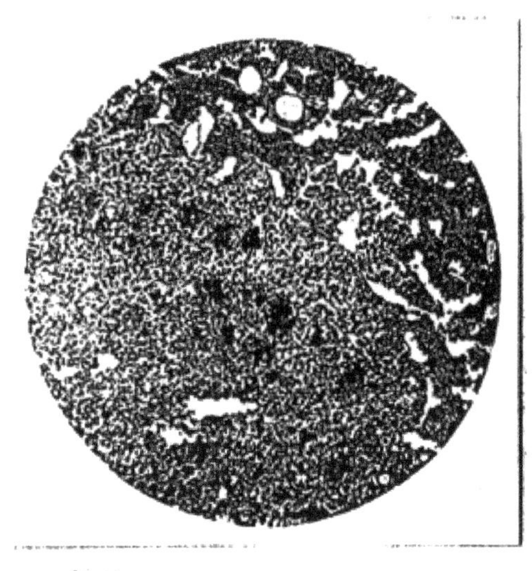

Diffuse round cell dissemination.

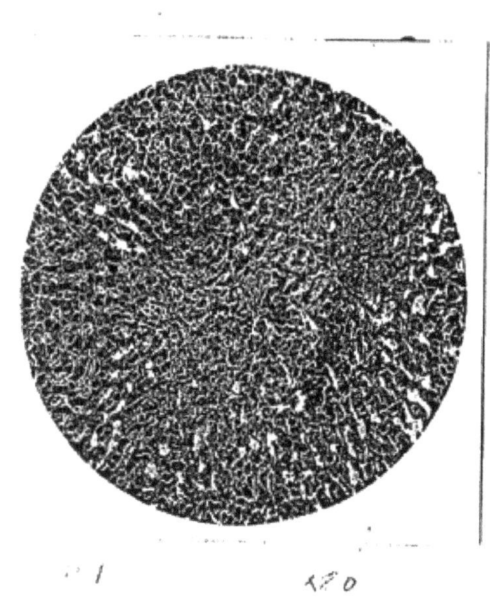

361

Field corn large necrosis.

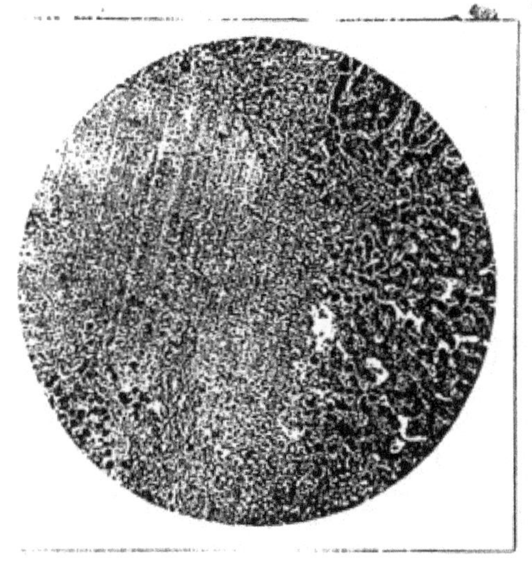

Field corn large necrosis.

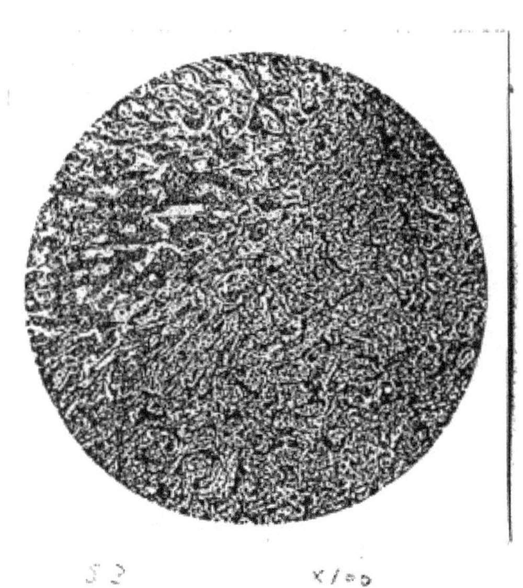

Supermiliary necrosis.

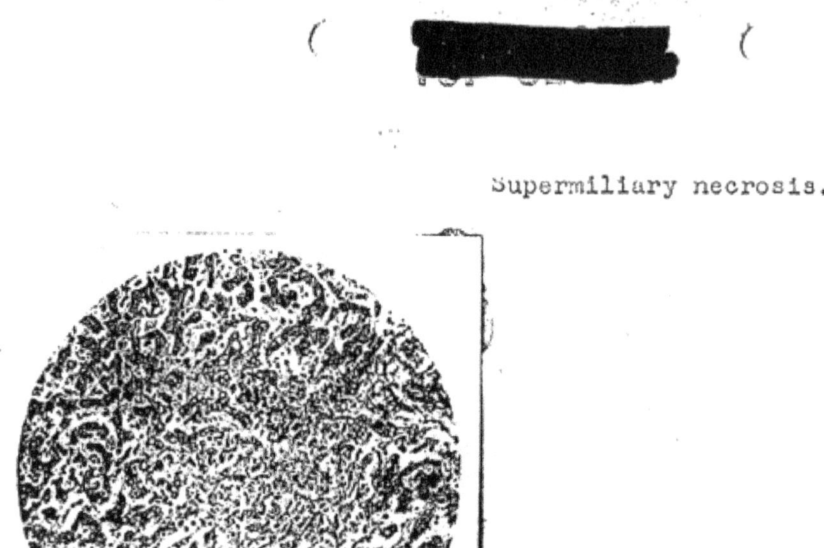

Supermiliary necrosis.

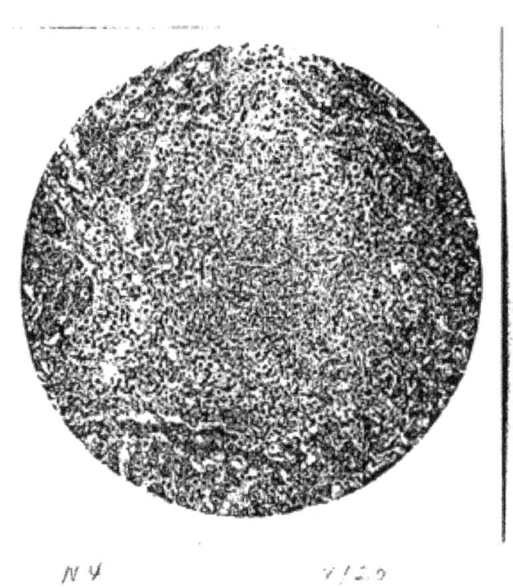

363

Submiliary necrosis with some bacterial dissemination, in high power.

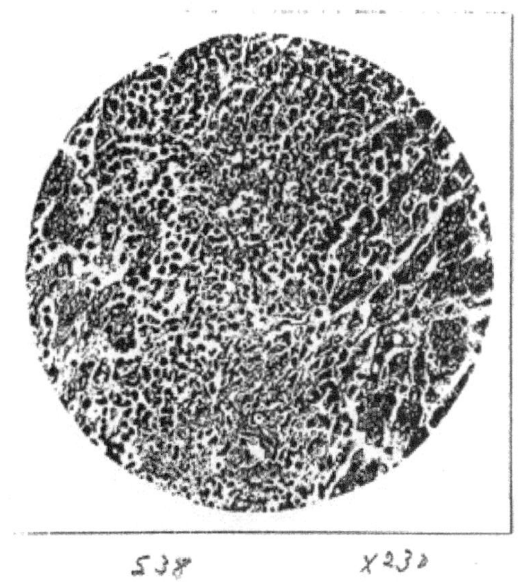

538 X230

364

Miliary knot in fresh stage.

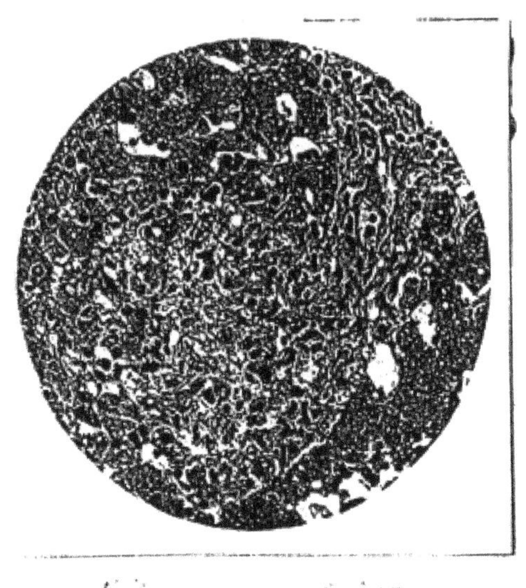

Miliary knot in leucocytic hemorrhagic form.

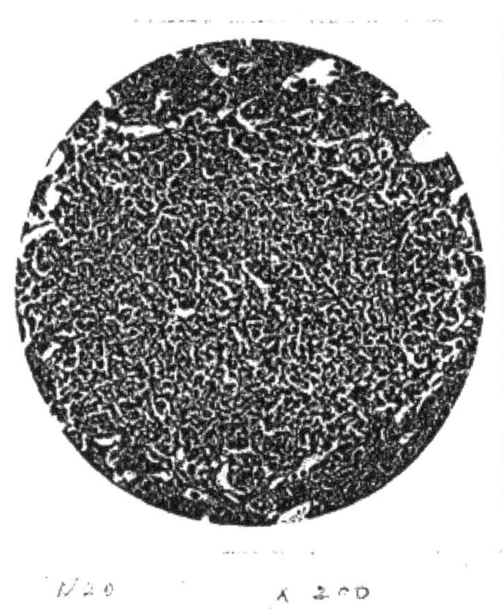

365

Submiliary necrosis.
In exudative form.

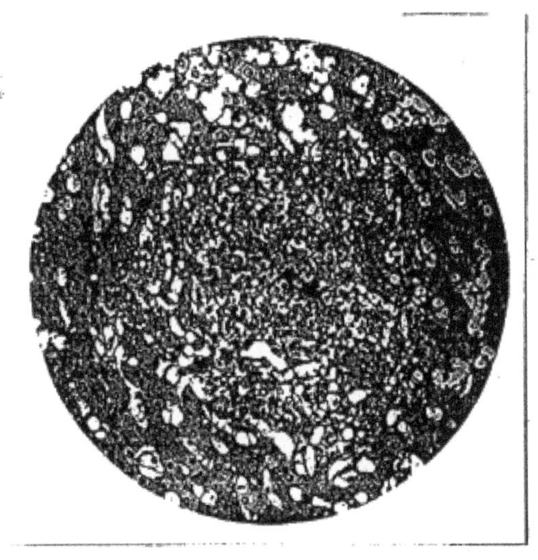

Submiliary necrosis.
In rather proliferative form.

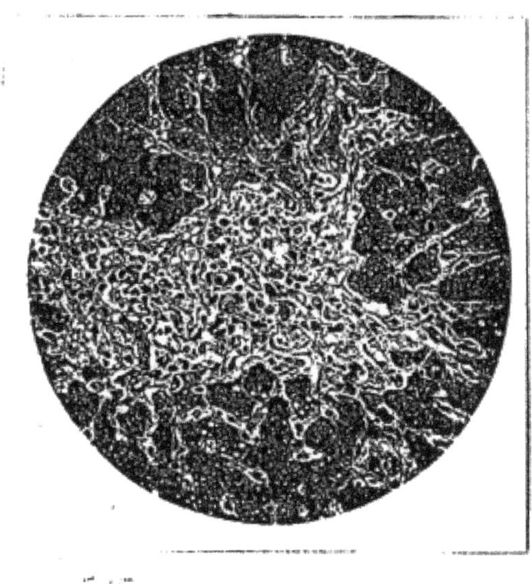

515

-366

Miliary knot in hemorrhagic form.

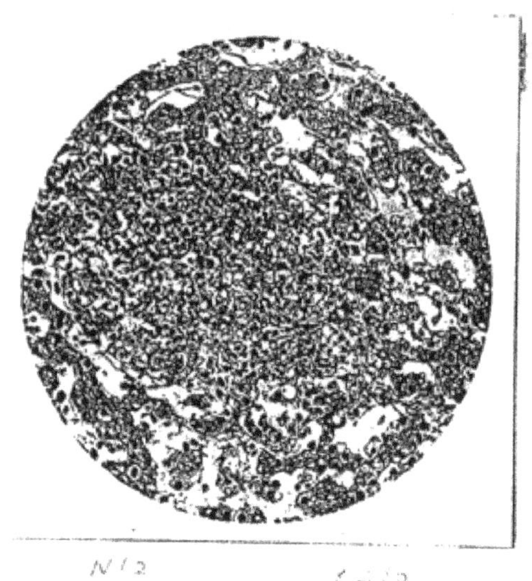

Miliary knot in hemorrhagic form.

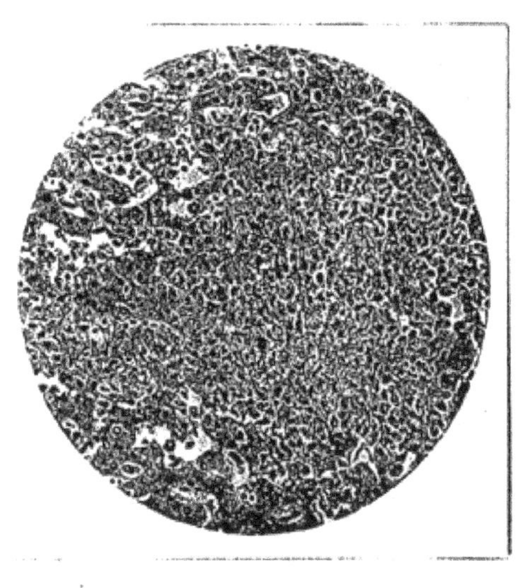

Submiliary necrosis.
in exudative form.

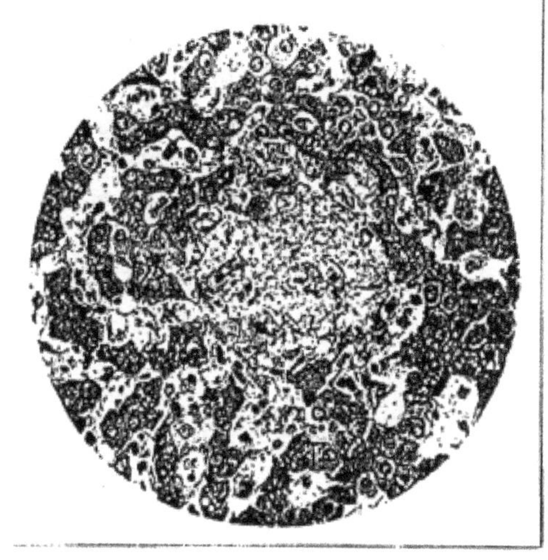

Submiliary necrosis.
in rather proliferative form.

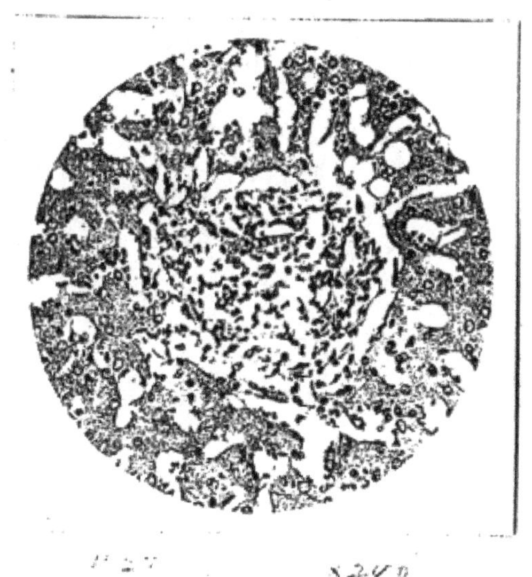

368

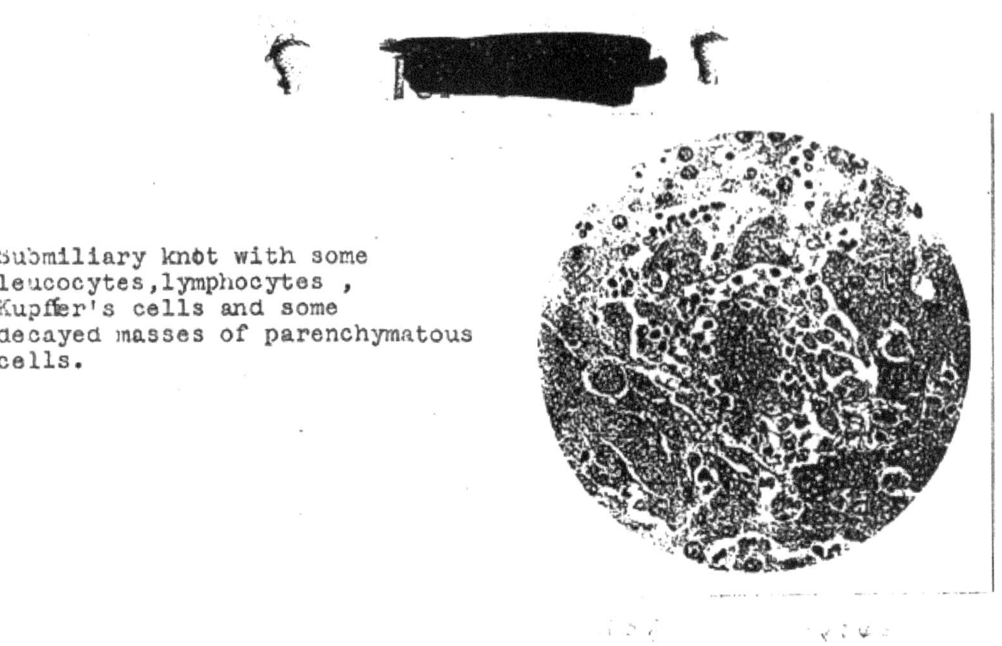

Submiliary knot with some leucocytes, lymphocytes , Kupffer's cells and some decayed masses of parenchymatous cells.

Submiliary knot.

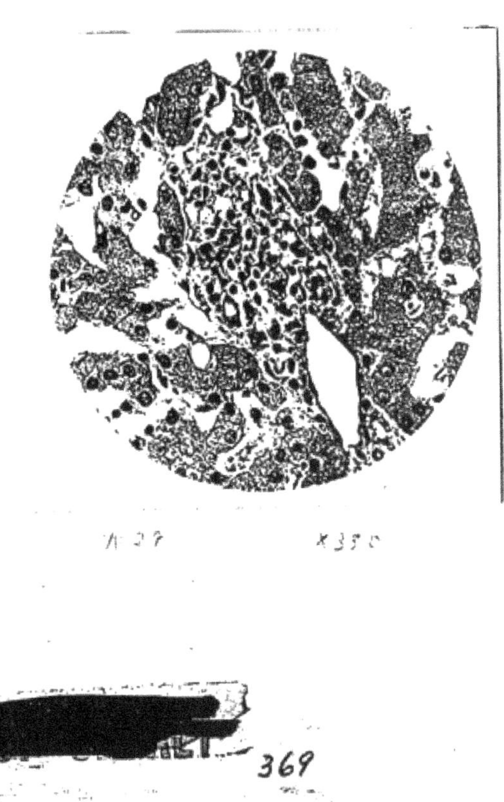

369

Stomach & Intestine

370

S T O M A C H.

(A) Microscop. Investigation.

I.

Rather atrophic glandular cells and slight catarth.

2.

No remarkable changes.

3.

No remarkable changes.

4.

Slight hyperplasia of lymphatic nodulus. Slight catarrh and slight round-cell-inifiltration in submucous tissues.

5.

Considerable congestion and multiple partial hemorrhages in T.propria with remarkable degeneration (cloudy swelling and vacuolar degeneration at hemorrhagic parts) of glandular cells.

Slight catarrh.

6.

Slight catarrh.

7.

Slight catarrh.

8.

No remarkable changes.

IO.

Slight hypersecretion.

— 371

I2.

Considerable congestion with partial hemorrhage and slight edematous swelling of mucous tissues. Slight hypersecretion.

I3.

Slight congestion, considerable edematous swelling of mucous tissues and rather atrophic glandular cells. Considerable congestion in submucous.

I4.

Slight edema, slight stasis of mucous tissues and rather atrophic glandular cells.

I5.

Slight swelling of mucous tissues and slight stasis of submucous tissues.

I6.

No remarkable changes.

I7.

No remarkable changes.

I8.

Slight congestion of mucous tissues and considerable congestion of submucous tissues.

I9.

Gastritis catarrhalis hypertrophicans and considerable congestion of mucous tissues.

372

20.

Post mortal changes. No remarkable changes.

2I.

Considerable congestion (some bacterial masses in blood-capillaries), considerable swelling of mucous tissues and slight hypersecretion.

23.

Slight hypersecretion.

26.

Gastritis catarrhalis hypertrophicans.

Slight hypertrophia of glandular cells and slight hypersecretion.

Considerable congestion of submucous tissues.

27.

Slight edematous swelling of mucous tissues and slight dissociation of glandular cell-arrangements.

29.

Slight congestion and slight hypersecretion of mucous tissues.

30.

Slight congestion of mucous tissues and slight degeneration (cloudy swelling) of glandular cells.

3I.

Almost normal, slight stasis and slight hypersecretion.

32.

Cloudy swelling of somewhat atrophic glandular cells and considerable congestion (with many leucocytes as capillary-contents) in submucous tissues.

373

([redacted] (

33.

Considerable congestion with partial hemorrhages and slight edematous swelling of mucous tissues.

34.

Slight hypersecretion.

36.

Gastritis catrrhalis levis and slight stasis of mucous tissues.

38.

Gastritis catarrhalis hypertrophicans. Hypertrophia of glandular cells with rather considerable catarrhalic masses and slight edematous swelling of mucous tissues.

40.

Considerable hypersecretion and no remarkable changes else.

42.

Slight congestion and slight hypersecretion.

44.

Rather atrophic glandular cells with considerable cloudy swelling and slight dissociation of glandular cell-arrangements.

46.

Almost mormal.

47.

Almost normal.

49.

Slight stasis and considerable congestion of submucous tissues. No remarkable changes else.

I.

S-2.

Slight hypersecretion with some desquamatied epithel cells and erythrocytes-leakages on the surface of mucous tissues.

S-3.

Slight hypersecretion with some desquamated epitheliar cells and slight stasis (at some places bacterial masses in capilaries) of mucous tissues.

S-4.

Slight stasis of mucous tissues.

S-5.

Hemorrhagic catarrhalic masses on the surface of mucous tissues. Considerable congestion and slight edematous swelling of mucous tissues and considerable cloudy or parenchymatous degeneration of glandular cells with somewhat dissociation of glandular cell-arrangements. Considerable congestion of submucous tissues.

S-6.

Gastritis catarrhalis with considerable hypersecretion. Very slight stasis.

S-8.

Considerable hyperplasia of mucous tissues with slight hypersecretion and slight stasis.

S-9.

Gastritis catarrhalis with considerable hypersecretion.

375

S-I0.

Gastritis catarrhalis hypertrophicans with hypertrophic glandular cells and considerable hypersecretions. Some desquamted epitheliar cells and mucous masses on the surface of mucous layers.

S-II.

Remarkable congestion with multiple diffuse or more or less localised hemorrhages in mucous tissues and severe perivascular bleeding in submucous tissues.

S-I2.

Remarkable congestion with remarkable localised hemorrhages and edmmatous swelling of mucous tissues. Slight hypersecretion of glandular cells. (bacterial masses in capillaries).

Considerable congestion of submucous tissues.

S-I4.

Considerable congestion (many leucocytes in capillaries), slight edematous swelling and ~~/slight edematous swelling~~ and slight hyperplasia of mucous tissues.

S-I5.

Considerable congestion (some leucocytes and some bacterial masses in capillaries), slight edema of mucous tissues and slight hypersecretion of glandular cells.

S-I9.

Almost normal.

[illegible]

[illegible]

376

S-22.

Edematous swelling of mucous with hyalinous swelling of blood-and lymph-capillary-walls and slight hyperplasia of plasma-cells and histiocytes in mucous tissues. Considerable atrophic glandular cells.

S-26.

Gastritis catarrhalis in medium degree, considerable hyperplasia of mucous tissues with some desquamated epithelial cells and catarrhalic masses on the surface of mucous layers. Slight stasis and considerable hypersecretion of glandular cells.

S-28.

Slight stasis with multiple localised hemorrhages in the upper layers of mucous tissues and slight edematous swelling and more or less increased round-cells in mucous tissues.

S-38.

Slight catarrh, no remarkable changes else.

377

SUMMARY.

(I)

The bird's eye-view of all investigated cases.

I. Rather atrophic glandular cells.

2. Almost normal.

3. Nomal.

4. Slight catarrh and some round-cell-infiltration in submucous tissues.

5. Considerable congestion and some multiple hemorrhages in mucous tissues.

6. Normal.

8. Normal.

9. Normal.

IO. Normal.

II. Considerable congestion and some locallised hemorrhages in mucous tissues.

I2. Rather atrophic glandular cells. Considerable congestion in submucous tissues.

I4. Rather atrophic glandular cells.

I5. Rather atrophic glandular cells.

I5. Normal.

I6. Normal.

I7. Normal.

378

I8. Considerable congestion in submucous tissues.

I9. Gastritis catarrhalis hypertrophicans and considerable congestion in submucous tissues.

20. Normal.

2I. Considerable congestion and some bacterial masses in capillaries.

23. Normal.

26. Slight Gastritis catarrhalis.

27. Normal.

29. Normal.

30. Normal.

3I. Normal.

32. Considerable congestion and many leucocytes in capillaries (in submucous tissues).

33. Considerable congestion and some localised hemorrhages in submucous tissues.

34. Normal.

36. Gastritis catarrhalis in slight degree.
Gastritis catarrhalis hypertrophicans.
Considerable hypersecretion.

42. Normal.

44. Rather atrophic glandular cells.

46. Normal.

47. Normal.

49. Considerable congestion in submucous tissues.

379

S-I. Missed. Uncertain.

S-2. Normàl.

S-3. Slight congestion and some bacterial masses in capillaries.

S-4. Normal.

S-5. Considerable congestion and edema in mucous tissues.
Hemorrhagic-catarrhalic masses on the surface of mucous tissues.

S-6. Gastritis catarrhalis.

S-8. Considerable hyperplasia of mucous tissues.

S-9. Gastritis catarrhalis.

S-I0. Gastritis catarrhalis hypertrphicans.

S-11. Remarkable congestion and multiple hemorrhages in mucous tissues.
Some perivascular hemorrhages in submucous tissues.

S-12. Remarkable congestion (some bacterial masses in capillaries) and multiple hemorrhages in submucous tissues.
Considerable congestion in submucous, tissues.

S-I4. Considerable congestion (some leucocytes in capillariess).

S-I5. Considerable congestion (some bacterial masses and some leucocytes in capillaries).

S-I9. Normal.

S-22. Edema and considerable congestion in mucous tissues.
Hyaline swelling of capillary-walls. Some histiocytes in mucous tissues.

S-26. Gastritis catarrhalis in medium degree.

S-28. Slight congestion and multiple localised hemorrhages in mucous sissues.

380

S-38. Slight catarrh.

---

(2)

Explaining of developing-mechanismus of pathological changes, based on all investigated 55 cases.

Plague-infection caused sometimes considerable congestion or some localised hemorrhages in mucous or submucous tissues.

	S-district	N-districts	total
a) Considerable congestion	5 cases.	5 cases.	IO cases.
with some leucocytes in capillaries.	2	I	3
with some bacterial masses in capillaries.	1	1	2
b) Remarkable congestion and some localised hemorrhages.	3 cases.	2 cases.	5 cases.
with some bacterial masses in capillaries.	1	0	1
c) With no remarkable reactive changes.	IO cases.	30 cases.	40 cases.
Total cases.	I8 cases.	37 cases	55 cases.

Therefore the main pathological findings are sometimes considerable congestion or furthermore sometimes some localised hemorrhages in mucous or sometimes submucous tissues.

381

SMALL INTESTINE

(A) Microscop. Investigation.

I.

Almost normal, slight hypersecretion.

2.

Considerable hypersecretion with some desquamated epithelial cells and catarrhalic masses and slight congestion of mucous tissues.

3.

Slight hypersecretion of mucous tissues. Slight hyperplasia of lymphatic nodulus with slight hyperplasia of reticulum cells and some bacterial masses in perifollicular capillaries.

4.

Slight hypersecretion and slight hyperplasia of lymphatic nodulus with considerable hyperplasia of reticulum cells (more or loss swollen reticulum cells).

5.

Considerable catarrh with some desquamated cells and catarrhalic masses and slight hyperplasia of lymphatic nodulus with slightly increased reticulum cells in germinative centers.

6.

Almost normal, slight hyperplasia of lymphatic nodulus and slight hypersecretion.

7.

Slight hypersecretion and slight congestion of mucous tissues. Slight hyperplasia of lymphatic nodulus with some increased reticulum cells.

382

8.

Slight hypersecretion and slight edematous swelling of mucous tissues.

9.

Slight hypersecretion and considerable congestion (with some leucocytes as capillaries-contents) of mucous tissues and lymphnodulus-capillaries.

Slight hyperplasia of lymphatic nodulus with slightly increased reticulum cells in germinative centers.

IO.

Slight hypersecretion, slight congestion and slight hyperplasia of lymphnodulus with some increased reticulum cells.

Considerable congestion of submucous tissues and considerable degeneration of ganglion cells in Auerbach's plexus.

II.

Considerable hypersecretion with some desquamated cells and ~~cat-~~ catarrhalic masses and slight edematous swelling of mucous tissues.

Considerable hyperplasia of lymph-nodulus with some perifollicular congestion with considerable congestion of follicular capillaries.

Considerable congestion of submucous tissues.

I2.

Enteritis catarrhalis. Considerable hypersecretion with massive desquamated cells and catarralic masses.

Considerable hyperplasia of lymphatic nodulus with some increased reticulum cells. Slight mucous congestion (with some leucocytes in capillaries) and slight submucous congestion with slight perivas-

383

cular round-cell-infiltrations.

I4.

Almost normal, considerable atrophia of mucous tissues.

I5.

Slight hypersecretion, slight congestion and slight hyperplasia of lymphatic nodulus.

I6.

Slight hypersecretion, considerable congestion and slight edema of mucous tissues and slight hyperplasia of reticulum cells in germinative centers.

I7.

Slight hypersecretion and slight edematous swelling of mucous tissues.

I8.

Considerable hypersecretion with massive desquamated cells and catarrahlic masses, considerable congestion with some localised miliary hemorrhages in mucous tissues and considerable swelling of mucous tissues. Some leucocytes (esp. eosinophilic cells) in mucous tissues. Slight hyperplasia and swelling of reticulum cells in germinative centers.

Considerable congestion (with some bacterial masses as capillaries-contents) of submucous tissues.

I8.

Duodenal parts.

Slight hypersecretion, slight edematous swelling and considerable

384

congestion (with some leucocytes and some bacterial masses as capillaries-contents).

Considerable congestion of submucous tissues.

I9.

Slight hypersecretion, considerable congestion and considerable swelling of mucous tissues.

20.

Almost normal. Slight hypersecretion.

2I.

Almost normal, rather atrophic glandular cells and slight hyperplasia and swelling of lymphatic nodulus with some increased reticulum cells.

23.

Almost normal.

24.

Almost normal.

26.

Almost normal. Slight hypersecretion.

29.

Considerable hypersecretion with some desquamated cells and catarrhalic masses and considerable hyperplasia of lymphatic nodulus with some increased reticulum cells.

Slight congestion (with some bacterial masses in capillaries) of submucous tissues.

30.

Enteritis follicularis. Slight congestion and remarkable hyper-

385

plasia of lymphatic nodulus with some increased reticulum cells in germinative cènters.

3I.

Slight hypersecretion, slight congestion, slight edema and slight hyperplasia of lymphatic nodulus.

32.

Considerable congestion (with some leucocytes and some bacterial masses in capillaries) and swelling of mucous tissues.

Considerable congestion of submucous tissues.

33.

Missed.

34.

Slight hypersecretion, slight swelling and slight hyperplasia of capillary endothel-cells with slight perivascular lymphocytes-infiltrations.

35.

Almsot normal.

36.

Slight hypersecretion, very slight congestion and slight congenital hyperplasia of lymphatic nodulus.

42.

Considerable hypersecretion, slight congestion and considerable hyperplasia and swelling of lymphatic nodulus with congestion of follicular capillaries.

Considerable congestion of submucous tissues.

386

44.

Almost normal.

46.

Almost normal, slight hypersecretion,

47.

Almost normal, slight hypersecretion.

49.

missed.

S-I. missed.

S-2. missed.

S-3.

Rather atrophic glandular cells and slight edematous swelling of mucous tissues with remarkable hyperplasia of lymphatic nodulus.

S-4.

Enteritis catarrhalis in medium degree, with massive desquamated epithelial cells and some catarrhalic masses on the mucous surfaces. Considerable congestion, slight edematous swelling and slight hyperplasia of lymphnodulus with some increased (and swollen) reticulum cells and considerable congestion of nodulus-capillaries.

Slight congestion (bacterial masses in capillaries) of submucous tissues.

S-4.

Duodoanl parts.

Slight hypersecretion and slight congestion.

387

S-5.

Slight congestion and slight edematous swelling of mucous tissues.

S-6.

missed.

S-7.

Enteritis catarrhalis in medium degree with remarkable desquamated epithelial cells and some catarrhalic masses. Slight congestion and slight reactive hyperplasia of lymphnodulus with some increased (and more or less swollen) reticulum cells.

Slight congestion (bacterial masses in capillaries) in submucous tissues and subserous tissues.

S-8.

Enteritis catarrhalis in medium degree with some desquamated epithelial cells and some catarrhalic masses on the mucous surface. Slight congestion and slight hyperplasia of lymphnodulus with some increased reticulum cells.

S-9.

Enteritis catarrhalis in medium degree with remarkable catarrhalic masses. Remarkable hypersecretion and slight congestion.

S-IO.

missed.

S-II.

Some desquamated epithelial cells and slight hypersecretion of glandular cells. Considerable congestion and slight hemorrhages in mucous tissues.

388

S-II.

Duodenal parts. Slight hypersecretion, considerable congestion and some localised hemorrhages in mucous tissues and considerable congestion in submucous tissues.

S-I2.

Enteritis catarrhalis in medium degree with remarkable hypersecretion of glandular cells and considerable congestion with slight edematous swelling of mucous tissues. Bacterial masses in capillaries. Slight hyperplasia of lymphnodulus with some increased reticulum cells and considerable congestion of submucous tissues.

S-I4.

Considerable congestion (with some leucocytes as capillaries-contents), considerable swelling of mucous tissues and slight congestion of submucous tiesues.

S-I5.

Slight Enteritis catarrhalis with some desquamated epithelial cells and catarrhalic masses on the mucous surface. Considerable congestion, considerable swelling and remarkable hyperplasia of lymphatic nodulus with remarkable congestion of nodulus-capillaries and remarkable increased germinative centers. Some leucocytes (esp. eosinophilic cells)-infiltration and at some places massive bacterial accumulations in lymphatic nodulus, esp. in germinative centers, which fall into bionecrosis, at some places due to bacterial dissemination.

Slight congestion and slight round cell infiltration in submucous tissues.

389

S-I9.

Slight hypersecretion with some desquamated epithelial cells and some catarrhalic masses. Slight edematous swelling and slight round-cell-infiltration in mucous tissues with rather atrophic glandular cells. Remarkable hyperplasia of lymphatic nodulus with slight congestion of nodulus-capillaries (some bacterial masses and some leucoytes as capillaries-contents).

S-22.

Enteritis catarrhalis in medium degree with considerable hypersecretion (some desquamated epitheial cells and some catarrhalic masses). Considerable congestion and slightly increased histiocytes and other proliferative cells (fibroplastic) in mucous tissues (rather cirrhotic).

Considerable reactive hyperplasia of lymphatic nodulus with considerable hyperplasia of germinative centers (more or less remarkable hyperplasia of reticulum cells, in somewhat edematous swelling and some lymphocytes and a little leucocytes).

Considerable congestion and remarkable hyperplasia of endothelial cells of blood-and lymph-capillaries. Remarkable hyalinous swelling (and thickening) of blood-vessels-walls and slight hyperplasia of connective tissues in mucous tissues.

Slight congestion and slight roun-cells (histiocytes and lymphocytes) -infiltration in submucous tissues.

S-26.

Enteritis catarrhalis in slight degree. Considerable hypersecretion, considerable congestion and slight edematous swelling of

390

mucous tissues.

S-28-

Slight hypersecretion, slight congestion and slight swelling of mucous tissues.

S-38.

Slight edematous swelling and slight congestion of muocus tissues with slight congestion of submucous tissues. Slight hyperplasia of lymphatic nodulus without any congestion.

No remarkable changes else.

391

(B) S U M M A R Y .

(I)

The bird's-eye views of all investigated cases.

I. Almost nornal.

2. Considerable hypersecretion.

3. Slight congestion with some bacterial masses in perifollicular capillaries.

4. Slight hyperplasia of lymph-nodulus.

5. Catarrh, slight hyperplasia of lymph-nodulus.

6. Almost normal.

7. Almost normal.

8. Almost normal.

9. Considerable congestion (with some leucocytes as capillary contents) in follicular and submucous capillaries.
Slight hyperplaisa of lymph-nodulus.

I0. Considerable congestion and slight hyperplaisa of lymphnodulus.

II. Considerable hypersecretion and considerable hyperplasia of lymph-nodulus (some increased reticulum cells), with perifollicular congestion

I2. Catarrh, considerable hyperplasia of lymph-nodulus (with some increased reticulum cells).

I4. Almost normal.

I5. Almost normal.

I6. Considerable congestion.

392

I7. Considerable congestion.

I8. Considerable hypersecretion and considerable congestion with some localised hemorrhages in submucous tissues.

I9.

Considerable congestion.

20. Almost normal.

2I. Almost normal, rather atrophic glandular cells.

23. Almost normal.

24. Almost normal.

26. Almost normal.

29. Considerable hypersecretion, Slight congestion (with some bacterial masses as capillaries contensts) in submucous tissues. Considerable hyperplasia of lymph-nodulus.

30. Enteritis follicularis.

3I. Slight hyperplasia of lymph-nodulus.

32. Considerable congestion with some leucocytes and some bacterial masses as capillaries contents.

33. Missed.

24. Slight congestion and slight perivascular round-cell-accumulation.

35. Almost normal.

36. Slight hyperplasia of lymph-nodulus.

42. Considerable hypersecretion, slight hyperplasia of lymph-nodulus with congested follicular capillaries. Considerable congestion in submucous tissues.

393

46. Almost normal.

49. Almost normal.

The bird's-eye views of all investigated cases.

S-I. Missed.

S-2. Considerable catarrh.

Considerable congestion and swelling of mucous tissues with

Considerable hyperplasia of lymph-nodulus with

remarkable congested follicular capillaries,

some hemorrhages, some bacterial masses-dissemination,

and some reactive increased reticulum cells in intense

cloudy swelling.

Considerable congestion, some perivascular bacterial accumulation and some increased histiocytes in submucous tissues.

S-3. Rather atrophic glandular cells.

Remarkable (congenital) hyperplasia of lymph-nodulus,

S-4. Considerable catarrh. Considerable congestion and slight hyperplasia of lymph-nodulus with some reactive increased reticulum cells in germinative centers and some congested follicular capillaries.

S-4. Duodenal parts: almost normal.

S-5. Almost normal.

S-6. Considerable catrarrh.

Slight congestion and slight reactive hyperplasia of lymphnodulus with some increased reticulum cells and congested follicular capillaries in mucous tissues.

395

Slight congestion (with some bacterial masses in capillaries) in submucous tissues.

S-8. Considerable catarrh and slight hyperplasia of lymph-nodulus with some reactive increased reticulum cells.

S-9. Considerable catarrh.

S-I0. Missed.

S-II. Considerable catarrh.

Considerable congestion, slight hemorrhages in mucous tissues.

Considerable congestion in submucous tissues.

S-I2. Considerable catarrh. Considerable congestion and some bacterial accumulation in mucous tissues and considerable congestion in submucous tissues.

Slight hyperplasia of lymph-nodulus (congenital).

S-I4. Considerable congestion (with some leucocytes as capillaries contents) in mucous tissues.

S-I5. Considerable catarrh. Considerable congestion of mucous capillaries.

Remarkable hyperplasia of lymph-nodulus with some reactive increase of reticulum cells, which fall into bionecrosis at some places, and some leucocytes and some bacterial masses-dissemination in follicular tissues.

Slight round-cell-infiltration in submucous tissues.

S-I9. Atrophic glandular cells. Slight round-cell-infiltration in mucous tissues.

396

S-22. Catarrh.

Considerable congestion and some histiocytes and fibroplasia in mucous tissues (rather scirrhous).

Condiderable hyperplasia of lymph-nodulus with reactive increased germinative centers and some lymphocytes and a little leucocytes in follicular tissues.

Considerable congestion and considerable increase of capillar endothel cells. Hyaline swelling or thickening of capillar walls.

Slight congestion and slight round-cell-dissemination in submucous tissues.

S-26. Considerable catrrh and considerable congestion in mucous tissues.

S-28. Almost normal.

S-?8. Almost mormal.

397

(2)

Frequency of pathological changes.

a) Plague-infection cause sometimes some reactive congestion in mucous or submucous tissues.

	S-District.	N-district.	total
Considerable congestion.	4 cases	5 cases	9 cases
", accompanied with some leucocytes in capillaries.	I	I	2
", accompanied with some bact. masses in capillaries.	2	3	5
", accompanied with some localised hemorrhages.	I	I	2.
with no remarkable congestion.	IO	27	37
total cases	I3	37	55

b) Plague-infection cause also sometimes some disturbances in lymph-nodulus.

	S-district	N-district	total
Slight hyperplasia of lymph-nodulus.	0 case	3 cases.	3 cases
(without any capillar congestion etc).			
Considerable follicular congestion.	I	2	3

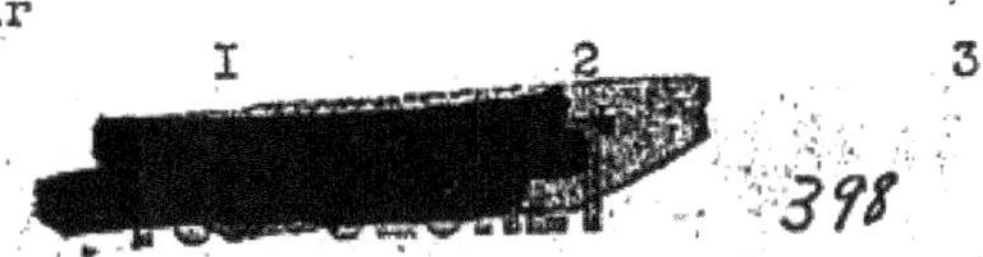

398

Follicular congestion and slight increase of reticulum cells.	I cases	0 cases	I cases
Follicular congestion with some leucocytes in capillaries and bionecrotic swelling of reticulum cells.	I	0	I
Slight hyperplasia of lymph-nodulus with some increased reticulum cells.	2	2	4
Considerable hyperplasia of capillary endothel-cells (chronic cases, 2I days).	I	0	I
Without any considerable hyperplasia of lymph-nods.	II	28	39
total cases	I6	37	55

(7)

Developing mechanismus of pathological changes.

Accordingly the general sketch of proceeding mechanismus of main pathological changes are as following:

a) At first to lymph-follicular tissues:

Plague-infection	Lymph-nodulus	
55 cases	without remarkable changes.	39 cases
	Slight follicular hyperplasia.	10 cases
	Follicular congestion.	3 cases

399

Acute Stage.	Folliculitis haemorrhagica.	
		I cases
	Folliculitis bio-necroticans.	I cases
Subacute Stage.	Some inflammatory reticulo-endotheliose. (2I-days)	I cases

b) Then occured the affection of mucous or submucous tissues.

Plague-infection ------	Mucous or submucous tissues.	
55 cases.	With no remarkable changes.	37 cases
Acute Stage.	With considerable capillary congestion, accompanied with some leucocytes or bacterial masses in capillaries.	I6 cases
	With some localised hemorrhages.	2 cases
Subacute Stage.	Considerable hyperplasia of capillary endothelial cells or histiocytes in submucous of mucous tissues. (2I days case).	I case

400

LARGE INTESTINE

(a) Microscop. Investigation.

I.

Almost normal, slight swelling of mucous tissues and rather atrophic glandular cells.

2.

Colitis catarrhalis in severe degree with massive desquamated epithelial cells and some catarrhalic masses. Remarkable congestion and round cells (plasma-cells, lymphocytes and some eosinophilic leucocytes) increase in mucous tissues. Extremely severe congestion and diffuse remarkable hemorrhages in subserous tissues and edematous swelling (with some bacterial masses) in subserous tissues.

3.

Colitis catarrhalis in medium degree with some desquamated epithelial cells and some catarrhalic masses on the mucous surface. Considerable congestion, slight edematous swelling and round-cells (lymphocytes and plasma cells) increase in mucous tissues.

Slight reactive hyperplasia of lymph-nodulus and considerable congestion of nodulus-capillaries.

4.

Slight submucous congestion and slight hyperplasia of lymph-nodulus. No remarkable changes else.

5.

Slight hypersecretion with some desquamated epithelial cells and some catarrhalic masses on the mucous surface. Slight congestion, slight edematous swelling and slight hyperplasia of lymph-nodulus with slight

401

congestion of nodulus-capillaries.

6.

Almost normal.

7.

Slight congestion, slight edematous swelling and slight hyperplasia of lymph-nodulus with reactive hyperplasia of germinative centres (swollen reticulum-cells and reticulum-fibres).

8.

Slight congestion and slight edematous swelling of mucous tissues.

9.

Colitis catarrhalis in medium degree with some desquamated epithelial cells and some catarrhlic masses on the mucous surface.

Considerable congestion and considerable edmeatous swelling of mucous tissues and considerable congestion of submucous tissues.

IO.

Slight congestion and slight edematous swelling of mucous tissues.

Considerable hypersecretion with some desquamated epithelial cells and some catarrhalic masses.

II. Almost normal.

I2.

Slight hypersecretion with some desquamated epithel. cells and some catarrhalic masses, and considerable congestion of mucous tissues.

Considerable hyperplasia of lymph-nodulus with remarkable congestion of nodulus-capillaries and partial miliary perivascular hemorrhages.

Considerable congestion and multiple miliary hemorrhages in submucous tissues and intermuscular tissues.

402

I4.

Slight submucous congestion and rather atrophic, hypoplastic glandular cells.

I5.

Colitis catrarrhlis with some desquamated epithel. cells and slight congestion of mucous tissues.

I6.

Slight edematous swelling and slight congestion of mucous tissues and rather atrophic glandular cells.

I7.

Slight edematous swelling and slight congestion of mucous tissues with atrophic glandular cells. Slight round-cell-infiltration in submucous tissues.

I8.

Slight hypersecretion with some desquamated epithel. cells and some catarrhalic masses and slight congestion with at some places localised miliary hemorrhages. Considerable congestion in submucous tissues.

I9.

Colitis catarrhalis hypertrophicans with considerable hypersecretion, considerable hypertrophia of glandular cells and considerable congestion in mucous tissues. Considerable congestion of nodulus-capillaries and submucous tissues.

20.

Almost normal, slight edema and slight congestion in mucous tissues.

2I.

Considerable congestion, slight edema and slight hyperplasia of

403

lymph-nodulus with considerable congestion of nodulus-capillaries. Considerable congestion of submucous tissues.

23.

Colitis catarrhalis in medium degree. Slight congestion and slight edema of mucous tissues.

24.

Almost normal, slight congestion and slight hyperplasia of lymph-nodulus with some swollen reticulum-fibres and reticulum-cells.

No remarkable changes else.

26.

Colitis catarrhalis with some desquamated epithel. cells and some catarrhalic masses. Considerable congestion in mucous tissues.

27.

Slight congestion and slight edema of mucous tissues and considerable congestion of submucous tissues.

29.

Almost normal, slight edema in mucous tissues.

30.

Almost nornal, slight congestion of mucous tissues.

3I.

Slight edema, slight congestion and rather atrophic glandular cells.

32.

Colitis catarrhalis in medium degree with some desquamated cells and catarrhalic masses on the mucous surface. Considerable congestion in submucous tissues.

33.

Colitis catarrhalis in medium degree with hypersecretion of glandular cells and considerable congestion with considerable edematous swelling of mucous tissues.

Considerable congestion and slight partial hemorrhages in submucous tissues.

33. (b)

Colitis catarrhalis in meduim degree with remarkable hypersecretion of glandular cells, remarkable congestion and slight edematous swelling of mucous tissues.

Remarkable congestion and remarkable diffuse hemorrhages in subserous tissues.

34.

Considerable congestion, considerable edema slight hypersecretion of glandular cells and round-cell-increase in mucous tissues with slight hyperplasia of lymph-nodulus, considerable congestion of nodulus-capillaries and slight hyperplasia and edematous swelling of reticulem-fibres and reticulum-cells.

35.

missed.

36.

Slight hypersecretion, considerable edematous swelling and round-cells-increase in mucous tissues and considerable congestion in submucous tissues.

38.

Slight congestion, slight edematous swelling and slight hypersecretion of glandular cells in mucous tissues. Considerable congestion with partial hemorrhages and slight perivascular round-cell-infiltration in

405

submucous tissues.

40.

Slight congestion and slight hypersecretion of mucous tissues with slight congestion in submucous tissues. Slight hyperplasia of lymph-nodulus with some swellen reticulum-cells.

42.

Considerable congestion, slight edematous swelling, slight hyper-secretion of glandular cells and slight hyperplasia of lymph-nodulus with remarkable congestion (bacterial masses in nodulus-capillaries) of nodulus-capillaries.

Remarkable congestion of submucous tissues.

44.

Almost normal and slight hypersecretion of glandular cells.

46.

Rather atrophic glandular cells and slight edematous swelling of mucous tissues.

47.

Slight hypersecretion of glandular cells, slight congestion and slight edematous swelling of mucous tissues

49. Missed.

406

S-I.

Very slight stasis and rather atrophic glandular cells with some desquamated epithel. cells on the mucous surface. Slightly increased round-cells in mucous tissues and considerable hyperplasia of lymphatic nodulus with slightly increased germinative centres.

S-2.

Colitis catarrhalis.

Considerable catarrh with some desquamted epithel. cells and catarrhalic masses on the mucous surface. Considerable stasis and slight hyperplasia of lymphatic nodulus with more or less reactive increased germinative centres (containing more or less swollen reticulum-cells and reticulum-fibres).

Considerable congestion in submucous tissues.

S-3.

Slight hypersecretion of glandular cells with some desquamated epithelcells and some mucous masses.

Considerable congestion in submucous tissues.

S-4.

Colitis catarrhalis levis. Considerable hypersecretion of glandular cells with some desquamated epithelial cells and catarrhalic masses on the mucous surface. Slightly increased round-cells in mucous tissues. Slight submucous congestion.

S-5.

Colitis catarrhalis levis. Slight hypersecretion of glandular cells. Considerable congestion and considerable edematous swelling and increased round cell (containing ~~some leucocytes, esp.~~ some eosiniphilic

1407

leucocytes)-infiltration in mucous tissues.

Considerable congestion and considerable perivasular leucocytes and round cell infiltration in submucous tissues with more or less remarkable swelling of Muscularis mucosa.

S-6.

Colitis catarrhalis levis. Some desquamated epithel. cells and catarrhalic masses on the mucous surface. Increased round cells in mucous tissues.

S-8.

Almost normal, slight congestion.

S-9.

Colitis catarrhalis levis. Remarkable hypersecretion of glandular cells with some desquamated epithel. cells and more or less slightly increased lymphatic nodulus (considerable congestion of nodulus-capillaries). Slight congestion in mucous tissues.

S-I0.

missed.

S-II.

Almost normal.

S-I2.

Colitis catarrhalis levis with slight hypersecretion of glandular cells and considerable congestion (some bacterial masses in capillaries) with slight hyperplasia of lymphatic nodulus.

S-I5.

Colitis catarrhalis. Considerable hypersecretion of glandular cells with some desquamated epithel-cells and catarrhalic masses on the mucous surface.

408

S-I9.

Almost normal.

S-22.

Colitis catarrhalis. Considerable hypersecretion of glandular cells with some desquamated epithel. cells and catarrhalice masses on the mucous surface. Considerable increased round cells, some histiocytes and some leucocytes in mucous tissues (rather scirrhous).

Considerable congestion and slightly hyalinously degenerated blood-and lymphocapillaries walls.

Slight hyperplasia of lymphatic nodulus with more or less increased histiocytes in germinative centres.

Considerable congestion and more or less hyalinously degenerative thickening of blood-vessels-walls in submucous tissues.

S-26.

Considerable congestion and slight hypersecretion of glandular cells with more or less increased round cells in mucous tissues.

S-28.

Considerable congestion and slight hypersecretion of mucous glandular cells with some desquamated epithel. cells and some catarrhalic masses on the mucous surface. Considerable cloudy swelling of glandular cells.

S-38.

Almost normal.

409

SUMMARY.

(I)

The bird's-eye-views of all investigated cases.

I. Almost normal, rather atrophic glandular cells.

2. Colitis catarrhalis in remarkable degree with remarkable congestion and some round-cell-infiltration in submucous tissues and remarkable congestion (some bacterial masses and leucocytes in capillaries), and some hemorrhages in subserous tissues.

3. Colitis catarrhalis in medium degree.
Considerable congestion and slight round-cell-infiltration in submucous tissues and slight hyperplasia of lymph-nodulus with congested nodulus-capillaries.

4. Slight congestion and no remarkable changes else.

5. Slight catarrh. Slight congestion and slight hyperplasia of lymph-nodulus with slightly congested nodulus-capillaries.

6. Almost normal.

7. Slight congestion and slight hyperplasia of lymph-nodulus with some swollen germinative centres.

8. Slight congestion and no remarkable changes else.

9. Considerable catarrh and considerable congestion in submucous tissues.

IO. Slight congestion and slight hypersecretion.

II. Almost normal.

I2. Slight hypersecretion and considerable congestion in submucous tissues.
Considerable swelling of lymph-nodulus with remarkable congested nodulus-

410

capillaries and following some miliary hemorrhages.

Considerable congestion and some miliary hemorrhages in subserous tissues.

I4. Atrophic glandular cells.

I5. Slight catarrh.

I6. Atrophic glandular cells.

I7. Atrophic glandular cells, slight congestion.

I8. Slight hypersecretion.

Considerable congestion and some miliary hemorrhages in submucous tissues.

I9. Considerable catarrh and some considerable congestion in submucous tissues.

20. Almost normal.

2I. Considerable congestion and slight hyperplasia of lymph-nodulus with considerable congested nodulus-capillaries.

23. Considerable catarrh.

24. Almost normal, slight hyperplasia of lymph-nodulus.

25. Catarrh. Considerable congestion.

27. Considerable congestion in submucous tissues.

29. Almost normal.

30. Almost normal.

3I. Almost normal and atrophic glandular cells.

32. Considerable catarrh and considerable congestion.

33. Considerable catarrh and congestion of submucous tissues.

Remarkable congestion and some diffuse hemorrhages in subserous tissues.

34. Considerable congestion and slight hyperplasia of lymph-nodulus with considerable congested nodulus-capillaries.

36. Slight hypersecretion and consid. congestion.

38. Considerable congestion, some localised hemorrhages and slight

411

round-cell-infiltration in submucous tissues.

40. Slight congestion and no remarkable changes else.

42. Considerable congestion and slight hyperplasia of lymph-nodulus with remarkable congested nodulus-capillaries.

Remarkable congestion in subserous tissues.

44. Almost normal.

46. Rather atrophic glandular cells.

47. Slight hypersecretion and slight congestion.

S-I. Rather atrophic glandular cells.

Considerable hyperplasia of lymph-nodulus with some reactive increased reticulum-cells.

S-2. Catarrh, considerable congestion and slight hyperplasia of lymph-nodulus with some reactive increased reticulum-cells.

S-3. Considerable congestion.

S-4. Catarrh in slight degree and slight round-cell-infiltration in submucous tissues.

S-5. Slight catarrh, considerable congestion, swelling and some round cell (containing some leucocytes, esp. eosinophilic cells) infiltration in submucous tissues.

Remarkable swelling of Muscularis mucosae.

S-6. Slight catarrh and some increased round-cell-dissemination in mucous tissues, due to catarrhalic changes.

S-8. Almost normal.

S-9- Considerable catarrh and slight hyperplasia of lymph-nodulus with some congested capillaries.

412

S-I0. Missed.

S-II- Almost normal.

S-I2. Catarrh. Considerable congestion (with some bacterial and leucocytic masses as capillaries contents) and slight hyperplaisia of lymph-nodulus in submucous tissues.

S-I5. Catarrh.

S-I9. Almost normal.

S-22- Catarrh.

Considerable congestion and considerable round-cell (with some histiocytes and some leucocytes)-dissemination in mucous and submucous tissues. Hyalinous swelling or degeneration of capillary walls.

Slight hyperplasia of lymph-nodulus with considerably increased reticulum-cells in germinative centres.

S-26. Considerable congestion and some round-cell-dissemination in mucous tissues.

S-28. Considerable congestion.

S-38. Almost normal.

---

(2)

a) Plague-infection cause sometimes considerable congestion and following disturbances in mucous or submucous tissues:

S-district N-district total.

413

Considerable congestion (sometimes accompanied with some leucocytes or bacterial masses in capillaries).	4 cases	I2 cases	I6 cases
Considerable congestion and some round-cell-infiltration. (sometimes, leucocytes).	I	2	3
Considerable congestion and some localised hemorrhages.	0	3	3
Considerable hyperplasia of histiocytes (chronic case).	I	0	I
With no remarkable changes.	I2	20	32
total cases.	I8	37	55

b) In lymph-nodulus, some changes around follicular capillaries :

with simple hyperpsia of lymph-nodulus. (slight increase of reticulum cells).	I	I	2
", accompanied with follicular congestion.	I	2	3
", accompanied with follicular hemorrhages.	0	I	I
Considerable hyperplasia of reticulam-cells (chronic case).	I	0	I
With no remarkable changes.	I5	33	48
total cases.	I8	37	55

414

General sketch of proceeding mechanismus of main pathological changes are as follows:

a) In mucous or submucous tissues:

Plague-infection ----------	Septicaemie metasis in capillaries in mucous or submucous tissues.	
	Considerable congestion, accompanied with some leucocytes or bacterial masses in capillaries.	I6 cases.
	Multiple localised hemorrhages.	3 cases.
	Some round-cell-infiltration	3 cases.

	Considerable hyperplasia of capillary endothel cells or histiocytes. (chronic case)	I case.

415

Hemorrhages in Peyer's lymphatic nodulus.

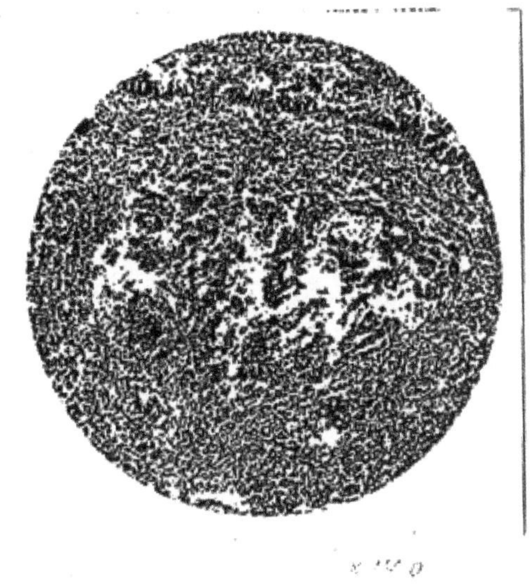

Bacterial accumulation and some necrotic changes in Peyer's lymphatic nodulus.

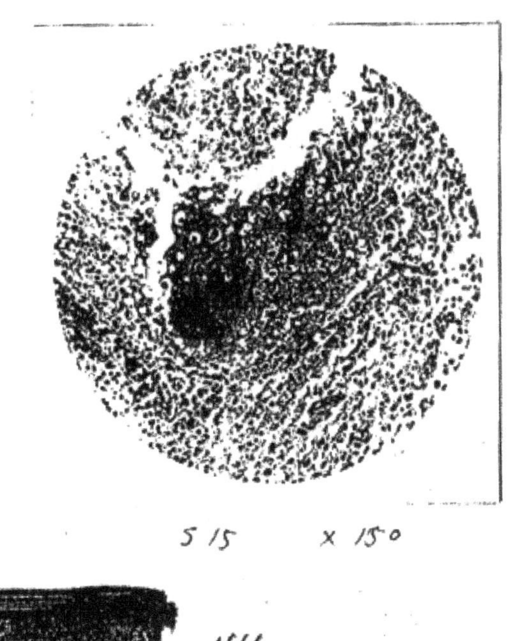

515 x 150

416

Bacterial accumulation and
some hemorrhages in T.propria.

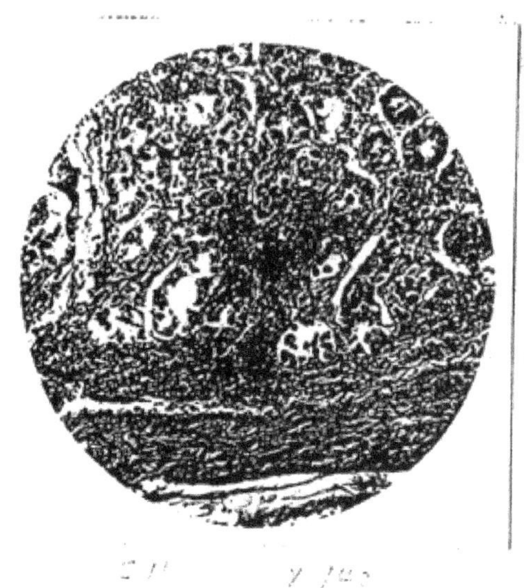

Bacterial accumulation and
some hemorrhages in T.propria.

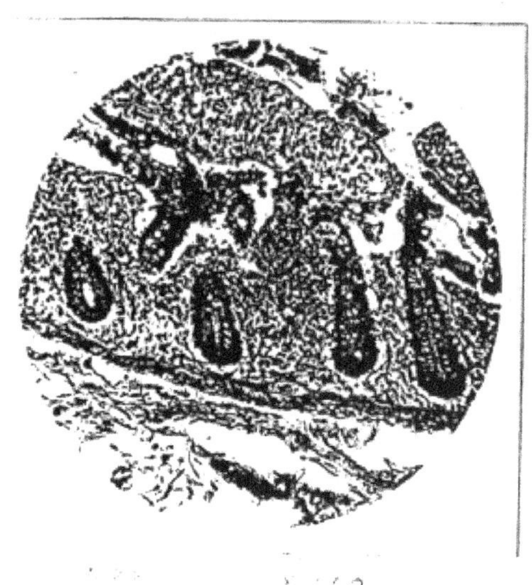

417

Some hemorrhagic leucocytic
places in mucous membrane.

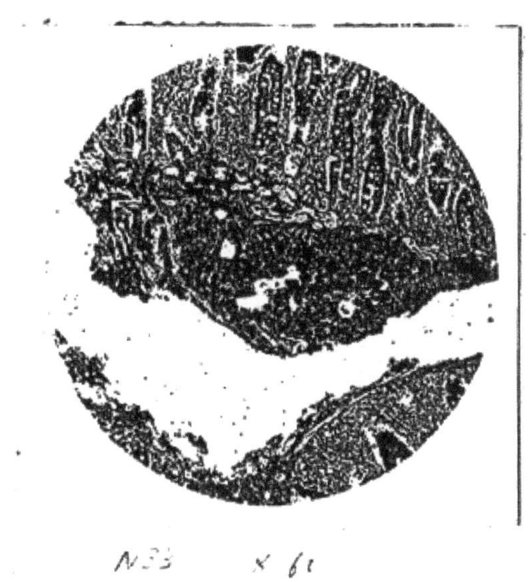

N33 × 61

Some hemorrhagic leucocytic
places in intermuscular tissues.

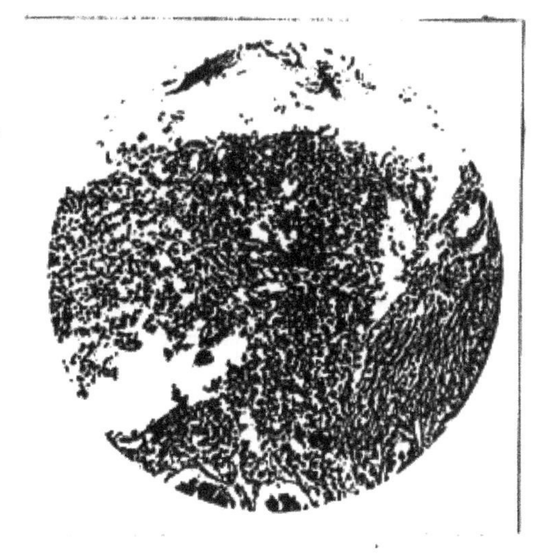

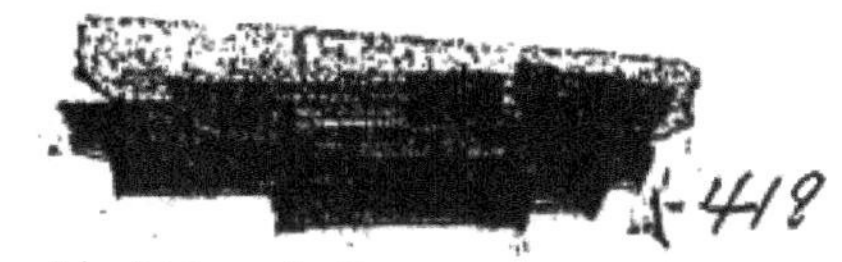

Spleen

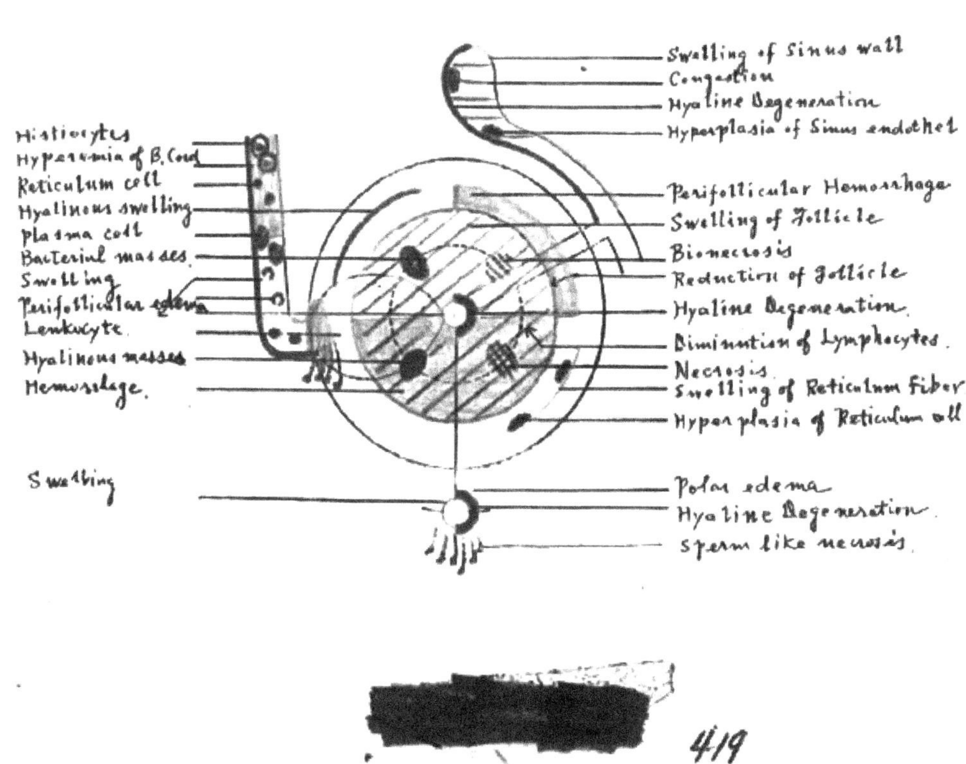
Histiocytes
Hyperaemia of B. Cord
Reticulum cell
Hyalinous swelling
plasma cell
Bacterial masses
Swelling
Perifollicular edema
Leukocyte
Hyalinous masses
Hemorrhage
Swelling
Swelling of Sinus wall
Congestion
Hyaline Degeneration
Hyperplasia of Sinus endothel
Perifollicular Hemorrhage
Swelling of Follicle
Bionecrosis
Reduction of Follicle
Hyaline Degeneration
Diminution of Lymphocytes
Necrosis
Swelling of Reticulum fiber
Hyperplasia of Reticulum cell
Polar edema
Hyaline Degeneration
sperm like necrosis

419

S P L E E N.

(A) Microscop. Investigation.

I.

1

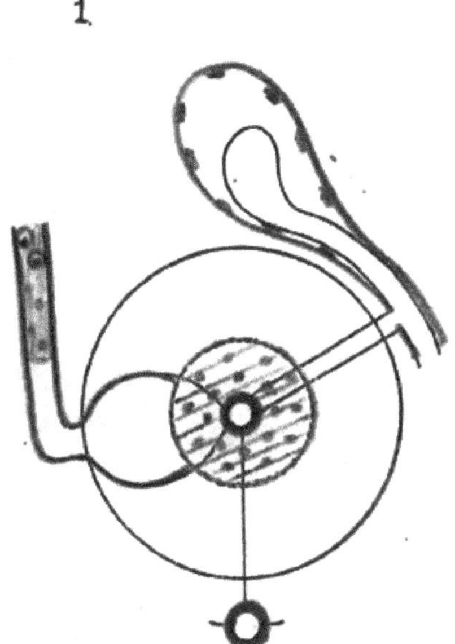

In follicles : swelling and hyaline degeneration of central artery-walls and slight edema with slight serous fluids in follicular tissues. Very slight increase of reticulum-cells.

In perifollicular portions : some increased reticulum-cells or some plasma-cells. Swelling and hyalinisation of penicillar artery-walls.

In sinuses : rather anemic and slight ectasia, accompnaied with some increased sinus endotheli al cells.

In fascicular cords : rich in reticulum-cells (and some splenocytes), with some leakage of erythrocytes.

2.

In follicles : Hyaline degeneration and some edematous swelling of central artery-walls.

Some peri-arterial edema and more or less remarkable hyaline degeneration of reticulum-fibres in follicular tissues.

Some peri-arterial edema and slight hemorrhages, accompanied with some hayline degeneration of reticulum-fibres and some karyorrhextic

420

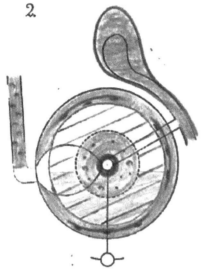

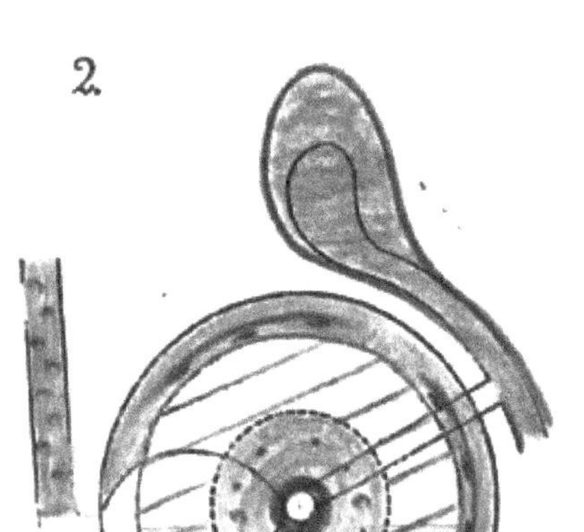

masses-accumulations.

In perifollicular portions : remarkable congestion and remarkable hemorrhages at perifollicular portions.

Hyalinisation of penicillar artery-walls.

In sinuses : remarkable congestion and edematous swelling of sinus walls and reticulum-fibres in fascicular tissues.

In fascicular cords : many leucocytes and myelocytes as exudative changes.

Degeneration and diminution of splenocytes and faciculer lymphocytes.

3.

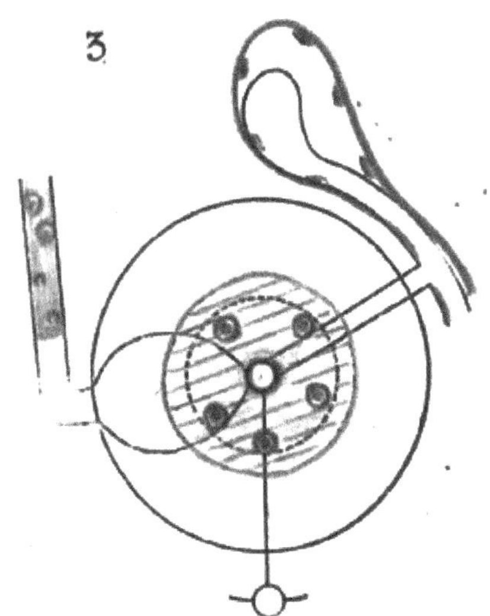

In follicles : Hyaline degeneration and slight edematous roughness of central artery-walls.

Slight edema and slight diminution of follicular lymphocytes and some slightly increases Reticulum-cells (most of them, in macor phagen-farm).

Hyalinisation of penicillar artery-walls.

In sinuses : rather anemic and slight ectasia, accompanied with some hyperplasia of sinus-endothelial cells and slight hyalinisation of sinus walls and reticulum-fibres in fascicular tissues.

4

In fascicular cords : some lymphocytes and degenerated reticulum-cells and a little other cells. Swelling of reticulum-fibres.

4.

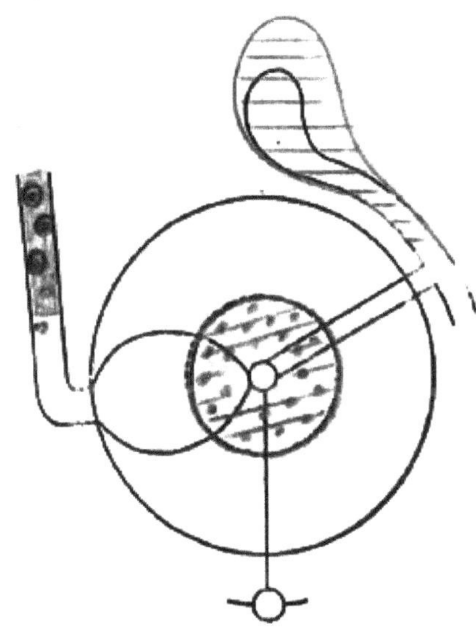

In follicles : swelling, roughness and some hyalinisation of central artery-walls. Slight edema, slight diminution of lymphocytes, some reticulum-cells(not swollen) and slight increased macrophagens. (pleticulum-cells, in macrophagen-form). swelling and roughness of panicillar artery-walls.

In sinuses : considerable congestion and some considerable swelling of sinus walls and reticulum-fibres in fascicular tissues.

In fascicular cords : Swelling of reticulum-fibres with some leucocytes and a few myelocytes. Some cloudy degenerated reticulum-cells.

5.

Intense reduction of follicles. Hyalinisation and more or less remarkable edematous swelling of central artery-walls.

422

5.

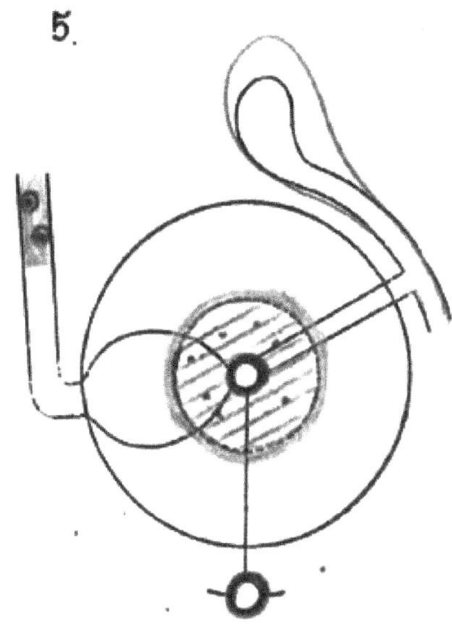

Partial edema (edematous swelling of basal tissues) and some or slight hemorrhages in follicular tissues. Diminution or some pyconotic changes of follicular lymphcocytes. Hyaline degeneration of penicillar artery-walls with some perifollicular edema and some perifollicular congestion or hemorrhages.

In sinuses : rather anemic and intensively exsudative with bionecrotic swelling of sinus walls and reticulum-fibres all over the fascicular tissues, due to some bacterial dissemination all over the fascicular tissues.

In fascicular cords : intensively exudative with some degenerated reticulum-cells (some of them in erythrophagy and some of them in intensely cloudy swelling or vacuolar degeneration) and more or less remarkable diminution of fascicular lymphocytes.

7.

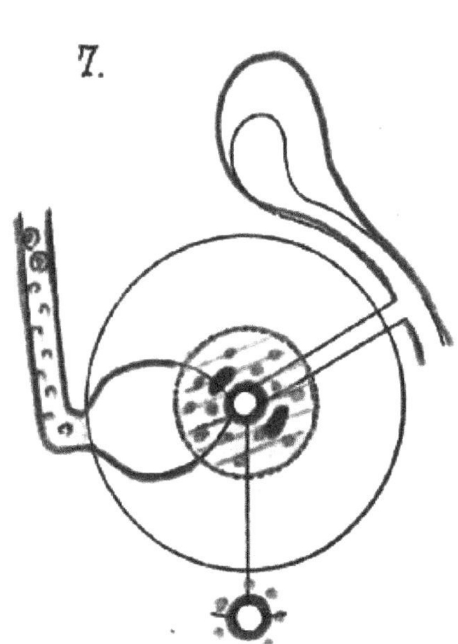

7.

Intense reduction of follicles and some hyaline degeneration or somewhat edematous swelling of central artery-walls.

Slight partial edema and slight diminution of follicular lymphocytes.

423

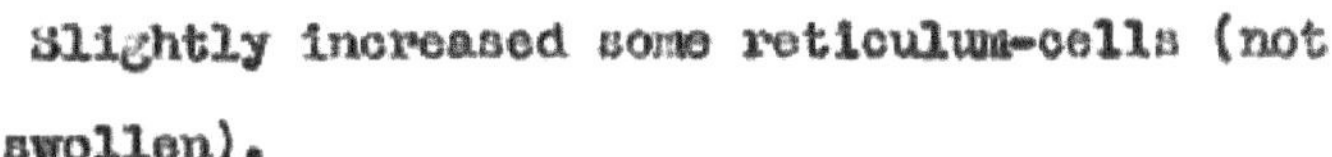

Slightly increased some reticulum-cells (not swollen).

In perifollicular tissues : Slight hyaline degeneration of penicillar artery-walls and some increased bright reticulum-cells at peripenicillar portions and accompanied with more or less remarkable perifollicular edematous swelling.

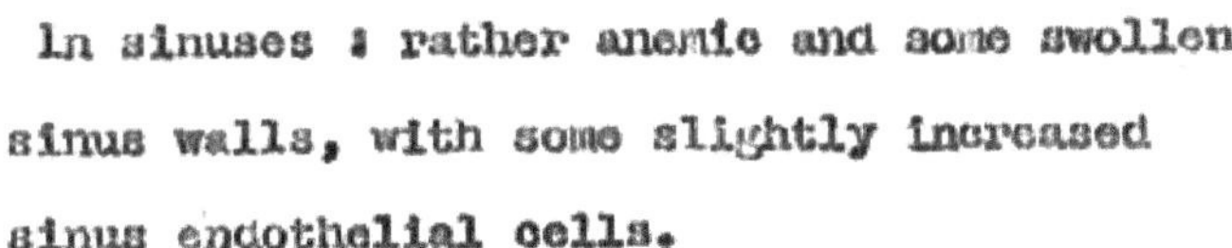

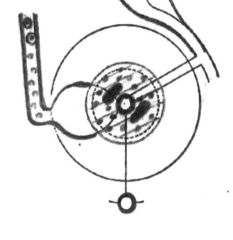

In sinuses : rather anemic and some swollen sinus walls, with some slightly increased sinus endothelial cells.

In fasciclar cords : many leucocytes and some myelocytes as esudative reactions. Some increased reticulum-cells in erythrophagy or intense cloudy swelling.

8.

Considerable reduction of follicles and intense hyalinisation and intense hyaline degeneration or edematous swelling of central artery-walls.

Some hyalinous masses accumulation at periarterial protions and slightly increased reticulum-cells.

424

In sinuses : rather anemic and swelling of sinus walls.

In fascicular cords : considerable swelling of reticular fibres and emigration of some leucocytes and some myelocytes, as exudative changes. Degenerated reticulum-cells and slight diminution of fascicular lymphocytes.

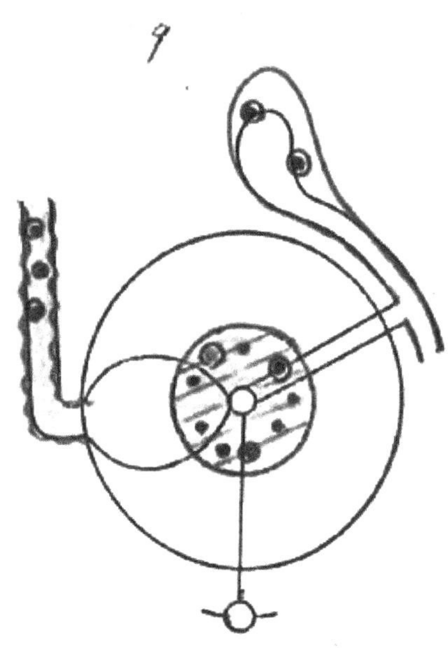

9.

Considerable reduction of follicles and slightly edematous swelling of central artery-walls.

Slight edema and some increased macrophagens in follicular tissues.

Slight edematous swelling of penicillar artery-walls with some perivascular (or peri-follicular) hyperplasia of reticulum-cells.

In sinuses : rather anemic and intense or bionecrotic swelling of sinus walls and reticulum-fibres in fascicular tissues, with a some bacterial dissemination all over the fascicular tissues.

Fascicular cords are generally poor in cellular elements.

Emigration of some leucocytes and some myelocytes, with some edematous swelling of

425

reticulum-fiber, as exudative changes.
More or less considerable hyperplasia and following degeneration of reticulum-cells (some of them in erythrophagy and some of them in intense degeneration). Intense diminution of fascicular lymphocytes.

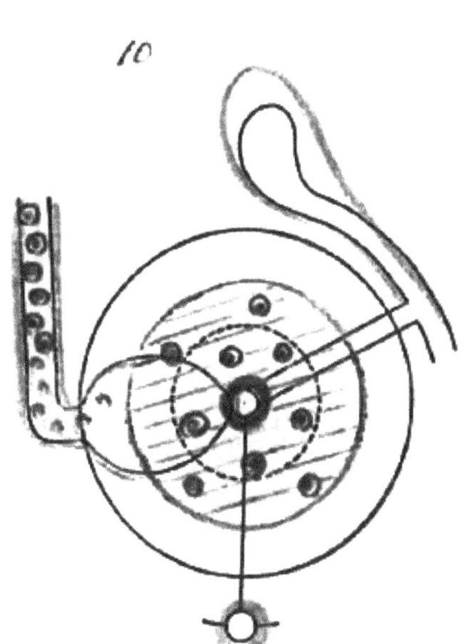

10.

Considerable reduction of follicles and hyaline degeneration or some edematous swelling of central·arterey-walls.

Considerable edema or some roughness, of basal tissues fibres in follicular tissues and some increased meticulum cells (in macrophagen-form).

Penicillary arteries with hyaline degeneration and some periarterial edematous swelling.

In sinuses : rather anemic with some or intense esudative changes, due to remarkable bacterial dissemination all over the fascicular tissues (bionecrotic swelling of sinus walls and reticulm-fibres).

In fascicular cords : with intense bionecrotic-esudative changes : emigration of some leucocytes and some myelocytes, with some bionecrotic swelling of reticulum-fibres.

426

11

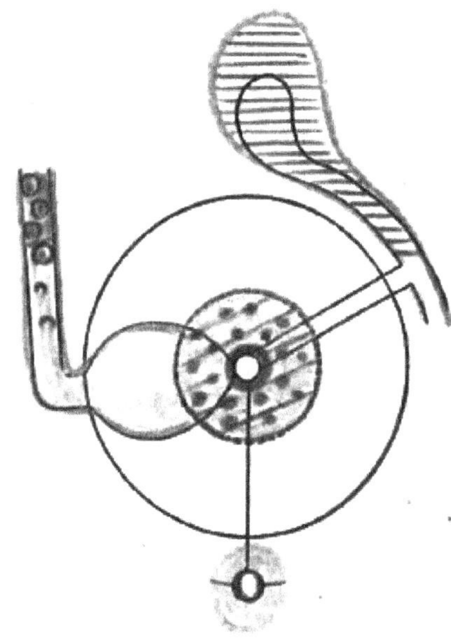

Reticulum-cells hyperplasied more or less remarkable, but fall into intensively cloudy swelling or vacuolar degeneration.

Some scattered plasma-cells.

11.

Intense reduction of follicles and slight hyaline degeneration or some edematous swelling of central artery-walls.

Slight edema (with some roughness of basal fibres in follicular tissues) and slight hemorrhages in follicular tissues.

In sinuses : with intense congestion with some edematous swelling of sinus walls.

In fascicular cords : with some exudative changes (some bacterial dissemination and intense edematous swelling of reticulum-fibres and emigration of some leucocytes and some myelocytes . Some degenerated lymphocytes.

12.

Considerable reduction of follicles and considerable hyaline degeneration or edematous swelling of central artery-walls.

427

12. Very slight edema in follicular tissues and some increased reticulum-cells in macrophagens -form.

In peri-follicular portions : edematous swelling of penicillar artery-walls and intense perifollicular (peri-vascular) edema with some serous fluids and some so-called sperma-like necrosis.

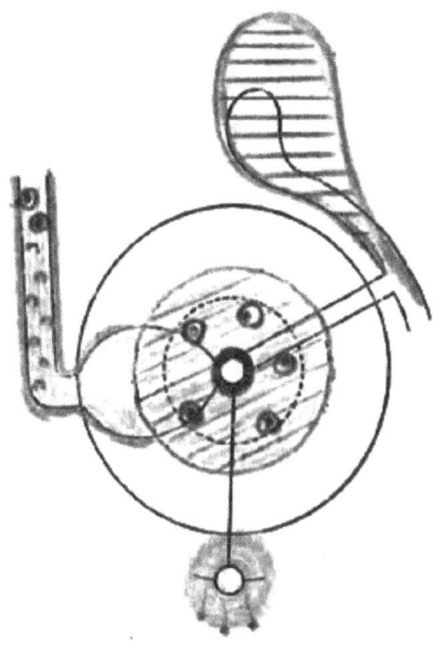

In sinuses : considerable congestion and considerable swelling of sinus walls and reticulum-fibres.

In fascicular cords ; with emigration of some leucocytes and a few myelocytes, and some bacterial dissemination all over the fascicular tissues.

Reticulum-cells hyperplasied slightly, but most of them fall into intense cloudy swelling or vacuolar degeneration.

13.

Intense reduction of follicles, and hyaline degeneration or some edematous swelling of central artery-walls.

Diffuse intense edema with cloudy or bionecrotically degenerated reticulum-cells or reticulum-fibres and some karyolytic masses in follicular tissues, accompanied with some

428

14

hemorrhages (at some places) and intense diminution of follicular lymphocytes.

In perifollicular tissues : with intense polar edema (intense edematous swelling of peri-penicillar arteries) and so-called sperma-like necrosis.

In sinuses : with considerable congestion and intense edematous swelling of sinus walls.

In fascicular cords : intense edematous swelling of reticulum-fibres with some sweous fluids and emigration of some leucocytes. Degenerated reticulum-cells and some karyorrhextic masses in fascicular tissues.

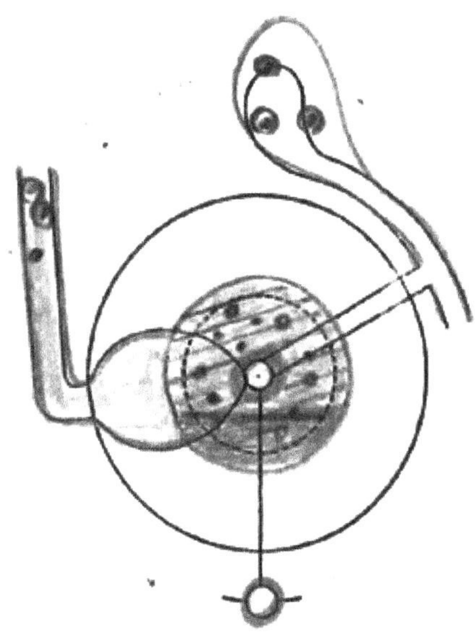

14.

Considerable reduction of follicles, and some edematous swelling of central artery-walls.

Very slight edematous swelling of basal fibres of follicular tissues and some increased reticulum-cells (not swollen). Slight hemorrhages at some places in follicular tissues.

Intense hyaline degeneration of penicillar artery-walls and somewhat edematously hyperplasied retiuclum-fibers.

439

In sinuses : slight and at some places considerable congestion with somewhat edematously swollen reticulum-fibres.

17 In fascicular cords : with some esudative changes (edematous swelling of reticulum-fibres) and emigration of some leucocytes and a few myelocytes.

Degenerated reticulum-cells.

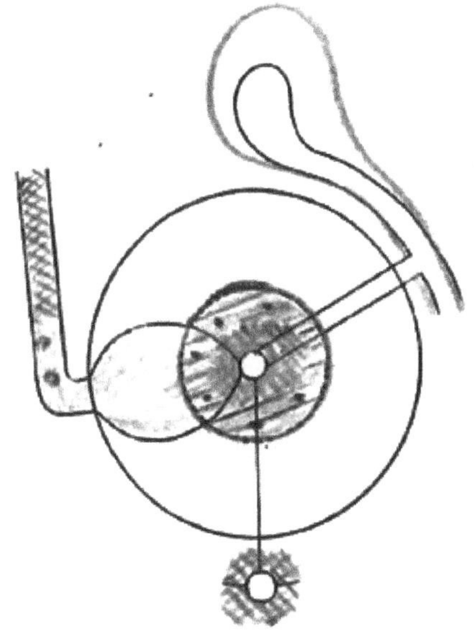

17.

In tense reduction of follicles and intense or bionecrotic swelling of central artery-wall.

Intense diffuse edematous swelling or bionecrotic changes all over the fascicular tissues with some bacterial accumulation and bionecrotic ruins of follicular cells (bionecrotic rouins of reticulum-cells and intense diminution of follicular lymphocytes).

At polar porttons : intense or bionecrotic swelling of penicillar artery-walls with intense peripenicillary edema (intense serous exudation).

and some bionecrotic changes.

430

In sinuses : rather anemic with intensively swellen reticulum-fibres and some bacterial didseminations.

18\. In fascicular cords : generally poor in cellular elements. Bionecrotic swelling of fascicular reticulum-fibres, intensively degenerated reticulum-cells and some leucocytes-emigration in fascicular tissues.

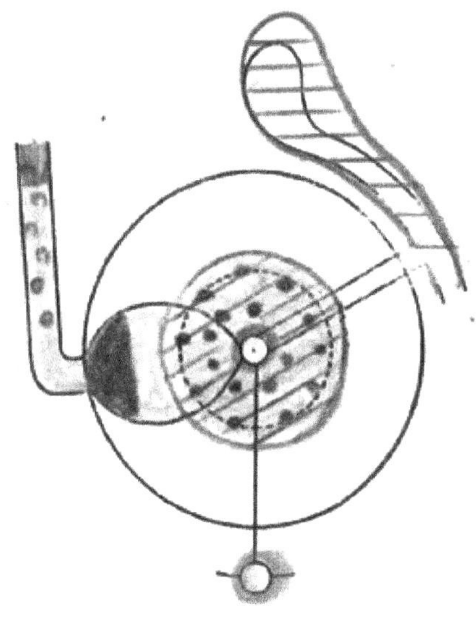

18\.

Considerable reduction of follicles and slight edematous swelling of central artery walls.

Slight swelling of basal fibres and some increased reticulum cells (not swollen).

Some edematous swelling of penicillar artery-walls.

In sinuses : considerable congestion and considerable edematous swelling of sinus walls and reticulum fibres in fascicular tissues.

In fascicular cords : plenty of bacterial dissemination all over the fascicular tissues and intense edematous swelling of fascicular reticulum-fibres. Some reticulum-cells in bacterial phagocytosis.

431

More or less remarkable emigration of leucocytes and some degenerated reticulum-cells.

19 Intense diminution of lymphocytes.

19.

Considerable reduction of follicles and some or slight edematous swelling of central artery-walls.

More or less remarkable increased reticulum-cells (and some histiocytes), with some hemorrhages and slight edematous swelling of basal fibres in follicular tissues.

Some roughness of penicillar artery-walls.

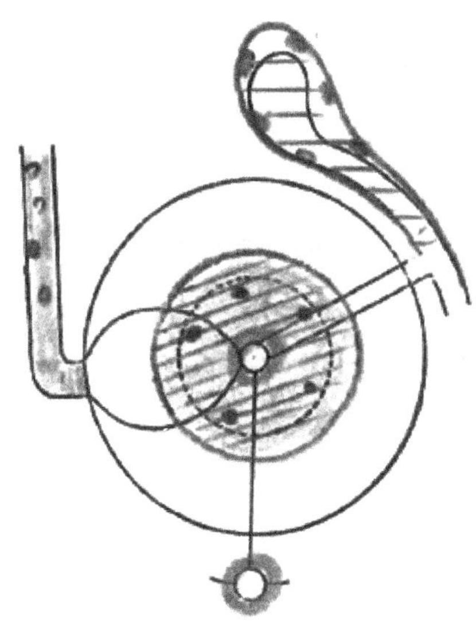

In sinuses : slight or at some places considerable congestion with some swollen reticulum-fibres and sinus walls. Some bacterial accumulation.

Slightly hyperplasied reticulum-fibres and reticulum cells. and some of them in bacterial phagocytosis.

In fascicular cords : some hyperplasia and swelling of reticulum-cells and reticulum-fibres. Slight emigration of leucocytes and some exudative changes (serous exudation).

20.

Intense reduction of follicles and intense edematous swelling of central artery-walls.

Intense diffuse edematous swelling of basal

432

20.

fibres and very slight hemorrhages in follicular tissues, with some increased reticulum-cells most of them in some macrophagen form.

Considerable diminution of follicular lymphocytes.

In perifollicular tissues : intense edematous swelling of penicillar artery walls and intense odematous swelling of periarterial tissues with some serous fluids.

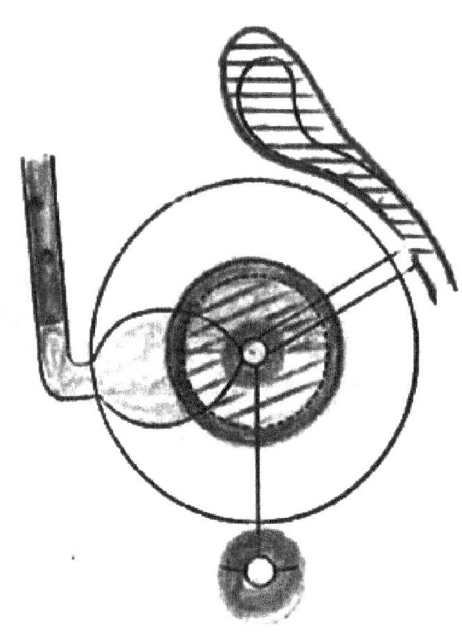

In sinuses : more or less considerable considarable congestion (esp. at perifollicular tissues) with some swollen reticulum fibres and sinus walls.

In fascicular cords : Intensively swollen reticulum-fibres and some degenerated reticulum cells.

At some places occured some supermiliary suppurative changes with plenty of leucocytes dissemination and decayed cellular masses or nuclear fragments-accumulation.

With hemorrhagic-exudative perifocal changes, not accompanied with proliferative hyperative hyperplasia of reticulum-fibres.

Many degenerated reticulum-cells,

433

21.

21

Considerable reduction of follicles and intense swelling or roughness of central artery-walls. Intense roughness of basal fibres and a few swollen retiuclum-cells (slight increase of reticulum-cells)

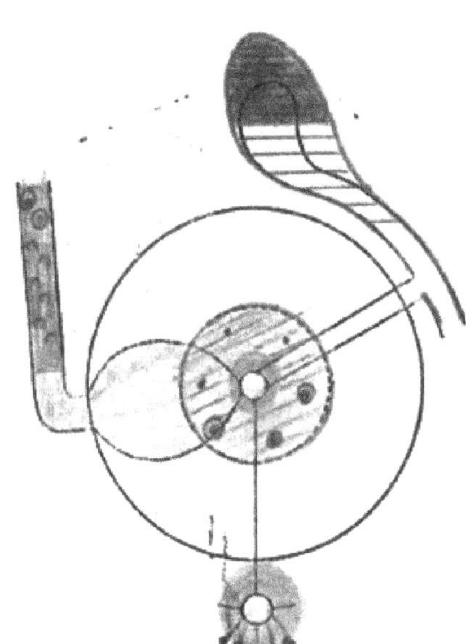

In perifollicular tissues : intense edematous swelling of penicillar artery walls with intense perifollicular edema and some sperma-like necrosis.

In sinuses : considerable congestion with considerable swelling of sinus walls and reticulum-fibres.

In fascicular cords : with some bacterial dissemination ell over the fascicular tissues and intense cloudy swelling or at some places bionecrotic changes of reticulum-fibres with some karyolytic masses.

Emigration of leucocytes, accompanied with intense degeneration or bionecrotic changes of reticulum-cells (with some karyolytic masses).

23.

Considerable reduction of follicles and intense edematous swelling of central artery-walls.

434

23.

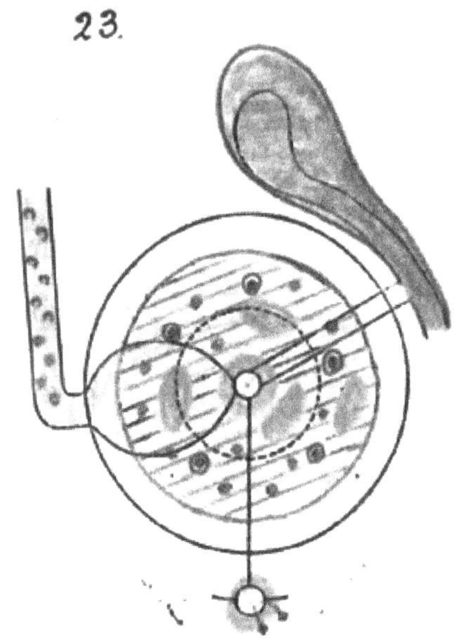

In follicles : intense periarterial edema with some serous fluids, slight hemorrhages and slight swelling of basal fibres. Some increased reticulum cells in macrophagen-form.

At polar portions : edematous swelling of penicillar artery-walls and intense exudative changes (with some serous fluids) and so-called sperma-like necrosis at perifollicular portions.

In sinuses : remarkable congestion and some swollen reticulum-fibres, and in fascicular cords, considerable swelling of basal fibres and condiderable emigration of leucocytes with some swollen degenerated reticulum-cells.

24

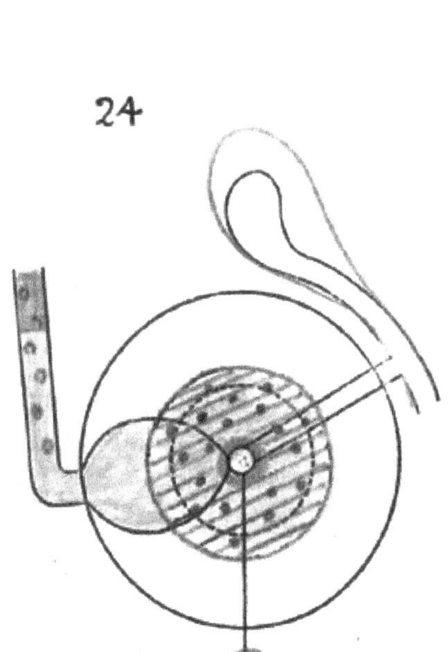

24.

Remarkable reduction of follicles and edematous swelling of central artery-walls.

In follicles : considerable swelling of basal fibres and intense diminution of (diffuse edema) slight hemorrhages, slight diminution of follicular lymphocytes and some swollen degenerated reticulum cells.

Edematous swelling of penicillar artery-walls.

In sinuses : considerable congestion or rather anemic at some places with some considerable swelling of sinus walls and reticulum-fibres.

435

In fascicular cords : intense swelling of reticulum-fibres with some bacterial dissemination all over the fascicular tissues, some emigration of some leucocytes (some of them, eosinophilic) and some swollen reticulum-cells in intense (vacuolar) degeneration.

26 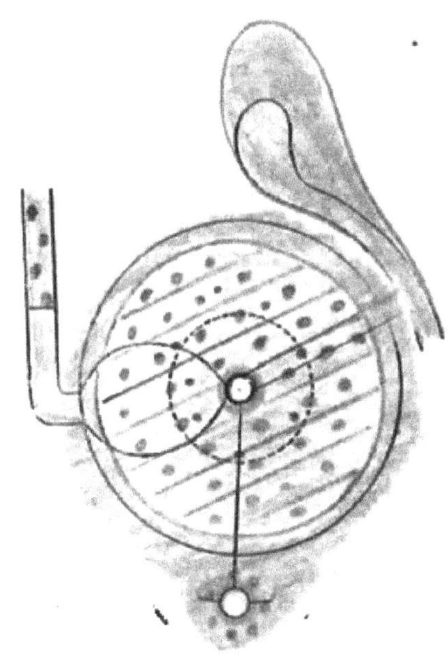

26.

Considerable reduction of follicles and edematous swelling of central artery-walls and edematous swelling (with slight hyaline degeneration) of central artery-walls.

In follicles : intense diffuse edema, remarkabl diminution of follicular lymphocytes and some degenerated reticulum-cells.

Remarkable perifollicular congestion and hemorrhages (leakage of erythrocytes in fascicular cords). Edematous swelling and roughness of penicillar artery walls and slight proliferation of reticulum-cells (and fibres) at periarterial or perifollicular portions.

In sinuses : extraordinary remarkable congestion and intense swelling of sinus walls and reticulum-fibres.

In fascicular cords : some serous fluids and poor in cellular elements with some degenerated reticulum cells,

 436

and (intense diminution of lymphocytes) due to flaky bacterial dissemination all over the fascicular tissues.

27

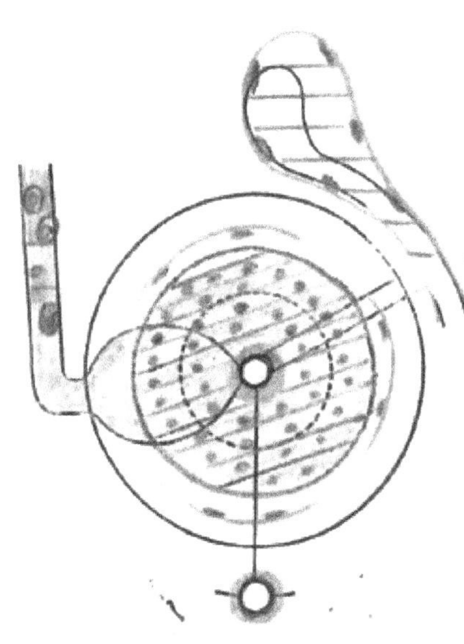

27. Slight reduction of follicles and some edematous swelling (with slight hyalinous degeneration) of central artery-walls.

In follicles : slight diminution of follicular lymphocytes and many reticulum-cells (not swollen or degenerated), esp. at perifollicular portions.

At polar portions : slight edematous swelling (and slight hyalinous degeneration) of penicillar artery-walls with considerable hyperplasia of reticulum-cells (and reticulum fibres).

In sinuses : rather anemic and considerable hyperplasia of reticulum-fibres and reticulum-cells.

In fascicular cords : considerable hyperplasia of reticulum-cells (and fibres) and proliferation of some plasma-cells.

28.

Considerable reduction of follicles and slight hyalinous degeneration (with slight edematous swelling) of central artery-walls.

437

29

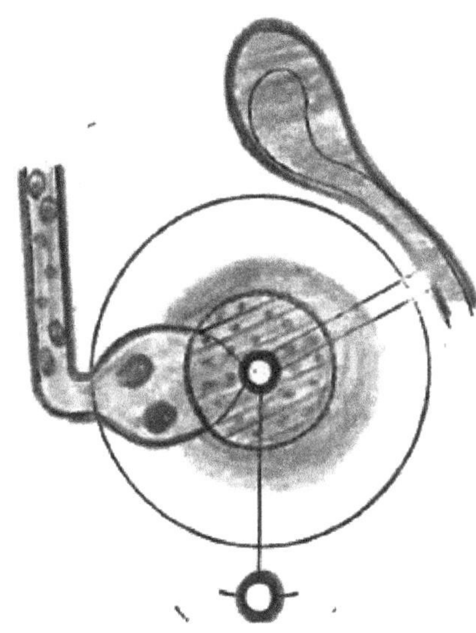

In follicles : considerable roughness of basal fibres, many hyalinous masses and slight hemorrhages. Considerable increased retiuclum cells (in intense cloudy swelling).

Slight hyalinous degeneration of penicillar artery-walls with slight hyperplasia of reticulum-cells (and fibres).

In sinuses : considerable swelling and intense and swelling (with some hyalinisation) of sinus walls and reticulum-fibres.

In fascicular cords : intense swelling of reticulum-fibres, emigration of some leucocytes, some increased reticulum cells (in intense cloudy swelling) and considerable diminution of fascicular lymphocytes.

Emigration of some plasma-cells.

30.

Intense reduction of follicles and swelling (with some hyalinisation) of central artery-walls.

In follicles : some hyalinous masses and slight hemorrhages with considerable edematous swelling of basal fibres and slight diminution of follicular lymphocytes.

Some reticulum-cells in cloudy degeneration.

438

30

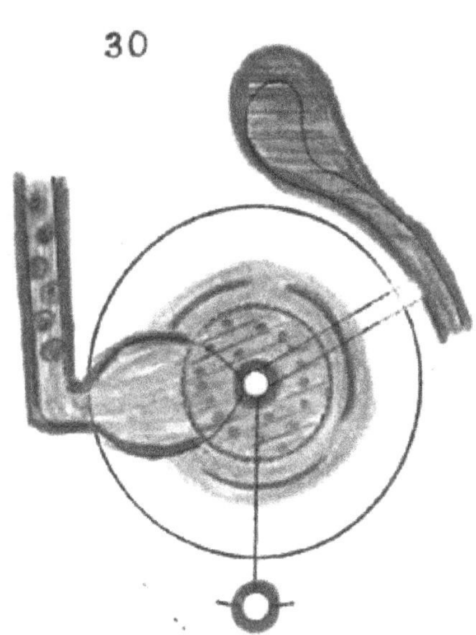

Some reticulum-cells in cloudy degeneration. Hyalinous degeneration of penicillar artery-walls and some perifollicular exudative changes.

In sinuses : more or less remarkable congestio and remarkable swelling of sinus walls and retiuclum-fibres.

In fascicular cords : intense swelling of reticulum-fibres with some serous fluids and emigration of some leucocytes, slightly increased reticulum-cells, some of them in erythrophagy and some of them intense cloudy degeneration. Remarkable diminution of fascicular lymphocytes.

31

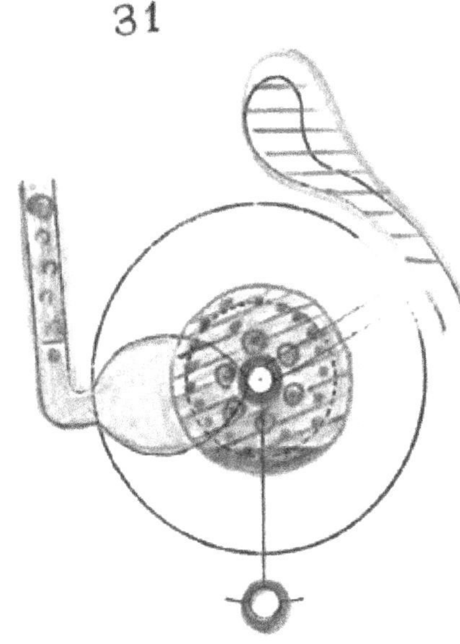

31.

Considerable reduction of follicles and intense edematous roughness (with some hyalinisation) of central artery-walls.

In follicles : considerable deposits of some hyalinous masses and considerable roughness of basal fibres with slightly increased retiulum-cells (in intense cloudy degeneration). Hyalinous swelling of penicillar artery-walls.

In sinuses : slight congestion and considerable edematous swelling of sinus walls and reticulum-fibres.

In fascicular cords : considerable edematous

39

swelling of reticulum fibres with emigration of some leucocytes. Some slightly increased retiuculum-cells, in remarkable cloudy swelling. At some places with supermiliary bionecrotic changes. Bionecrotic swelling of reticulum fibres with plenty of leucocytes-emigration, plenty of karyolytic masses, some decayed or amorphous masses with exudative-hemorrhagic perifocal reactions.

33

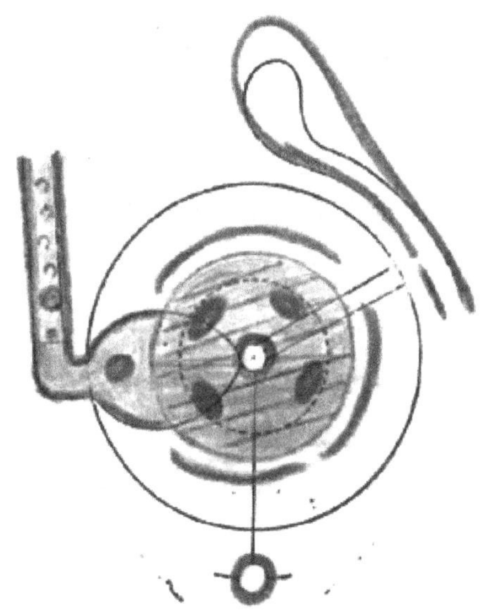

33.

Considerable reduction of follicles and edematous swelling (with some hyalinisation) of central artery-walls.

In follicles : considerable roughness of basal fibres with slight hemorrhages, deposits of some hyalinous messes and some degenerated reticulum-cells.

In sinuses : slight congestion and slight swelling of reticulum-fibres.

In fascicular cords : considerable swelling of reticulum-fibres, not increased reticulum-cells (most of them in intense cloudy degeneration) and emigration of some leucocytes.

At polar portions : some hyalinisation of penicillar artery-walls, not accompanied with proliferative changes.

 440

35

35.

Considerable reduction of follicles and some edematous swelling (with slight hyalinisation) of central atery-walls.

In follicles : remarkable roughness of basal fibres (diffuse edema) with considerable diminution of follicular lymphocytes and slightly increased reticulum-cells (some of them, histiocytes-like form).

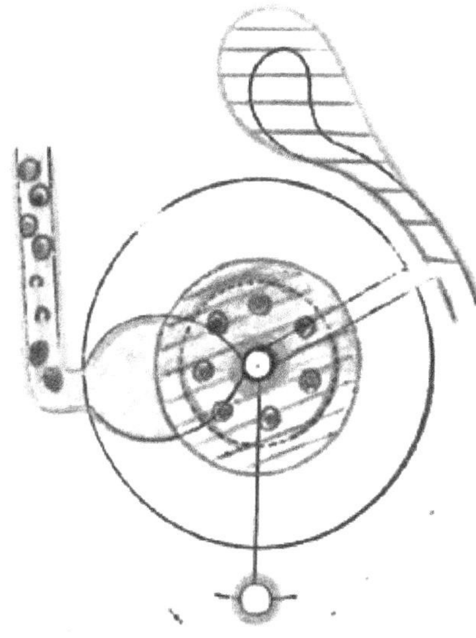

Edematous swelling of penicillar artery-walls.

In sinuses. slight congestion and some swollen reticulum-fibres and sinus walls.

In fascicular cords : considerable or remarkable edematous swelling of reticulum-fibres with some slightly increased reticulum-sells (most of them in cloudy degeneration). Some plasma -cells.

Intense reduction of follicles and intense edematous swelling of central artery-walls.

36.

In follicles : intense roughness of basal fibres (intense diffuse edema) with remarkable diminution of follicular lymphocytes and some remained reticulum-cells(most of them in

441

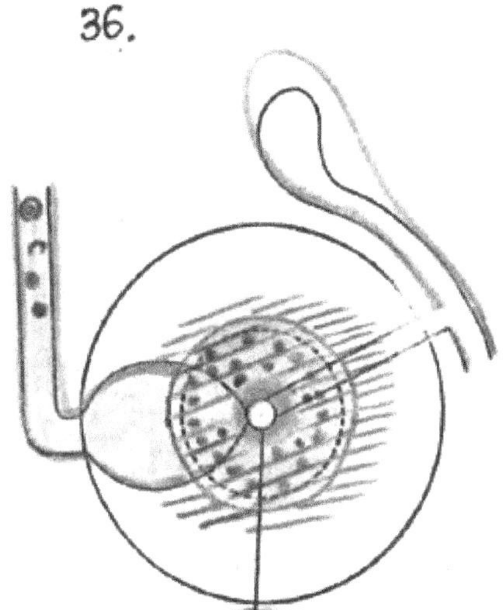

intense cloudy degeneration).

Intense edematous swelling of penicillar artery-walls and some periarterial exudative changes. (some perifollicular congestion, hemorrhages and edema).

In sinuses : slight congestion and intense swelling of sinus walls and reticulum-fibres with slight bacterial accumulations.

In fascicular cords : intense edematous swelling of reticulum-fibres with slight bacterial accumulation at some places and some leucocytes -emigration.

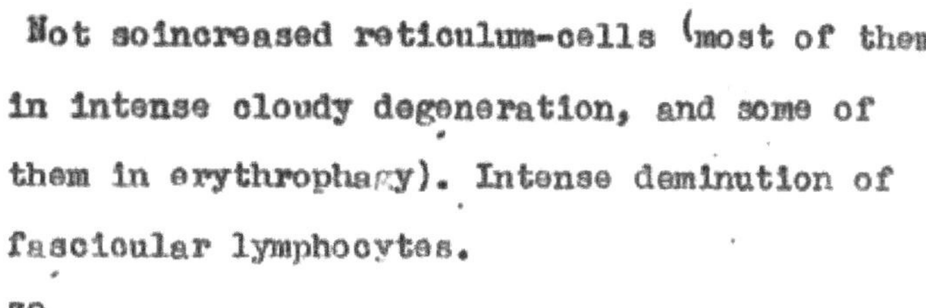
Not soincreased reticulum-cells (most of them in intense cloudy degeneration, and some of them in erythrophagy). Intense deminution of fascicular lymphocytes.

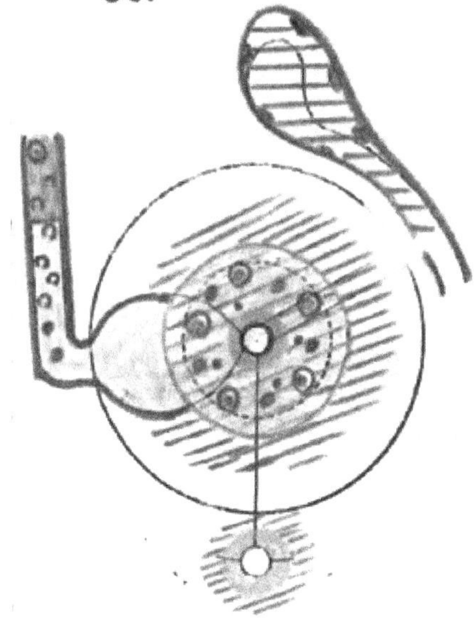

38.

Considerable reduction of follicles and edematous swelling of central artery-walls.

In follicles : remarkable roughness of basal fibres (intense edema) with some karyolytic masses and slight diminution of lymphocytes and remarkable hyperplasia of reticulum-cells (some of them, histiocyteslike), esp. at periarterial portion.

442

40

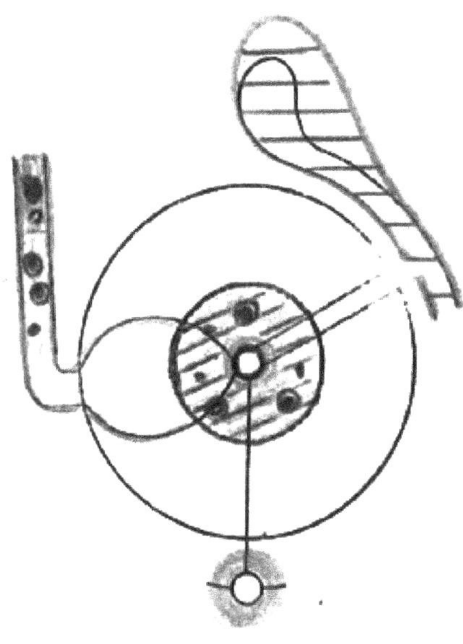

Some edematous swelling of penicillar artery-walls and some perifollicular congestion and nemorrhages.

In sinuses : considerable congestion with intense edema and edematous swelling of sinus walls and reticulum-fibres.

In fascicular cords : some serous fluids and edematous swelling of reticulum-fibres with plenty of leucocytes-emigrations and some bacterial dissemination some (slightly increased) reticulum-cells (most of them in intense swelling and degeneration).

40.

Intense reduction of follicles and intense edematous swelling (with some hyalinisation) of central artery-walls.

In follicles : remarkable roughness of basal fibres with deposits of some hyalinious masses and edematous swelling of reticulum-cells.

Slight diminution of follicular lymphocytes and some (slightly increased) reticulum-cells (most of them in cloudy degneration).

Edematous sweling of penicillar artery-walls and some perifollicular edema.

In sinuses : slight congestion and some

443

swollen reticulum-fibres.

In fascicular cords : considerable swelling of reticulum-fibres with some considerably increased-reticulum cells and some plasma-cells. With some leucocytes and a few myelocytes.

42

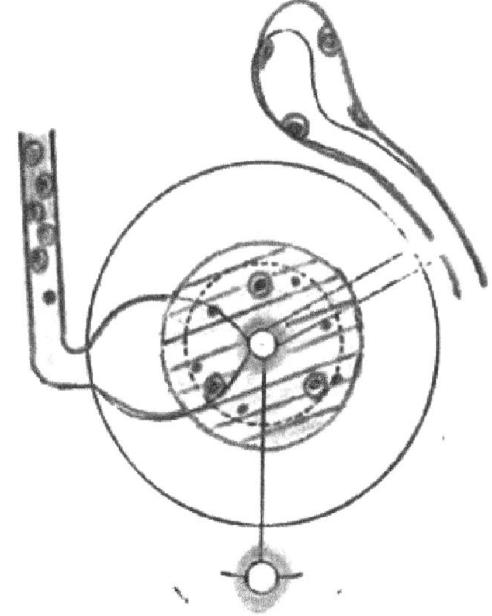

42.

Intense reduction of follicles and edematous swelling of central artery-walls.

In follicles : intense roughness of basal fibres and intense edematous swelling of reticulum-cells, with slight hemorrhages and considerable diminution of follicular lymphocytes. Considerably increased reticulum-cells (some of them in histiocytes-like form).

At polar portions : edematous swelling of pnenicillar artery-walls.

In sinuses : slight congestion with some swelling (with slight hyalinisation) of sinus walls, and considerable hyperplasia of sinus endothelial cells (some of them in histiocytes-like form).

In fascicular cords : considerable hyperplasia of reticulum-cells (some of them in histiocytes-like form) and some plasma-cells. Considerable diminution of fascicular lymphocytes.

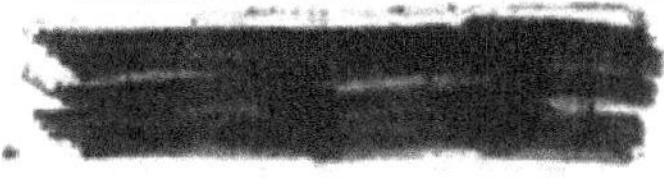

445

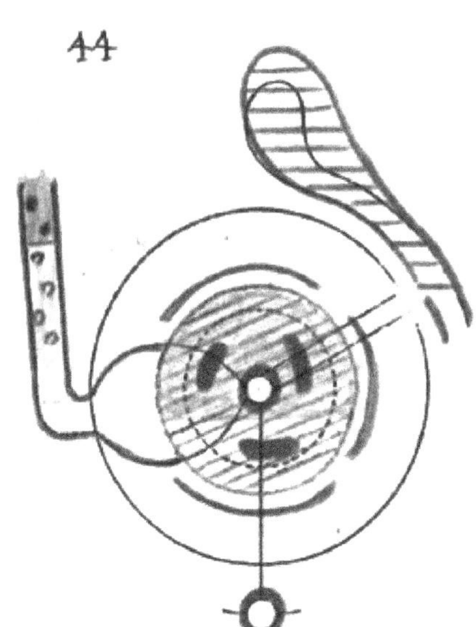

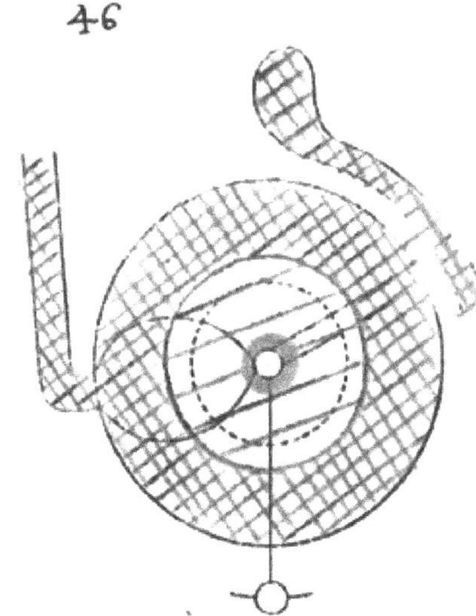

44.

Considerable reduction of follicles and emematous roughness (with some hyalinisation) of central artery-walls.

In follicles : some edematous roughness of basal fibres with deposits of some hyalinous masses and slight hemorrhages. Slight or considerable diminution of follicular lymphocytes.

Considerable edematous swelling of penicillar artery-walls.

In sinuses : considerable congestion and considerable edematous swelling of sinus walls and reticulum-fibres.

In fascicular cords : considerable emigration of leucocytes (with a few myelocytes) and intense edematous swelling of reticulum-fibres. Some degenerated reticulum-cells.

46.

Intense reduction of follicles and intense edematous swelling of central artery-walls.

In follicles : remarkable roughness of basal fibres and slight hemorrhages with intense diminution of follicular lymphocytes. Some remained reticulum-cells (most of them in intense cloudy degeneration).

Intense post mortal changes all over the

446

fascicular tissues : not increased reticlum -cells (in cloudy degeneration), and intense swelling of reticulum-fibres. Without emigration of leucocytes.

47 47.

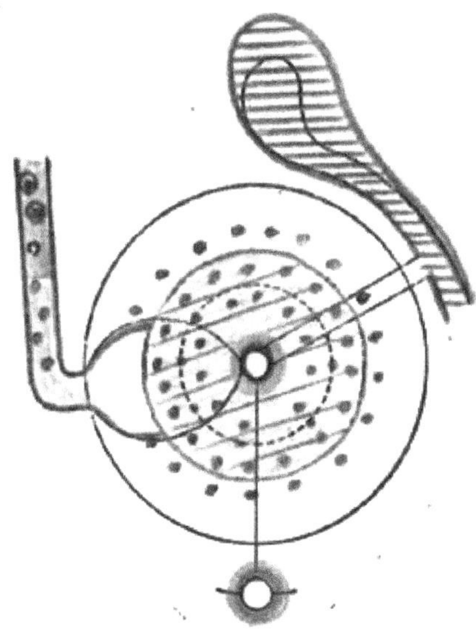

Considerable reduction of follicles and considerable swelling (with some hyalinisation) of central artery-walls.

In follicles : slight roughness of basal fibres with slight hemorrhages and some deposits of some hyalinous masses. Remarkable hyperplasia of feticulum-cells at periarterial protion with remarkable hyperplasia of reticulum-fibres, esp. at perifollicular portion.

Hyalinous swelling of penicillar artery-walls.

In sinuses : considerable congestion and considerable hyperplasia of reticulum-fibres and sinus endothelial cells (with slight hyalinisation).

In fascicular cords : considerable swelling and considerable hyperplasia of reticulum-fibres and reticulum-cells. esp. at peritrabecular portion.

Emigration of a little leucocytes.

447

49.

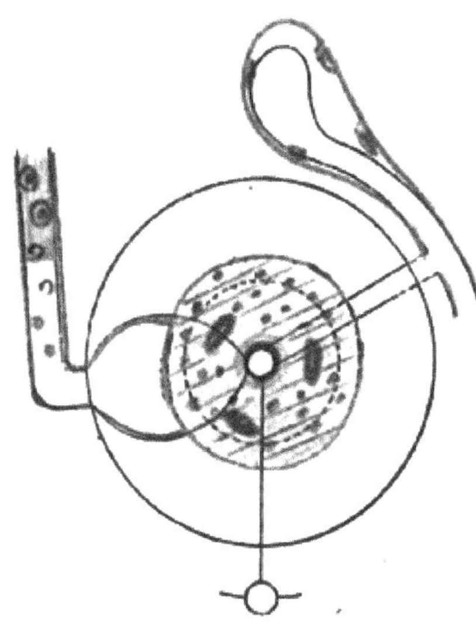

49.

Considerable reduction of follicles and some haylinous degeneration of central artery-walls.

In follicles : slight roughness of basal fibres with deposits of some hyalinous masses and slight diminution of follicular lymphocytes.

Some reticulum-cells (most of them, not swollen).

In sinuses : rather anemic with slight proliferation (and hyalinisation) of reticulum-fibres.

In fascicular cords : slightly increased reticulum-fibres and-cells.

With a few leucocytes.

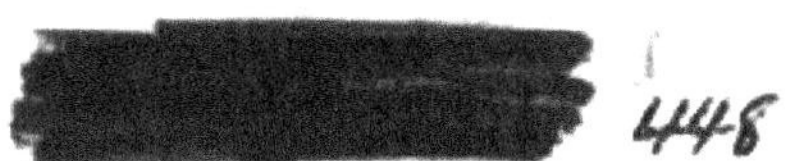

448

S P L E E N

A) Microscopical Investigation

S.1.

S 1.

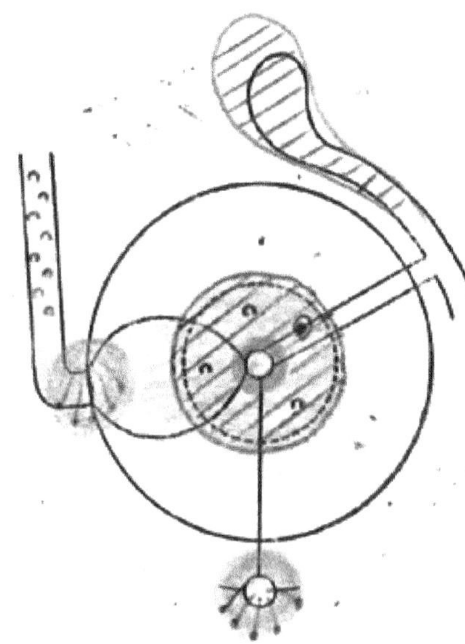

Remarkable reduction of follicles with considerable edematous swelling of central artery-walls. In follicles, severe edema, some leucocytes with myeloic metaplasia, some hyperplssied reticulum-cells(macrophages), which fall into severe cloudy swelling, severe edematous swelling of reticulum-fibres and severe diminution of follicular lymphocytes.

Remarkable polar edema(some serous exudation and our so-called sperma-like severedegeneration of heticulum-cells).

In pulpa-meshes, diffuse severe edema with bionecrotic swelling of reticulum-fibres (and -cells)or some masses. Some leucodytes with myeloic metaplasia and considerable congestion in sinuses.

S 2.

Considerable reduction of follicles with considerable edematous swelling of central and penicilliary artery-walls. In follicles,con-

449

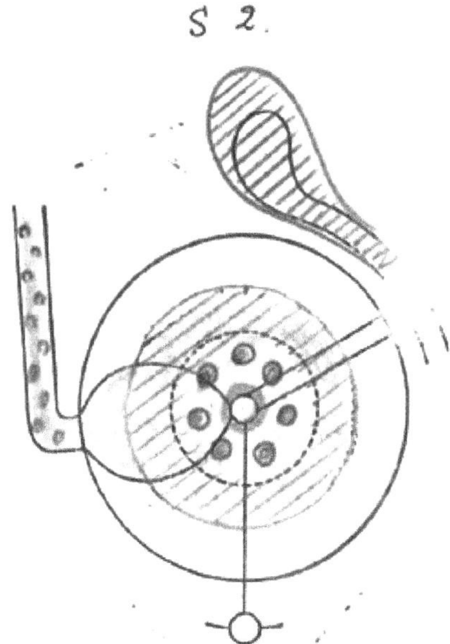

iderable edema, some karyorrhexi masses and some hyperplasied macrophages in germinative centers(M-form germinative centers).

Considerable diminution of follicular lymphocytes.

In pulpa-meshes, consideravle diffuse edema with cloudy swollen reticulum-cells and -fibres Some leucocytes,some karyorrhexis masses with myeloic metaplasia, some hyperplasied reticulum-cells in severe cloudy swelling and consideravle congestion in sinuses.

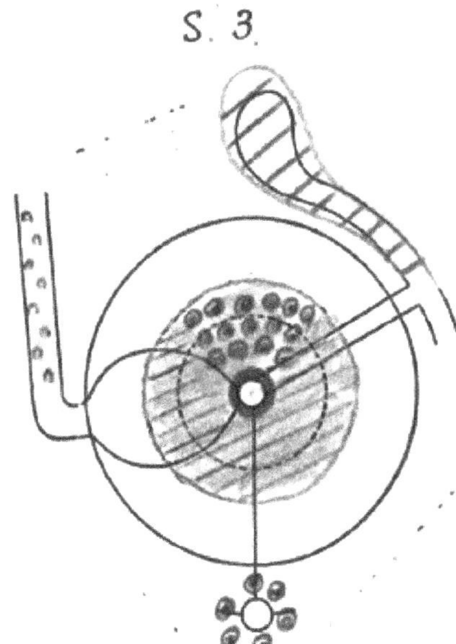

S.3.

Considerable reduction of follicles and considerable edematous or hyalinous swelling of central and penicilliary artery-walls.

In follicles, diffuse considerable edema, considerable diminution of lymphocytes and consideravle hyperplasia of reticulum-cells at some places in follicles and at polar portions(polar proloferation of reticulum-cells

In pulpa-meshes, severe diffuse edema, bionecrotic swelling of sinus-walls and reticulum-fibres, some leucocytes with slight myeloic metaplasia, and consideravle hyperplasia of reticulum-cells,which fall into severe cloudy swelling, slight congestion in sinuses.

450

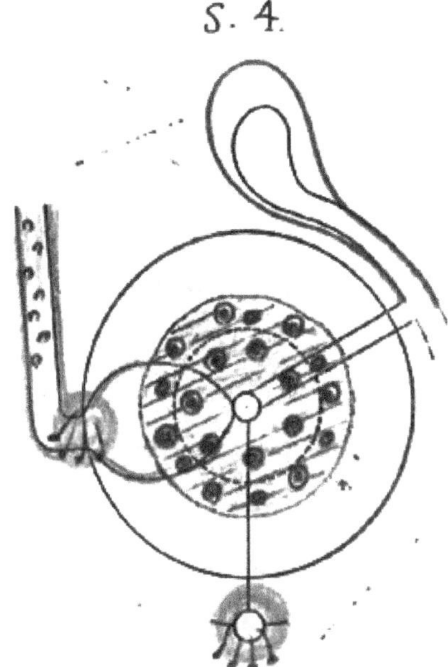

S. 4.

Comdiderable reduction of follicles with consideravle edematous swelling of central and penicilliary artery-walls.

In follicles, slight edema, swollen reticulum-fibres, slight haemorrhages, considerable diminution of follicular lymphocytes and some increased reticulum-cells or macrophages.

Severe edema and mutiple miliary necrosis with so-called sperma-like severe degeneration.

In pulpa-meshes, severe edema wirh intense edematous swelling of reticulum-fibres, some leucocytes and considerable congestion in sinuses.

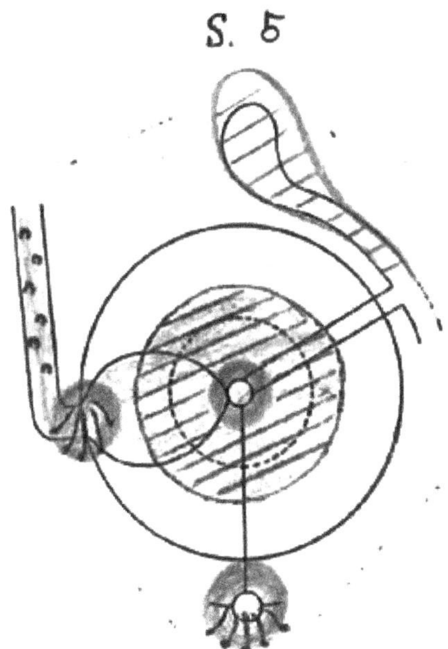

S. 5.

Condiderable reduction of follicles with consideravle edematous or hyalinous swelling of central and penicilliary artery-walls.

In follicles, considerable edema and bionecrotic swelling of reticulum-fibres with considerable diminution of follicular lymphocytes.

Intense polar edema and multiple polar necrosis with so-called sperma-like degeneration.

451

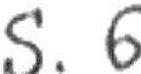

S. 6

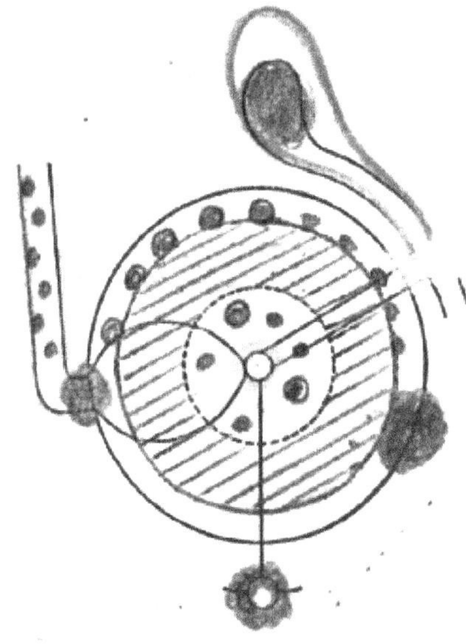

In pulpa-meshes, severe edema with severe swelling of reticulum-cells and -fibres, some leucocytes and slight congestion in sinuses.

S 6.

Slight reduction of follicles with considerable edematous swelling of central artery-walls.

In follicles, intense edema with remarkable or bionecrotic swelling of reticulum-fibres (and -cells), some leucocytes, considerable diminution of follicular lymphocytes and some increased reticulum-cells, esp. at polar portions.

At polar portions, multiple bacterial accumulation with submiliary necrosis and some edema, accompanied with some increased reticulum-cells, as proloferative reactions.

In pulpa-meshes, diffuse intense edema with severe swelling of sinus-walls and bionecrotic swelling of reticulum-fibres, some leucocytes with myeloic metaplasia, and some increased reticulum-cells in severe cloudy swelling.

S. 8.

Remarkable reduction of follicles with severe

452

S 8.

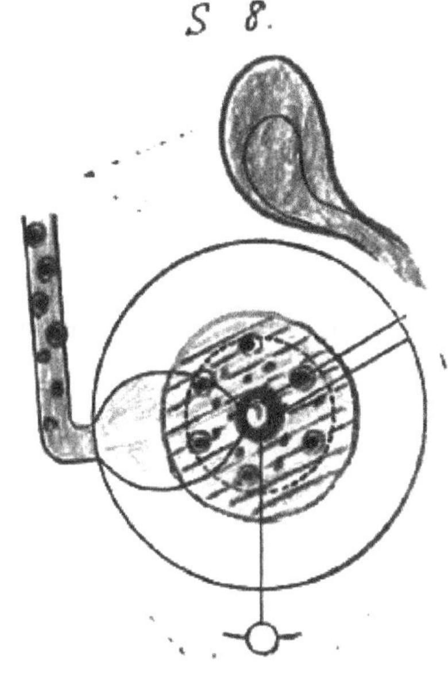

edematous or hyaline swelling of central and penicilliar artery-walls.

In follicles, considerable diffuse edema, considerable hemorrhages ,edematous swelling of reticulum-fibres and considerable increased reticulum-cells with erythrophagy and severe diminution of follicular lymphocytes.

In pulpa-meshes, remarkable congestion in sinuses with slight swelling reticulum -cells in cloudy swelling with some erythrophagy and severe diminution of lymphocytes.

S. 9

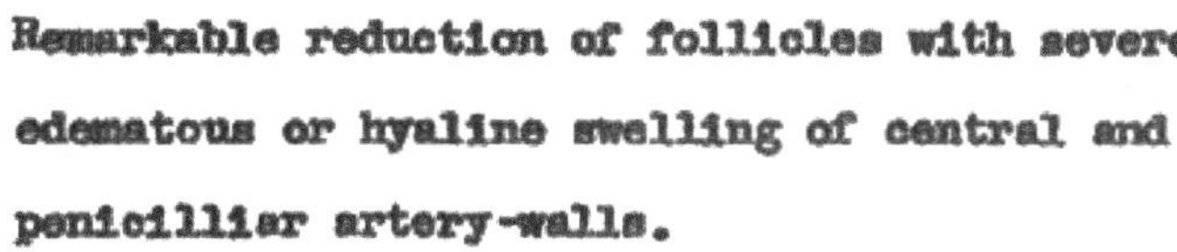

Remarkable reduction of follicles with severe edematous or hyaline swelling of central and penicilliar artery-walls.

In follicles, considrable diffuse edema, considerable localised hemorrhages and some increased reticulum-cells or macrophages in cloudy swelling.

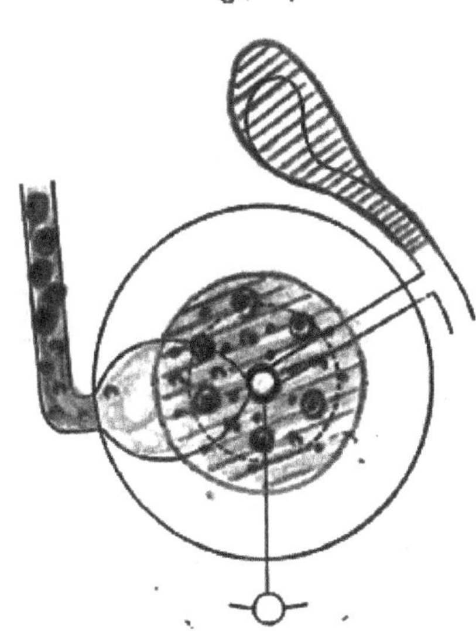

In pulpa-meshes, remarkable congestion in sinuses with slight swelling of sinus-walls and reticulum-fibres, some leucocytes, considerable diminution of lymphocytes and some inreased reticulum-cells with erythrophagy in cloudy swelling.

453

S. 10

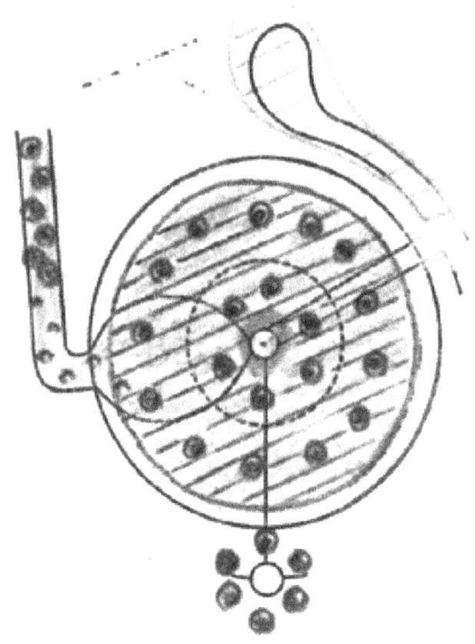

S. 11

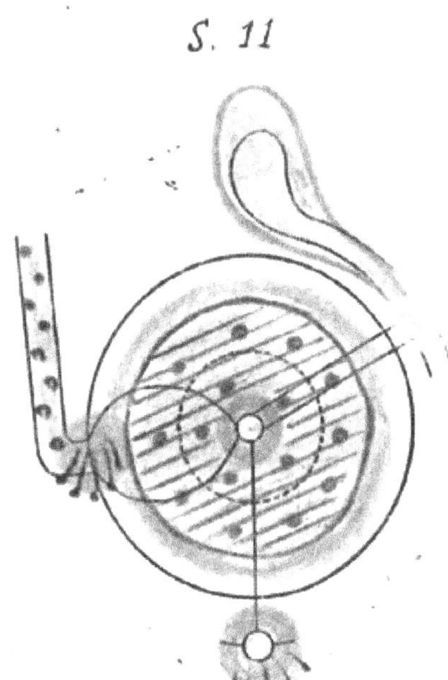

Some bacterial masses in arterioles and sinuses.

S.10.

Slight reduction of follicles with considerable edematous or hyaline swelling of central artery-walls. In follicles, slight edema, slight considerable diminution of follicular lymphocytes and considerable increased reticulum-cells or macrophages.

At polar portion, or at some places some bacterial accumulations and considerably increased reticulumcells.

In pulpa-meshes, considerable edema with swollen reticulum-fibres and -cells, some leucocytes with slight myeloic metaplasia, multiple submiliary necrosis and on the other hands slightly increased reticulum-cells or macrophages. Slight congestion in sinuses.

S.11.

Considerable reduction of follicles with considerable edematous swelling of central artery-walls.

In follicles, severest edema with intense polar edema, intense edematous swelling of reticulum-fibres(and reticulum-cells),

454

S. 12

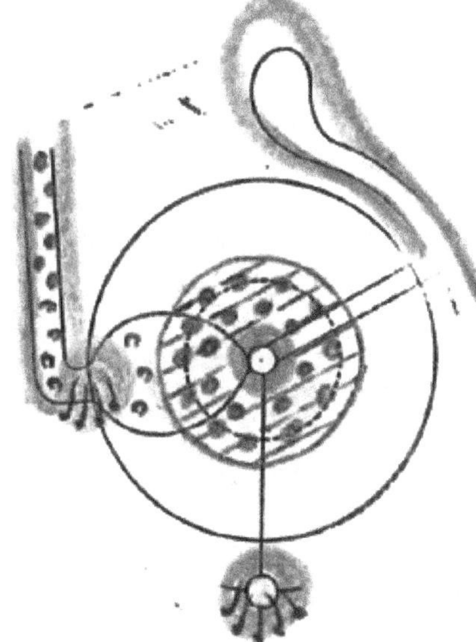

severe diminution of follicular lymphocytes and some increased reticulum-cells or macrophages, in cloudy swelling.

In polar portions, intense edema with so-called sperma-like, severe degeneration of reticulum-cells.

In pulpa-meshes, remarkable congestion in sinuses with severe swelling of reticulum-fibres or -cells, some leucocytes and considerable edema in contract fasciculi.

S. 12.

Follicles:edematous swelling of central artery-walls. Intense diffuse edema in follicular tissues, acco,panied with some increased reticulum-cells(in intense cloudy swelling) and some bionecrotic masses.

In perifollicular tissues:intense edema with a large quantity of serous fluids and typical sperma-like necrosis.

In sinuses: slight congestion and intense edematous swelling of sinus-walls and reticulum-fibres,all over the splenal tissues.

In fascicular cords: some leucocytes and some degenerated reticulum-cells, accompanied with considerable diminution of fascicular

455

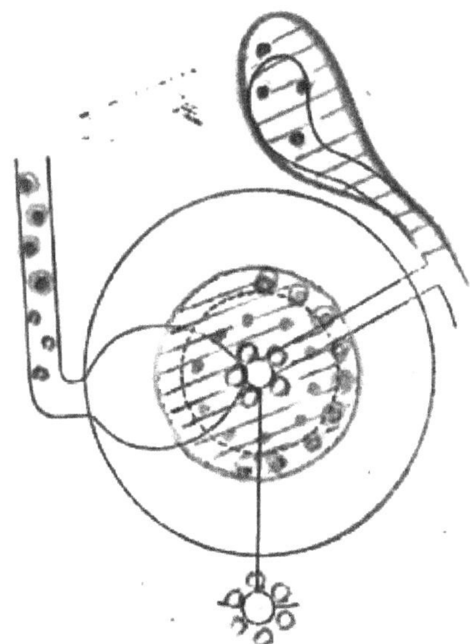

lymphocytes.

S 14.

In follicules:edematous swelling of central artery-wall. Some increased reticulum-cells, most of them, in bright macrophagen-like form, in follicular tissues.

In perifollicular tissues: remarkavle increase of epitheloid cells.

In sinuses:slight congestion and slight hyalinisation fo sinus-walls and reticulum-fibres, accompanied with remarkably increased epitheloid cells and some reticulum-cells in macrophagens-form.

In fascucular cords; more or less remarkable increase of reticulum-cells, some epitheloid cells, some macrophagens and some plasma-cells (some diminution of fascicular lymphocytes).

These increase of reticulum-cells or epitheloid cells suggest some acquirement of immunity Hemorrhagic-exudative changes with some bacterial dissemination all over the splenal tissues.

S 15.

In follicules;intensive edematous swelling or roughness of central artery-walls and intensively diffuse edematous swelling of

456

S 15

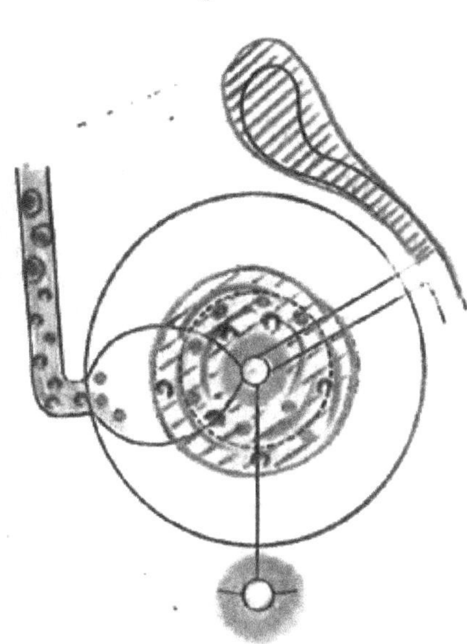

of riticulum-fibres in follicular tissues (serous fluids and some leucocytes in follicles)

In perifollicular tissues; intensively edematous swelling with a large quantity of serous fluids.

In sinuses; intense stasis in sinus all over the splenal tissues and intense edematous swelling of sinus-walls and reticukum-fibtes in fascicular tissues.

In fascicular cords; some leucocytes, some degenerated splenocuѣes (in vasular degeneration) and a little plasma-cells and macrophagnes.

S. 22

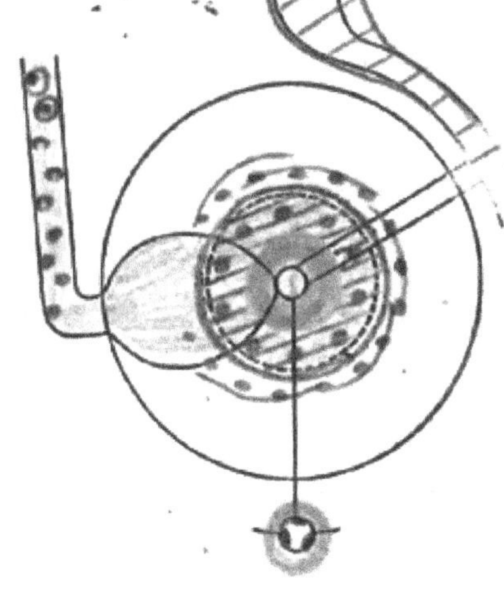

S. 22.

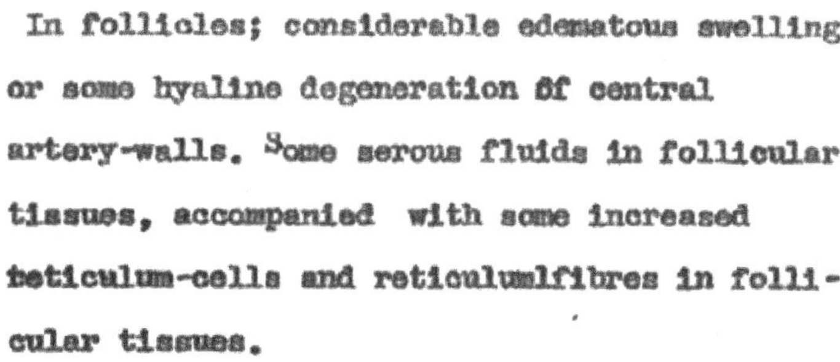

In follicles; considerable edematous swelling or some hyaline degeneration of central artery-walls. Some serous fluids in follicular tissues, accompanied with some increased beticulum-cells and reticulumlfibres in follicular tissues.

In perifollicular tissues; remarkable hyperplasia of reticulum-cells, accompanied with exudative changes on the other hand.

slight hyalinisation of penicillar artery-walls, accompanied with consgderable

457

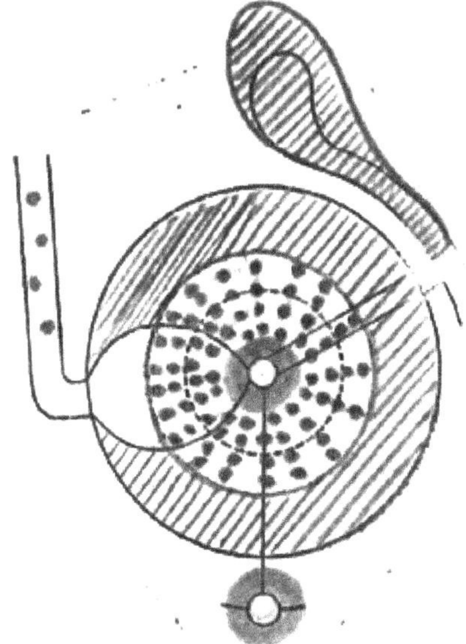

hyperplasia of endothelial cells and peri-adventitial reticulum-cells.

In sinuses; intense stasis with massive increased reticulum-cells and endothelial cells of sinus-walls.

In fasciclea massive increased reticulum-cells histiocytes and more or less remarkable increased plasma-cells(inflammatory reticuloendotheliosis), accompanied with some leucocytes, some myelocytes-emigration and some other exudative changes on the other hand.

The proloferative reactions suggest some aquirement of immunity.

S. 26.

In follicles; edematous swelling or intense roughness of central artery-walls. Intense edema with abandant serous fluids all over the follicular tissues and intense diminution o follicular lymphocytes.

In perifollicular tissues; with intense congestion and some hemorrhages and intense edema at peripenicillar portions.

In sinuses; intense congestion and intense edematous swelling of sinus-walls and reti-

459

S. 19

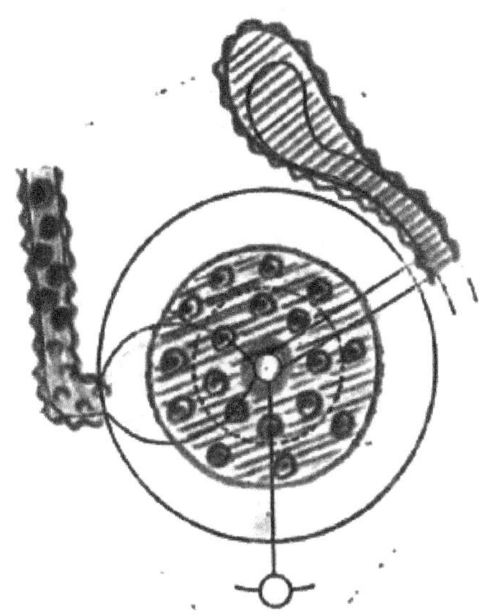

culum-fibres all over the fascucular tissues.

In fascicules; intense edema and some hemorrhages,(some leakage of erythrocytes in fascicular cords),with intense diminution of fascicular lymphocytes and a little reticulum-cells(diminution of and degeneration of reticulum-cells).

S. 19.

Considerable reduction of follicles with severe edematous swelling of central artery-walls. In follicles, severe edema, considerable hemorrhages, considerable swelling of reticulum-fibres and some hyperplasied reticulum-cells or macrophagens in intense cloudy swelling.

In pulpa-meshes; considerable congestion in sinuses with severe the most swelling of sinus-walls and bionecrotic swelling of reticulum-fibres,some leucocytes,some plasma-cells, some reticulum-cells or macrophages in contract fasciculi and considerable diminution of lymphaocytes.

S 28.

Considerable reduction of follicles with considerable edematous swelling of central artery-walls.

S. 28

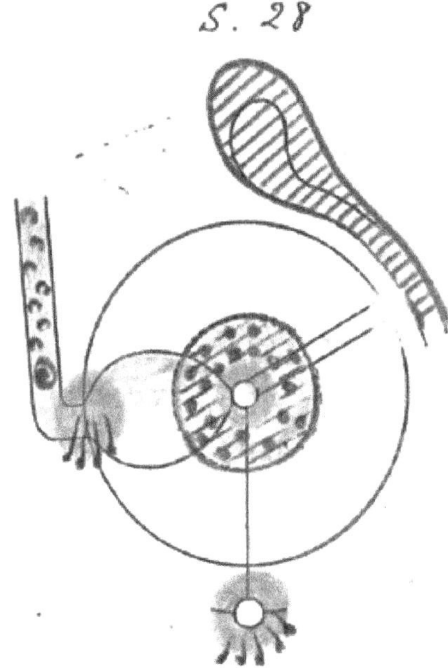

In follicles, some diffuse edema and some increased reticulum-cells in cloudy swelling.

At polar portions, intense edema and multiple polar submiliary necrosis with so-called sperma-like degeneration of reticulum-cells.

In pulpa-meshes, considerable edema, some leucocytes and some reticulum-cells in cloudy swelling in fasciculi, accompanied with considerable dimination of lymphocytes.

S 38.

Severe reduction of follicles with severe bionecrotic swelling of central artery-walls.

S. 38

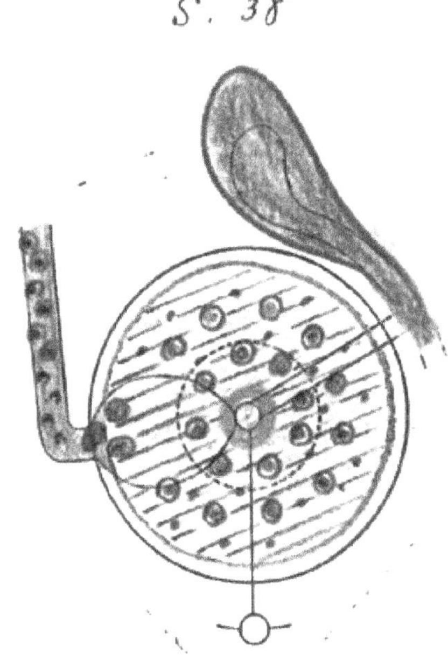

In follicles, severe diffuse edema, plenty karyolytic masses, slight hemorrhages and severe diminution of follicular lymphocytes.

In pulpa-meshes, some considerable increased reticulum-cells or macrophagem in intense cloudy swelling.

In pulpa-meshes, the most severe diffuse edema with bionecrotic swelling of reticulum-fibres and -cells, and plenty karyolytic masses, some slightly increased reticulum-cells in severe or bionecrotic swelling, some leucocytes and considerable diminution of lymphocytes, accompanied with diffuse remarkable

 460

large necrosis, at some places.
Folliculitis suppurativa totalis et fasci-culitis necroticans.(total necrotic ruins of some follicles with bacterial accumulations and following more diffuse large necrosis, due to bacterial dissemination in pulpa-meshes).

461

(B) SUMMARY

(1)

The birdseye views of all splenar changes of all investigated cases are as following :

462

The bird's eye view of all investigated cases.

1.	Angio-Folliculitis exsudativa.	Exudative changes in severe degree.
	Fasciculitis exsudativa.	Exudative changes in severe degree.
2.	Angio-Folliculitis haemorrhagico-exsudativa.	Hemorrhagic changes in medium degree. Exudative changes in severe degree. with slight proliferative tendency. with some bion ecrotic changes. with leucocites emigration in slight degree.
	Fasciculitis exsudativa.	Exudative changes in severedegree. with leucocytes dissemination in severe degree. with some myeloic metaplasia.
3.	Angio-Folliculitis exsudativa.	Exudative changes in severe degree.
	Fasciculitis exsudativa.	Exudative changes in severe degree. with leucocytes dissemination in slight degree.
4.	Angio-Folliculitis exsudativa.	Exudative changes in severe degree.
	Fasciculitis exsudativa.	Exudative changes in severe degree. with leucocytes dissemination in slight degree. with some myeloic metaplasia.
5.	Angio-Folliculitis haemorrhagico-exsudativa.	Hemorrhagic changes in slight degree. Exudative changes in severe degree.
	Fasciculitis exsudativa.	Exudative changes in severe degree.
7.	Angio-Folliculitis exsudativa.	Exudative changes in severe degree.
	Fasciculitis exsudativa.	Exudative changes in severe degree. with leucocytes dissemination in severe degree. with some myeloic metaplasia.
8.	Angio-Folliculitis exsudativa.	Exudative changes in medium degree.
	Fasciculitis exsudativa.	Exudativa changes in severe degree. with leucocytes dissemination in severe degree. with some myeloic metaplasia.

463

9.

Angio-Follicilitis exsudativa. Exudative changes in medium degree. with slight proliferative tendency.

Fasciculitis exsudativa. Exudative changes in severe degree. with leucocytes dissemination in slight degree.

10.

Angio-Folliculitis exsudativa. Exudative changes in severe degree. with slight proliferative tendency.

Fasciculitis exsudativa. Exudative changes in severe degree. with leicocytes dissemination in sefere degree. with some myeloic metaplasia.

11.

Angio-Folliculitis haemorrhagico-exsudativa. Hemorrhagic changes in slight degree. Exudative changes in severe degree.

Fasciculitis exsudativa. Exudative changes in severe degree. with leucocytes dissemination in slight degree. with some myeloic metaplasia.

12.

Angio-Folliculitis exsudativa. Exudative changes in severe degree. with leucocytes emigration in slight degree. with polar edema. with polar miliar necrosis. (Sperm like necrosis.)

Fasciculitis exsudativa. Exudative changes in severe degree. with leucocytes dissemination in severe degree. with some miliary necrosis. (Sperm like necrosis.) with some myeloic metaplasia.

14.

Angio-Folliculitis haemorrhagico-exdudativa. Hemorrhagic changes in medium degree Exudative changes in severe degree. with polar edema.

Fasciculitis exsudativa. Exudative changes in severe degree. with leucocytes dissemination in slight degree. with some myeloic metaplasia.

16.

Angio-Folliculitis haemorrhagico-exsudativa. Hemorrhagic changes in slight degree Exudative changes in severe degree.

464

Fasciculitis exsudativa. exudative changes in severe degree. with leucocytes dissemination in severe degree. with some mueloic metaplasia.

17.

Angio-Folliculitis exsudativa. Exudativa changes in severe degree. with some bionecrosis. with polar edema. with polar miliary bionecrosis

Fasciculitis exsudativa. Exudative changes in severe degree. with some bionecrosis. with leucocytes dissemination in slight degree.

18.

Angio-Folliculitis exsudativa. Exudative changes in severe degree.. with polar edema. with polar some miliary necrosis.

Fasciculitis exsudativa. Exudative changes in severe degree. with leucocytes d issemination in slight degree. with som e miliary bionecrosis

---

19.

Angio-Folliculitis exsudativa. Exudative changes in medium degree.

Fasciculitis exsudativa. Exudative changes in medium degree. with leucocytes dissemination in slight degree.

20.

Angio-Folliculitis haemorrhagico-exsudativa. Hemorrhagic changes in slight degree. Exudative changes in medium degree. with polar hemorrhage.

Fasciculitis exsudativa. Exudative changes in medium degree. with leucocytes dissemination in slight degree.

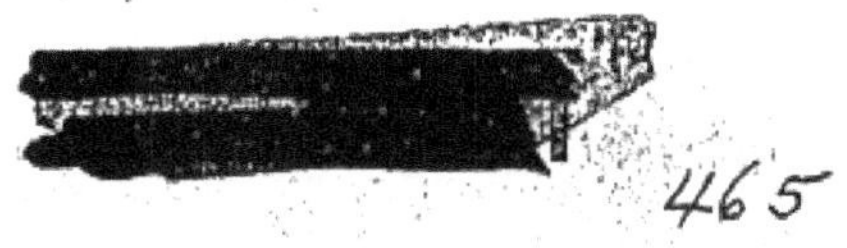

465

21. Angio-Folliculitis haemorrhagico exsudativa.	Hemorrhagic changes in slight degree. Exudative changes in severe degree. with polar edema. with polar miliary necrosis ((Sperm like necrosis) with leucocytes emigration in slight degree.
Fasciculitis exsudativa.	Exudativa changes in severe degree. with leucocytes dissemination in severe degree. withn some miliary necrosis.
23. Angio-Folliculitis hemorrhagico-exsudativa.	Hemorrhagic changes in slight degree. Exudative changes in severe degree. with polar edema. with polar miliary necrosis.
Fasciculitis exsudativa.	Exudative changes in severe degree. with leucocytes dissemination in severe degree. with some myeloic metaplasia. with some miliary necrosis.
24. Angio-Folliculitis haemorrhagico-exsudativa.	Hemorrhagic changes in slight degree. Exudative changes in severe degree. with polar edema.
Fasciculitus exsudativa.	Exudative changes in severe degree. with leucocytes dissemination in medium degree. with some myeloic metaplasia.
26. Angio-Folliculitis haemorrhagico-exsudativa.	Hemorrhagic changes in slight degree Exudative changes in medium degree. with slight proliferative tendency. (Reticulum cell) with polar hemorrhage.
Fasciculitis exsudativa.	Exud ative changes in severe degree. with leucocytes dissemination in slight degree.
27. Angio-Folliculitis haemorrhagico-exsudativa.	Hemorrhagic changes in slight degree Exudative changes in medium degree. with slight proliferative tendency.
Fasciculitis exsudativa.	Exudative changes in severe degree. with slight pro,liferative tendency.
29. Angio- Folliculitis haemorrhagico-exsudativa.	Hemorrhagic changes in severedegree

466

	Exudative changes in severe degree. with polar plasma cell reaction.
Fasciculitis exsudativa.	Exudative changes in severe degree. with leukocytes dissemination in slight degree. with slight proliferative tendency.-

---

30.

Angio-Folliculitis haemorrhagico-Exsudativa.	Hemorrhagic changes in medium degree. Exudative changes in severe degree.
Fasciculitis exsudativa.	Exudative changes in severe degree. with slight proliferative tendency. with leucocytes dissemination in slight degree. with some myeloic metaplasis.

31.

Angio-Folliculitis haemorrhagico-exsudativa.	Hemorrhagic changes in slight degree. Exudative changes in severe degree. with slight proliferative tendency.
Fasciculitis exsudativa.	Exudative changes in severe degree. with leucocytes dissemination in medium degree. with slight proliferative tendency.

33.

Angio-Folliculitis haemorrhagico-exsudativa.	Hemorrhagic changes in medium degree. Exudative changes in severe degree.
Fasciculitis exsudativa.	Exudativa changes in severe degree. with leucocytes dissemination in medium degree.

35.

Angio-Folliculitis haemor rhagico-exsudativa.	Hemorrhagic changes in slight degree. Exudative changes in medium degree. with polar hemorrhage. with polar plasma cell reaction. with slight proliferative tendency.
Fasciculitis exsudativa.	Exudative changes in severe degree. with leucocytes dissemination in slight degree. with plasma cell reaction.

467

36.

Angio-Folliculitis exsudativa.	Exudativa changes in severe degree. with polar edema. with polar hemorrhage.
Fasciculitis Exsudativa.	Exudativa changes in severe degree. with leucocytes dissemination in slight degree.

38.

Angio-Folliculitis exsudativa.	Exudative changes in severe degree. with slight proliferative tendency. with polar edema.
Fasciculitis exsudativa.	exudative changes in severe degree. with leucocytes disse mination in severe degree.

40.

Angio-Folliculitis haemorrhagico-exsudativa.	Hemorrhagic changes in slig t degree. Exudative changes in severe degree. with slight proliferative tendency. with polar edema. with polar hemorrhage.
Fasciculitis exsudativa.	Exudative changes in severe degree. with leucocytes dissemination in slight degree. with some myeloic metaplasia.

42.

Angio-Folliculitis haemorrhagico-exsudativa.	Hemorrhagic changes in slight degree. Exudative changes in severe degree. with polar hemorrhage. with slight proliferative tendency. with polar plasma cell reaction.
Fasciculitis exsudativa.	Exudative changes in severe degree. with proliferative tendency. with some plasma cell reaction.

44.

Angio-Folliculitis haemorrhagico-exsudativa.	H emorrhagic changes in slight degree. Exudative changes in medium degree.
Fasciculitis exsudativa.	Exudative changes in medium degree. with leucocytes dissemination in medium degree. with some myeloic metaplasia.

468

46.	
Angio-Folliculitis exsudativa.	Exudativa changes in severe degree. with diffuse bionecrotic changes.
Fasciculitis necroticans.	Necrotic changes in severe degree. with diffuse necrotic and bionecrotic changes.
47.	
Angio-Folliculitis haemorrhagico-Exsudativa.	Hemorrhagic changes in slight degree. Exudative changes in sever e degree. with proliferative tendency(Reticulum-cell).
Fasciculitis exsudativa.	Exudative changes in sever e degree. with leucocytes dissemination in slight degree.
49.	
Angio-Folliculitis haemorrhagico-exsudativa.	Hemorrhagic changes in slight degree. Exudative changes in severe degree. with slight proliferative tendency. (Reticulum cell)
Fasciculitis exsudativa.	Exudative changes in severe degree. with leucocytes dissemination in slight degree.
S 1.	
Angio-Folliculitis exsudativa.	Exudative changes in severe degree. with leucocytes emigration in slight degree. with polar edema. with polar miliary necrosis. (Sperm like necrosis).
Fasciculitis exsu dativa.	Exudative changes in severe degree. with leucocytes dissemination in severe degree. with some myeloic metaplasia, withnsome miliary necrosis. (Sperm like necrosis).
S 2.	
Angio-Folliculitis haemorrhagico-exsudativa.	H emorrhagic changes in slight degree. Exudative changes in severe degree. with slight proliferative tendency.
Fasciculitis exsudativa.	Exudative changes in severe degree. with leucocyted dissemination in slight degree. with some myeloic metaplasia.

469

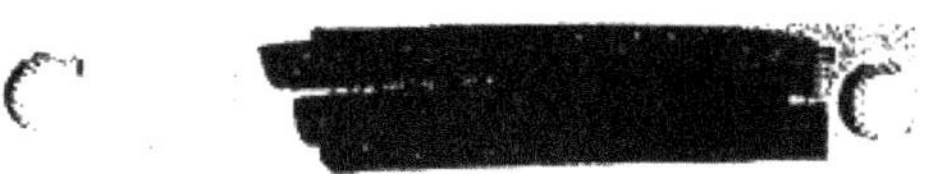

S 3.

Angio-Folliculitis exsudativa.	Exudative changes in severe degree. with slight proliferative tendency.
Fasciculitis exsudativa.	Exudative changes in severe degree. with leucocytes dissemination in severe degree. with some myeloic metaplasia.

S-4.

Angio-Folliculitis exsudativa.	exudative changes in severe degree. with leucocytes emigration in slight degree. with polar edema. with polar miliary necrosis. (Sperm like necrosis)
Fasciculitis exsudativa.	Exudative changes in severe degree. with leucocytes dissemination in severe degree. with some miliary bionecrosis.

S-5.

Angio-Folliculitis haemorrhagico-exsudativa.	Hemorrhagic changes in slight degree. Exudative changes in severe degree. with polar edema. with polar miliary necrosis. (Sperm like necrosis)
Fasciculitis exsudativa.	Exudative changes in severe degree. with leucocytes dossemination in severe degree. with some myeloic metaplasia. with some miliary necrosis.

S-6.

Angio-Folliculitis exsudativa.	Exudative changes in medium degree.
Fasciculitis exsudativa.	Exudative changes in severe degree. with leucocytes dissemination in slight degree. with some myeloic metaplasia.

S-8.

Angio-Folliculitis haemorrhagico-exsudativa .	Hemorrhagic changes in slight degree. Exudative changes in medium degree. with slight proliferative tendency.
Fasciculitis exsudativa.	Exudative changes in medium degree. with leucocytes dissemination in medium degree.

470

S-9.	
Angio-Folliculitis haemorrhagico-exsudativa.	Hemorrhagic changes in slight degree. Exudative changes in medium degree. with slight proliferative tendency.
Fasciculitis exsudativa.	Exudative changes in medium degree. with leucocytes dissemination in medium degree. with slight proliferative tendency.
S-10.	
Angio-Folliculitis exsudativa.	Exudative changes in severe degree. with slight proliferative tendency.
Fasciculitis exsudativa.	Exudative changes in severe degree. with slight proliferative tendency. with leucocytes dissemination in severe degree. with some myeloic metaplasia.
S-11.	
Angio-Folliculitis Haemorrhagico-exsudativa.	Hemorrhagic changes in slight degree. Exudative changes in severe degree. with polar edema. with polar miliary necrosis. (Sperm like necrosis).
Fasciculitis exsudativa.	Exudative changes in severe degree. with leucocytes dissemination in medium degree. with some myeloic metaplasia. with some miliary necrosis. (Sperm like necrosis)
S-12.	
Angio-Folliculitis exsudativa.	Exudative changes in severe degree. with polar edema. with some miliary necrosis. (Sperm like necrosis).
Fasciculitis exsudativa.	Exuda tive changes in severe degree. with leucocytes dissemination in medium de gree. with some miliary necrosis. (Sperm like necrosis).

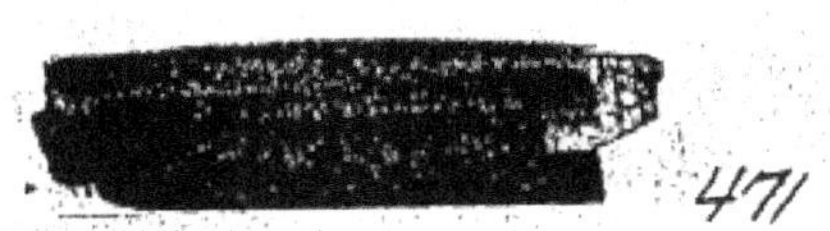

471

S-14.

Angio-Folliculitis Exsudativa.	Exudative changes in severe degree. with polar edema.
Fasciculitis exsudativa.	Exudative changes in severe degree. with leucocytes dissemination in slight degree.

S-15.

Angio-Folliculitis haemorrhagico-exsudativa.	Hemorrhagic changes in medium degree. Exudative changes in severe degree. with leucocytes emigration in slight degree,
Fasciculitis exsudaiva.	Exudative changes in severe degree. with leucocytes dissemination in severe degree. with some myeloic metaplasia. with some plasma cell reaction.

S-19.

Angio-Folliculitis E sudativa.	Exudative changes in severe degree. with slight proliferative tendency. with polar edema. with polar plasma cell reaction.
Fasciculitis exsudativa.	Exudative changes in severe degree. with leucocytes dissemination in medium degree. with some plasma cell reaction. with slight proliferative tendency.

S-22.

Ang io-Folliculitis Exsudativa.	Exudative changes in medium degree. with slight proliferative tendency.
Fasciculitis exsudativa.	Exudative changes in medium degree. with slight proliferative tendency. with leucocytes dissemination in slight degree. with some myeloic metaplasia.

472

S-26.

Angio-Folliculitis exsudativa.	Exudative changes in severe degree. with slight proliferative tendency. with polar edema.
Fasciculitis exsudativa.	Exudative changes in severe degree.

S-28.

Angio-Folliculitis haemorrhagico-exsudativa.	Hemorrhagic changes in slight degree. Exydative changes in severe d egree. with polar edema. with polar miliary necrosis.
Fasciculitis exsudativa.	Exudative changes in severe degree. with leucocytes dissemination in medium degree. with some myeloic metaplasia. with some miliary bionecrosis.

S-38.

Angio-Folliculitis haemorrhagico-exsudativa.	Hemorrhagic changes in slight degree. Exudative changes in medium degree. with slight proliferative tendency. with some necrosis. with leucocytes emigration in slight degree and severe degree.
Fasciculitis exsudativa.	Exudative changes in severe degree. with slight proliferative tende-ncy. with leucocytes dissemination in medium degree.

473

(2)

A) Disturbances of follicules.

1) Disturbances of A.centralis.

Hyalinous or edematous swelling of walls of A.centralis.

in slight degree. 0 cases.

in medium degree. 17 cases.

in severe degree. 38 cases.
(necrotic swelling)

2) Disturbances of perivascular and follicular tissues.

Angio-folliculitis exsudativa. 53 cases.

in slight degree.
(edema in perivascular tissues)
0 cases.

in medium degree.
(diffuse edema in follicular tissues).
13 cases.
in severe degree. 40 cases.

Angio-folliculitis haemorrhgico-exsudativa.
(Angio-folliculitis exsudativa with some hemorrhages)

29 cases.

in slight degree. 23 cases.

in medium degree. 5 cases.

in severe degree. 1 cases.

Angio-folliculitis exsudativa with leucocytes-emigration.

7 cases.

in slight degree. 6 cases.

474

in medium degree. 0 cases.

in severe degree. 1 cases.

with myeloic metaplasia. 0 cases.

Angio-folliculitis exsudativa with miliary necrosis. 4 cases.

in exudative form. 2 cases.

in exudative-hemorrhggic form. 2 cases.

in exudative form with slight proliferative tendency. 0 cases.

Angio-folliculitis with remarkable our so-called"polar changes". 39 cases.

with remarkable polar edema. 19 cases.

with remarkable polar hemorrhages 6 cases.

with some polar miliary necrosis 7 cases.

bionecrosis 3 cases.

with considerable polar cases.

plasma cells reaction 4 cases.

with some proliferative polar reaction 5 cases.

Angio-folliculitis exsudativa with slight proliferative tendency. 21 cases.

475

B) Disturbances of Billoth's cords.

3) Disturbances of pulpa-meshes.

Fasciculitis exsudativa	52	cases.
in slight degree.	0	cases.
in medium degree.	6	cases.
in severe degree.	46	cases.

Fasciculitis exsudativa with so-called "blood-sea".
(Fasciculitis haemorrhagbo-exsudativa).

	4	cases.
in slight degree.	1	cases.
in medium degree.	3	cases.
in severe degree.	0	cases.

Fasciculitis exsudativa with leucocytes-dissemination.
(Fasciculitis sero-purulenta or haemorrhagio-purulenta).

	47	cases.
in slight degree.	20	cases.
in medium degree.	13	cases.
in severe degree.	14	cases.
with myeloic metaplasia	24	cases.

Fasciculitis exsudativa with miliary necrosis.

	11	cases,
in slight exudative form.	0	cases.

476

in consid. exudative form. 0 cases.

in severe exudative form. 11 cases.

in exudative form, with slight proliferative tendency. 0 cases.

with some bacterial dissemination 13 cases.

Fasciculitis exsudativa with slight proliferative tendency. 10 cases.

4) Classification of splenal changes, according to concept "Folliculo-fasciculitis".

Folliculo-fasciculitis exsudativa. 53 cases.

in slight degree. 0 cases.

in medium degree. 6 cases.

in severe degree. 47 cases.

Folliculo-fasciculitis haemorrhagico-exsudativa. 29 cases.

in slight degree. 23 cases.

in medium degree. 5 cases.

in severe degree. 1 cases.

Folliculo-fasciculitis sero-purulenta or haemorrhagico-purulenta. 46 cases.

477

in slight degree. 20 cases.

in medium degree. 12 cases.

in severe degree. 14 cases.

with myeloic metaplasia. 24 cases.

Folliculo-fasciculitis exsudativa with some miliary necrosis. 13 cases.

in exudative form. 6 cases.

in hemorrhagic-exudative form 7 cases.

with some bacterial dissemination 13 cases.

in exudative form, but with slight proliferative tendency. 0 cases.

Follicul-fasciculitis exsudativa with slight proliferative tendency. 10 cases.

Disturbances and frequency of pathological changes in every section of "splenon" are as above described.

The main pathological findings are severe exudative or hemorrhagic-exudative changes, accompanied sometimes with remarkable miliary necrosis formation or bacterial dissemination.

478

SPLEEN

			N 1	N 2	N 3	N 4	N 5	N 7	N 8	N 9	N 10	N 11	N 12	N 14	N 15	N 17	N 18	N 19	N 20	N 21
Capsule	Thickness		↑++	↑+++	↓÷	↑++	↑	↑++	↑+·	↑++	↑—	↑+	↓÷	↑++	↑+	↑++	↑++	↑++	N	↓÷
	Curve		—	(+)	÷	+	↑	—	—	—	—	+	—	—	+	—	÷	÷	÷	—
Trabeculae	Thickness		↑+	N	↑÷	↑++	↑++	↑++	↑+·	↑+	↑÷	↑+·	↓÷	↑++	↑+	↑++	↑++	↑++	↑+	↓+·
	Blood Vessels	Congestion	+	+	+	+	+·	÷	÷	÷	+	÷	÷	+	+·	+	÷	÷	+·	+·
		Swelling of Walls	+·	++	++	+	++	++	++	+	+·	++	+·	++	++	+	++	+·	+	+·
		Loosening of Walls	+·	++	++	+	+	+	++	+	+	++	++	++	(++)	+	++	++	+	+·
		Hyaline Degeneration	+·	+	+·	÷	+·	++	++	+·	+·	÷	÷	+	++·	÷	+	÷	÷	÷
Reticulum	Hyperplasia		÷	÷	÷	÷	÷	—	—	—	—	—	—	—	÷	—	÷	—	—	—
	Swelling		+·	+	+	+	+·	÷	+	÷	÷	÷	÷	+	(++)	+	+·	÷	+	÷
	Hyaline Degeneration		+·	+	÷	÷	+	÷	+	++	÷	÷	÷	÷	+	÷	÷	÷	÷	—
	Hyperplasia of Reticular Cells	in Follicles	+	÷	÷	+	÷	+·	+	÷	÷	+	+	÷	+·	÷	+·	÷	÷	+·
		Perifollicular	+·	÷	+	÷	—	÷	÷	+	÷	÷	÷	÷	+	÷	+	÷	÷	÷
		Peritrabecular	÷	÷	÷	÷	—	÷	÷	÷	÷	÷	÷	÷	+	÷	÷	÷	÷	÷
Follicles	Size		↓+++	↓+·	↓++	↓+++	↓++·	↓+++	↓+++	↓+++	↓++	↓+++	↓++·	↓++	↓++·	↓+++	↓++	↓++	↓++	↓(+++)
	Number		↓+++	↓++	↓++	↓+++	↓++	↓++	↓++	↓+++	↓++	↓++	↓++	↓++	↓++	↓++	↓++	↓++	↓++·	↓+++
	Decrease of Lymphocytes		++	+++	+·	++	++	++	++	+++	++	++	++	++	++	++	++	+·	++	++
	Edema	in Follicles	++	++	++	++	++	++	+·	+	++	+++	++	++	++	++	++	+·	++	+++
		Perifollicular	+++	++	++	++	++	++	+·	+	++	+++	++	++	++	++	++	+·	++	+++
	Hemorrhage	in Follicles	÷	+·	÷	÷	÷	÷	÷	÷	÷	÷	÷	+	+	—	÷	÷	÷	÷
		Perifollicular	÷	+++	÷	÷	+	÷	÷	÷	÷	÷	÷	+	+	—	÷	÷	÷	÷
	Histiocytes	in Follicular	÷	÷	÷	÷	÷	—	÷	÷	+	—	÷	—	—	—	—	÷	÷	÷
		Perifollicular	÷	÷	÷	÷	÷	—	÷	÷	+	—	÷	—	—	—	—	÷	÷	÷
	Central Artery	Congestion	÷	++	÷	÷	÷	÷	÷	÷	÷	÷	÷	÷	÷	÷	÷	÷	÷	÷
		Endothelium Swelling	÷	÷	+	÷	++	++	+	+	++	+	+	++	+	÷	+	+	+	÷
		Endothelium Hyperplasia	—	—	—	—	—	—	—	—	—	—	—	—	—	—	—	—	—	—
		Endothelium Desquamation	÷	÷	+	÷	++	+·	+·	+	+·	+·	+	+	÷	+	÷	+	÷	÷
		Walls Swelling	+++	+·	++	+++	+++	++	+++	+·	++	++	+·	++	+++	++	+·	++·	+++	+++
		Walls Loosening	+++	++	++	+++	+·	+	+	+	+	+	÷	++·	+	+·	++	++·	++	+++
		Walls Hyaline Degeneration	++	++	+	+	++	+++	+++	+	+·	+	+·	÷	+++	+	÷	÷	÷	÷
	Exist of Germinating Center		—	—	—	—	—	—	—	—	—	—	—	—	—	—	—	—	—	—
	Necrosis	central	—	—	—	—	—	—	—	—	—	—	—	—	—	+	—	—	—	—
		peripheral	—	—	—	—	—	—	—	—	—	—	—	—	—	—	—	—	—	—
Venous Sinuses	Width		+++	++	+++	+·	+·	++	++	+·	+	++	+·	+	++	+·	+	+·	+·	++
	Cavernous Sinuses		+	+	+	+	—	—	—	+	+	+	—	—	—	—	—	—	++	+
	Congestion		÷	++	÷	+	÷	÷	—	÷	÷	+·	+	÷	(+·)	÷	+	÷	+	++
	Cellular Inclusion	Leucocytes	—	+	—	÷	—	÷	÷	÷	÷	÷	÷	—	÷	÷	÷	÷	—	÷
		Lymphocytes	÷	÷	÷	—	÷	÷	÷	÷	÷	÷	÷	÷	÷	÷	÷	÷	÷	÷
		Histiocytic Cells	÷	÷	—	÷	÷	÷	÷	÷	+	÷	÷	÷	÷	—	—	—	—	—
	Endothelium	Hyperplasia	+	—	+	—	—	—	—	—	—	—	—	—	—	—	—	+	—	—
		Resolution	÷	÷	÷	÷	+	÷	÷	÷	—	+	÷	—	—	++	÷	÷	÷	÷
		Phagocytosis	+	+	+	+	+	+	+	++	+	+	+	+	+	—	+	÷	+	+
Billroth's Cord	Edema		++	++	+·	++	++	+·	++	++	++	+++	+++	+++	++	++	++	+·	+·	++
	Congestion		+	++	+·	+	÷	÷	÷	÷	÷	÷	÷	÷	+	÷	÷	÷	(+·)	++
	Necrosis		—	—	—	—	—	—	—	—	÷	—	+	—	—	+	—	—	—	+
	Decrease of Lymphocytes		++	++	+·	++	++	+++	+·	+++	+++	+++	++·	÷	++	+++	++	++	++	+++
	Leucocytes		—	++	÷	÷	—	++	+·	÷	+·	÷	+·	÷	++	÷	+	÷	÷	+·
	Plasma Cells		—	—	—	—	—	—	—	—	÷	—	—	—	—	—	—	÷	—	—
	Splenocytes		÷	÷	÷	÷	÷	÷	÷	÷	+·	+	÷	÷	÷	—	—	÷	÷	÷
	Reticular Cells		+	÷	+	÷	—	÷	÷	÷	—	÷	—	÷	+	—	÷	+	÷	÷
Hemosiderosis			÷	÷	÷	÷	—	—	—	÷	÷	÷	÷	÷	÷	—	—	÷	—	—

479

SPLEEN

	N 23	N 24	N 26	N 27	N 29	N 30	N 31	N 33	N 35	N 36	N 38	N 40	N 42	N 44	N 46	N 47	N 49
Capsule – Thickness	↑++	↓++	↓+:	↑++	↑÷	↓÷	↑÷	↓∸	↑++	↑÷	↓++	↑+:	↑+:	↓+++	↑++:	↑++	↑+++
Capsule – Curve	∸	∸	∸	+	∸	∸	∸	—	∸	÷	∸	÷	÷	∸	÷	÷	+
Trabeculae – Thickness	↑+	↓+	↑+	↑+	↑∸	↑÷	↑+	↓∸	↑+	↑+	↑+	↑+	↑+	↓+++	↑++:	↑∸	↑+
Trabeculae – Blood Vessels – Congestion	++	÷	++	+	++	+++	+	(+++)	÷	+:	+:	+++	+	+	÷	+	÷
Trabeculae – Blood Vessels – Swelling of Walls	+	+++	++	++	++	+:	+:	++	++	++	++	++:	++	+	++	+++	++
Trabeculae – Blood Vessels – Loosening of Walls	+	++	++	+:	++	+	++	+:	++	++	++	++:	++	++	++	++	+
Trabeculae – Blood Vessels – Hyaline Degeneration	∸	÷	÷	+	++	++	+	++	+	∸	+	+:	++	+:	÷	+	++
Reticulum – Hyperplasia	—	—	—	∸	∸	∸	—	∸	∸	—	∸	∸	÷	—	—	∸	—
Reticulum – Swelling	++	+:	++	+	++	+:	÷	+:	+:	+:	++	++	+	÷	+:	++	+
Reticulum – Hyaline Degeneration	—	—	—	+	++	++:	∸	+++	∸	—	∸	+:	+:	+	+	÷	∸
Reticulum – Hyperplasia of Reticular Cells – in Follicles	+:	÷	+++	+:	+	+	÷	÷	÷	÷	÷	+	÷	∸	—	+++	+
Reticulum – Hyperplasia of Reticular Cells – perifollicular	÷	∸	+	+++	+:	—	÷	÷	∸	∸	+	÷	÷	∸	—	++++	∸
Reticulum – Hyperplasia of Reticular Cells – peritrabecular	∸	∸	÷	÷	+	—	∸	∸	∸	∸	∸	∸	∸	∸	—	+	∸
Follicles – Size	↓+:	↓+++	↓+:	↓++	↓+++	(++++)	↓+++	↓++:	↓++:	↓+++	↓+++	↓+++	↓+++	↓+++	↓+++	↓++:	↓+++
Follicles – Number	↓+++	↓+++	↓++	↓++	↓+++	↓+++	↓++	↓+++	↓+++	↓+++	↓++	↓++:	↓+++	↓++	↓+++	↓++	↓+
Follicles – Decrease of Lymphocytes	+++	++	+++	++	++	+:	++	+++	+++	++:	++	++:	++	+:	+++	+++	++
Follicles – Edema – in Follicles	+++	+++	++:	+:	++	++	++	++	++	+++	++	++	+++	+:	++	++:	++
Follicles – Edema – perifollicular	+++	+++	++:	+:	++	++	++	++	++	+++	++	++	+++	+:	++	+++	++
Follicles – Hemorrhage – in Follicles	÷	÷	÷	∸	++	++	÷	+:	∸	∸	∸	∸	÷	÷	∸	÷	÷
Follicles – Hemorrhage – perifollicular	÷	÷	÷	÷	++	++	∸	+:	∸	∸	∸	∸	÷	÷	∸	÷	÷
Follicles – Histiocytes – in Follicles	÷	∸	—	∸	∸	∸	÷	∸	÷	∸	÷	∸	∸	∸	∸	∸	—
Follicles – Histiocytes – perifollicular	÷	∸	—	∸	∸	∸	÷	∸	÷	∸	÷	∸	÷	+	∸	—	—
Follicles – Central Artery – Congestion	÷	∸	∸	∸	÷	∸	∸	÷	∸	∸	∸	∸	∸	∸	∸	∸	∸
Follicles – Central Artery – Endothelium – Swelling	+	+	+:	++	++	++	+:	+	+:	÷	—	+	+:	+	+:	—	+:
Follicles – Central Artery – Endothelium – Hyperplasia	—	—	—	—	—	—	—	—	∸	—	—	÷	—	—	—	—	÷
Follicles – Central Artery – Endothelium – Desquamation	÷	+	+	+	+	+	+	÷	÷	÷	∸	÷	∸	∸	++	÷	∸
Follicles – Central Artery – Walls – Swelling	+++	++:	+++	++	++:	+:	+:	+:	+:	+++	++	++	++	++	++	++:	+:
Follicles – Central Artery – Walls – Loosening	+:	++:	++	++	÷	÷	+	+	++	+	(+++)	++	+++	÷	++	++	++
Follicles – Central Artery – Walls – Hyaline Degeneration	∸	∸	÷	+	+++	++	++	+:	÷	—	+	÷	∸	++	÷	÷	∸
Follicles – Exist of Germinating Center	—	—	—	—	—	—	—	—	—	∸	—	—	—	—	—	—	—
Follicles – Necrosis – central	—	—	—	—	—	—	—	—	—	—	—	—	—	—	÷	—	—
Follicles – Necrosis – peripheral	—	—	—	—	—	—	—	—	—	—	—	—	—	—	++	—	—
Venous Sinuses – Width	++	+++	++	+	+:	+:	+	+++	++:	++:	+	+:	+	+	+	+	++
Venous Sinuses – Cavernous Sinuses	+	+	+	+	—	—	—	—	—	—	—	+	—	—	—	—	+
Venous Sinuses – Congestion	++	÷	++	÷	++	++	+	∸	+	∸	+	÷	÷	÷	÷	+:	÷
Venous Sinuses – Cellular Inclusion – Leucocytes	∸	∸	—	—	—	—	—	—	—	—	∸	—	—	∸	+	—	—
Venous Sinuses – Cellular Inclusion – Lymphocytes	∸	∸	∸	∸	∸	∸	∸	∸	÷	∸	÷	∸	∸	÷	|	∸	∸
Venous Sinuses – Cellular Inclusion – Histiocytic Cells	∸	∸	∸	∸	∸	∸	÷	∸	÷	∸	—	∸	÷	∸	|	∸	∸
Venous Sinuses – Endothelium – Hyperplasia	—	—	—	+:	—	—	—	—	—	—	÷	—	+	—	|	+	+
Venous Sinuses – Endothelium – Resolution	+	÷	+	—	—	—	÷	÷	÷	+	∸	∸	∸	∸	|	÷	∸
Venous Sinuses – Endothelium – Phagocytosis	+	+	+	+	+	+	+	+	+	+	+	+	+	+	|	+	+
Billroth's Cord – Edema	+++	++	++++	++	++	+++	++	++	+++	+++	+++	++	+:	+:	+	++	++
Billroth's Cord – Congestion	÷	÷	(+)	÷	++	+:	+	+:	∸	∸	∸	÷	÷	÷	|	+	+
Billroth's Cord – Necrosis	∸	—	—	—	—	—	—	—	—	—	—	—	—	—	|	—	—
Billroth's Cord – Decrease of Lymphocytes	+++	++	++++	++	++	+++	++	++	++	+++	+:	++	++	+	|	+++	++
Billroth's Cord – Leucocytes	+:	+	∸	—	∸	—	÷	+	—	∸	+:	∸	—	+	|	∸	÷
Billroth's Cord – Plasma Cells	—	—	—	∸	—	—	—	—	÷	—	∸	∸	÷	∸	|	—	—
Billroth's Cord – Splenocytes	∸	∸	—	∸	∸	+	+:	∸	∸	∸	∸	÷	+:	÷	|	÷	∸
Billroth's Cord – Reticular Cells	+	÷	÷	÷	∸	∸	÷	∸	∸	∸	÷	∸	—	∸	|	+	÷
Hemosiderosis	—	∸	+	∸	∸	+:	∸	∸	∸	∸	∸	∸	∸	∸	|	÷	∸

480

SPLEEN

			S 1	S 2	S 3	S 4	S 5	S 6	S 8	S 9	S 10	S 11	S 12	S 14	S 15	S 19	S 22	S 26	S 28	S 38
Capsule	Thickness		↓++	↓+	↓÷	N	N	↓÷	↑++	↑++	↑++̈	↑++̈	↑+++	↑++	↑+̈	↓++	↑+	↑÷	|	↓÷
Capsule	Curve		—	—	÷	÷	÷	—	—	—	—	—	++	—	÷	÷	—	—	|	+̈
Trabeculae	Thickness		↓++	↓+	↓+̈	N	↓+	↓÷	↑++	↑++	↑+	↑++	↑+̈	↓÷	↑+	↓+	↑+	↑+	↑÷	↑÷
Trabeculae	Blood vessels	Congestion	÷	÷	(+++)	(++̈)	÷	+̈	+	+	++	++	++	++	+̈	+̈	++	+̈	++	÷
Trabeculae	Blood vessels	Swelling of Walls	÷	+	+̈	+	+	+	++	+̈	+̈	++	++	+̈	++	+++	++	++	+++	++
Trabeculae	Blood vessels	Loosening of Walls	÷	÷	+̈	÷	+	+	+	+	+	++	++	+	++	++	+	+++	+++	++
Trabeculae	Blood vessels	Hyaline Degeneration	—	—	÷	÷	÷	÷	++	+̈	+̈	+	—	—	+	++	—	÷	+	+
Reticulum	Hyperplasia		—	—	—	÷	—	÷	÷	÷	—	—	—	—	—	÷	÷	—	—	÷
Reticulum	Swelling		++	++	++	+̈	+	+	+̈	+	+̈	++	+++	+̈	+̈	++	+̈	++	+	+̈
Reticulum	Hyaline Degeneration		—	—	÷	÷	÷	—	++	+	÷	—	—	÷	—	÷	÷	—	—	÷
Reticulum	Hyperplasia of Reticular Cells	in Follicles	÷	÷	÷	+	÷	÷	÷	—	÷	+++	++̈	+	+	÷	÷	+++	+	÷
Reticulum	Hyperplasia of Reticular Cells	Perifollicular	÷	+	—	÷	÷	÷	÷	—	÷	+̈	÷	+	÷	÷	+	÷	÷	+
Reticulum	Hyperplasia of Reticular Cells	Peritrabecular	÷	÷	—	÷	÷	÷	—	—	÷	++	+̈	+	÷	÷	÷	÷	÷	÷
Follicles	Size		↓+++	↓+̈	↓++	↓+++	↓+++	↓+	↓+++	↓+++	↓+	↓+̈	↓+++	↓+++	↓+++	↓++	↓(+++)	↓++	↓+++	↓(+)
Follicles	Number		↓+++	↓+	↓++	↓++	↓+++	↓+	↓+++	↓+++	↓+	↓+̈	↓+++	↓+++	↓+++	↓++	↓+̈	↓++	↓+++	↓+
Follicles	Decrease of Lymphocytes		+++	+	++	+++	++	+	+++	++̈	++	+++	+++	++	++̈	++	+̈	+++	+++	+++
Follicles	Edema	in Follicles	+++	+̈	++	+	+̈	+	+	+	++	+̈	+++	++	++	+++	+̈	+++	+̈	++
Follicles	Edema	Perifollicular	++	++	++	++	+̈	+	+	+	++	+̈	+++	++	++	+++	++	+++	+̈	+++
Follicles	Hemorrhage	in Follicles	÷	÷	÷	÷	÷	÷	÷	+	÷	÷	÷	÷	÷	+̈	÷	—	++	÷
Follicles	Hemorrhage	Perifollicular	÷	÷	÷	—	—	—	++	++	÷	÷	÷	÷	+	+̈	÷	+̈	+̈	+
Follicles	Histiocytes	in Follicles	÷	(+)	+	+̈	÷	—	+̈	+	++	÷	+̈	÷	÷	+̈	÷	—	÷	++
Follicles	Histiocytes	Perifollicular	÷	÷	++	++	÷	÷	+̈	+	++	÷	+̈	÷	÷	+̈	÷	—	÷	++
Follicles	Central Artery	Congestion	÷	÷	÷	÷	÷	÷	÷	÷	÷	÷	÷	÷	÷	÷	—	÷	÷	÷
Follicles	Central Artery Endothelium	Swelling	+	+	+	+	÷	÷	÷	÷	÷	+	+	+	+	++	++	++	++	+̈
Follicles	Central Artery Endothelium	Hyperplasia	—	÷	—	—	—	—	—	—	—	—	—	—	—	—	—	—	—	—
Follicles	Central Artery Endothelium	Desquamation	+	÷	÷	÷	÷	÷	÷	÷	÷	+	+	÷	+	+̈	+++	++	+	+
Follicles	Central Artery Walls	Swelling	+	+	+	+	++	++	++	++	++	+++	++	++	++	+++	++++	+++	++	++
Follicles	Central Artery Walls	Loosening	÷	+	+̈	+̈	+	+	++	++	++	+++	++	+̈	++̈	+++	++++	++	++	++
Follicles	Central Artery Walls	Hyaline Degeneration	—	—	÷	÷	(+++)	—	++	++	+̈	+	—	÷	÷	++	—	—	+	+
Follicles	Exist of Germinating Center		—	+	—	—	—	(+)	—	—	—	—	—	—	—	—	—	—	—	—
Follicles	Necrosis	Central	—	—	—	—	—	—	—	—	—	—	—	—	+	—	—	—	—	+
Follicles	Necrosis	Peripheral	—	—	—	—	—	—	—	—	—	—	—	—	—	—	—	—	—	+
Venous Sinuses	Width		+	++	++	+̈	+	+	++	++	+	++	+	+	+	+	+	++	+̈	+̈
Venous Sinuses	Cavernous Sinuses		—	+	+	++	+	—	+	+	+	+̈	—	—	+	+	—	+	+	+
Venous Sinuses	Congestion		+	+̈	÷	÷	÷	+	÷	÷	÷	+̈	(+)	÷	++	+̈	÷	+̈	+	++
Venous Sinuses	Cellular Inclusion	Leucocytes	+	÷	+	÷	÷	÷	÷	÷	÷	÷	|	—	÷	+	÷	—	+	÷
Venous Sinuses	Cellular Inclusion	Lymphocytes	÷	÷	÷	÷	÷	÷	÷	÷	÷	÷	|	÷	÷	÷	÷	÷	÷	÷
Venous Sinuses	Cellular Inclusion	Histiocytic Cells	÷	÷	÷	÷	÷	÷	+	÷	÷	÷	|	÷	÷	+	÷	—	÷	+
Venous Sinuses	Endothelium	Hyperplasia	—	÷	—	—	—	++	—	—	+	+	—	—	—	—	—	—	—	—
Venous Sinuses	Endothelium	Resolution	÷	+	++	+	+	—	—	—	—	—	+	÷	÷	+++	—	+++	+	++
Venous Sinuses	Endothelium	Phagocytosis	—	÷	+	+	+	—	++	++	+	+	—	÷	+	++	÷	—	++	++
Billroth's Cord	Edema		++++	+++	++	+̈	+̈	++	+	+	++	++	+++	++	++	++	++	++++	+++	++
Billroth's Cord	Congestion		÷	÷	÷	÷	÷	÷	++	+̈	÷	÷	÷	÷	+	+̈	÷	÷	++	++
Billroth's Cord	Necrosis		+	÷	+	+	+	—	+	—	—	(+)	++	—	—	+	—	—	++	++
Billroth's Cord	Decrease of Lymphocytes		++	+̈	++	++	+̈	+	++	++	++	+++	+++	++	++	+++	++	+++	+̈	++
Billroth's Cord	Leucocytes		++	+̈	++	+̈	++	÷	+̈	+̈	+̈	+	+̈	—	+̈	+	+	—	++	+
Billroth's Cord	Plasma Cells		—	—	—	—	—	—	|	—	—	—	—	—	÷	÷	—	—	—	÷
Billroth's Cord	Splenocytes		÷	÷	+	÷	÷	÷	+̈	+̈	+̈	+	—	÷	÷	+̈	+	—	÷	+̈
Billroth's Cord	Reticular Cells		÷	+	—	÷	÷	+	—	—	+	+̈	+̈	+	÷	÷	+	÷	+	+̈
	Hemosiderosis		÷	÷	÷	÷	÷	÷	—	—	—	—	÷	—	+̈	÷	—	—	÷	+̈

481

Typical polar edema.
Intense edematous swelling of
penicillar artery wall and
intense edematous swelling of
peri-penicillar artery tissues.

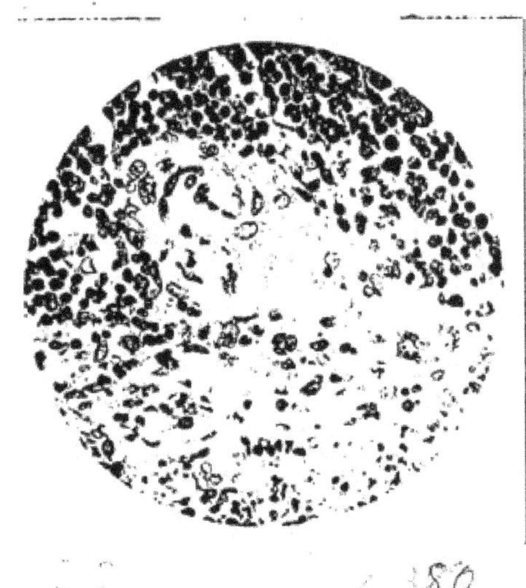

x 380

Folliculitis exsudativa with intense
exudative changes in follicle and
intense hemorhages at perifollicular
tissues(our so-called polar hemorhhgges).

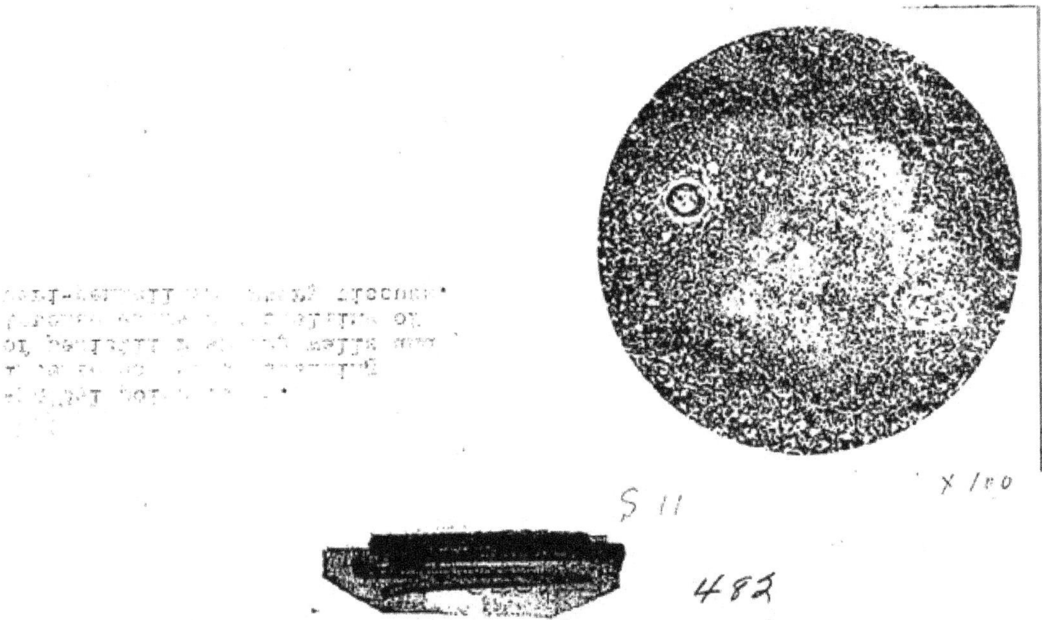

x 100

S 11

482

The most intense exudative

necrotic changes in fascucular tissues.

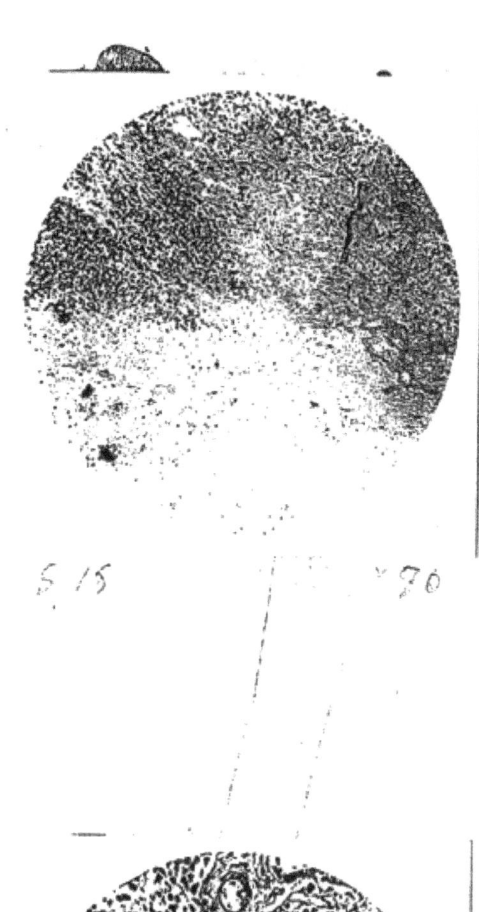

Intense bionecrotic changes in fascicular cords.

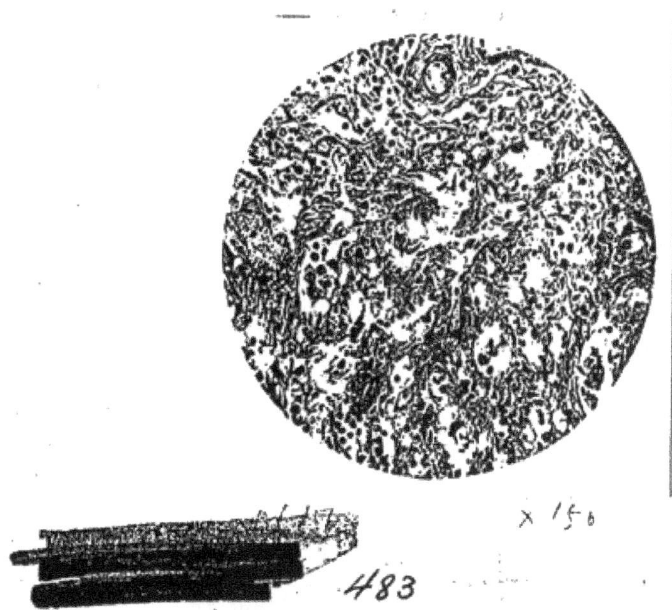

Hyalinous swelling of trabecle blood vessel.

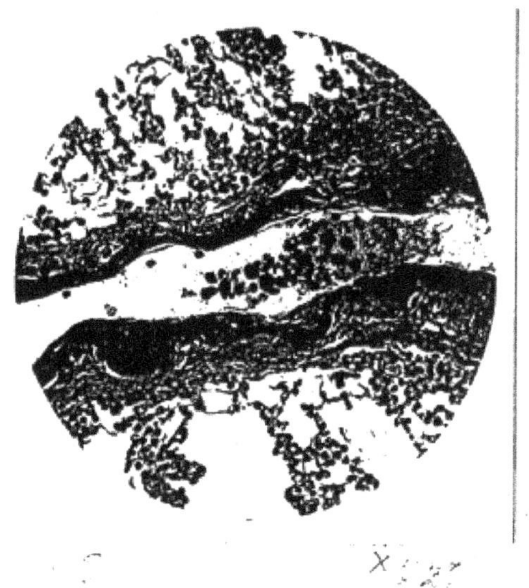

Hyaline degeneratiom of trabecle artery, accompanied with hyaline droplets formation.

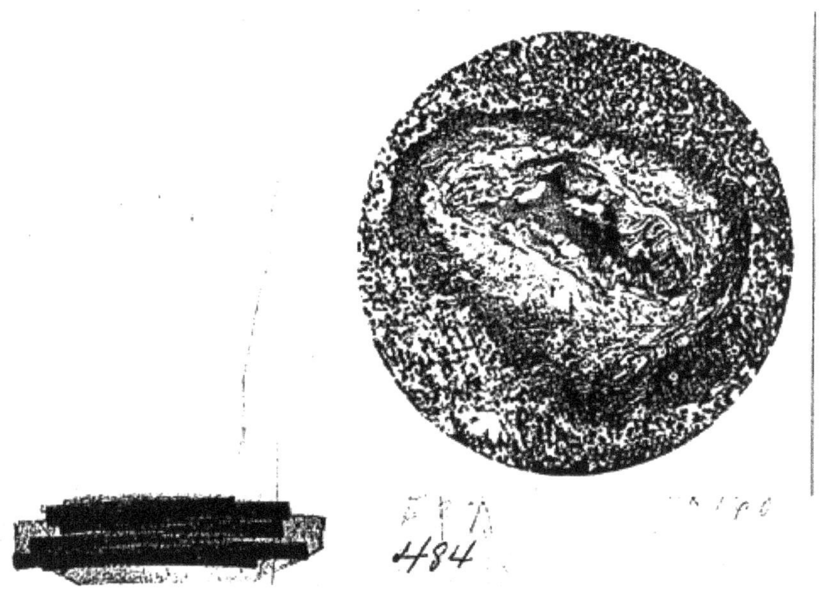

So-called sperma like necrosis, at perifollicular portion.

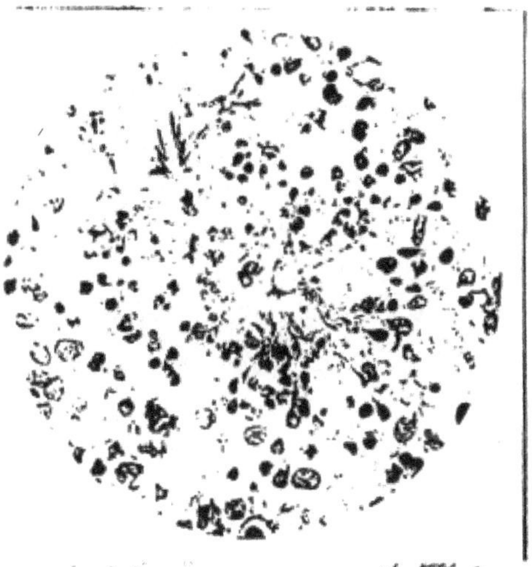

S 12 × 580

S 12 × 720

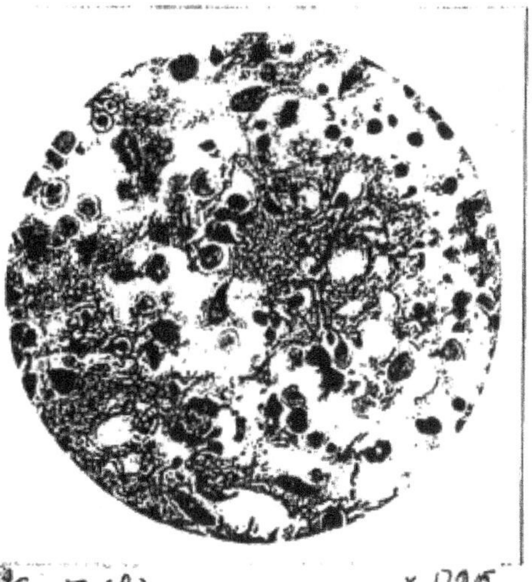

S 5 (b) × 720
485

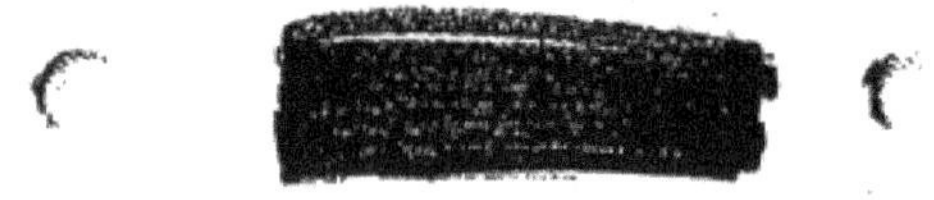

Edematous swelling of penicillar artery.

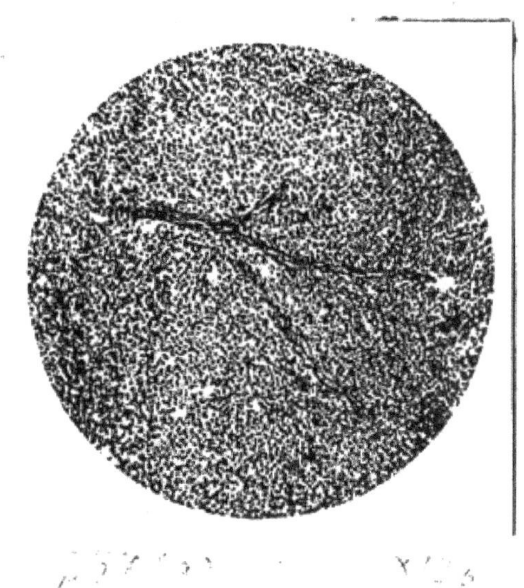

[illegible]

Hyalinous swelling of penicillar aretery.

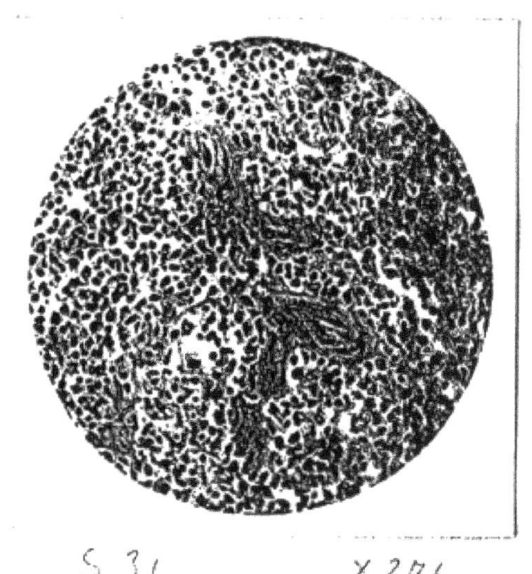

S 31 X 276

486

Edematous swelling and loosening of
central artery walls. and
serous exduation at perivascular tissues.

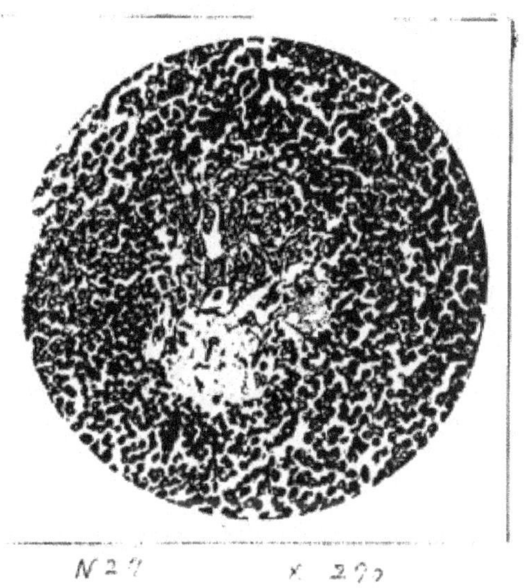

Proliferative reaction around A.radiolat
Some increased reticulum cells and
some increased adventitia cells.

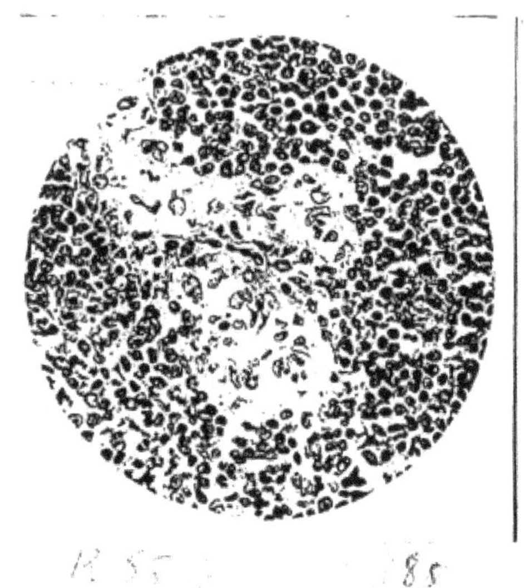

Hyalinnously degenerated follicle.

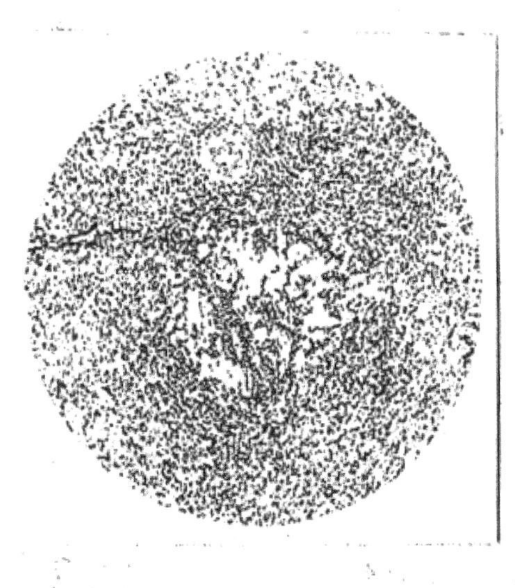

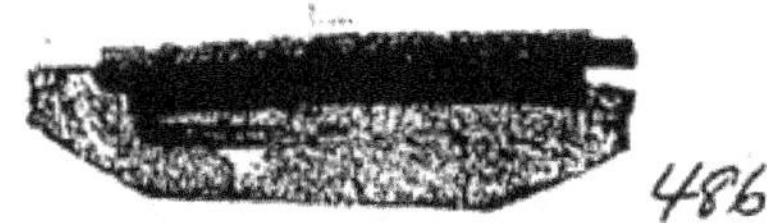

486

Angio-folliculitis exsudativo-suppurativa.
Edematous swelling of central artery walls.
Some exudative leucocytic changes in follicle.

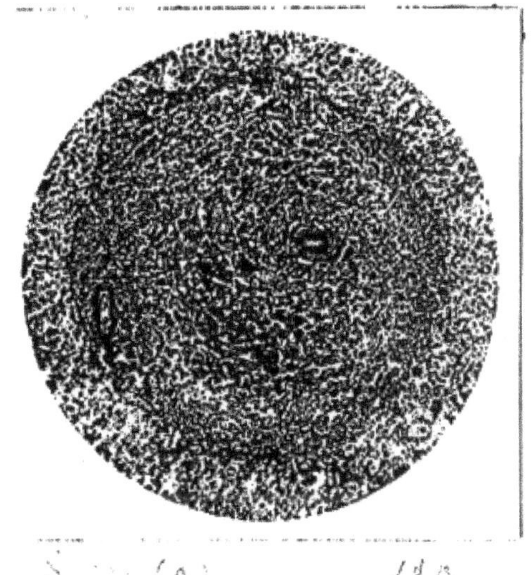

Angio-Folliculitis exsudativo-suppurativa.
Hyalinous swelling of central artery wall.
Some leucocytic changes in follicle.

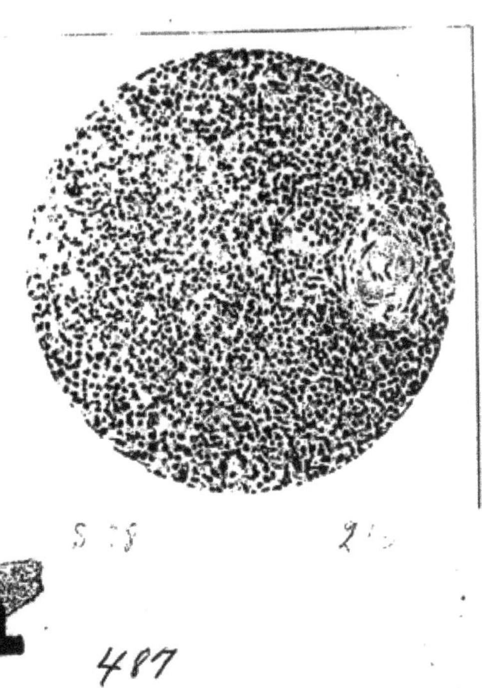

487

Remarkable hyperplasia of reticulum cells and reticulum gibresm at perifollicular portion.

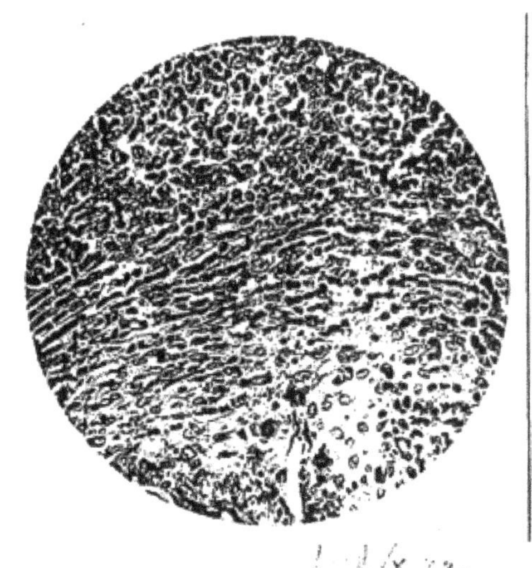

Plasma cell reaction, in high power. At perofolliculara pobtion.

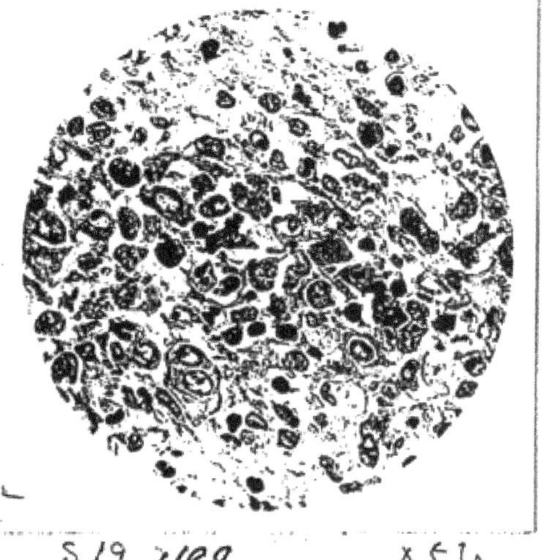

S19 488 X530

Lymphocytes accumlation at subendothelial layer of trabecle vein.

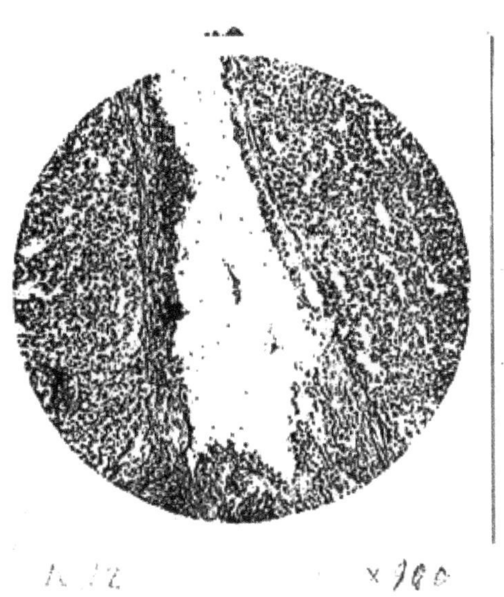

N 12 ×100

Lymphocytes accumulation in trabecle.

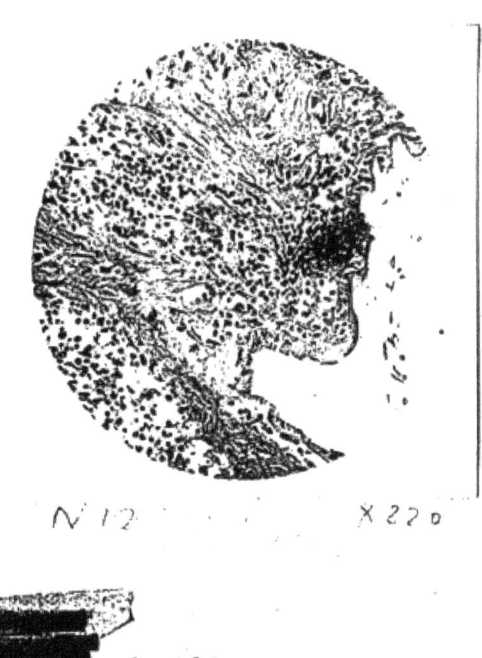

N 12 ×220

489

Hyperplasiae of endothelial cells
of sinus.

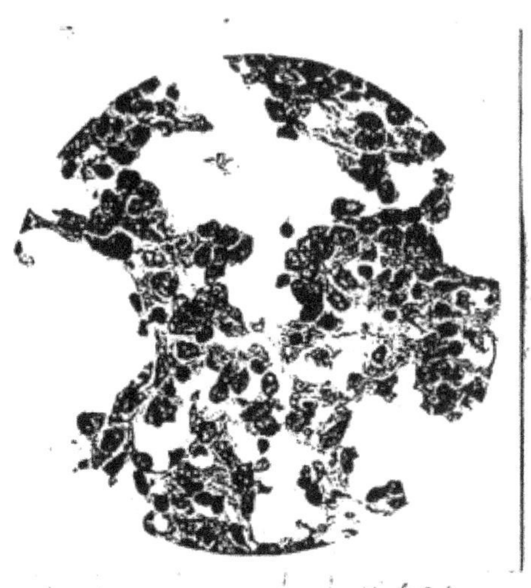

Hyperplasia of endothelial cells

of sinus and megakaryocyte.

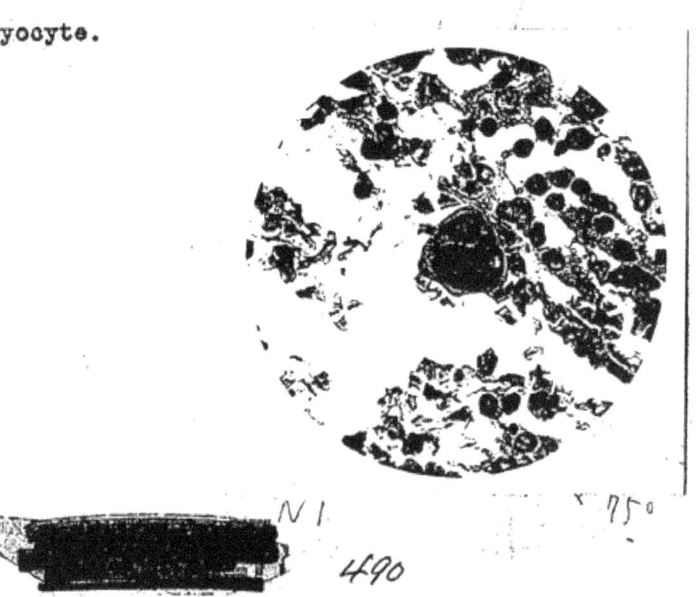

Hyalinous swelling of reticulum
fibers and reticulum cells at
perifollicular portion,
accompanied with slight proliferative
tendency.

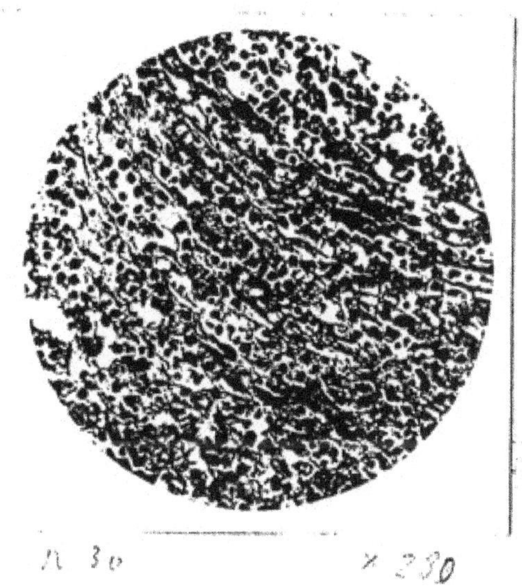

Lymphnode

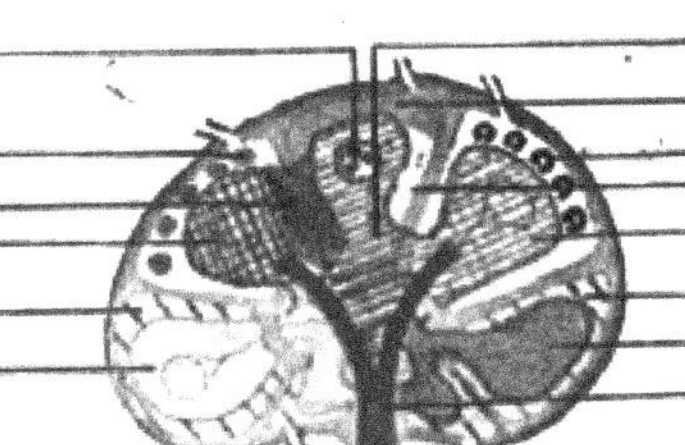
Hyperplasia of Germ center
Hyperplasia of Reticulum cell
Sinus congestion
Necrosis of follicle
Normal sinus
Exudation
No remarkable changes
Bacterial accumlation
Leukocytes dissemination
Sinus Exudation
Bionecrosis of Follicle
Sinus catarrh
Hemorrhage of Follicle
Congestion

442

LYMPH - NODE.

(A) Microscop. Investigation .

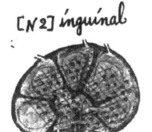

[N2] inguinal

3. Inguinal : quaill-egg large.
Intenst Pericapsulitis with remarkable congestion and plenty of leucocytes as capillary contents, severe hemorrhages and edema.
Some bacterial masses in capillaries.
Follicular tissues in severe inflammation ; intense hemorrhagic necrotic changes all over the follicular tissues with plenty leucocytes and erythrocytes (hemorrhages).

[N2] axillar

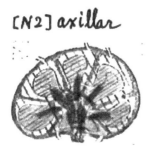

2. Axillar : pea-large.
Considerable Pericapsulitis with some congestion and perivascular hemorrhages.
Peripheral sinus with some bionecrotically swollen reticulum-cells and some leucocytes.
Medullary tissues with intenst congestion, severe edematous swelling and some leucocytes -emigration and
Follicular tissues with slight swelling and slight reduction.

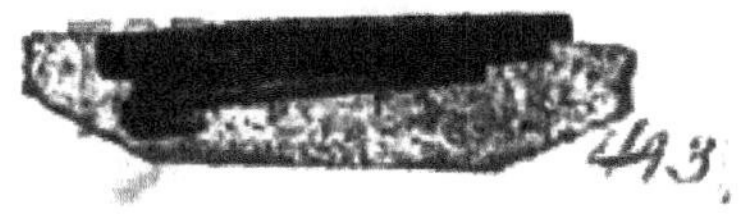

443

[N3] mesenterial

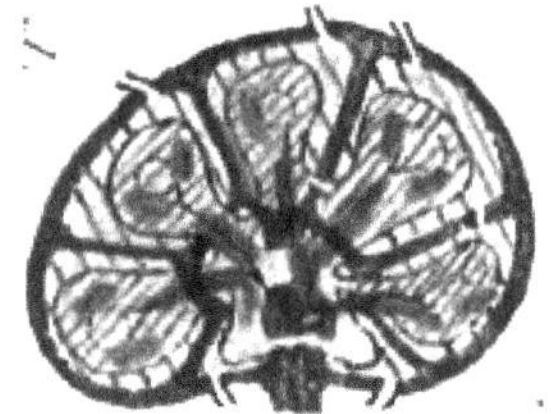

[N3] peribronchial

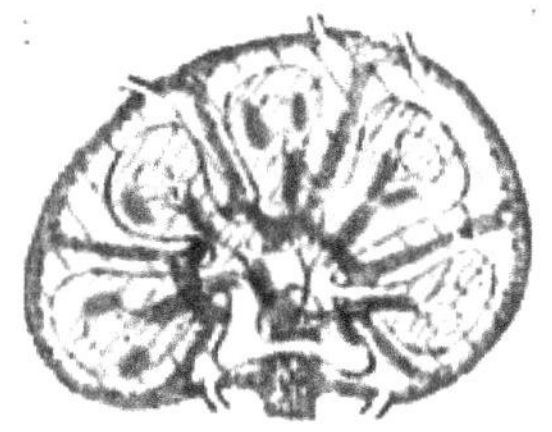

[N3]

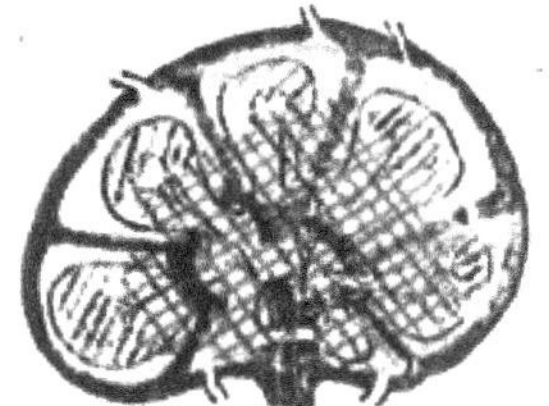

[N4] axillar

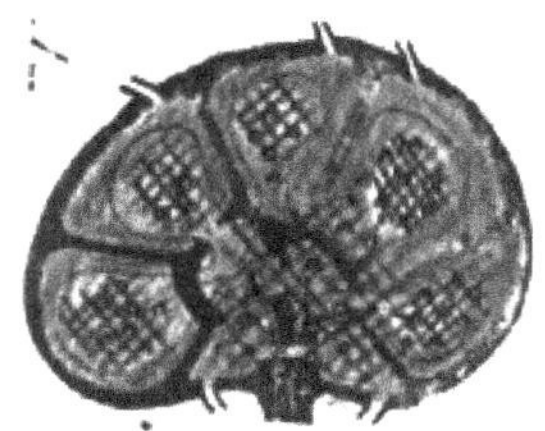

3. Mesenterial :

Medullary and follicular tissues with considerable congestion and some leucocytes, accompanied with considerable swelling of reticulum fibres.

3. Peribronchial :

Pericapsulitis and the same as above mentioned changes in follicular tissues.

3.

Lymphadenitis caseosa with some ginat cells.

4. Axillaris :

Pericapsular tissues with remarkable congestion (bionecrotic swelling of vessel-walls and some bacterial masses as capillary contents).

Medullary tissues with diffuse severe hemorrhages, plenty leucocytes dissemination and severe or bionecrotic swelling of medullary tissues.

Follicular tissues with total necrosis : plenty leucocytes-dissemination and severe diffuse hemorrhages.

4.

Peribronchial :

Peripheral sinus with slight catarrh and

444

[N4] peribronchial

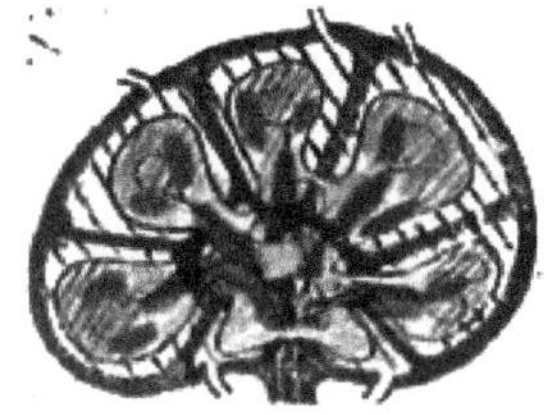

[N4] ileocecal

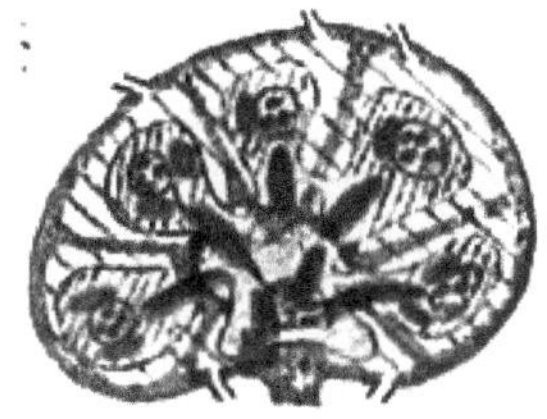

[N4] Mesenterial

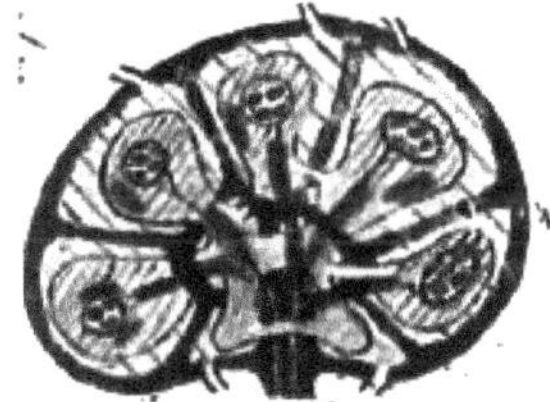

[N5] peribronchial

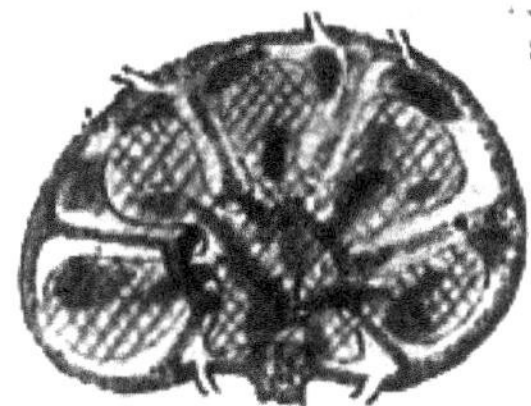

some leucocytes.

Medullary tissues with considerable congestion, remarkable edema and some increased cloudy swellen reticulum cells and

Follicular tissues with cloudy swelling and considerable congestion, accompanied with slight diminution of lymphocytes.

4.

Ileocecal : field corn-large.

Peripheral sinus with slight catarrh, medullary tissues with considerable congestion and considerable edematous swelling and follicular tissues with the same changes (congestion and edema).

Germinative centres with some increased reticulum-cells in cloudy swelling.

4. Mesenterial : Tapioca-large.

With the same changes, as avobe mentioned.

5. Peribronchial : pea-large.

Peripheral sinus with considerable homorhages and some bacterial masses, medullary tissues with remarkable congestion, some bacterial dissemination and bionecrotic swelling of medullary tissues.

Accompanied with some diffuse hemorrhages at

[N7] inguinal

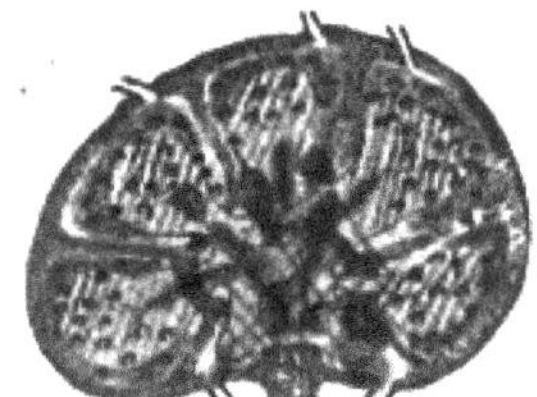

some places.

7. Inguinal : pea-large.

Slight pericapsular congestion and slight edema.

Peripheral sinus with considerable leucocytes and bacterial masses, accompanied with bionecrotic swelling of reticulum-fibres.

Medullary tissues with remarkable congestion, necrotic ruins of capillary-walls, bionecrotic swelling of follicular tissues, with some bacterial dissemination and diffuse hemorrhages. Follicular tissues with severe edema with plenty leucocytes and severe edema.

[N7] mesenterial

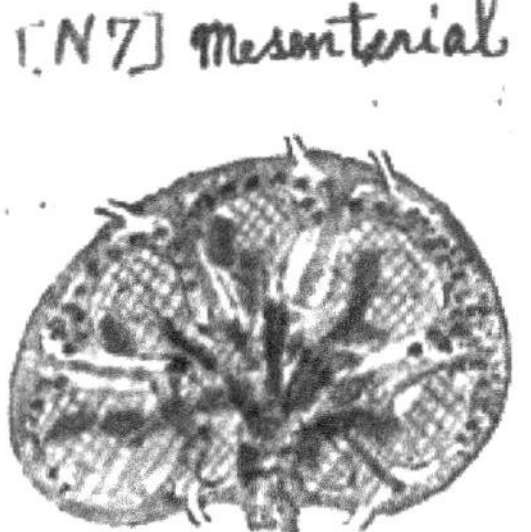

7. Mesenterial : pea-large.

Peripheral sinus with the same changes as above mentioned.

Medullary tissues with remarkable congestion, bionecrotic swelling of capillary walls, perivascular more or less diffuse bacterial dissemination and severe bionecrotic swelling of medullary tissues and follicular tissues with remarkable congestion, severe bionerotic swelling of reticulum fibres and more or less diffuse perivascular bacterial dissemination.

496

[N 8] Submaxillar (right)

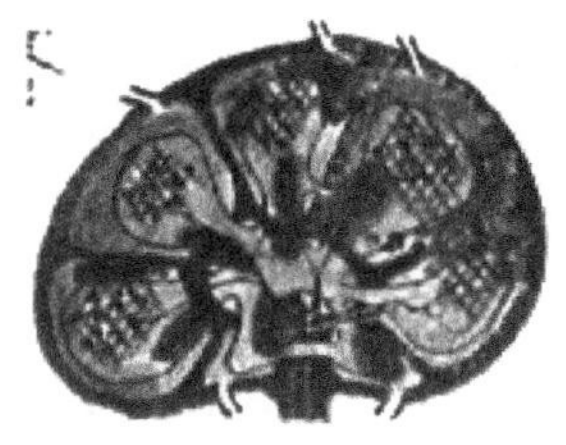

8. Submaxillaris (r) :

Considerable pericapsular congestion and peripheral sinus with intense hemorrhages and medullary tissues with considerable bacterial dissemination, plenty leucocytes, some lymphocytes and severe edematous swelling.

Follicular tissues with the same leucocytic -necrotic changes.

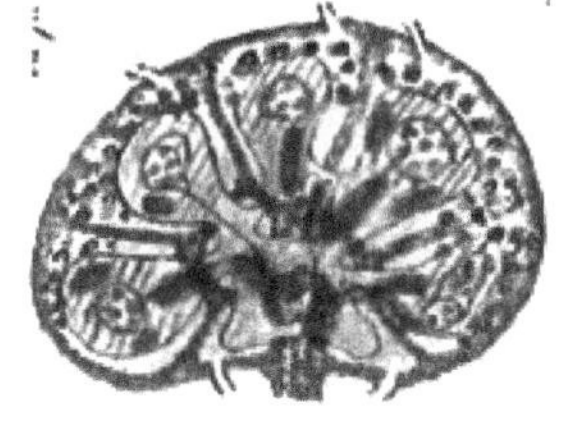

8. Submaxillaris (L).

Peripheral sinus with some leucocytes, some reticulum-cells in cloudy swelling and Medullary tissues with remarkable congestion, considerable edema, some increased reticulum cells in cloudy swelling and considerable edema.

[N8] peribronchial

Follicular tissues with considerable congestion and some increased reticulum-cells in cloudy swelling, accompanied with slight diminution of lymphocytes. Germinative centres with some increased reticulum-cells in intense cloudy swelling.

8. Peribronchial : pea-large.

Peripheral sinus with some hemorrhages and some bacterial masses.

Medullary tissues with intense congestion,

497

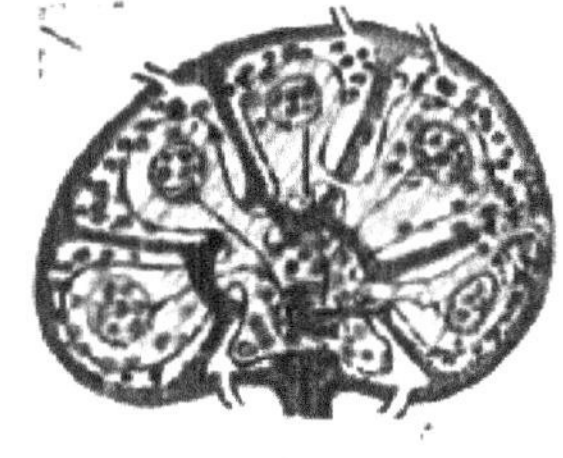

bionecrotic swelling, and diffus hemorrhages.
Follicular tissues with severe edematous swelling of reticulum cells, considerable reduction of follicular tissues and intense diminution of lymphocytes.

9.

Mesenterial : fiald-corn large.
Peripheral sinus with slight catarrh, slightly increased reticulum cells, some lymphocytes and a few leucocytes.
Medullary tissues with considerable hyperplasia of reticulum-cells.
Follicular tissues with slight swelling and slightly increased reticulum cells.
Germinative centres with the same changes.

9. Inguinal : missed.

10. Submaxillaris : quaill-egg large.
Pericapsular tissues with considerable congestion and some bacterial-dissemination.
Medullary tissues with considerable congestion, perivascular hemorrhages and severe edema with some bacterial dissemination.
Follicular tissues with some leucocytes, diffuse flaky bacterial dissemination, and severe bionecrotic swelling, accompanied

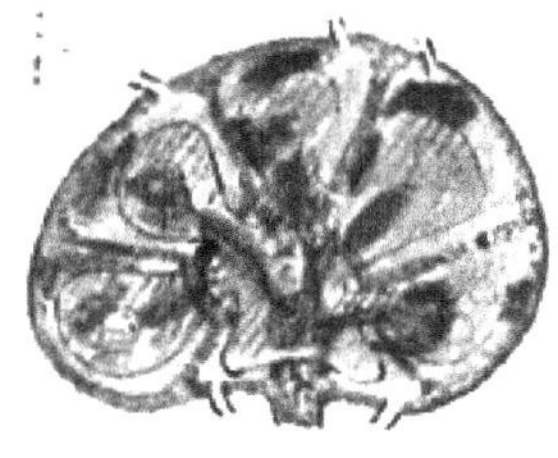

498

[N10] Submaxillar

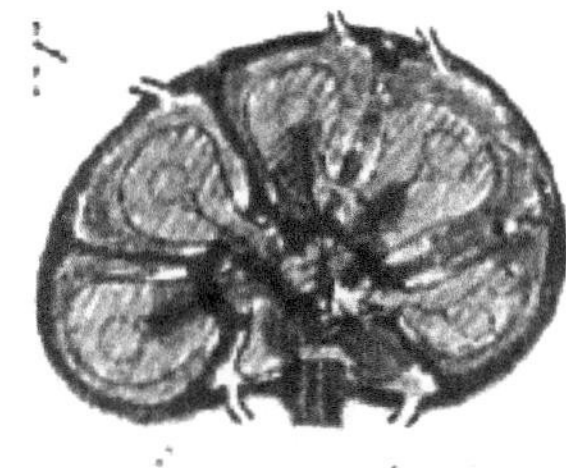

[N10] Peribronchial

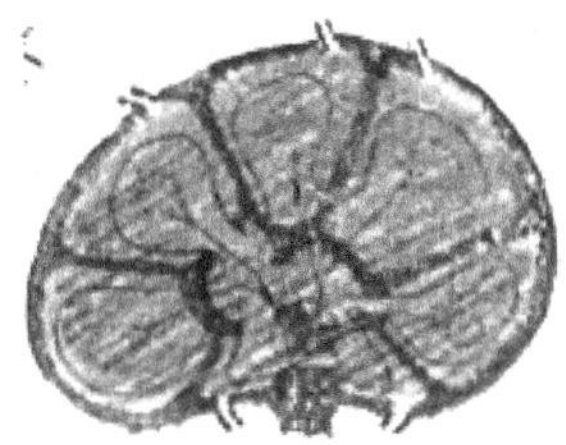

[N 11] inguinal

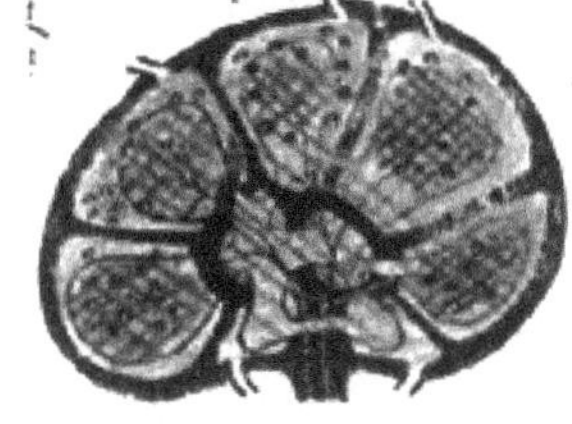

[N 11] Retroperitoneal

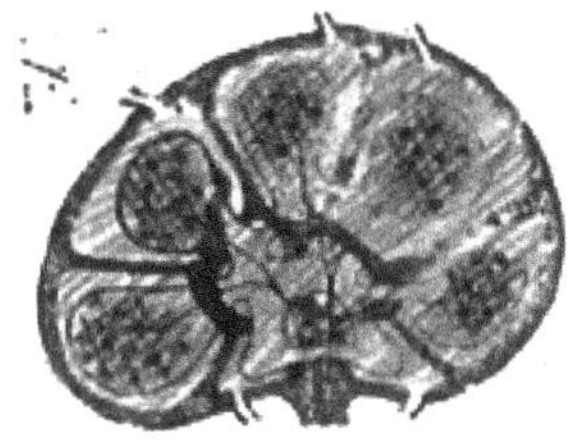

with diminish of lymphocytes.

10. Submaxillaris (I) : Quaill-egg large.

with the same changes.

10. Peribronchial : pea-large.

Pericapsular tissues with considerable congestion.

Peripheral sinus with plenty leucocytes, flaky bacterial masses and some bionecrotic swollen reticulum-cells.

Medullary tissues with remarkable congestion, bionecrotic ruins of capillary-walls, severe edema with diffuse bacterial dissemination and slightly increased reticulm-cells in intense cloudy swelling.

Follicular tissues with the same changes (leucocytic and hemorrhagic changes).

10. Peribronchial :

The most intense total hemorrhagic changes all over the follicular tissues, without any cellular structures.

11. Inguinal : Pigeon-egg large.

Pericapsular tissues with some arterioles in necrotic changes : necrotic ruins of walls, due to bacterial dissemination and plenty leucocytes in blood-vessels, and perivascular diffuse intense hemorrhagic-leucocytic infil-

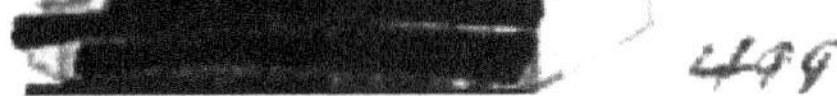

449

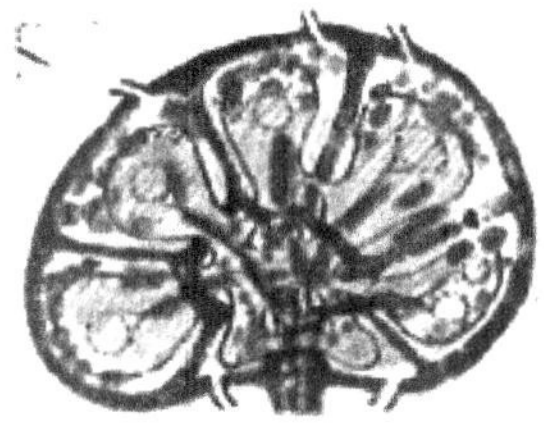

trations.

Follicular tissues in complete necrosis with plenty leucocytes and intense diffuse hemorrhages.

11. Retroperitoneal :

with the same changes : the most Intense Pericapsulitis with sëvere diffuse hemorrhagic-serous-leucocytic inflammation and follicular tissues with same hemorrhagic -leucocytic necrosis all over the tissues.

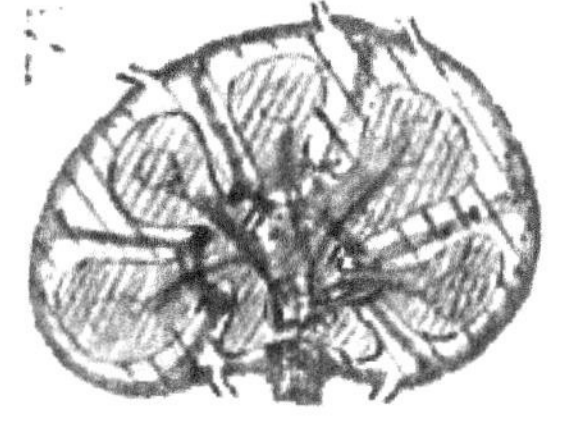

11. Peribronchial : sugar-corn large.

11. Peribronchial : Field corn-large.

Peripheral sinus with massive bacterial and plenty leucocytes dissemination and bionecroti ruins of reticulum-fibres.

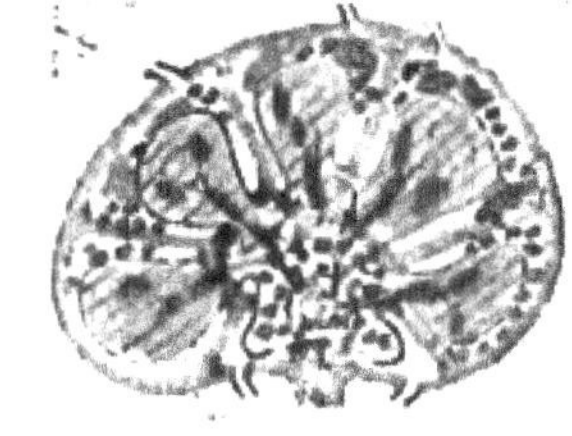

Medullary tissues with considerable congestion edema and some increased reticulum-cells in intense cloudy swelling with some leucocytes.

Follicular tissues with plenty leucocytes and bacterial accumulation, accompanied with severe edematous swelling in some follicles an some considerable reduction in some follicles.

12. Peribronchial : Tapioca-large.

Slight catarrh in peripheral sinus and slight congestion with some partial hemorrhages in medullary tissues. Slight edema and slight

506

[N14] mesenterial

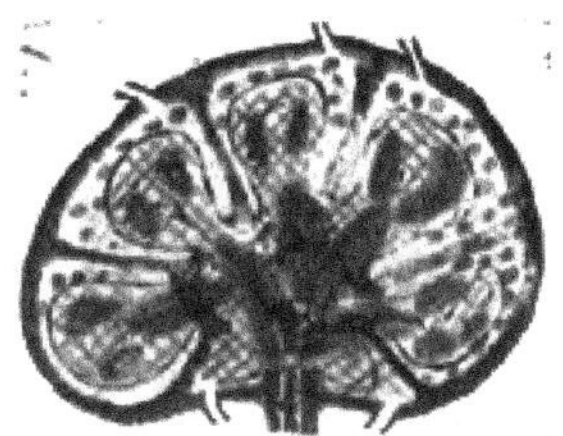

diminution of lymphocytes in follicular tiss-ues.

12. Peribronchial : Sugar-corr large.

Peripheral sinus with remarkable hyperplasia of reticulum-cells (cell by cell), in cloudy swelling and some bacterial masses, accompanied with intense hemosiderin deposits.

Medullary tissues with remarkable hyperplasia of reticulum-cells in intense cloudy swelling, and bionecrotic swelling of reticulum-fibres with some bacterial accumulations.

Follicular tissues with considerable conges-tion and edema.

[N 14] peribronchial

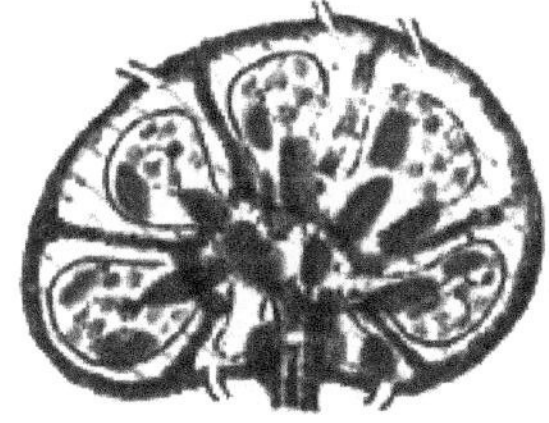

14. Mesenterial : Sugar-corn large.

Peripheral sinus with slight catarrh : some swollen reticulum-cells and some lymphocytes.

Medullary tissues with severe congestion, severe swelling of capillary walls, and diffus intense bionecrotic swelling with some bacterial accumulations.

Follicular tissues with intense bionecrotic swelling with some bacterial accumulations and at some places necrotic ruins of follicul-ar tissues with some leucocytes and severe diminish of lymphocytes.

501

[N14] heart-sack

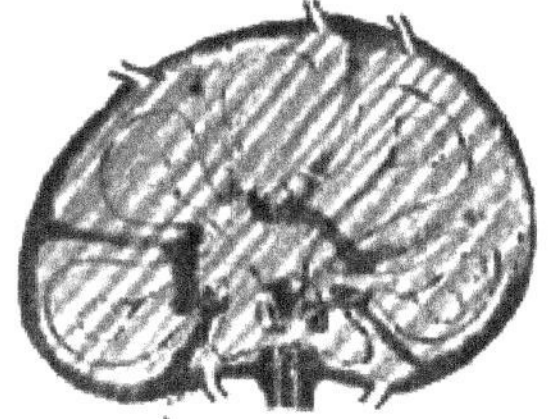

At some remained follicles with intense congestion and edema.

14. Peribronchial : pea-large.

Intense congestion in medullary and follicular tissues, with slightly increased reticulum--cells. No remarkable changes else.

[N15] peribronchial

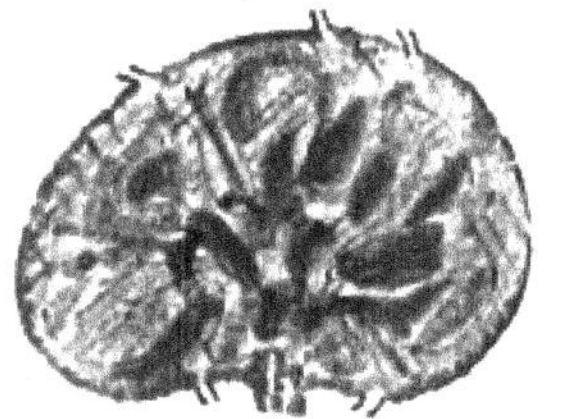

14. Inguinal (r) : pea-large.

Totally hemorrhagic all over the follicular tissues.

15. Peribronchial : Sugar-corn large.

Follicular tissues with considerable congestion, slight localised hemorrhgae and some bacterial accumulation.

[N15] peribronchial (at bifulcation)

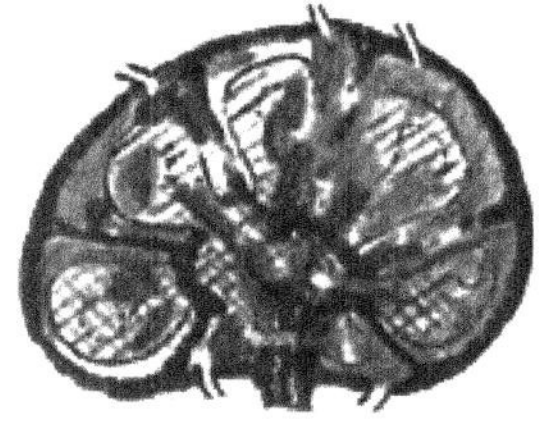

15. Peribronchial (at bifulcation) : fibld-cor large.

Pericapsular tissues with considerable congestion, some leucocytes-emigration, some bacterial accumulation and considerable perivascular edema.

[N16] peribronchial

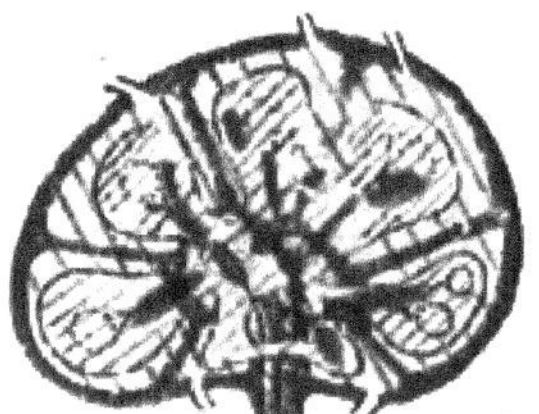

Peripheral sinus with remarkable hemorrhages, some leucocytes and bacterial accumulation and necrotic ruins of reticulum-fibres.

Medullary tissues with intense congestion, bionecrotic swelling of capillary walls, severe bionecrotic edema with plenty bacteria dissemination.

502

[N16] inguinal

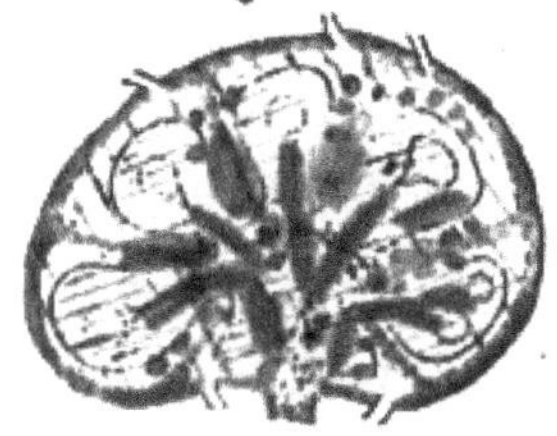

Follicular tissues, some places with the same changes and some places with severe congestion and edema, accompanied with slight diminution of lymphocytes.

16. Peribronchial : tapioca-large.

Medullary tisseus with considerable congestion and some edema.

[N16] mesenterial

16. Inguinal : pea-large.

Considerable congestion and slight hyperplasia of reticulum-cells.

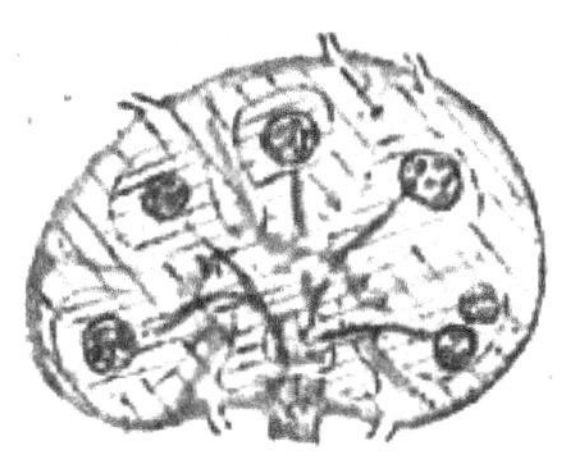

16. Mesenterial : field-corn large.

Slight catarrh of sinus and slight hyperplasia of germinative centres with some increased reticulum-cells.

16. Mesenterial (Radix) :

[N16] M-root

Medullary tissues with remarkable congestion (with slight hemorrhages) and considerable edema.

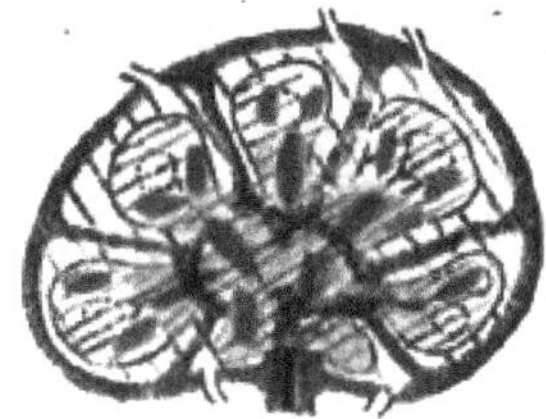

17. Ileocecal : pea-large.

Medullary tissues with considerable congestion and edema, No remarkable changes else.

17. Mesenterial :

Medullary tissues with remarkable congestion and considerable swelling.

503

[N17] ileocecal

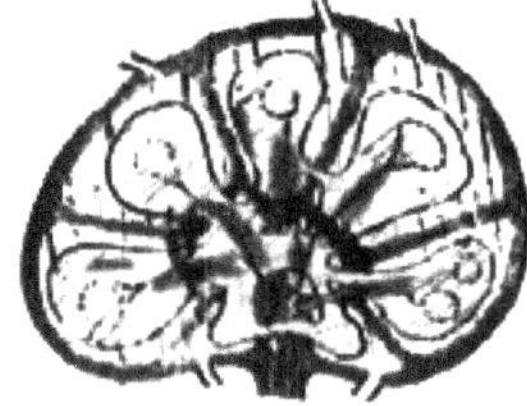

[N17] mesenterial

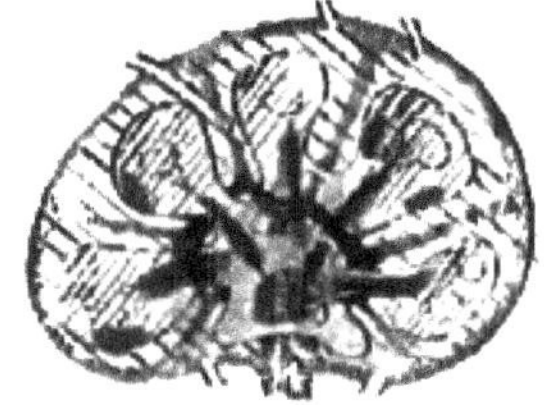

[N17] Hilus

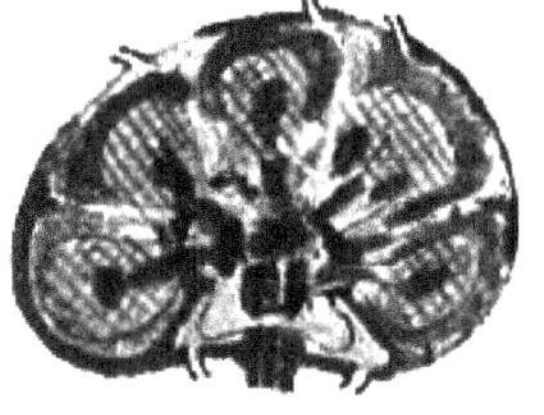

[N19] peribronchial

17. Lung-hilus : field-corn large.

Pericapsular tissues with remarkable congestion, diffuse intense hemorrhages, severe edema and intense leucocytes-dissemination.

Peripheral sinus with some leucocytes and intense bacterial accumulation.

Medullary tissues with remarkable congestion and intense swelling.

Follicular tissues with remarkable leucocytes-accumulation, more or lessextensive edematous swelling with flaky bacterial dissemination and multiple rather diffuse necrosis.

19. Peribronchial : field-corn large.

Pericapsular tissues with considerable congestion, peripheral sinus with plenty bacterial or necrotic masses.

Medullary tissues with some bacetrial masses at some places necrotic swelling of tissues.

Intense bionecrotic swelling of remained medullary tissues with considerable congestion, at some places considerable hemorrhages, and some erythrocytes- and leucocytes-emigrations.

Follicular tissues with considerable edema, slight hyperpasia of reticulum cells in intense cloudy swelling and some bacterial

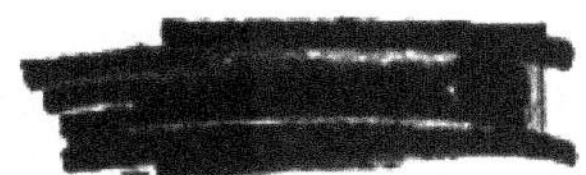

[N19] mesenterial

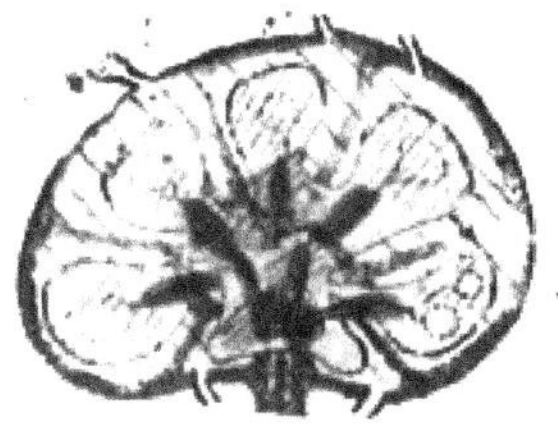

disseminations.

19. Mesenterial : field-corn large.

Medullary tissues with considerable congestion, edematous swelling of capillary walls, slight perivascular hemorrhages and edematous swelling of medullary tissues.

[N20] axillar

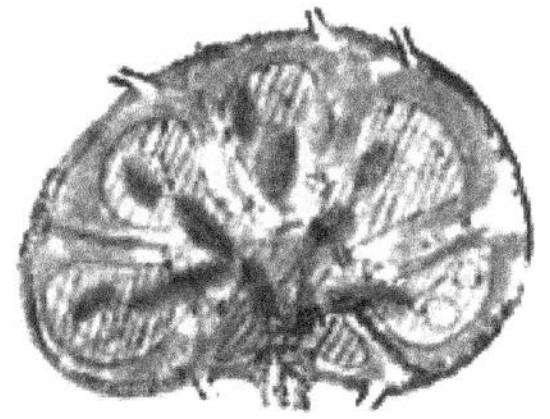

20. Axillaris : pea-large.

Peripheral sinus with considerable congestion, some reticulum cells in cloudy swelling, Medullary tissues with intense congestion, severe swelling of capillary walls, considerable hemorrhages and considerable edema. Follicular tissues with considerable congestion and edema, with some reticulum cells in cloudy swelling.

[N21] periaortal

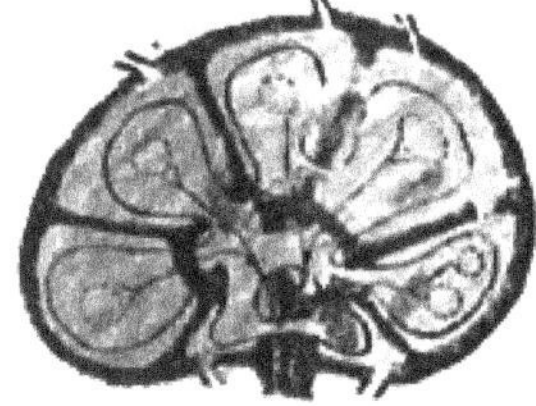

21. Peri-aortal : Sugar-corn large.

Severe congestion with some bacterial masses, intense swelling of vessel-walls, diffuse hemorrhages and at some places considerable bacterial accumulation, diffuse edematous swelling and some bacterial dissemination.

[N21] peribronchial

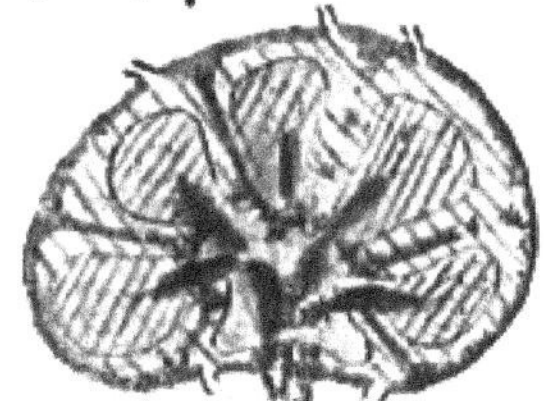

21. Peribronchial : Sugar-corn large.

Pericapsular tissues with intense congestion with some bacterial masses and considerable edematous swelling.

505

[N21] inguinal

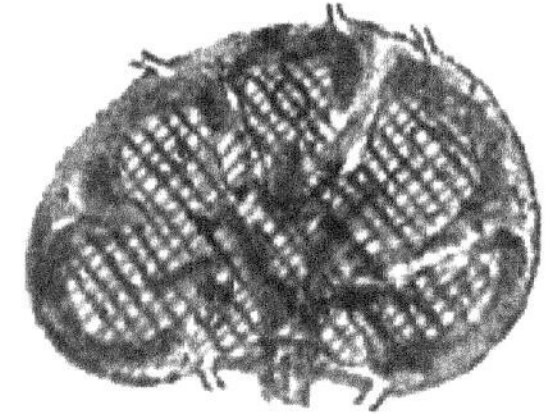

Peripheral tissues with slight catarrh.
Medullary tissues with considerable congestion, some increased reticulum cells and slight edematous swelling of tissues.
Follicular tissues with slight swelling.

21. Inguinal : sugar-corn large.
Pericapsular tissues with remarkable inflamation : remarkable congestion with some bacterial masses and plenty leucocytes, bionecrotic ruins of capillary-walls, perivascular considerable edema and some leucocytes-emigrations, considerable hemorrhages and some bacterial dissemination.
Follicular tissues with total necrotic-homorrhagic changes all over the follicular tissues : flary bacterial dissemination, some leucocytes emigration and intense reduction or diminish of follicular tissues, remarkable congestion of remained blood-vessels and severe odematous swelling of remained tissues.

[N23] peribronchial

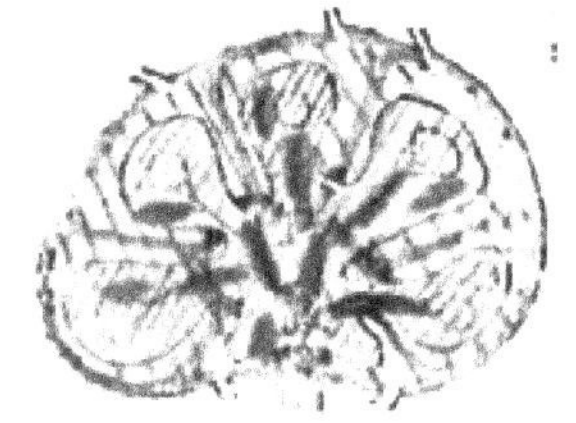

23. Peribronchial : Sugar-corn large.
Peripheral sinus with slight catarrh .
Medulary tissues with considerable congestion and slight edema.
Follicular tissues with slight congestion and slight edematous swelling.

[N24] peribronchial

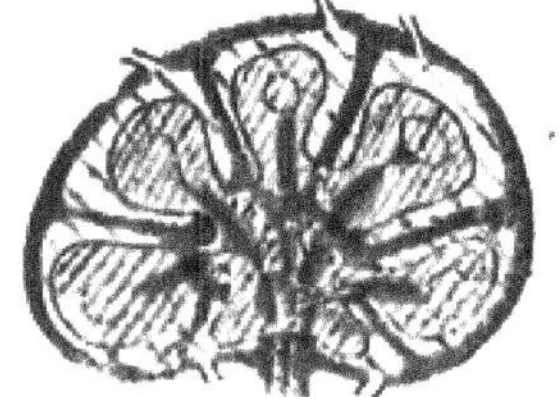

506

[N24] peribronchial

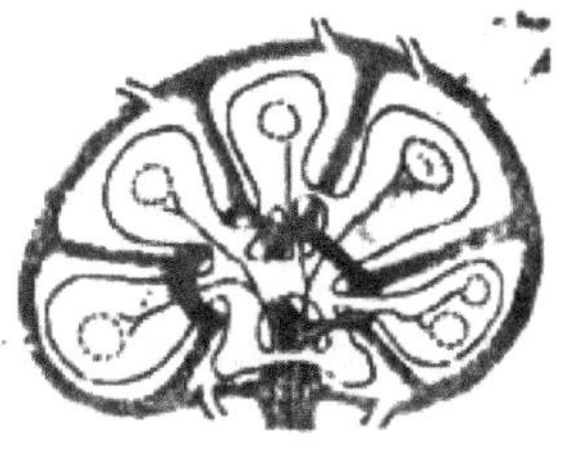

24. Peribronchial : Sugar-corn large.
Medullary tissues with considerable congestion and no remarkable changes else.

24. Mesenterial : Sugar-corn large.
Medullary tissues with considerable congestion, slight hyperplasia of reticulum-cells and slight swelling of tissues.

[N24] mesenterial

26. Peribronchial : some sugar-cornlage lymph-nodulus.
Pericapsular tissues with considerable congestion.
Follicular tissues with intense hemorrhagic--leucocytic-necrotic changes all over the follicular tissues : multiple rather diffuse hemorrhagic leucocytic or necrotic places with intense bacterial dissemination.
Remarkable congestion and edematous swelling of remained tissues.

[N26] peribronchial

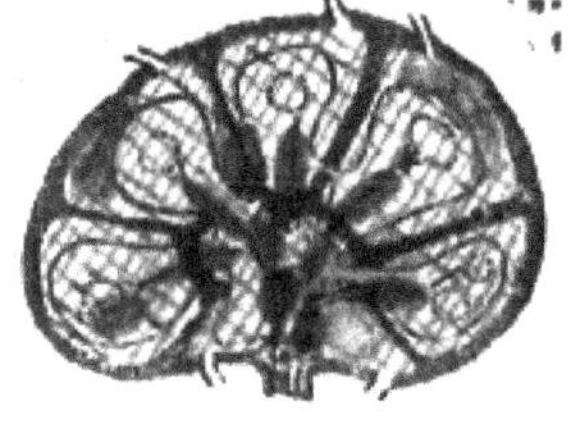

26. Retroperitoneal : field-corn large.
Pericapsular tissues with intenst inflammation :severe serous exudation, diffuse hemorrhages and diffuse bacterial dissemination with some leucocytes. Blood-vessels with necrotic swelling of walls and plenty bacterial accumulation.

[N26] Retroperitoneal

Intense hemorrhagic-necrotic changes all

507

[N26] inguinal

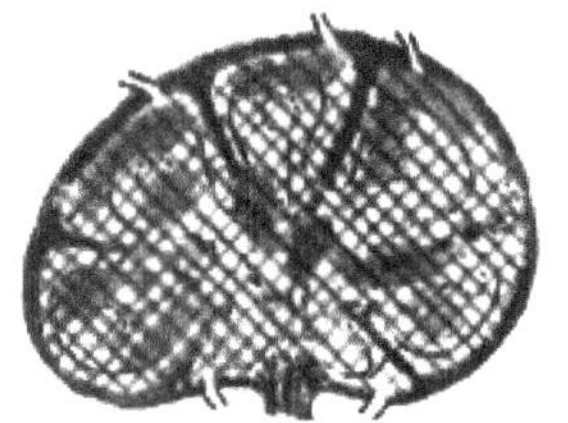

over the follicular tissues: with flaky bacterial dissemination and diffues structureless places. Remarkable congestion , hemorrhages and severe edema of remained tissues.

26. Inguinal : Field-corn large.

[N26] inguinal

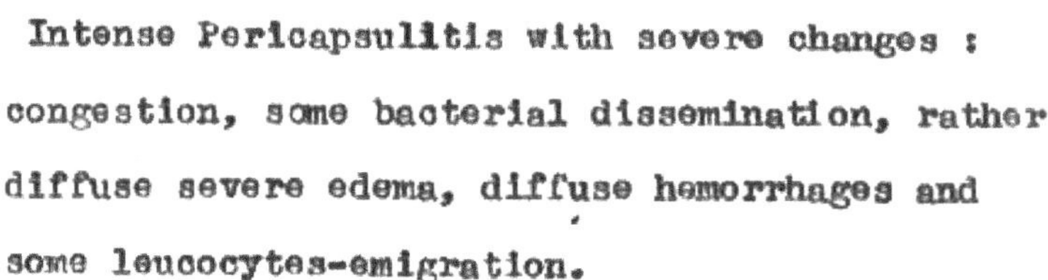

Intense Pericapsulitis with severe changes : congestion, some bacterial dissemination, rather diffuse severe edema, diffuse hemorrhages and some leucocytes-emigration.

Follicular tissues : flaky bacterial dissemination or at someplaces intense leucocytes-emigration.

26. Inguinal : pea-large.

[N27] peribronchial

Intense Pericapsulitis with intense diffuse hemorrhagic - necrotic changes all over the follicular tissues.

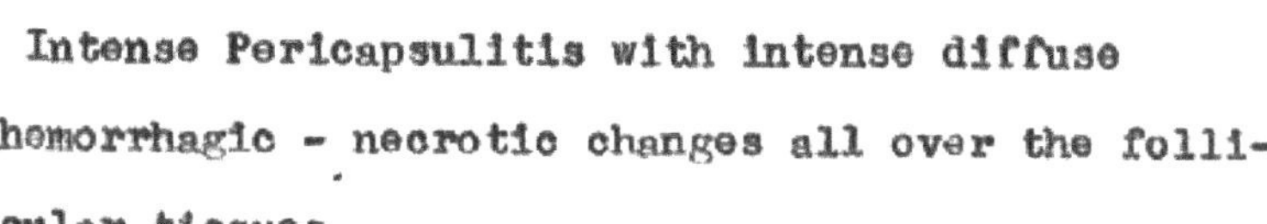

26. Mesenterial : pea-large.

Follicular tissues with considerable congestion and some edematous swelling.

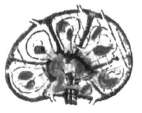

27. Peribronchial : pea-large.

[N27] mesenterial

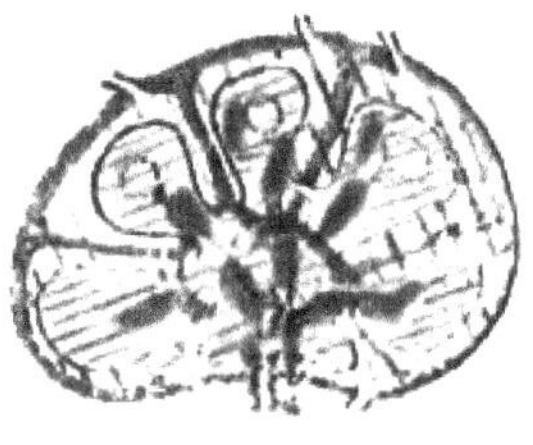

Intense and diffuse hemorrhages and intense edema of medullary tissues, remarkable congestion and multiple localised hemorrhages of follicular tissues. Severe reduction of follicular tissues with some leucocytes emigration and some diminution of lymphocytes.

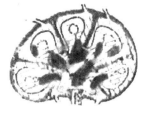

508

[N30] mesenterial

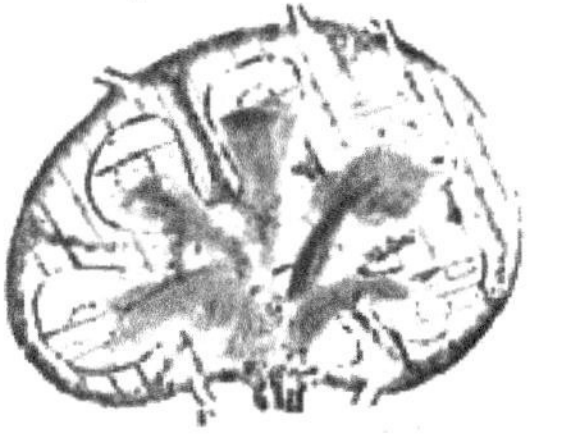

27. Mesenterial : pea-large.
Considerable congeotion and edematous swelling of medullary and follicular tissues.

[N31] mesenterial

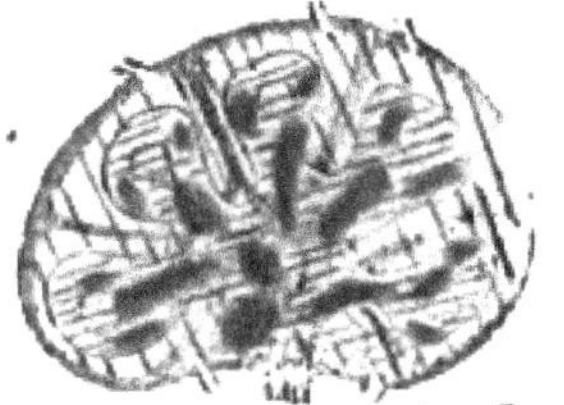

30. Mesenterial : Sugar-corn large.
Severe hemorrhages of pericapsular tissues.

31. Mesenterial : Sugar-corn large.
Considerable congestion and edematous swelling of medullary and follicular tissues, with some increased reticulum-cells in cloudy swelling.

[N31] inguinal

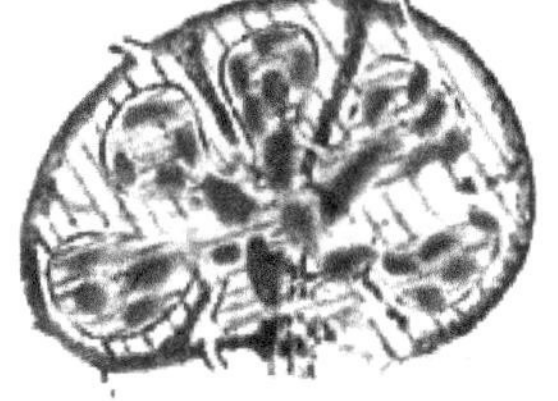

31. Inguinal : Field-corn large.
Considerable congestion and edematous swelling of medullary tissues and slight swelling and reduction of follicular tissues.

[N32] peribronchial

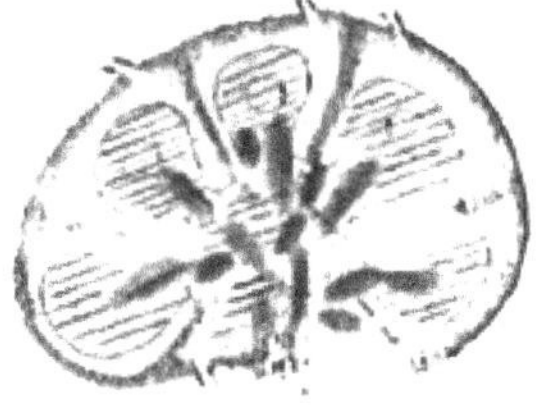

32. Peribronchial : some sugar-corn large nodulus.
Peripheral sinus with abandant serous fluids and some reticulum cells in bionecrotic swelling.
Medullary tissues with intense congestion and some bacterial disseminations scattered at some places.
Follicular tissues with slight reduction and slight swelling.

[N33] Retroperitoneal

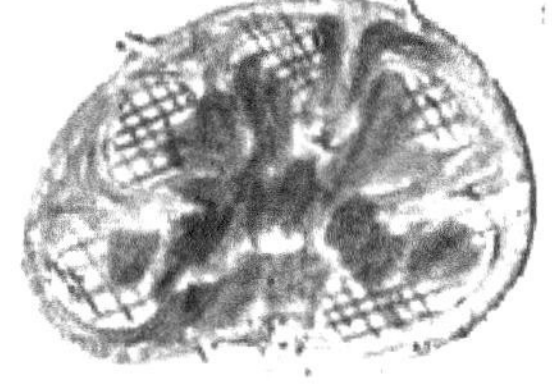

33. Retroperitoneal : Field-corn large.
Pericapsular tissues with severes inflammatory changes : some blood-vessels with plenty leucocytes and bacterial masses, necrotic ruined vessels

509

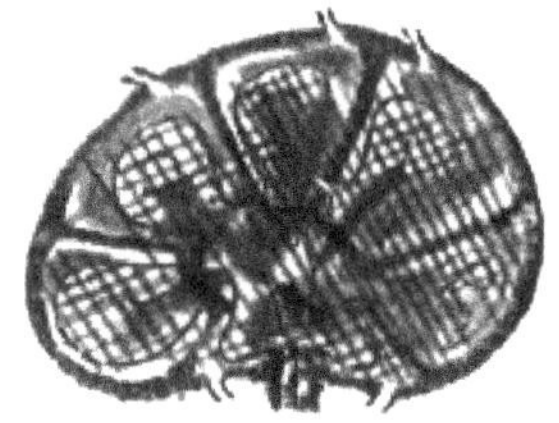

with plenty leucocytes and bacterial masses, severe perivascular hemorrhages and bacterial dissemination all over the neighbouring fatty tissues.

Follicular tissues : completely in hemorrhagic -necrotic changes with flaky bacterial disseminati(o)ns.

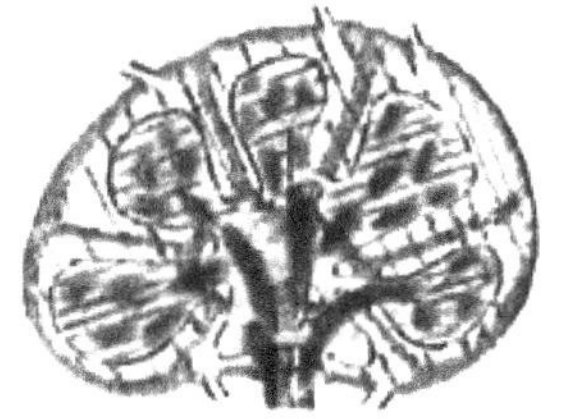

33. Inguinal : Quaill-egg large.

With the same changes : some blood-vessels in necrotic process and intense perivascular exudative-hemorrhagic-leucocytic changes in pericapsular tissues and complete necrotic-leucocytic changes all over the follicular tissues with plenty bacterial disseminations.

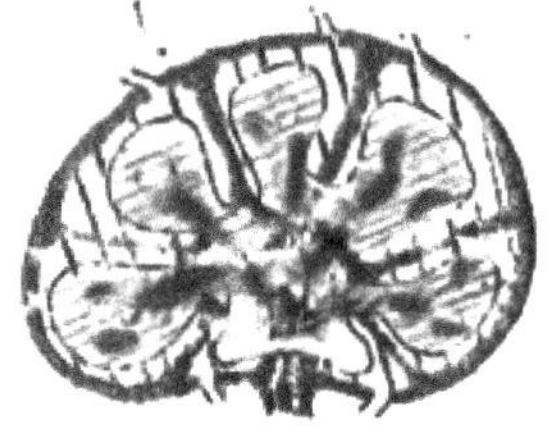

33. Peribronchial : Sugar-corn large.

Pericapsular tissues with slight congestion and medullary or follicular tissues with considerable congestion and some perivascular hemorrhages, accompanied with diffuse edematous swelling of tissues.

Slight reduction of follicular tissues.

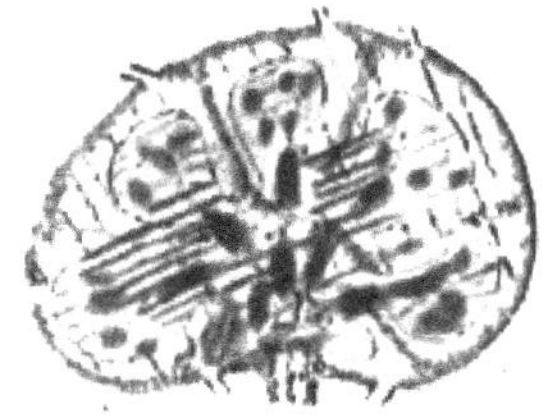

33. Mesenterial : Sugar-corn large.

Considerable congestion and some slight hemorrhages in medullary or follicular tissues with

510

[N 34] axillar

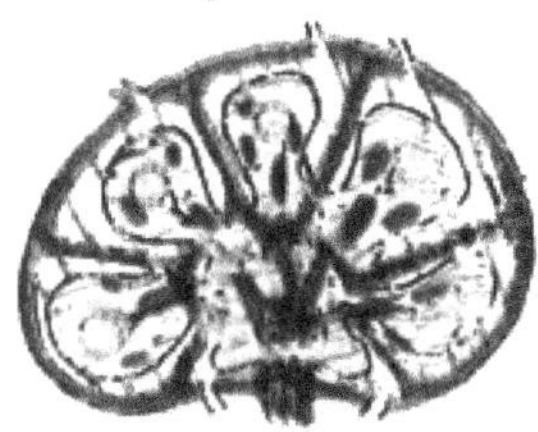

some increased reticulum cells in severe cloudy swelling. Slight edema of follicular tissues.

33. Mesenterial : Sugar-corn large.

With the same changes. Considerable congestion and multiple hemorrhages in medullary or follicular tissues with considerable edematous swelling and some increased reticulum cells in cloudy swelling.

[N 34] submaxillar

34. Axillar : pea large.

Peripheral sinus with some swollen reticulum fibres and some lymphocytes.

[N 34] mesenterial

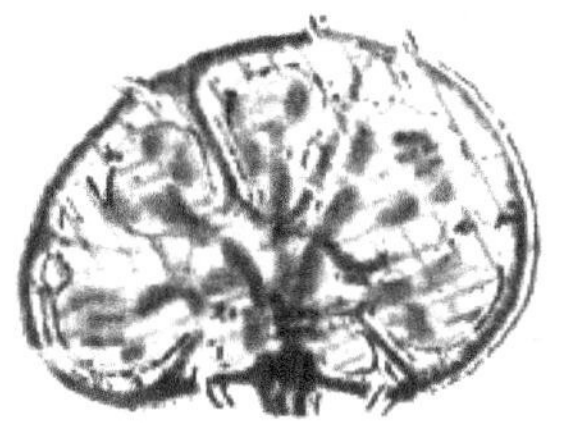

Medullary tissues with some considerable congestion with some leucocytes as capillary contents, slight perivascular edema, some increased reticulum cells in intense cloudy swelling.

Follicular tissues with considerable congestion, edema and some increased reticulum cells in intense cloudy swelling.

[N 34] peribronchial

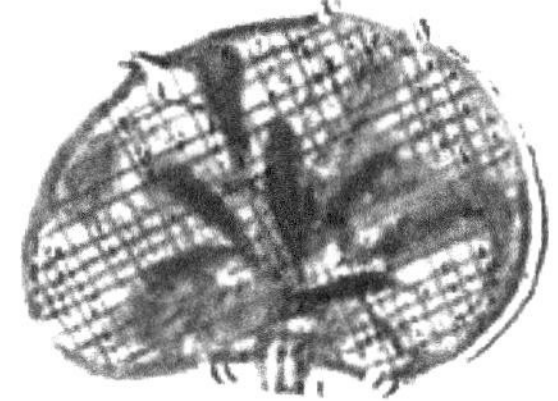

34. Submaxillaris : Field-corn large.

Medullary tissues with considerable congestion in swelling and Follicular tissues with slight diminution of lymphocytes and some increased reticulum cells in cloudy swelling.

34. Mesenterial : Sugar-corn large.

With the same changes.

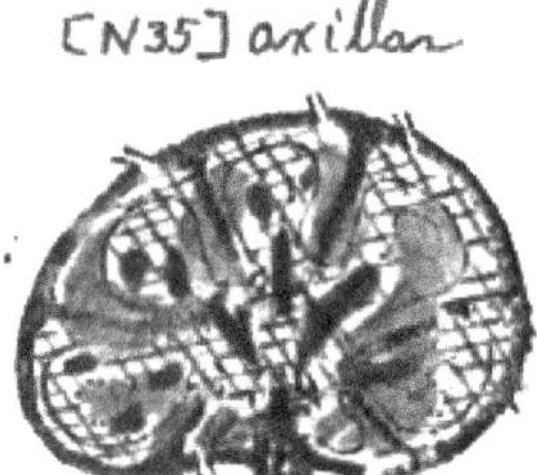

Medullary tissues with considerable congestion and some increased reticulum cells in cloudy swelling and edema.

Follicular tissues with slight diminution of lymphocytes and some increased reticulum cells in cloudy swelling.

Germinative centres with some increased reticulum cells.

35. Peribronchial : Sugar - corn large.

Pericapsular tissues : some blood-vessels with necrotic changes, (plenty leucocytes and bacterial masses as capillary contents and necrotic ruins of walls) and intense perivascular inflammatory changes (diffuse hemorrhages, plenty leucocytes-dissemination and flaky bacterial emigration) in fatty tissues.

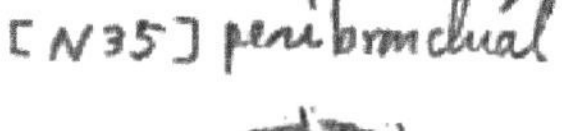

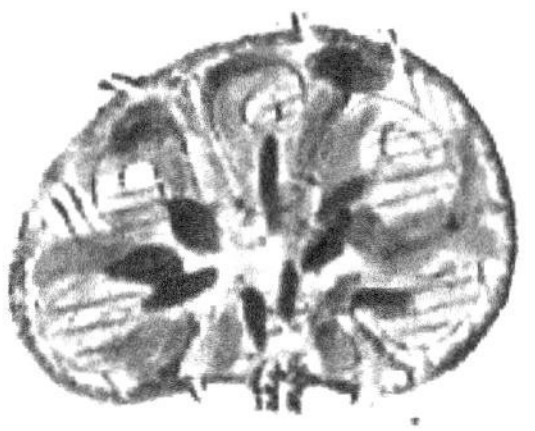

Follicular tissues in complete ruins : total hemorrhages and necrotic changes all over the follicular tissues.

35. Peribronchial : pea-large.

Peripheral sinus with some bacterial masses, some leucocytes and bionecrotic swollen reticulum fibres.

512

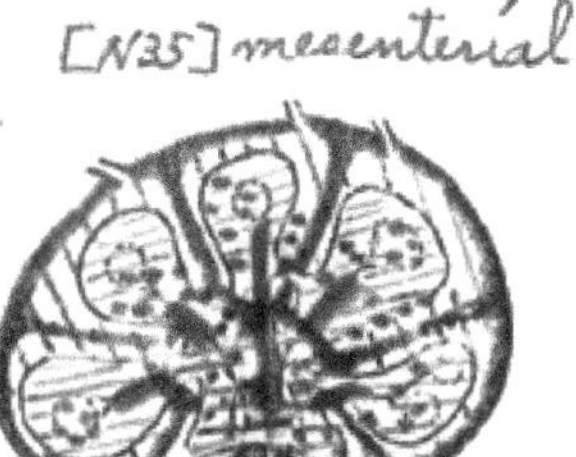

Medullary tissues with considerable congestion, muliple hemorrhages and intense edematous swelling of tissues.

Follicular tissues with the same changes : Considerable congestion, multiple hemorrhages and intense edema with some retiuclum cells in intense cloudy swelling.

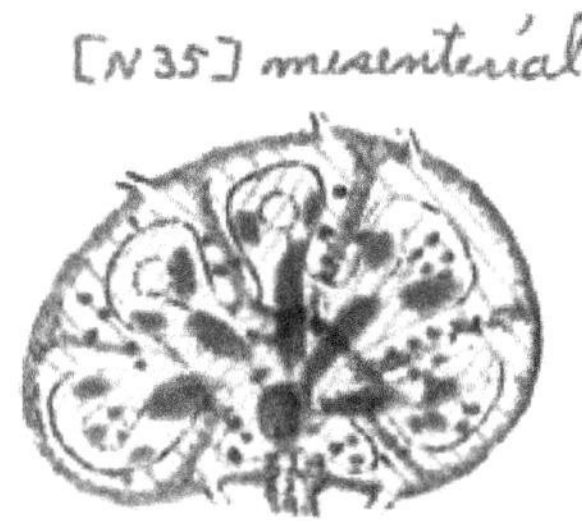

35. Mesenterial : pea-large.

Considerable congestion and considerable hyperplasia of reticulum cells in cloudy swelling. No remarkable changes else.

35. Mesenterial : pea-large.

Considerable congestion and slight hyperplasia of reticulum cells, which are in cloudy swelling.

Follicular tissues with the same changes.

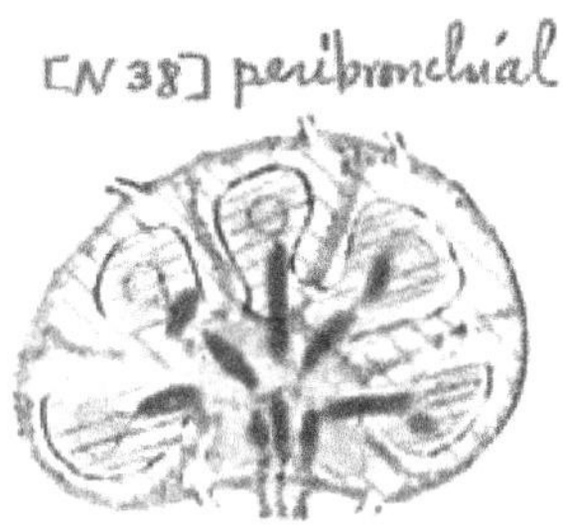

38. Peribronchial : Sugar-corn large.

Intense edema and considerable congestion of medullary tissues with slight diminution of follicular lymphocytes.

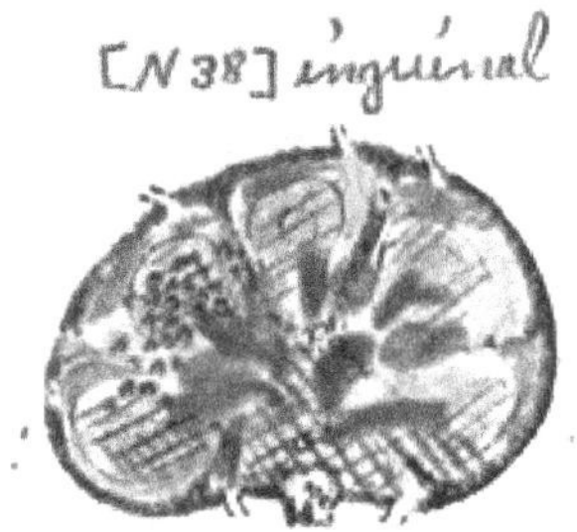

38. Ileocecal fatty tissues with multiple hemorrhagic places.

38. Inguinal : guaill-egg large.

Pericapsular tissues with considerable congestion, slight multiple hemorrhages and some bacterial disseminations.

Peripheral sinus with remarkable exudation with

-513

fibrinous masses, some bacterial dissemination and some swollen reticulum fibres.

Medullary tissues with intense congestion and with massive fibrinous secretion and, intense edematous swelling and some increased reticulum cells in cloudy swelling with at some places bionecrotic swelling, and at some places plenty leucocytes-accumulations.

Medullary tissues with intense congestion with massive fibrinous masses, intense edematous swelling and some increased reticulum cells in cloudy swelling, at some places with plenty leucocytes-disseminations and at some places with plenty bacterial accumulation.

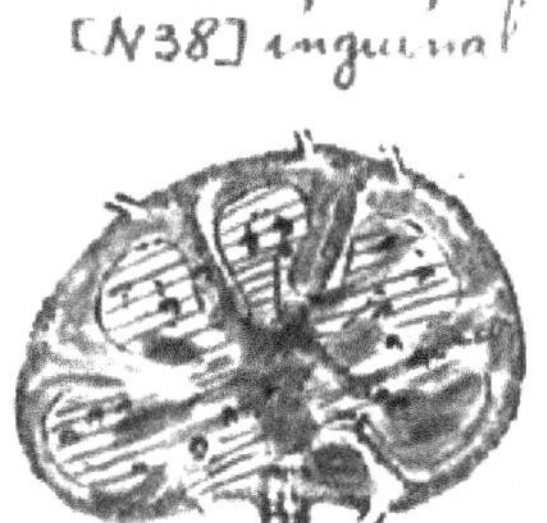

Remarkable congestion of remained capillaries.

38. Retroperitoneal : some field-corn large nodulus.

Intense hemorrhagic-necrotic changes in peri-capsular tissues : some blood-vessels in nocrotic changes with plenty leucocytes as contenst and necrotic ruins of walls, intense diffuse hemorrhagic leucocytic infiltration all over the neighbouring fatty tidsues.

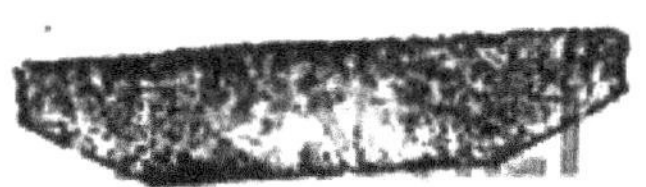

514

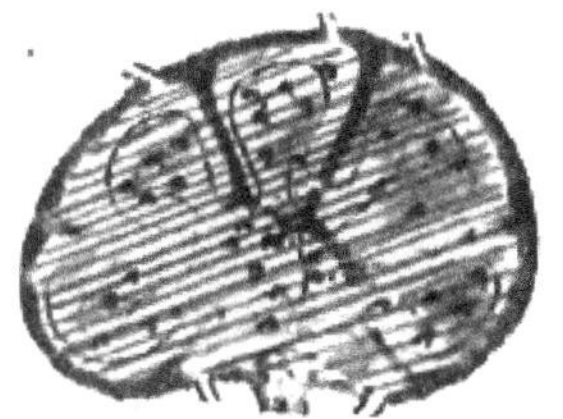

Intense hemorrhagic changes all over the follicular tissues with flaky bacterial dissemination and some leucocytes-accumulations.

38. Inguinal :

With the same changes.

40. Retroperitoneal : quaill-egg large.

Pericapsular tissue in hemorrhagic-necrotic changes with some blood-vessels in ruining processes (plenty leucocytes-accumulation as contents and necrotic ruins of walls). Intense perivascular hemorrhages with leucocytic changes all over the follicular tissues.

515

[N40] inguinal

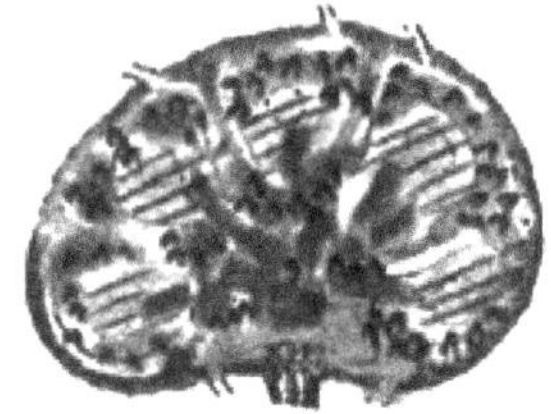

40. Inguinal : quail-egg large.

Pericapsular tissues with the same changes : severe congestion and severe and diffuse perivascular hemorrhagic and leucocytic infiltration, accompanied with swevere edema and some bacterial disseminations.

Capsules with severe inflammatory changes : intense congestion and some leucocytes emigration.

[N40] femolar

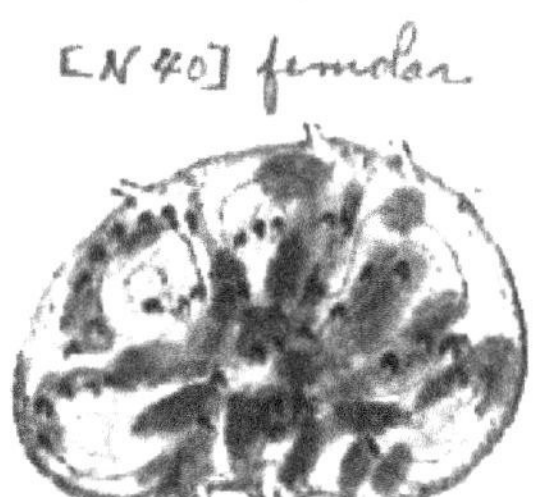

Peripheral sinus with plenty leucocytes, and flaky bacterial accumulation, and necrotic swelling of reticulum-fibres.

Medullary sinus with intensee congestion, multiple intense hemorrhages, severe bionecrotic swelling of reticulum fibres with plenty leucocytes and flaky bacterial dissemination.

Follicular tissues with remarkable reduction of follicular tissues, and intense deminution of lymphocytes and intense edematous swelling of reticulum-fibres.

[N40] peribronchial

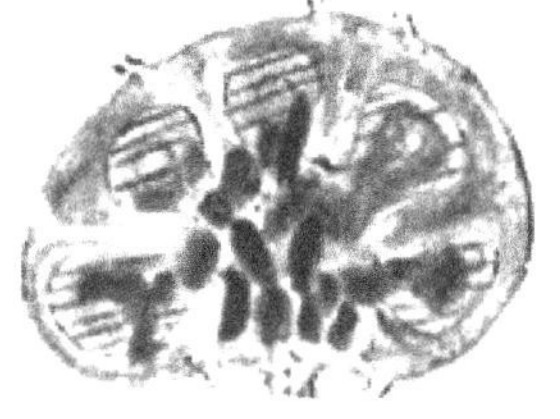

40. Femolaris : Field-corn large.

With the same changes. Severe exudative-hemorrhagic-leucocytic inflammation.

40. Peribronchial : pea-large.

Peripheral sinus with plenty bacterial and some

316

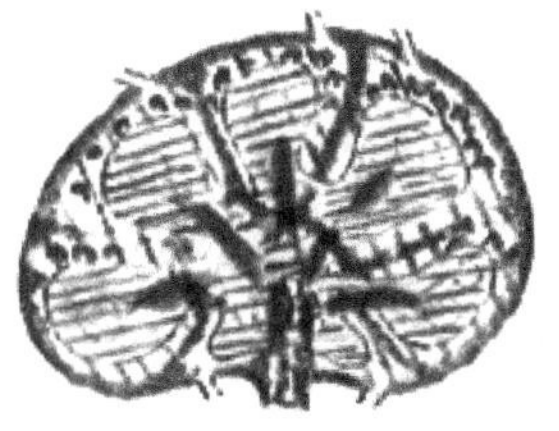

leucocytes accumulation.

Medullary tissues with considerable congestion, plenty bacterial dissemination, severe edematous swelling of reticulum-fibres.

Follicular tissues with plenty leucocytes and bacterial dissemination, severe edema of reticulum-fibres and intense reduction of follicular tissues.

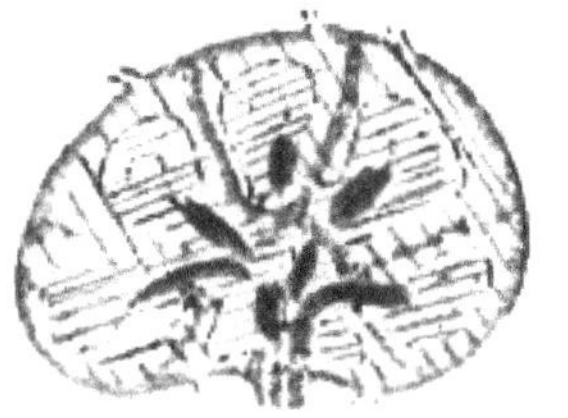

42. Mesenterial :
Considerable congestion.

42. Mesenterial : Sugar-corn large.

Pericapsular tissues with considerable congestion and edema.

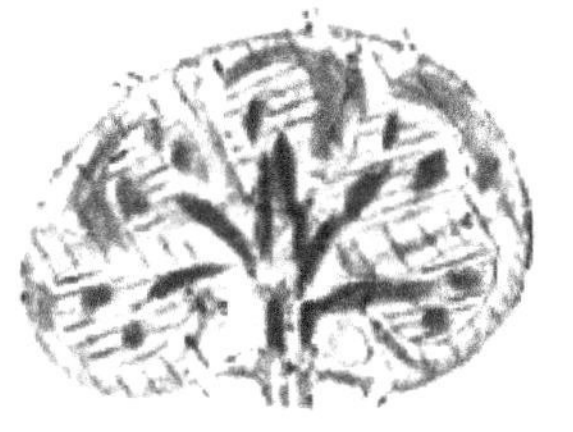

Peripheral sinus with considerable catarrh with some increased reticulum cells, slight hemorrhages and some leucocytes.

Medullar tissues with considerable congestion, slight edema, some increased reticulum cells.

Follicular tissues with slight edema and slight congestion.

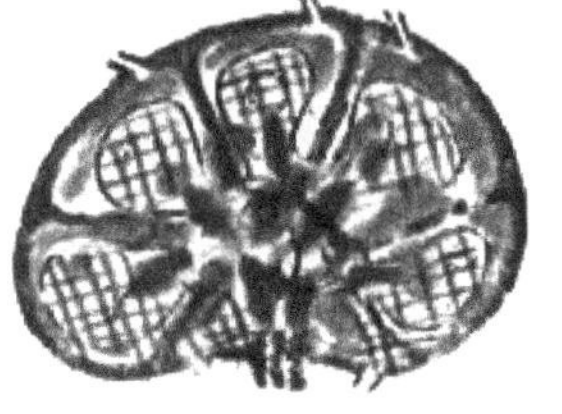

42. Submaxillar : Eield-corn large.

Co~~m~~mpletely necrotic changes all over the follicular tissues with necrotic decay of all follicular tissues and flaky diffuse bacterial dissemination.

517

[N44] mesenterial

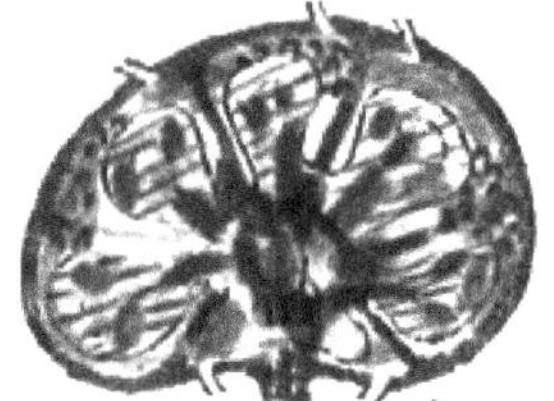

Remarkable congestion of remained blood-vessels and perivascular severe inflammatory changes ; necrotic-hemorrhagic changes.

44. Mesenterial : some pea-large lymph-nodulus. Pericapsular tissues with slight congestion. Peripheaal tissues with some bacterial masses, some hemorrhages, some leucocytes accumulation .

[N44] mesenterial

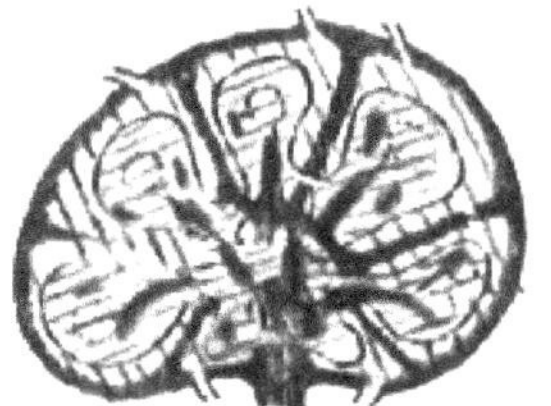

Medullary tissues with considerable congestion, edema with some bacterial dissemination and bionecrotic swelling of reticulum cells, Follicular tissues with intense swelling, edema, congestion and some reduction of follicular tissues.

44. Mesenterial : Sugar-corn large.
Peripheral sinus with some catarrh.
Medullary tissues with some congestion, slight edema and some increased reticulum cells. Follicular tissues with slight congestion and slight edema.

[N46] axillar

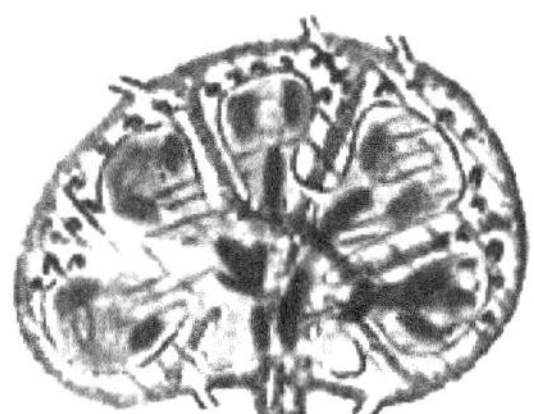

46. Axillaris : pea-large.
Poripheral sinus with some leuocytes and some cloudy swelling of reticulum cells.
Follicular tissues with considerable congestion, slight edema, some leucocytes emigration and some hemorrhages.

518

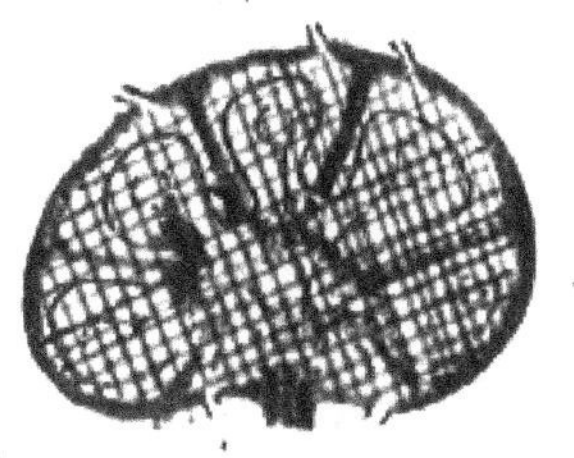

46. Peribronchial pea-large.

Pericapsular tissues with slight hemorrhages and complete necrotic changes all over the follciular tissues.

49. Peribronchial : Sugar-corn large.

Pericapsular tissues with slight congestion. Peripheral sinus with considerable swerous exudation, some leucocytes accumulations and bionecrotic swelling of reticulum-fibres.

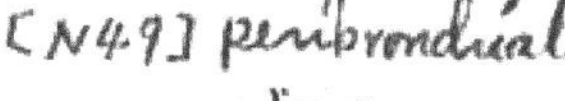

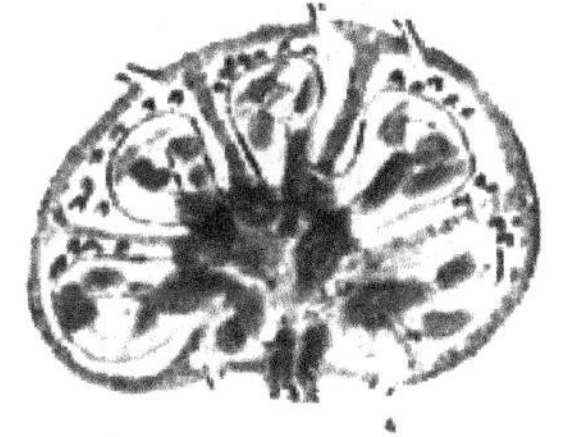

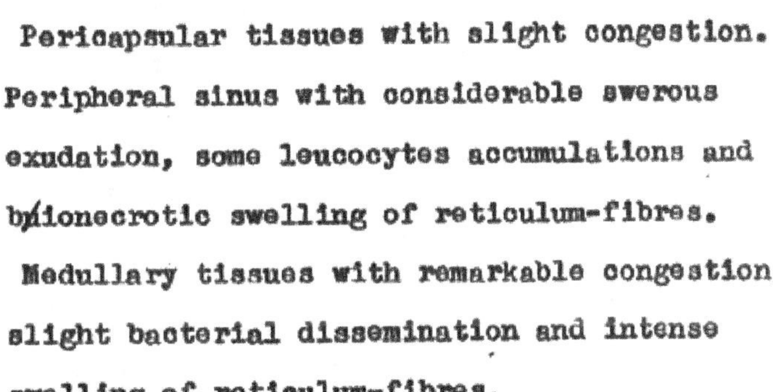

Medullary tissues with remarkable congestion, slight bacterial dissemination and intense swelling of reticulum-fibres.

Follicular tissues with considerable congestion, slight perivascular hemorrhages, slight bacterial accumulation and intense swelling of follicular tissues, accompanied with some diminution of lymphocytes.

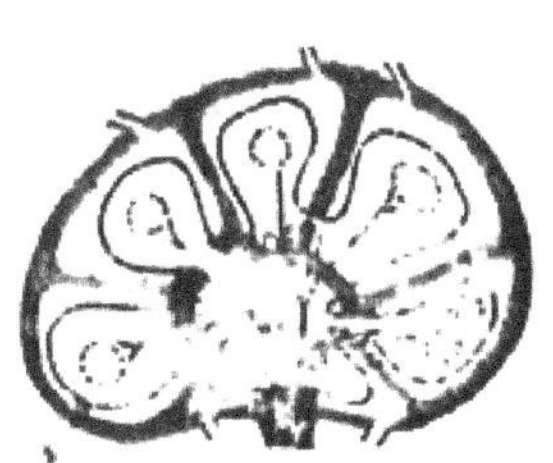

S-I. Peribronchilal : Some pea-lare lymph-nodes. No pericapsular changes. Slight catarrh of peripheral sinus (with some reticulum cells) and considerable congestion and slight hyper-plasia of medullary sinus. Slight reduction and swelling of follicular tissues with slight hyperplasia of capillary endothel-cells.

[S1] peribronchial

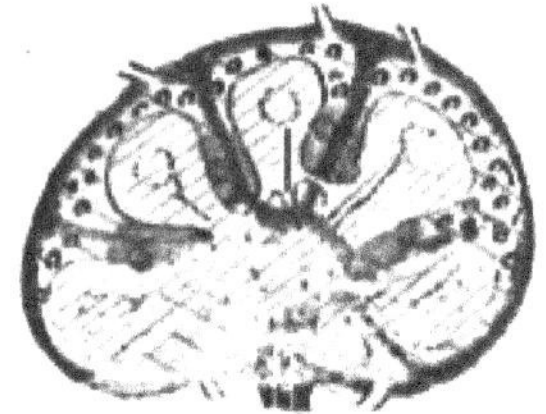

Germinative centres in solid form, with some swollen reticulum cells.

I. Mesenterial : No remarkable changes.

2. Peribronchial : some pea-large lymph-nodes. No Pericapsulitis and no considerable catarrh of peipheral sinus.

Remarkable congestion and diffuse hemorrhages in medulary sinus.

[S1] mesenterial

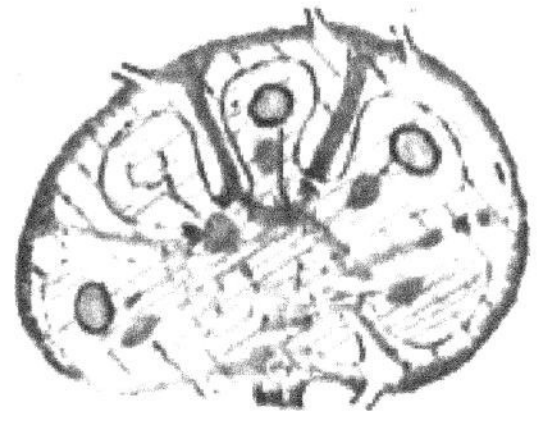

Slight swelling of follicular tissues without significant diminution of lymphocytes. Slight swelling of capillary endothel-cells and germinative centres with some swollen reticulum cells.

2. Mesenterial : Sugar-corn large.

Considerable congestion and considerable hemorrhages with intense swelling of ca illa ry endothel-cells, in medullary sinus.

[S2] peribronchial

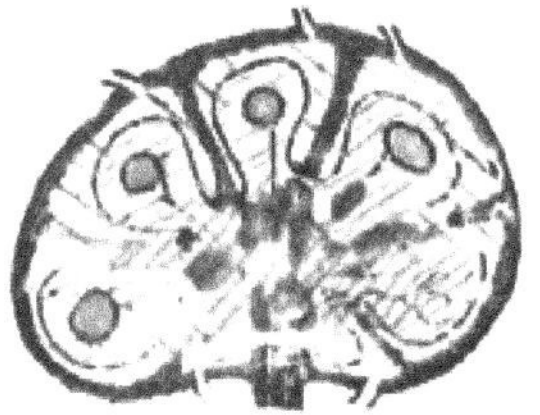

Slight swelling of follicula r tissues and germinative centres with some swollen reticulum cells.

3. Retroperitoneal : some quaill-egg large lymph-nodes.

52

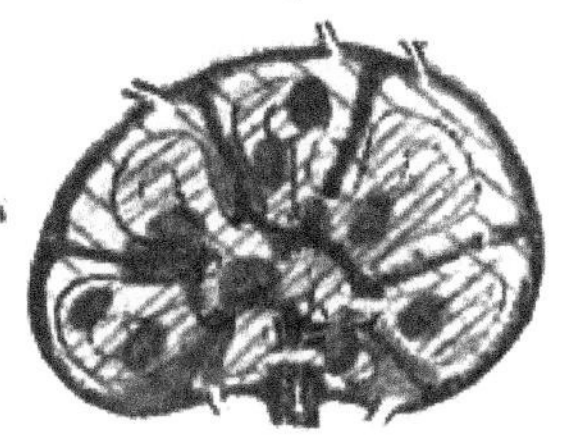

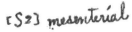

Severe pericapsular inflammation with intesnse congestion, due to necrotic swelling of capillary walls, remarkable diffuse hemorrhages and plenty bacterial masses in capillaries.

Plenty bacterial masses and karyorrhextic masses in peripheral sinus and diffuse, intense hemorrhagic-necrotic ruins of all follicular masses : remarkable congestion and diffuse hemorrhages with necrotic ruins of capillary walls, some leucocytes in medullary tissues, intense bacterial accumulation and necrotic ruins of greater parts of follicles and intense reduction of follicular tissues and lymphocytes.

[S 3] Retroperitoneal

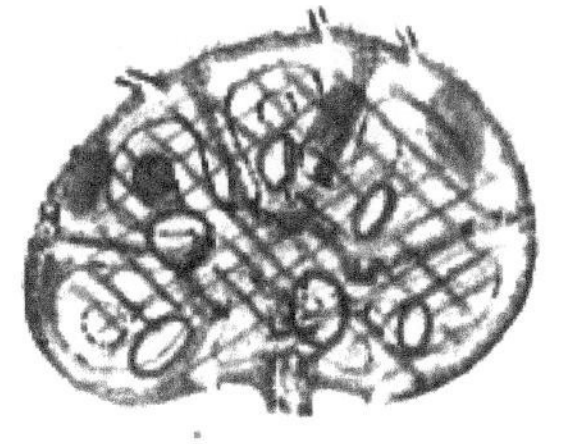

S-3. Peribronchial (at bifulcation-portion) : pea-large.

The same, hemorrhagic-necrotic inflammation.

[S 3] Bifulcation-portion

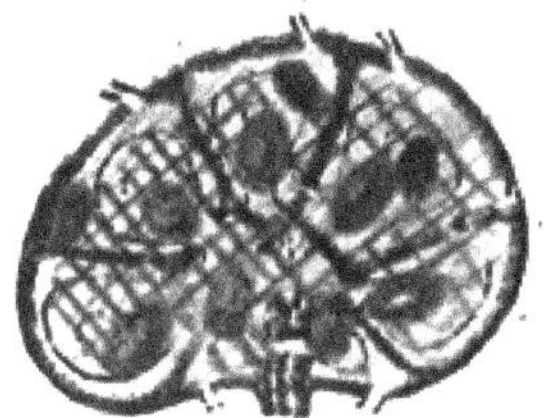

S-4. Lymph-nods at bifulcations-portions.

Considerable pericapsular inflammation with considerable congestion and some leucocytes -disseminations.

In peripheral sinus, ome bacterial masses and some swollen reticulum cells, and in medullary sinus, considerable or remarkable congestion, severe perivascular edema, bionecrotic swelling

521

[S4] Bifulcation-portion

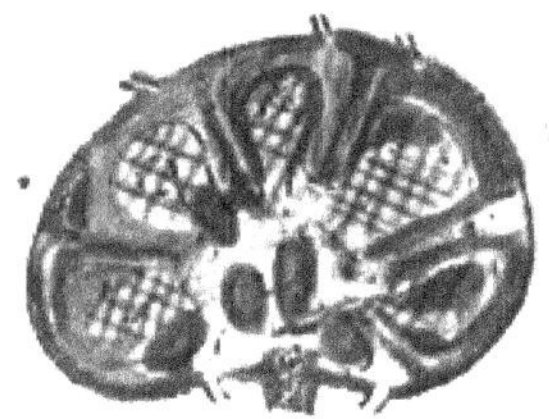

of reticulum-fibres with some pycnotic masses and some leucocytes and at some places some bacterial disseminations.

In follicular tissues ; remarkable congestion and bionecrotic swelling of reticulum-finres with some localised or rather diffuse bacterial dissemination, accompanied with some leucocytes, severe reduction of follicular tissues and severe edematous swelling of reticulum-fibres.

S-4. Peribronchial : Sugar-corn large.

Severe Peri-capsulitis and capsulitis with severe congestion and diffuse hemorrhages, due to necrotic swelling of capillaries walls.

[S4] peribronchial

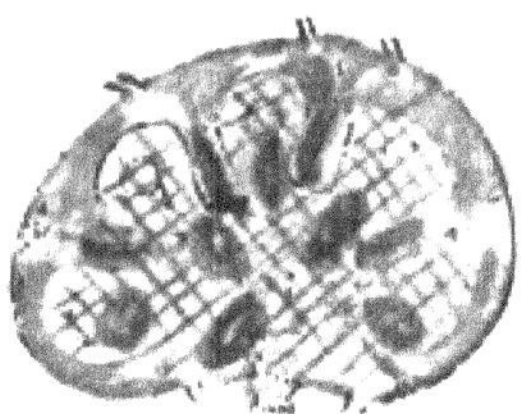

In peripheral sinus : plenty bacterial and karyolytic masses, plenty leucocytes and some necrotic reticulum cells.

In medullary sinus, intenst congestion, diffuse hemorrhages, intenst bionecrotic or necrotic swelling of medullary tissues, due to necrotic ruins of capillary-walls with plenty bacterial disseminations.

In follicular tissues, the same, hemorrhagic-necrotic changes.

Namely, intense hemorrhagic-necrotic changes all over the follicular tissues.

S-5. I inguinal : Some sugar-corn large nodui-

522

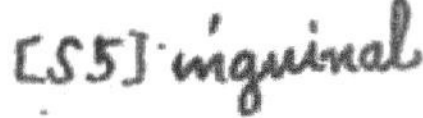

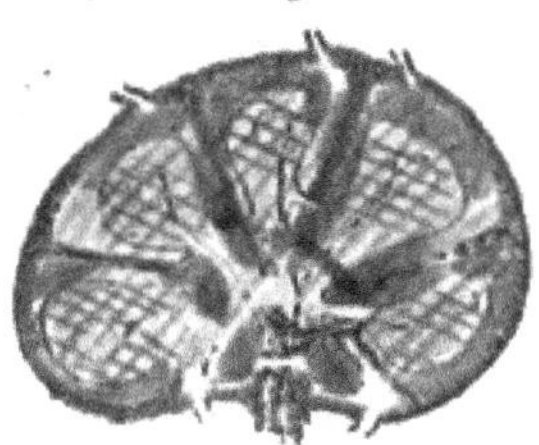

us.

Severe diffuse pericapsular inflammation with diffuse hemorrhages, leucocytes disseminations and remarkable bacterial accumulations.
Severe diffuse hemorrhagic-necrotic inflamatory changes all over the follicular tissues with the same changes, as above mentioned.

S-5. Retroperitoneal : Qauill-egg large.

Severe Pericapsulitis with severe congestion, hemorrhages and some bacterial disseminations.

In peripheral sinus with massive bacterial accumulation, some leucocytes and diffuse hemorrhagic masses.

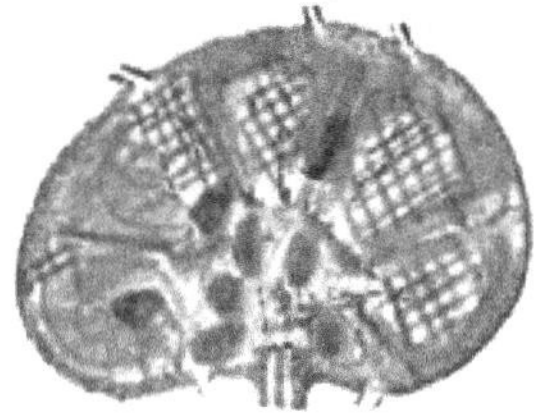

Medullary sinus and folliculat tissues with the same hemorrhagic necrotic changes all over the tissues : remarkable congestion, blonecrotic ruins of capillary walls, remarkable diffuse hemorrhages, bionecrotic or necrotic swelling of reticulum fibres with plenty leucocytes and bacterial disseminations.

S-5. Mesenterial : Sugar-corn large.

Considerable pericapsular congestion.
Peripheral sinus with some bionecrotically swollen reticulum cells, some leucocytes and slight bacetrial accumulation.

523

[S5] mesenterial

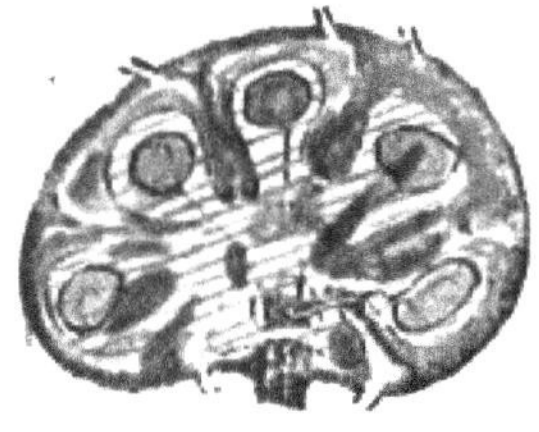

Medullary sinus with considerable congestion, considerable hemorrhages, and intense edematous swelling of reticulum fibres with some leucocytes-dissemination.

Follicular tissues with considerable congestion, swelling and slight diminution of lymphocytes.

S-5. Peribronchial : Sugar-corn large.

Slight Pericapsulitis, peripheral sinus with some bionecrotically swellen reticulum cells and some erythrocytes.

[S 5] peribronchial

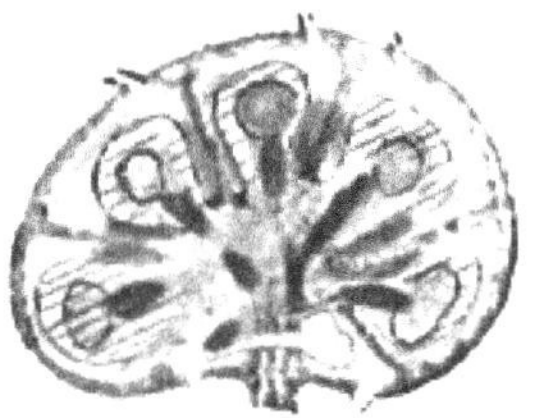

Medullary tissues with remarkable congestion, severe edematous swelling with some leucocytes -accumulations and slight hemorrhages.

Follicular tissues with considerable congestion, swelling, slight reduction of follicular tissues with some germinative centres, accompanied with some swollen cloudy reticulum cells.

S-6. Submaxillar : Qauill-egg large.

Severe Pericapsulitis with remarkable congestion and diffuse intense hemorrhages in fatty tissues.

Follicular tissues fall into totally hemorrhagic-necrptic changes : with multiple supermiliary necrosis in follicular tissues with plenty leucocytes and flaky bacterial dissemination,

524

[S6] submaxillar

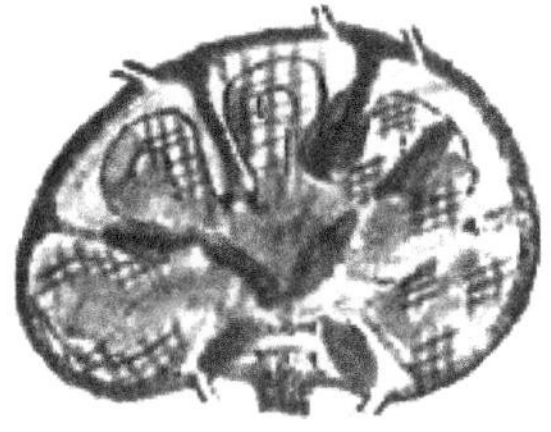

[S6] mesenterial

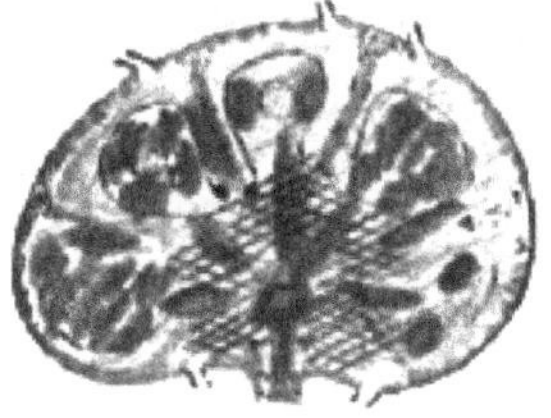

[S6] peribronchial

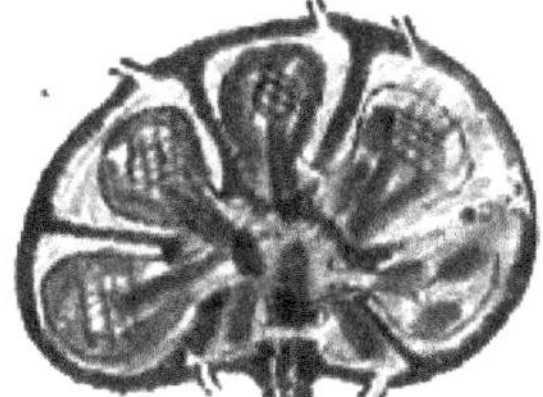

accompanied with multiple more or less diffuse hemorrhages and bionecrotic swelling of medullary tissues.

S-6. Mesenterail : Sugar-corn large.

Considerable congestion of pericapsular tissues, severe hemorrhages with some leucocytes and bionecrotic swollen reticulum cells in peripheral sinus, remarkable congestion, more or less diffuse hemorrhages, due to bionecrotic ruins of capillary walls, multiple submiliary necrosis with some bacterial accumulatios, and leucocytes-dissemination with bionecrotic swelling of medullary tissues in medullary and follicular tissues.

S-6. Peribronchial : Sugar-corn large.

With the same changes, as avobe mentioned.

Lymphadenitis necroticans partialis.

S-8. Submaxillaris. Sugar-corn large.

Severe Pericapsulitis with some leucocytes -emigration and slight congestion.

Considerable catarrh of peipheral sinus with some leucocytes and some cloudy swollen reticulum cells.

Considerable congestion, some bacterial accumulation with severe oedematous swelling of medullary tissues and

535

[S8] submaxillar

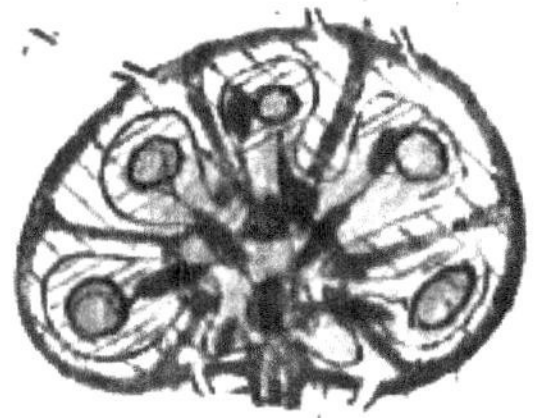

considerable congestion, swelling and some bacterial accumulations of follicular tissues with some swollen germinative centres, which have some cloudy swollen reticulum cells.

S-8. Peribronchial : Sugar-corn large.

Anthracosis. No pericapsular inflammation.

Peripheral in total ruins with plenty bacterial and necrotic masses.

[S8] peribronchial

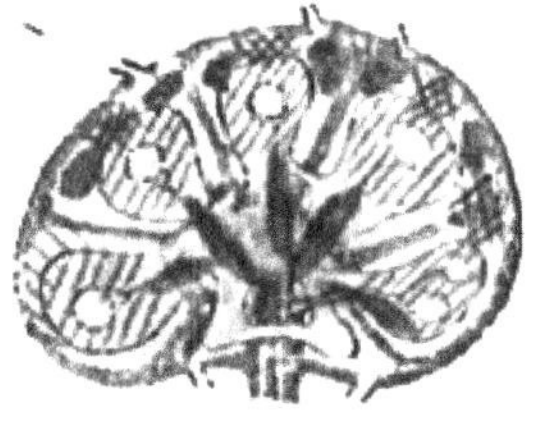

Medullary tissues in considerable edematous swelling with cloudy swollen reticulum cells and-fibres, accompanied with considerable congestion. (with some leucocytes as capillary -contents).

Follicular tissues in slight reduction with some swollen cloudy reticulum cells.

S-8. Mesenterial : Sugar-corn large.

[S8] mesenterial

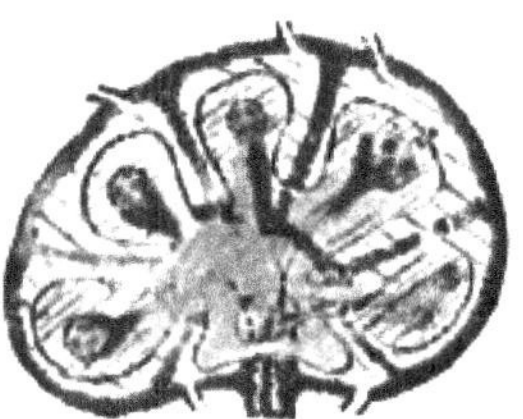

Medullary tissues with considerable swelling and some increased reticulum cells.

Follicular tissues in slight reduction with some germinative centres, which have some slightly increased reticulum cells. Slight congestion in germinative centres.

No significant changes else.

S-9. Peribronchial : Sugar-corn large.

Peripheral sinus with some leucocytes, some

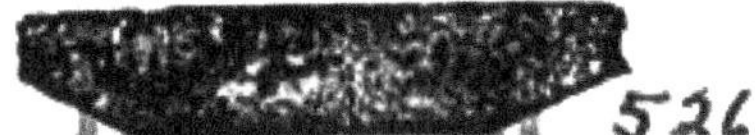

526

[S9] mesenterial

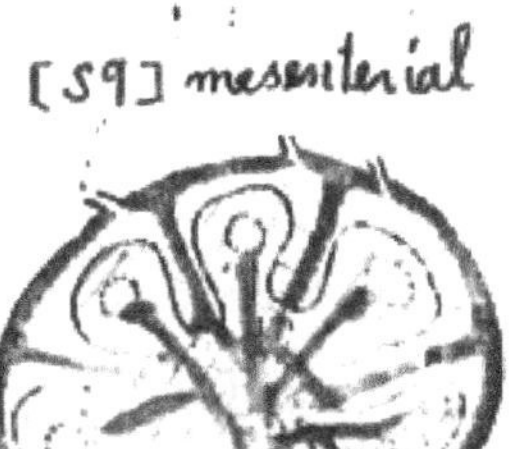

bacterial masses and bionecrotically swollen reticulum cells.

Medullary sinus with the same changes : considerable leucocytes dissemination, some bacterial masses and severe edematous swelling of reticulumfibres and-cells.

Follicular tissues in slight reduction with slightly swollen reticulum fibres and no remarkable changes else.

S-9. Mesenterial : No remarkable changes.

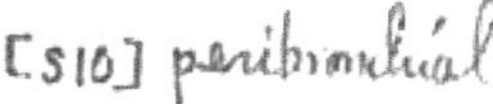

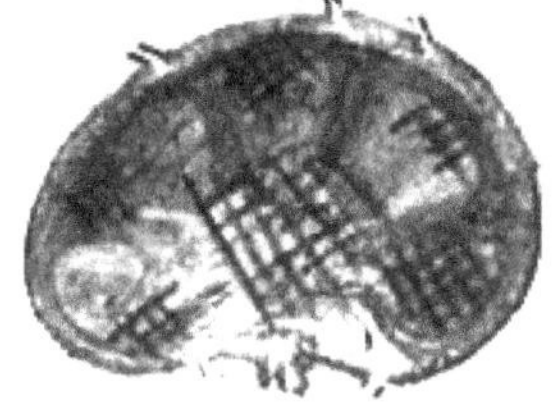

S-10. Peribronchial : Sugar-corn-large.

Pericapsular tissues with considerable congestion.

Peripheral sinus with plenty bacterial and necrotic masses.

Follicular tissues in total necrosis : with flaky bacterial and plenty necrotic-leucocytes dissemination all over the follicular tissues (with intense congestion of remained capillaries).

S-11. Peribronchial : Sugar-corn large.

Capsular tissues with considerable congestion.

Peripheral sinus with more or less diffuse

537

S.11 peribronchial

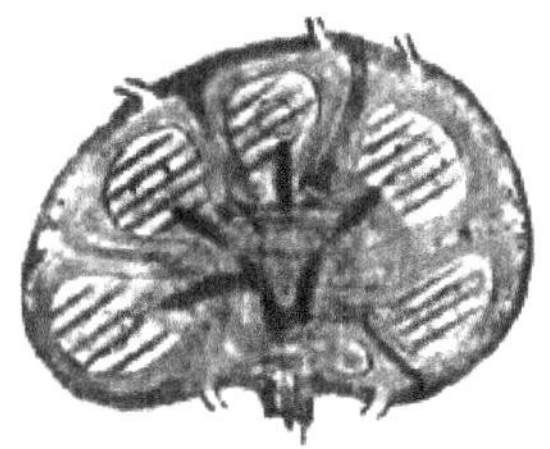

S.11 Inguinal

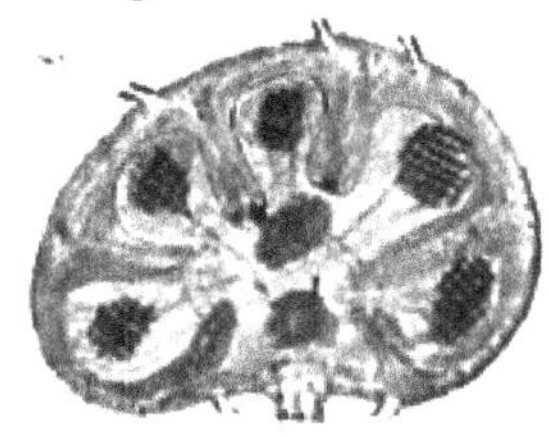

S 12. Mesenterial

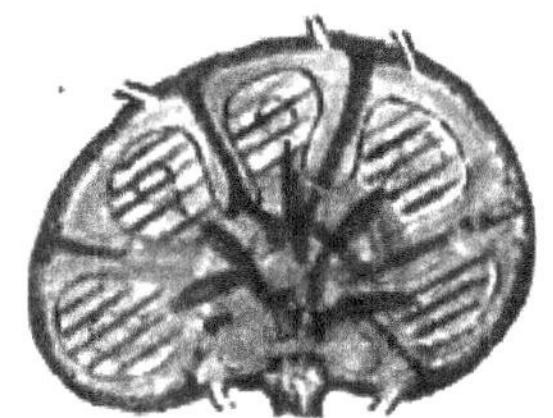

hemorrhages, some leucocytes and diminished reticulum-fibres.
Medullary tissues with remarkable congestion, diffuse hemorrhages and swollen reticulum-fibres and-cells.
Follicular tissues in slight edema and slight reduction.

S11. Inguinal : Some sugar-corn large nodulus.
Capsular tissues with considerable congestion.
Peripheral sinus with plenty bacterial masses, some hemorrhages and decayed cell-masses.
Medullary tissues with intenste diffuse hemorrhages and flaky bacterial dissemination with some leucocytes all over the tissues and follicular tissues with intense diffuse necrosis and diffuse hemorrhages with some leucocytes. Germinative centres with total necrosis.

S-12. Mesenterial :
Peripheral sinus with massive erythrocytes, bionecrotically swollen reticulum cells and severe edematous swelling of reticulum-fibres.
Medullary tissues with severe congestion, considerable hemorrhages, severe edema of tissues and considerable hyperplasia of

528

S.14. Axillaris

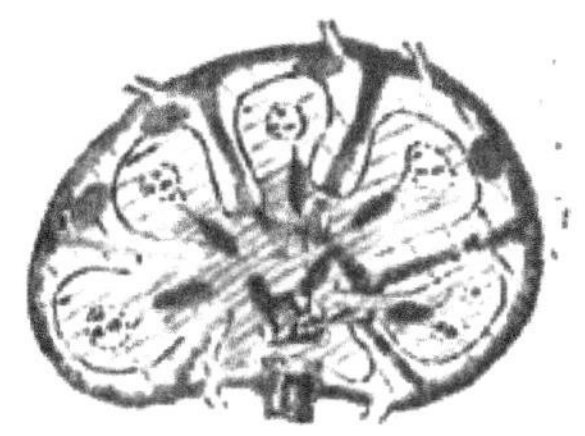

S14 Mesenterial

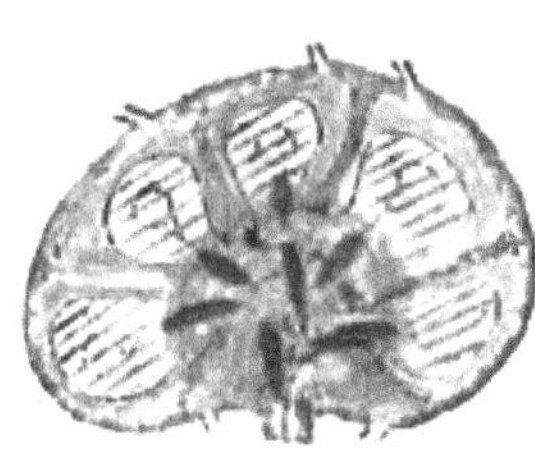

reticulum cells in intense cloudy swelling. Follcicular tissues with considerable swelling and reduction.

S-14. Axillaris : some quaill-egg large lymph-nodes.

Pericapsular tissues with considerable congestion and some leucocytes.

Peripheral sinus with some leucocytes, some erythrocytes, some swollen cloudy reticulum cells, and some bacterial masses.

Medullary tissues with considerable congestion, more or less diffuse hemorrhages, severe swelling of tissues and some cloudy swollen reticulum cells.

Follicular tissues with considerable swelling and slight reduction with some germinative centres which have some swollen reticulum cells.

14. Mesenterial : sugar - corn large.

Pericapsular tissues with considerable congestion.

Peripheral sinus with some leucocytes, massive erythrocytes and some bionecrotic ally swollen

S 15 Peribronchial

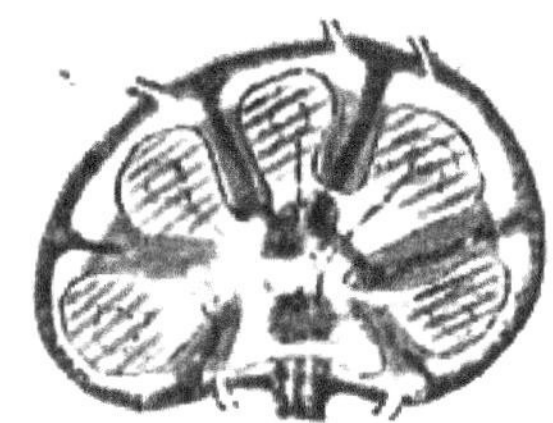

reticulum cells.

Medullary tissues with severe congestion, more or less diffuse hemorrhages, bionecrotic swelling of tissues with some leucocytes and some increased reticulum cells in severe cloudy swelling.

Follicular tissues with slight swelling and slight reduction.

S-15. Peribronchiall: Sugar-corn large.

Peripheral sinus in slight catarrh : with some reticulum cells.

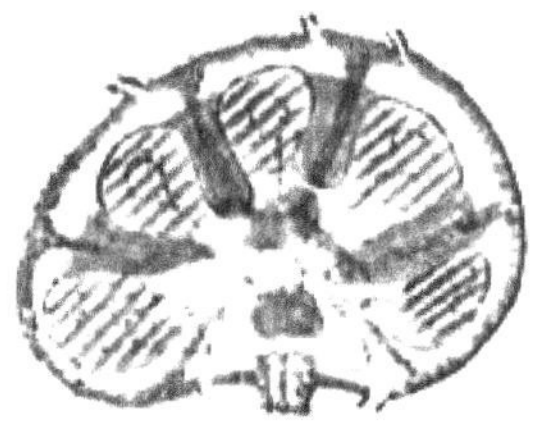

Medullary sinus with considerable congestion, with some leucocytes as capillary contents, and considerable edematous swelling of reticulum-fibres.

Follicular tissues with slight reduction and slight swelling.

S-15. Retroperitoneal : quaill-egg large.

Pericapsular tissues with considerable inflammation : with congestion and some leucocytes emigration.

Peripheral sinus in slight catarrh : with some reticulum cells.

Medullary sinus with considerable congestion (some leucocytes as capillary contents) and severe edematous swelling of reticulum fibres.

530

S.15 Mesenterial

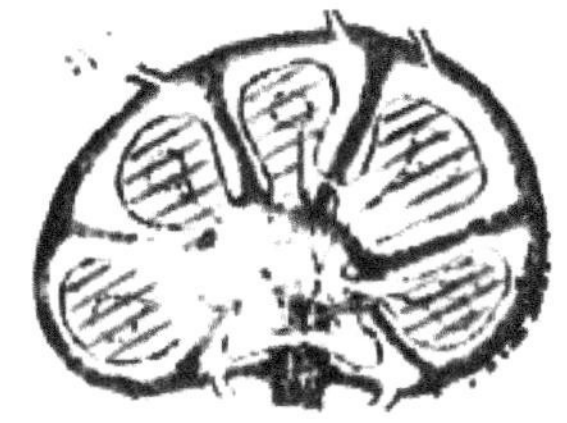

Follicular tissues with considerable swelling of reticulum-fibres and slight diminution of follicular lymphocytes and some germinative centres with some swollen reticulum cells.

15. Mesenterial : Sugar-corn large.

Medullary tissues with intense swelling with fibrinous separations, considerable congestion and remarkable diffuse leucocytes disseminations.

S 19 Mesenterial

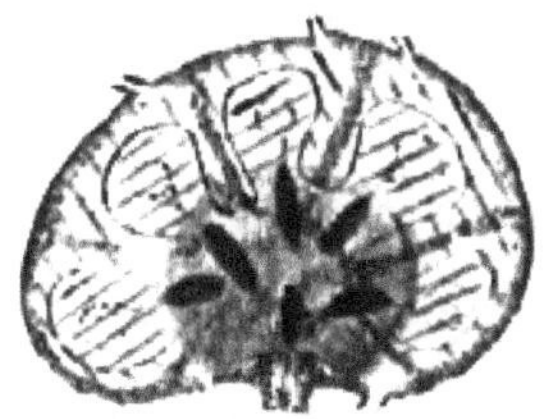

Follicular tissues with remarkable reduction, intense deminution of lymphocytes and considerable leucocytes-emigrations.

S-19. Peribronchial : pea-large.

Slight pericapsular congestion, slight catarrh in peripheral sinus and considerable congestion in medullary tissues.

S 22. Mesenterial

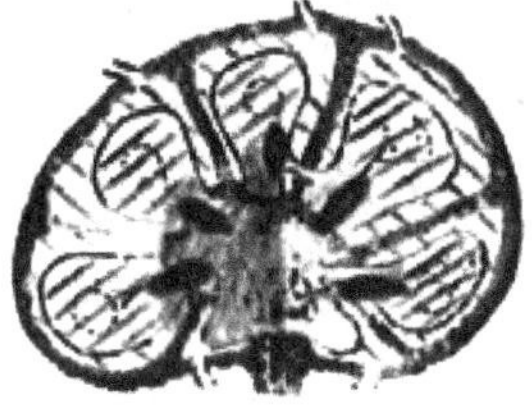

Slight edema in follicular tissues, with slight reduction of follicular lymphocytes.

S-19. Mesenterial : Sugar-corn large.

Slight catarrh of peripheral sinus, considerable congestion, considerable hemorrhages and edema of medullary sinus, slight edema in follicular tissues and slight diminution of follicular lymphocytes.

531

S.22. Submaxillar

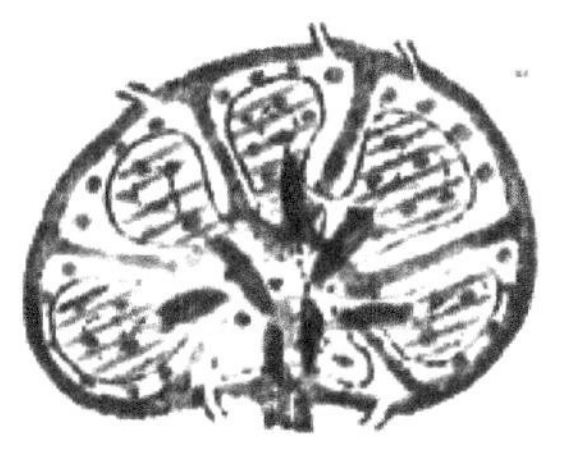

S-22. Mesenterial : submaxillaris, some pea large lymph-nodes.

Slight catarrh in peripheral sinus with considerable hyperplasia of reticulum cells, considerable congestion and some oralised hemorrhages.

Slight swelling of medullary tissues and slight reduction of follicular tissues.

S-22. Submaxillaris : some pea large lymph-noculus.

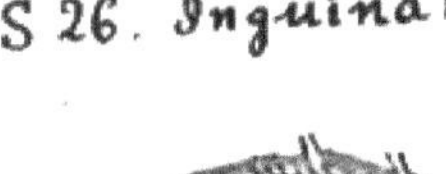

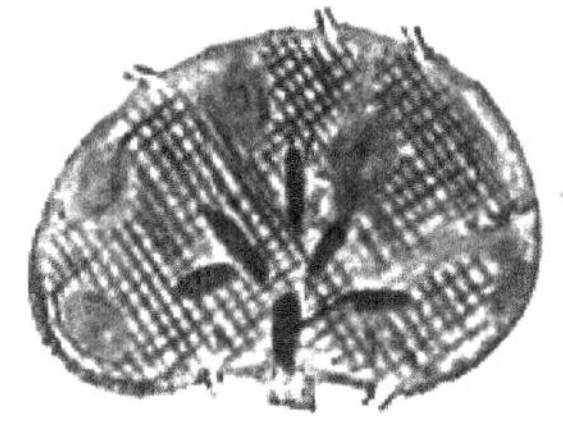

Peripheral sinus in intense catarrh : remarkable hyperplasia of reticulum cells and capillary endothel-cells (so-called inflammtory endotheliosis), accompaneid with some leucocytes-dissemination.

Medullary tissues with intense hyperplasia of reticulum cells and capillary endothel-cells, accompanied with considerable congestion and some leucocytes-dissemination.

Follicular tissues in remarkable reduction, due to intense hyperplasia of reticulum cells and reticulum fibres, accompanied with remarkable diminution of follicular lymphocytes (so-called inflammtory endotheliosis).

S-26. Inguinal : quaill-egg large.

S.28. Inguinal

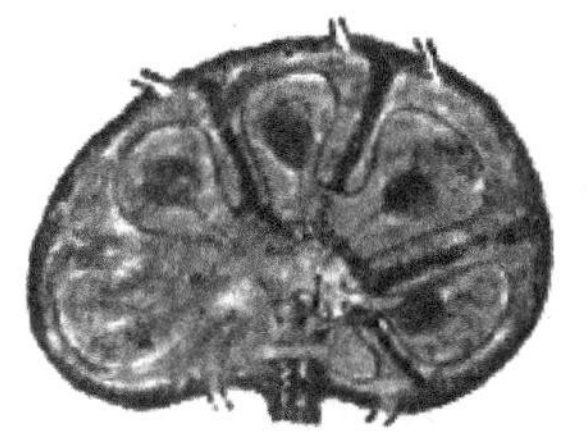

S.28. Peribronchial

Intense Pericapsulitis with flaky bacterial dissemination and intense leucocytic-necrotic changes all over the pericapsular fatty tissues, accompanied with necrotic ruin of blood-vessel-walls, due to plenty bacterial accumulation.

Intense diffuse hemorrhagic-leucocytic inflammation all over the follicular tissues : with flaky bacterial dissemination, diffuse necrosis, intense ruins of capillary walls, remarkable diffuse hemorrhages and intense diminution of lymphocytes.

S-28. Inguinal : some sugar-corn large lymph-nodes.

Severe Pericapsulitis with diffuse intense heomrrhages and diffuse flaky bacterial dissemination, esp. at perivascular portions.

Some blood-vessels with intense ruins of walls and plenty bacterial masses as contents.

Peripheral sinus with plenty and flaky bacterial masses and total diminish of cellular components.

Follicular tissues with intenst diffuse (all

533

S.28. Mesenterial.

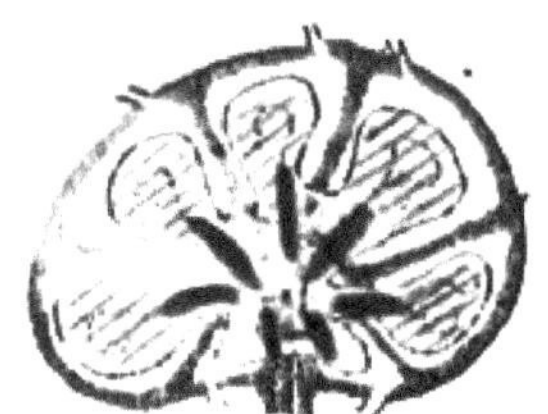

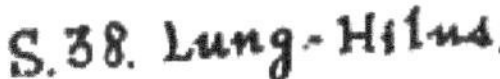

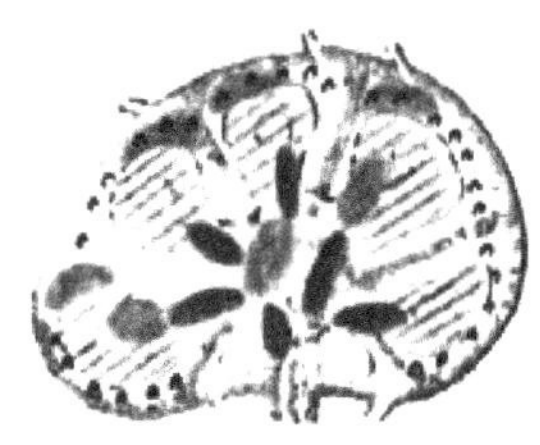

over the follicular tissues) hemorrhages with some leucocytes and some bacterial masses and total diminish of cellular components.

S-28. Peribronchial : sugar-corn large.

Pericapsular tissues with considerable congestion.

Peripheral sinus in considerable catarrh : with considerable hyperplasia of reticulum cells (in cloudy swelling) with some erythrophagocytosis,

Medullary tissues with intense congestion (some bacterial masses as capillary-contents) and severe swelling of medullary tissues.

Follicular tissues with slight reduction and slight diminution of lymphocytes.

S-28. Mesenterial : Sugar-corn large.

Pericapsular tissues with considerable congestion, considerable hemorrhages and some leucocytes-emigrations.

Medullary tissues with remarkable congestion and intense swelling.

Follicular tissues with considerable congestion, considerable swelling and considerable reduction of lymphocytes. Germinative centers in solid-form.

534

S. 38. peribronchial

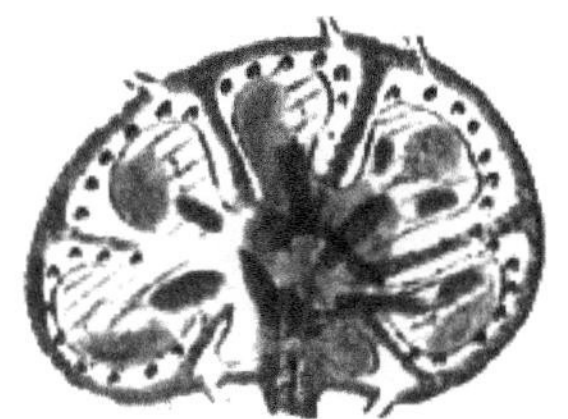

S-38. Lung-hilus : quaill-egglarge.

Considerable Pericapsulitis with considerable congestion and some leucocytes-emigrations. Peripheral sinus with considerable leucocytes -accumulation, some bacterial masses and some cloudy swollen reticulum cells.

Medullary tissues with considerable congestion, intense swelling of medullary tissues and some bacterial dissemination.

Follicular tissues with intense swelling.

S-38. Peribronchial : Sugar-corn large.

Considerable Pericapsulitis with consid. congestion and some leucocytes. Peripheral sinus with considerable leucocytes-accumulation, some hemorrhages and some bionecrotically swollen reticulum cells.

Medullary tissues with remarkable congestion, severe edematous swelling and some hemorrhages.

Follicular tissues with considerable congestion, severe serlling, and slight diminution of lymphocytes.

Lymph-nodes in remarkable congestion and swelling.

535

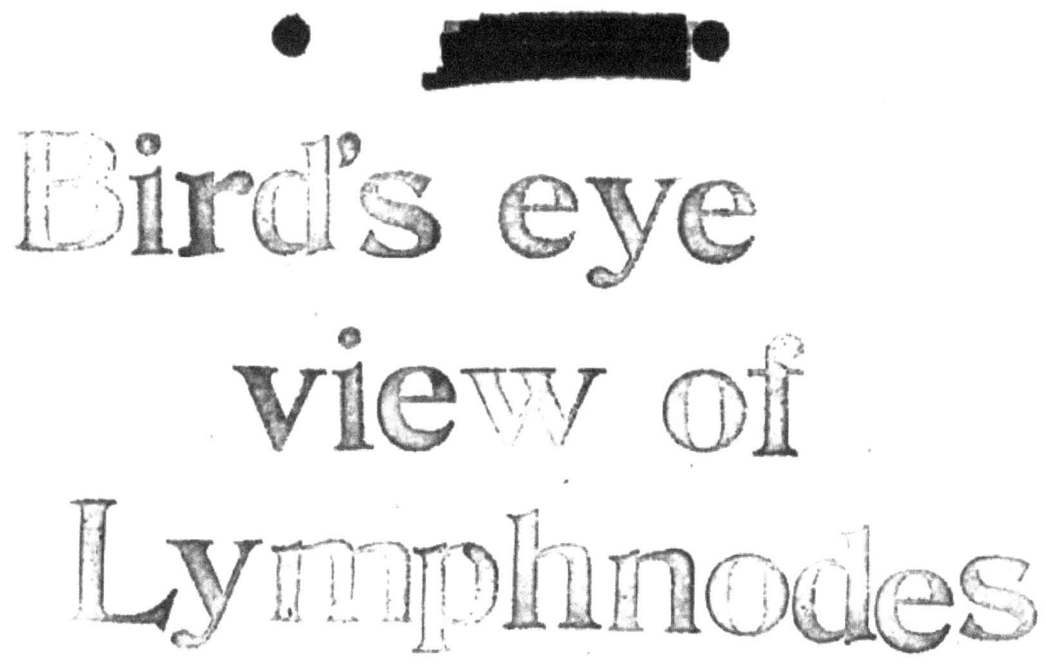
Bird's eye
view of
Lymphnodes

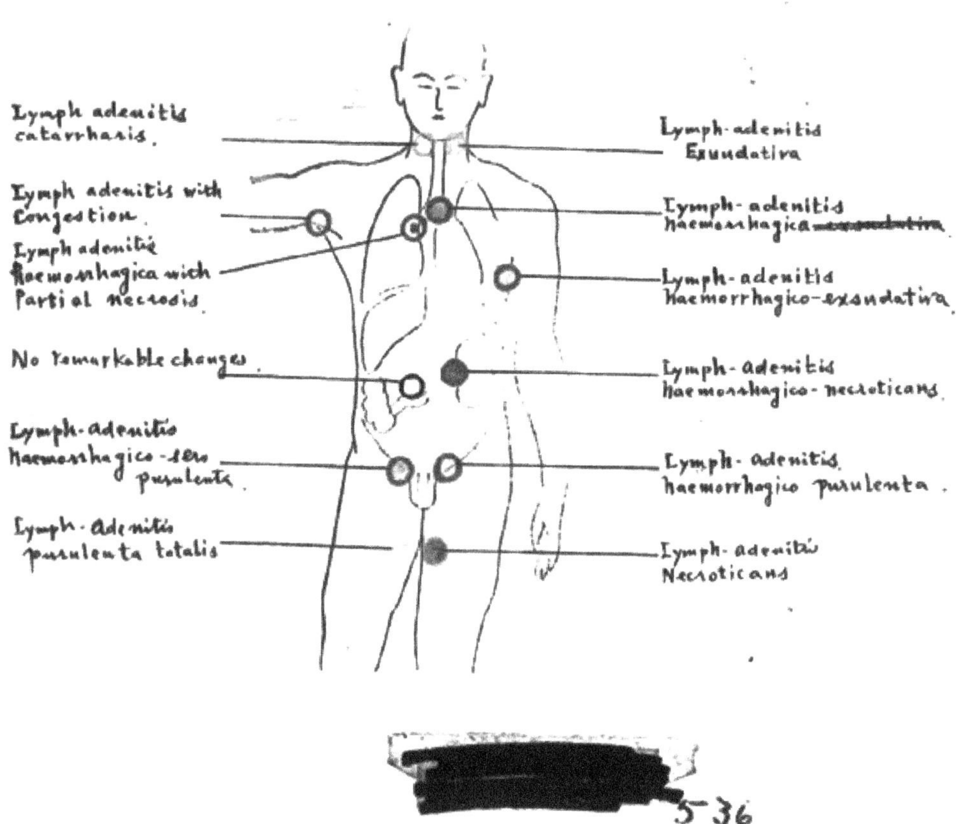
Lymph adenitis catarrhalis.
Lymph-adenitis Exsudativa
Lymph adenitis with Congestion.
Lymph-adenitis haemorrhagica
Lymph adenitis haemorrhagica with partial necrosis.
Lymph-adenitis Haemorrhagico-exsudativa.
No remarkable changes.
Lymph-adenitis haemorrhagico-necroticans.
Lymph-adenitis haemorrhagico-sero purulenta.
Lymph-adenitis haemorrhagico purulenta.
Lymph-Adenitis purulenta totalis
Lymph-adenitis Necroticans
5 36

SUMMARY.
(I)

The bird's-eye view of all investigated cases.

I. Axillaris (l) L. hemorrhagica totalis.
Peribronchial. L. hemorrhagico-purulenta.

2. Axillaris.(r) L. hemorrhagico-purulenta.

Inguinal. (r) L. hemorrhagico-purulenta, with plenty leucocytes and some bacterial masses in follicular tissues.

Medenterial. Catarrh and slight congestion.

3. Axillaris (r). L. hemorrhagica.

Mesenterial. L. acuta with considerable congestion in follicular tissues.

Peribronchial, L. acuta with considerable congestion. and some bacterial dissemination.

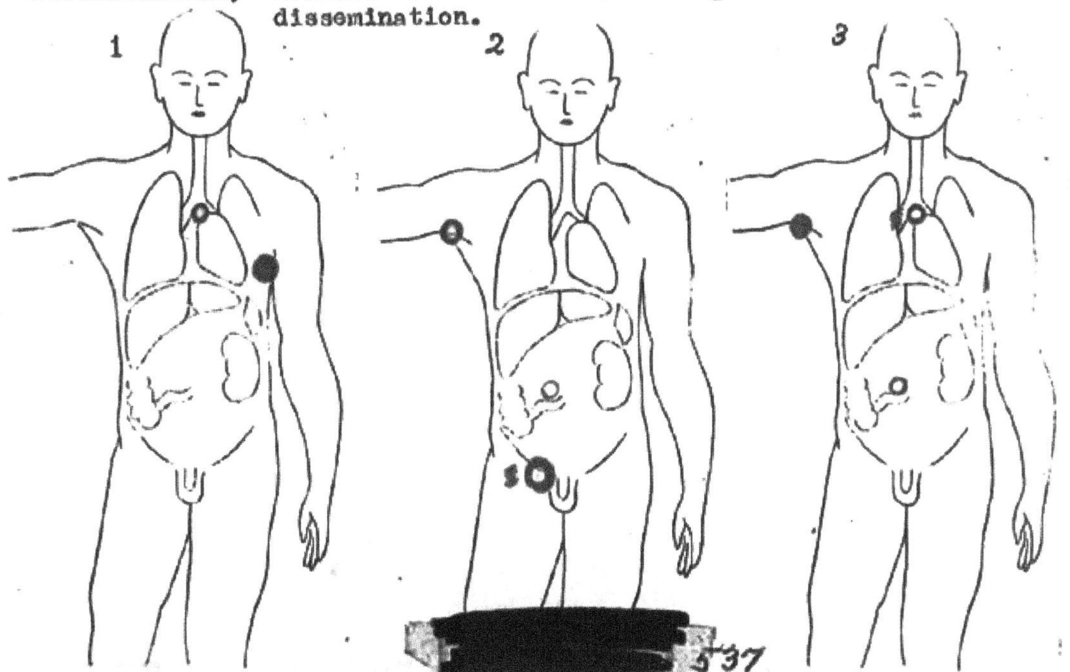

4. Axillaris (r).	L. hemorrhagico-purulenta with severe hemorrhages, plenty leucocytes and partial necrosis.
Peribronchial.	Slight catarrh with some leucocyte and consid. congestion in follicular tissues.
Ileocoecal.	Slight catarrh and considerable congestion.
Mesenterial.	Slight catarrh and considerable congestion.
Retroperitoneal.	Intense congestion, necrotic ruins of follicular capillary walls and intense perivascular hemorrhages exudation and leucocytes-dissemination.
Inguinal.	Catarrh and considerable congestion.

4

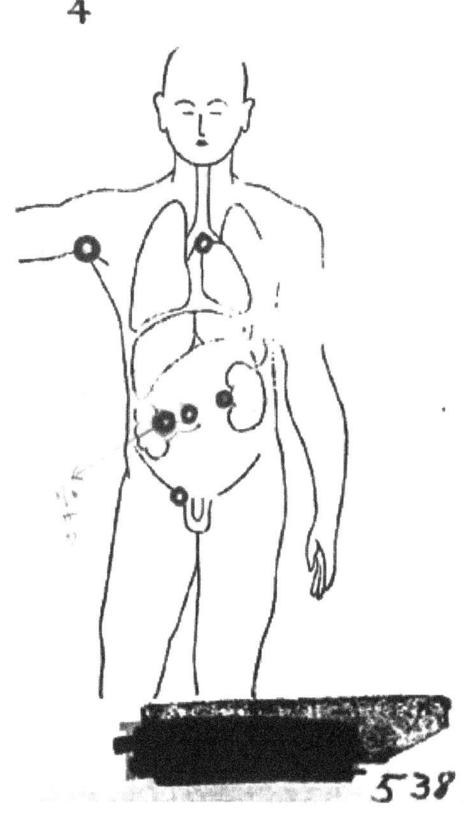

538

5. Inguinal.	L. necroticans totoalis.
Peribronchial	L. hemorrhagico-necroticans, with some bacterial masses, some hemorrhages and partial necorosis.
Retroperitoneal.	Intense congestion and some hemorrhages.
6. Sepsis.	Without any sighificant changes of lymph-nods.
Mesenterial.	Sinus-catarrh.

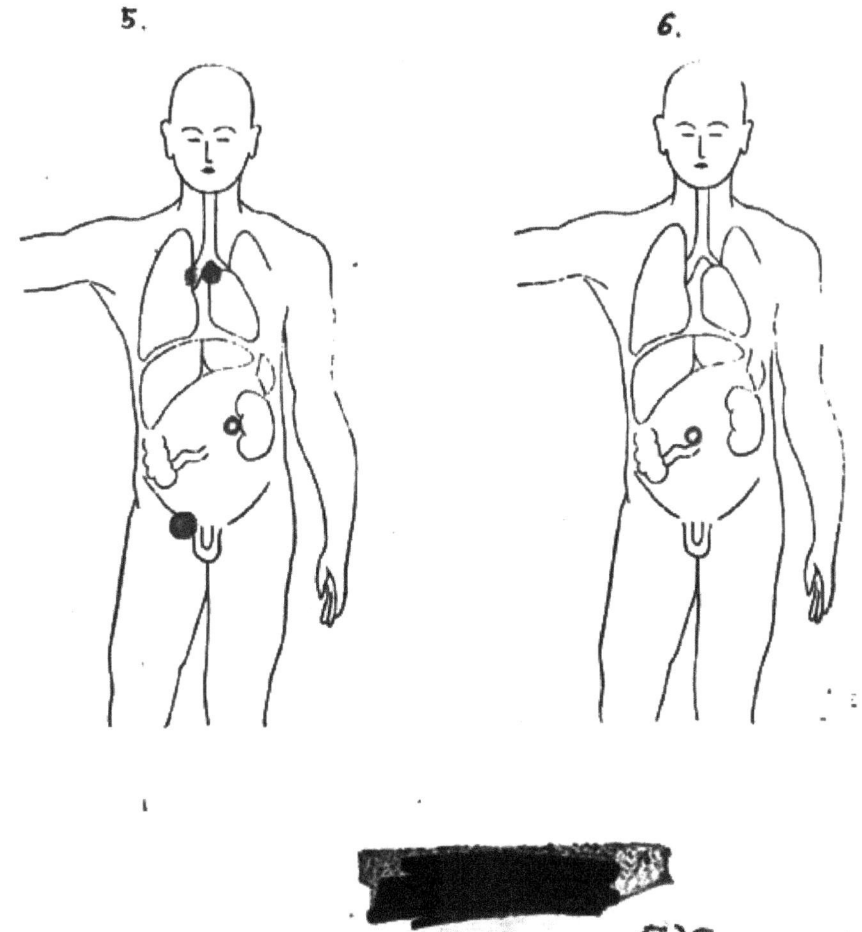

539

7. Inguinal.	L. hemorrhagica. Intense congestion, diffuse hemorrhages and some bacterial dissemination.
Mesenterial.	L. hemorrhagica with diffuse hemorrhages and diffuse bacterial dissemination.
Cervicalis (1).	catarrh and considerable congestion.
8. Submaxillaris.	L. hemorrhagico-purulenta. with diffuse bacterial dissemination.
Submaxillaris.	L. acuta with intense congestion and edema.
Peribronchial.	L. haemorrhagica with diffuse hemorrhages, some bacterial disseminat, and bionecrotic swelling of follicular tissues.
Retroperitoneal.	Intense congestion, dnultiple hemorrhages and some bacterial dissemination.

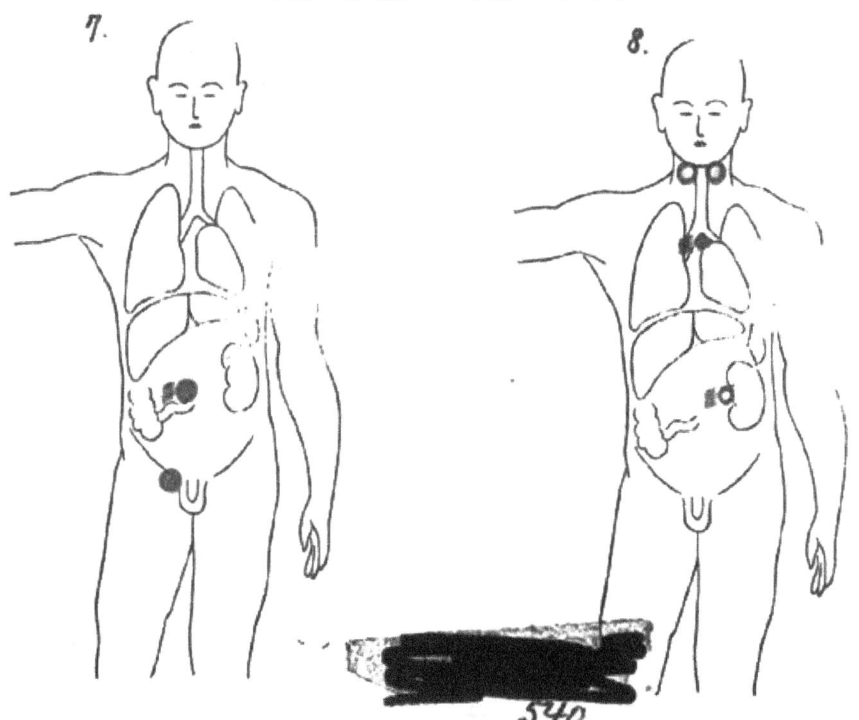

540

9. Inguinal. (1)	L. hemorrhagico-purulenta totalis, with consid. congestion, some hemorrhages and diffuse bacterial dissemination.
Mesenterial.	L. catarrhalis.
10. Submaxillaris.	L. hemorrhagica, with consid. congestion multiple hemorrhages and diffuse bacterial dissemination.
Submaxillaris.	L. hemorrhagica with the some changes.
Peribronchial.	L. hemorrhagico-purulenta with remarkable congestion and plenty of bact. dissemin.
Peribronchial.	L. hemorrhagico-purulenta totalis with the same changes.
Mesenterial.	Catarrh.

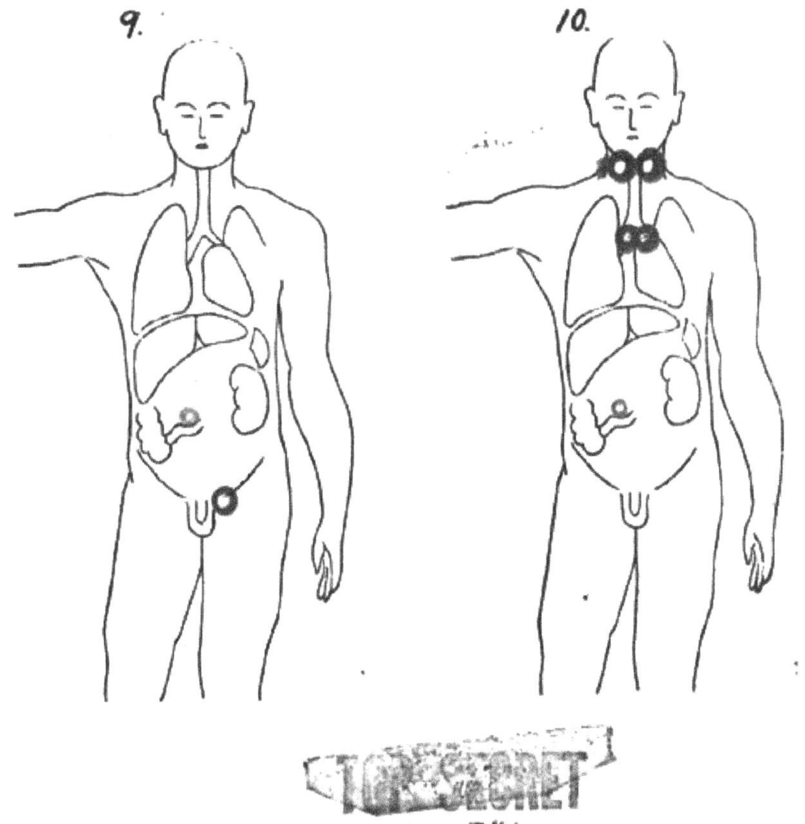

541

11. Inguinal.	Intense Pericapsulitis.
	L.hemorrhagico-necroticans totalis.
Retroperitoneal.	L.hemorrhagico-sero-purulenta totalis.
	Intense Pericapsulitis.
Peribronchial.	L.purulenta with some bacterial dissemin. and plenty of leucocytes.
Mesenterial.	Catarrh, intense congestion multiple hemorrhages and leucocytes-dissemination.

11

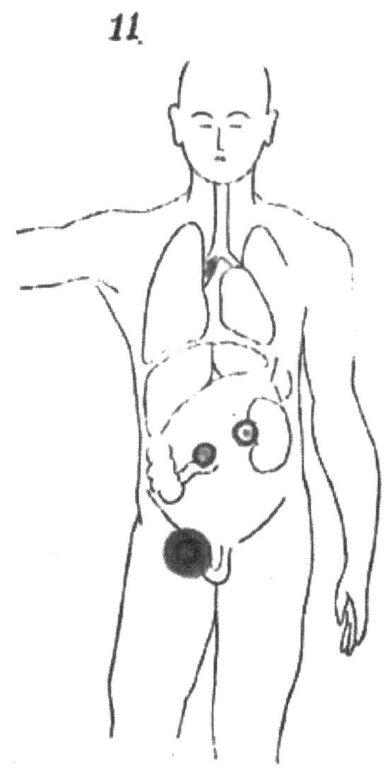

542

12. Submaxillaris. (1)	L.hemorrhagico-purulenta totalis.
Peribronchial.	L. catarrhalis acuta with consider. congestion, some bacterial dissemin. and remarkable increase of reticulum cells.
Mesenterial.	L. catarrhalis acuta with considerable congest. and slight hemorrhages.
Inguinal.	Catarrh with some bacterial masses in capillaries.

12.

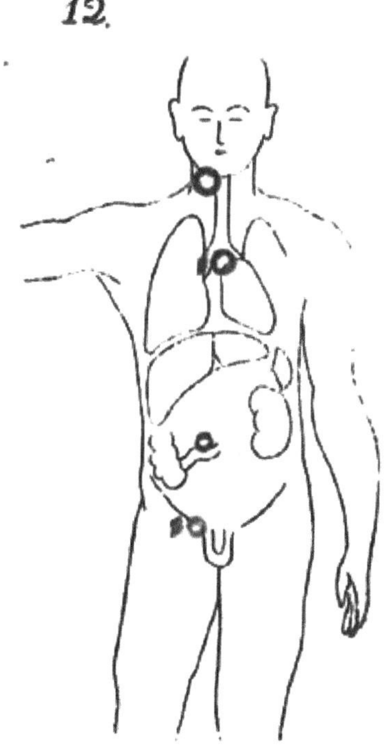

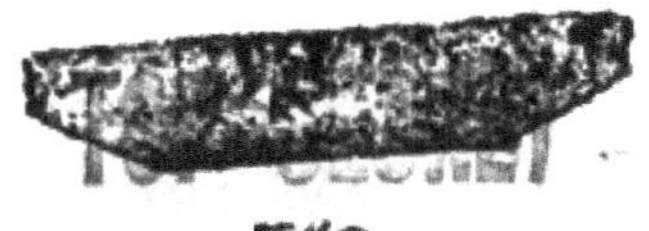

543

14.	Inguinal (r).	L. hemorrhagico-necrotifans totalis.
	Mesenterial.	L. catarrhalis acuta with consid congestion, some bact.dissemin. and bionecrotic swelling of reticulum fibres.
	Peribronchial.	Catarrh and intense congestion in follicular tissues.
	Peribronchial. (Bifulcatio)	L.hemorrhagica totalis.
15.	Peribronchial.	L. acuta with multiple localised hemorrhages and some bact. dissemination.
	Peribronchial.	L. hemorrhagico-purulenta with some bacterial dissemination.
	Inguinal (r).	L. hemorrhagico-purulenta.

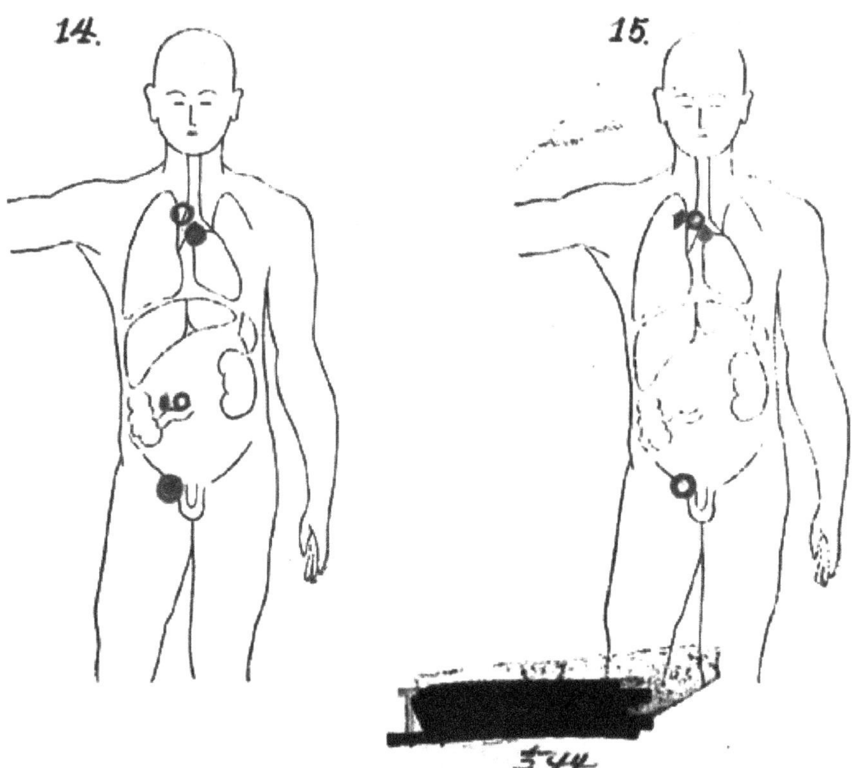

344

16. Axillaris. L. haemorrhagica acuta. Intense congestion.
Inguinal. L. haemorrhagica acuta with intense congestion.
Mesenterial. L. haemorrhagica with intense congestion.
Mesenterial. L.haemorrhggica acuta with intense congestion and edema (radix)
Peribronchial.L. acuta with cons. congestion.
17. Inguinal(l).L.acuta with consi. congestion.
Inguinal.(r).L. acuta with intense congestion.
Mesenterial. L. acuta with intense congestion.
Lung-hilus. Intense Pericapsulitis with hemorrhagic -exudative changes and
L. haemorrhagico(totalis) and necroticans(partial).
Peribronchial. Catarrh, intense congestion and slight hemorrhages.
18. Inguinal(r).L. haemorrhagico-necroticans totalis.
Retroperitoneal. L. haemorrhagico-necroticans totalis.
Retroperitoneal. Intense Pericapsulitis and inter-muscular abscesses.

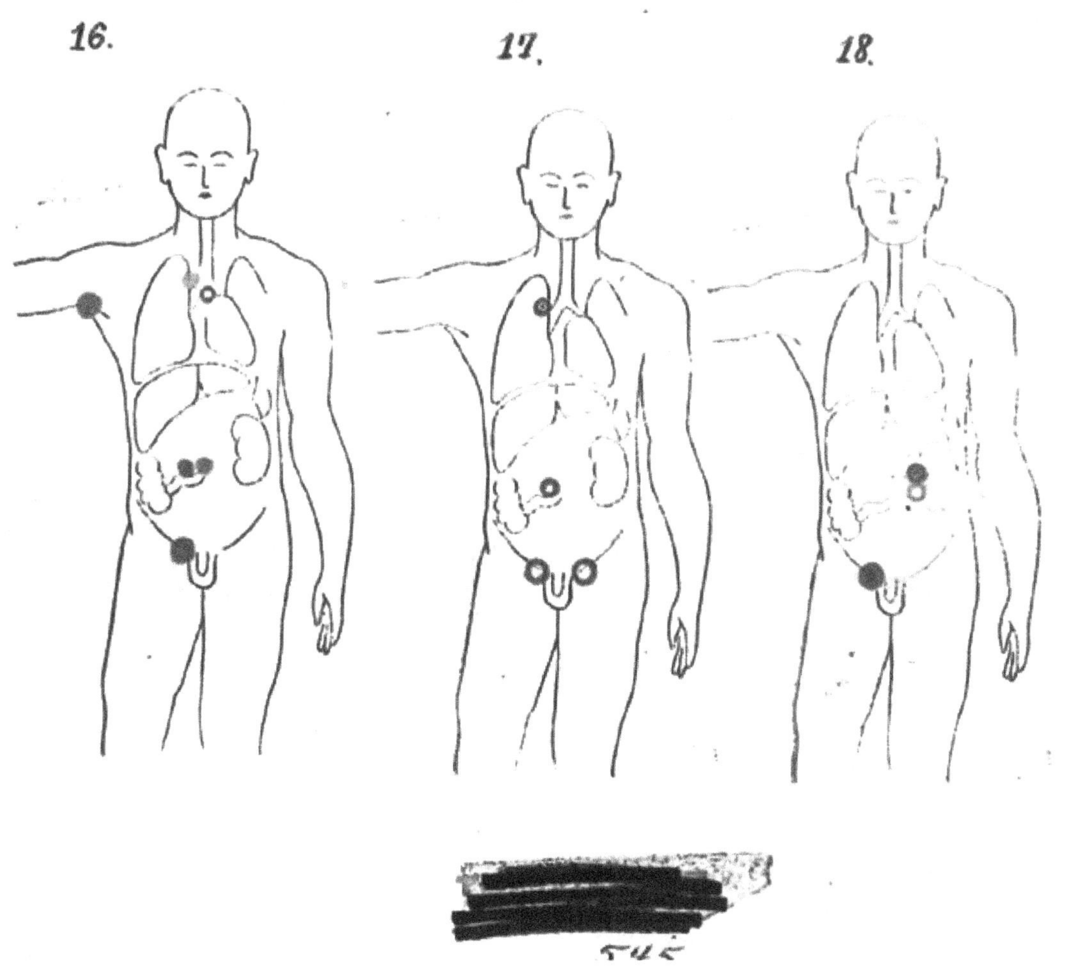

545

19. Axillaris(r). L.haemorrhagico-purulenta totalis.
    Peribronchial. L. haemorrhagico-purulenta with some bacterial dissemination, some hemorrhages and some leucocytes accumulation.
    Inguinal(l). L. haemorrhagica totalis.
    Mesenterial. L. acuta with considerable congestion and slight perivascular hemorrhages.
20. Axillaris(r). Intense Pericapsulitis with intense congestion and consid. hemorrhages.
    L. exsudativo-haemorrhagica with intense congestion and considerable hemorrhages.
    Inguinal(l). Catarrh and considerable congestion.
    Mesenterial. Catarrh and considerable congestion.

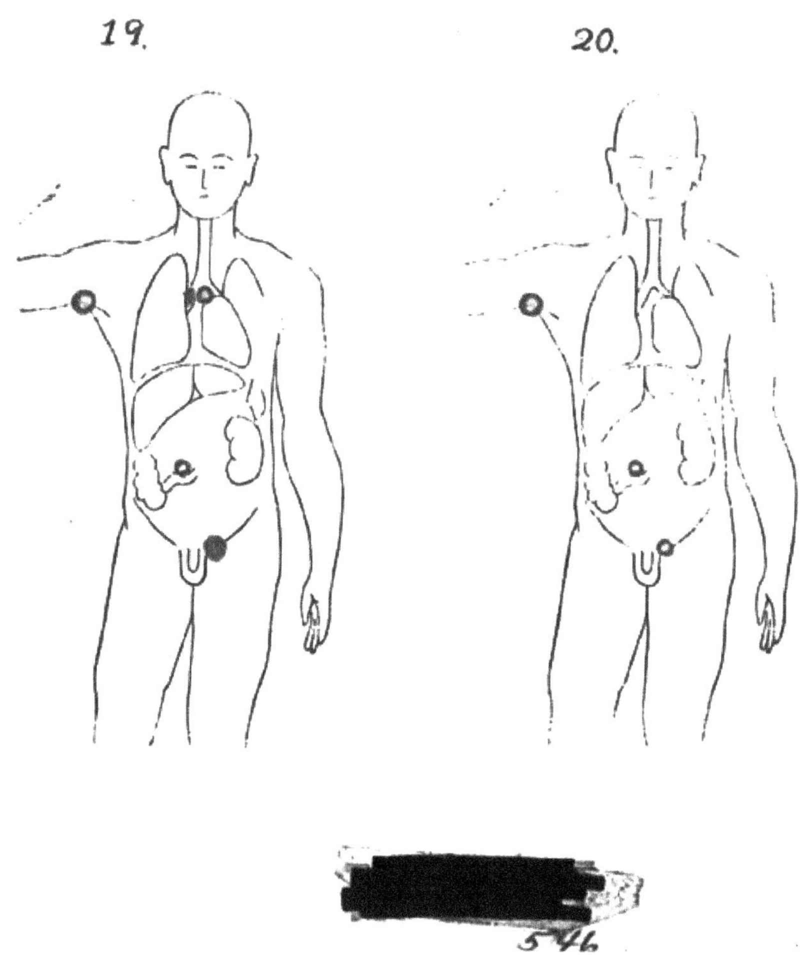

546

21. Inguinal(r). L.haemorrhagico-exsudativa totalis with some bact. disseminati on.
Peribronchial. L. haemorrhagico-exsudativa with some bacterial masses.
Peribronchial. L. acuta with considerable congestion and Intense Pericapsulitis with severe congestion and some bact. dissemination.
Retroperitonea;. L.haemorrhagica totalis with intense Pericapsulitis with diffuse hemorrhages.
Cervicalis(r). Catarrh and congestion.
Axillaris(r). Catarrh and congestion.

23. Peribonchial. L. catarrhalis levis.
Mesenteria;. No remarkavle changes.

24. Inguinal(r). L. purulenta gravis totalis.
Mesenterial. L.acuta with considerable congestion.
Peribronchial L. acuta with considerable congestion.

25. Sepsis. No remarkable swelling of lymph-nods, anywhere.

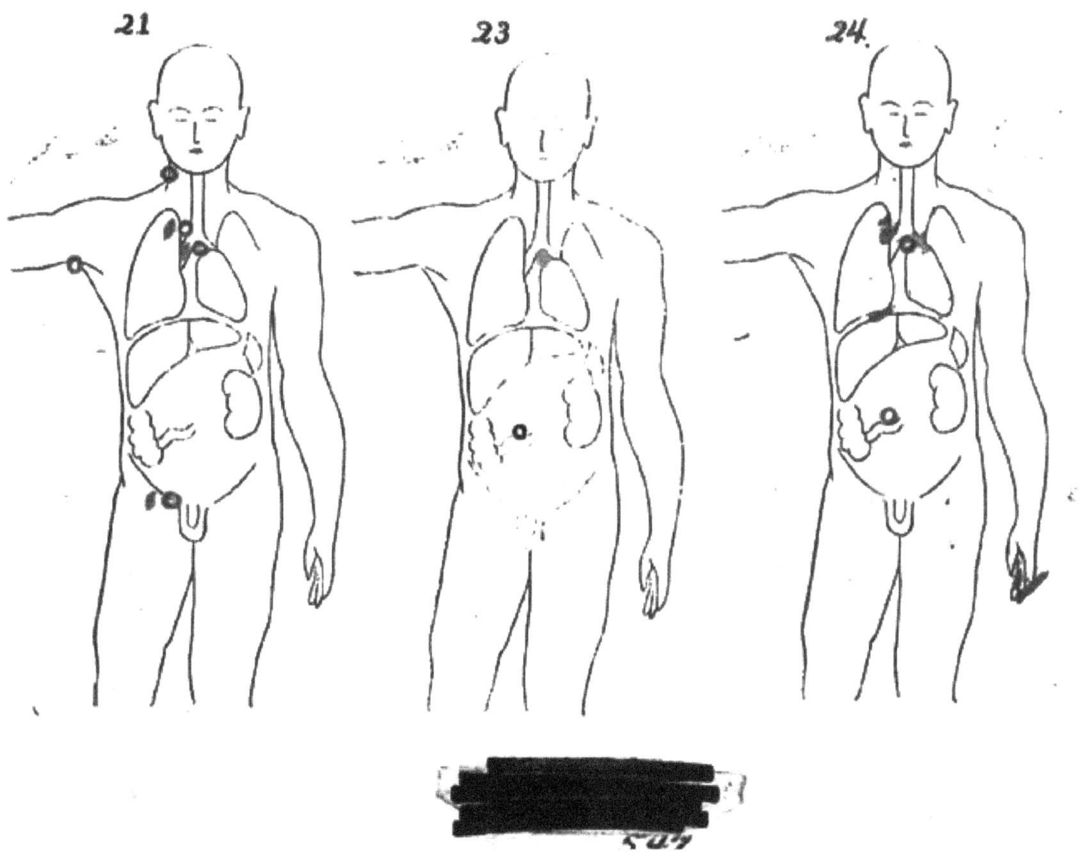

26. Inguinal(r).L. haemorrhagica totalis.
Inguinal(l).L. haemorrhaigca totalis.
Retroperitoneal. L.haemorrhagico-necroticans totalis and intense Pericapsulitis with diffuse hemorrhages.
Peribronchial. L.haemorrhagico-purulenta et necroticans partialis, with plenty bacterial dissemination.

27. Peribronchial. L.haemorrhagica totalis.
Mesenterial. L. acuta with considerable congestion.

29. Inguinal(r). Lymph-nodulus post extripatio.
Cerivalis. Catarrh and congestion.
Peribronchial. Catarrh and slight congestion.

30. Axillaris(r). L.haemorrhagico-necroticans totalis.
Axillaris(l). L. acuta with intense congestion and swelling.
Inguinal(r). L. acuta with intense congestion,
Inguinal(r), L. acuta with intense congestion.
Mesenterial. Intense Pericapsulitis with some hemorrhages.
L.acuta with intense congestion.
Peribronchial. L.haemorrhagico-necroticans.

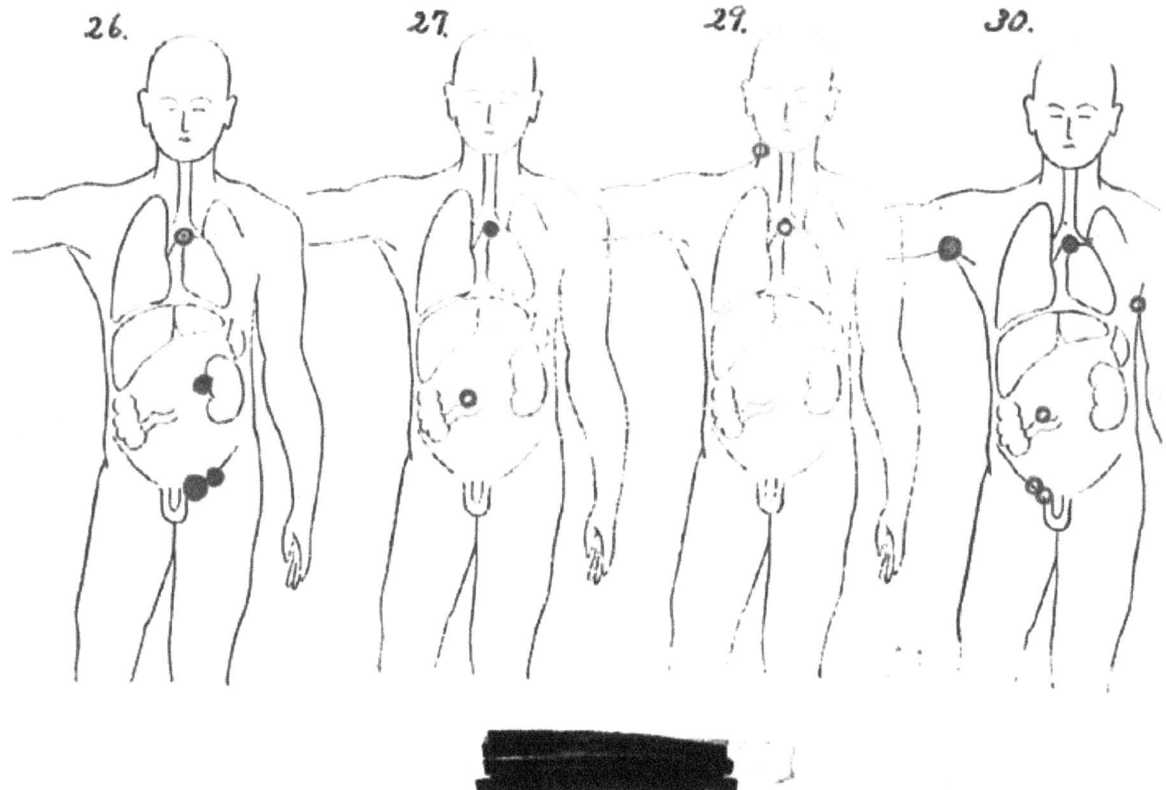

31. Axillaris(l).	L.haemorrhagico-necroticans totalis.
Mesenterial.	Some congestion.
Inguinal.	Considerable congestion in follicur tissues.
Peribronchial.	L. haemorrhagico-necroticans partialis.
32. Inguinal. (sepsis).	L. acuta with consid. congestion and scattered bacterial disseminations.
Peribronchial.	Catarrh and intense follicular congestion.
33. Inguinal(r).	L. haemorrhagico-exsudativeo-purulenta totalis. Intense Pericapsulitis with diffuse hemorrhages. Intense cutanous edema and hyperemia.
Retroperitoneal.	L.haemorrhagico.necroticans totalis. Intense Pericapsulitis with diffuse hemorrhages.
Peribronchial.	L. acuta with considerable congestion and partial hemorrhages.
Mesenterial.	L. acuta with consid. congestion adn multiple hemorrhages.

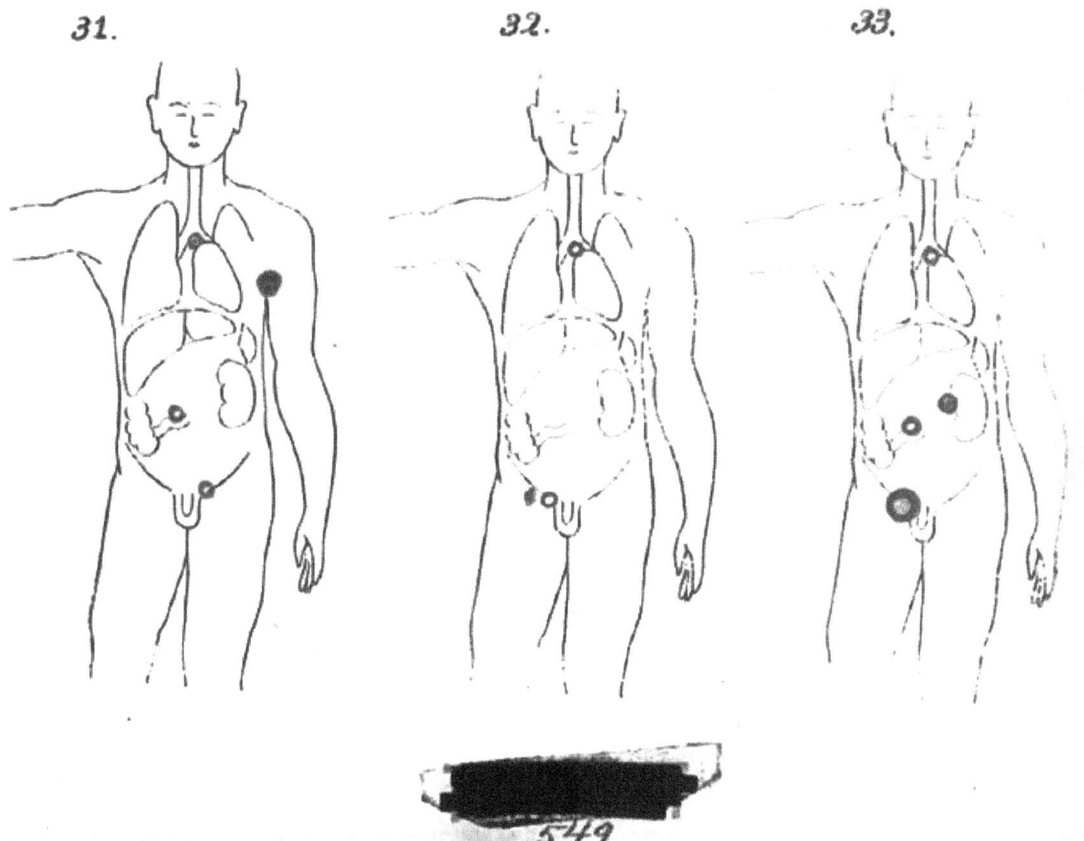

549

34. Axill aris(r),	L. haemorrhagico-necroticans totalis.
Submaxillaris(r)	L. acuta haemorrhagica with consid. congestion and some partial hemorrhages and leucocytes accumul.
Inguinal.	Considerable congestion in follicular tissues.
Mesenterial.	Considerable congestion,
Peribronchial.	Catarrh and follicular congestion.
35. Axillaris(l).	L. haemorrhagico-necroticans totalis.
Peribronchial.	Intense Pericapsulitis with some leucocytes and bacterica dissemination. L. haemorrhagica with multiple hemorrhages, consid. congestion and edema.
Mesenterial.	L. acuta with considerable congestion,
36. Supra-clavicular.	L. necroticans totalis.
Infraclavicular	L. necroticans totalis.
Axillaris(r).	L. necroticans totalis.
Peribronchial.	L. haemorrhagico.necroticans partialis.

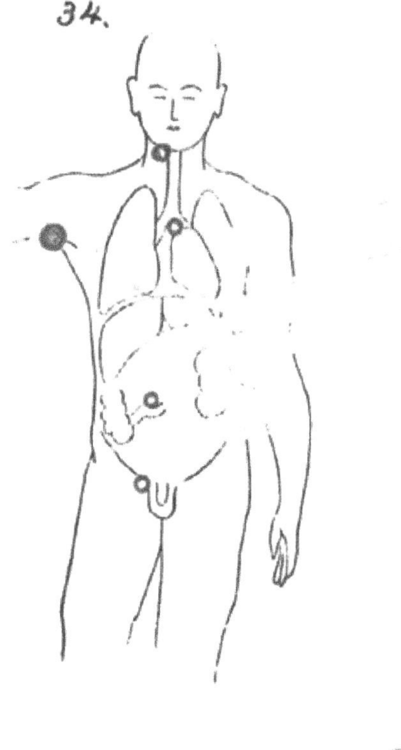

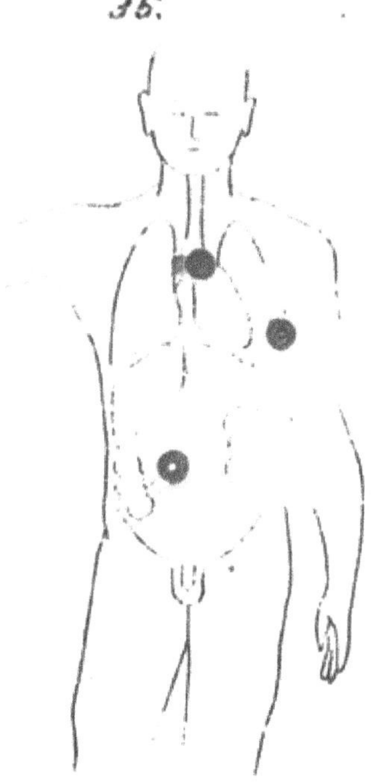

38. Inguinal(r). L.(hemorrhagico)-sero-purulenta with intense congestion,plenty of leucocytes-emigration and remarkable exudation.
    Retroperitoneal. L. haemorrhagico-necroticans with flaky bacterial dissemination.
    Intense Pericapsulitis with diffuse hemorrhages.
    Mesenterial. L. acuta haemorrhagica partialis.
    Peribronchilaris Intense congestion in follicular tissues.

40. Inguinal(r). L. haemorrhagico-sero-purulenta totalis.
    Phlegmons of adjacent cutaneous tissues.
    Retroperitoneal. L. haemorrhagico-purulenta and intense Pericapsulitis,with diffuse hemorrhages totalis.
    Axillaris(l). L. haemorrhagica acuta with consid. congestion and some partial hemorrhages.
    Axillaris(r). L. haemorrhagica acuta with consid. congestion and some partial hemorrhages.
    Peribronchial. L. haemorrhagico-purulenta with cons. congestion, partial hemorrhages and plenty bacterial dissemination
    Mesentrial. L. acuta. with considerable congestion, edema and some leucocytes-dissemination,

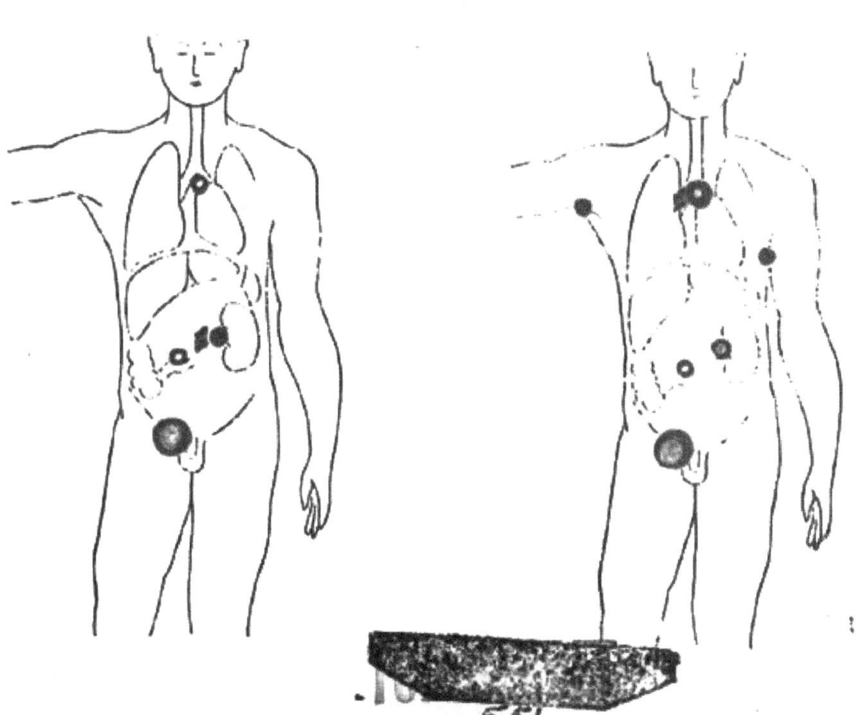

541

42. Inguinal. Post operatio. Phlegmons of adjacent cutaneous tissues.
Retroperitoneal. L.haemorrhagico.necroticans totalis and intense Pericapsulitis with diffuse hemorrhages.
Mesanterial. Considerable congestion.
Submaxillaris. L. haemorrhagco-necroticans totalis.

44. Axillaris(r). L. haemorrhagico.necroticans partialis.
Inguianl(l). L. catarrhalis acuta with consi. congestion.
Inguinal(r). With the same changes.
Mesenterial. L. acuta catarrhalis et haemorrhagica with some hemorrhages, some leucocytes and bacterial dissemination and edematous swelling.

42

44

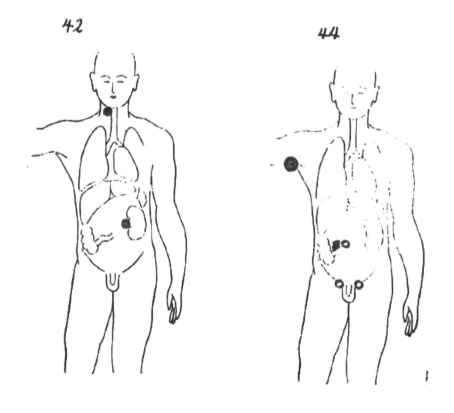

46. Axillaris(r). Edema and intense congestion of cutaneous tissues. L.haemorrhagico-purulents in medium degree, with consid. congestion and localised hemorrhages and some leucocytes-dissemination.
    Peribronchial. L.(haemorrhagico)-necroticans totalis.

47. Axillaris(r). L.haemorrhagico-necroticans totalis.
    Axillaris(l). L. haemorrhagico-necroticans totalis.
    Cervidalis. L.haemorrhagico-necrotácand totalis.
    Mesenterial. L. catarrhalis acuta with consid. congestion.

49. Cervicalis . L.haemorrhagica partialis with intense congestion and partial hemorrhages.
    Peribronchial. L.haemorrhagica partialis with intense congestion, some localised hemorrhages, serous exudation and some leucocytes and bacterial dissemination.

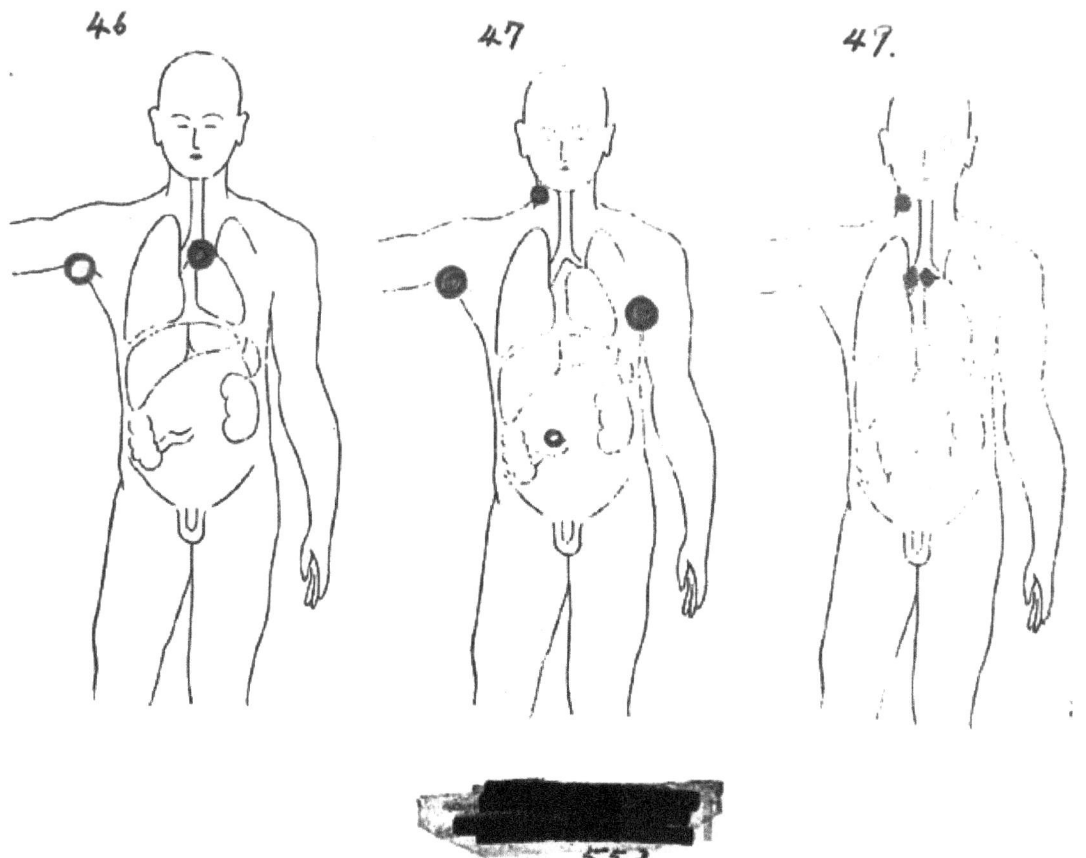

553

S-I.	Peribronchial.	L. catarrhalis with conisderable congestion.
	Mesenterial.	Normal.
S-2.	Inguinal (r).	L. haemorrhagica with intense congestion and some localised hemorrhages.
	Inguinal (l).	With the same changes.
	Mesenterial.	With the same changes.
	Peribronchial.	L. haemorrhagica with intense congestion and diffuse hemorrhages.
	Cervicalis.	L. haemorrhagica with intense congestion and diffuse hemorrhages.
	Axillaris. (r)	The same changes.
S-3.	Inguinal (r).	L. haemorrhagico-sero-purulenta totalis.
	Retro-peritoneal.	Intense periadenitis with diffuse hemorrhages and flaky bacterial dissemination.
	Mesenterial.	L. catarrhalis with consid. congestion.
	Peribronchial.	L. haemorrhagico-necroticans totalis.
	Peribronchial. (Bifulcation).	L. haemorrhagico-necroticans totalis.
	Cervicalis (l).	L. haemorrhagico-necroticans partialis.

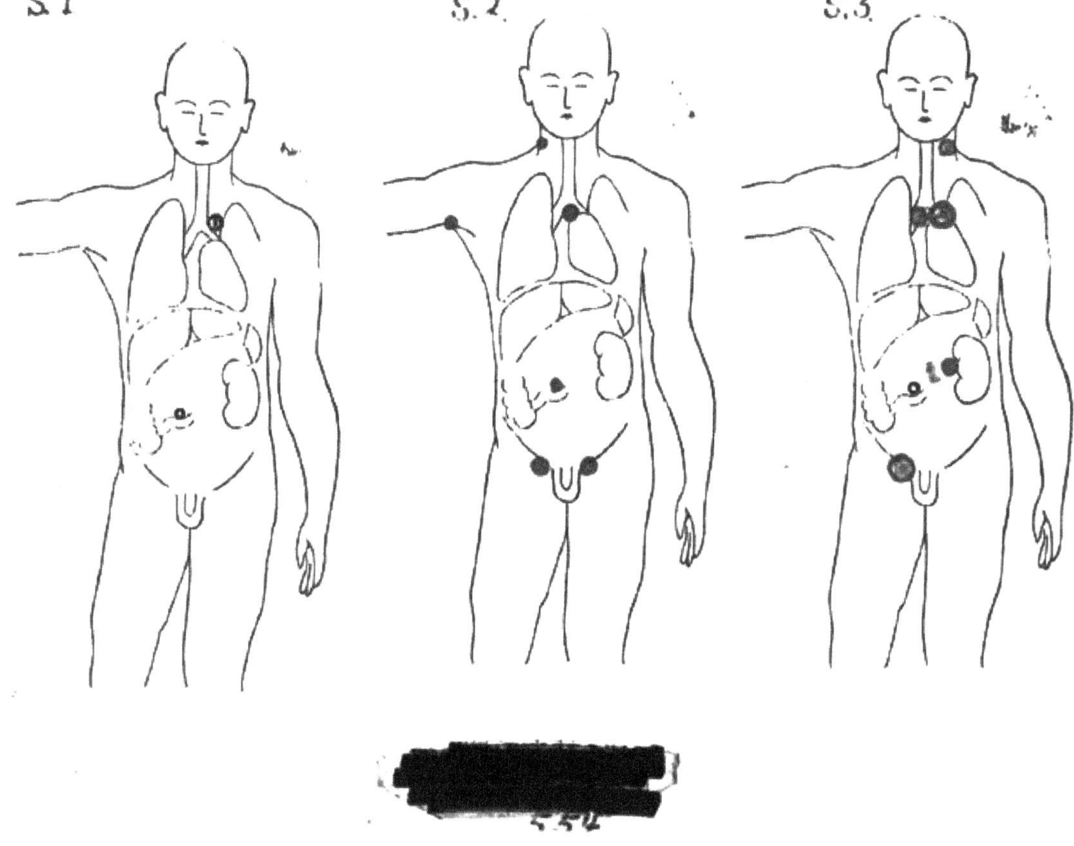

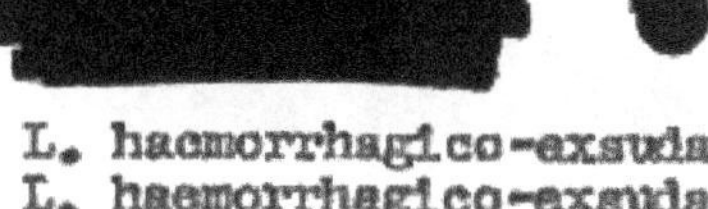

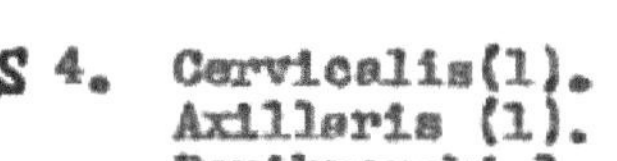

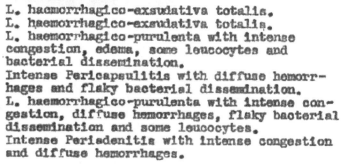

S 4.	
Cervicalis(1).	L. haemorrhagico-exsudativa totalis.
Axillaris (1).	L. haemorrhagico-exsudativa totalis.
Peribronchial.	L. haemorrhagico-purulenta with intense congestion, edema, some leucocytes and bacterial dissemination. Intense Pericapsulitis with diffuse hemorrhages and flaky bacterial dissemination.
Peribronchial. (bifulcation).	L. haemorrhagico-purulenta with intense congestion, diffuse hemorrhages, flaky bacterial dissemination and some leucocytes. Intense Periadenitis with intense congestion and diffuse hemorrhages.

S. 4

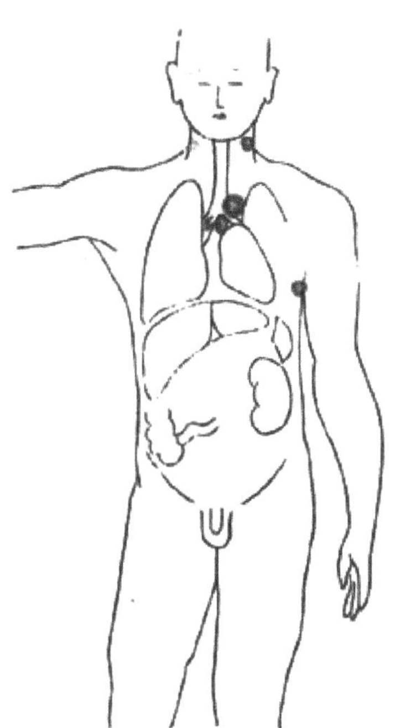

555

S-5.	Inguinal (l).	L. haemorrhagico-necroticans totalis with intense Pericapsulitis (diffuse hemorrhages).
	Retro-peritoneal.	Intense Pericapsulitis with diffuse hemmorrhages L. haemorrhagico-necroticans totalis.
	Mesenterial.	L. haemorrhagico-purulenta partialis with considerable congestion, some localised hemorrhages, some leucocytes and some bacterial dissemination.
	Peribronchial.	Slight Pericapsulitis with L. haemorrhagica partialis with intense congestion and some leucocytes dissemination.
	Cervicalis.	Catarrh and follicular congestion.
S-6.	Axillaris (r).	L. haemorrhagica with intense congestion and diffuse hemorrhages. Slight Pericapuslitis with some congestion.
	Submaxillaris.	L. haemorrhagico-necroticans totalis and intense Pericapsulitis with diffuse hemorrhages.
	Peribronchial.	L. haemorrhagico-necroticans partialis.
	Mesenterial.	L. haemorrhagico-necroticans with some leucocytes dissemination, some bacterial accumulation and some miliary necrosis.
	Cervicalis.	L. haemorrhagico-necroticans.

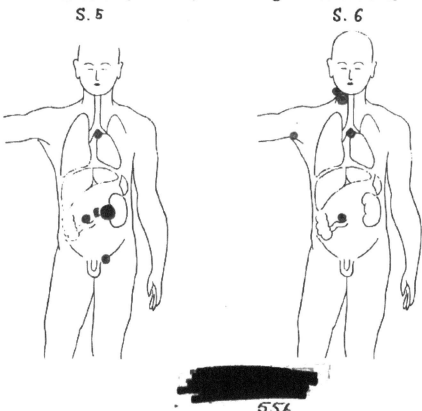

S. 5　　　　S. 6

S-8.	Axillaris (r).	Intense Pericapsulitis with some leucocytes-dissimin. L. catarrhalis acuta with some congestion and some bacterial dissemination.
	Submaxillaris (r, l).	(S. haemorrhagico-necroticans partialis with some leucocytes dissemination.
	Inguinal (r, l).	L. acuta with consid. congestion and some hemorrhages.
	Mesenterial.	Considerable congestion and slight catarrh.
	Peribronchial.	L. haemorrhagico-necroticans partialis.
S-9.	Peribronchial.	L. acuta with considerable congestion, some leucocytes and some bacterial dissemination.
	Mesenterial.	Almost normal.

S. 8.

S. 9.

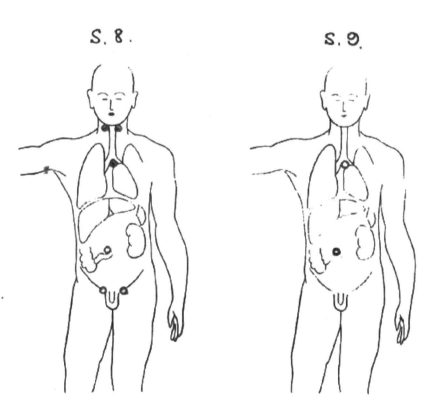

S-IO.	Axillaris (r).	L. purulenta with plenty leucocytes.
	Axillaris (l).	L. purulenta with plenty leucocytes. Intense Peri-capsulitis with flaky bact-dissemin.
	Inguinal (r).	L. purulenta with intense congestion and some leucocytes and some bact. dissemination.
	Inguinal (l).	With the same changes.
	Mesenterial.	L. catarrhalis with consid. congestion.
S-II.	Inguinal (r).	L. haemorrhagica totalis and necroticans partial.
	Retro-Peritoneal.	With the same changes with interse Pericapsulitis (diffuse hemorrhages).
	Mesenterial.	L. acuta with intense congestion, some leucocytes and some bact-dissemination.
	Axillaris (r).	L. haemorrhagico-purulenta with intense congestion, diffuse hemorrhages and edema.
	Peribronchial.	L. haemorrhagica with intense congestion and diffuse hemorrhages.

S. 10.

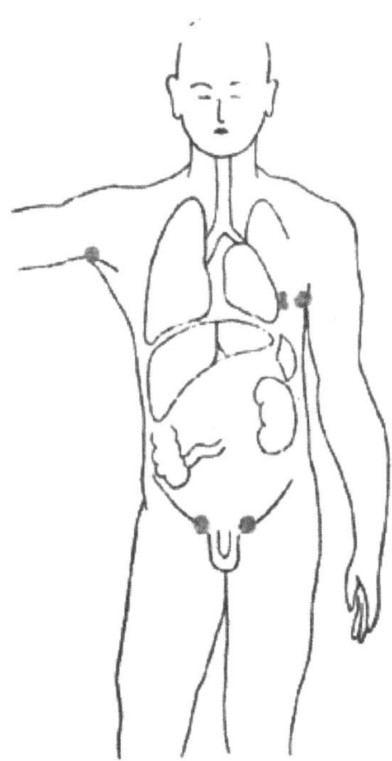

S. 11

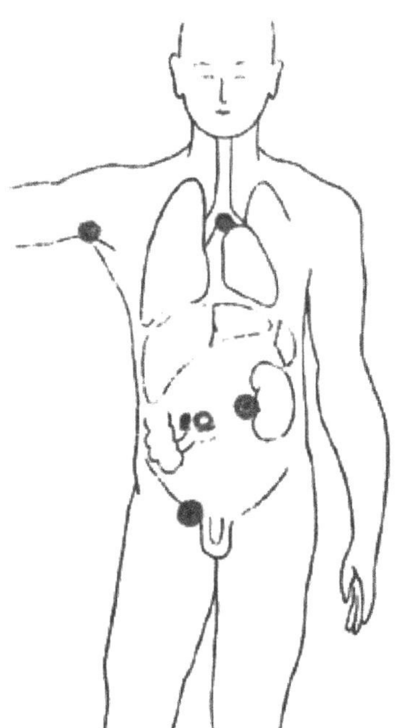

S-I2.	Inguinal (l).	L. haemorrhagico-purulenta totalis and intense Periadenitis.
	Inguinal (r).	L. haemorrhagico-purulenta totalis.
	Mesenterial.	L. haemorrhagica with intense congestion and diffuse hemorrhages.
	Peribronchial.	L. haemorrhagica.
S-I4.	Axillaris (l).	L. haemorrhagica with consid congestion and diffuse hemorrhages and some leucocytes-disseminat. Intense Pericapualitis.
	Axillatis (r).	With the same changes.
	Meserterial.	L. haemorrhagica partialis with intense congest. and diffuse hemorrhages.
	Peribronchial.	L. haemorrhagica partialis.

S. 12.

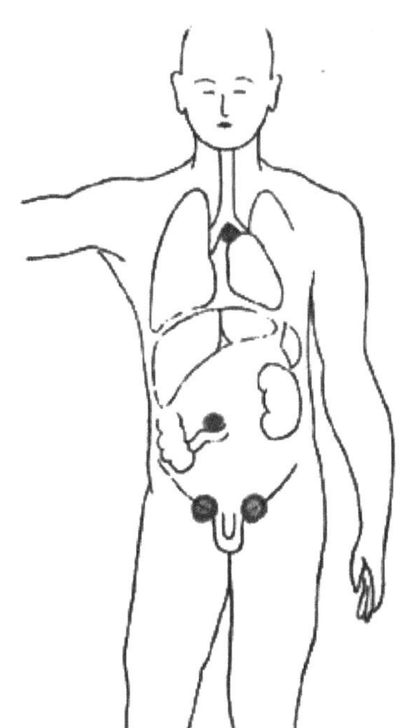

S. 14.

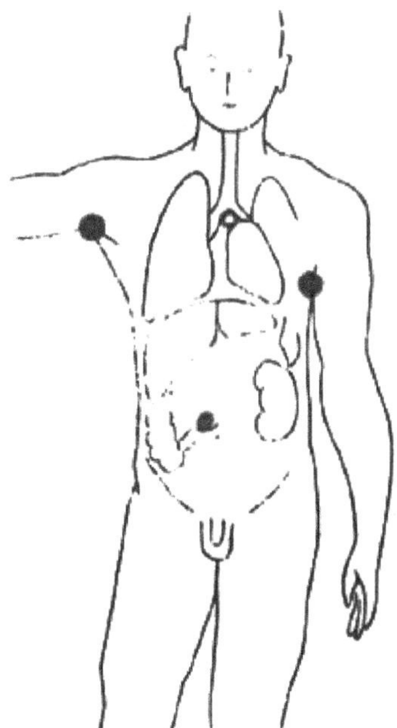

559

S-I5.	Inguinal (l).	L. haemorrhagica-purulenta totalis and intense Pericapsulitis.
	Retro-Peritoneal.	With the same changesand intense Pericapsulitis.
	Mesenterial.	L. purulenta with diffuse leucocytes -disseminat.
	Peribronchial.	L. catarrhalis levis with considerable congest. and some leucocytes-dissemination.
	Parathgreiodeal.	L. haemorrhagico-necroticans grabis.
S-I9.	Mesenterial.	L. catarrhalis with consid-congestion and considerable hemorrhages.
	Inguinal (l).	L. catarrhalis with considerable congestion.
	Inguinal (r).	L. haemorrhagico-purulenta with intense peribocal exudation.
	Peribronchial.	Catarrh and follicular congestion with some bacterial dissemination.

S.15.

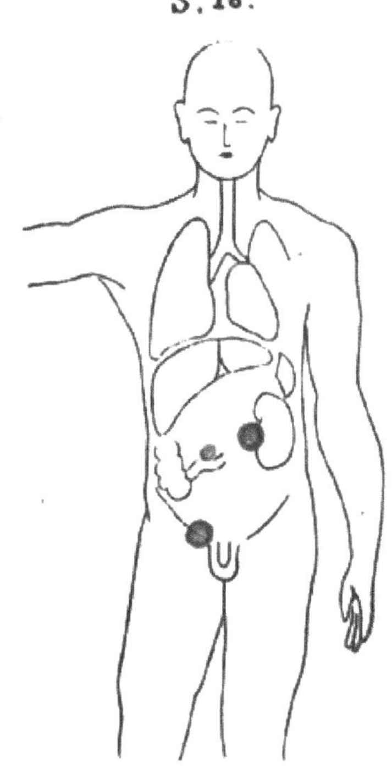

S.19.

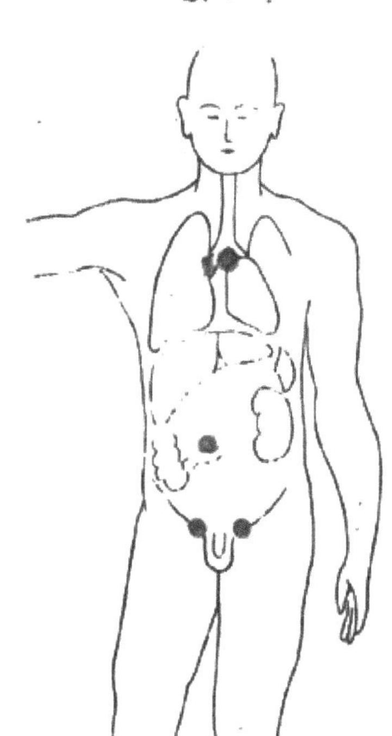

566

S-22.	Submaxillaris (l).	L. catarrhalis with inflammatory reticuloendotheliose (intense hyperplaisa of reticulumcells).
	Submaxillaris (r).	With the same changes. Muscular absecss in r. Submaxillar portion.
	Mesenterial.	Considerable congestion, slight hemorrhages and consid. hyperplasia of reticulum cells.
	Peribronchial.	L. catarrhalis with hyperplasia of reticulum cells.
	Inguinal (r, l).	Sinus-reticulosis.
	Axillaris (r, l).	Sinus-reticulosis.
S 26.	Phlegmon at l- femoral portion.	
	Femoral and Inguinal (l).	L. haemorrhagico-necro-purulenta totalis with diffuse hemorrhages, diffuse necorosis and diffuse bacterial dissemination.
	Retro-Peritoneal.	With the same changes and intense pericapsular congestion and hemorrhages.

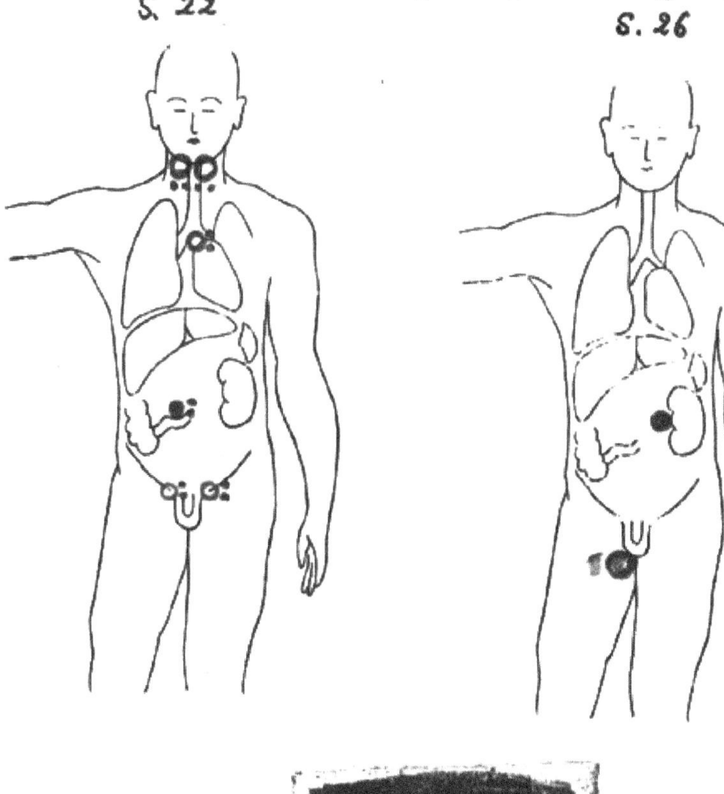

S-28.	Inguinal (r).	L. haemorrhagica totalis and intense.
	Femoral (r).	Pericapsulitis with diffuse hemorrhages.
	Mesenterial.	With the same changes.
	Mesenterial.	Pericapsulitis with some leucocytes and somewhat diffuse hemorrhages.
		L. acuta with intense congestion and edema.
	Peribronchial.	L. acuta with intense congestion (some bact. in capillares) and some leucocytes dissemin. Considerable catarrhalic changes.
S-38.	Lung-hilus.	L. acuta purulenta with considerable congestion and some bacterial dissemination. Considerable Pericapsulitis with some leucocytes-dissemination.
	Peribronchial.	L. haemorrhagica with intense congestion and some hemorrhages and some leucocytes-dissemination. Pericapsulitis with some congestion, and some leucocytes dissemination.
	Mesenterial.	Catarrh and follicular congestion.

S. 28

S. 38

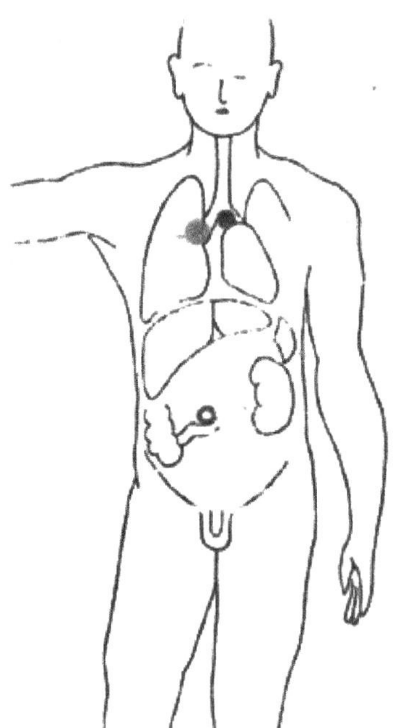

Diffuse hemorrhagic exudative changes all over the follicular tissues.

Some large germinative centers in intense exudative changes.

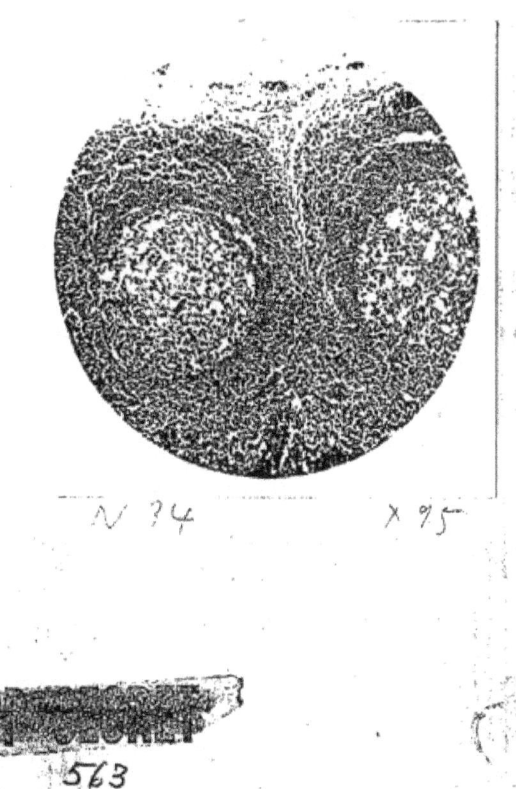

N 34　　x 95

563

Severe congestion of vas afference, A accompanied with some hemorrhagic changes.

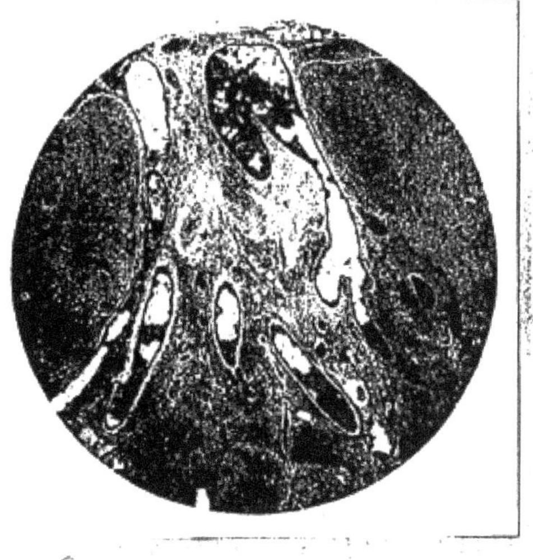

5.28 ×20

The same in high power, Bacterial accumulation, plenty of leucocytes and some lymphocytes in blood vessel.

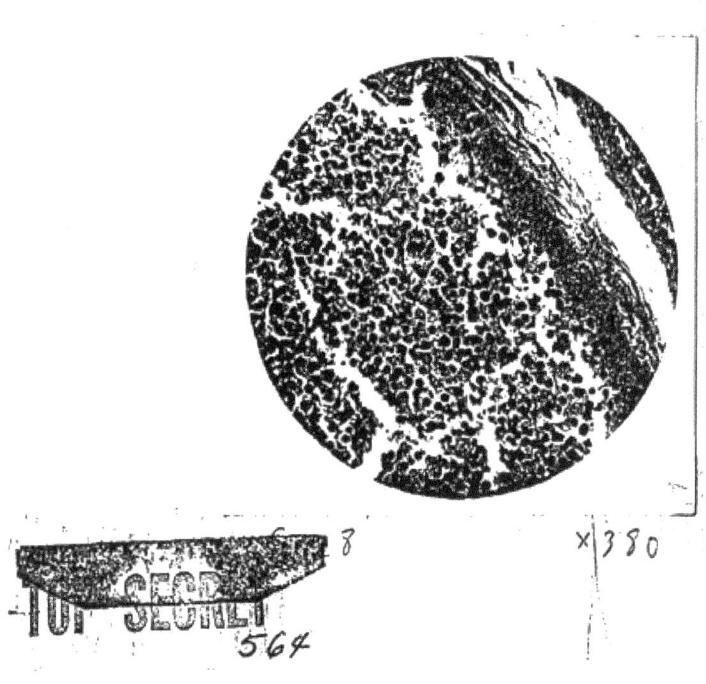

×380

TOP SECRET

564

So-called blood-sea, in
high power.

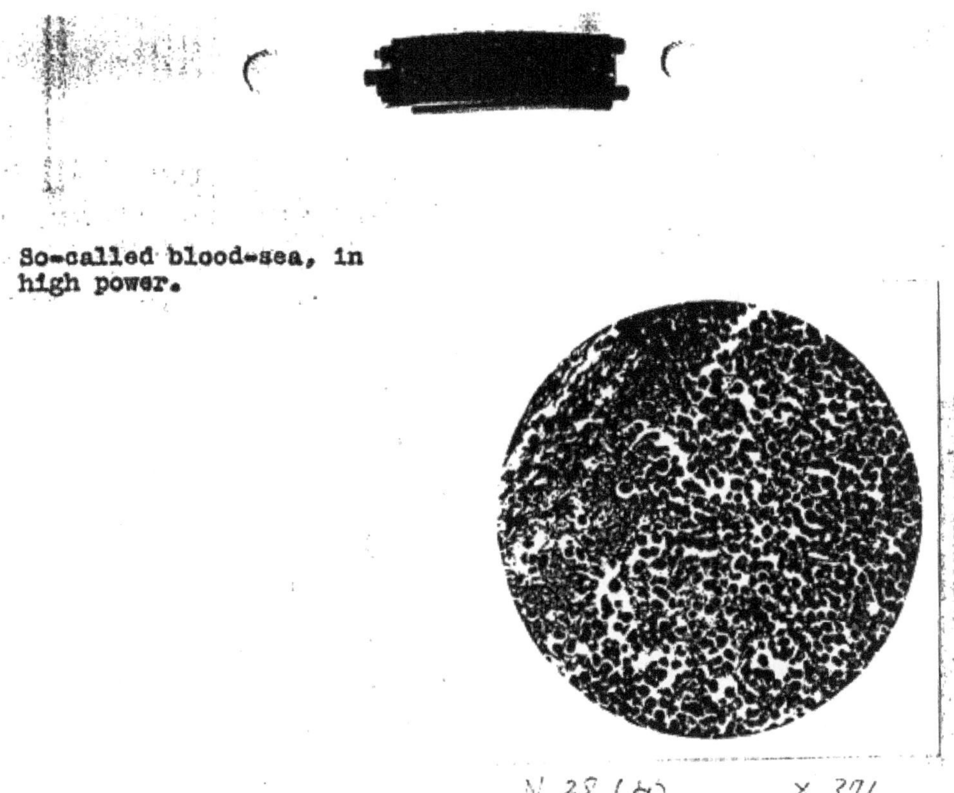

N 28 (a) X 376

So-called blood sea, accompanied
with hyalinous swealling of reticulum
fibers.

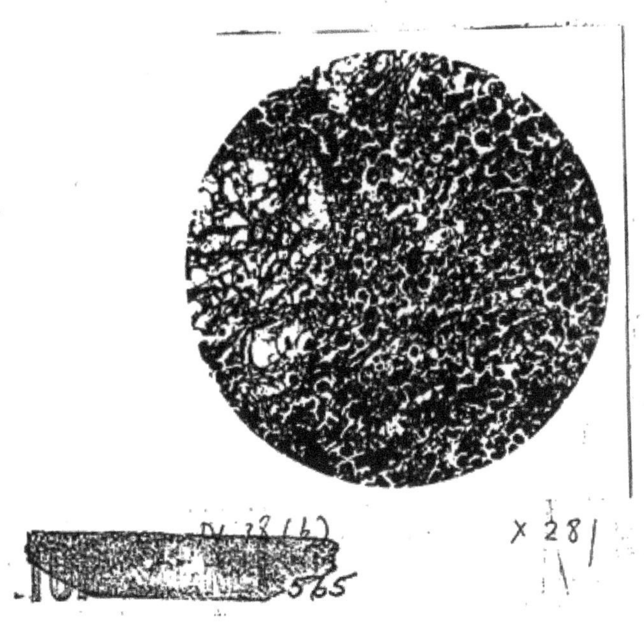

Stasis in sinuses, accompanied with erythrophagy.

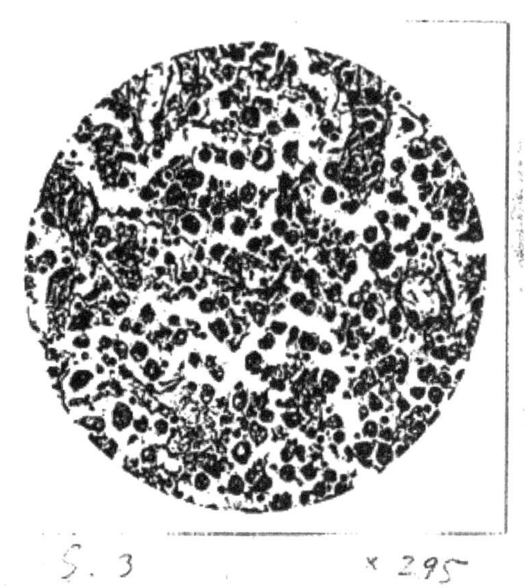

Stasis in sinuses, accompanied with erythrophagy.

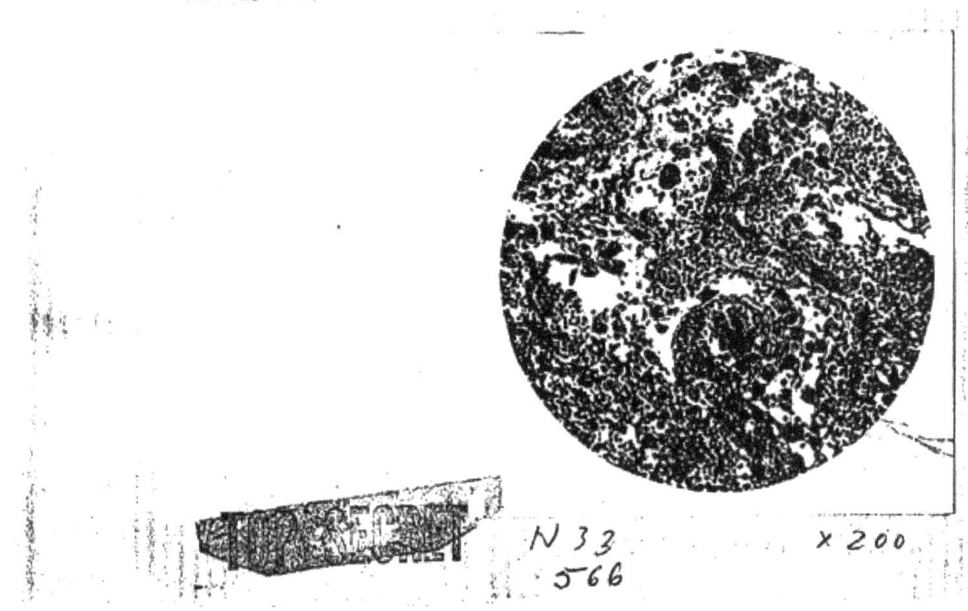

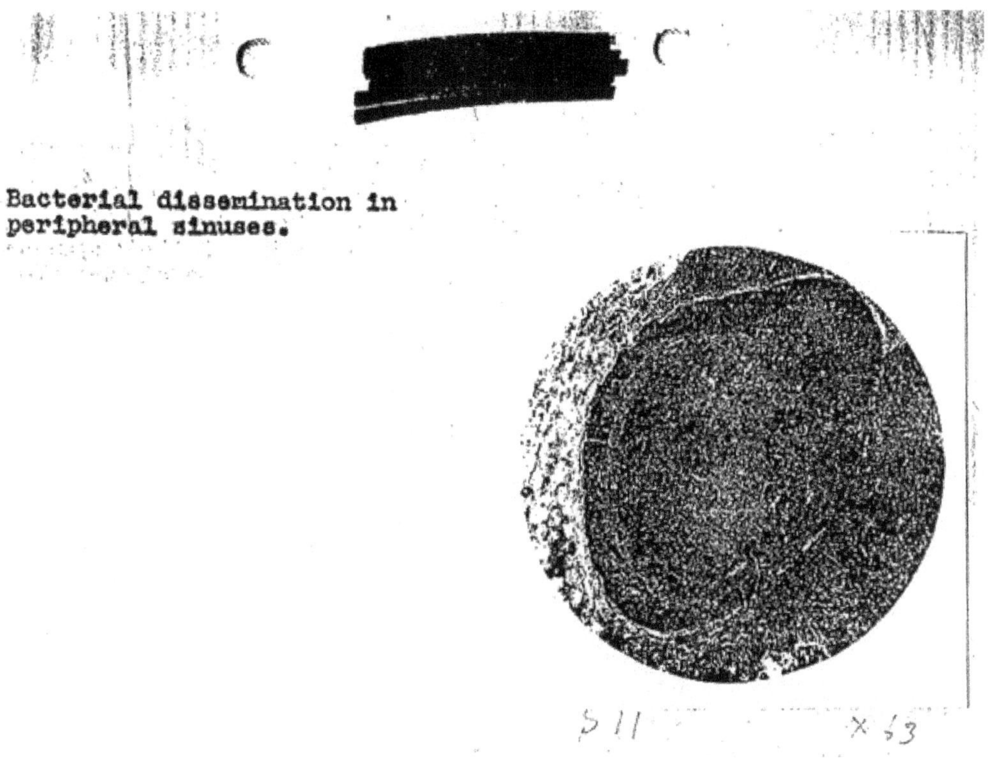

Bacterial dissemination in peripheral sinuses.

Bacterial dissemination in follicular tissues.

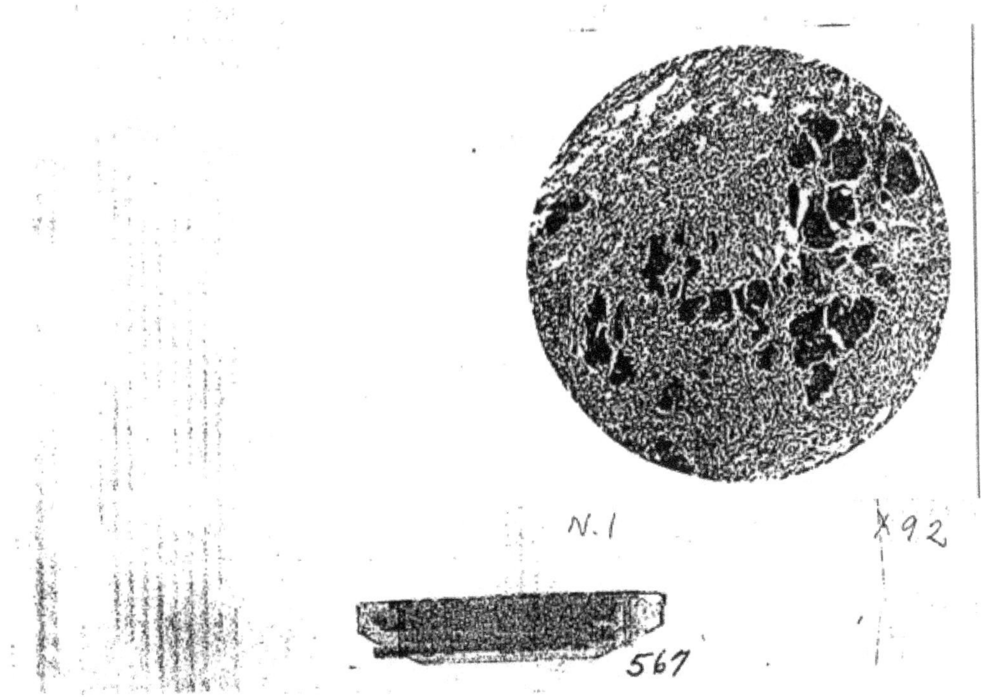

Bacterial dissemination all over the follicular tissues.

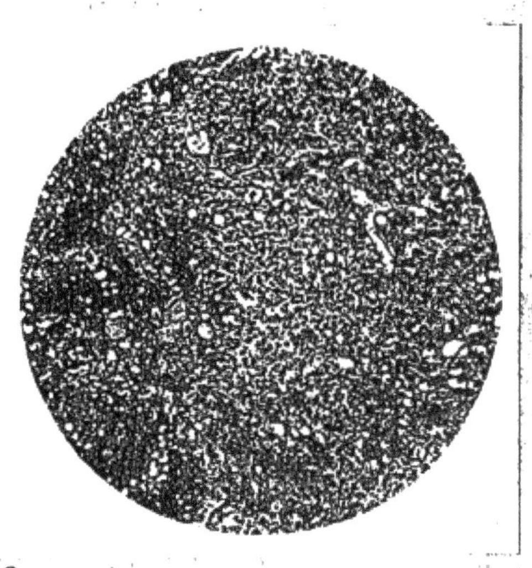

Diffuse intence exudative changes all over the follicular tissues.

N.10 ×95

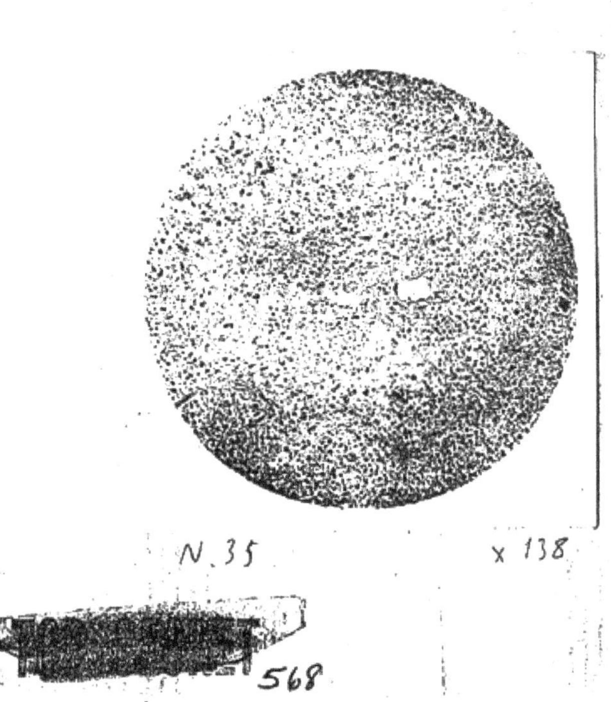

N.35 ×138

568

Exudative changes in fascicular tisses, accompanied with some serous fluids, some fibrinous masses, some leucocytes and some histiocytes.

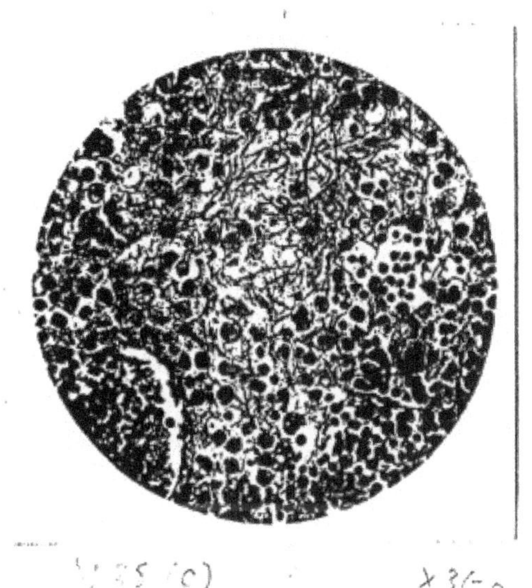

Cell proliferation at sinus walls.

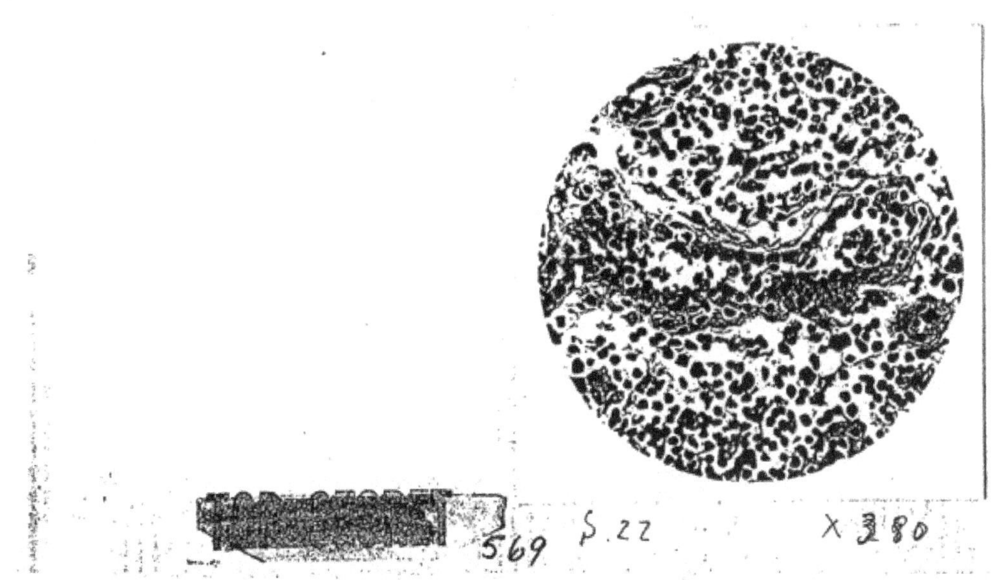

Hyperplasia of histiocytes and some plasma cells in sinuses.

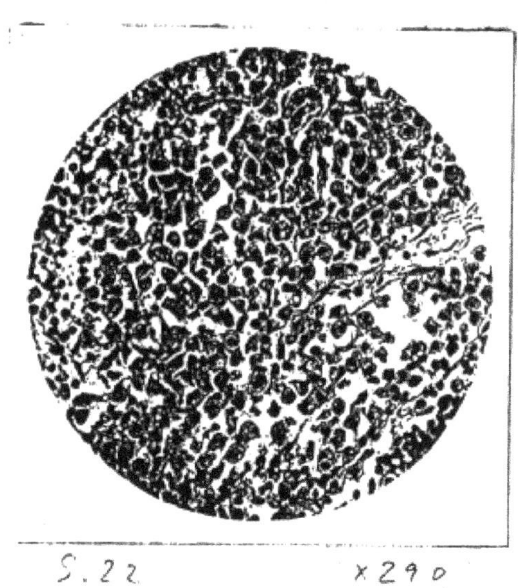

S.22 x290

Plasma cell reaction, in high power.

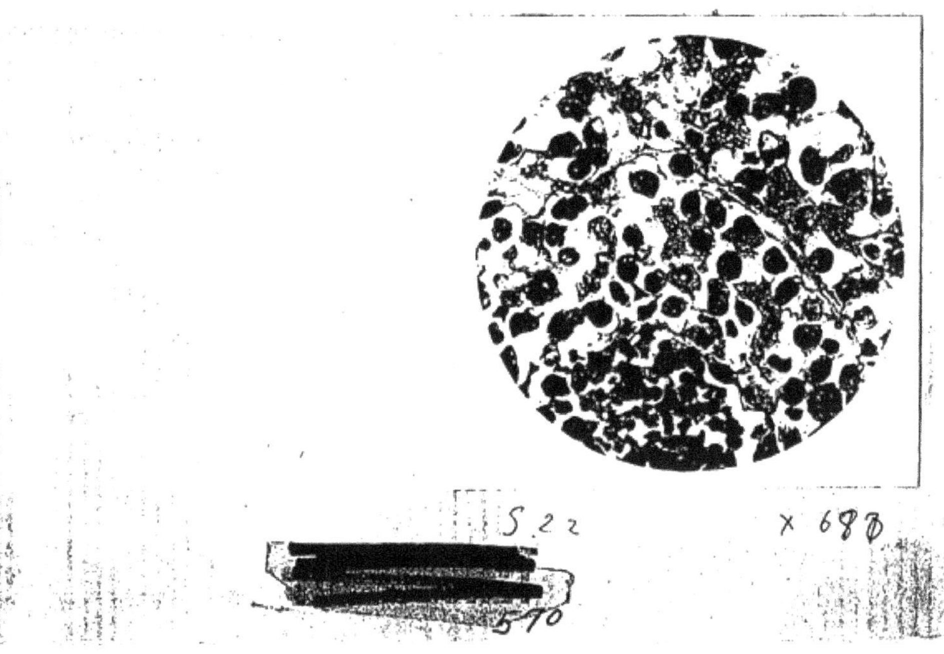

S.22 x 680

570

Kidney

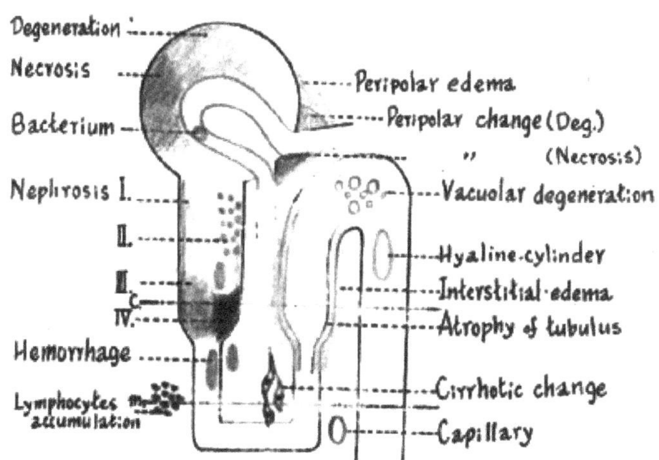
Degeneration
Necrosis
Bacterium
Nephrosis I.
II.
III.
C
IV.
Hemorrhage
Lymphocytes accumulation
Peripolar edema
Peripolar change (Deg.)
" (Necrosis)
Vacuolar degeneration
Hyaline cylinder
Interstitial edema
Atrophy of tubulus
Cirrhotic change
Capillary

571

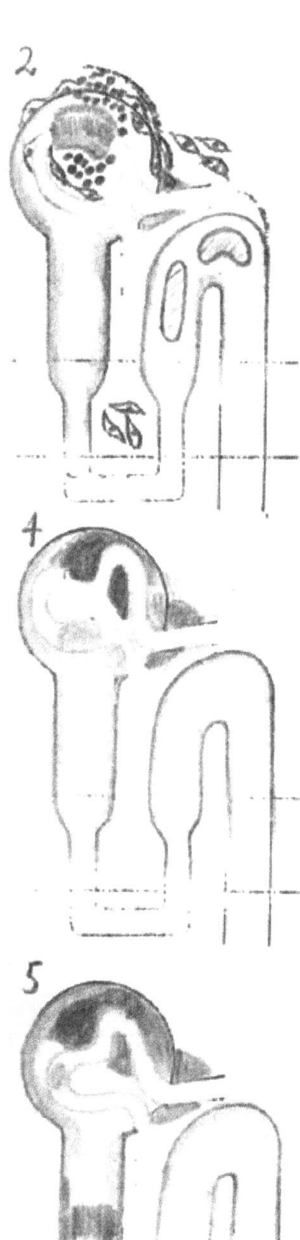

K I D N E Y

(A) Microscopical Investigation

1.

Slight Glomerulo-nephrosis with slight our so-called peripolar changes.

Nephrosis in I. degree, at some places in III. degree.

2.

Slight Glomerulo-nephrosis and Nephrosis in I degree, accompanied with some round-cell-infiltration.

At some places, it shows Nephritis subacuta with some hyalinously degenerated glomerular loops, some round-cell-infiltration, slight increase of connective tissues and many hyaline cylinders in tubuli.

4.

Slight Glomerulo-nephrosis with slight peripolar changes.

At some places, it shows our so-called Glomerulo-nephrosis bionecroticans with bionecrotic or sometimes necrotic swelling of glomerular loops, hyaline or fibrinous casts in glomerular capillaries and some peripolar changes.

4.

Slight Glomerulonephrosis with slight peripolar changes.

Nephrosis in I degree.

5.

Our so-called Glomerulonephrosis bionecroticans with bionecrotic or sometimes necrotic swelling of glomerular loops, hyaline or fibrinous casts in glomerular capillaries and some slight peripolar changes.

572

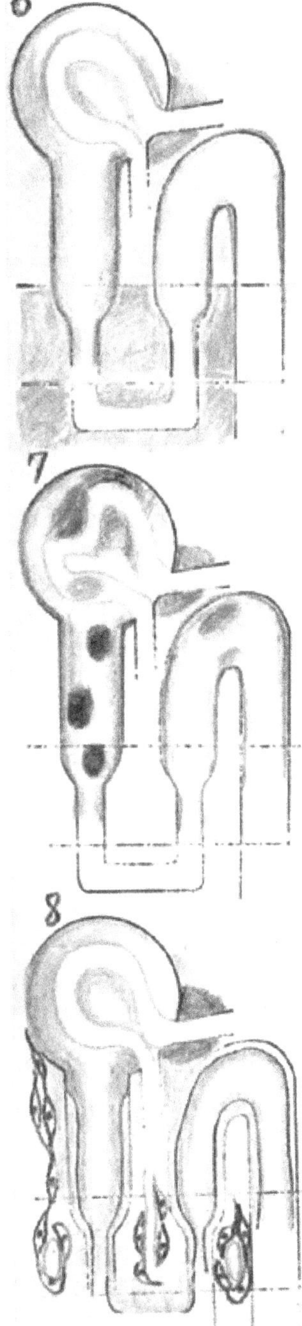

Nephrosis in I degree, at some places in III, degree.

6.

Slight glomerulo-nephrosis with slight peripolar changes.

Nephrosis in I degree, some times in III. degree: accompanied with some edema in cortal tissues and conspicious edema in medullary tissues.

7.

Glomerulo-nephrosis bionecroticans with bionecrotic or necrotic swelling of glomerular loops, some hyaline or fibrinous casts in glomerular capillaries and some slight peripolar changes.

Nephrosis in I. degree, sometimes in III. degree: with some miliary necrosis of renal tubulus (mainly at Tubulus contortus I).

8.

Considerable Glomerulo-nephrosis with some considerable peripolar changes.

Nephrosis in I. degree, sometimes accompanied with perivascular cirrhotic changes: considerable edema, slight increase of connective tissues and some atrophic or degenerated tubulis.

9.

Slight Glomerulo-nephrosis with considerable peripolar changes.

Nephrosis in I. degree.

10.

Considerable Glomerulo-nephrosis with slight peri-

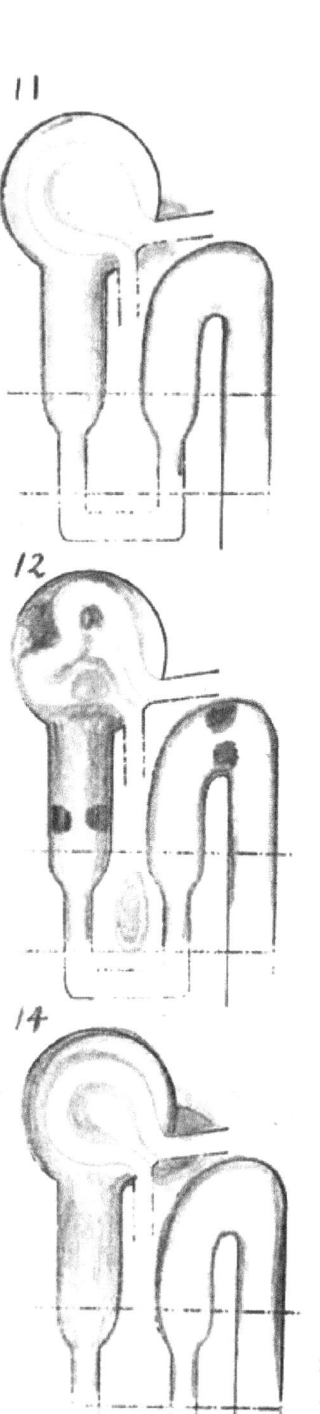

polar changes.

Nephrosis in I. degree.

11.

Slight Glomerulo-nephrosis with slight peripolar changes.

Nephrosis in I. degree.

12.

Our so-called Glomerulo-nephrosis bionecroticans with bionecrotic or necrotic swelling of glomerular loops, coagulated hyaline or some fibrinous masses in glomerular capillaries and considerable peripolar changes.

Nephrosis in I degree, sometimes in III. degree:
Some times with some hyaline cylinders in small blood-vessels or capillaries.

14.

Considerable Glomerulo-nephrosis with slight peripolar changes.

Nephrosis in I. degree.

15.

Slight Glomerulo-nephrosis with slight peripolar changes.

Nephrosis in I. degree.

16.

Slight Glomeruo-nephrosis with considerable peripolar changes.

Nephrosis in I. degree.

TOP SECRET 574

17.

Slight Glomerulo-nephrosis with slight peri-polar changes.

Nephrosis in I. degree.

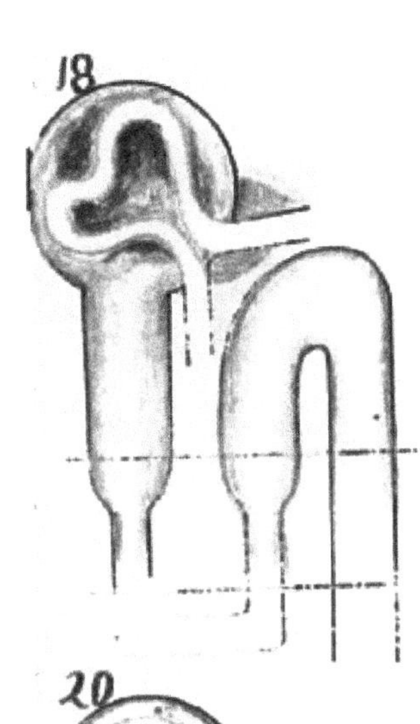

18.

Our so-called Glomerulo-nephrosis bionecroticans with intense necrotic swelling of all glomerular loops and some peripolar changes.

Nephrosis in I. degree.

19.

Slight Glomerulo-nephrosis with slight peripolar changes.

Nephrosis in I. degree with slight round-cell-infiltration.

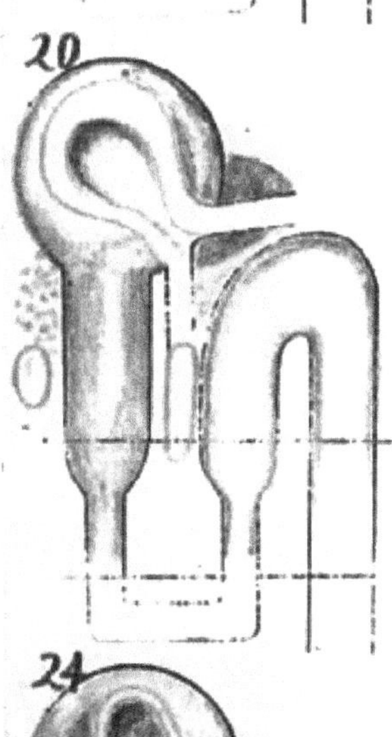

20.

Slight Glomerulo-nephrosis (rather in degener[illegible]t d form) with some peripolar changes.

Nephrosis in I. degree with conspicious congestion and some hemorrhages in cortical tissues.

24

23.

Slight Glomerulo-nephrosis with slight peripolar changes.

Nephrosis in I. degree.

24.

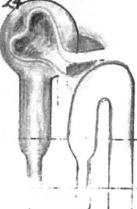

Our so-called Glomerulo-nephrosis bionecroticans (bionecrotic swelling of glomerular loops, which are [illegible] state) and slight peripolar changes.

Nephrosis in I. degree.

575

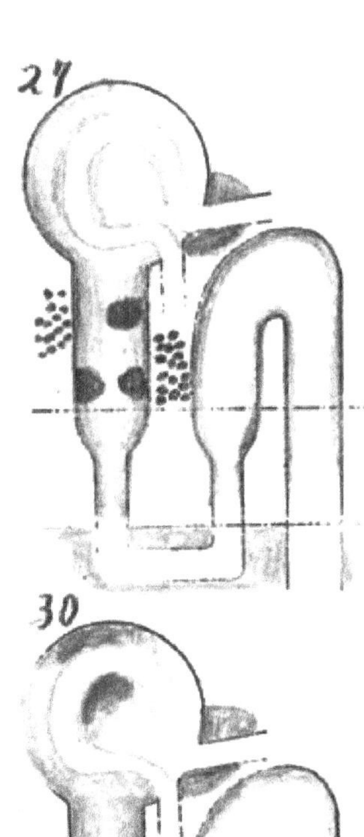

26.

Considerable Glomerulo-nephrosis and some peripolar changes.

Slight nephrosis in I. degree.

27.

Considerable Glomerulo-nephrosis with considerable peripolar changes.

Nephrosis in I. degree, sometimes in III. degree; with slight round-cell-infiltration in cortical tissues and conspicious edema in medullar tissues.

29.

Considerable Glomerulo-nephrosis with some peripolar changes.

Nephrosis in I-degree.

30.

Our so-called Glomerulo-nephrosis bionecroticans with slight peripolar changes.

Nephrosis in I. degree, sometimes in III. degree.

31.

Some Glomerulo-nephrosis with some peripolar changes.

Nephrosis in I. degree, sometimes in III. degree.

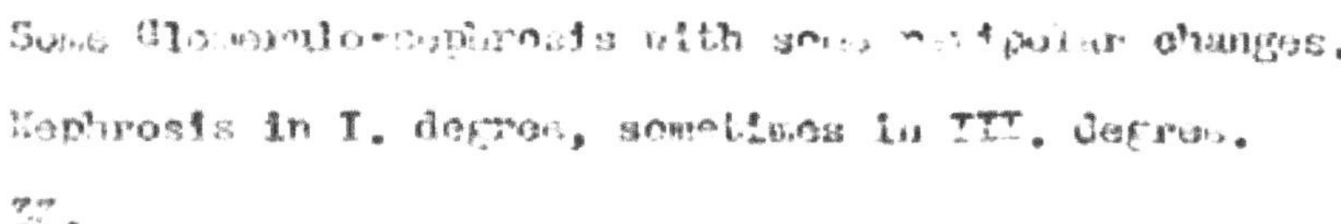

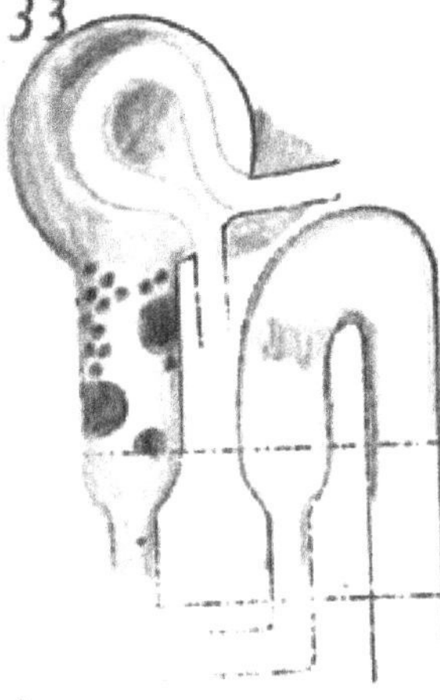

32.

Our so-called Glomerulo-nephrosis bionecroticans with some peripolar changes.

Nephrosis in I. degree, sometimes in III. degree with conspicious hyaline-droplets degeneration of renal tubulis (II degree of Nephrosis).

576

34.

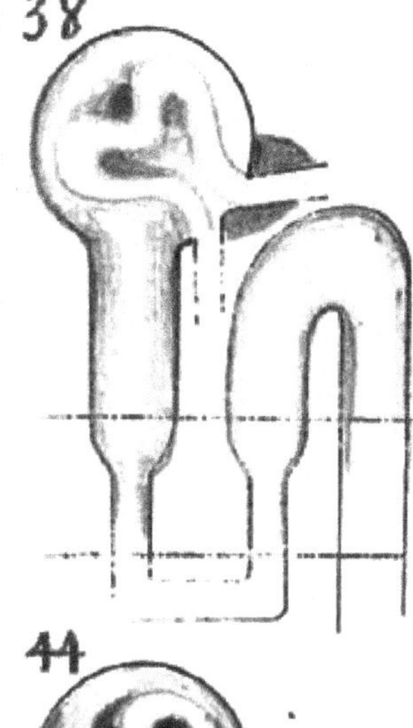

Slight Glomerul-nephrosis with some peripolar changes.

Nephrosis in I. degfee.

35.

Slight Glomerulo-nephrosis and some peripolar changes.

Nephrosis in I. degree.

36.

Slight Glomerulo-nephrosis with some peripolar changes.

Nephrosis in I. degree.

38.

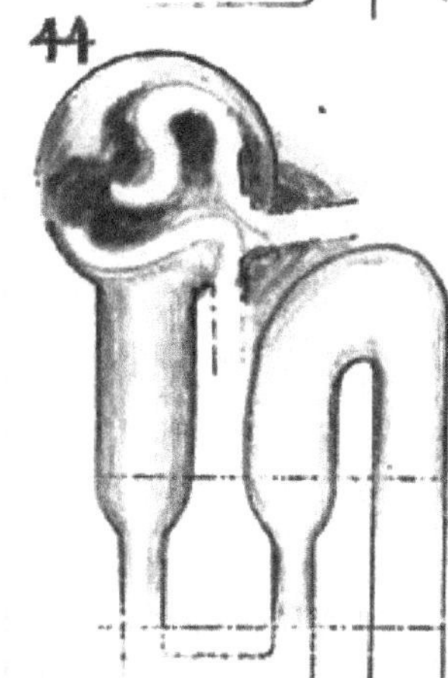

So-called Glomerulo-nephrosis bionecroticans with some degenerated glomerular loops. Slight peripolar changes.

Nephrosis in I. degree.

40.

Some Glomerulo-nephrosis with slight peripolar changes.

Nephrosis in I. degree.

42.

Some Glomorulo-nephrosis with slight peripolar changes.

Nephrosis in I. degree.

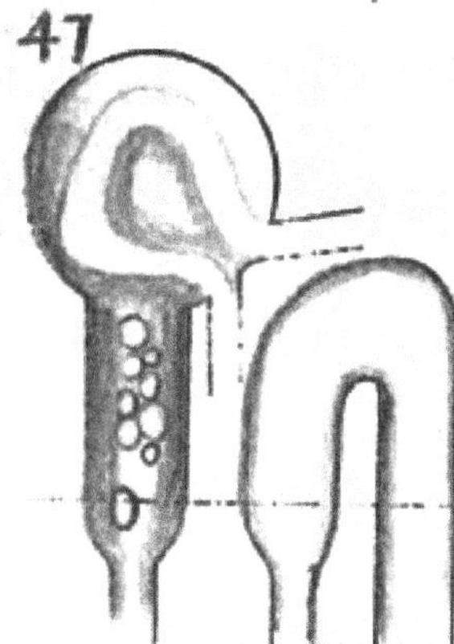

44.

Our so-called Glomerulo-nephrosis bionecroticans with intense degerated glomeruler loops and some peripoler changes.

Nephrosis in I. degree.

47.

Slight Glomerulo-nephrosis with slight peripolar changes.

Nephrosis in I. degree with some conspicious vacuolar

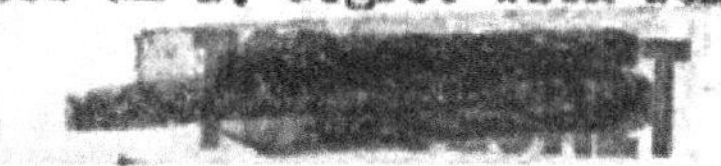

577

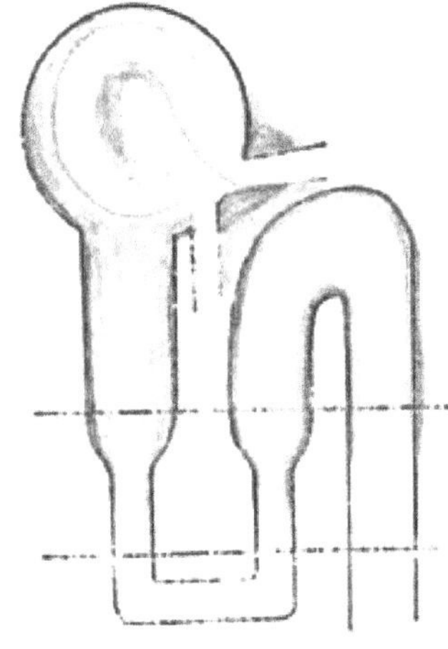

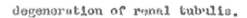

degeneration of renal tubulis.

49. Considerable Glomerulo-nephrosis with slight peripolar changes.

Nephrosis in I. degree.

578

S-1.

Considerable Glomerulo-nephrosis with considerable peripolar changes.

Nephrosis in I. degree.

S-2

Slight Glomerulo-nephrosis with slight peripolar changes.

Nephrosis in I. degree.

S-3.

Considerable Glomerulo-nephrosis with some peripolar changes.

Nephrosis in I. degree, sometimes in III. degree.

S-4.

Considerable Glomerulo-nephrosis with intense peripolar changes.

Nephrosis in I. degree.

S-5.

Considerable Glomerulo-nephrosis with some peripolar changes.

Nephrosis in I.degree, at some places with Nephritis interstitialis: some round-cell-infiltration, considerable edema and slight or considerable increase of connective tissues.

S-6.

Slight Glomerulo-nephrosis with some peripolar changes.

Nephrosis in I degree.

S-8.

579

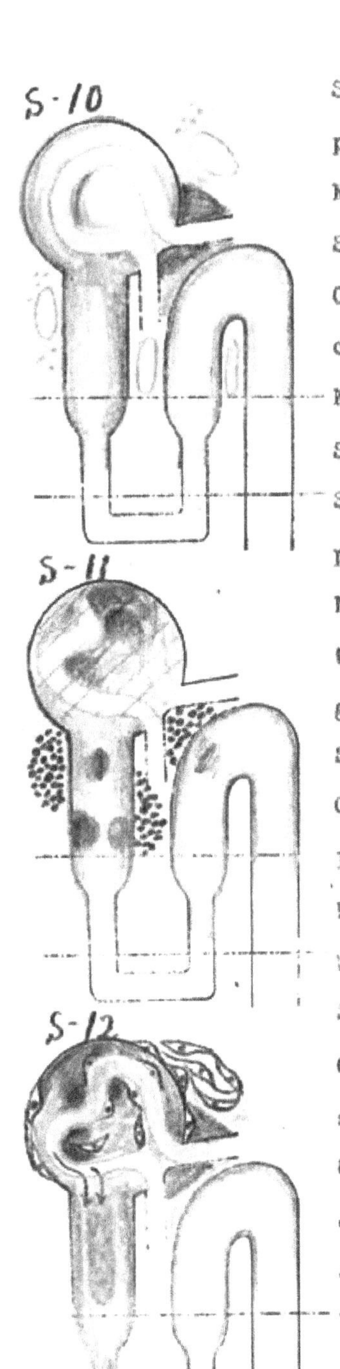

Slight or considerable Glomerulo-nephrosis with some peripolar changes.

Nephrosis in I. degree.

S-9.

Considerable Glomerulo-nephrosis with some peripolar changes.

Nephrosis in I. degree.

S-10.

Slight or considerable Glomerulo-nephrosis with some peripolar changes.

Nephrosis in I. degree with intense capillar congestion in cortical tissues and scattered some hemorrhages.

S-11.

Glomerulo-nephrosis bionecroticans with some peripolar changes and some hyalinous degenerated glomeruli.

Nephrosis in I. degree, sometimes in III. degree.

With some round-cell-infiltration in cortical tissues.

S-12.

Glomerulo-nephrosis bionecroticans and at some places subchronica, with slight peripolar changes.

Glomerulo-nephritis subchronica haemorrhagica.

S-14.

Some Glomerulo-nephrosis with slight peripolar changes.

Nephrosis in I. degree with massive hyaline cylinders in renal tubulis and some hemorrhages in medullar tissues.

580

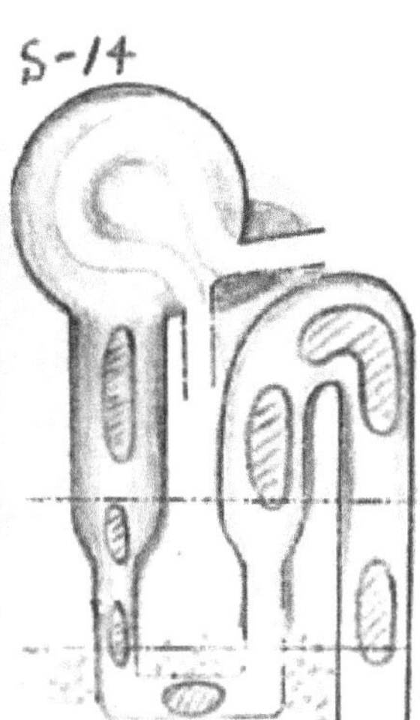

S-15.

Some Glomerulo-nephrosis with some peripolar changes.

Nephrosis in I. degree.

S-16.

Glomerulo-nephrosis bionecroticans with some peripolar changes.

Nephrosis in I. degree.

S-16.

Glomerulo-nephrosis bionecroticans with some peripolar changes.

Nephrosis in I. degree, sometimes in III. degree.

S-22

S-22.

Slight Glomerulo-nephrosis with some peripolar changes.

Nephrosis in I. degree with some remarkable round-
cell-accumulation (granulom-formation with some lymphocytes and histiocytes);

S-26.

Some Glomerulo-nephrosis with some peripolar changes.

Nephrosis in I. degree.

S-28

S-28.

Considerable Glomerulo-nephrosis with some peripolar
changes.

Nephrosis in I. degree with some considerable edema
in interstitiums.

S-38.

Some Glomerulo-nephrosis with some peripolar changes.

Nephrosis in I. degree.

581

(B) SUMMARY

a) Tubular changes.

Generally occured more or less intense cloudy swelling and sometimes hyaline-droplets formation or bionecrotic swelling of tubular epitheliums.

Generally with some coagulated protein-masses in tubular spaces and sometimes with some hyaline cylinders in Henle's loops or its following renal tubulus, and sometimes accompanied with some fibrinous or calcinated masses or some erythrocytes in tubular spaces.

x) On Nephrosis.

Nephrosis I. degree.		45 cases
II. degree.		1 case
III. degree.		
	with some bionecrotic swelling.	9 cases.
	with some necrotic changes.	6 cases.

All microscopically investigated cases. 63 cases.

x). On pathological tubular contents.

	Protein-masses	Hyaline subst.	Calcinated subst.	Erythrocytes
In slight degree.	6 cases	0	0 case	1 case
In medium degree.	50 cases	1 case	0 case	0
Inssevere degree.	7 cases	2 cases	0 case	0

b) Glomerular changes.

I classified 3 types of glomerular changes, so as following.

582

1) Generally occured so-called "Glomerulo-nephrosis, Randerath's", with some edematous swelling of capillary-walls of glomerular loops, swelling or slight increase of capillary-walls-cells of glomerular loops and some serous exsudation in Bowmann's spaces.

2) Sometimes occured our so-called "Glomerulonephrosis bionecroticans", with homogenous or (bio) necrotic swelling of capillary-walls. Intense degeneration or degenerative changes (intense degeneration, bionecrotic swelling or some diminution) of capillary-wall-cells and sometimes edematous swelling of walls of afferent blood-vessels (with hyaline masses in blood-vessels).

3) Intermediate form with edematous swelling of capillary walls and some degenerations of capillary-wall-cells.

x) On Glomerulo-nephrosis.

Glomerulo-nephrosis Randerath's.		
In slight degree.	16	cases.
In medium degree.	18	cases.
In severe degree.	9	cases.
Glomerulo-nephrosis bio-necroticans.	17	cases.

x) On our so-called "Polar changes".

In slight degree.	28	cases
In medium degree.	27	cases.

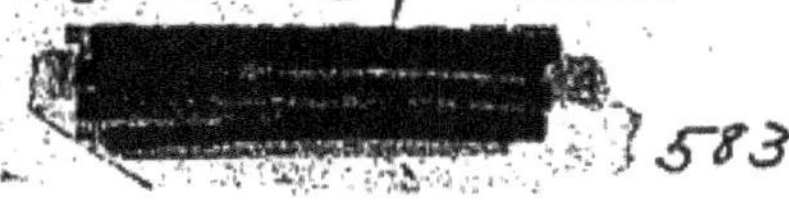

583

In intense degree. / cases.

---

c) Interstitium.

Generally with more or less intense capillary congestion, some perivascular edema, and sometimes localised or blood-sea like diffuse hemorrhages in interstitium.

Generallyccloudy degeneration and sometimes slight or knoty hyperplasia of capillary-wall-cells).

Some cases are accompanied with some perivascular round-cell-infiltration and I case in chronic course, with remarkable lymphocytic-histiocytic accumulation.

Hemorrhages.

In slight degree.	/	cases.
In medium degree.	2	cases.
In severe degree.	0	cases.

Round-cell-accumulation.

In slight degree.	2	cases
In intense degree.	3	cases.

Accordingly the main pathological changes are Glomerulo-nephrosis (sometimes Glomerulo-nephrosis bionecroticans) with some complicated sign.

584

On polar changes:

Our so-called polar portions of kidney fall within like periglomerular areas at afferent portions of blood-vessels,bounded with 2 blood-vessels (V.afferens and defferens) and intercalary portion of tubulus and equipped with special cellular arrangements with neuro-myo-angio-epitheliar segments, which belong to so-called diffuse endocrinic system.

These areas are very chemoreceptoric, and able to regulate blood-quantity in glomeruli and furthermore favorite-seats of varous inflammatory changes.

Noxae, advanced hematogenously to kidney, cause inflammatory changes firstly at afferent portions, due to their chemoreceptroic properties, then at glomeruli and sometimes at V. defferens.

Thus occured inflammatory changes angio-vasculally at perivascular portions in Δ-areas.

These noxae are filtrated at glomerular loops,then excreted in tubulus with nephrosis and some of them absorbed again mainly at intercalary portions of tubulus, accompanied with considerable degeneration of tubular eitheliar cells and some peribubular inflammatory changes in neighbouring Δ-areas.

Thus occured inflammatory changes epitheliogenously at peritubular portions in Δ-areas.

Δ-areas are very sensitive to inflammatory changes, which occured in 2 manners, a)angiovasculally at perivascular portions with mesenchymal reactions and b)epitheliogenously at peribubular potions with epitheliogenous reactions and accomoanied with various complicated changes, due to chemoreceptoric and regenerative properties of these

585

intercalary portions.

In -areas, inflammatory changes apt to be occured and if occured, in 2 manners,not only with mesenchymal reactions but also with epitheliogenous reactions.

Such special cellular arragements with mesenchymal and epitheliar segments which belong to diffuse endocrinic system, are expected to exist in each organgs(for example, dissovery of "lung-island" by us) and inflammatory changes of these portions are named by us "polar changes" of each organs.

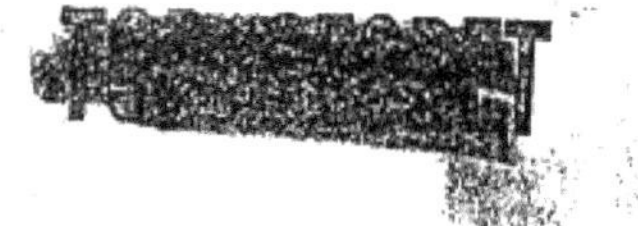

586

KIDNEY

			N 1	N 2	N 3	N 4	N 5	N 6	N 7	N 8	N 9	N 10	N 11	N 12	N 14	N 15	N 16	N 17	N 18	N 19
Glomeruli	Glomerular Loop	Dilatation	÷	+	+·	∸	÷	+·	÷	+·	÷	+·	÷	÷	+·	÷	∸	÷	+	+
	Capillary-Walls	Swelling	÷	÷	÷	÷	+·	÷	+	+·	÷	+·	+	++	+·	÷	÷	÷	+	+
		Deposition of Hyaline or Albuminoid Substance	÷	÷	÷	÷	+·	÷	+	+·	÷	+·	÷	++·	+	÷	÷	÷	+	÷
	Changes of Nuclei	Increase of Nuclei	∸	∸	÷	−	⊢	∸	−	∸	∸	∸	∸	⊢	−	∸	÷	÷	∸	∸
		Swelling	+	+	++·	+	÷	÷	+	÷	+	÷	++·	∸	+	+	++	+	+·	+
		Pyknosis	+	∸	∸	∸	+	÷	÷	÷	÷	÷	∸	÷	÷	∸	÷	÷	∸	÷
	Contents of Capillaries	Erythrocytes	+	++·	+·	+·	++·	+·	÷	÷	÷	+·	++·	∸	+·	+·	+·	÷	+·	+·
		Round Cells	÷	∸	∸	∸	∸	∸	∸	∸	∸	∸	∸	∸	÷	∸	∸	∸	÷	∸
	Bowman's Lumen	Dilatation	∸	∸	∸	÷	÷	÷	∸	÷	∸	∸	−	÷	÷	∸	∸	÷	÷	∸
		Hyaline or Albuminoid Casts	∸	+	÷	÷	÷	∸	∸	÷	∸	∸	∸	÷	÷	÷	∸	÷	÷	∸
		Penetrative Fluid	∸	+	÷	÷	÷	∸	∸	÷	∸	∸	∸	÷	÷	÷	∸	∸	÷	∸
	Epithelium of Bowman's Capsule	Cloudy Swelling	÷	÷	∸	∸	÷	∸	∸	∸	∸	∸	∸	∸	÷	∸	∸	÷	∸	∸
		Proliferation	−	−	÷	−	−	−	−	−	−	−	−	−	−	−	−	−	−	−
	Bowman's Capsules	Swelling	÷	÷	÷	÷	+	÷	÷	+	÷	+	÷	÷	+	÷	÷	÷	÷	+
		Hyaline Degeneration	−	−	÷	−	−	∸	∸	−	−	∸	÷	−	−	÷	÷	∸	∸	÷
	Vasa afferentia	Congestion	+	+·	+	÷	+·	÷	÷	÷	÷	+·	(++)	÷	+	+·	(+·)	+	÷	+·
	Endomelial Cells	Swelling	÷	+	÷	÷	÷	÷	∸	∸	÷	∸	+	÷	÷	+	+·	÷	+	÷
		Proliferation	∸	÷	+	∸	∸	+	−	∸	+	∸	÷	∸	∸	÷	(+)	∸	(÷)	÷
		Desquamation	∸	−	∸	−	−	∸	−	−	−	∸	÷	∸	−	∸	∸	∸	∸	÷
	Media	Swelling	+	÷	÷	÷	÷	÷	+	÷	÷	+	÷	÷	+	÷	÷	÷	÷	÷
		Hyaline Degeneration	∸	−	−	−	−	−	÷	−	÷	∸	−	−	−	∸	−	−	−	−
		Tendency to Necrosis	∸	−	−	−	−	−	÷	−	−	−	−	−	−	(÷)	−	−	−	−
	Adventitial Cells	Swelling	+	÷	÷	÷	÷	÷	∸	∸	÷	∸	+	÷	÷	+	+·	÷	+	∸
		Proliferation	∸	÷	+	∸	∸	+	−	∸	+	∸	÷	∸	∸	÷	(+)	÷	(÷)	÷
	Adjoining Portion	Peripolar Edema	+	÷	÷	÷	÷	+	+·	÷	÷	+	+	÷	+	÷	+	+	+	÷
		Appearance of „Polkissen"	∸	+	+	∸	∸	(+)	∸	∸	+	∸	∸	(+)	∸	∸	(+)	∸	∸	(+)
		Macula densa	∸	+	∸	∸	∸	∸	∸	∸	+	∸	∸	(+)	∸	∸	+	∸	∸	(+)
Parenchym	Tubules Epithelium	Cloudy Swelling	++·	++	+·	+·	++	++	++	+·	+·	++	++·	+·	+·	+·	+·	++	++	+·
		Hyaline Droplet Degeneration	−	−	−	−	−	−	−	−	−	−	−	−	−	−	−	−	−	−
		Vacuolar Degeneration	÷	÷	∸	÷	(+)	÷	(++)	(+)	∸	(+·)	(+)	(+)	+	(÷)	(÷)	÷	÷	÷
		Fatty Degeneration	∸	∸	−	∸	(÷)	∸	(+)	(÷)	∸	∸	÷	(÷)	÷	∸	∸	÷	∸	∸
		Necrosis	÷	−	−	(÷)	÷	(+)	(++)	−	−	−	−	+	−	−	−	÷	−	−
		Degenerations of Nuclei	+	+	+	+	∸	+	+	÷	÷	+	÷	+	÷	∸	∸	+	+	÷
	Tubules Contents	Cloudy or Massive Albuminoid Substance	∸	∸	÷	÷	∸	+	++	÷	+·	÷	∸	+·	+·	+	∸	+	+	÷
		Fibrinous Substance	−	−	−	−	(+)	−	+	−	−	−	−	−	−	−	−	−	−	−
		Hyaline or Colloid Cylinder	(+)	(+)	(++)	−	(+)	(+)	(+)	(+)	−	−	(+)	(+)	(+)	(++)	−	−	(+)	−
		Various Calcium Casts	−	−	−	−	−	−	−	−	−	−	−	−	−	−	(+)	(+)	(+)	−
		Erythrocytes	−	−	−	−	−	−	+	−	−	−	(+)	−	−	−	−	−	−	−
Interstitium	Congestion	Cortex	+++	+·	+	+·	++	+	+·	÷	+	++·	++·	+·	++	++	+·	++·	+	+·
		Medulla	+·	+·	÷	++·	+++	÷	+·	+	÷	+·	++	+·	++	++	+·	++	(+)	+·
	Edema	Cortex	+	+	+	÷	+	+·	(+·)	(++)	+	÷	÷	+	(+·)	÷	÷	+·	÷	÷
		Medulla	++	+·	+·	+·	+·	+++	+·	++·	+·	+·	+	+	+++	+·	+	++	(+)	+
	Hemorrhage	Cortex	−	−	−	−	−	−	−	−	−	−	−	−	−	−	−	−	−	−
		Medulla	−	−	−	−	−	−	−	−	−	−	−	−	(+)	−	−	−	−	−
	Round Cell Infiltration	Cortex	−	−	(++)	−	−	−	−	∸	−	∸	−	−	÷	−	−	−	−	÷
		Medulla	−	÷	−	−	−	−	−	−	−	−	−	−	−	÷	−	−	−	−
	Vessel Walls	Hyaline Degeneration	∸	∸	÷	−	÷	÷	∸	÷	∸	÷	∸	∸	÷	÷	−	÷	÷	∸
		Tendency to Necrosis	−	−	∸	÷	∸	∸	−	−	−	∸	∸	∸	∸	−	−	∸	−	÷
		Proliferation of Adventitial Cells	∸	÷	+	÷	−	∸	+	∸	∸	∸	÷	∸	÷	(+)	+	∸	∸	∸
Colonies of Bacterium			+	−	+	∸	−	−	−	−	−	−	−	−	−	−	−	−	−	−

587

KIDNEY

			N 20	N 23	N 24	N 26	N 29	N 30	N 31	N 32	N 33	N 34	N 35	N 36	N 38	N 40	N 42	N 44	N 47	N 49
Glomeruli	Glomerular Loop	Dilatation	÷	÷	÷	+	÷	÷	÷	+	+	+:	+	÷	+	+:	÷	÷	+:	+
	Capillary-Walls	Swelling	+:	÷	++	+	÷	++	+	(+++)	++	+	+	÷	++	÷	÷	(+++)	÷	(+)
		Deposition of Hyaline or Albuminoid Subsutance	+	÷	++	÷	÷	++	÷	(+++)	++	÷	÷	∸	++	÷	∸	(+++)	÷	(+)
	Changes of Nuclei	Increase of Nuclei	−	∸	⊢	∸	÷	⊢	∸	⊢	⊢	÷	÷	÷	∸	÷	∸	∸	÷	∸
		Swelling	∸	+	÷	+:	+	∸	÷	÷	÷	+:	+	+	+:	+:	÷	+	+:	+
		Pyknosis	++	÷	+	÷	∸	+	∸	+	++	∸	÷	∸	÷	∸	÷	÷	∸	÷
	Contents of Capillaries	Erythrocytes	+	+	+:	+	(+++)	+:	++	÷	+:	++:	+:	++	+:	+:	+:	++	+:	++
		Round Cells	∸	∸	∸	∸	∸	∸	∸	∸	∸	∸	∸	∸	∸	∸	∸	∸	∸	∸
	Bowman's Lumen	Dilatation	∸	∸	∸	∸	∸	∸	∸	÷	−	∸	÷	÷	−	÷	∸	∸	∸	∸
		Hyaline or Albuminoid Casts	÷	∸	∸	÷	÷	∸	÷	÷	∸	÷	∸	÷	÷	÷	÷	∸	∸	∸
		Penetrative Fluid	÷	∸	∸	÷	∸	∸	∸	−	−	∸	∸	∸	∸	∸	∸	−	∸	∸
	Epithelium of Bowman's Capsule	Cloudy Swelling	÷	∸	∸	∸	∸	∸	∸	∸	∸	÷	∸	∸	−	∸	∸	÷	÷	÷
		Proliferation	−	−	−	−	−	−	−	−	−	−	−	−	−	−	−	−	−	−
	Bowman's Capsules	Swelling	+	÷	+	+	÷	÷	+	÷	+:	÷	÷	÷	÷	÷	÷	÷	÷	÷
		Hyaline Degeneration	−	−	+	÷	÷	÷	÷	÷	÷	∸	∸	∸	∸	∸	∸	∸	−	÷
	Vasa afferentia	Congestion	÷	+	+:	÷	++	÷	(+++)	÷	÷	++	+	+:	+	+	+	+:	−	÷
	Endothelial Cells	Swelling	∸	÷	∸	+	÷	÷	÷	÷	∸	+	+	+	∸	÷	÷	+	+	+:
		Proliferation	∸	∸	÷	÷	÷	∸	÷	∸	∸	÷	÷	÷	∸	÷	∸	÷	÷	∸
		Desquamation	−	∸	∸	∸	∸	−	−	−	−	∸	∸	∸	−	∸	−	∸	∸	−
	Media	Swelling	+	÷	+	+	+	+	+	÷	+	÷	÷	+	÷	÷	+	÷	÷	+
		Hyaline Degeneration	−	−	−	−	∸	∸	∸	−	∸	−	∸	−	∸	−	−	∸	−	−
		Tendency to Necrosis	−	−	−	−	−	∸	∸	−	∸	−	−	−	∸	−	−	∸	−	−
	Adventitial Cells	Swelling	∸	÷	÷	+	÷	÷	÷	÷	∸	+	÷	+	∸	÷	÷	+	÷	∸
		Proliferation	∸	∸	∸	÷	÷	∸	÷	∸	∸	÷	∸	÷	∸	÷	÷	÷	÷	∸
	Adjoining Portion	Peripolar Edema	+	÷	÷	+	+	÷	+	÷	+	÷	÷	+	+	+	+	+	÷	+
		Appearance of "Polkissen"	∸	∸	÷	∸	∸	∸	∸	∸	∸	(÷)	∸	∸	∸	÷	∸	(÷)	∸	∸
		Macula densa	∸	∸	∸	(÷)	∸	∸	(÷)	∸	∸	(÷)	(+)	∸	−	∸	∸	∸	∸	∸
Parenchyma	Tubules Epithelium	Cloudy Swelling	++:	+:	++:	+:	+:	++	+:	+:	(+++)	++	+:	+:	++:	+:	+:	+:	++	+:
		Hyaline Droplet Degeneration	−	−	−	−	−	−	−	−	+++	−	−	−	−	−	−	−	−	−
		Vacuolar Degeneration	∸	÷	+	+	(+:)	÷	(+)	∸	÷	(+)	+:	∸	(÷)	(+:)	(+)	∸	(+++)	÷
		Fatty Degeneration	−	∸	÷	÷	(+)	∸	÷	−	∸	(÷)	÷	−	∸	(+)	(÷)	−	(+)	∸
		Necrosis	∸	−	∸	−	−	÷	−	÷	(+)	−	−	∸	∸	∸	−	∸	−	−
		Degenerations of Nuclei	+	∸	÷	+	÷	÷	∸	÷	÷	÷	÷	÷	+	÷	÷	÷	÷	÷
	Tubules Contents	Cloudy or Massive Albuminoid Substance	+	÷	+:	+	+:	÷	+:	+	(+:)	+:	+:	+	(+++)	(+)	+:	+:	++	+:
		Fibrinous Substance	−	−	−	−	−	−	−	−	−	−	+	−	−	−	−	−	−	−
		Hyaline or Colloid Cylinder	(+)	(+)	(+)	(+)	(+)	−	−	(+)	(+)	−	−	(+)	(+++)	(+)	−	−	(+)	−
		Various Calcium Casts	(+)	−	−	−	−	−	−	−	++	−	−	−	−	−	−	−	−	−
		Erythrocytes	−	−	÷	+	÷	÷	−	−	+	−	−	(+)	(+)	−	−	−	(+)	−
Interstitium	Congestion	Cortex	+++	+:	+:	+:	++	(+:)	+++	+	++:	+++	+:	++:	++	+:	+:	+:	(+++)	+
		Medulla	+	+:	+	+:	+++	÷	++:	÷	+:	++:	+:	++	++	++	+	+:	+:	÷
	Edema	Cortex	+:	÷	÷	+	÷	÷	÷	+:	+	÷	+	+	+	÷	+	÷	+	÷
		Medulla	+:	+	+	+:	+	+:	+	+	÷	+	+:	+:	+:	+:	+	+:	+	+
	Hemorrhage	Cortex	+++	−	−	−	−	−	(÷)	−	−	−	−	−	−	−	−	−	−	−
		Medulla	−	−	−	−	−	−	−	−	−	−	−	−	−	−	−	−	−	−
	Round Cell Infiltration	Cortex	−	−	−	∸	−	−	−	−	−	÷	−	−	−	−	−	−	−	−
		Medulla	−	−	−	−	−	−	−	−	−	−	−	−	−	÷	−	−	−	−
	Vessel-Walls	Hyaline Degeneration	∸	÷	∸	∸	∸	÷	∸	÷	÷	∸	∸	∸	÷	−	−	∸	−	∸
		Tendency to Necrosis	∸	∸	−	∸	∸	−	−	−	−	−	÷	∸	÷	−	−	−	−	−
		Proliferation of Adventitial Cells	∸	∸	÷	÷	∸	∸	÷	∸	∸	÷	∸	+	∸	∸	∸	∸	∸	∸
	Colonies of Bacterium		−	−	−	−	−	−	−	−	−	−	−	∸	−	÷	∸	÷	−	−

588

KIDNEY

			S 1	S 2	S 3	S 4	S 5	S 6	S 8	S 9	S 10	S 11	S 12	S 14	S 15	S 19	S 22	S 26	S 28	S 38
Glomeruli – Glomerular Loop		Dilatation	+	÷	+	+	+	÷	÷	÷	+	÷	+	+	+	+	+	+	+	+
	Capillary-Walls	Swelling	÷	÷	+	+	÷	÷	÷	+	÷	+	(+++)	÷	÷	+	÷	+	+	÷
		Deposition of Hyaline or Albuminoid Substance	÷	(÷)	+	+	÷	÷	÷	+	÷	+	(+++)	÷	÷	÷	÷	÷	+	÷
	Changes of Nuclei	Increase of Nuclei	+	÷	⊢	÷	÷	÷	−	+	−	⊢	⊢	÷	−	÷	÷	÷	−	÷
		Swelling	++	++	÷	++	++	++	+	÷	+	+	−	++	+	++	++	++	+	+
		Pyknosis	−	−	+	−	−	−	÷	−	÷	÷	÷	÷	÷	−	−	−	÷	−
	Contents of Capillaries	Erythrocytes	+	++	+	++	++	+	+	++	+	+	+	+	+	+	+	+	+	++
		Round Cells	−	−	÷	÷	÷	÷	÷	−	÷	−	−	−	−	−	−	−	−	−
Glomeruli	Bowman's Lumen	Dilatation	÷	−	−	÷	÷	÷	÷	−	÷	÷	−	÷	−	÷	−	÷	−	÷
		Hyaline or Albuminoid Casts	÷	÷	÷	−	−	−	÷	÷	+	÷	÷	+	÷	÷	−	÷	÷	÷
		Penetrative Fluid	÷	−	÷	−	−	−	÷	÷	−	−	−	÷	−	÷	÷	−	−	÷
	Epithelium of Bowman's Capsule	Cloudy Swelling	−	−	÷	÷	−	−	−	−	−	÷	−	÷	−	+	−	−	−	÷
		Proliferation	÷	−	−	−	−	−	−	−	−	−	−	−	−	÷	−	−	−	(÷)
	Bowman's Capsules	Swelling	÷	÷	÷	+	÷	÷	+	+	÷	÷	÷	+	÷	÷	÷	÷	÷	÷
		Hyaline Degeneration	−	−	−	−	−	−	÷	÷	−	÷	−	−	÷	÷	−	−	−	÷
Glomeruli – Vasa afferentia		Congestion	+	+	÷	÷	(+++)	+	÷	++	÷	++	+	+	÷	+	÷	+	+	++
	Endothelial Cells	Swelling	+	÷	−	+	+	+	÷	÷	÷	÷	−	÷	÷	÷	+	÷	−	÷
		Proliferation	+	−	÷	+	÷	÷	−	÷	−	÷	−	−	÷	−	÷	+	−	÷
		Desquamation	−	−	−	−	−	−	−	−	−	−	−	−	−	÷	−	−	−	−
	Media	Swelling	÷	÷	÷	(+++)	÷	÷	÷	÷	÷	÷	÷	÷	÷	+	÷	÷	÷	÷
		Hyaline Degeneration	−	−	−	+	−	−	−	−	−	+	−	−	−	÷	−	−	−	−
		Tendency to Necrosis	−	−	−	(+++)	−	−	−	−	−	(+)	÷	−	−	÷	−	−	−	−
	Adventitial Cells	Swelling	+	÷	÷	+	+	+	÷	÷	÷	÷	÷	÷	÷	÷	+	+	÷	÷
		Proliferation	+	−	÷	+	÷	÷	−	−	÷	÷	÷	÷	÷	−	÷	÷	÷	÷
	Adjoining Portion	Peripolar Edema	÷	÷	÷	+	+	+	÷	+	+	÷	÷	+	÷	++	+	÷	÷	÷
		Appearance of "Polkissen"	+	−	−	++	÷	+	−	−	÷	−	−	−	−	−	−	−	−	(÷)
		Macula densa	+	−	−	÷	÷	+	−	−	−	−	−	−	−	−	−	−	−	−
Parenchyma – Tubules	Epithelium	Cloudy Swelling	+	+	++	+	+	+	+	+	+	+	+	+	+	+	++	++	++	++
		Hyaline Degeneration	−	−	−	−	−	−	−	−	−	−	−	−	−	−	−	−	−	−
		Vacuolar Degeneration	÷	−	÷	÷	(+)	−	−	−	+	÷	÷	−	(+)	++	(+)	(÷)	−	(÷)
		Fatty Degeneration	−	−	−	−	(÷)	−	−	−	÷	÷	÷	−	÷	+	(÷)	−	−	−
		Necrosis	−	−	+	−	−	−	−	−	−	÷	÷	−	−	−	−	−	−	−
		Degenerations of Nuclei	÷	÷	+	÷	÷	÷	÷	÷	÷	+	÷	÷	÷	÷	÷	÷	÷	÷
	Contents	Cloudy or Massive Albuminoid Substance	÷	+	÷	+	+	+	÷	+	+	+	+	+	÷	+	+	+	+	+
		Fibrinous Substance	−	−	−	−	(++)	−	−	−	−	−	−	−	−	−	−	−	−	−
		Hyaline or Colloid Cylinder	(+)	(+)	(+)	(++)	(+)	(+)	(+)	(+++)	(+)	+	(+)	+++	+	(+)	(+)	(+)	(++)	(÷)
		Various Calcium Casts	−	(+)	−	−	−	−	−	−	−	−	(+)	−	−	−	−	−	−	−
		Erythrocytes	−	(÷)	−	(+)	(+)	−	−	−	−	−	−	−	−	(+)	−	−	−	−
Interstitium	Congestion	Cortex	+	++	÷	+	+	+	++	++	++	+	+	+	+	+	++	+	+	++
		Medulla	+	++	÷	+	+	++	++	++	+++	++	+	+++	+	(+)	÷	++	+++	+++
	Edema	Cortex	+	÷	+	÷	+	÷	+	+	+	+	+	+	+	(++)	+	÷	+	+
		Medulla	+	+	++	+	+	+	++	++	++	+	+	+	+	++	+	+	++	+
	Hemorrhage	Cortex	−	−	−	−	−	−	−	−	÷	−	+++	−	−	(+)	−	−	−	−
		Medulla	−	−	−	−	−	−	−	−	−	−	−	+++	−	−	−	−	−	−
	Round Cell Infiltration	Cortex	−	−	−	−	(+)	−	÷	+	÷	+	(++)	−	−	(+)	+	−	−	−
		Medulla	−	−	−	−	÷	−	−	÷	(÷)	−	−	−	−	÷	+	−	−	−
	Vessel Walls	Hyaline Degeneration	÷	−	÷	+	÷	−	÷	÷	−	−	÷	÷	−	(+)	−	−	−	−
		Tendency to Necrosis	÷	−	−	(+)	÷	÷	÷	−	÷	÷	−	÷	−	(÷)	−	−	−	−
		Proliferation of Adventitial Cells	+	+	−	÷	÷	÷	÷	÷	÷	−	−	÷	−	−	+	÷	÷	÷
Colonies of Bacterium			+	+!	+	÷	−	−	−	−	−	−	+	−	−	+	−	−	−	−

589

Myolysis (intanse edematous swelling) of vasa afference.

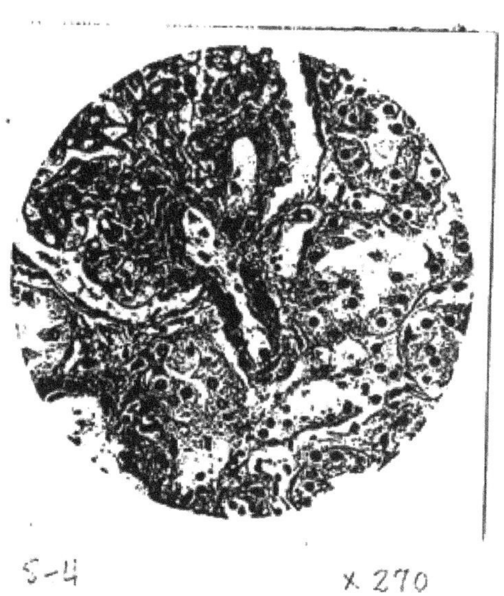

S-4 x 270

590

Hyalinous net-work masses in V.afferense.

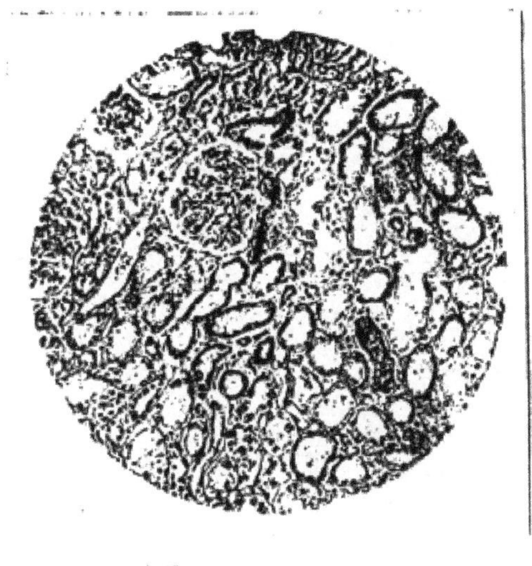

N-7

Typical peripolar changes, with so-called edematous swollen " pol-kissen " .

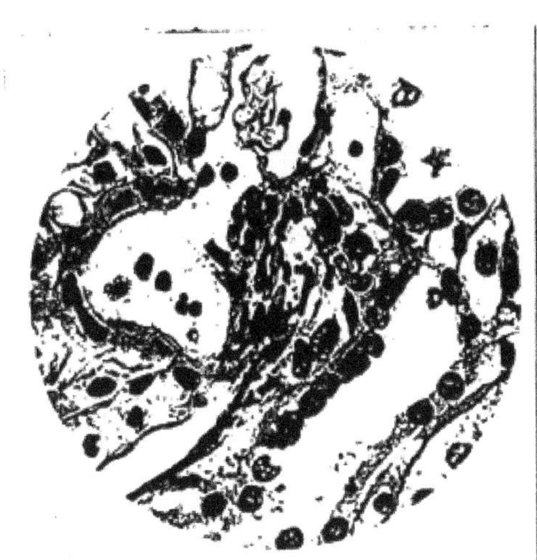

S-4

Nephritis interstitialis with some leucocytes accumulation.

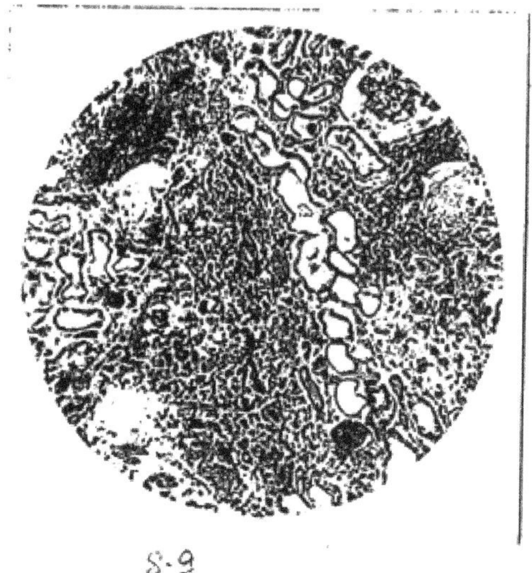

S-9

592

Glomerulo-nephritis necroticans, accompanied degeneration of walls of V.afferense.

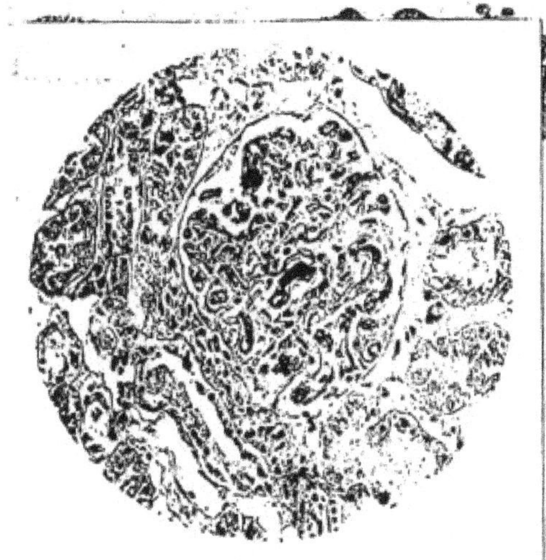

N-21

Glmmerulo-nephritis necroticans, with abandant albuminous masses in Tubulus contortus II.
Remarkable so-called " polar edema".

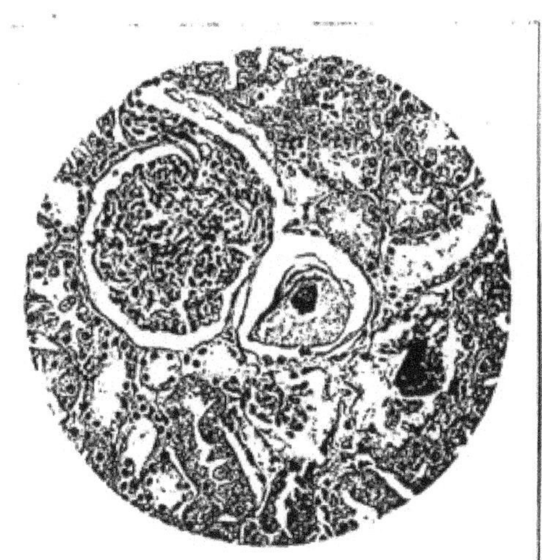

N-18

593

Pancreas

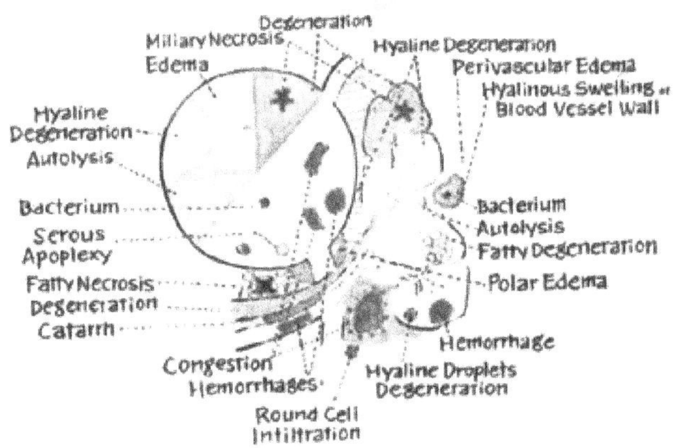

594

P A N C R E A S

(A) Microscopical Investigation.

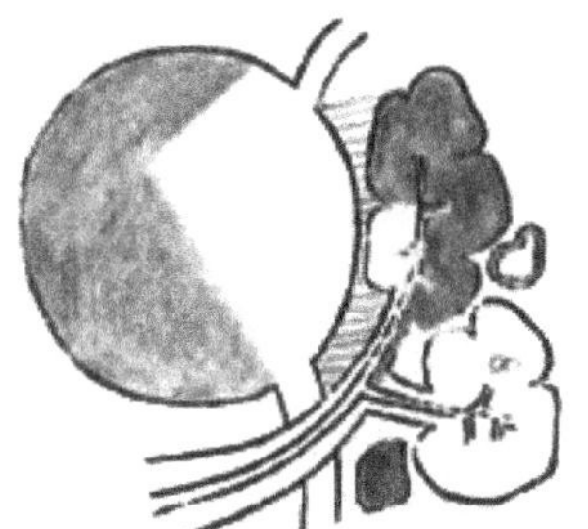

S-I.

Slight congestion (some eosinophilic leucocytes as contents) with edematous swelling of vessel-walls. Slight cloudy swelling of parenchymatous cells and slight swelling and anisocytosis of island-cells.

S-2.

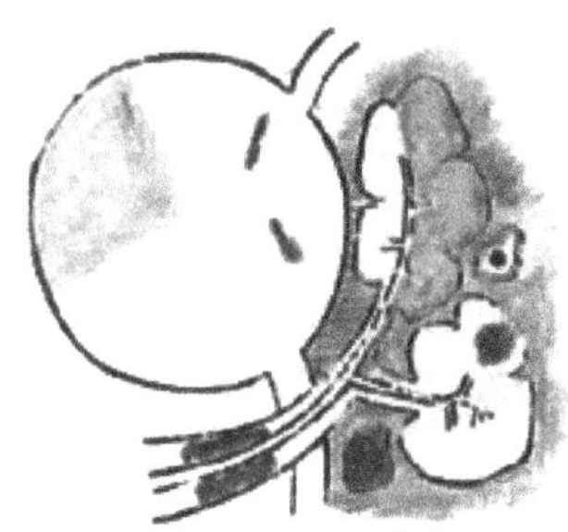

Remarkable congestion (some leucocytes, esp. eosinophilic cells and bacterial masses as contents) and remarkable multiple diffuse hemorrhages in interstitial tissues. Intense hyaline degeneration of blood-vessel-walls and perivasculer edema. Intense cloudy swelling or at some places vacuolar degeneration of parenchymatous cells. Considerable congestion with edematous swelling of endothelial cells of island-capillaries and considerable cloudy swelling of island-cells.

S-3.

Considerable congestion (some leucocytes, esp. eosinophilic cells) and fibrinous and bacterial masses as capillaries contents), hyalinous swe-

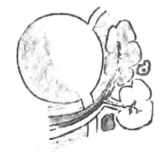

595

lling of vessel-walls and perivascular edema and swelling of interstitial tissues. Considerable congestion of acinus-capillaries and more or less considerable swelling and slight hyperplasia of basal membrane. Considerable cloudy swelling of rather atrophic parenchymatous cells. Slight congestion of island-capillaries and swelling and anisocytosis of island-cells.

S-4.

Remarkable congestion with hyalinous swelling of vessel-walls and slight perivascular hemorrhages and perivascular round-cell-accumulations at some portions. Intense cloudy swelling or vacuolar degeneration of parenchyatous cells (extremly intense pycnotic cells at perivascular portions) and some cell-groups with hyalinous degeneration.

Slight congestion and slight swelling of endothelial cells of island-capillaries with cloudy swelling of island cells.

S-5.

Remarkable congestion (some leucocytes and eosinophilic cells as contents), with hyalinous swelling of vessel-walls and considerable perivascular edematous swelling and sligh hemorrhagie per diapedision in interstitial tissues.

596

Considerable congestion of acinus-capillaries and slight partial hemorrhages. Cloudy swelling of parenchymatous cells, esp. intense pycnotic cells at perivascular portions.

Slight congestion of island- capillaries and remarkable bleeding of some islands (our so-called island-apoplexy). Cloudy swelling and anisocytosis of island-cells.

Catarrh of efferent ducts.

S-6.

Remarkable congestion (some leucocytes and eosinophilic cells as contents) with hyalinous swelling of vessel-walls and slight perivasculer swelling in interstitial tissues and remarkable congestion of acinus-capillaries. Considerable cloudy swelling, at some places remarkable hyaline degeneration and at perivasculer portions intense pycnosis of parenchymatous cells.

Considerable congestion, swelling of endothelial cells of island-capilla-ries with multiple partial hemorrhages and cloudy swelling of island-cells.

S-8.

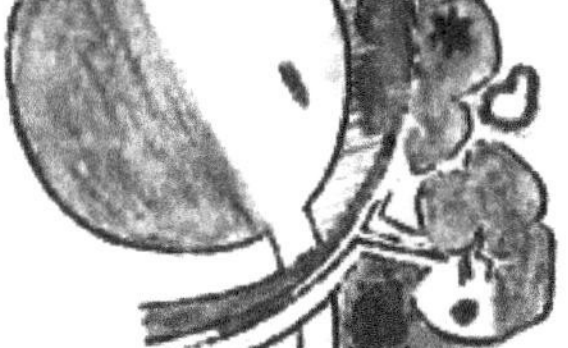

Slight congestion, slight hyalinous swelling of vessel-walls and edematous swelling of perivascu-lar tissues. Intense cloudy swelling of parenchym-atous cells, hyaline-droplets in some acinus and

597

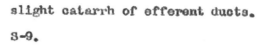

slight catarrh of efferent ducts.

S-9.

Considerable congestion with hyalinous swelling of vessel-walls, perivascular edematous swelling and multiple localised hemorrhages in interstitial tissues. Considerable congestion of acinus-capillaries and slight hemorrhages in some island. Cloudy swelling of parenchymatous cells and island-cells.

Increase of fatty cells in acinus.

S-II.

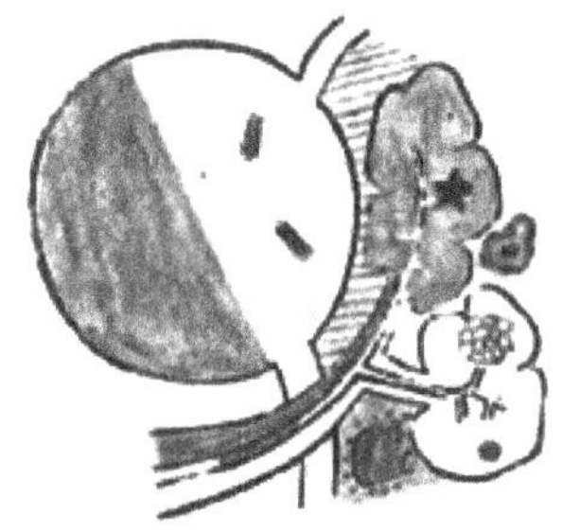

Remarkable congestion (some leucocytes, eosinophilic cells and bacterial masses as contents) with intense hyalinous swelling of vessel-walls, perivascular edematous swelling and perivascular remarkable diffuse hemorrhages in interstitial tissues.

Considerable congestion of acinus-capillaries and intense cloudy swelling and intense pycnosis of rather atrophic glandular cells.

Hyaline-droplets in some acinus and at some places bionecrotic ruins of parenchymatous cells, due to toxicosis.

Slight congestion, severe swelling of capillary-wall cells and intense cloudy swelling of island-cells.

598

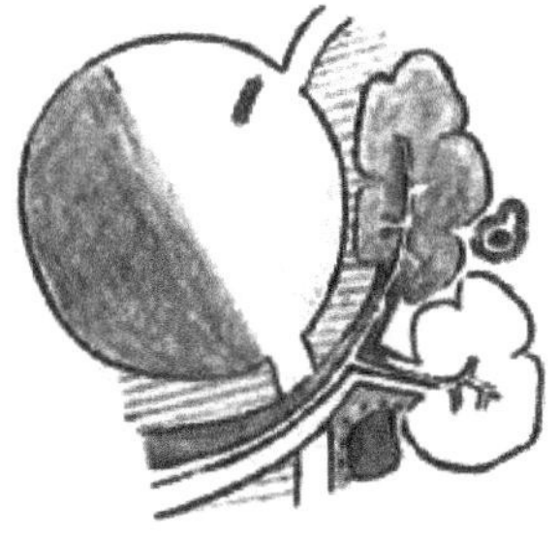

S-I2.

Slight congestion (some leucocytes and bacterial masses as contents) and slight hyalinous swelling of vessel-walls.

Remarkable cloudy swelling of parenchymatous cells and island cells.

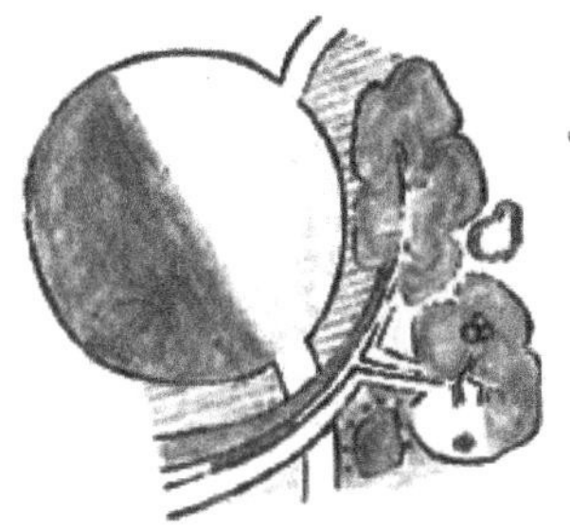

S-I4.

Slight congestion with slight hyalinous swelling of vessel-walls and slight parital hemorrhages in interstitum. Severe clouding and severe swelling (at some acinuses, hyaline-droplets) of parenchymatous cells and island cells.

S-I5.

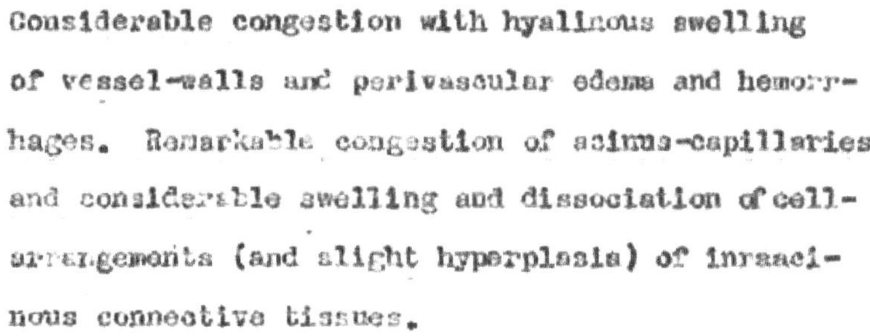

Considerable congestion with hyalinous swelling of vessel-walls and perivascular edema and hemorrhages. Remarkable congestion of acinus-capillaries and considerable swelling and dissociation of cell-arrangements (and slight hyperplasia) of inraacinous connective tissues.

Considerable cloudy swelling of rather atrophic glandular cells.

Slight congestion of island-capillaries and intense cloudy swelling of island-cells.

S-I7.

Slight congestion (some leucocytes and eosinophilic cells as contents) with hyalinous swelling of

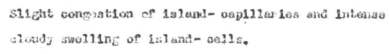

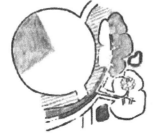

579

vessel-walls and slight perivascular edema in interstitium. Slight congestion of acinus-capillaries and considerable swelling and hyperplasia of inraacinous connective tissues. Intense cloudy swelling of parenchymatous cells and increase of fatty cells in acinuses.

Considerable swelling and considerable hyperplasia of island cells. (with swelling and slight hyperplasia of capillary endothelial cells).

S-21.

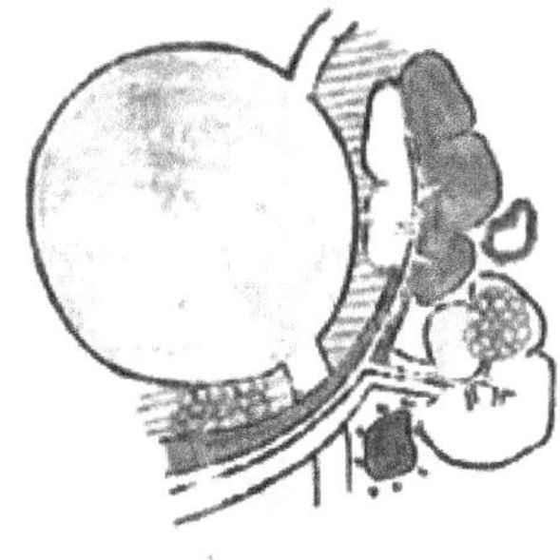

Hyalinous swelling of vessel-walls and slight hyperplasia of intraacinous connective tissues with slight dissociation of cellarrangements.

Increase of fatty cells in acinuses.

Slight cloudy swelling of parenchymatous cells.

S-22.

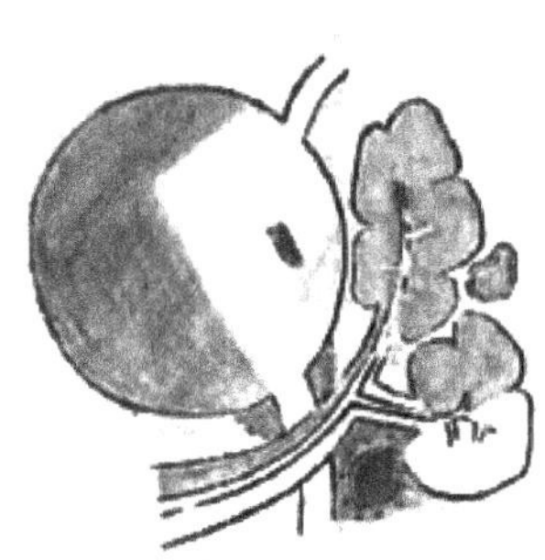

Very slight congestion and considerable perivascular round-cell-infiltration (with some histiocytes infiltration) in interacinous connective tissues and considerable hyperplasia of endothelial cell of acinus-capillaries with considerable hyperplasia of intraacinous connective tissues.

Intense cloudy swelling or vacuolar degeneration of parenchymatous cells and severe cloudy swelling or severe vacuolar degeneration of island-cells

600

with slight hyporplesia of endothelial cells of island-capillaries.

Vacuolar degeneration of nerve bundles in acinus and considerable edema at [illegible] socalled polar portions of islands.

S-20.

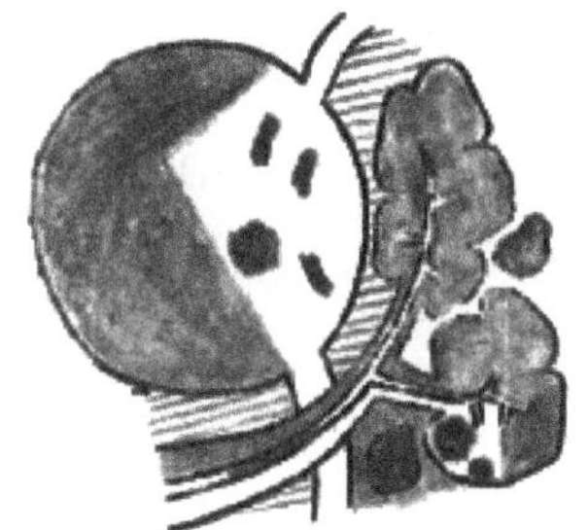

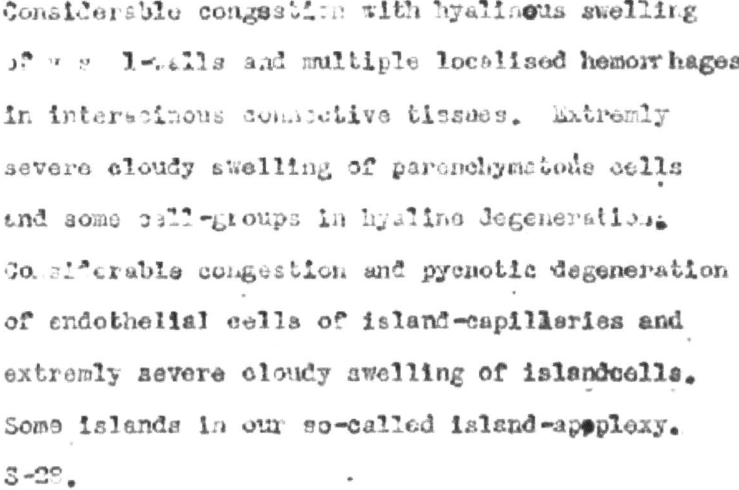

Considerable congestion with hyalinous swelling of [illegible]l-walls and multiple localised hemorrhages in interacinous connective tissues. Extremly severe cloudy swelling of parenchymatous cells and some cell-groups in hyaline degeneration.

Considerable congestion and pycnotic degeneration of endothelial cells of island-capillaries and extremly severe cloudy swelling of islandcells.

Some islands in our so-called island-apoplexy.

S-29.

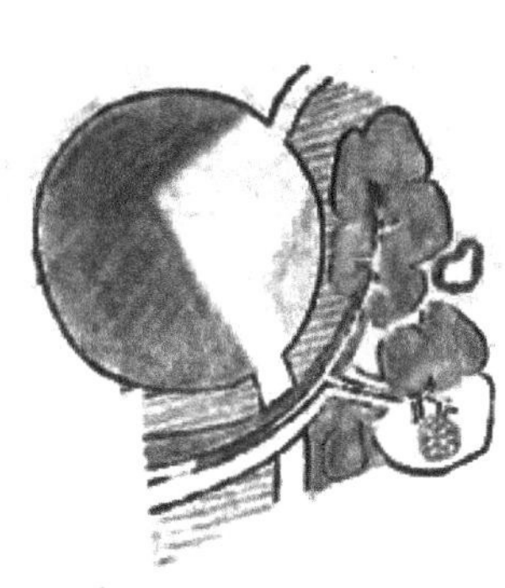

Slight congestion (some leucocytes and eosinophilic cells as contents) with hyalinous swelling of vessel-walls and perivascular edema and considerable localised hemorrhages in interacinous tissues. Severe swelling of intraacinous connective tissues and severe cloudy swelling of parenchymatous cells.

Hyaline-droplets (erythrocytes?) in nerve-bundles in acinuses.

Severe cloudy swelling and anisocytosis of island-cells.

601

S-38.

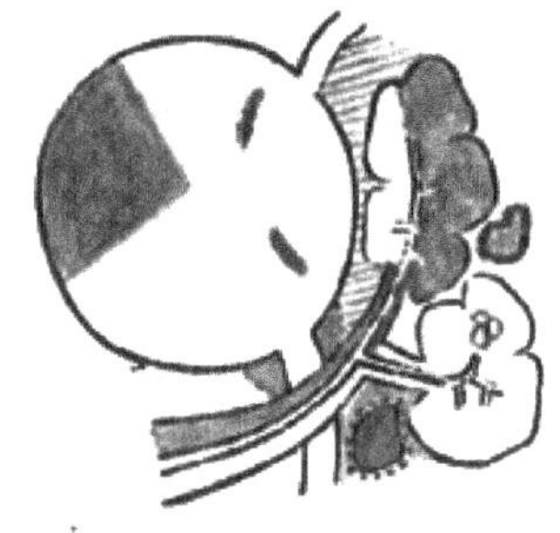

Considerable congestion with hyalinous swelling of vessel-walls and slight perivascular edematous swelling. Considerable congestion of acinus-capillaries and considerable cloudy swelling of parenchymatous cells, at some places (slight hemorrhagic parts), vacuolar degeneration and considerable congestion of island-capillaries, accompanied with cloudy swelling of island-cells and considerable remarkable our socalled polar edema.

2.

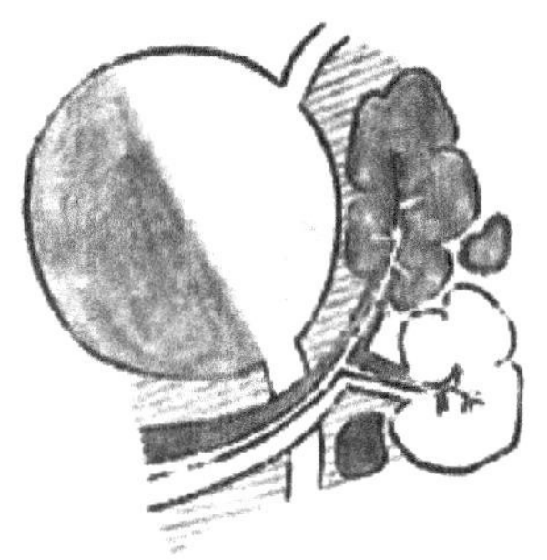

Slight congestion with considerable hyalinous swelling of vessel-walls and severe cloudy swelling or vacuolar degeneration of parenchymatous cells and island-cells.

3.

missed.

4.

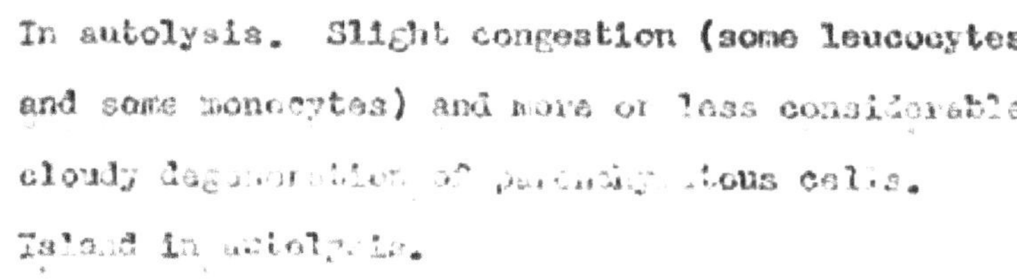

In autolysis. Slight congestion (some leucocytes and some monocytes) and more or less considerable cloudy degeneration of parenchymatous cells. Island in autolysis.

5. missed.

6.

Considerable congestion with remarkable hyalinous

602

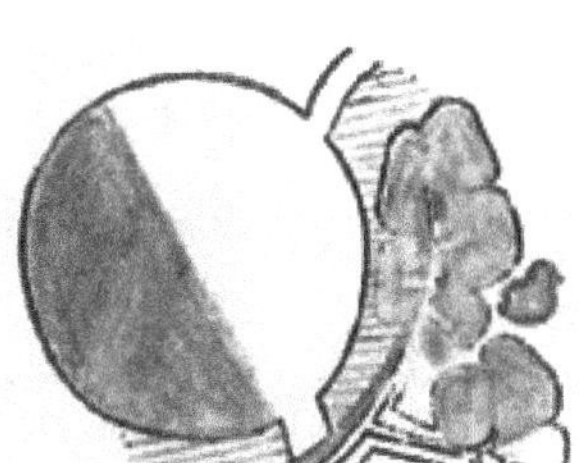

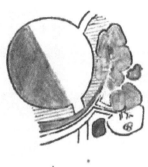

swelling of vessel-walls and remarkable cloudy degeneration, of parenchymatous cells, esp. at pericapillary portions,

Remarkable swelling of endothelial cells of island-capillaries and severe cloudy swelling of island-cells.

7.

Severely atrophic glandular cells and remarkable cloudy swelling of glandular cells and island cells.

8.

Slight congestion with hyalinous swelling of vessel-walls and swelling and slight hyperplasia of intraacinous connective tissues, accompanied with cloudy swelling of parenchymatous cells. Remarkable increase of fatty cells in acinuses and at some acinuses some glandular cells are now being metamorphosed to fatty cells.

9.

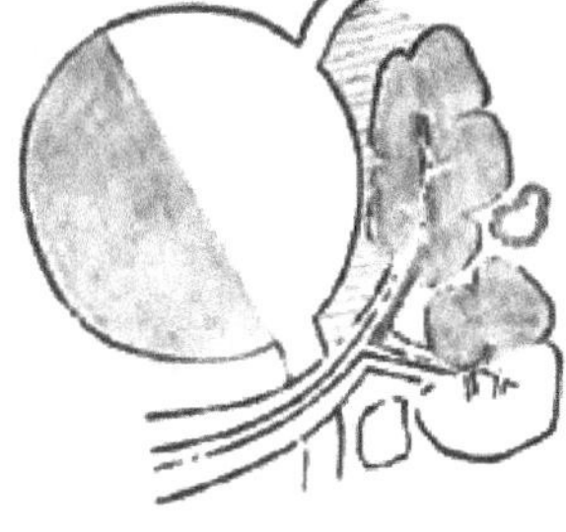

Hyaline degeneration of blood-vessel-walls, remarkable swelling of parenchymatous cells and remarkable swelling with slight hyperplasia of island-cells,

10.

Slight congestion with slight hyaline swelling of vessel-walls and multiple localised hemorrha-

603

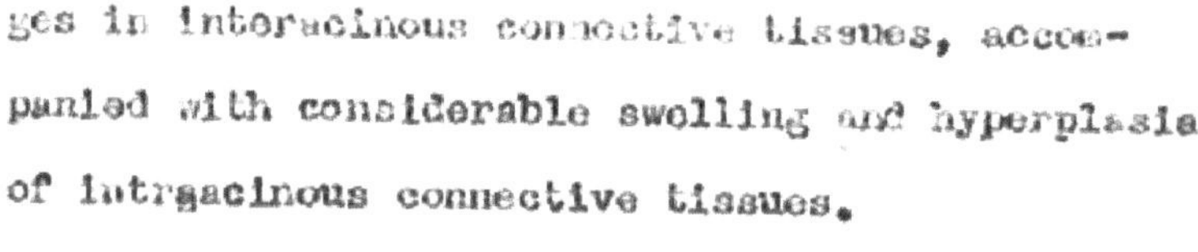

ges in interacinous connective tissues, accompanied with considerable swelling and hyperplasia of intrgacinous connective tissues.

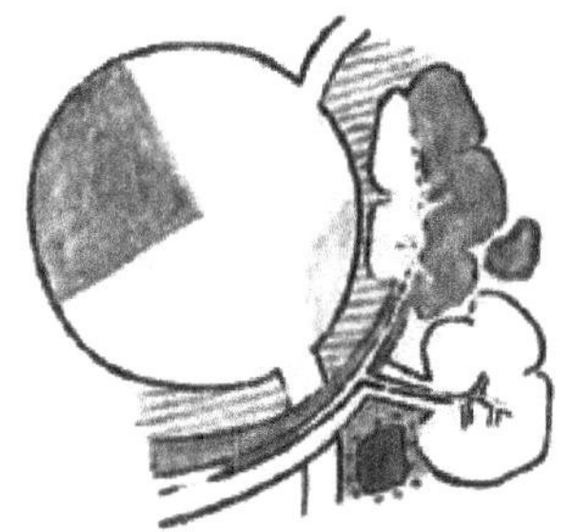

Rather atrophic glandular cells with considerable cloudy swelling and at some places vacuolar degeneration.

II.

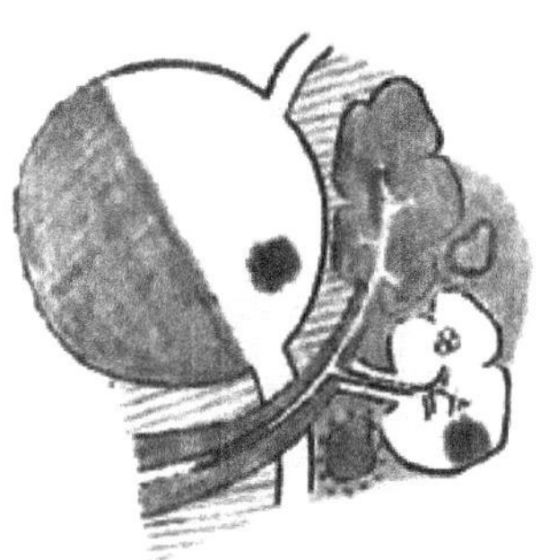

Remarkable congestion with hyalinous swelling of vessel-walls and multiple localised hemorrhages in interacinous connective tissues and considerable cloudy swelling of parenchymatous cells.

Slight congestion of island-capillaries and at some places typical island-apoplexy. Considerable swelling of endothelial cells of island-capillaries and remarkable cloudy swelling of island-cells.

I4.

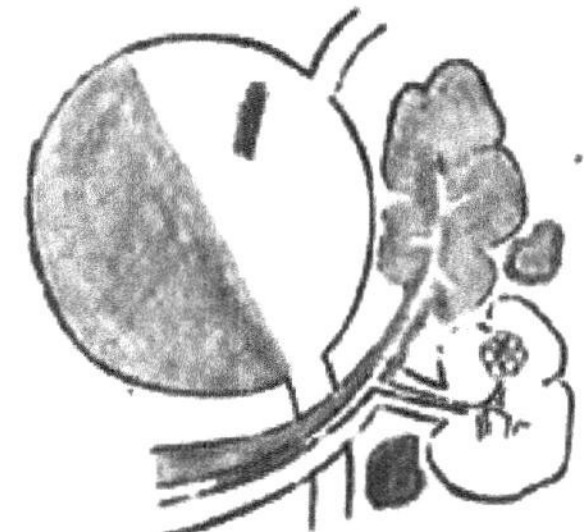

Considerable congestion with slight hyalinous swelling of vessel-walls and remarkable cloudy swelling, at some places vacuolar degeneration of parenchymatous cells. Considerable swelling and pycnotic degeneration of endothelial cells of island-capillaries, accompanied with considerable swelling of island-cells.

I5.

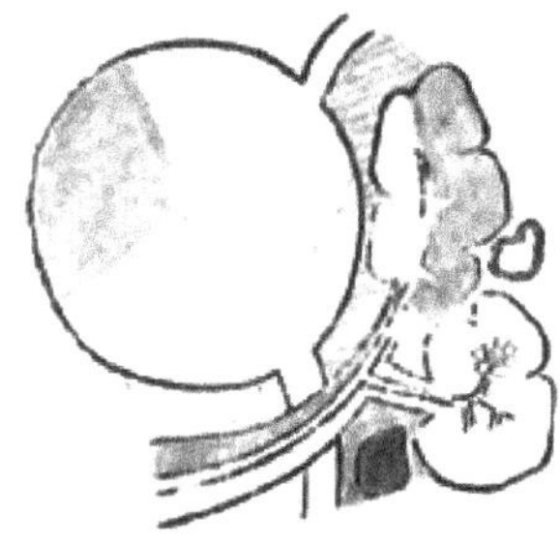

Considerable congestion with hyalinous swelling of vessel-walls and slight hemorrhagia per dia-

604

podisis in interacinous connective tissues.
Considerable swelling of parenchymatous cells and island cells. Increase of fatty cells in acinus.

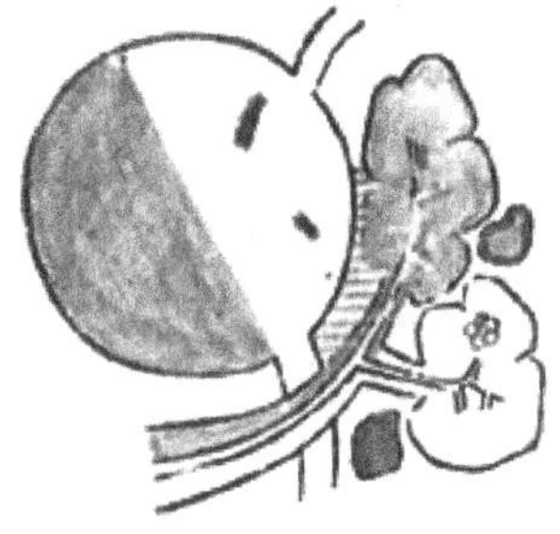

18.

Slight congestion (some leucocytes and eosinophilic cells) with slight hyalinous swelling of vessel-walls and slight cloudy swelling of parenchymatous cells.
Considerable swelling of endothelial cells of island-capillaries and slight swelling of island-cells.

20.

No remarkable changes, except atrophic glandular cells in post mortal changes.

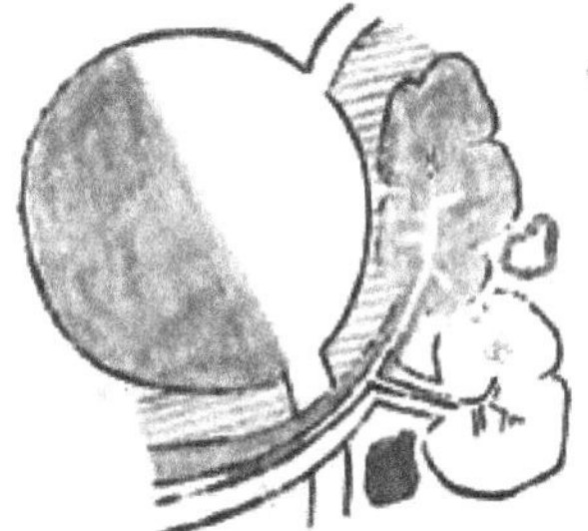

21.

Slight congestion with slight hyalinous swelling of vessel-walls and remarkable cloudy swelling or, at some places vacuolar degenerations.

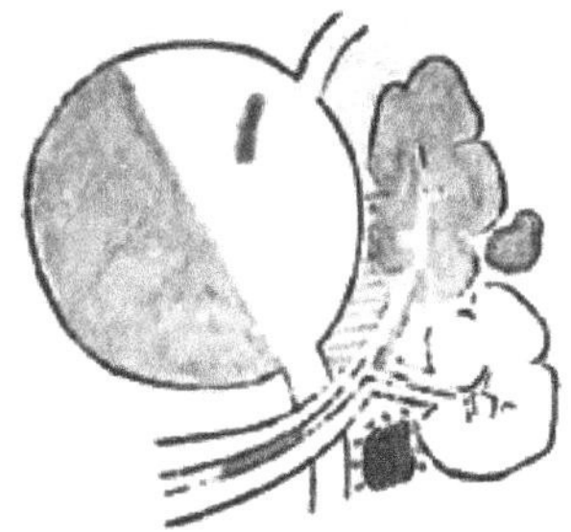

24.

Slight congestion with slight hyalinous swelling of vessel-walls and remarkable swelling of parenchymatous cells, accompanied with cloudy degeneration and anisocytosis of island-cells.

26.

Slight congestion with slight perivascular round-

605

cell-accumulations in interacinous connective tissues and slight congestion of intraacinous capillaries, with slight swelling and slight hyperplasia of intraacinous connective tissues. Remarkable cloudy swelling of parenchymatous cells and also remarkable swelling and hyperplasia of island cells. Hyperplasia of endothelial cells of island-capillaries.

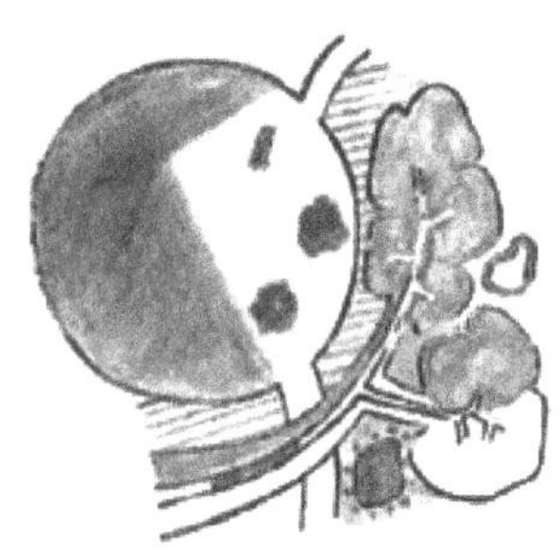

27.

Considerable congetion with hyaline swelling of vessel-walls and slight cloudy swelling of parenchymatous cells.

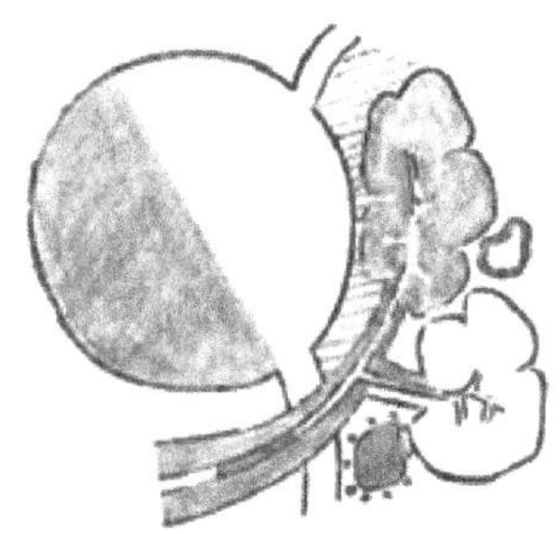

Increase of endothelial cells of island capillaries and remarkable swelling of island-cells.
Hydropic swelling of island-cells.

29.

Slight congestion with hyalinous swelling of vessel-walls, accompanied with slight swelling and slight hyperplasia of intraacinous connective tissues and considerable swelling and at some places remarkable vacuolar degeneration of rather atrophic glandular cells.

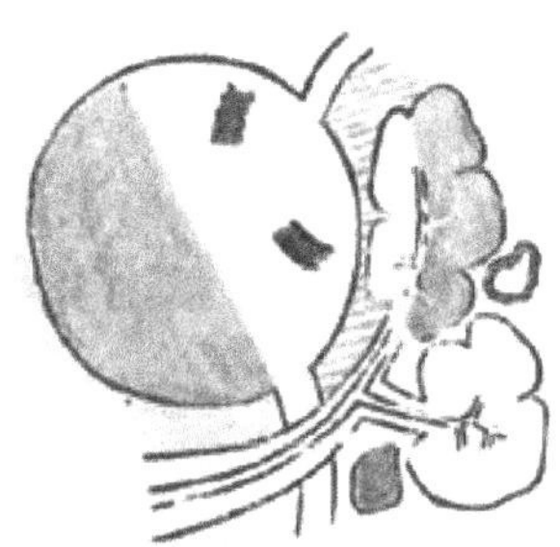

Slight congestion and slight swelling of endothelial cells of island-capillaries, accompanied with considerable cloudy swelling of island-cells.

30.

Slight congestion with slight hyalinous swelling

606

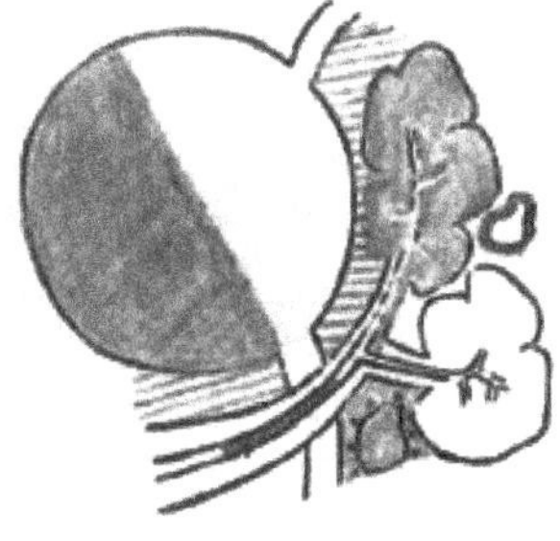

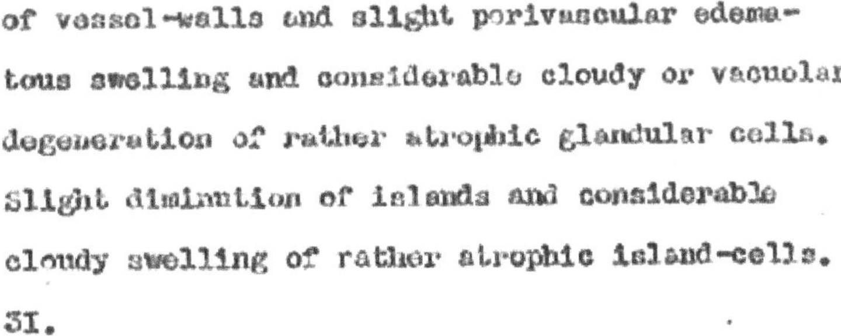

of vessel-walls and slight perivascular edematous swelling and considerable cloudy or vacuolar degeneration of rather atrophic glandular cells.

Slight diminution of islands and considerable cloudy swelling of rather atrophic island-cells.

31.

Slight congestion with slight hyalinous swelling of vessel-walls and slight swelling or slight hyperplasia of interacinous connective tissues, accompanied with considerable dissociation of cell-arrangements and considerable cloudy swelling of parenchymatous cells.

Considerable swelling of endothelial cells of island-capillaries and cloudy swelling of island cells.

Increase of fatty cells in acinuses.

33.

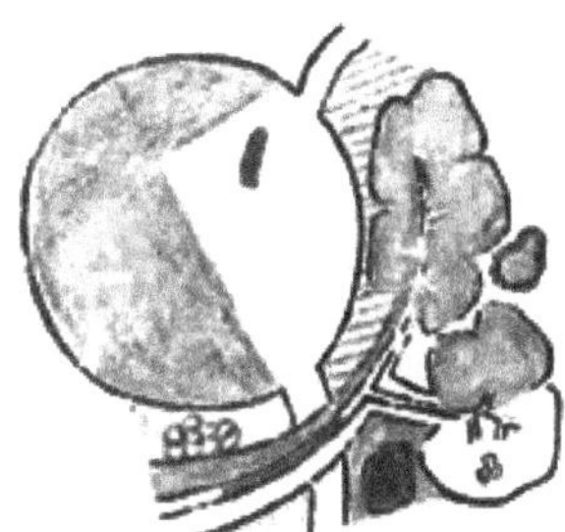

Considerable congestion with hyalinous swelling of vessel-walls and multiple slight localised hemorrhages in interacinous connective tissues and considerable cloudy or at some places vacuolar degeneration of parenchymatous cells.

34.

Considerable congestion with hyalinous swelling of vessel-walls and considerable congestion of intraacinous capillaries, accompanied with

607

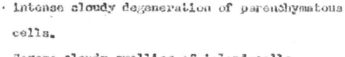

intense cloudy degeneration of parenchymatous cells.

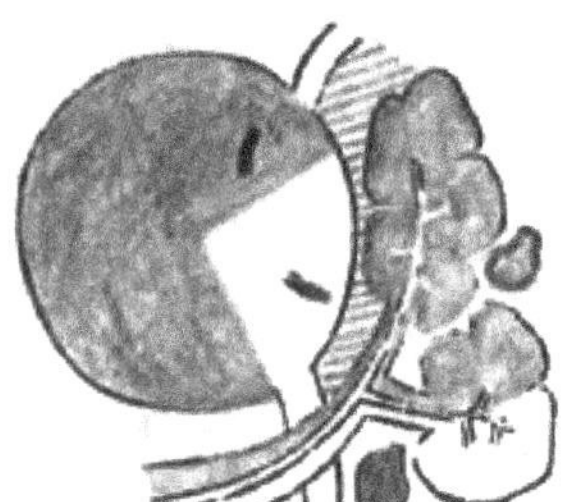

Severe cloudy swelling of island-cells.

35.

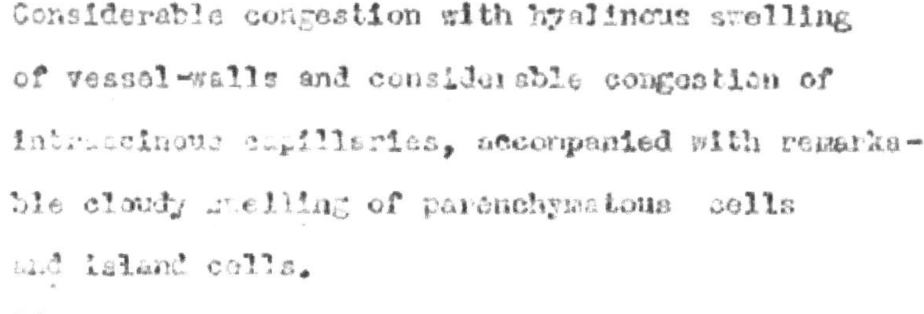

Considerable congestion with hyalinous swelling of vessel-walls and considerable congestion of intraacinous capillaries, accompanied with remarkable cloudy swelling of parenchymatous cells and island cells.

36.

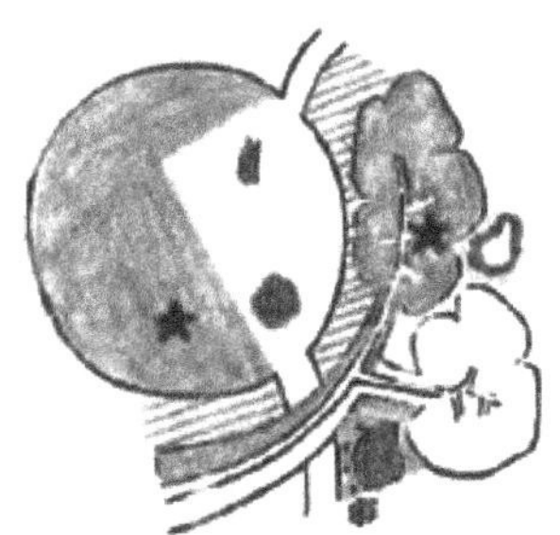

Slight congestion with slight hyalinous swelling of vessel-walls and slight perivascular bleeding and considerable round cell accumulations in interacinous connective tissues.

Severe cloudy swelling of parenchymatous cells and island-cells.

40.

Slight congestion with slight hyalinous swelling of vessel-walls and very slight perivascular round cell accumulation in interacinous connective tissues. Considerable cloudy swelling or vacuolar degeneration of parenchymal cells and island-cells.

42.

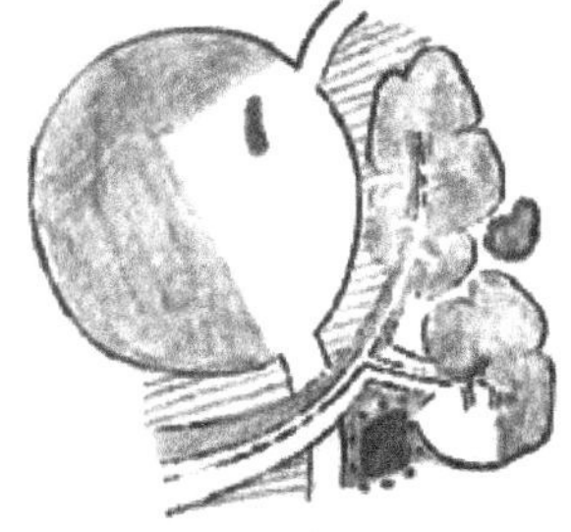

Considerable congestion with hyalinous swelling of vessel-walls and multiple localized hemorrhages in interacinous tissues and intraacinous tissues.

608

Considerable cloudy swelling of parenchymatous cells and vacuolar degeneration in bundles of nerves.

44.

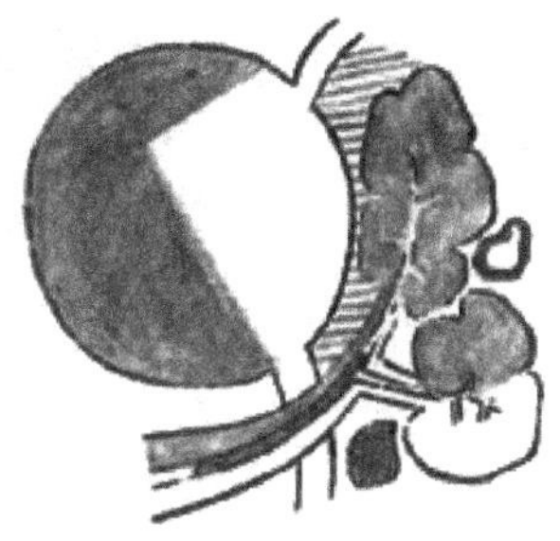

No remarkable changes. Slight congestion with very slight hyalinous swelling of vessel-walls and slight cloudy swelling of parenchymatous cells and island-cells.

46.

Post mortal changes.

47.

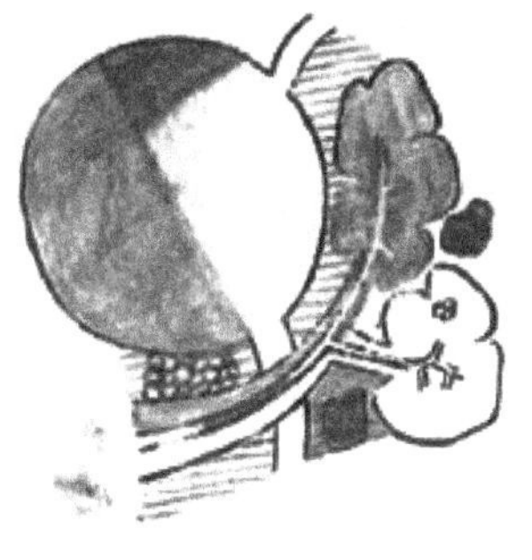

Considerable congestion with hyalinous swelling of vessel-walls and very slight hemorrahgia per diapedisin. Considerable cloudy swelling or vacuolar degeneration of rather atrophic glandular cells and island-cells.

Increase of fatty cells in acinus and slight catarrh of efferent ducts.

49.

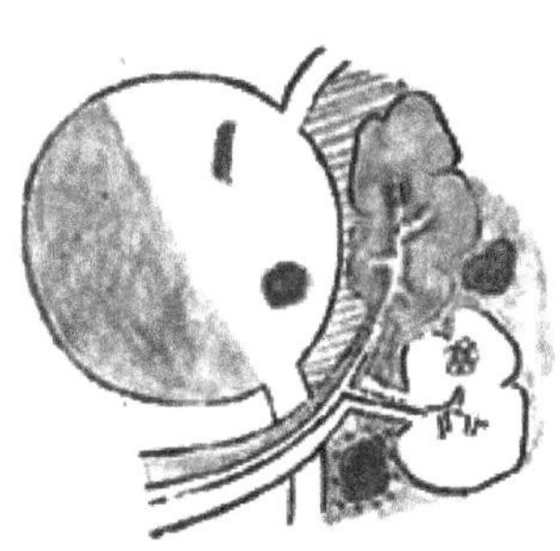

Remarkable congestion with hyalinous swelling of vessel-walls and multiple slight localised hemorrhages in interacinous tissues and considerable congestion of intraacinous capillaries.

Slight congestion and considerable swelling of endothelial cells of island-capillaries, accompanied with at some places our so-called island-apoplexy and considerable cloudy swelling of island-cells.

609

(B) SUMMARY

(I).

Histological observation of all investigated 46 cases.

A). Acinus.

I) In the most cases, with some congestion of inter- and intra-acinous capillaries.

Congestion in slight degree. 6 cases.
in medium degree. 21 cases.
in severe degree. 17 cases.

Congestion with hyalinous swelling or degeneration of capillary walls. 30 cases.

Congestion, accompanied with consid. perivascular edema. 15 cases.

Congestion, accompanied with slight perivascular hemorrhages. 30 cases.

Congestion, accompanied with some perivascular round cell accumulations (some leucocytes, lymphocytes, plasma cells and some histiocytes). 24 cases.

2) After that, occured some degenerative changes of parenchymatous cells, esp. at pericapillar protions.

With cloudy swelling of parenchymal cells.
in slight degree. 9 case.
in medium degree. 21 cases.
in severe degree. 15 cases.
with hyalinous degeneration. 2 case.
with hyaline-droplets formation. 5 cases.

610

vacuolar degeneration. 38 cases.

Accordingly it shows generally some considerable parenchymatous degeneration and sometimes some remarkable changes with hyalinous degeneration, hyaline-droplets formation or vacuolar degeneration in acinuses.

B) Islands.

I). Sometimes, with considerable congestion of island-capillaries.

Congestion in considerable degree 2 cases.

Congestion in remarkable degree, accompanied with edematous swelling of capillary-walls. I cases.

Congestion with our so-called "polar edema". I case.

Congestion with our so-called "serous apoplexy of islands." 0 case.

Congestion with our so-called "(hemorrhagic) apoplexy of islands". Il cases.

2). Sometimes some degenerative changes of islands-cells.

with rather atrophic cells. I5 cases.

with cloudy swelling. 45 cases.

with slight vacuolar degeneration. I2 cases.

611

PANCREAS

			N 2	N 6	N 7	N 8	N 9	N 10	N 11	N 14	N 15	N 16	N 18	N 21	N 24	N 26	N 27	N 30	N 31	N 33	N 34	N 35	N 36
Acinus	Size		↓	↓	↓	↓	↓	↓	↓	↓	↓	↓	↓	↓	↓	↓	↓	↓	↓	↓	↓	↓	↓
	Dissociation		−	−	−	−	−	−	−	−	−	−	−	−	−	−	−	−	−	−	−	−	−
	Necrosis		−	−	÷	−	−	−	−	−	−	−	−	−	−	−	−	−	−	−	−	−	÷
Parenchyma	Clouding		++	++·	++	++	++	+	++	++	+	++·	++	++	++	++·	++	++	++	++·	++:	++:	++
	Swelling		+	++·	+	+	++·	÷	++	+	+	++·	+·	+	+++	++·	++	+	+	++	++·	++:	+
	Zymogen Granules		−	+·	÷	+	−	+·	++	−	+	+·	÷	−	+·	÷	÷	−	++	+·	+	−	−
	Honeycombed Degeneration		+·	−	++	−	−	++:	+	−	−	(+)	÷	++	÷	(+·)	−	÷	+·	÷	+·	+	+·
	Changes of Nuclei	Swelling	−	−	−	−	−	−	−	−	−	−	−	−	−	−	−	−	−	−	−	−	−
		Pyknosis	+	(+·)	(++·)	+·	++	+	+	+	(+·)	(++)	+·	(+++)	+·	+	+	++·	+	+·	(++:)	+·	++·
		Karyolysis	÷	−	÷	−	−	÷	−	−	−	−	÷	+·	−	÷	÷	+	−	÷	+	÷	+
	Hyperplasia of Centroacinar Cells		−	−	−	−	−	−	−	−	−	−	−	−	−	−	−	−	−	−	−	−	−
	Dsq of Epithelium of Efferent Ducts		−	−	÷	−	−	−	−	−	−	−	−	÷	−	−	÷	÷	−	÷	−	−	−
Interstitium	Edema		+·	÷	++	++	++·	+·	+	−	+·	+	÷	++	+	+	÷	+	+·	+:	+·	++:	+·
	Contents of Capillaries	Erythrocytes	++	++·	−	++	−	++	++	++	++	++	++	++÷	++·	+·	+·	÷	++	++	++·	++:	+
		Leucocytes	÷	÷	÷	÷	−	÷	÷	−	+	+	÷	÷	÷	÷	÷	÷	÷	÷	+:	−	÷
		Lymphocytes	÷	+	−	+	−	÷	÷	−	+·	+·	+	÷	÷	÷	÷	÷	÷	÷	+·	−	÷
	Hemorrhage		−	−	−	−	−	−	++·	−	÷	−	−	−	−	+:	−	−	+	−	÷	−	÷
	Infiltration	Leucocytes	−	−	−	−	−	−	÷	−	−	−	−	−	÷	−	÷	÷	÷	−	÷	−	(+·)
		Lymphocytes	−	−	−	−	−	−	−	−	−	−	−	−	−	−	−	−	−	−	−	−	−
	Proliferation	Plasma Cells	−	−	−	−	−	÷	−	−	−	−	−	÷	−	−	−	−	−	−	−	−	−
		Histiocytes	−	−	÷	−	−	÷	÷	−	−	−	−	−	÷	−	÷	÷	÷	−	−	−	−
		Capillary Wall Cells	−	−	−	−	−	−	−	−	−	−	−	−	−	−	−	−	−	−	−	−	−
Langerhans's Island	Number		↓÷	↑	↓++	↑	↓÷	↓÷	↑	↓+	N	N	↑	↓++	↓÷	↓÷	↓+	↓++	↓÷	↓++·	↓+:	↓÷	↓÷
	Atrophia		÷	+	++	÷	−	÷	÷	+	÷	÷	÷	+	+·	+	−	−	+	+	+	÷	−
	Necrosis		−	−	−	−	−	−	−	−	−	−	−	−	−	÷	−	−	−	−	−	−	+
	Parenchymal Cells	Size	↓÷	↓+	↓++	↓÷	N	↑	↓÷	↓++	↓÷	↓+	↓+	↓+	↓+	↓÷	↓÷	↓++	↓+	↓+:	↓+:	↓+	N
		Clouding	++	++	++	++	++	+	++	++	+	++	++	++	++	++·	++	++	++·	++·	++·	++:	++
		Swelling	++	++	++	+	++·	÷	++	+	+	++	++	++	++	++·	++	+	++·	++·	++·	++:	++·
		Honeycombed Degeneration	+	−	+	−	−	−	−	−	÷	÷	÷	+	÷	+	(+:)	−	÷	÷	÷	÷	÷
		Changes of Nuclei: Swelling	−	−	−	−	−	−	−	−	−	−	−	−	−	−	−	−	−	−	−	−	−
		Changes of Nuclei: Pyknosis	÷	++	++·	+	++	++·	−	÷	+·	(++)	(+·)	++:	++	+·	+·	++:	+	(++)	(++)	÷	(+)
		Changes of Nuclei: Karyolysis	−	−	−	−	−	−	−	−	−	−	−	+·	−	−	−	÷	−	−	−	÷	−
	Congestion of Capillaries		−	−	−	+	−	−	−	÷	−	÷	÷	−	÷	÷	−	−	÷	÷	+	+	÷
	Hemorrhage		−	−	÷	+	−	−	−	−	−	−	−	−	−	+:	−	−	+	−	−	−	÷
	Hyperplasia of Capillary Wall Cells		−	÷	−	−	−	−	−	−	−	−	÷	−	−	−	−	−	÷	÷	÷	÷	÷

612

PANCREAS

		N 40	N 42	N 44	N 47	N 49	S 1	S 2	S 3	S 4	S 5	S 6	S 8	S 9	S 11	S 12	S 14	S 15	S 22	S 26	S 28	S 38
Acinus	Size	↓	↓	↓	↓	↓	↓	↓	↓	↓	↓	↓	↓	↓	↓	↓	↓	↓	↓	↓	↓	↓
	Dissociation	—	—	—	—	—	—	—	—	—	—	—	—	—	—	—	—	—	—	—	—	—
	Necrosis	—	—	—	—	—	—	—	—	—	—	—	+	—	—	—	—	—	—	—	—	—
Parenchyma	Clouding	⧺:	⧻:	⧻:	⧺	⧺	+:	+	⧺	+:	+	⧺	⧻:	⧻:	⧺	⧺	⧻:	⧺	⧺:	⧻:	⧺:	+
	Swelling	⧺	⧺:	⧺	⧺	⧺	+:	+	+	+:	+	⧺	⧻:	+	(⧺)	⧺	⧻:	+	⧺:	⧻:	⧺:	+
	Zymogen Granules	÷	÷	—	—	÷	—	—	—	+:	⧺	÷	—	—	—	÷	—	+:	+:	+:	—	+:
	Honeycombed Degeneration	+	+	—	—	÷	—	+	—	—	—	—	+:	÷	+	+	÷	—	+:	⧻:	⧻:	+
	Changes of Nuclei: Swelling	—	—	—	—	—	—	—	—	—	—	—	+	—	—	—	—	—	—	—	—	—
	Changes of Nuclei: Pyknosis	+	+	⧻:	(⧺:)	(⧺)	+	÷	⧺:	+	÷	+	+	+	⧺	÷	÷	⧺	⧺	+:	⧺:	+
	Changes of Nuclei: Karyolysis	÷	÷	—	—	—	÷	+	+	—	÷	—	÷	—	+:	÷	—	—	—	—	—	—
	Hyperplasia of Centroacinar Cells	—	—	—	—	—	—	—	—	—	—	—	—	—	—	—	—	—	—	—	—	—
	Dsq. of Epithelium of Efferent Ducts	—	—	+	—	—	—	—	+	÷	+:	÷	÷	—	÷	—	÷	÷	—	—	+	—
Interstitium	Edema	÷	(+)	+	+:	+	—	—	—	—	—	—	+	÷	+	+	(⧻)	⧺	⧺:	—	⧺	+
	Contents of Capillaries: Erythrocytes	⧺	⧺:	+:	⧻:	⧺:	⧺	⧺	+:	⧺	(+:)	⧺	+:	+:	(⧻)	⧺	+:	⧺	+:	⧺:	+:	⧺:
	Contents of Capillaries: Leucocytes	÷	—	—	÷	÷	÷	÷	—	(+:)	÷	+	÷	÷	÷	÷	+	÷	÷	+:	÷	÷
	Contents of Capillaries: Lymphocytes	÷	—	—	+	÷	—	—	—	—	—	—	÷	+	÷	÷	+	+	÷	+:	÷	÷
	Hemorrhage	—	÷	—	—	(⧻)	—	⧻:	—	÷	+	⧺	+	÷	+	—	÷	+	÷	+	÷	÷
	Infiltration: Leucocytes	—	—	—	—	—	—	+	—	—	—	—	—	—	—	—	—	÷	÷	—	—	—
	Infiltration: Lymphocytes	÷	÷	—	—	—	—	+:	—	—	—	—	÷	÷	—	÷	÷	÷	÷	—	—	÷
	Proliferation: Plasma Cells	—	—	—	—	—	—	—	—	—	—	—	—	—	—	÷	÷	—	—	—	—	÷
	Proliferation: Histiocytes	÷	÷	—	—	÷	—	—	—	—	—	—	÷	÷	—	÷	÷	÷	+	—	—	+
	Proliferation: Capillary Wall Cells	—	—	—	—	—	—	—	—	—	—	—	—	—	—	—	—	—	—	—	—	—
Langerhans's Island	Number	↓÷	↓+:	↓⧺:	↓+:	↓÷	N	N	↓+	↓÷	↓÷	↑	↓÷	↓+	↓+	↓÷	↓÷	↓÷	↓÷	↓÷	↓+:	↓÷
	Atrophia	—	—	—	—	—	÷	÷	+	÷	÷	÷	÷	—	+	+	÷	÷	—	+	÷	+
	Necrosis	—	—	—	—	—	—	—	⧺	—	—	—	—	—	—	—	—	—	—	—	—	—
	Parenchymal Cells: Size	N	↓+	↓+	↓÷	↓÷	↓÷	↓÷	↓+	↓÷	↓÷	↓÷	↓÷	↓+	↓+	↓+	↓÷	↓÷	↓÷	↓+	↓÷	↓+
	Parenchymal Cells: Clouding	⧺:	⧺:	⧺:	⧺:	⧺	⧺	+	⧺	⧺	⧺	+:	⧺	⧺	⧺	⧺	⧺	⧺	⧺:	⧺:	⧺:	+
	Parenchymal Cells: Swelling	⧺:	⧺:	⧺:	⧺	⧺	⧺	+	+	⧺	⧺	⧺	⧺	⧺	(⧻)	+	+	+	⧺:	⧺:	⧺:	÷
	Parenchymal Cells: Honeycombed Degeneration	÷	÷	—	—	—	—	—	+	—	—	—	÷	÷	+	÷	—	÷	+:	+:	+	÷
	Parenchymal Cells: Changes of Nuclei: Swelling	—	—	—	—	—	—	—	—	—	—	—	—	—	—	—	—	—	—	—	—	—
	Parenchymal Cells: Changes of Nuclei: Pyknosis	÷	+	⧺	÷	(⧻)	⧺	÷	⧺	+	÷	+	⧺:	+	⧺	+	—	⧺	+	+:	+:	+:
	Parenchymal Cells: Changes of Nuclei: Karyolysis	—	—	—	—	—	—	—	⧺	—	—	—	—	—	+	—	—	—	—	÷	—	—
	Congestion of Capillaries	+	÷	—	—	÷	—	+	—	+	+	+:	÷	+	(+)	÷	—	+	÷	+:	—	+
	Hemorrhage	—	—	—	—	+	—	—	—	—	+	—	—	+	—	—	—	—	—	+	—	—
	Hyperplasia of Capillary Wall Cells	÷	—	—	÷	+:	—	—	—	—	—	—	—	—	—	—	—	÷	—	+	—	—

613

Cloudy swelling and intense bionecrotic changes of parenchymatous cells.

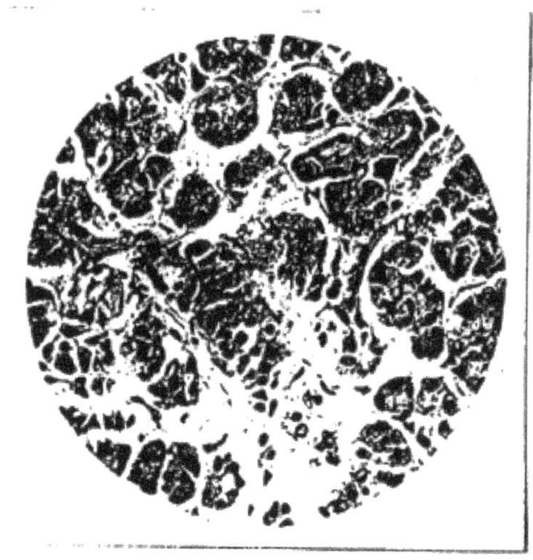

614

Intense edema (bio-necrotic changes) at perivascular portion.

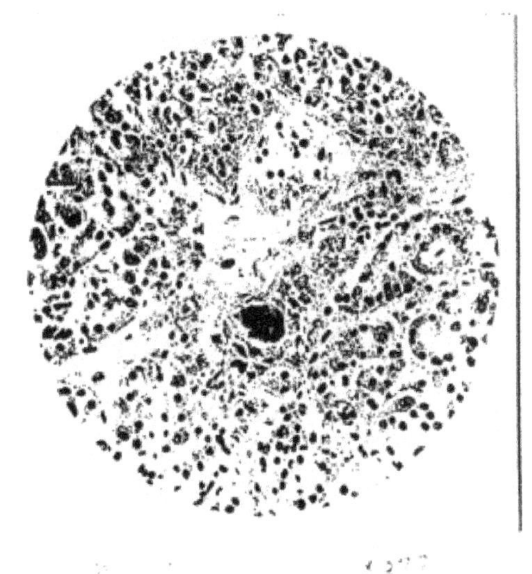

Intense edema (bio-necrotic changes) at perivascular portion.

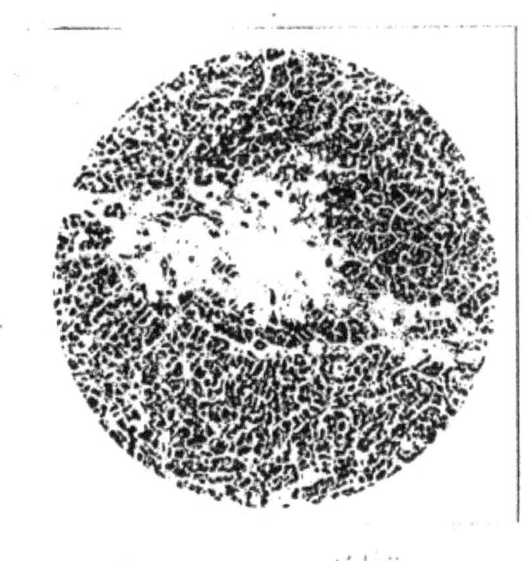

615

Hemorrhages in intra-acinous tissues, in high power.

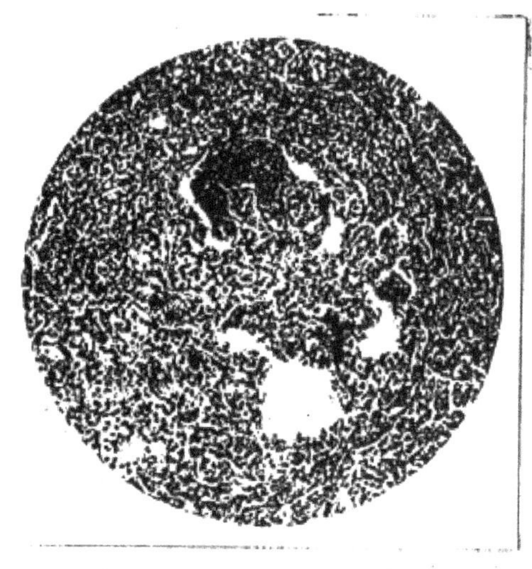

P.N. 11.

Hemorrhages in intra-acinous tissues, in high power.

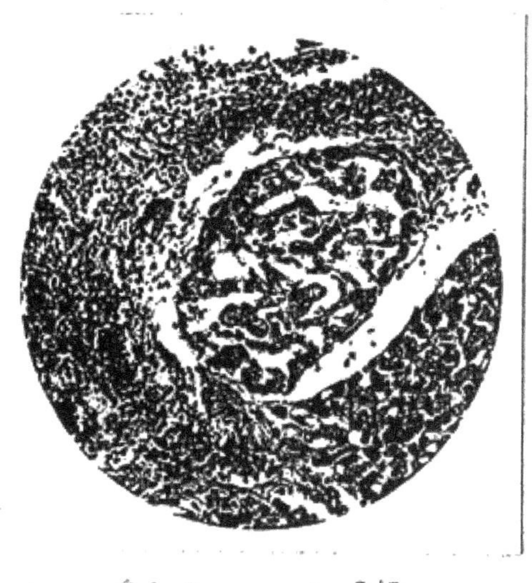

P.S. 2 x 210

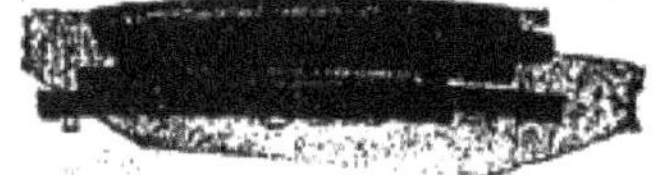

616

Intese atrophy of island.

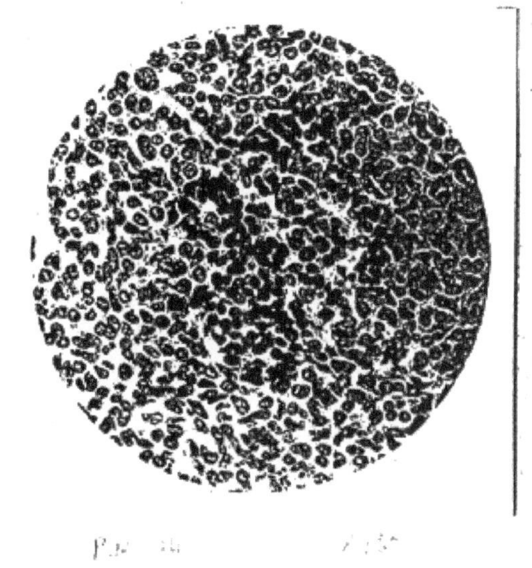

Intese edenatous swelling of island.

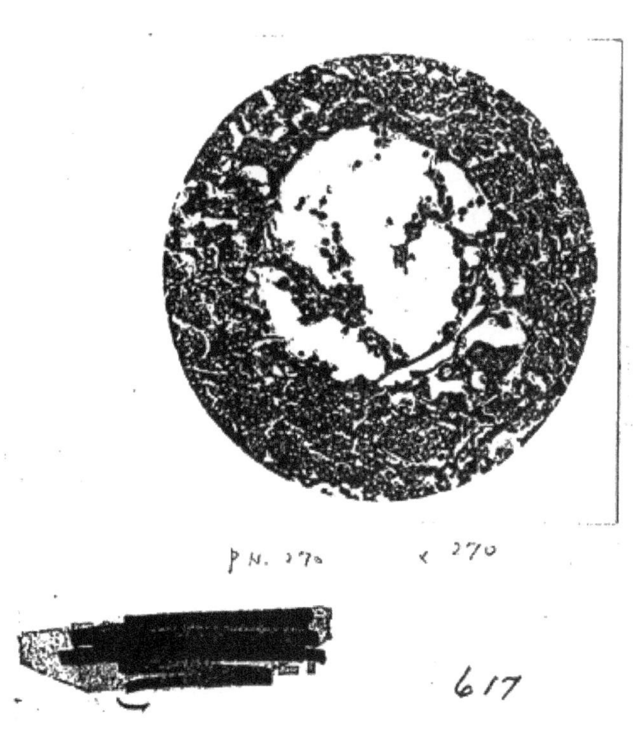

P N. 270　　× 270

617

Diffuse hemorrhages in intra-acinous tissues.

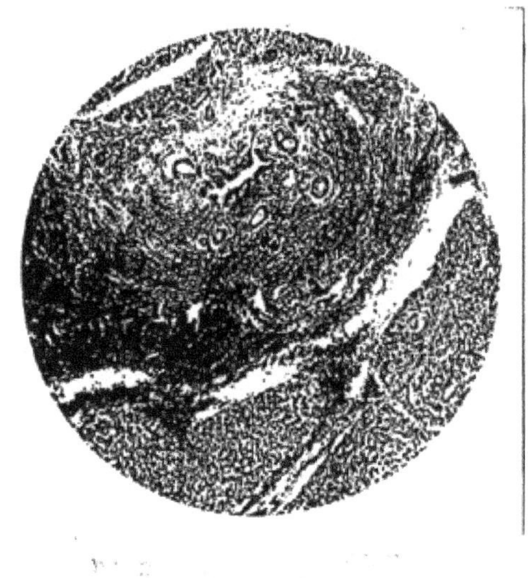

Congestion and some leucocytes in capillary. Slight perivascular round cell infiltration.

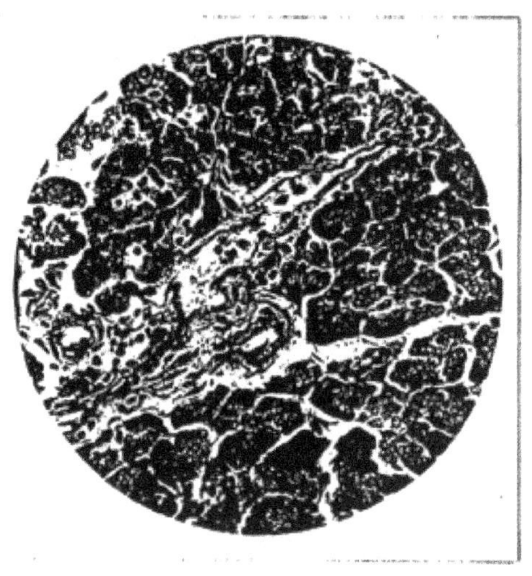

618

Intense congestion of island-capillary.
Intense degneration of island-cells.

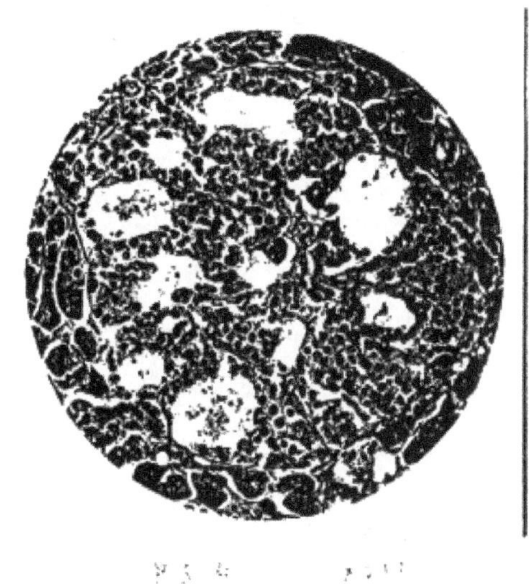

Intense hemorrhages in island (apoplexy of island).

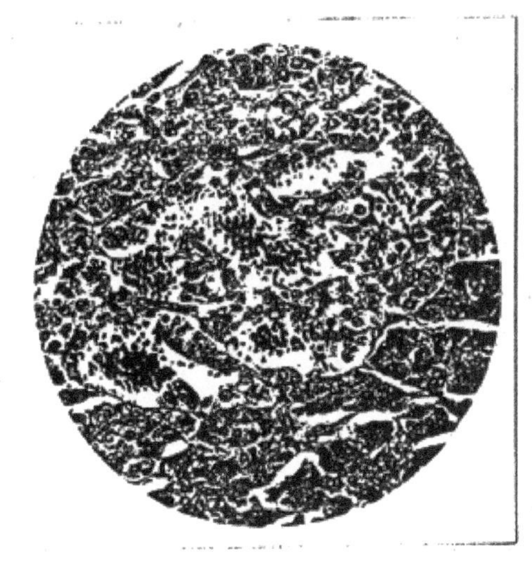

619

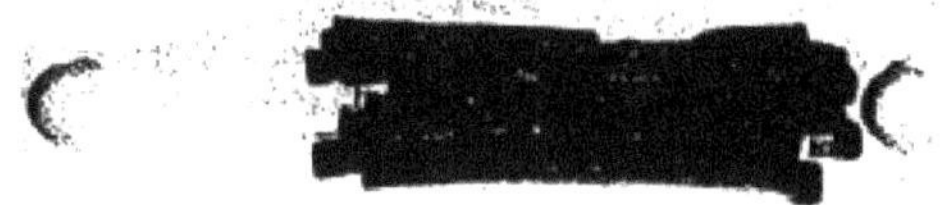

Congestion and edematous swelling of island.

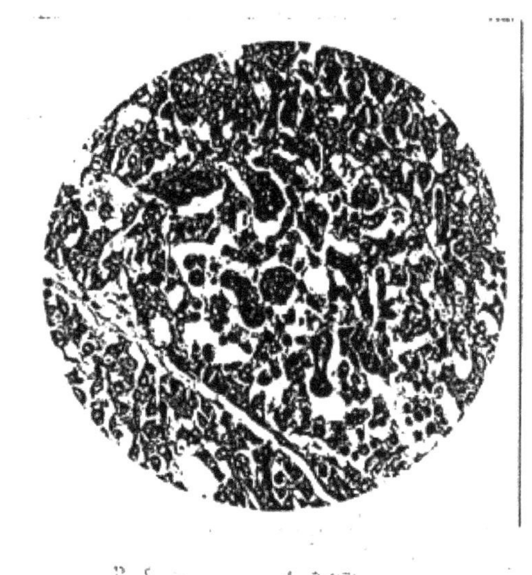

Degeneration of nervous bundle.

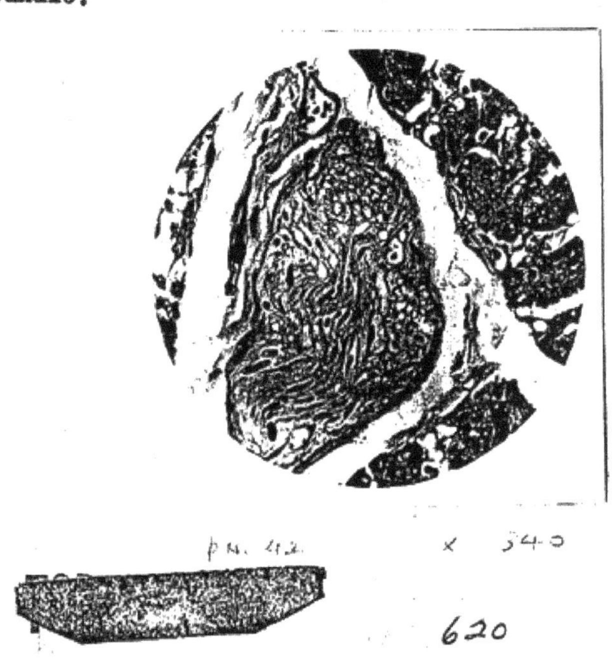

620

Perivascular round cell
infiltration.

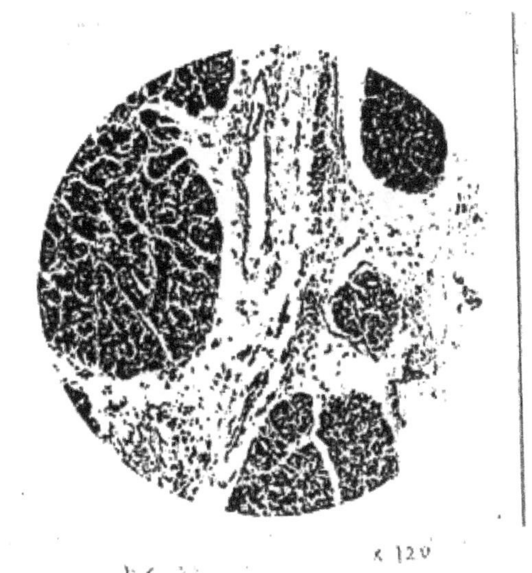

Perivascular round cell
infiltration.

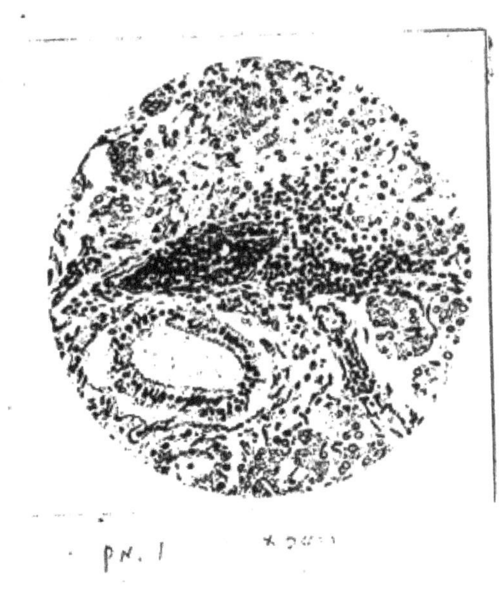

621

Suprarenal

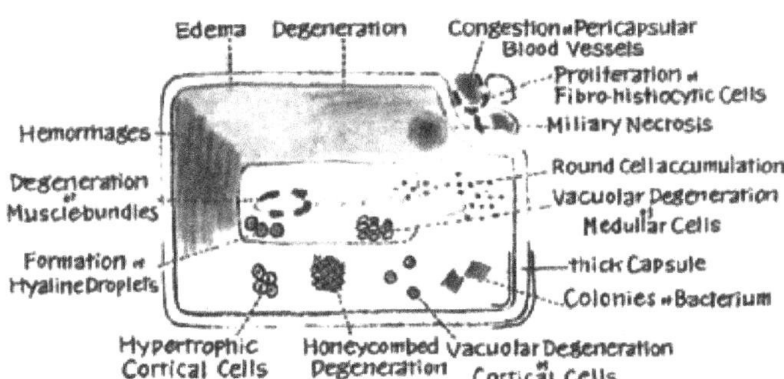
Edema
Degeneration
Congestion of Pericapsular Blood Vessels
Proliferation of Fibro-histiocytic Cells
Miliary Necrosis
Hemorrhages
Round Cell accumulation
Degeneration of Muscle bundles
Vacuolar Degeneration of Medullar Cells
Formation of Hyaline Droplets
thick Capsule
Colonies of Bacterium
Hypertrophic Cortical Cells
Honeycombed Degeneration
Vacuolar Degeneration of Cortical Cells

632

SUPRA-RENAL GLAND

A) Microscopical Investigation.

1.

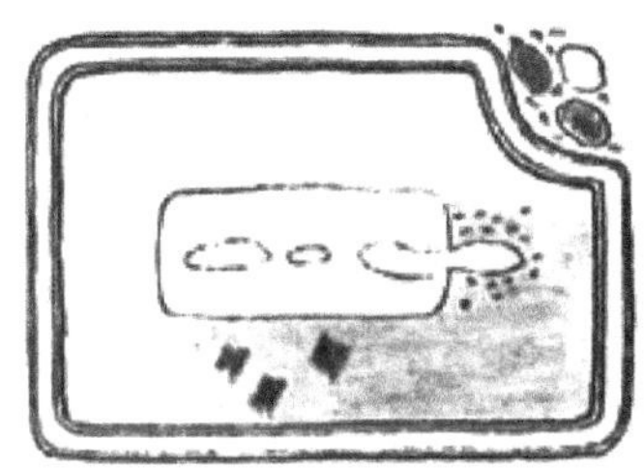

With thick capsules.

Epinephritis seros III : considerable atrophia, dissociation and remarkable degeneration of cortical cells, accompanied with confused arrangements of capillaries, due to serous exudation and edematous swelling of capillary walls.

Considerable reduction of Z.glomerulosa.

Some round-cell-accumulation in Z. reticularis, esp. around central veins and some bacterial embolus in coritcal capillaries.

2.

Remarkable degenerated cortical cells in 2 types :
a) bright and more or less swollen protoplasma with bright nuclei and b) eosinophilic and more or less smaller protoplasma with chromatin-rich nuclei.

Honeycombed degeneration of some cortical cells.

Severe congestion in all layers of cortical tissues, esp. in Z. reticularis and at some places of medullar tisses.

623

Considerable hemorrhages in Z. reticularis and edematous swelling of muscle-fibres of central vein-walls. Some bacillus-embolus in cortical capillaries.

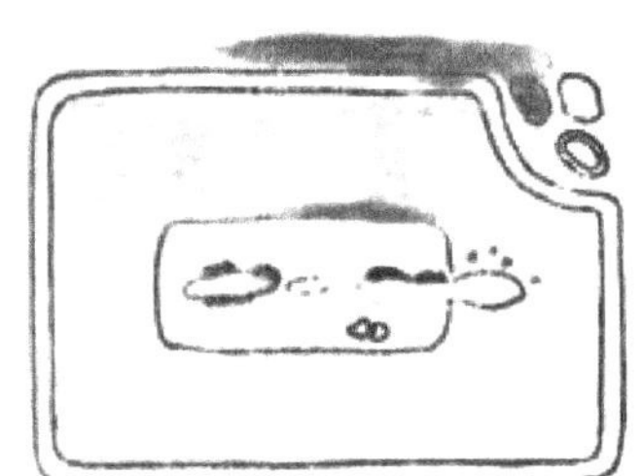

3.

Atrophia and dissociation of cortical cells and hemorrhages with slight small-round-cell-accumulation in Z.

reticuaris, esp. around central veins.

5.

Some blood-vessels with some desquamated endothelial cells in pericapsular tissues.

Remarkable fat-deposits at some places of cortical tissues.

Atrophia, dissociation and degeneration of cortical cells, accompanied with multiple localised hemorrhages in Z. fasciculata and Z. reticularis and bionecrotic ruins of adjacenty cortical cells.

6.

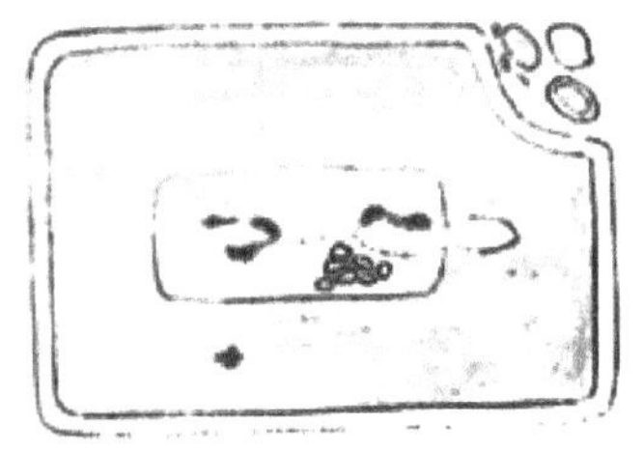

Considerable clouding of cortical cells with chromatin-rich or pycnotic nuclei. Cellular arrangements of cortical cells with remarkable

624

lumina-formation in Z. fasciculata.

Edematous swelling of muscle-fibres of central vein-walls and some bacterial dissemination in cortical tissues.

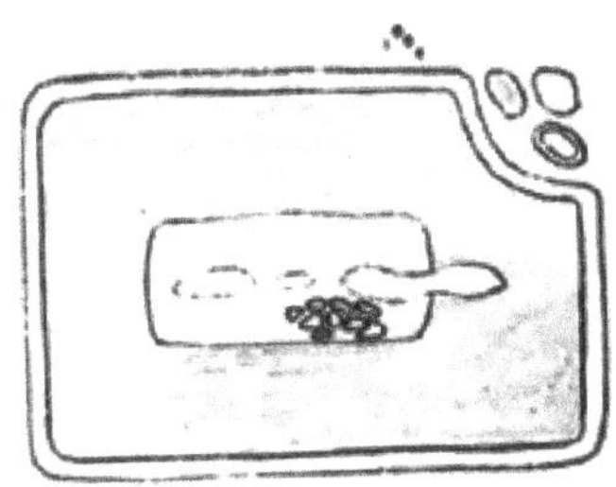

IO.

Many degenerated cortical cells with chromatin-rich nuclei.

Remarkable congestion in Z. reticularis and edematous swelling of muscle fibres of central vein-walls.

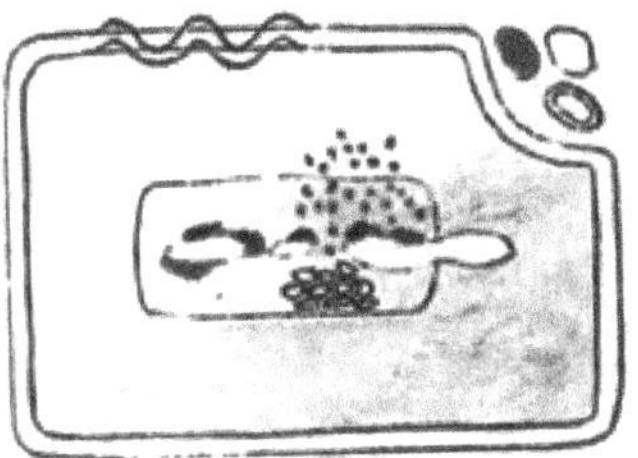

II.

Atrophic capsules with some folds formation.

Clouding of cortical cells with many more or less intense nuclear changes (pycnosis, karyorrhexis and karyolysis) in Z. reticularis.

Medullar cell in ruining processes with some nuclear changes : karyorrhexis etc.

Plasma-cells-accumulation around medullary capillaries and intense degeneration of muscles fibres of central vein walls.

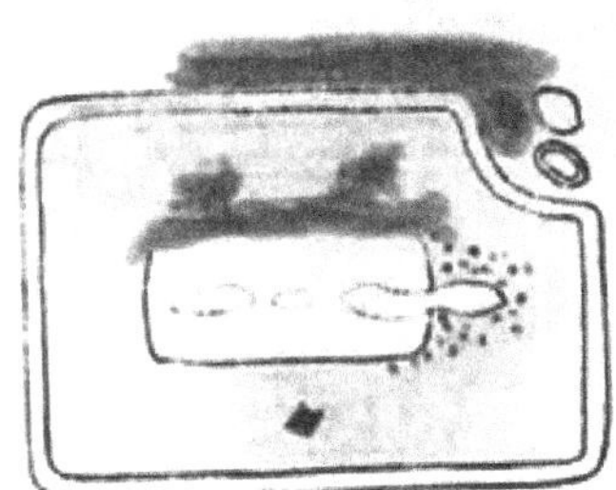

I2.

Epinephritis serosa II.

Hemorrhages in Z. fasciculata and Z. reticularis.

Small-round-cell-accumulation in Z. reticularis.

625

esp. around central veins. Some bacillus embolus in cortical capillaries.

I4.

Epinephritis serosa II or III (partially).
Remarkable hemorrhages in Z. reticulris and some, round-cells-accumulation in Z. reticularis, esp. around central veins.
Intense degeneration of muscle fibres of central vein-walls.

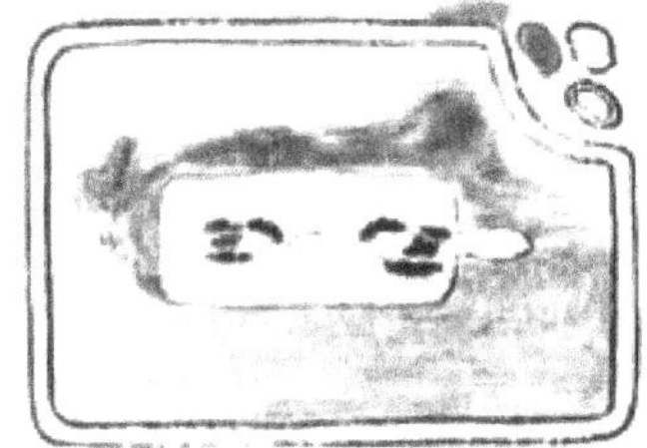

I5.

With some cell groups of hypertrophic cortical cells.
Diffuse hemorrhages in Z. reticularis and Z. fasciculata, accompanied with the ruining processes adjacent cortical cells.
Edematous swelling of muscle fibres of central vein-walls.
Some bacilus-embolus in cortical capillaries.

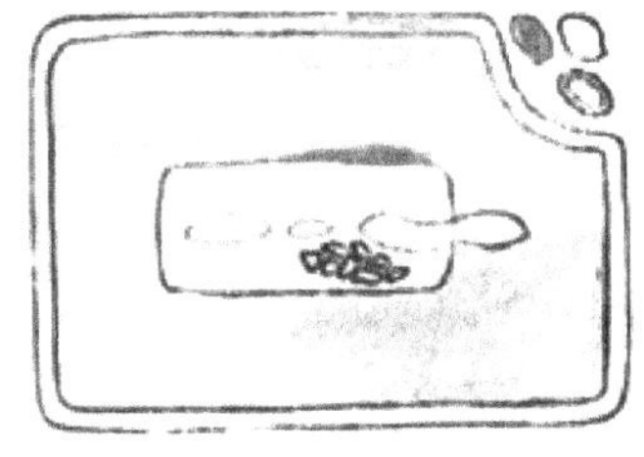

I6.

At some places, intense atrophia and degeneration of cortical cells with pycnotic nuclei.
Considerable congestion in Z. reticularis and Z. fasciculata (partially).

I7.

Diffuse congestion in Z. reticularis and Z. fasciculata and multiple localised in medullar

TOP SECRET

626

tissues.

Remarkable degeneration of muscle fibres of central vein-walls and some localised perivascular hemorrhages.

Degeneration of nervous cells, in medullar tissues and some bacillusembolus in cortical capillaries.

18.

Pericapsuler tissues with some blood-vessels, containing some bacillus and plenty of leucocytes.

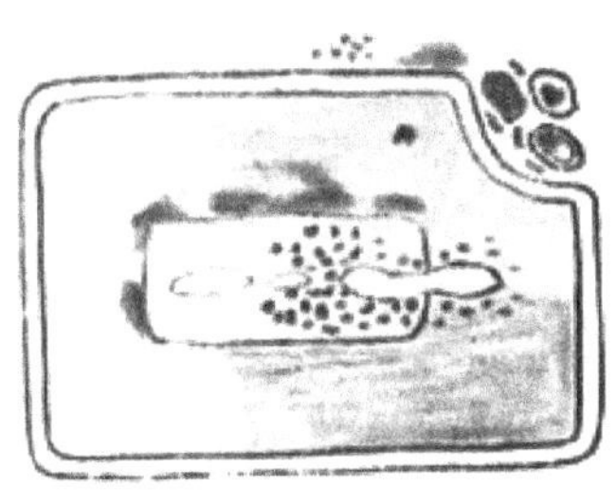

Remarkable degenerated cortical cells in 2 types, as described in No. 2.

Considerable congestion with some increased endothelial cells and some round-cell-accumulation in Z. reticularis and Z. fasciculata.

Remarkable round-cells-accumulation in medullar tissues.

Some bacillus-embolus in cortical capillaries.

19.

Degeneration of cortical cells with pycnotic nuclei and some honeycombed degeneration of cortical cells.

Considerable congestion in all layers of cortical tissues and some medullar tissues and some hemorrhagic places in cortical tissues.

Degeneration of muscle fibres of central vein-walls.

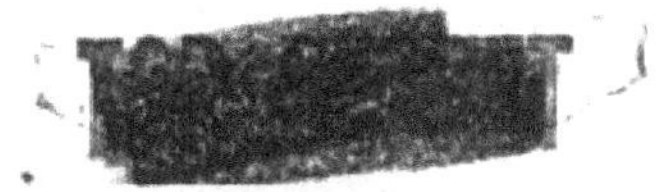

627

20.

Intense subcapsular congestion and Epinephritis serosa II : remarkable congestion with some increased epithelial cells and remarkable hemorrhages in Z. fasciculata and Z reticularis.

Edematous swelling and degeneration of muscle fibres of ~~cortical~~ central vein-walls.

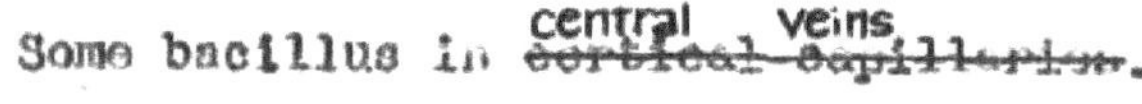

Some bacillus in ~~cortical capillaries~~ central veins.

21.

Epinephritis serosa II or III (partially).

Some hemorrhages in Z, reticularis and Z. fasciculta (partially).

Edematous swelling and degeneration of muscle fibres of central vein-walls.

23.

Many degenerated cotical cells with karyolytic nuclei.

Considerable congestion and some hemorrhages in Z. reticularis.

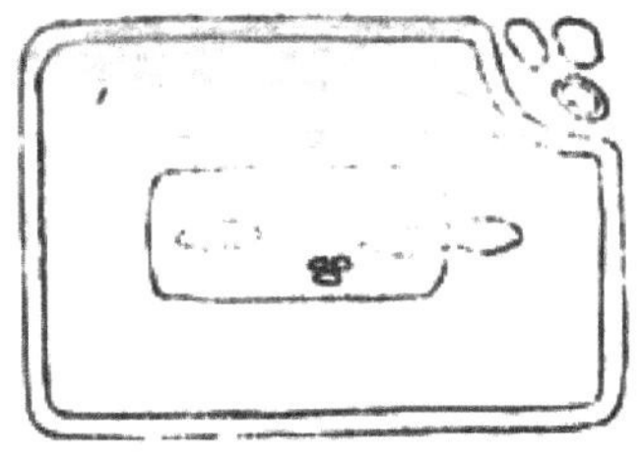

24.

Edema, atrophia, dissocciation and degeneration of cortical cells with pycnotic nuclei.

2C.

Remarkable degeneration of cortical cells in

629

2 types; as mentioned in No. 2 case.
Considerable congestion in Z. reticularis and Z. fasciculata, and some localised hemorrhages in Z. fasciculata.
Multiple small-round-cell-accumulation in Z. reticularis and degeneration of muscle fibres of central vein-walls.

Some bacillus in cortical capillarities.

29.

Epinephritis serosa II or III (a partially).
Multiple honeycombed degeneration in Z. fasciculata and intense diffuse hemorrhages in Z. reticularis, accompanied with small-round-cell-accumulation in Z. fasciculata, etc.

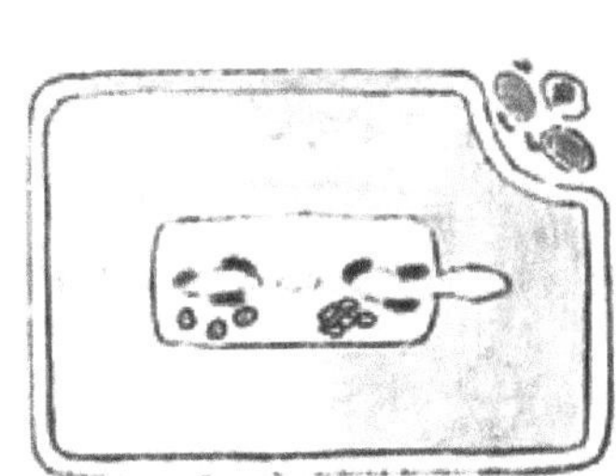

30.

Epinephritis serosa II.
Intense degeneration of nervous cells in medullar tissues and degeneration of muscle fibres of central vein-walls.

31.

Many degenerated cortical cells with chromatin-rich nuclei.
Intense congestion and some homorrhages in subcapsular cortical and medullar tissues.

629

32.

Epinephritis serasa II or III (partially).

Some hemorrhages in Z. reticularis and some bacillus in cortical capillaries.

33.

Atrophic capsules with folds formation.

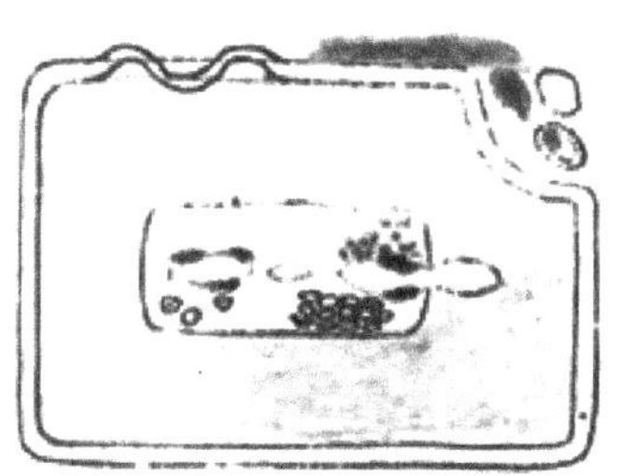

Many degenerated cortical cells with pycnotic or chromatin-rich nuclei.

Some round-cell-accumulation in medullar tissues, esp. around central veins.

Considerable degeneration of muscle fibres of central vein-walls.

34.

Epinehritis serosa II (partially).

Some hemorrhages in Z. reticularis and remarkable small-round-cell (containing some plasma-cells)-accumulation in medullar tissues.

Some degenerated nervous cells.

35.

Some degenerated cortical cells with chromatin-rich or pynotic nuclei.

Intense congestion and some hemorrhages in Z. reticularis and edematous swelling of muscle fibres

630

of central vein-walls.

36.

Epinephritis serosa II or III (partially).

Diffuse hemorrhages in Z. reticularis and Z. fasciculata.

38.

Many degenerated cortical cells with chromatin-rich or pycnotic nuclei.

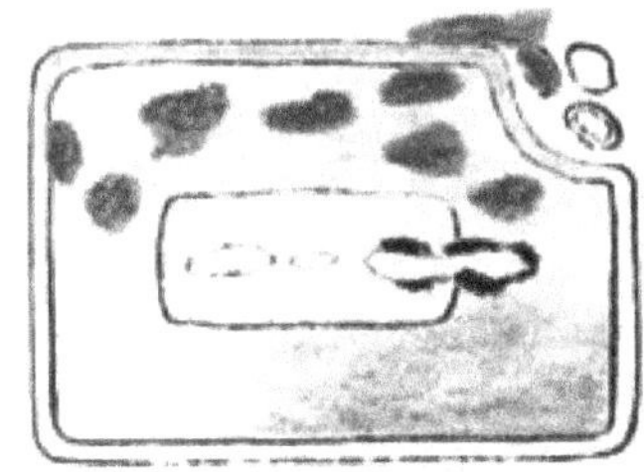

Multiple localised, intense hemorrhages in subcapsular and fascicular tissues.

Edema and some degeneration of muscle fibres of central vein-walls.

40.

Epinephritis serosa II with intense edema of cortical tissues.

Some hemorrhages in Z. reticularis and multiple round-cell-accumulation in Z. reticularis and Z. fasciculata.

Remarkable hyaline-droplets formation in medullar tissues.

42.

Epinephritis serosa II.

Honeycombed degeneration in Z. fasciculata.

631

Multiple localised hemorrhages in Z. reticularis and Z. fasciculata with some small-round-cell-accumulation in Z. reticulris, esp. around central veins.

Intense degeneration (hyaline degneration or intense swelling) of muscle fibres of central vein-walls.

47.

Binephritis serosa II.

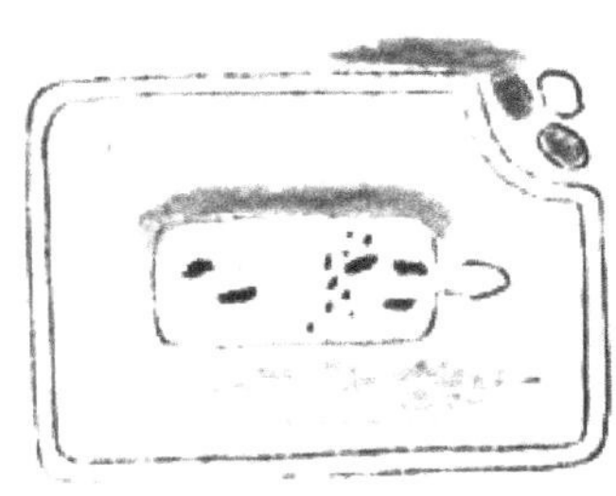

Honeycombed degeneration of medullar cells and more or less remarkable swelling and edema of muscle-fibres of central vein-walls.

Some bacillus-embolus in subcapsular capillaries and some laucocytos accumulation in cortical capillaries.

49.

Epinephritis serosa III.

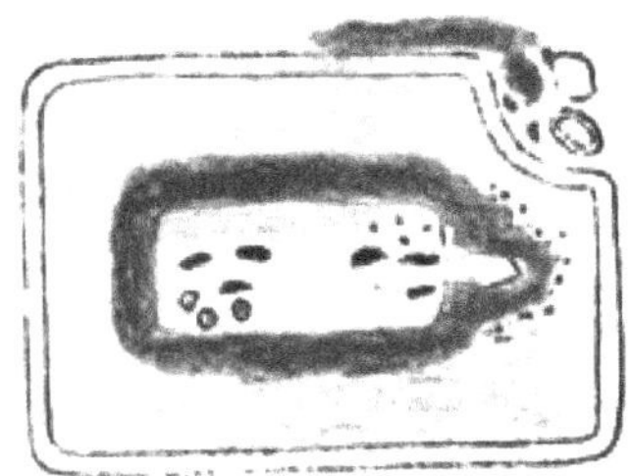

Hyaline degeneration of blood-vessel-walls ~~and~~ of perivascular tissues. (vascular corrected to caps)

Diffuse, intense hemorrhages in Z. reticularis and some round cell-accumulation in Z. reticularis.

Anisonuclei of medullar cells and somewhat degeneration of muscle fibres of central vein-walls.

632

S-I.

Many degenerated cortical cells in 2 types, as mentioned in No. 2 case.

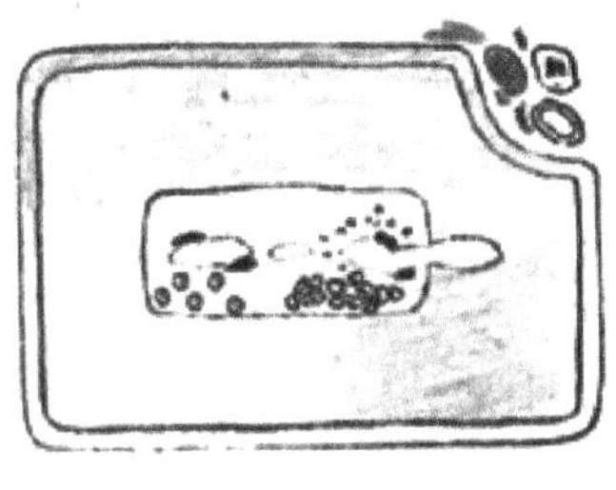

Remarkable congestion and dilatation of subcapsular capillaries with some bacterial masses, some leucocytes, some lymphocytes and some monocytes in capillaries.

Some considerable congestion (with some increased endothelial cells) of cortical capillaries and some small-round-cell-accumulation in medullar tissues, esp. around central veins.

Some degeneration of muscle fibres of central vein walls.

S-2.

Many degenerated cortical cells in 2 types, as mentioned in No. 2 case.

Remarkable congestion at some places of subcapsular capillaries and considerable congestion in Z. reticularis, esp. around central-veins.

S-4.

Considerable leucocytes-and monocytes-accumulation in pericapsular and subcapsular capillaries and considerable edema in cortical tissues.

Some increase of endothelial cells of cortical

633

capillaries and scattered plasma-cells dissemination in cortical tissues.

Considerable leucocytes-and monocytes-accumulation in small blood-vessels of medullar tissues with some plasma-cells and some round-cells accumulation in medullar tissues.

Honeycombed degeneration of medullar cells. Considerable edema and degeneration of muscle fibres of central vein-walls.

Some bacillus-embolus in ~~medullar~~ cortical capillaries.

S-5.

Many degenerated cortical cells in 2 types, as mentioned in No. 2 case.

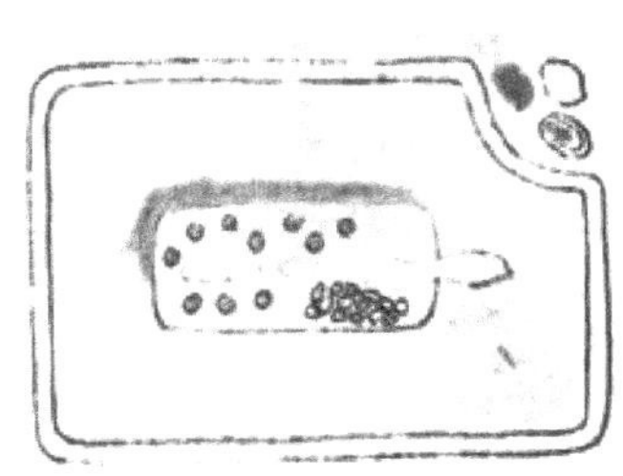

Considerable fatty deposits at some plases of cortical tissues.

Considerable congestion and some hemorrhages in Z. retcularis (with some leucocytes and monocytes accumulation as capillary contents) and in Z. fasciculata.

S-8.

Atrophia, clouding and degeneration of cortical cells (some of them in remarkable brown pigments atrophia).

Remarkable hyperplasia of capillar endothelial cells.

-634

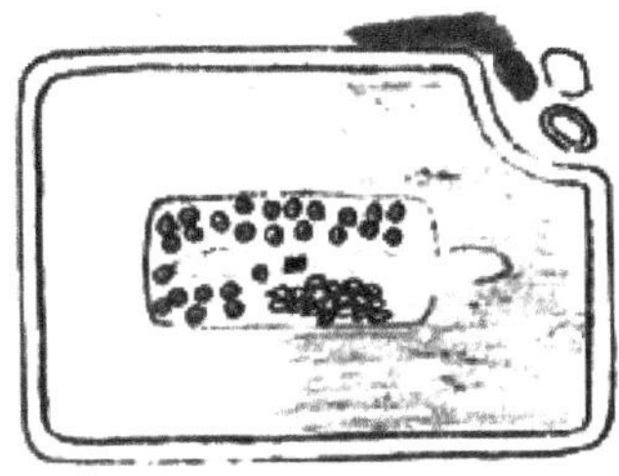

Intense hyaline droplets formation in medullar tissues and some bacillus-embolus in medullar capillaries, accompanied with some perivascular leucocytes and some lymphocytes accumulations.

S-9.

Swelling of capsules and considerable congestion of subcapsular tissues.

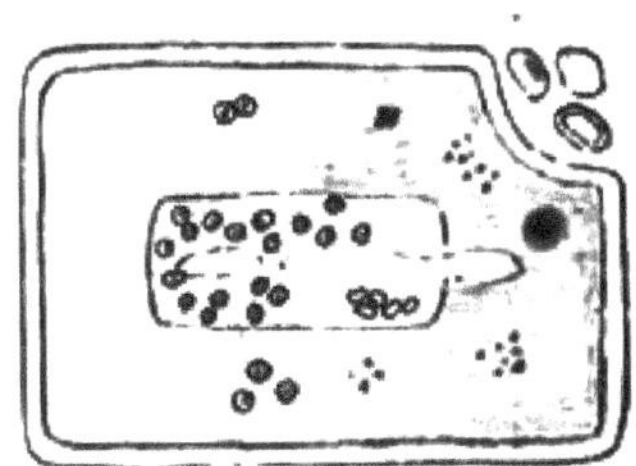

Many degenerated cortical cells with pycnotic nuclei and some vacuolar degeneration of cortical cells or some places in slight honeycombed degeneration.

Some miliar bionecrotic places in Z. fasciculata and some cell groups of hypertrophic cortical cells.

Considerable increase of endothelial cells of cortical capillaries.

Remarkable hyaline-droplets formation in medullar tissues and some bacterial masses in cortical capillaries.

S-10.

[illegible] 11:

Considerable congestion with some increased endothelial cells and some haemorrhages in Z. fasciculata and Z. reticularis, accompanied with some

635

small-round-cells accumulation in Z. reticularis and Z. glomerulosa.

Some anisonuclei of medullar cells and some bacterial masses in cortical capillaries.

S-11.

Considerable fatty deposits at some places of cortical tissues and multiple localised, more or less diffuse hemorrhages in all layers of cortical tissues, accompanied with some bacterial dissemination and following bionecrotic ruins of cortical cells.

Some small-round-cell accumulation in all layers of cortical tissues and medullar tissues.

S-14.

Subcapsular congestion and many degenerated cortical cells in 2 types, as described in No. 2 case or furthermore some vacuolar degeneration of cortical cells.

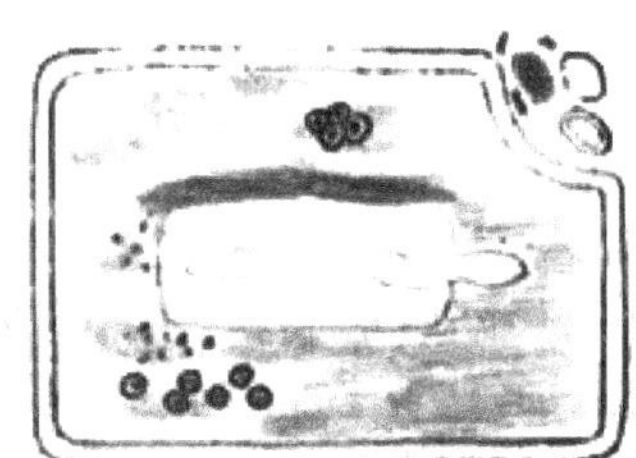

Considerable congestion (with some leucocytes accumulation in capillaries, some of them eosinophilic) in all layers of cortical tissues and some perivascular hemorrhages in Z. reticularis, accompanied with some small-round-cell accumulation (containing some eosinophilic leucocytes) in Z. reticularis.

636

S-I5.

Epinephritis serosa II.

Many leucocytes in cortical capillaries and some hemorrhages in Z.reticularis with some increased endothelial cells.

Some round-cell-accumulation in Z. reticularis and edematous swelling of muscle fibres of central vein-walls.

S-22.

Remarkable histiocytes-accumulation at some places of capsules and considerable subcapsular congestion.

Some considerable fatty deposits at some places of Z. glomerulosa and some cell groups of hypertrophic cortical cells.

Considerable congestion in Z. fasciculata (partially at some places) and Z. reticularis (all over the tissues), accompanied some hemorrhages in Z. reticularis.

Remarkable hyperplasia of capillar endothelial cells (some of them in erythrophagy) in cortial capillaries.

Considerable swelling and degeneration of muscle fibres of central vein-walls.

637

S-26.

Many degenerated cortical cells in 2 types, as mentioned in No. 2 case.
Some localised hemorrhages in Z. reticularis with some inreased endothelial cells, of capillaries.
Considerable fatty deposits at some places of cortical tissues and considerable medullar congestion.

S-28.

Considerable swelling of capsule and subcapsular congestion.
Epinephritis serosa II or III (partially).
Considerable hemorrhages in Z. fasciculata and some fatty deposits at some places of Z. fasciculata.
Severe edematous swelling and degeneration of muscle fibres of central vein-walls and some bacillus-embolus in cortical capillaries.

638

(B) S U M M A R Y .

Histological investigation of 45 micro-slices.

Pericapsular, tissues :

Generally with considerable congestion and somewhat perivascular hemorrhages (17 cases in medium degree).

Leucocytes or lymphocytes emigration, scarecely.

Some histiocytes accumulation in chronic course. (No. S-22).

Capsules :

Generally with edematous swelling (2 cases of them in severe degree).

Some cases with slight hemorrhages and cell infiltration.

Cortex:

Generally with remarkable diminution of fatty contents in cortical cell-protoplasma (splitting of fatty drops and protoplasma with dark and homogenous tone) and some cases with considerable fatty deposits in some cortical cell groups.

With hypertrophic cell groups in 6 cases of more or less chronic course.

With vacuolar degeneration (Dietrich's) in 5 cases.

With slight honeycombed degeneration (Dietrich's) in 7 cases.

Cell arrangements with lumina-formation. in 28 cases.

in severe degree in 2 cases of them.

639

With degenerated cortical cells in 2 types : a) bright and more or less swollen protoplasma with bright nuclei and b) eosinophilic and more or less smaller protoplasma with chromatin-rich nuclei.

in 8 cases.

With degenerated cortical cells with remarkable pycnotic or hyperchromatic nuclei,

in I4 cases.

with miliary necrocis. in I cases.

Generally with considerable edema of cortical tissues.

in slight degree.	in	6	cases.
in medium degree.	in	29	cases.
in severe degree.	in	9	cases.

By classification of all cases, according to concept " Epinephritis serosa " :

Epinephritis serosa I.	in	27	cases.
II.	in	I5	cases.
III.	in	2	cases.

In most cases with some congestion in subcapsular or reticular tissues and in several cases with remarkable congestion in all layers of cortical tissues.

With many leucocytes as capillary contents.	in	7	cases.
With many lymphocytes as capillary contents.	in	2	cases.

TOP SECRET

640

C [redacted]

with some bacterial masses in capillaries, without any cell-reaction). in 6 cases.

With some hyperplasied endothelial cells (esp. capillaries of reticular tissues). in I4 cases.

With more or less considerable hemorrhages (esp in Z. reticularis). in almost cases.

in medium degree in 8 cases.

in severe degree in 22 ccases.

With multiple localised (sharply bounded) hemorrhages. in a few cases.

With localised small-round-cell-accumulation (mainly in Z. reticularis). in I8 cases.

Medullar tissues : (34 cases)

Generally with some edema.

With vacuolar degeneration. in all cases, except I cases.

With hyaline droplets formation of medullar cells. in 28 cases

Items :

in slight degree. 9 cases.

in medium degree. I2 cases.

in severe degree. 7 cases.

With anisonuclei of medullar cells. in a few cases.

With considerable small-round-cell-accumulation. in II cases.

(With plasma-cells accumulation in I cases.).

TOP SECRET 641

Generally with some changes of muscle fibres of central vein-walls(edematous swelling, hyaline or sometimes vacuolar degeneration, and fragmentation).

With more or less considerable degeneration of nervous cells. in some cases.

642

SUPRARENAL

			N 1	N 2	N 3	N 5	N 8	N 10	N 11	N 12	N 14	N 15	N 16	N 17	N 18	N 19	N 20	N 21	N 23	N 24	N 26	N 29	N 30	N 31	N 32
Serous Inflammation			III	I	I	I	I	I	I	II	II	I	I	I	I	I	II	II	I	I	I	II	II	I	II
Pericapsular Tissues	Congestion		+·	++	+	++	÷	÷	+	+	++	+	+	+·	+·	+·	++	+	++	÷	+	+·	++	++	++
Pericapsular Tissues	Hemorrhage		(÷)	++	++	÷	(÷)	(÷)	÷	++·	++	÷	÷	+++	÷	++	+	+	++	÷	÷	÷	÷	++	+
Pericapsular Tissues	Infiltration	Leucocytes	—	—	—	—	÷	—	—	+·	—	—	—	÷	—	—	—	—	÷	—	—	—	—	—	—
Pericapsular Tissues	Infiltration	Lymphocytes	÷	(÷)	÷	(÷)	÷	(+)	—	÷	(+)	÷	÷	(÷)	+	÷	(÷)	÷	÷	÷	(÷)	÷	÷	÷	÷
Pericapsular Tissues	Infiltration	Histiocytic Cells	++	÷	÷	÷	+	÷	÷	÷	(+++)	÷	÷	++	+	÷	÷	÷	÷	÷	÷	+	+	÷	÷
Capsule	Edema		÷	(+)	÷	÷	÷	÷	÷	+	÷	+	÷	+	÷	+	++	++	÷	++	++	+	+·	++	÷
Capsule	Hemorrhage		(÷)	÷	÷	—	÷	(÷)	—	÷	(÷)	—	—	÷	÷	÷	—	÷	÷	—	÷	÷	—	++	—
Capsule	Cellular Infiltration		+	÷	÷	—	—	÷	—	—	(÷)	÷	—	÷	—	—	—	—	—	—	—	÷	—	—	—
Cortical Parenchyma	Decrease of Fat		+++	++·	+++	++	++·	++·	+++	+++	++·	++	++	+·	++·	++	+++	+++	+++	+++	++·	+++	+++	+++	+++
Cortical Parenchyma	Atrophia		++	÷	++	(+)	+	÷	—	++·	(+++)	(+++)	+	+	÷	+	++·	+++	÷	+	÷	++·	++·	÷	+++
Cortical Parenchyma	Hypertrophia		—	—	—	—	—	—	÷	—	—	—	(+)	—	—	÷	—	—	—	—	—	—	—	—	—
Cortical Parenchyma	Dissociation		++·	÷	++	(+++)	÷	—	—	+++	++·	÷	÷	÷	÷	—	++·	++·	—	+·	÷	++·	+++	÷	+++
Cortical Parenchyma	Splitting of Lipoid-drops (Dietrich)		+++	++·	+++	++	++·	++·	+++	+++	+++	(+++)	(++·)	+	++·	++·	+++	+++	++·	+++	++·	+++	+++	+++	++·
Cortical Parenchyma	Vacuolar Degeneration (")		—	÷	—	—	—	—	(÷)	—	—	—	—	—	—	—	—	—	—	—	—	—	—	(÷)	—
Cortical Parenchyma	Honeycombed Degenerat (")		—	++	(÷)	—	—	—	—	—	—	—	—	—	÷	(+)	—	—	—	—	—	++	—	—	—
Cortical Parenchyma	Lumina Formation		÷	÷	÷	÷	++	÷	÷	—	÷	—	—	÷	÷	÷	÷	÷	—	—	—	—	—	+	—
Cortical Parenchyma	Brown Pigment		++	÷	+	÷	++·	+	(++)	÷	÷	—	÷	÷	÷	÷	÷	(+++)	+·	—	+	÷	÷	—	+
Cortical Parenchyma	Changes of Nuclei	Pyknosis	÷	+·	÷	÷	(+++)	++	+	÷	÷	+	÷	÷	++	++	÷	÷	÷	÷	+	+	÷	+	÷
Cortical Parenchyma	Changes of Nuclei	Karyolysis	++	+·	÷	÷	+	+·	++	+	+·	+·	+	+·	+	÷	+	+	+·	÷	÷	+	÷	÷	+·
Cortical Parenchyma	Changes of Nuclei	Disappearance	++	÷	÷	+	+·	+	÷	+	+	÷	+	+·	÷	÷	+	+·	÷	÷	÷	++·	+	÷	+·
Cortical Interstice	Edema		++	+·	++	++	++	++	÷	++	++	++	++	+	++	++	+++	++·	+·	+·	++	++	++·	++	++
Cortical Interstice	Congestion of Subcapsular Blood V.		÷	++·	÷	+	÷	+	+	÷	÷	+	+	+·	+	++	+++	÷	÷	÷	+·	+·	—	++	÷
Cortical Interstice	Contents	Erythrocytes	|	+++	+	+	÷	++	++	++	÷	+·	+	+·	+·	(++·)	++	+	+·	÷	+	+·	|	++·	÷
Cortical Interstice	Contents	Leucocytes	|	÷	(÷)	—	÷	(÷)	—	÷	—	÷	÷	(÷)	÷	—	÷	÷	÷	(÷)	—	÷	(÷)	÷	—
Cortical Interstice	Contents	Lymphocytes	|	÷	(÷)	÷	÷	+	÷	+	(÷)	+	÷	÷	÷	÷	÷	÷	+	÷	÷	÷	(+)	÷	÷
Cortical Interstice	Contents	Monocytes	|	÷	(+)	÷	÷	÷	(÷)	÷	(÷)	÷	÷	÷	÷	÷	÷	÷	÷	÷	÷	—	(+)	÷	÷
Cortical Interstice	Hemorrhage		|	++	+	++	÷	÷	÷	++	++·	÷	++·	+·	++	+·	+++	+·	+	(÷)	++	+++	|	+++	+
Cortical Interstice	Circumscribed Round Cell Infilt.		+·	—	÷	—	—	÷	+	+·	+	—	÷	÷	+	—	÷	÷	÷	—	+·	+	(÷)	—	—
Cortical Interstice	Hyperplasia of Vessel Wall Cells		—	—	÷	÷	÷	÷	÷	—	—	÷	÷	—	+	÷	+	÷	÷	÷	÷	+	÷	÷	÷
Cortical Interstice	Bacterium		++	+	—	—	÷	—	—	+	—	—	—	+	÷	—	÷	—	—	÷	+	—	—	—	÷
Medulla	Parenchyma	Hyalin-drops	|	+	—	|	—	÷	÷	|	÷	÷	—	(÷)	÷	÷	—	÷	|	÷	(++)	÷	+	++·	|
Medulla	Parenchyma	Vacuolar Degen.	|	++·	+	|	++	++	++	|	+	++	+	÷	÷	+	+	+·	|	+	++·	(+)	+·	++·	|
Medulla	Edema		|	+	+	|	+	+	+	|	+·	+	+·	+·	+	++	++	++	|	+	+·	÷	+	++	|
Medulla	Congestion		|	(+++)	÷	|	÷	÷	++	|	÷	+	÷	+	÷	(++)	+	÷	|	—	++	÷	—	++	|
Medulla	Hemorrhage		|	÷	(÷)	|	÷	÷	÷	|	÷	—	—	(+)	÷	÷	÷	÷	|	—	÷	÷	—	+	|
Medulla	Circumscribed Round Cell Infiltration		|	÷	÷	|	÷	÷	(+·)	|	÷	—	÷	÷	++	—	+·	÷	|	—	÷	÷	÷	+	|

643

SUPRARENAL

			N 33	N 34	N 35	N 36	N 38	N 40	N 42	N 47	N 49	S 1	S 2	S 4	S 5	S 8	S 9	S 10	S 11	S 14	S 15	S 22	S 26	S 28
Serous Inflammation			I	II	I	II	I	II	II	II	III	I	I	I	I	I	I	II	I	−	II	I	I	II
Pericapsular Tissues	Congestion		+:	+	++	+	+	++	++	++	+	+	++	+:	+:	+	÷	++:	++	+	÷	++	÷	++:
	Hemorrhage		+	++:	÷	++	+	÷	++	+	+	÷	+:	(∸)	÷	+	∸	+:	++:	∸	+:	+:	∸	++
	Infiltration	Leucocytes	−	÷	−	(∸)	−	−	−	−	−	−	−	−	−	∸	−	−	(+)	−	∸	(∸)	−	−
		Lymphocytes	∸	∸	÷	∸	(÷)	∸	∸	∸	÷	÷	−	++	(+)	∸	∸	(+)	÷	÷	∸	∸	∸	∸
		Histiocytic Cells	+	÷	+:	÷	∸	÷	÷	÷	+	+	÷	÷	∸	÷	∸	++	∸	+	÷	+:	∸	∸
Capsule	Edema		+:	++	++	÷	++	+	++	+++	+	++	÷	++	÷	÷	∸	+	+	∸	+:	∸	+++	∸
	Hemorrhage		−	÷	∸	∸	÷	∸	∸	÷	∸	÷	∸	−	∸	−	∸	−	−	∸	÷	+	∸	∸
	Cellular Infiltration		−	−	(÷)	−	−	∸	−	−	−	−	−	−	∸	−	−	∸	−	∸	÷	+	∸	∸
Cortical Parenchyma	Decrease of Fat		++	++	++:	++:	+:	+++	++:	+++	+++	+++	+++	++:	++	+++	+++	++:	(++)	+++	+++	++:	++:	++:
	Atrophia		+	++	+	+++	+	+	+:	++	+++	÷	÷	+	+	(++:)	∸	(++:)	(++:)	−	++	∸	∸	++:
	Hypertrophia		−	−	−	−	−	−	−	−	−	−	−	(+)	−	−	∸	−	−	÷	−	÷	−	−
	Dissociation		−	+	∸	+++	−	÷	+:	+	+++	−	−	+:	∸	(+)	∸	++	+:	∸	++	−	−	(+++)
	Splitting of Lipoid-drops (Dietrich)		++:	++:	++:	++:	(++:)	+++	+++	++:	+++	+++	++:	+++	++	+++	+++	+++	+++	+++	+++	++:	++:	++:
	Vacuolar Degenerat. (〃)		−	−	−	−	−	−	−	−	−	−	−	−	−	−	÷	−	−	+	−	−	−	−
	Honeycombed Degen. (〃)		−	−	−	−	−	−	++	−	−	−	−	−	−	−	∸	−	−	−	−	−	−	−
	Lumina Formation		−	−	+	−	−	∸	++	∸	∸	∸	∸	(∸)	+	∸	÷	+	−	(∸)	−	∸	−	−
	Brown Pigment		∸	∸	÷	++	+	++	+	+	(++)	∸	−	++	+	++	+	+	+:	÷	∸	−	÷	++
	Changes of Nuclei	Pyknosis	+	∸	+:	−	++	÷	+:	+:	÷	++	+:	−	++	∸	+	∸	+	+:	∸	÷	++	÷
		Karyolysis	÷	+:	+	+:	+	+	+	+:	+:	÷	÷	+:	÷	+:	+:	+:	+	÷	+	+:	÷	+
		Disappearance	∸	÷	÷	+	+	(++)	+:	+:	+	∸	−	+:	÷	(+)	+	+	(÷)	÷	÷	∸	∸	+
Cortical Interstice	Edema		++	++	++:	++	++	++:	++:	+++	++	++	(++)	(++:)	++	+	+	++	+:	∸	++:	÷	++	++
	Congestion of Subcapsular Blood V.		+:	+:	++	+	+:	++	++	∸	+:	+++	(+++)	++:	+	++	+:	+:	++	++	+:	++	+	++
		Erythrocytes	(+)	+:	++:	1	++	++	+	÷	÷	+:	++:	+	++:	+	(+)	+	+	+	+:	++	+:	+
		Leucocytes	÷	(∸)	∸	−	(∸)	−	−	+	−	++	+	+	++	÷	÷	−	+	++	++	(∸)	(∸)	∸
		Lymphocytes	∸	÷	÷	÷	÷	÷	∸	÷	÷	+:	÷	÷	÷	∸	∸	∸	+:	÷	∸	÷	÷	÷
		Monocytes	∸	∸	÷	∸	∸	∸	∸	∸	∸	++	∸	+:	+	−	+	÷	∸	∸	÷	∸	(∸)	÷
	Hemorrhage		∸	+:	+	++	+++	++	++	+	++++	(∸)	∸	÷	+	∸	∸	+	+++	÷	+	+:	+:	+:
	Circumscribed Round Cell Infiltration		−	−	(+)	−	(÷)	++:	+	∸	+:	∸	+	∸	−	+	+:	+	++	+	+	∸	−	−
	Hyperplasia of Vessel Wall Cells		∸	+	+	∸	∸	∸	∸	∸	÷	+:	∸	+	∸	++	+	+	÷	+	+	(+)	+	÷
	Bacterium		−	−	−	−	−	−	−	−	−	−	−	−	−	−	−	−	−	−	−	−	−	−
Medulla	Parenchyma	Hyalin-drops	+	÷	∸	+	+	(+++)	+	−	+	+:	ǀ	∸	+:	+++	++:	∸	÷	ǀ	ǀ	−	+	ǀ
		Vacuolar Degen.	++	++	++	ǀ	ǀ	++:	++	−	÷	++	ǀ	+	++	++	+	+	∸	ǀ	ǀ	∸	++	ǀ
	Edema		++	++	+:	ǀ	ǀ	++:	++	÷	+	+	ǀ	+	+:	+	∸	÷	÷	ǀ	ǀ	÷	+:	ǀ
	Congestion		+	÷	+:	ǀ	ǀ	+	+	÷	+:	+	ǀ	+	+	+	(+:)	∸	÷	ǀ	ǀ	÷	++	ǀ
	Hemorrhage		−	(∸)	∸	ǀ	ǀ	−	÷	∸	÷	∸	ǀ	∸	∸	∸	∸	−	÷	ǀ	ǀ	∸	÷	ǀ
	Circumscribed Round Cell Infiltration		+	++	∸	ǀ	ǀ	÷	−	+	÷	+	ǀ	+	∸	÷	∸	+	++	ǀ	ǀ	∸	÷	ǀ

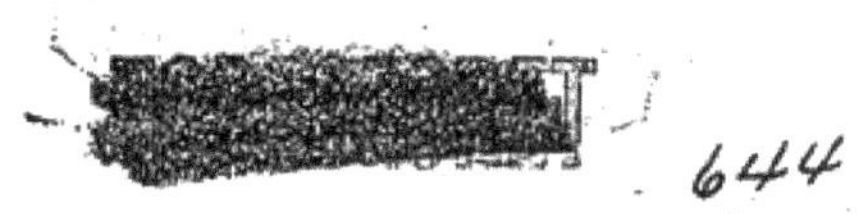

644

Some localised hemorrhages in cortical tissues.

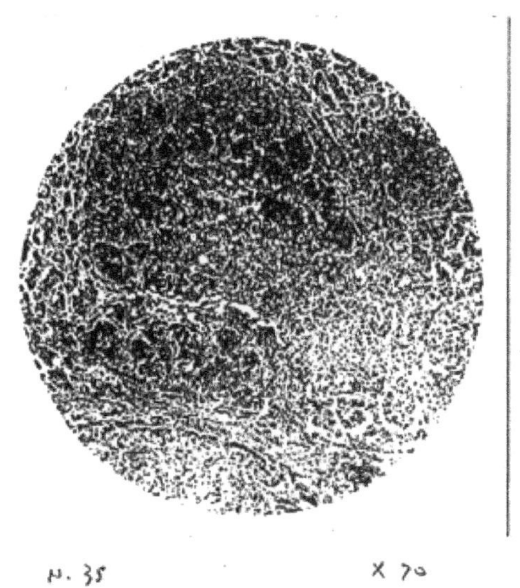

Diffuse hemorrhages in Z.reticularis.

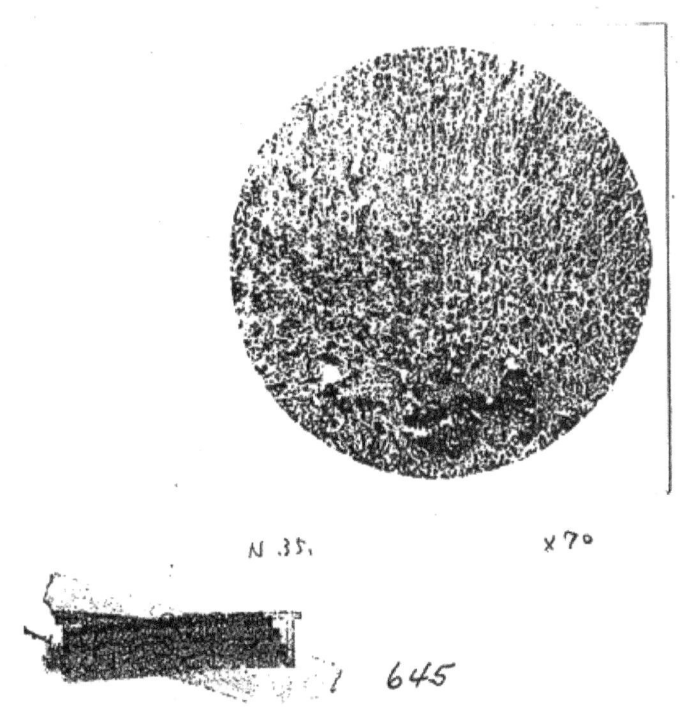

Epinephritis III.

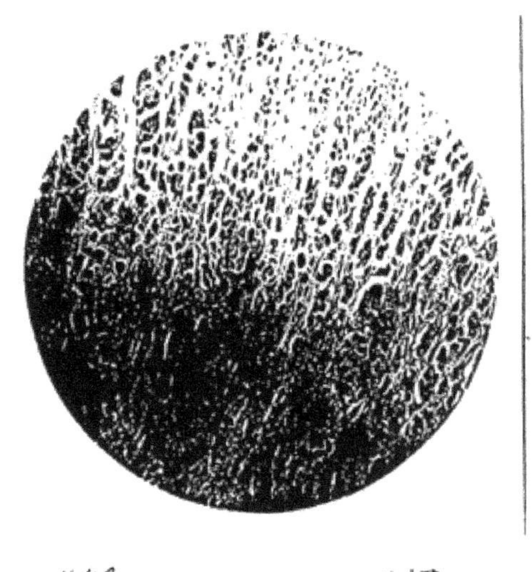

N 49.　　　× 150

Round cell dissemination in
cortical tissues.

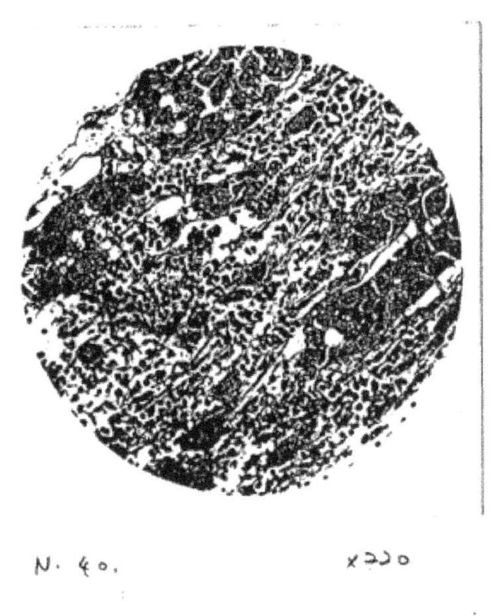

N. 40.　　　x220

646

Bacterial accumulation in capillary and intense degeneration of cortical cells.

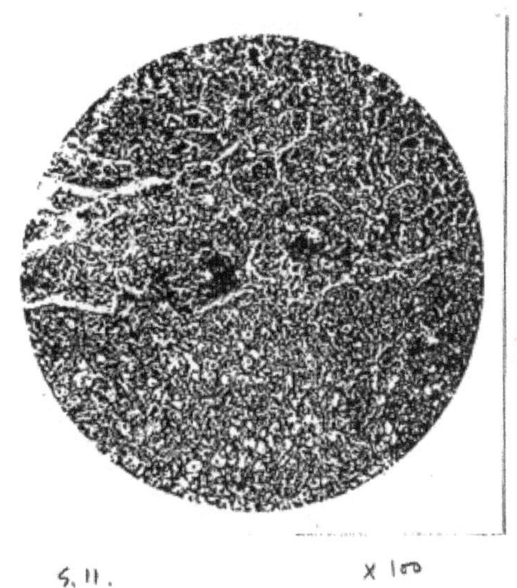

S. 11.　　x 100

Bacterial accumulation and some localised hemorrhages, accompanied with intense degeneration of cortical cells.

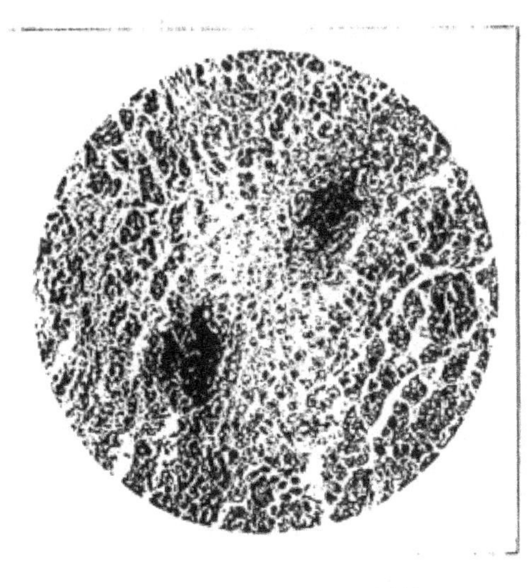

N. 1　　x 110

647

Honeycombed degeneration of cortical cells.

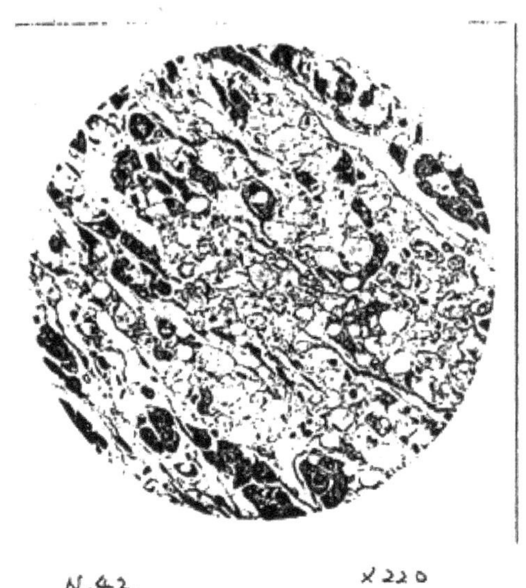

N.42. ×220

Intense degeneration of cortical cells, with our so-called 2 typed cells.

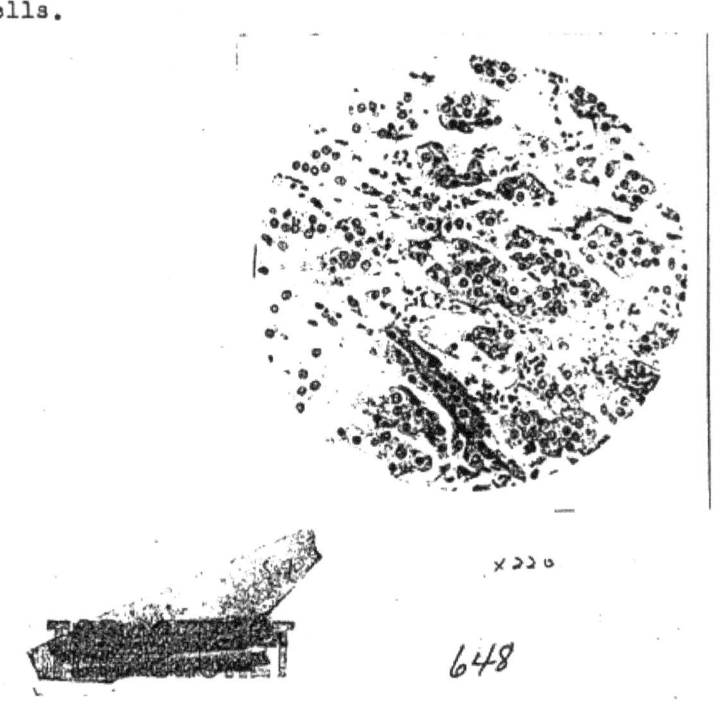

×220

648

Thyroid

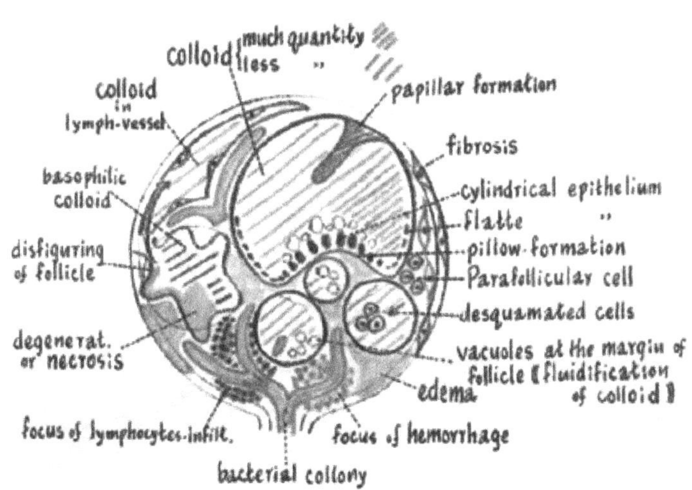
Colloid much quantity
less ,,
papillar formation
Colloid in lymph-vessel
fibrosis
basophilic colloid
cylindrical epithelium
flatte ,,
disfiguring of follicle
pillow-formation
Parafollicular cell
desquamated cells
degenerat. or necrosis
vacuoles at the margin of follicle (fluidification of colloid)
edema
focus of lymphocytes-infilt.
focus of hemorrhage
bacterial collony

649

THYROID.

(A) Microscop. Investigation.

1

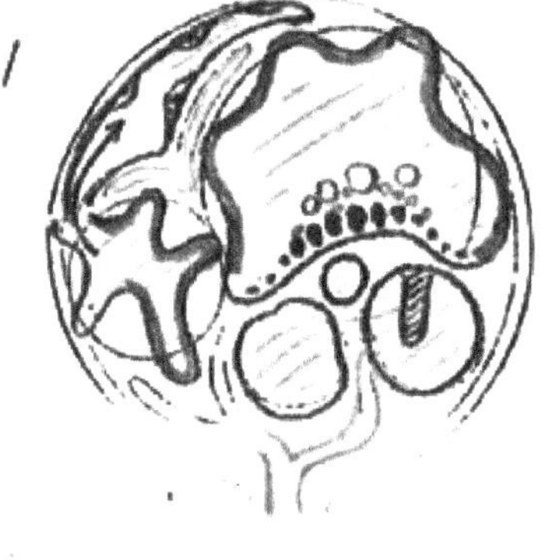

I.

Most of follicles are degenerative with some signs of follicular collapse. Slight colloidal accumulation in lymph-sinusoids.

At some places, rather regenerative with some pillow-like or papillar increase of epitheliums.

3

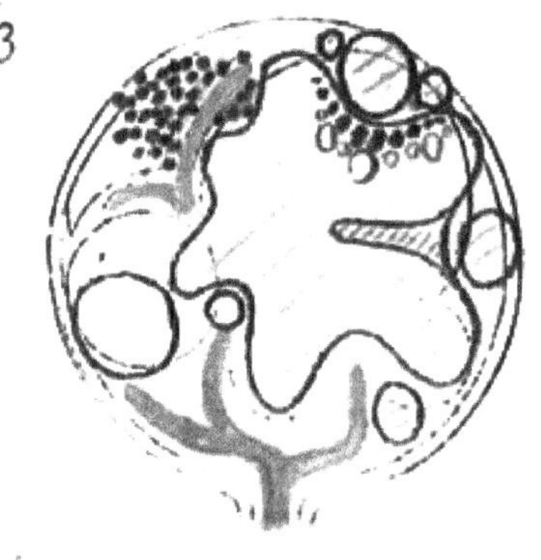

3.

Most of follicles are large or sacky dilatated and accompanied with many micro-follicles around them (so-called satellite-follicles). Here and there some pillow-like or papillar increase of epitheliums and considerable congestion and some round-cell-accumulation.

4

4.

Intense folliclar collapse. All follicles are small and their pycnotic epitheliums are dissociated or desquamated extremely.

Colloidal masses in follicles are fluidificated or could be rarely recognized.

Slight congestion and slight perivascular round-cell-Infiltration.

650

7 7.

Thyroid with many small follicles in collapse, all over the tissues: (flat, thin, pycnotic epithel cells and their dissociation or desquamation).

Colloidal masses are fluidificated or rarely recognized.

More or less considerable edema, swelling of capillary-walls (with some bacterial masses in capillaries), perivascular edema, congestion and slight round-cell-accumulation.

8.

Struma diffusa colloides proliferans(papillaris

.

Remarkable pillow-like or papillar increase of epitheliums with a large quantity of colloidal masses in caves and intense capillar congestion.

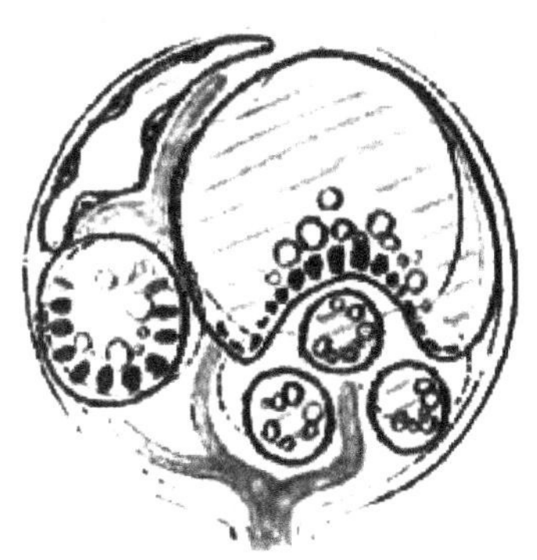

There is one lobulus with many small micro-follicles in activated state : with flat, cuboidal pitheliums , envolving many granules in cell-protoplasma and chromatin-rich nuclei.

Colloidal masses in these micro-follicles are fluidificated or rarely recognized, accompanied with some colloidal accumulation in lymphsinuseids. Considerable capillar congestion.

651

10

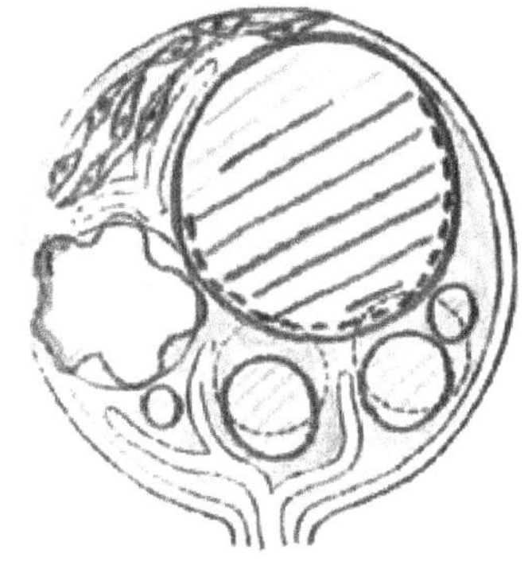

11

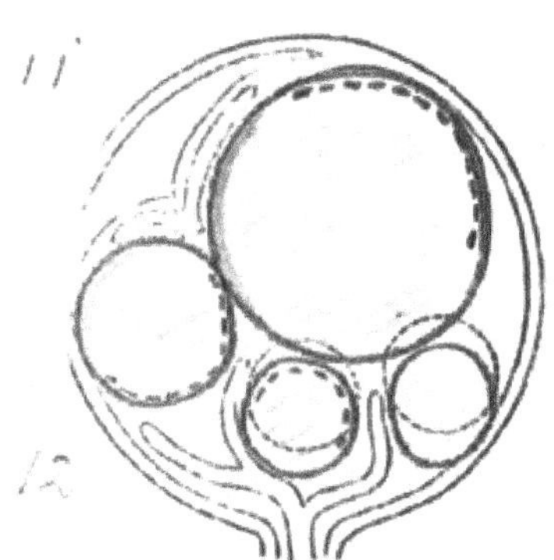

12

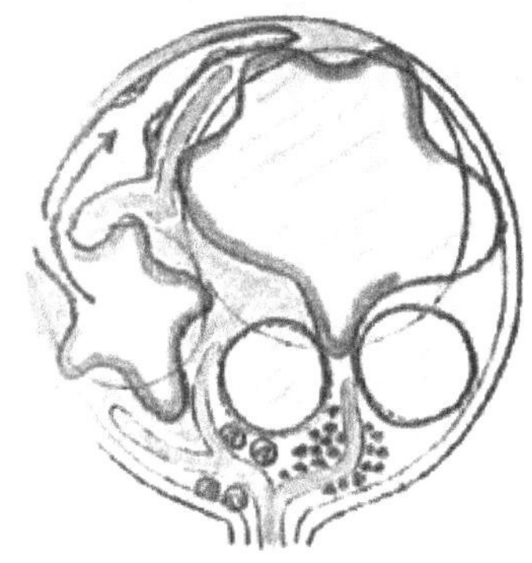

10.

Most of follicles with flat epitheliums and thick or basophilic colloidal masses. Some follicles are broken into many microfollicles with somewhat degenerated epitheliums and thick colloids.

~~Some increased connective tissues and edema.~~

Slight atrophy of follicles , slight fibrosis and edema.

11.

Atrophic follicles (in inactivitated state), with some slight degenerated epitheliums and thick colloidal masses.

12.

Thyroid in follicular collapse with somewhat degenerated epitheliums. (At some places, papillar increase of epitheliums).

Colloidal masses in lymphsinusoids and remarkeble edema.

Considerable congestion and some localised cell-infiltration (lymphocytes, leucocytes and their fragments).

14.

Follicles with pillow-like or papillar increase

652

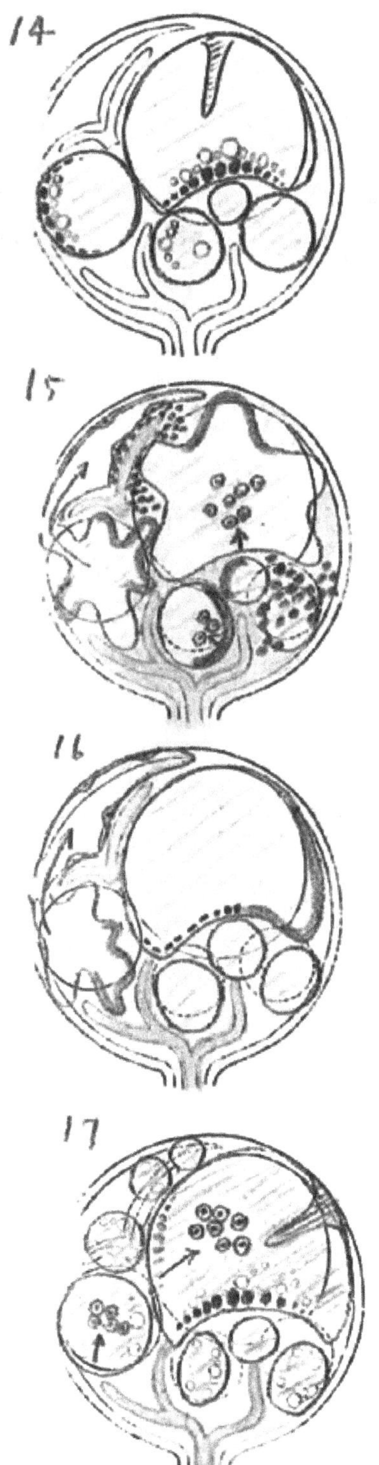

of epitheliums and some signs of slight hyper-secretion : flat or cuboidal epitheliums with some small vacuoles at the apical parts of cell-protoplasma and chromatin-rich nuclei.
Considerable congestion.

15.

Follicular collapse with some signs of intense degeneration:
pycnosis and desquamation (to form solid-cell-groups at some places) of epitheliums.
Swelling and edema in interstitium with considerable congestion and localised round-cell-infiltration.

16.

Struma diffusa colloides non-proliferans.
With follicular collapse : degenerated epitheliums (pycnosis and Karyorrhexis) and pouring out of colloidal masses into lymphsinusoids.
Considerable congestion.

17.

Struma colloides proliferans.
Papillar or pillow-like increase and multiplication of epitheliums (tend to desquamate) with

 653

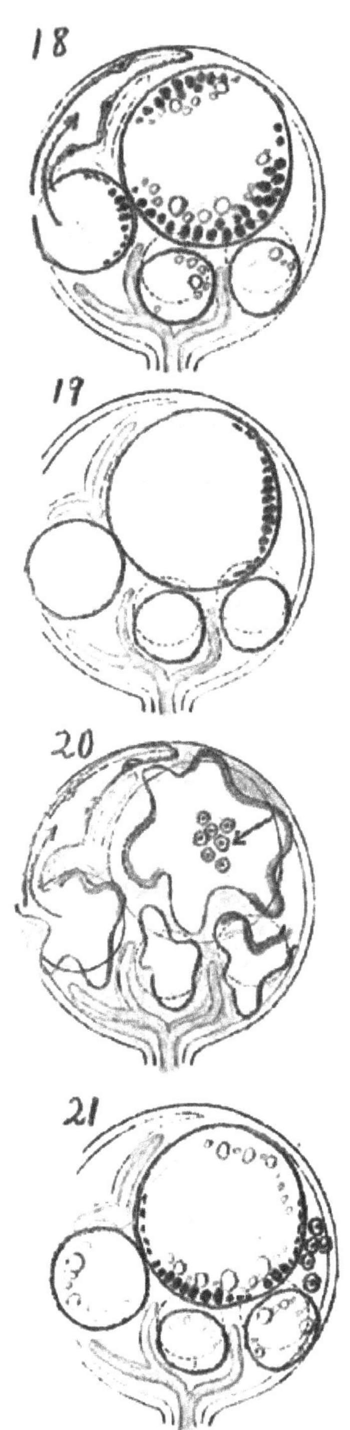

a large cystic follicles, involving a large quantity of colloidal masses. These satellite -follicles show some cell-activities. Considerable congestion.

18.

Follicles with cuboidal or cylindrical increase and multiplication of epithel cells. Remarkable congestion and some colloidal accumulation in lymphsinusoids.

19.

Slight congestion, slight multiplication of epitheliums and no remarkable changes else.

20.

Follicular collapse with degenerated epitheliums (degeneration, dissociation and desquamation) and some in terstitial changes (intense congestion and intense edema. Some colloidal accumulation in lymphsinusoids).

21.

Considerable congestion and some signs of cellular activities : cuboidal epitheliums and a large quantity of [illegible] with some [illegible] of cases.

[illegible] of [illegible] -follicular cells.

654

23

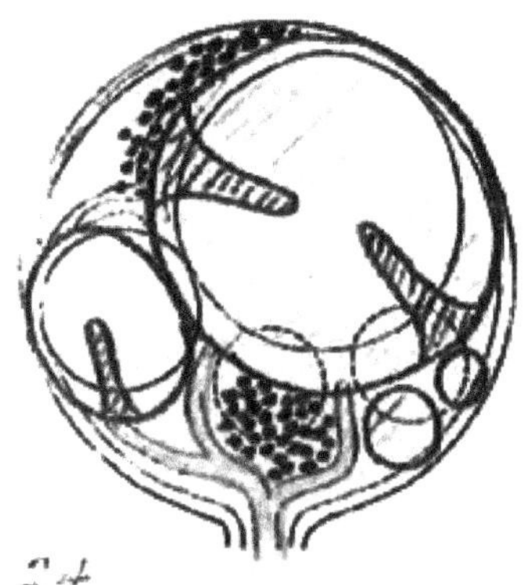

24

26

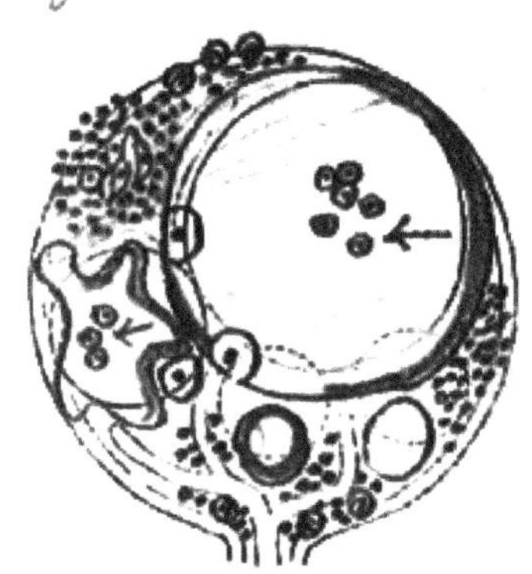

23.

Struma colloides nodosa macrofollicularis papillaris.

Cystic follicles with a large quantity of colloidal masses.

Slight congestion and some lymphocytes-accumulation around the cysts.

(with some lymphatic nodulus).

24.

Thyroid with many small or micro-follicles, equipped with degenerated epitheliums : severe degeneration and desquamation.

Diminishing of colloidal masses or bad-staining of remained colloids.

Slight fibrosis, some round-cell-accumulation and slight localised hemorrhages.

26.

Struma diffusa colloides macrofollicularis.

Macrofollicles with some degenerated epithelium (degeneration, pycnosis, and desquamation. Sometimes seceded to form giant-cells, solid -cell-groups and furthermore small follicles).

Among these degenerated small follicles exist some lymphocytes-infiltration with some

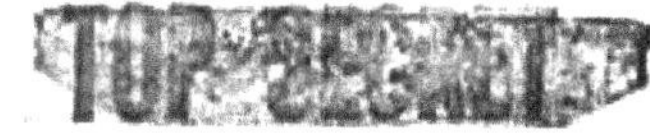

655

lymphatic nodulus (germinative centres with some increased reticulum-cells) and some slight leucocytes-emigrations.

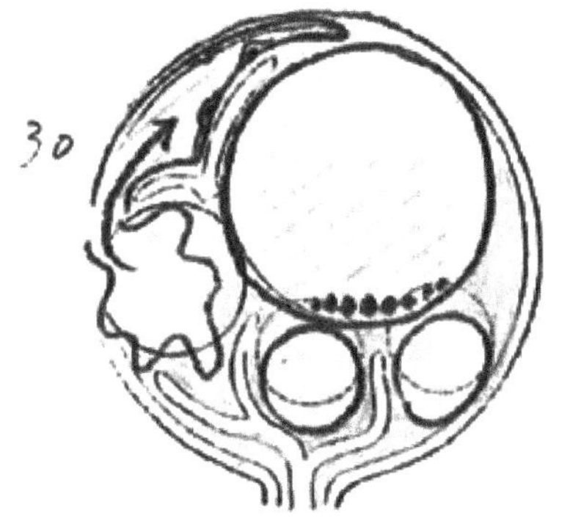

30.

Atrophic follicles with cuboidal or cylindrical epitheliums.

Colloid flow out from follicles into lymphsinusoids. Slight edema.

31

31.

Intense atrophy of lobuli. Small follicles with degenerated epitheliums (degeneration, dissociation and desquamtion).

Intense diminution of colloidal masses and remained colloids are vacuolar or granular. Edematous stroma.

32

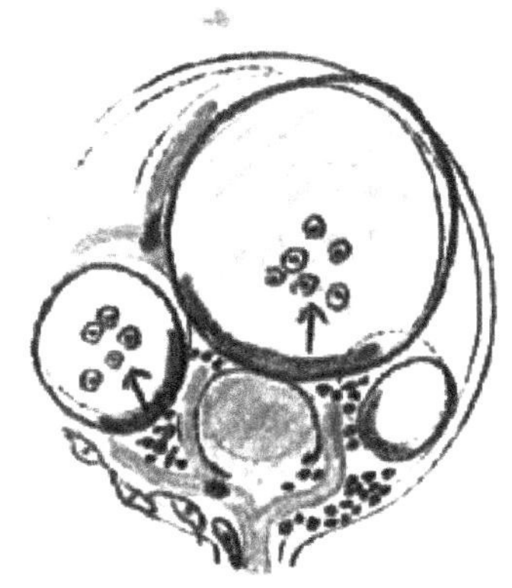

32.

Struma colloides macrofollicularis.

Inactive form of lobuli with some degenerated flat epitheliums and a large quantity of stayed colloids.

In one follicle lobulus, a focus of considerable congestion, somewhat obsolete hemorrhages, (some bacterial masses as capillary contents),

and round-cell or histiocytes-accumulation, accompanied with some intensively degenerated and desquamated epitheliums around the focus.

33.

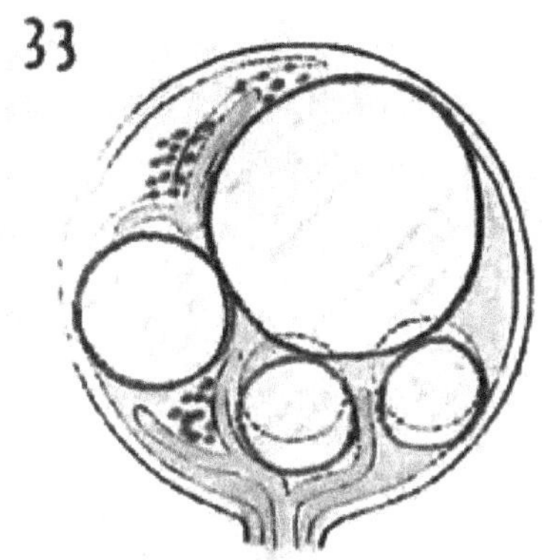

Considerable congestion, oedema and some round-cell-infiltration.

34. Struma parenchymatosa levis in degenerative state.

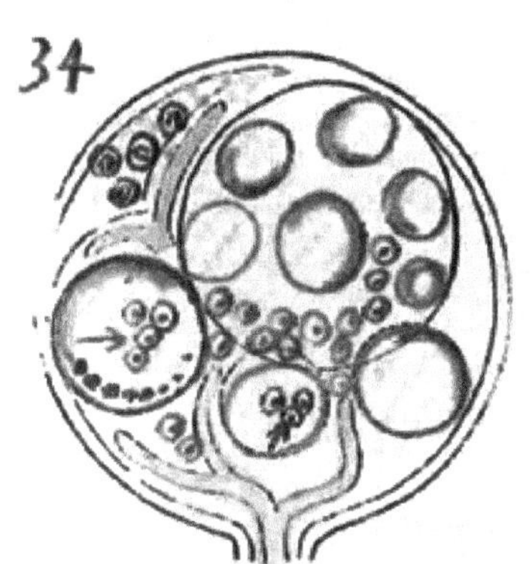

Small follicles with some cuboidal epithel. cells in intense degeneration: degeneration, dissociation and desquamation (sometimes, to form some solid-cell-groups).

Intense congestion and some cell-infiltration (erythrocytes and leucocytes).

35.

Struma colloides diffusa.

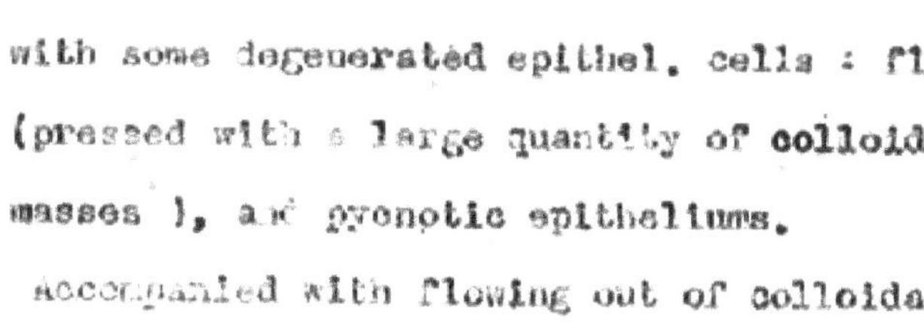

with some degenerated epithel. cells : flat (pressed with a large quantity of colloidal masses), and pyenotic epitheliums.

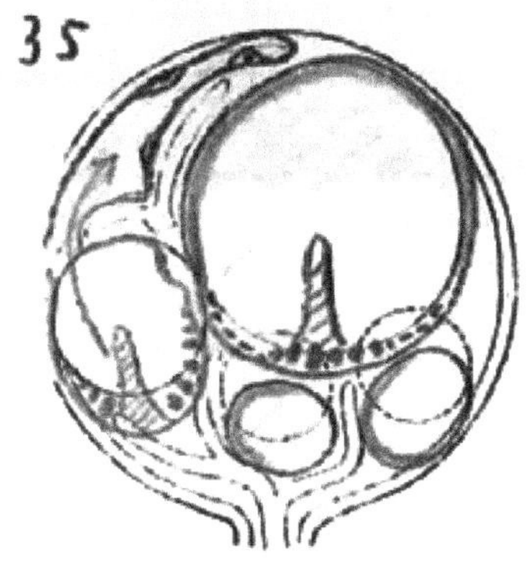

Accompanied with flowing out of colloidal masses from follicles to lymph-sinusoids.

At some places, papillar increase or some multiplication of epithel cells.

36.

Atrophic follicles with flat or pyenotic

657

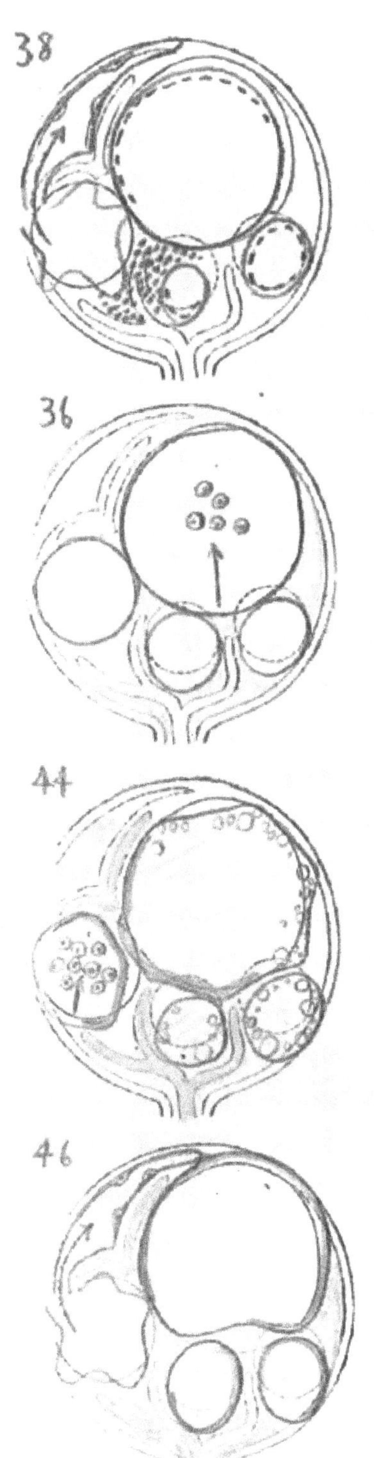

epithel.cells, accompanied with flowing out of colloidal masses from follicles to lymph-vessels at some places.

Some lymphocytes-accumulations.

36.

Slight edema, slight desquamation and no remarkable changes else.

44.

Small follicles in polygonal form with intensively degenerated epitheliums : intense degeneration, pycnosis, intense desquamation.

Some follicles are filled with desquamated epithel.cells.

Intense congestion and slight hemorrhages.

Considerable diminution of colloidal masses with some remained colloidal masses (with some vacuole-formation).

46.

Flat epitheliums with some signs of degeneration, pycnosis and slight desquamation, pressed with a large quantity of colloidal masses.

Slight congestion, some interstitial edema and some colloidal accumulation in lymph-vessels.

658

47.

47 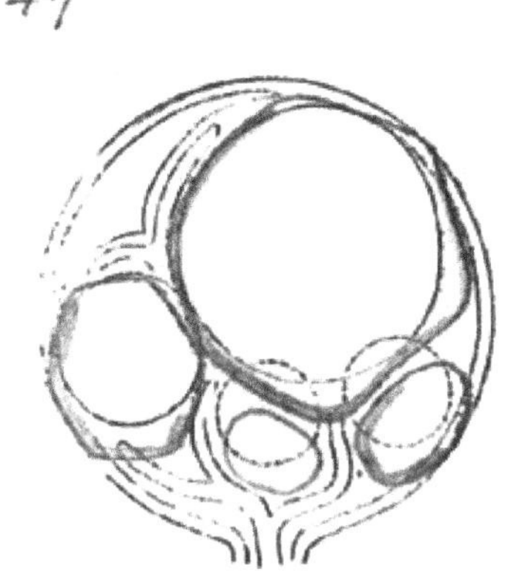

Large or polygonal follicles, reserved with a large quantity of colloidal masses. Epitheliums are pressed with some degenerative signs. No remarkable changes else.

S-1.

S-1 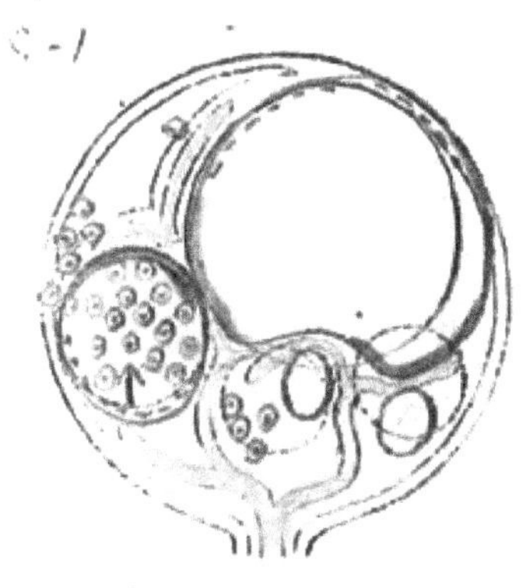

Generally thyroid with large follicles, equipped with flat epitheliums and abandant colloidal masses. At some places ~~with~~ polygonal (and atrophic) follicles with pycnotic or some desquamated epithel.cells (epithel.cell desquamate into cavities to form at some places solid-cell-groups), accompanied with some new-capillaries formations and considerable congestion of subepitheliar capillaries. These are some signs of degenerative changes.

S-3.

Generally thyroid with large follicles in inactivated state: flat epitheliums with pycnotic nuclei, desquamated epitheliums, abandant colloidal masses and flowing out of colloidal masses into lymphsinusoids and considerable capillar congestion.

At some places it shows some regenerative changes : pillow-like or papillar arrangement of epithel.cells.

659

S-4

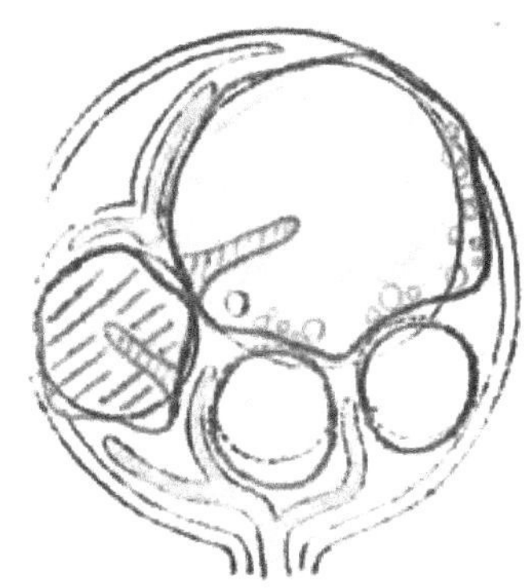

S-4.

Thyrsoid in inactivated state. Many polymorphic follicles with basophilic colloids in some follicles, are accompanied with considerable capillar congestion.

At some places with slight pillow-like arrangememnt of epitheliums, as slight regenerative changes.

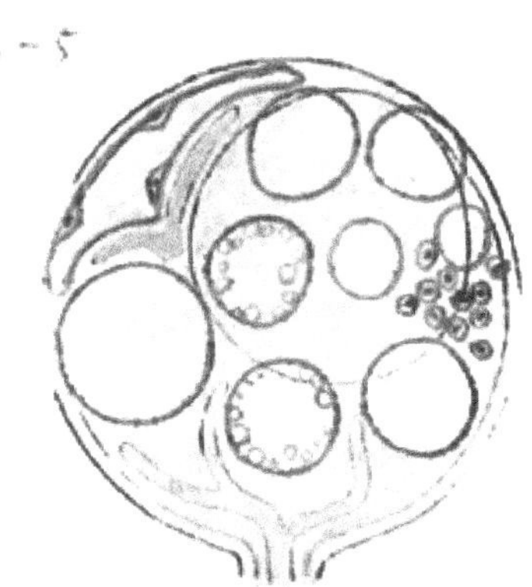

S-5.

Struma parenchymatosa levis with many small or micro-follicles, equipped with flat, cuboidal epitheliums which involve many granules and many vacuoles, esp. at the apical parts of themselves protoplasma (signs of increased resorptions).

Accompanied with intense congestion of subepithelial capillaries and remarkable fluidification or diminishing of colloidal masses.

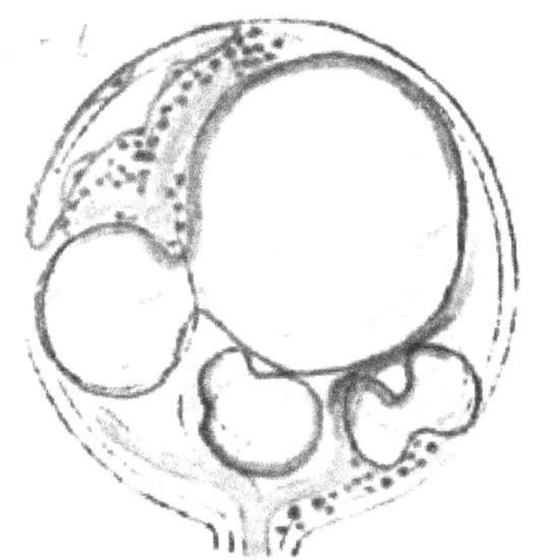

6.

Follicular collapse.

Generally follicles in alveolar form with some-things of atrophy of lobuli : epitheliums are flat and pressed with abundant reserved colloidal masses.

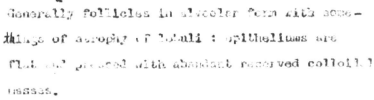

660

These collapsed follicles are surrounded with congested capillaries and some lymphocytes-infiltration.

In interstitium, some colloidal masses in lymphsinusoids and diffuse lymphocytes-infiltration.

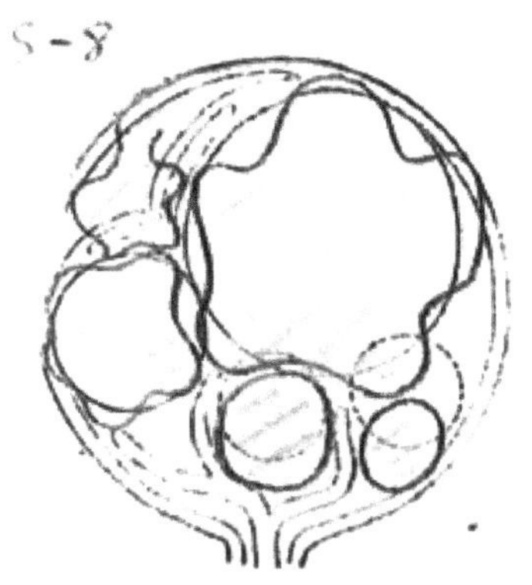

S-8.

Here and there many collapsed follicles : flat epitheliums and abandant colloidal masses. Without any signs of hypersecretions.

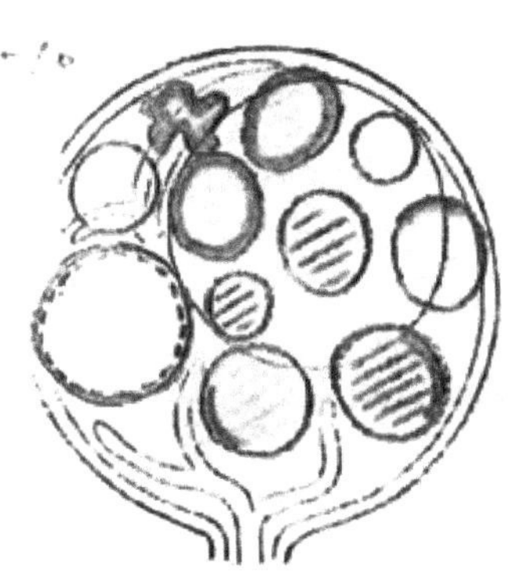

S-10.

Struma parenchymatosa levis with many small or micro-follicles all over the tissues ; these are somewhat regressive with flat, pycnotic and cloudy swoln epitheliums and basophilic colloidal masses.

without any regenerative sighs (for example pillow-like arrangemant of epithel.cells).

Rather anemic.

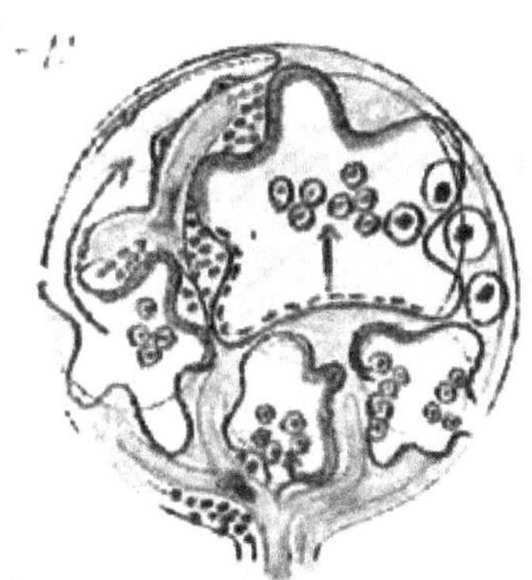

S-11.

Folliclar collapse.

Folliclar collapse with extensive degeneration of epitheliums : thin, flat, pycnoitc or karyolytic cells and their intense desquamation.

661

CONFIDENTIAL

(some of them are turned into giant cells in caves of follicles and in stroma).

The walls of many follicles are destroyed ~~and accompanied with flowing out of colloidal masses in lymphsinusoids.~~

Extensive congestion (and some bacterial masses in capillaries) and severe edema.

Some lymphocytes-accumulation at perivascular-portion and abandant colloidal masses in lymphsinusoids near the collapsed follicles.

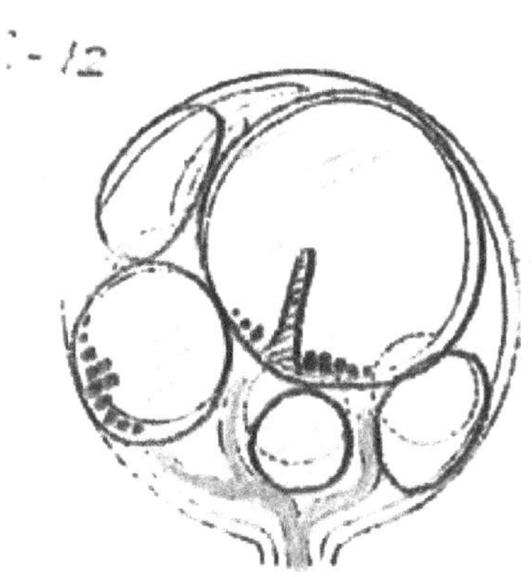

S-12.

Struma diffusa colloides. Most of follicles are large-cystic and epitheliums of them are flat and pressed with a large quantity of colloidal masses.

At some places with papillar increase or multiplication of epitheliums.

Slight congestion in stroma.

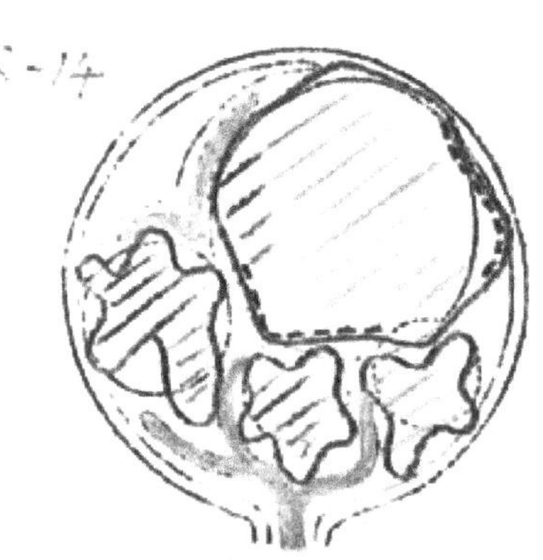

S-14.

Severe collapse of follicles.

[illegible] with polymorphic follicles with flat, pycnotic or thin epitheliums and abandant basophilic colloidal masses, accompanied with considerable capillary congestion.

662

S-18.

Some superm ficiary haemorrhagic places with a large quantity of necrotic masses (diffuse necrosis) and some bacterial-and leucocytes -dissemination in focus and considerable leucocytic-hemorrhagic changes in perifocal parts. Without any proliferative signs (increase of phagocytic cells).

S-15

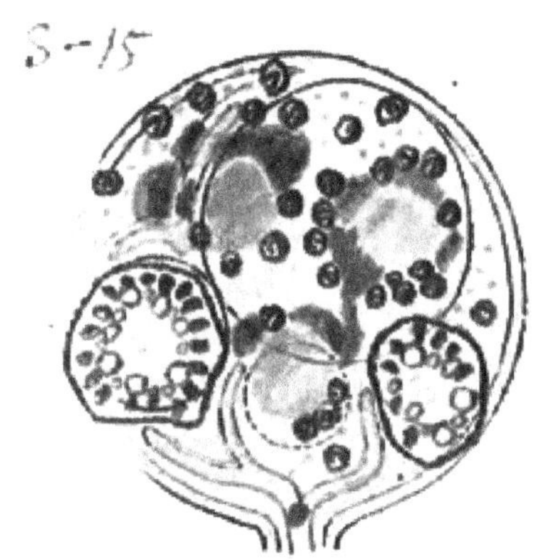

In other general tissues with some signs of hyperfunction: polymorphic follicles with high, fatt epithliums, involving some vacuoles at the apical parts of cell-protoplasms and remarkable fluidification of colloidal masses, accompanied with considerable congestion (regeneration and hyperfunction).

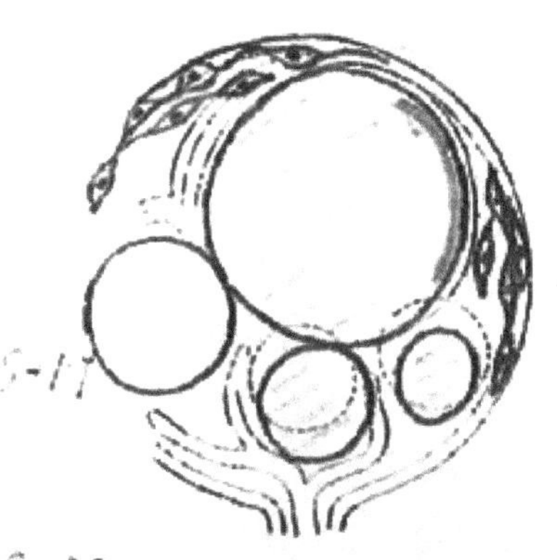

S-17

S-19.

Slight atrophy of follicles and slight fibrosis. Thyroid in inactivated state.

S-22

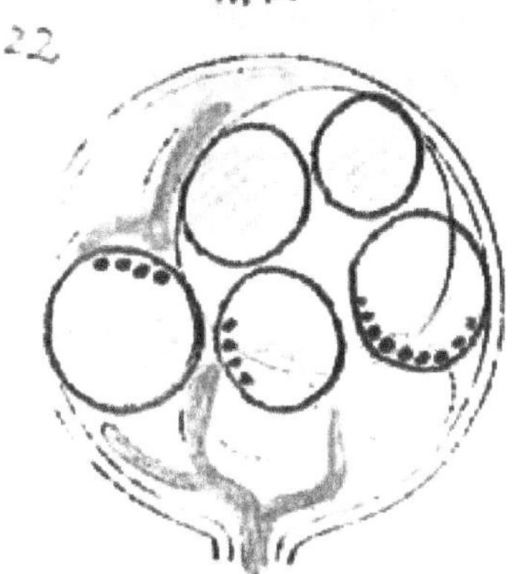

S-22.

Thyroid with many small follicles, equipped with cuboidal epitheliums and good-stained colloids. Considerable congestion and no remarkable changes else.

S-2[illegible].

Epitheliums are flat and pressed with a large

663

S-26

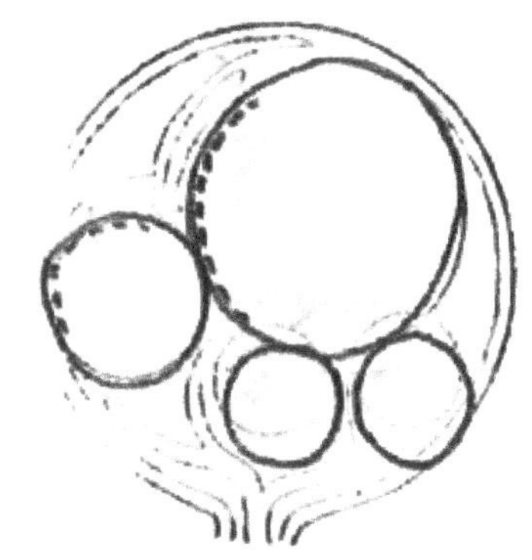

quantity of colloidal masses. Rather anemic and without any signs of activity.

S-28.

Thyr@oid with large or polygonal follicles ; epitheliums are flat or cuboidal and tend to fall into pycnosis. Considerable congestion (some places, some bacterial masses in capillaries) and some colloidal masses in lymphsinusoids.

S-28

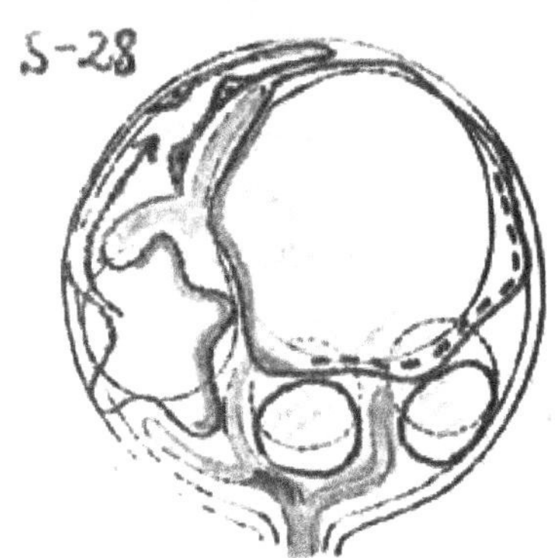

664

B) S U M M A R Y.

(I).

The birds-eye-view of all investigated cases.

Changes, due to infection.	Ground-disease.
1. Slight follicular collapse. (with slight regeneration).	
2. Slight hyperplasia of follicular epithel. cells. Some round-cell-infiltration.	Satellite - follicles.
4. Intense follicular collapse.	
7. Intense follicular collapse.	
8. Activated state. Intense congestion.	Struma diffuse colloides proliferans.
10. Slight congestion. Atrophic follicles.	
11. Inactivated state.	Atrophic follicles.
12. Folliclar collapse. Consid.congestion.	
14. Slight hyperplasia of follicular epithel. cells. Considerable congestion.	
15. Folliclar collapse. Considerable congestion.	
16. Degenerated state. Considerable congestion.	Struma colloidles non-proliferans.
17. Activated state. Considerable congestion.	Struma collidles prolif. S~~t~~atellite follicles

 665

No.	Findings	Diagnosis
18.	Activated state. Intense congestion.	
19.	Slight activated state. Slight congestion.	
20.	Folliclar collapse.	
21.	Acitvated state. Considerable congestion.	
23.	Slight congestion and slight round-cell-infiltration.	struma colloides nodosa macrofollicul.
24.	Folliclar collapse.	Satellite follicles.
25.	Degenerated state. Slight leucocytes-emigrations.	Diffuse Struma colloid. macrofollicularis. Some lymph-nodulus with germinative centres.
30.	Inactivated state. Atrophic follicles.	Atrophic follicles.
31.	Degenerated state.	Intense atrophic follicles.
32.	Inactivated state.	Struma colloid.macrofollic.
33.	Considerable congestion Some round-cell-infiltration.	
34.	Degenerated state.	Struma parenchym.levis.
35.	Degenerated state.	Struma colloid,diffusa.
36.	Inactivated state.	
38.	Some lymphocytes-accumulat. Inactivated state.	Atrophic follicles.
44.	Folliclar collapse.	

666

CONFIDENTIAL

46. Degenerated state. Slight congestion.

47. Slight degeneration.

S-1. Degenerated state.

S-3. Inactivated state.
(slight increase of folliclar epitheliums).

S-4. Inactivated state.
(slight increase of folliclar epitheliums).

S-5. Activated state. Intense congestion. Struma parenchym.levis.

S-6. Folliclar cellapse.
Considerable congestion and some lymphocytes-accumulation.

S-8. Folliclar collapse.

S-10. Degenerated. rather anemic. Struma parenchym.levis.

S-11. Folliclar collapse.
Intense congestion with some bacterial masses.
Some lymphocytes-accumulation.

S-12. Slight degenerated state. Struma colloid, diffusa.
Slight congestion.

S-15. Supermiliary hemorrhagic necrosis(with bacterial and leucocytic dissemination).

S-19. Inactivated state. Folliclar atrophia.
Slight fibrosis.

S-22. Almost normal.
Considerable congestion.

S-26. Inactivated state. Rather anemic.

S-28. Degenerated state.
Considerable congestion.

667

(2)

Therfore, the frequency of pathological changes in all cases are as following:

	N-district.	S-district	Total
Statical state. (inactivated state).	6	5	11
Slight activated state. (in regenerative form).	9	1	10
(Accomapnied with lymphocytes-accumulat.)	(3)		
Degenerated state.	7	4	11
Follicular collapse.	8	4	12
(with intense acute disfiguring.)	(2)		
Supermiliary hemorrhagic necrosis.	0	1	1
All invetsgated cases	30	15	45

Namely, the first one-fourth cases are ih not activated, statical state, second one-fourth cases are slightly actvated with somewhat congestion and slight hyperplasia of folliclar epitheliums, next

668

CONFIDENTIAL

one-fourth cases are considerably degenerated with some signs of folliclar degeneration and the last one-fourth cases are in folliclar collapse with severe folliclar disturbances.

In I case (No. 15,), occured acute Thyreoiditis with some supermiliary hemorrhagic necrosis.

CONFIDENTIAL 669

CONFIDENTIAL

(3).

The general sketch of progresses in thyreoid.

¼ - cases. (II cases)	Not activated, statical state		
¼ - cases. (10 cases)	Slightly activated state.	with	slight lymphocytes accumulation. 3 cases of them.
¼ - cases. (11 cases)	Degenerated state.	with	slight leucocytes emigration. 1 cases of them.
¼ - cases. (12 cases)	Folliclar collapse.		
(1 cases)	Thyreoiditis acuta with hemarrhagic necrosis.		

CONFIDENTIAL

670

CONFIDENTIAL

THYROID

			N 1	N 3	N 4	N 7	N 8	N 10	N 11	N 12	N 14	N 15	N 16	N 17	N 18	N 19	N 20	N 21	N 23	N 24	N 26	N 30	N 31	N 32	N 33
Parenchyma	Follicles	Large Follicles	+	++	−	−	++	+	+	+	+	÷	+++	+++	+	+	++	+	+++	−	++	+	÷	++	+
		Small Follicles	÷	+	++	++	+	+	+	+	+	+	+	÷	+	+	+	+	+	++	+	+	++	÷	+
		Cysts	−	−	−	−	−	−	−	−	−	−	+	++	−	−	÷	−	++	−	÷	−	−	−	−
		Microfollicles	−	÷	++	++	÷	÷	÷	÷	÷	÷	÷	÷	+	÷	+	+	÷	+	÷	÷	+	−	÷
		Ruin	÷	÷	++	+++	÷	÷	÷	÷	÷	+	(+)	++	−	(+)	++	÷	÷	+	++	−	++	÷	÷
	Epithelium	flat	+	+	+	+	+	++	+	÷	÷	+	++	+	÷	÷	+	÷	++	÷	+	÷	+	++	+
		Cuboidal	+	+	+	+	+	÷	÷	++	++	+	(+)	++	++	+	+	++	+	+	+	+	÷	÷	÷
		Cylindrical	(+)	(+)	−	−	(++)	÷	÷	÷	÷	(+)	(÷)	(++)	(++)	÷	÷	+	(+)	÷	(+)	÷	÷	−	−
		Papilla Formation	+	÷	−	−	++	÷	÷	÷	+	+	(÷)	++	÷	÷	÷	÷	++	÷	+	÷	÷	−	÷
		Pillow Formation	+	+	−	−	+++	÷	÷	÷	+	÷	(+)	++	+	÷	÷	+	+	÷	(+)	÷	−	−	÷
		Solid Cell Groups	+	÷	++	+	−	+	+	+	÷	+	÷	+	÷	−	+	+	÷	+	+	+	++	÷	÷
		Trabecular Arrangement	−	−	−	−	−	−	÷	−	−	÷	÷	−	−	−	−	−	−	−	−	−	−	−	−
		Sack Formation	(+)	+	−	−	−	÷	÷	÷	÷	÷	÷	÷	−	−	÷	−	÷	+	÷	+	÷	−	−
		Desquamation	÷	+	++	+++	(+)	÷	(+)	(+)	+	(+)	+	++	+	(+)	++	÷	(++)	++	+	÷	++	÷	÷
	Changes of Nuclei	Pyknosis etc.	÷	÷	+	+	÷	÷	÷	−	−	÷	++	÷	−	÷	÷	÷	+	+	+	÷	+	÷	÷
		Increase of Chromatin	(+)	(÷)	÷	−	+	÷	÷	+	++	÷	÷	+	+	÷	÷	+	÷	÷	÷	÷	÷	÷	÷
		Karyolysis & rrnexis	÷	÷	÷	÷	÷	÷	÷	−	−	÷	++	÷	÷	÷	÷	÷	÷	+	÷	÷	÷	÷	÷
	Colloid	Quantity	↑+	↑+	↓++	↓+	↑+	↓÷	↑÷	−	−	↓÷	↑++	↑++	↑÷	↑÷	↑÷	−	↑+++	↓++	↑+	↓÷	↓++	↑++	−
		Vacuoles	÷	÷	÷	÷	+	÷	÷	÷	+	÷	÷	++	−	÷	+	+	÷	++	+	÷	++	÷	÷
		Fluidification	−	−	÷	+	÷	−	÷	÷	÷	÷	÷	++	÷	÷	÷	+	÷	++	÷	÷	++	÷	÷
Stroma		Edema	+	÷	+	++	÷	÷	+	÷	÷	++	++	++	+	+	++	+	÷	÷	÷	+	+	÷	÷
		Hyaline Degeneration	÷	−	−	−	−	÷	÷	−	−	÷	−	−	−	−	−	−	−	−	−	÷	−	−	÷
		Fibrosis	÷	÷	−	÷	−	÷	÷	÷	÷	÷	÷	−	−	−	−	−	÷	+	÷	÷	÷	(÷)	−
		Colloid in Lymph-Vessels	+	÷	÷	÷	(+)	−	−	÷	÷	++	++	+	+	÷	+++	+	÷	÷	÷	++	+	−	÷
		Hemorrhage	−	÷	÷	÷	(÷)	−	÷	÷	÷	−	÷	(+)	(+)	(÷)	|	|	|	(+)	÷	−	|	(+++)	−
		Round Cell Infiltration	+	(+)	(÷)	÷	−	−	−	(+)	−	(+)	÷	÷	−	÷	÷	−	÷	÷	++	−	−	(÷)	−
	Blood Vessels – Contents	Congestion	÷	++	+	+	++	÷	÷	+	+	+	++	+	+++	+	+++	+	+	+	++	÷	+	++	+++
		Lymphocytes	÷	+	÷	÷	÷	÷	÷	÷	÷	÷	÷	÷	÷	÷	÷	÷	+	÷	+	÷	÷	÷	÷
		Leucocytes	−	+	÷	÷	÷	÷	÷	+	−	++	÷	÷	÷	÷	÷	÷	÷	÷	÷	÷	÷	÷	÷
		Fibrin	−	÷	−	−	÷	−	−	−	−	−	−	−	−	−	−	−	−	−	−	−	−	−	−
	Blood Vessels	Increase of Endothelium	−	÷	÷	÷	÷	÷	÷	÷	÷	÷	−	−	÷	÷	÷	÷	÷	÷	÷	÷	÷	÷	÷
		Degeneration of Endothelium	+	÷	÷	÷	÷	÷	÷	+	÷	÷	+	÷	÷	÷	÷	+	÷	÷	+	÷	+	÷	÷
		Swelling of Walls	÷	÷	+	+	+	+	÷	÷	÷	+	+	÷	÷	+	+	+	÷	+	÷	+	+	÷	÷
	Lymphoid Focus	Lymphocytes	|	÷	|	|	|	|	|	|	|	|	|	|	|	|	|	|	|	|	++	|	|	|	|
		Plasma Cells	|	−	|	|	|	|	|	|	|	|	|	|	|	|	|	|	|	|	−	|	|	|	|
		Germinating Center	|	−	|	|	|	|	|	|	|	|	|	|	|	|	|	|	|	|	−	|	|	|	|

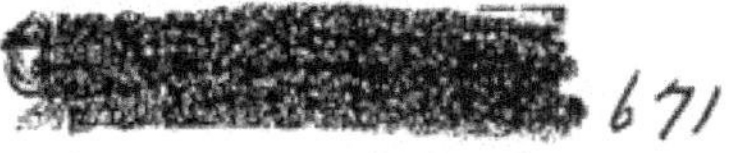
671

CONFIDENTIAL

THYROID

			N 34	N 35	N 36	N 38	N 44	N 46	N 47	S 1	S 3	S 4	S 5	S 6	S 8	S 10	S 11	S 12	S 14	S 15	S 19	S 22	S 26	S 28
Parenchyma	Follicles	Large Follicles	÷	++	+	+	÷	+	+	++	++	+	÷	+	+	÷	+	++	+	÷	+	÷	++	++
		Small Follicles	++	+	+	+	++	+	÷	÷	÷	+	++	+	+	++	+	÷	+	+	+	++	+	÷
		Cysts	−	−	−	−	−	−	−	−	−	−	−	−	−	−	−	−	−	−	−	−	(+)	−
		Microfollicles	++	÷	−	−	+	÷	÷	÷	÷	÷	÷	÷	−	+	÷	÷	÷	÷	−	+	−	−
		Ruin	+	÷	+	(+)	++	+	÷	−	−	−	−	++	+	+	++	÷	÷	(++)	|	−	−	−
	Epithelium	flat	÷	+	+	++	+	++	++	++	+	+	÷	++	++	+	+	++	+	÷	|	÷	++	+
		Cuboidal	++	(+)	+	÷	+	÷	÷	(+)	+	+	++	÷	÷	+	+	+	+	+	|	++	÷	+
		Cylindrical	+	(+)	÷	÷	−	÷	−	−	÷	÷	+	−	−	÷	−	(+)	−	++	|	÷	−	−
		Papilla Formation	÷	(+)	÷	÷	÷	−	(+)	÷	(+)	+	÷	÷	−	÷	÷	(+)	÷	÷	÷	−	÷	−
		Pillow Formation	÷	(+)	−	−	÷	−	−	−	(+)	÷	÷	−	−	−	−	−	÷	−	−	−	−	−
		Solid Cell Groups	++	÷	÷	÷	+	÷	÷	−	−	−	÷	++	÷	÷	+	−	÷	÷	|	+	÷	−
		Trabecular Arrangement	−	−	−	−	−	−	−	−	−	−	−	−	−	−	−	−	−	−	−	−	−	−
		Sack Formation	÷	(+)	−	+	−	÷	÷	−	+	÷	÷	+	÷	÷	÷	−	−	+	−	−	÷	−
		Desquamation	++	÷	÷	÷	++	÷	÷	÷	(+)	(+)	+	+	÷	÷	++	(+)	÷	+	÷	÷	÷	÷
	Changes of Nuclei	Pyknosis etc.	÷	÷	+	+	+	+	+	÷	÷	÷	÷	+	+	+	+	÷	+	÷	|	÷	+	÷
		Increase of Chromatin	÷	÷	÷	÷	÷	−	−	÷	÷	÷	+	÷	−	÷	÷	÷	÷	÷	−	÷	÷	÷
		Karyolysis & -rrhexis	÷	÷	÷	÷	÷	÷	+	÷	÷	÷	÷	÷	+	÷	÷	÷	÷	÷	−	÷	÷	÷
	Colloid	Quantity	+++	+++	−	+÷	++	++	++	++	+++	−	÷	+÷	−	+÷	+÷	++	−	+++	−	÷	++	++
		Vacuoles	+	−	−	÷	++	−	+	÷	÷	÷	++	+	−	÷	−	÷	−	++	−	−	−	−
		Fluidification	+	−	÷	÷	++	−	−	÷	−	−	++	÷	−	÷	÷	÷	−	++	−	÷	−	−
Stroma		Edema	÷	−	+	÷	+	+++	−	÷	÷	−	(÷)	+	÷	+	++	÷	(+)	(++)	÷	÷	÷	÷
		Hyaline Degeneration	−	−	−	−	−	÷	−	÷	÷	−	−	−	−	−	÷	−	−	−	−	−	−	−
		Fibrosis	−	−	−	÷	÷	−	÷	−	÷	−	÷	÷	−	+	−	(÷)	÷	−	÷	÷	÷	−
		Colloid in Lymph-Vessels	÷	(++)	÷	(+)	+	++	−	÷	+	−	(+)	+	÷	−	++	÷	(÷)	+	−	−	−	÷
		Hemorrhage	÷	−	÷	−	÷	−	−	−	÷	−	−	|	−	−	−	−	−	+++	−	−	−	−
		Round Cell Infiltration	−	−	−	(+)	(÷)	−	−	−	÷	−	(÷)	+	−	−	÷	÷	÷	÷	−	÷	−	−
	Blood Vessels – Contents	Congestion	+++	÷	+	÷	+++	÷	÷	÷	++	÷	+	+	÷	÷	++	+	÷	++	÷	÷	÷	++
		Lymphocytes	÷	÷	÷	÷	÷	÷	÷	÷	÷	÷	÷	+	÷	÷	+	÷	÷	÷	|	÷	÷	÷
		Leucocytes	÷	÷	÷	÷	÷	÷	÷	÷	÷	÷	÷	÷	÷	+	÷	÷	+	+	|	÷	÷	÷
		Fibrin	−	−	−	−	−	÷	−	−	−	−	−	−	−	−	−	−	−	−	−	−	−	−
	Blood Vessels	Increase of Endothelium	÷	÷	÷	÷	÷	−	÷	÷	÷	÷	÷	÷	÷	÷	÷	÷	÷	+	÷	÷	÷	÷
		Degeneration of Endothelium	÷	÷	÷	+	+	+	÷	÷	÷	÷	÷	÷	÷	÷	+	÷	÷	÷	|	÷	÷	÷
		Swelling of Walls	÷	÷	÷	÷	÷	++	÷	÷	÷	÷	÷	÷	÷	+	+	÷	+	+	÷	÷	÷	÷
	Lymphoid Focus	Lymphocytes	|	|	|	|	|	|	|	|	|	|	|	|	|	|	+	|	|	|	|	|	|	|
		Plasma Cells	|	|	|	|	|	|	|	|	|	|	|	|	|	|	−	|	|	|	|	|	|	|
		Germinating Center	|	|	|	|	|	|	|	|	|	|	|	|	|	|	−	|	|	|	|	|	|	|

672

N-3 Papillar increase of follicular epitheliums, in high power.
x160

S N-12 Active follicles, with multiplication of follicular epitheliums. Accompanied with some follicular congestion.
x 295

673

C.J. Active follicles, with some follicular congestion.

x75

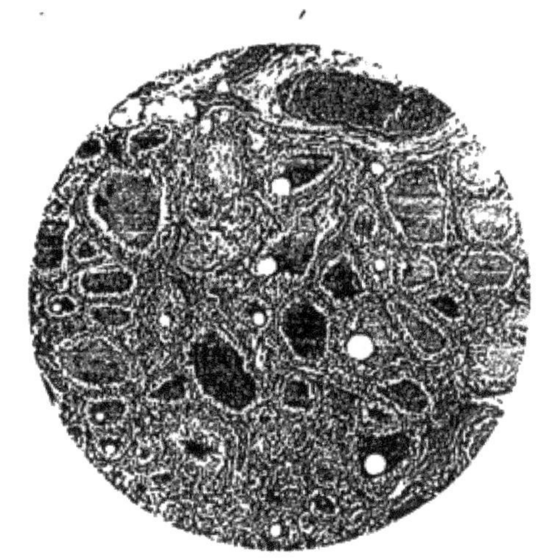

S.I. Active follicles, with some follicular congestion.

x75

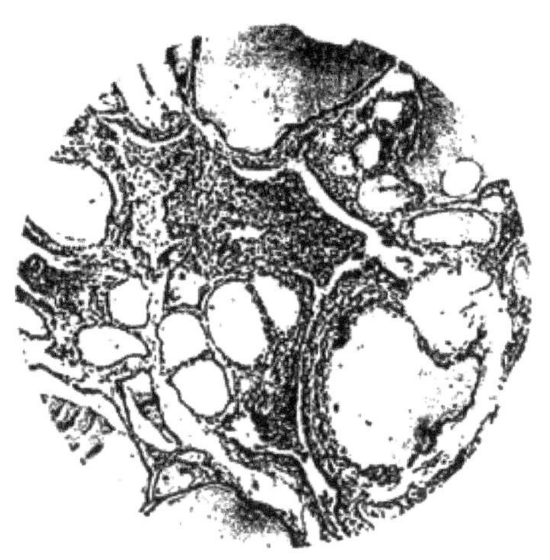

674

Group of active micro-follicles, with slight follicular congestion.

x130

Pillow-like or papillar increase of follicular epitheliums.

x64

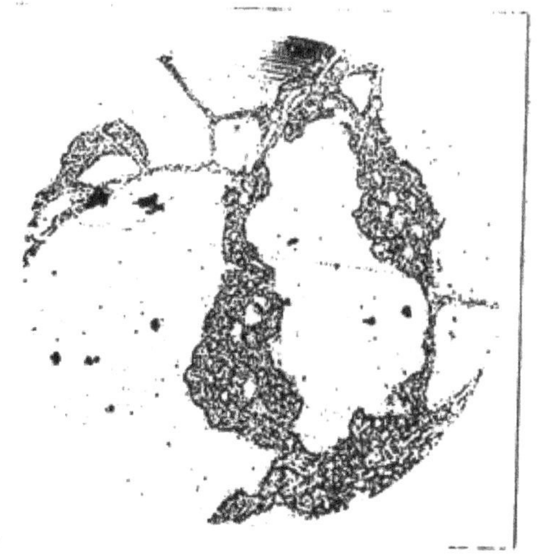

675

S-15 Intense follicular congestion and some diffuse hemorrhages.

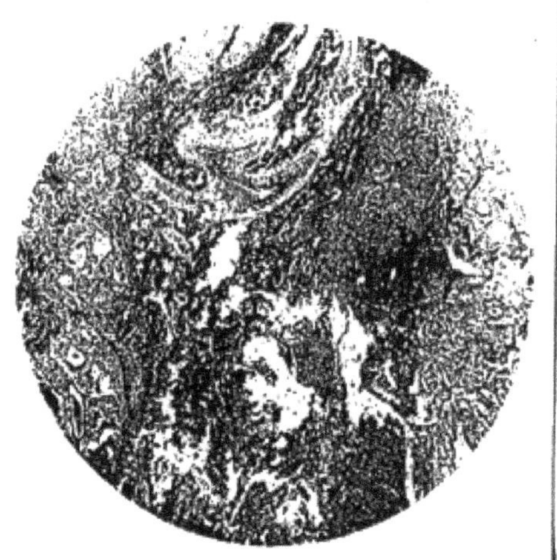

Hemorrhages, in high power.

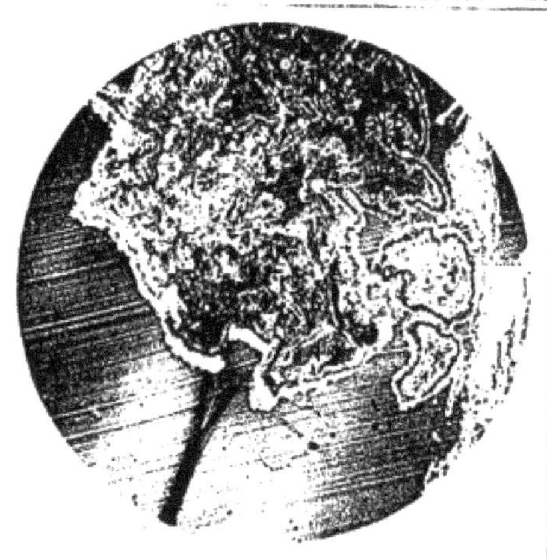

N-32 Obsolete hemorrhages, in high power.

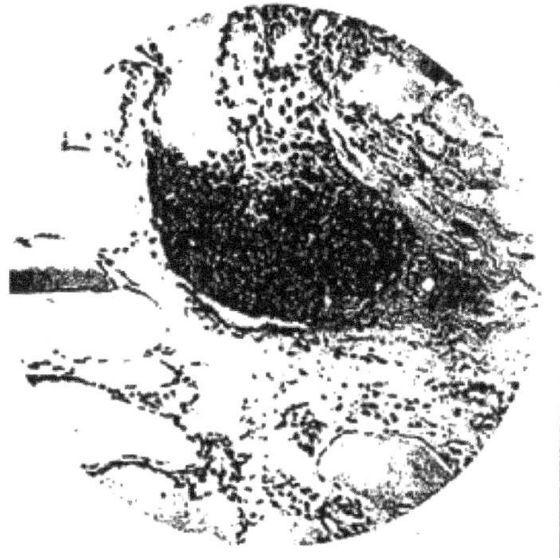

CONFIDENTIAL
TOP SECRET
676

S.30 Follicular collapse.
×78

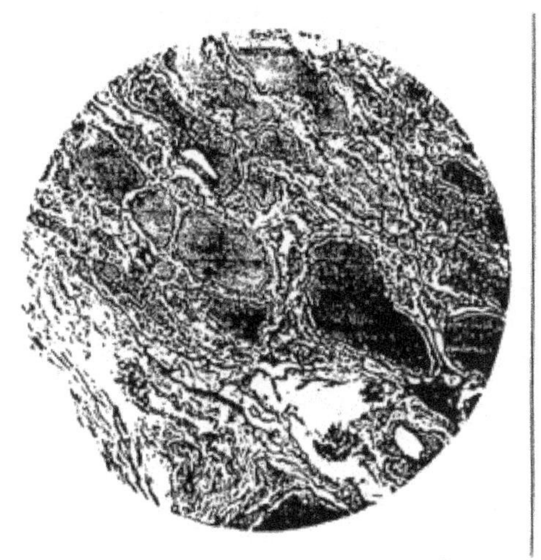

S. N.38 Follicular collapse, accompanied with some lymphocytes-infiltration.
×116

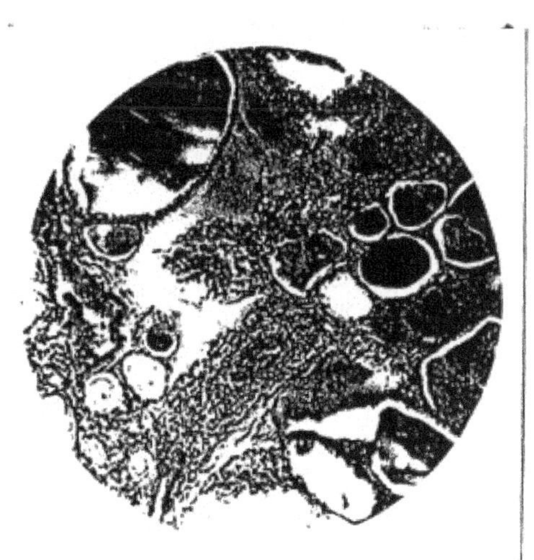

677

S.6 Intense follicular collapse (follicles in ruins) and lymphocytes-infiltration around follicles.

CONFIDENTIAL

×62

S.8 Lymphocytes-infiltration and appearance of some giant cells.

×270

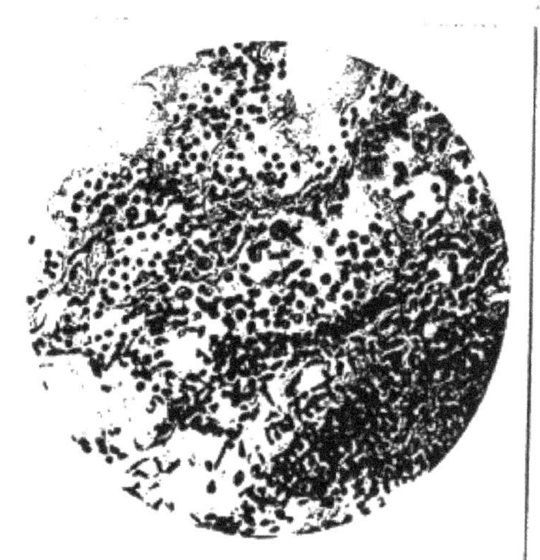

CONFIDENTIAL

678

N.44 Dissociation and degeneration of follicular epitheliums, due to interstitiar edema and some follicular congestion.

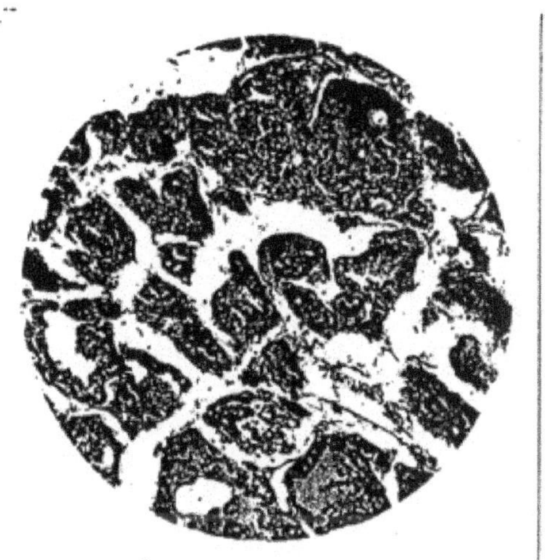

N.10 Atrophy of loblus.
×130

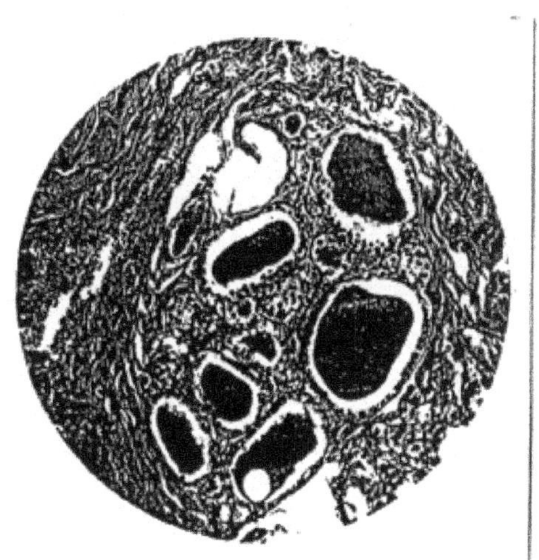

679

N 23 Intese collapse of follicles
and diffuse lymphocytes-dissemnation.

CONFIDENTIAL

x 65

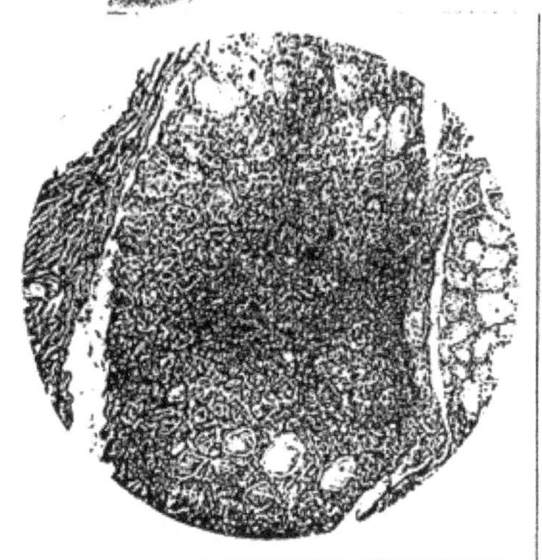

N 26 Intese collpse of some micro-follicles
and diffuse lymphocytes infiltration.

x 105

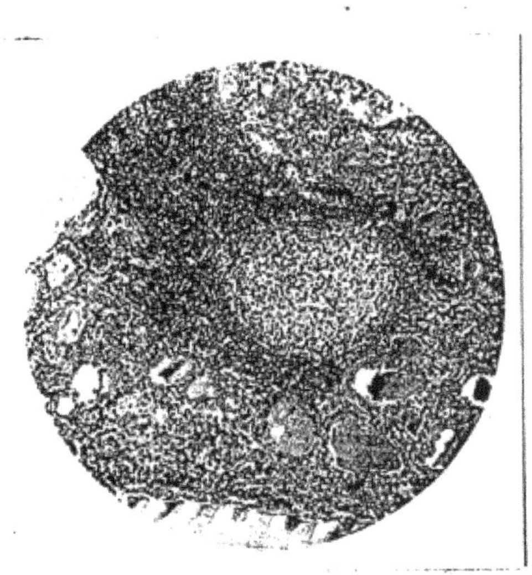

CONFIDENTIAL

650

CONFIDENTIAL

N.44 Follicular collapse, in high power.
Desquamation and degeneration of follicular epitheliums.

×110

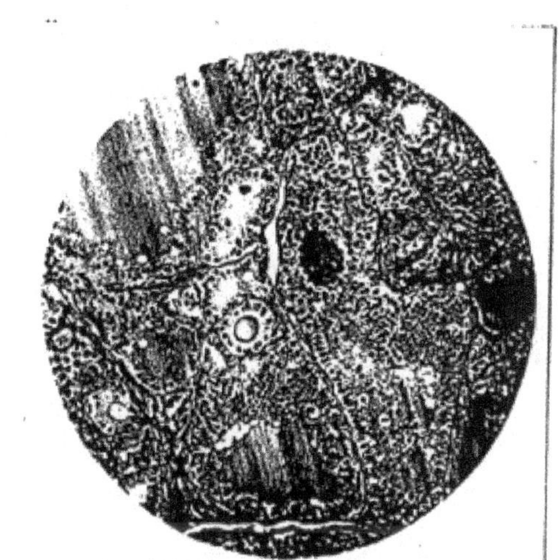

N.15 Follicular collapse, in high power.
Dissociation of follicular epitheliums and some colloidal masses in lymphsinusoid.

×160

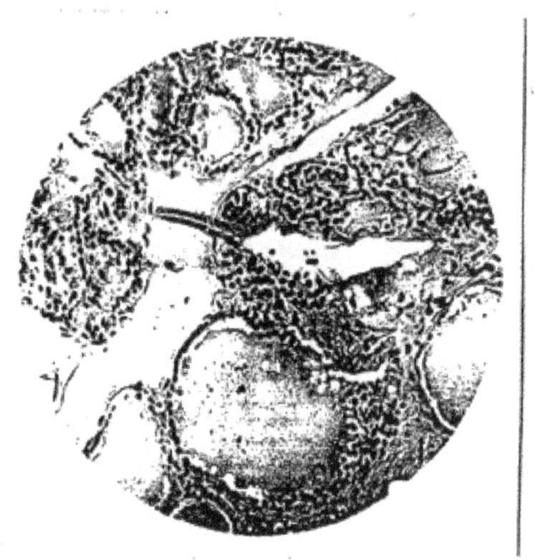

CONFIDENTIAL

681

CONFIDENTIAL
Thymus

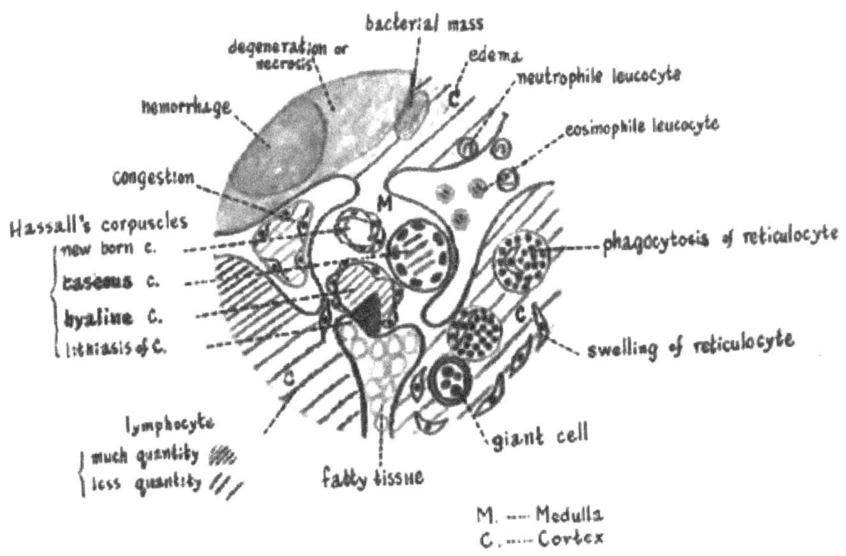
bacterial mass
degeneration or necrosis
edema
neutrophile leucocyte
hemorrhage
eosinophile leucocyte
congestion
M
C
Hassall's corpuscles
new born c.
caseous c.
hyaline c.
lithiasis of c.
phagocytosis of reticulocyte
swelling of reticulocyte
lymphocyte
much quantity
less quantity
fatty tissue
giant cell
M. ---- Medulla
C. ---- Cortex

CONFIDENTIAL
682

THYMUS.

(A) Microscop. Investigation.

S.I.

Remarkable edema and congestion. Here and there are recognized many focuses of the localised necrosis (involving many bacterial colonies).

Slight hemorrhages in and around the focus of necrosis.

Pycnosis and karyorrhexis of lymphocytes and reticulum-cells.

Hassall's corpuscles are generally regressive : most of them are caseous corpuscles which tend to softening, especially at the focus of necrosis.

The lymphatic nodulus in cortex disappear completely.

S.15.

Considerable congestion and edema. Lymphocytes--infiltrate diffusely into the medullary tissues (accidental involution III) and tend to fall in pycnosis.

Swelling and considerable phagocytosis of reticulum cells are remarkable.

As for the Hassall's corpuscles : most of them show the rather progressive changes : namely

683

appearance of new born corpuscles and some activation of reticulum-cells around them. Accompanied with some leucocytes (and thier fragments) in the spaces of some corpuscles.

S.10.

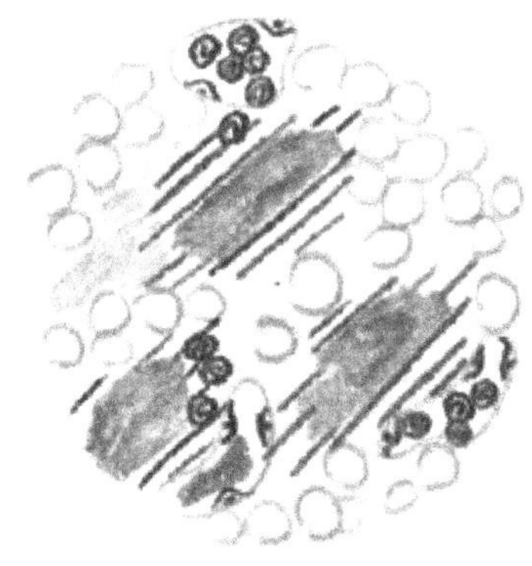

Remarkable increase of fatty tissues and intense injuries of reticulum-cells and lymphocytes : pycnosis and other nuclear changes.

Medulla and corte are not distinguished each other (accidental involution II) and Hassall's corpuscles are not recognized.

Attend to some remarkable focus of necrosis, consisted of the decayed epithelialiums and pycnotic leucocytes, lymphocytes and some bacterial masses, which are accompanied with remarkable hemorrhages.

Intense injuries of blood-vessels, which involve many leucocytes and some bacterial masses.

N.4.

Accidental involution I., with slight degenerative changes (slight diminution of lymphocytes in cortical tisseus. But medulla are certified from cortex).

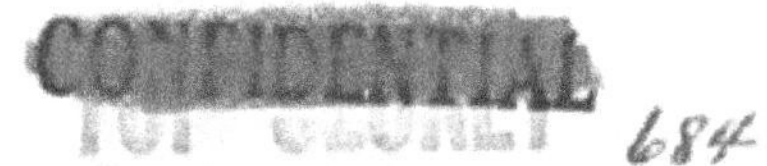
CONFIDENTIAL 684

Reticulum-cells in cortical tissues swell and sometimes phagocytise lymphocytes.

Many young corpuscles, consisted of a few reticulum-cells and appearance of some giant cells.

Slight congestion.

N.34.

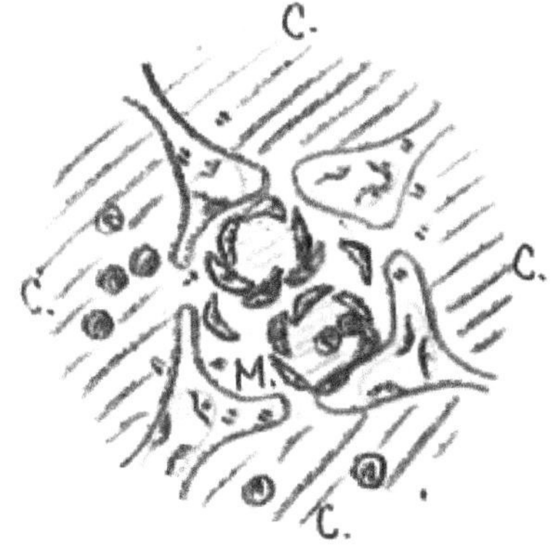

Cortical and medullar tissues are distinguished each other distinctly.

In inter-and intra-lobular connective tissues, considerable congestion, some histiocytes- and some leucocytes (some of them, eosniophilic cells)- infiltration.

Hassall's corpuscles are generally small and involve some hyaline masses and some leucocytes -fragments, accompanied with some activation of reticulum-cells around them.

N. 42.

Considerable reduction of parenchymatous tissues, due to remarkable increase of fatty tissues and some increased connective tissues.

In the latter, remarkable congestion and remarkable edema.

685

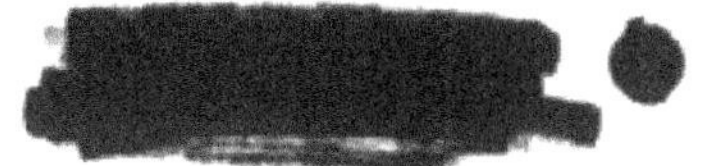

Small hyaline corpuscles tend to sometimes desolation (softening or organ eating).

Considerable decrease of lymphocytes and considerable serous exudation and some leucocytes-infiltrations.

Remarkable injurines of blood-vessel-walls with desquamation of endothelial cells, vacuolar degeneration of media and perivascular serous exudation.

N.44.

Extraordinary intense congestion, intense perivascular oedematous swelling and diffuse leucocytes and bacterial dissemination all over the follicular tissues.

Many Hassall's corpusclces with many concentrated hyalinous masses.

Some of them tend to lithiasis.

Some eosinophilic cells in capillaries and in connective tissues.

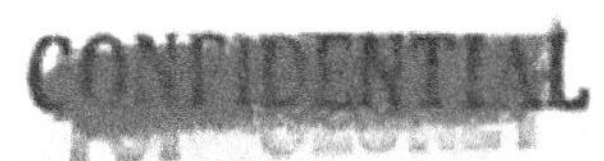

686

(B) S U M M A R Y

Stroma : Considerable congestion and sonsiderable edema (in 3 cases in the highest degree) with more or less leucocytes infiltration and eosinophilia(in 2 cases).

Parenchyma : Decrease and considerable degenerative cjanges of lymphocytes; pycnosis, karyorrheix and other nuclear changes. Lymphocytes-infiltration reversely in medullar tissues, in 2 cases, (accidental vinvolution II),or diffuse dissemination all over medullar and cortical tissues in 2 cases(accidental invoultion III). Swelling and considerable phagocytosis of teticulum cells and appearance of giant cells in 2 cases.

Hassall's Corpuscle : Many hyaline or caseous corpuscle, which incline rather to regress(lithiasis and organizing in 1 case), but sometimes reactive new born corpuscles which involve leucocytic cells and are surrounded with active reticulum cells.
Bacterial masses as capillary content or in parenchymatous tissues in 3 cases, around which necrotic parenchymatous tissues and leucocytes infiltration are recognised.

In short , there are bacterial necrotic changes in 2 cases in severe grad and in 2 cases in slight grade, and reactive changes which involve active retuculum cells(in 2 cases in consideragle grade and in 1 case in slight grade).

687

CONFIDENTIAL

N-44 Intense congestion and edema. Accomaanied with lithiasis of Hassal's corpuscle.

x 48

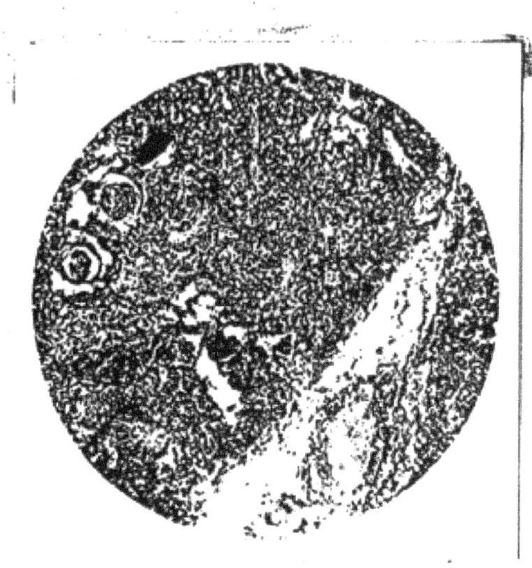

Reticulocytes aound hyaline Hassal's corpuscle.

x 325

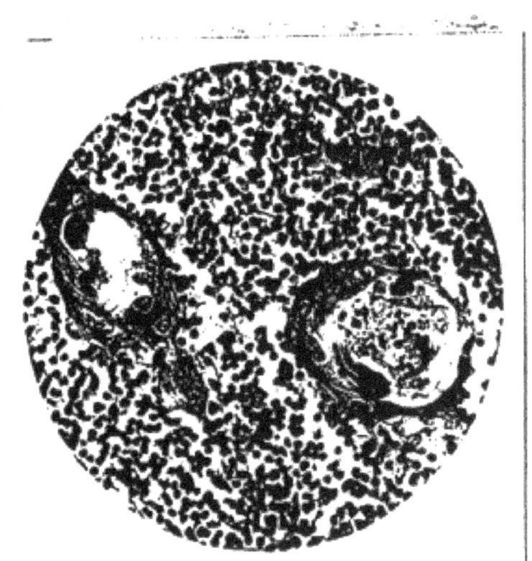

CONFIDENTIAL

688

CONFIDENTIAL

Rather diffues necrosis.

x57

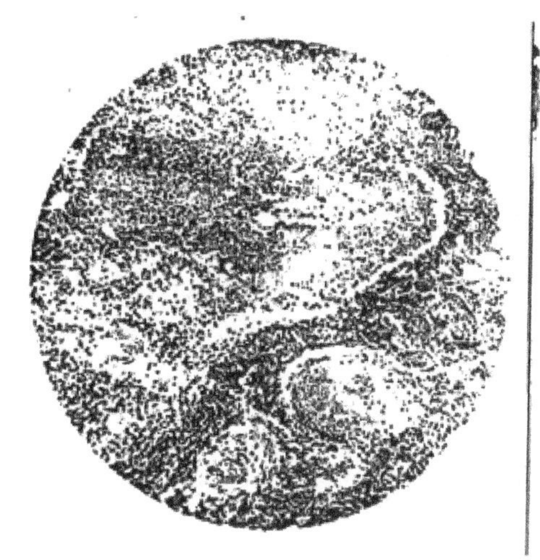

Necrosis in trabecular parenchyma.

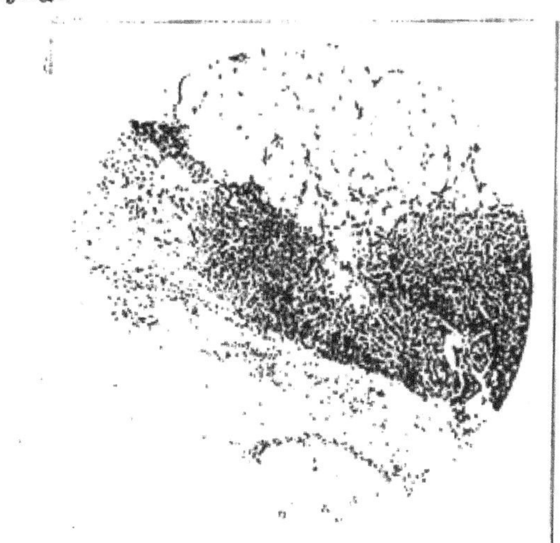

689

CONFIDENTIAL

S-15 Phagocytic reticulocytes group.
×325

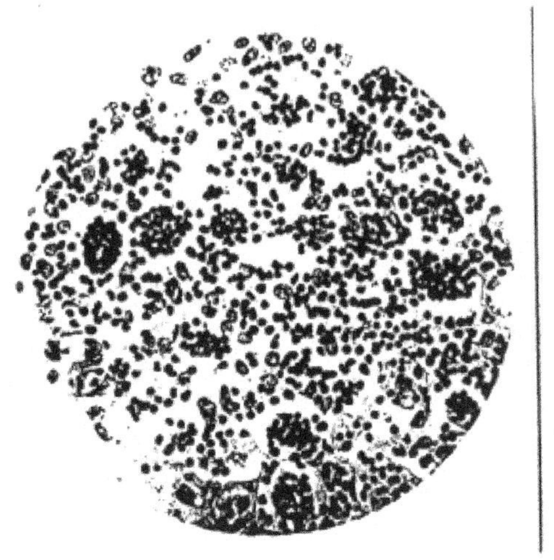

CONFIDENTIAL

690

Testis

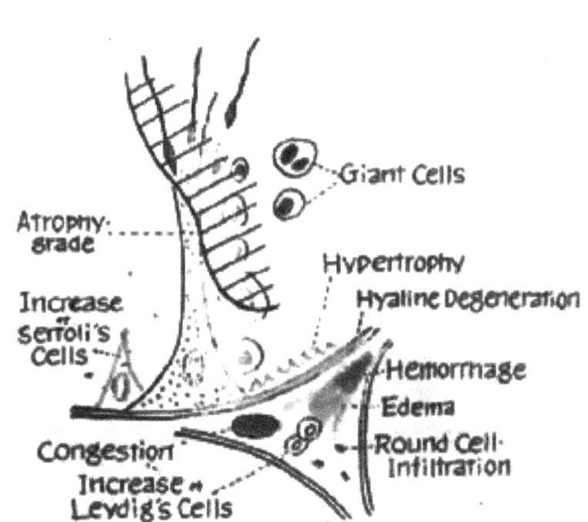
Giant Cells
Atrophy grade
Hypertrophy
Hyaline Degeneration
Increase of Sertoli's Cells
Hemorrhage
Edema
Congestion
Round Cell Infiltration
Increase of Leydig's Cells

CONFIDENTIAL
691

TESTICLE

A) Microscopical Investigation

a) Parenchyma.

	Reduction of Tubulus	Atrophia testis	Hypertrophia or Hyaline degeneration of T.propria.	Formation of Giant cells	Hyperplasia of Sertoli's cells
N-5	I.	II	−	∸	N
N-18	−	I.	÷	−	N
N-19	I.	I.	∸	−	N
N-21	−	I.	−	∸	N

b) Stroma.

	Congestion	Hemorrhages	Round cell infiltration	Swelling or Roughness	Increase of Leydig's cells.
N-5	+	∸	∸	÷	÷
N-18	+	++	+	∸	N
N-19	+	−	∸	÷	N
N-21	++	−	∸	−	N

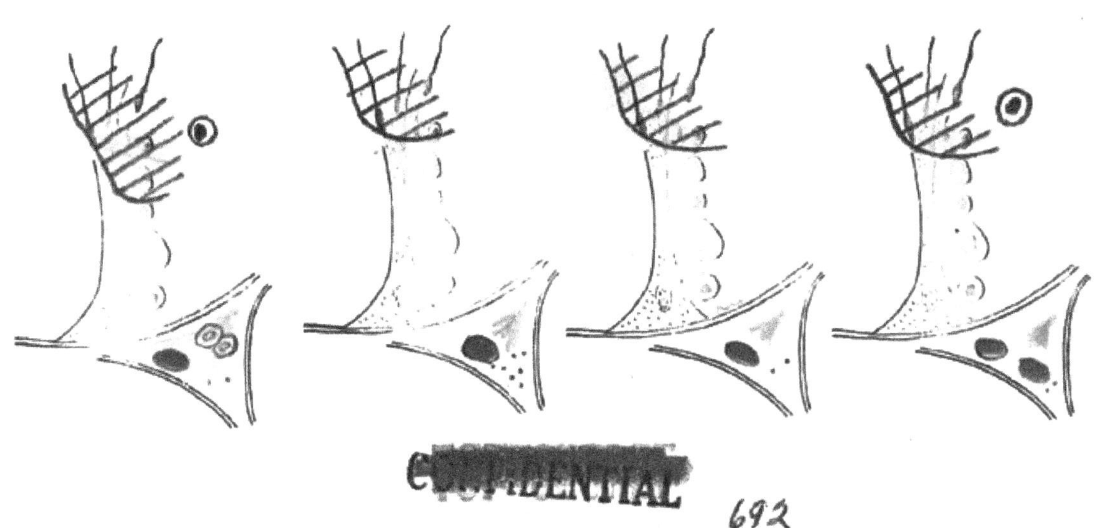

CONFIDENTIAL

a) Parenchyma.

	Reduction of Tubulus	Atrophia testis	Hypertrophia or Hyaline degeneration of T.propria.	Formation of Giant cells	Hyperplasia of Sertoli's cells
N-24	Ⅲ.	—	—	—	⧺
N-27	Ⅲ.	—	⧺	∸	÷
N-35	~Ⅰ.	Ⅱ.	∸	÷	N
N-42	~Ⅰ.	Ⅲ.	—	—	N

b) Stroma.

	Congestion	Hemorrhages	Roud cell infiltration	Swelling or Roughness	Increase of Leydig's cells.
N-24	⧺	—	∸	—	↓
N-27	÷	—	—	÷	↓
N-35	∸	+	+	—	N
N-42	∸	∸	∸	∸	N

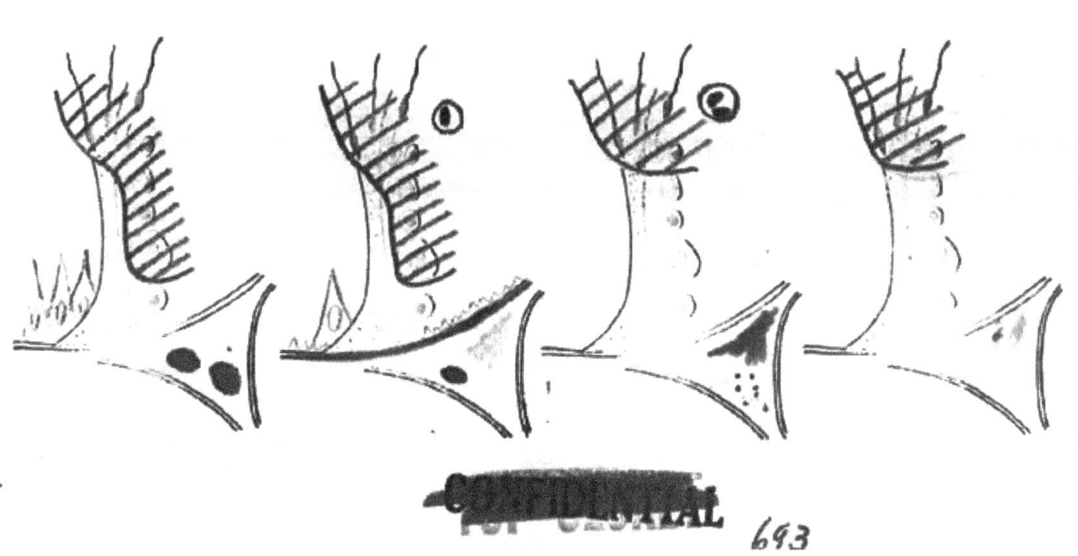

CONFIDENTIAL

693

a) Parenchyma.

	Reduction of Tubulus	Atrophia testis	Hypertrophia or Hyaline degeneration of T.propria.	Formation of Giant cells	Hyperplasia of Sertoli's cells
N-46	—	II.	÷	+	N
N-49	~I.	II.	÷	÷	N
S-4	III.	III.	—	—	+
S-8	I.	I	++	÷	N

b) Stroma.

	Congestion	Hemorrhages	Round cell infiltration	Swelling or Roughness	Increase of Leydig's cells.
N-46	÷	—	±	÷	N
N-49	+	—	÷	÷	N
S-4	÷	—	÷	÷	N
S-8	+	—	÷	÷	N

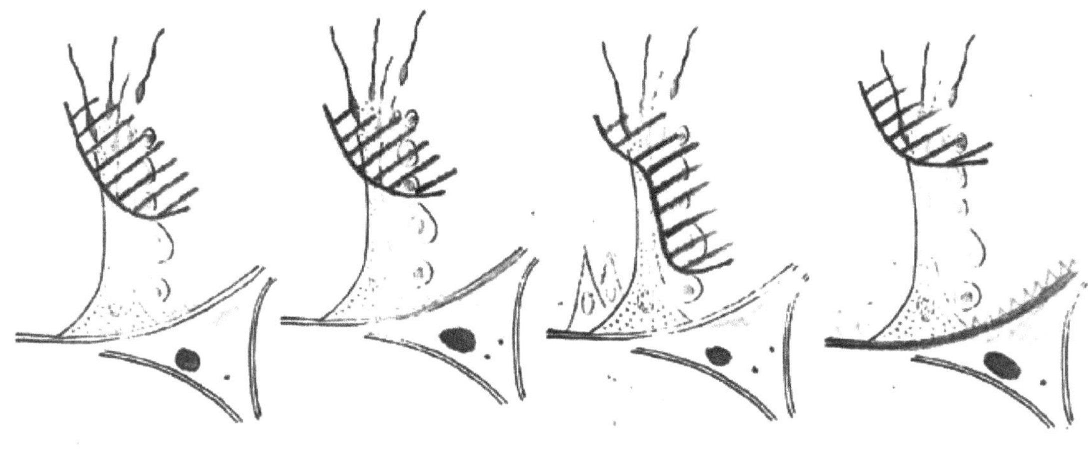

694

a) Parenchyma.

CONFIDENTIAL

	Reduction of Tubulus	Atrophia testis	Hypertrophia or Hyaline degeneration of T.propria.	Formationn of Giant cells	Hyperplasia of Sertoli's cells
S-9	I.	I.	++	∸	N
S-11	I.	II.	+	+	N
S-15	~I.	I.	∸	∸	N
S-26	—	I.	∸	++	N

b) Stroma.

	Congestion	Hemorrhage	Round cell infiltration	Swelling or Roughness	Increase of Leydig'scells.
S-9	÷	—	—	∸	÷
S-11	+	∸	∸	∸	÷
S-15	∸	—	÷	—	÷
S-26	+	—	∸	—	+

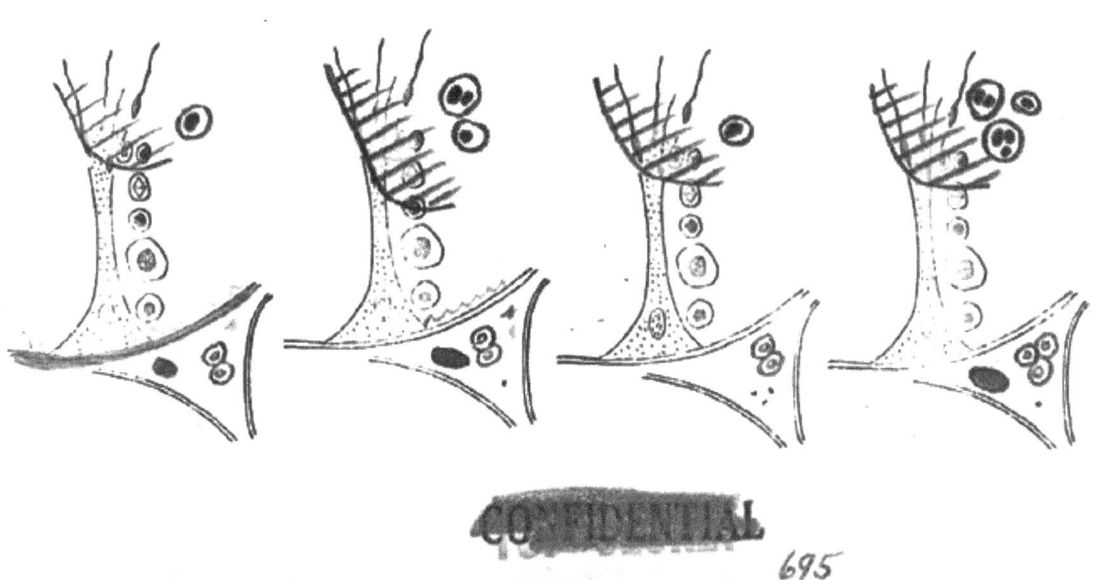

CONFIDENTIAL

695

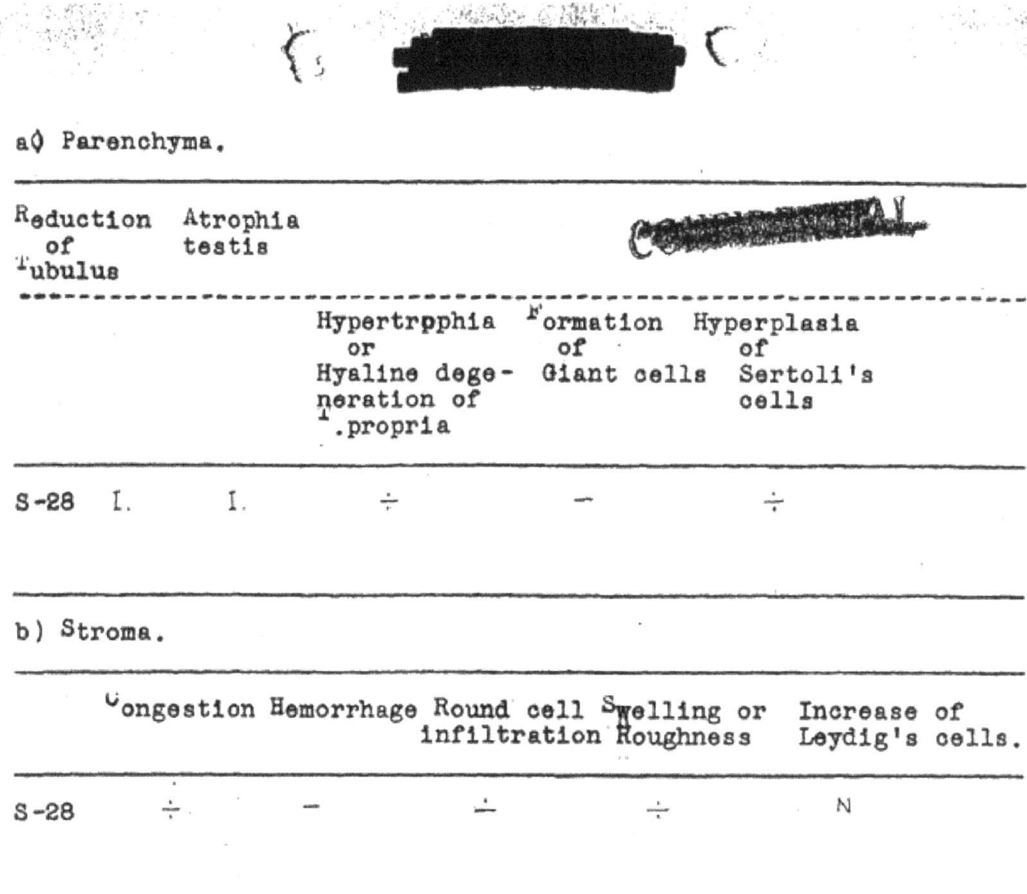

a) Parenchyma.

	Reduction of Tubulus	Atrophia testis	Hypertrpphia or Hyaline degeneration of T.propria	Formation of Giant cells	Hyperplasia of Sertoli's cells
S-28	I.	I.	÷	−	÷

b) Stroma.

	Congestion	Hemorrhage	Round cell infiltration	Swelling or Roughness	Increase of Leydig's cells.
S-28	÷	−	∸	÷	N

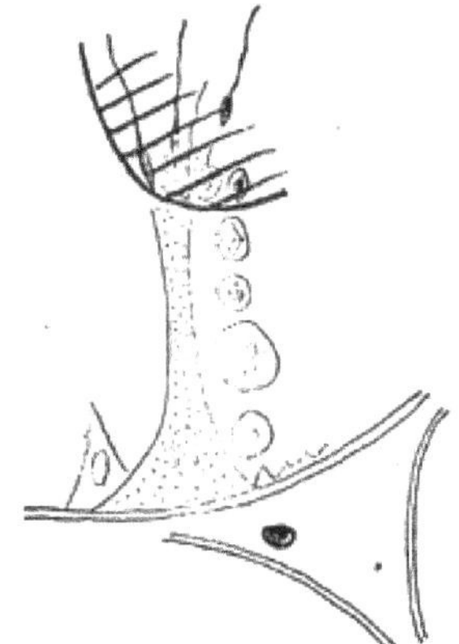

CONFIDENTIAL

696

B) S U M M A R Y

(I)

Our classification of "disturbance of spermatopoietic process".

a) On the "Atrophia testis".

Atrophia testis I. Pyknotic spermatozoa.
Relative increase of prespermatids and spermatids.

Atrophia testis II. Degeneration of prespermatids and spermatids with somewhat considerable excoriation or sometimes giant cell-formation (as sighs of degeneration).

Atrophia testis 111. Remarkable degenerqtion of prespermatids and spermatids.

Atrophia testis IV. Remarkable degeneration or sometimes complete diminishment of spermatocytes.
Degeneration and sometimes irregular cell-arrangement of spermatogonien.

Atrophia testis V. Complete diminishment of spermatic cells.
Remarkable swelling and hyaline degeneration of T. propria of tubuli seminiferi.

b) On the reduction of tubuli seminiferi.

Reduction 1 Diameter of tubulus seminiferus is reduced to $\frac{3}{4}$ of normal. (slight atrophia).

Reduction 11. Reduced to $\frac{1}{2}$. (medium atrophia).

Reduction 111. Reduced to $\frac{1}{4}$. (severe atrophia).

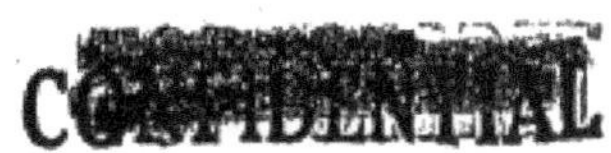

697

(2) CONFIDENTIAL

Generally infection causes some disturbances of spermatopoietic process:

Atrophia testis 1. 8 cases.

" 11. 5 cases.

" 111. 2 cases.

Reduction of tubuli seminiferi

1. 10 cases.

" 11. 0 case.

" 111. 3 cases.

Sometimes accompanied with giant cell-formation of spermatids amd prespermatids, as degenerative sighs.

11 cases.

Generally infection causes some congestion.

Congestion in slight degree. 7 cases.

" in medium degree. 2 cases.

Sometimes hemorrhages and edema ininterstitial tissues.

Hemorrhages in slight degree. 4 cases.

" in medium degree. 2 cases.

Edema in slight degree. 11 cases.

Accompanied with sometimes some round cell-infiltration.

in slight degree. 13 cases.

in medium degree. 2 cases.

Leydig's cells. Sometimes increase.

in slight degree. 4 cases.

in medium degree. 1 case.

sometime decrease

CONFIDENTIAL 698

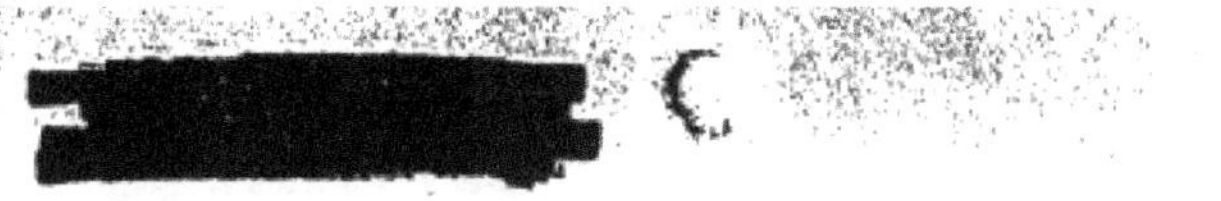

CONFIDENTIAL

in slight degree. 1 case.

in medium degree. 1 case.

in normal state 10 cases.

699

TESTIS

	N 5	N 18	N 19	N 21	N 24	N 27	N 35	N 42	N 46	N 49	S 4	S 8	S 9	S 11	S 15	S 26	S 28
Tubuli seminiferi: Grade of Reduction	+	±	+	−	+++	+++	±	+	±	±	+++	+	+	+	±	±	+
Tubuli seminiferi: T. propria: Thickening	−	±	±	−	−	++	±	−	±	±	−	++	++	+	±	±	±
Tubuli seminiferi: T. propria: Fibrous Degeneration	±	±	±	−	−	−	±	±	−	−	−	−	−	±	±	±	±
Tubuli seminiferi: T. propria: Hyaline Degeneration	−	−	−	−	−	++	−	−	±	+	−	++	++	−	−	±	±
Tubuli seminiferi: Serroli's Cells: Quantity	N	N	N	N	↑++	↑±	N	N	N	N	↑+	N	N	N	N	N	↑±
Tubuli seminiferi: Serroli's Cells: Degeneration	−	−	−	−	−	±	−	±	−	−	−	−	−	−	−	−	±
Tubuli seminiferi: Spermatogonien: Quantity	N	N	N	N	N	↓+	N	N	N	N	N	N	N	N	N	N	N
Tubuli seminiferi: Spermatogonien: Degeneration	−	−	±	−	±	++	−	±	−	−	±	−	−	−	−	−	−
Tubuli seminiferi: Spermatocytes: Quantity	N	N	N	N	↓+++	↓++	N	N	N	N	↓++	N	N	N	N	N	N
Tubuli seminiferi: Spermatocytes: Degeneration	+	±	±	−	−	+++	+	+	+	±	++	−	−	±	±	±	±
Tubuli seminiferi: Prespermatids: Quantity	↓±	N	N	↑±	↓+++	↓++	↓+	↓++	↑±	N	↓+++	↑±	↑±	↓±	N	↑±	↑±
Tubuli seminiferi: Prespermatids: Degeneration	+	+	+	−	−	+++	++	+	++	+	+++	−	−	+	±	±	±
Tubuli seminiferi: Spermatids: Quantity	↓+	↑±	↓+	↑±	↓+++	↓+++	↓+	↓++	↑±	N	↓+++	↑±	↑±	↓±	N	N	↑±
Tubuli seminiferi: Spermatids: Degeneration	+	+	+	−	−	+++	++	+	++	+	+++	±	−	+	±	±	±
Tubuli seminiferi: Spermatozoa: Quantity	↓±	↓±	↓±	N	↓+++	↓+++	↓++	↓++	↓++	N	↓+++	↑±	↑±	↓±	N	N	↓±
Tubuli seminiferi: Spermatozoa: Degeneration	+	±	±	±	−	+++	++	+++	+++	+	+++	±	±	++	+	±	±
Tubuli seminiferi: Giant Cells	±	−	−	±	±	±	±	−	+	±	±	±	±	+	+	++	−
Stroma: Congestion	+	+	+	++	++	±	±	±	±	+	±	+	±	+	±	+	±
Stroma: Edema	±	±	±	−	−	±	−	−	±	±	±	±	±	±	−	−	±
Stroma: Hemorrhage	±	++	−	−	−	−	+	±	−	−	±	−	−	±	−	−	−
Stroma: Round Cell Infiltration	±	+	±	±	±	−	+	±	±	±	±	±	−	±	±	±	±
Stroma: Increase of Connective Tissue	−	−	−	−	−	−	−	−	−	−	±	−	−	−	±	±	−
Stroma: Vessel Wall: Degeneration of Endothelium	±	+	±	±	±	±	−	±	±	+	±	±	±	+	+	±	±
Stroma: Vessel Wall: Hyaline Degeneration	±	±	±	+	±	±	±	−	−	±	−	±	−	−	±	++	±
Stroma: Vessel Wall: Swelling	±	±	±	−	−	−	±	±	±	−	±	−	±	±	±	±	±
Stroma: Leydig's Cells: Quantity	↑±	N	N	N	↓+	↓±	N	N	N	N	N	N	↑±	↑±	↑±	↑+	N
Stroma: Leydig's Cells: Yellow Granules	++	++	+	±	−	−	+	+	+	±	−	++	+	+	+	+	±
T. albuginea / T. vasculosa: Congestion	|	±	+	++	+	+	±	±	|	++	±	+	+	++	±	++	|
T. albuginea / T. vasculosa: Hemorrhage	|	±	−	−	−	−	±	−	|	−	−	−	−	−	−	−	|
T. albuginea / T. vasculosa: Round Cell Infiltration	|	+	±	+	±	±	±	±	|	±	±	−	−	±	±	±	|
T. albuginea / T. vasculosa: Degeneration of Vessel Endothelium	|	+	±	±	±	±	±	±	|	±	±	±	−	+	+	±	|
T. albuginea / T. vasculosa: Increase of Connective Tissue	|	−	−	±	−	−	−	−	|	−	±	−	−	−	−	−	|
Grade of Atrophy	II	I	I	I	−	−	II	III	II	II	III	I	I	II	I	I	I

N=normal

700

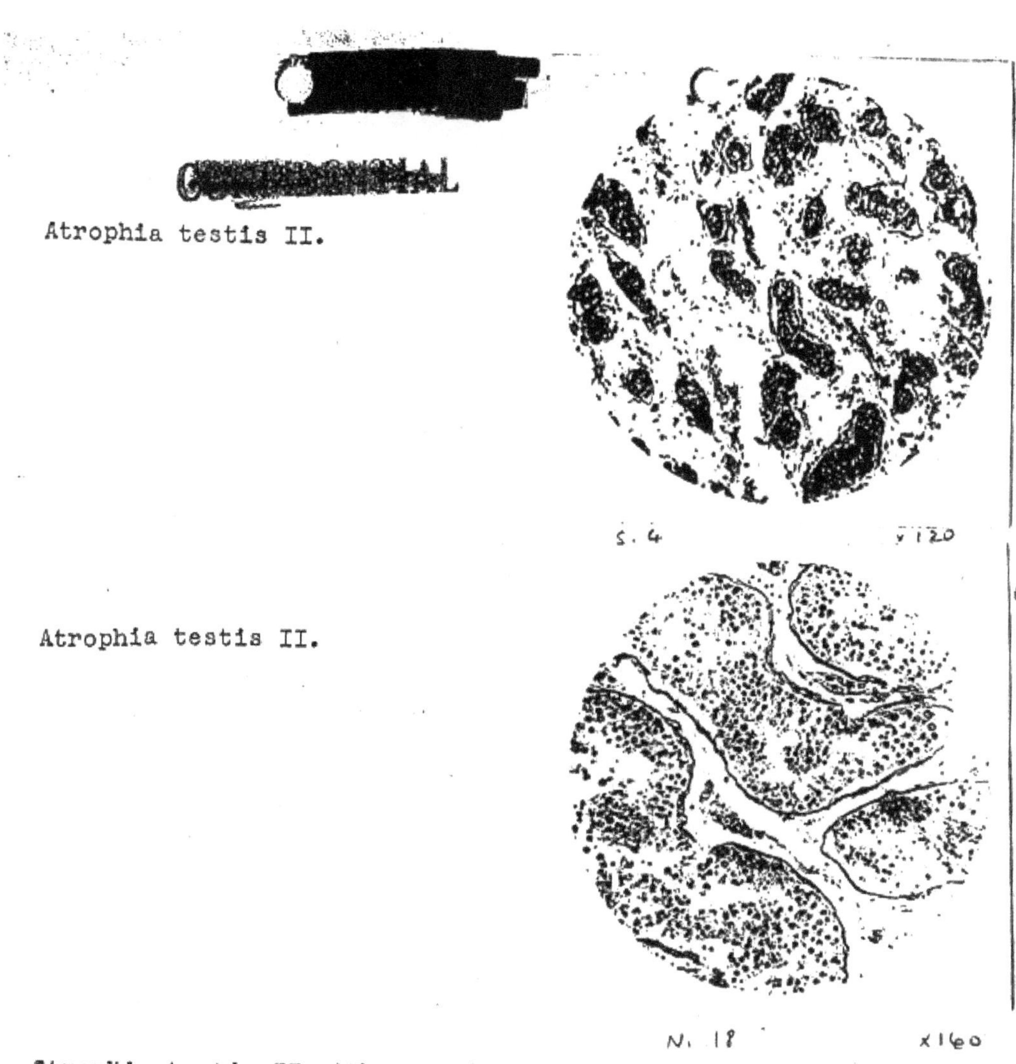

Atrophia testis II.

Atrophia testis II.

Atrophia testis II,with some degenerative signs
(giant cell formation)

Pituitary body

702

PITUITARY-BODY.

(A) Microscop. Investigation

N. 2.

Pituitaritis serosa. Slight congestion and slight dissociation of parenchymatous cell arrangements with more or less considerably degenerated parenchymatous cells.

N. 2I.

Considerable congestion with some leucocytes as capillary contents and miliary localised fresh hemorrhages (bionecrtic ruins of parenchymatous cells at hemorrhagic parts). Slight edematous swelling of subendotheliar tissues and slight dissociation of parenchymatous cell arrangements with considerably degenerated parenchymatous cells.

N. 23.

Slight congestion with some leucocytes as capillary contents and cloudy swelling of rather atrophic glandular cells.

N. 26.

Considerable congestion with some leucocytes and some bacterial masses as capillary contents and edematous swelling of subendotheliar layers with slight dissociation of cellular arrangements. Cloudy swelling or vacuolar degeneration of rather atrophic glandular (esp. basophilic) cells.

703

N. 29.

Considerable congestion and edematous swelling of subendotheliar layers. Cloudy swelling of rather atrophic glandular (esp. basophilic cells) cells.

N. 31.

Slight congestion, slight parenchymatous cloudy swelling and slight dissociation of cell-arrangements.

N. 34.

Post mortal changes.

Considerable congestion, with some leucocytes as capillary contents and remarkable subendotheliar swelling with slight dissociation of glandular cell-arrangements.

More or less remarkable cloudy swelling of parenchymatous cells.

N. 35.

Considerable congestion with some leucocytes, swelling of capillary-endothelial cells and more or less considerabley cloudy swelling of parenchymatous cells.

N. 36.

Considerable congestion with some leucocytes, subendotheliar swelling and more or less considerable cloudy swelling of parenchymatous cells.

N. 38.

Intense congestion (with some bacterial masses in capillaries) and Atrophic glandular cells with slight parenchymatous degeneration. Some submiliary hemorrhages in posterior lobe.

N. 40.

Intense congestion, intense edema and slight erythrocytes-leakages in

CONFIDENTIAL

anterior lobe.

Some parenchymatous degeneration.

Considerable congestion and slight hemorrhages in posterior lobe.

N. 42.

Intense pericapsular hemorrhages and intense congestion, (with some bacterial masses in capillaries) edema and slight hemorrhages in anterior lobe.

Considerable parenchymatous degeneration.

Considerable congestion and some hemorrhages in posterior lobe.

N. 46.

Slight congestion, considerable edema and some parenchymatous degeneration in anterior lobe.

Considerable congestion and slight erythrocytes-leakages in posterior lobe.

N. 44.

Considerable congestion with some leucocytes, subendotheliar swelling and swelling of capillary endothelial cells with slight dissociation of glandular cell arrangements. More or less remarkable cloudy swelling of glandular cells.

N. 49.

More or less severe congestion with submiliary localised hemorrhages and edematous swelling of subendotheliar tissues with slight dissociation of cellular arrangements.

More or less remarkable cloudy degeneration of parenchymatous cells (esp. basophilic cells).

In neuro-pituitary parts, considerable congestion and partial hemorrhages with slight perivascular round cell accumulation.

CONFIDENTIAL 705

CONFIDENTIAL

S. 38.

More or less remarkable congestion with some leucocytes, edematous swelling of subendotheliar layers and swelling of capillary endothelial cells. Remarkable cloudy swelling of parenchymatous cells.

706

(B) SUMMARY

A) Anterior lobe.

I) Generally with some capillary congestion.

in slight degree. 4 cases.

in medium degree. 7 cases.

in severe degree. 5 cases.

with some leucocytes as capillary contensts.

8 cases.

with some bacterial masses as capillary contents.

3 cases.

with some perivasular hemorrhages.

3 cases.

Hemorrhages in pericapsular tissues.

1 cases.

2) Then occured some signs of so-called serous inflammation.

with considerable subendotheliar edema. 7 cases.

with some dissociation of cellular arrangements.

7 cases.

with some degenerative swelling of capillary endothelial cells (swelling, clouding and desquamation). 3 case.

3) Then it shows some degenerative changes of parenchymatous cells, esp. at perivascular portions.

Cloudy swelling in slight degree. 1 cases.

in medium degree. 7 cases.

in severe degree. 6 cases.

707

CONFIDENTIAL

Cloudy swelling with considerable vacuolar degeneration.

1 cases.

B) Posterior lobe.

Sometimes with considerable congestion and following changes.

Considerable congestion. 1 cases.

", with some perivascular hemorrhages. 3 cases.

", with slight hyperplasia of neuroglia cells.

0 cases.

Accordingly, the main significant changes are considerable Pituitaritis serosa (congestion, serous exsudation and some hemorrhages and some parenchymatous degeneration).

Pituitaritis serosa.	I.	2 case.
	II.	5 cases.
	III.	4 cases.
	IV.	1 cases.

708

PITUITARY BODY

			N 2	N 21	N 23	N 26	N 29	N 31	N 34	N 35	N 36	N 38	S 38
Capsule		Congestion	∸	−	∸	∸	+	+	÷	|	+	++	+
		Edema	+	++	++	+	+	+	÷	|	++	+++	+
		Hemorrhage	−	+	÷	+	+	+	∸	|	+	++	÷
		Round Cell Infiltration	−	−	−	+	∸	∸	∸	|	∸	++	∸
Adenohypophysis		Congestion	÷	++	+	++	++	+	++	+	+	++	++
		Edema	+	÷	+	++	+	+	++	++	+++	+++	++
		Hemorrhage	−	++	++	∸	+	−	∸	−	+	−	−
		Round Cell Infiltration	∸	∸	−	−	−	∸	−	∸	∸	−	−
	Chromophobe Cells	Atrophy	+	−	+	+	∸	−	−	−	−	+	−
		Degeneration	÷	−	+	+	+	∸	∸	−	−	÷	∸
		Changes of Nuclei: Pyknosis	∸	−	∸	−	−	−	−	−	−	−	−
		Changes of Nuclei: Karyorrhexis	−	−	−	−	−	−	−	−	−	−	−
		Changes of Nuclei: Karyolysis	∸	−	∸	÷	∸	∸	∸	−	−	+	∸
	Eosinophile Cells	Atrophy	+	−	+	+	∸	−	−	−	−	+	−
		Degeneration	+	+	+	++	+	+	++	+	+	+	++
		Changes of Nuclei: Pyknosis	∸	÷	∸	+	+	+	−	+	−	∸	++
		Changes of Nuclei: Karyorhexis	−	−	−	−	−	∸	+	−	−	∸	−
		Changes of Nuclei: Karyolysis	+	+	+	+	+	+	+	+	+	+	+
	Basophile Cells	Atrophy	+	−	∸	+	∸	−	−	−	−	+	−
		Degeneration	+	+	+	++	++	+	++	+	+	+	+
		Changes of Nuclei: Pyknosis	∸	−	−	+	+	+	−	−	−	−	−
		Changes of Nuclei: Karyorrhexis	−	−	−	−	−	−	+	−	−	−	−
		Changes of Nuclei: Karyolysis	+	+	+	+	++	+	+	+	+	+	+
		Necrosis	−	−	−	−	−	−	−	−	−	−	−
Neurohypophysis		Congestion	−	÷	|	+	∸	+	|	−	+	++	+
		Edema	+	+	|	+	÷	+	|	+	+	+++	+
		Hemorrhage	−	∸	|	+	−	+	|	∸	+	+++	+
		Round Cell Infiltration	−	∸	|	∸	−	÷	|	−	∸	++	+
Pars intermedia		Color of Colloid	V.	V.	|	V.	|	V.	|	|	V.	|	R.
		Vacuoles in Colloid	+	+	|	+	|	+	|	|	+	|	−
		Desquamation of Epithelium	−	+	|	−	|	+	|	|	+	|	−
		Hemorrhage	−	−	|	−	|	−	|	|	−	|	−
		Round Cell Infiltration	−	−	|	−	|	−	|	|	−	|	−

V. = violet
R. = red

709

C ████ C

CONFIDENTIAL

Congestion and edema at perivascular and subepithelial layers.
Intense degeneration of parenchymatous cells.

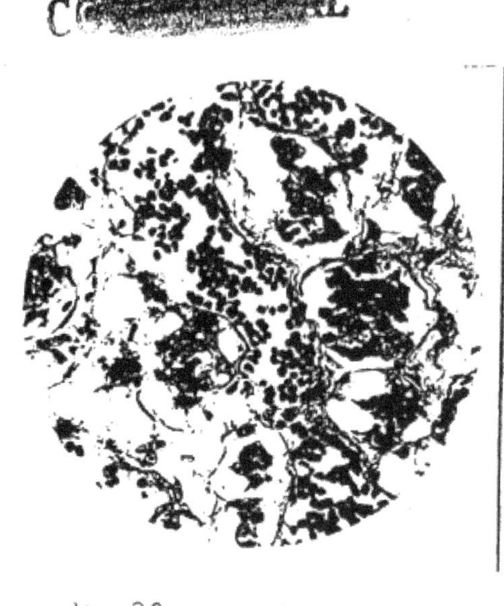

N-38 x330

Congestion, edematous swelling of subepithelial layer and cloudy swelling of parenchymatous cells.

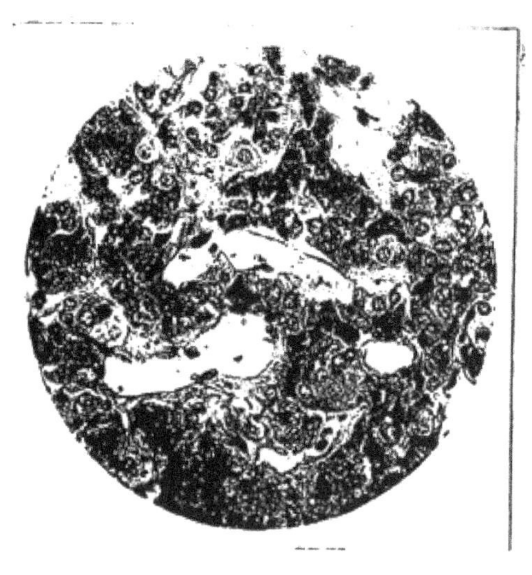

N-38 x130

CONFIDENTIAL

710

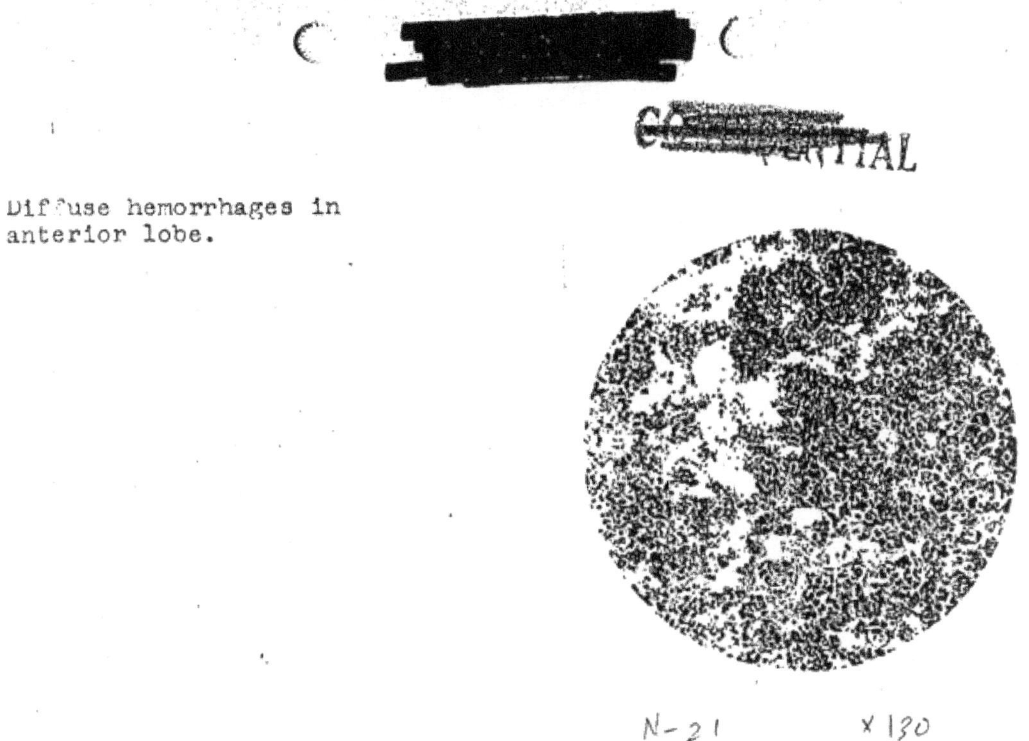

CONFIDENTIAL

Diffuse hemorrhages in anterior lobe.

N-21　　x130

Diffuse hemorrhages in posterior lobe.

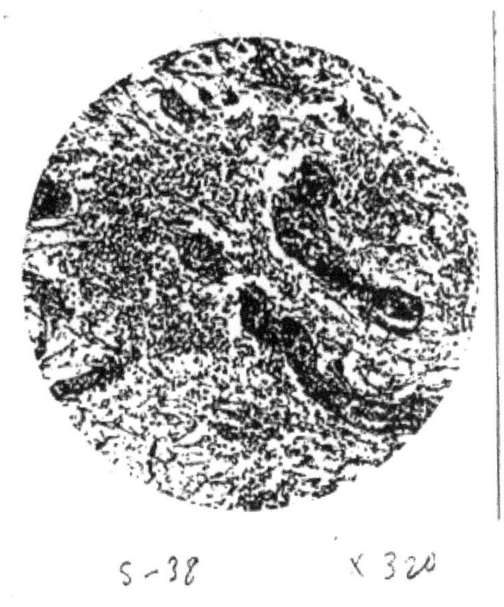

S-38　　x320

CONFIDENTIAL　711

Skin

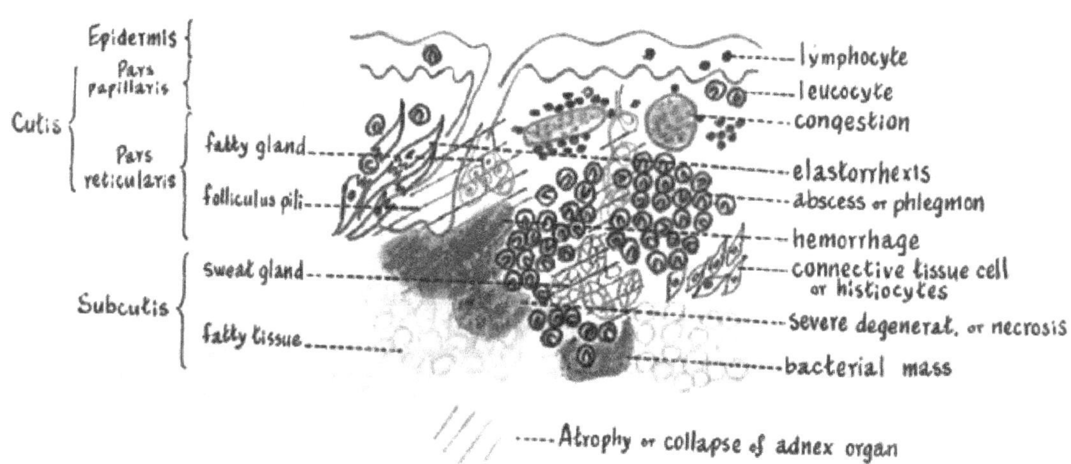
Epidermis
Pars papillaris
Cutis
Pars reticularis
fatty gland
folliculus pili
sweat gland
Subcutis
fatty tissue
lymphocyte
leucocyte
congestion
elastorrhexis
abscess or phlegmon
hemorrhage
connective tissue cell or histiocytes
severe degenerat. or necrosis
bacterial mass
Atrophy or collapse of adnex organ

CONFIDENTIAL

712

CONFIDENTIAL

S K I N

(A) Microscop. Investigation.

~~e-e~~

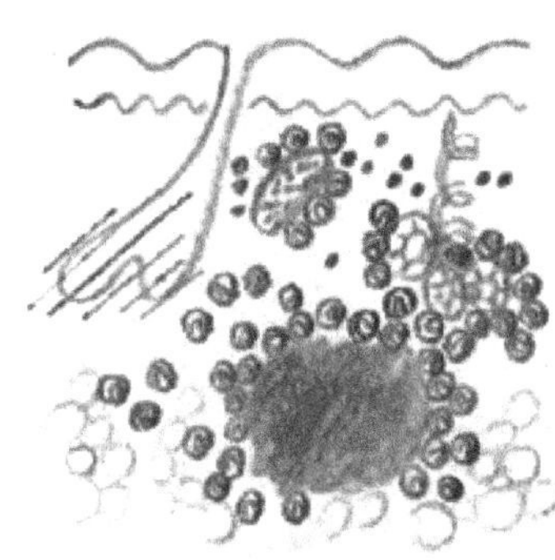

S. I4.(a)(Skin of r-forearm).

Intense hemorrhages in subcutaneous tissues (plenty of erythrocytes and fragments of leucocytes).

At the perifocal tissues of these hemorrhagic places, occured intense phlegmons with plenty of leucocytes-migrations.

In cutis, occured diffuse leucocytes (and some lymphocytes)- emigration, esp. along the blood-vessels and sweat glands.

Atrophy of Folliculus pili.

S14(b)

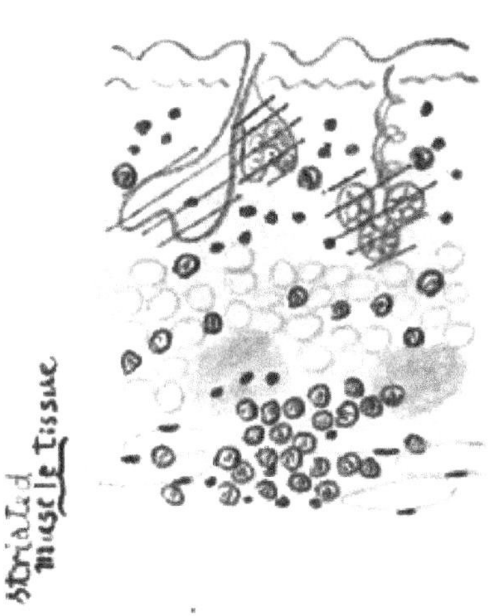

S. I4 (b). (Skin of l-forearm).

Diffuse phlegmonous infiltration of leucocytes (and some lymphocytes) in striated muscle tissues, which lie under ~~the~~ the subcutis, accompanied with some hemorrhages at perivascular portions.

Diffuse leucocytes (and some lymphocytes)-infiltration in cutaneous and subcutaneous tissues.

Atrophy of the adnex-organs.

S. I5. (Skin of l-thigh).

Diffuse phlegmonous infiltration of leucocytes in all layers of skin, and esp. in the muscle

CONFIDENTIAL 413

CONFIDENTIAL

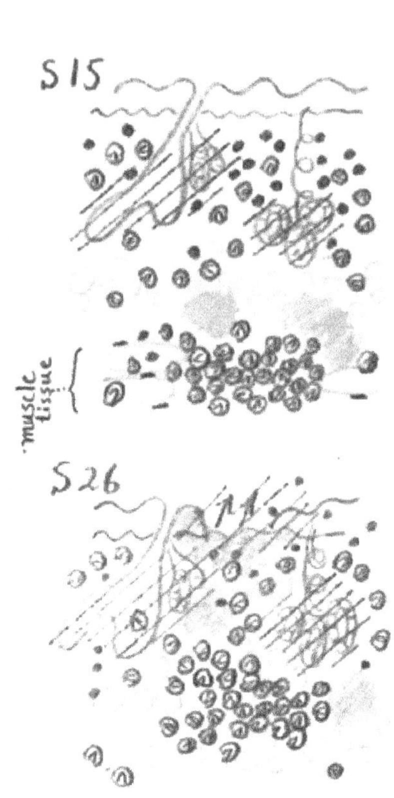

tissues, which lie under the subcutis, accompanied with multiple hemorrhages in muscle tissues.

Rather anemic in cutaneous tissues.

Atrophy of adnex-organs..

S. 26. (Skin of abdominal region).

Abscesses in cutaneous and subcutaneous tissues, in which many hemorrhagic focus are recognized.

.Intense degeneration of epidermis and cutaneous tissues.

Collapse of adnex-organs.

N. 2. (Skin of r-forearm).

Diffuse phlegmone-us infiltration in subcutaneous tissues, ~~accompnied~~

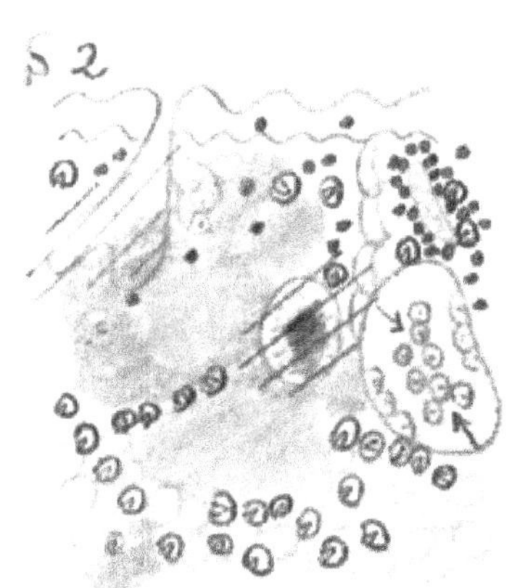

S-2 (Skin of mamma).

The most diffuse, intense hemorrhages, accompanied with leucocytic and necrotic changes all over the investigated areas.

Necrotic ruins of glands. Some remained glands are filled with massive desquamated epitheliums, some serous fluids, decayed masses and some round cells.

Here and there multiple perivascular round-cell-accumulation.

With massive fibrinous separation and multiple localised hemorrhagic or leucocytic infiltra-

CONFIDENTIAL

714

tion along the blood-vessels.

N7

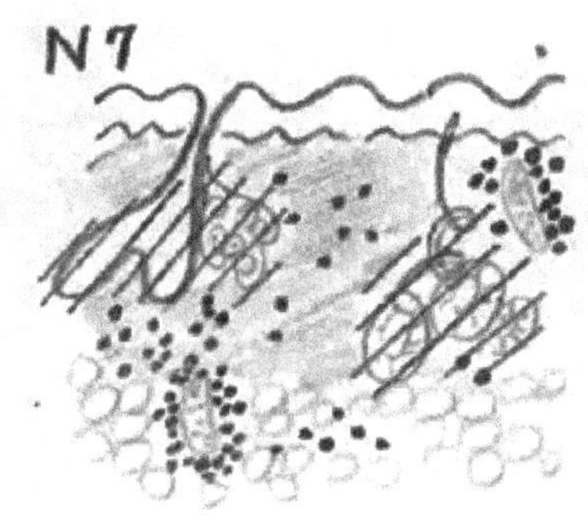

In the cutis, occured intense congestion, slight hemorrhages and some round-cell-infiltration at perivascular portions.

Collapse of adnex-organs.

N. 7. (eye-lid).

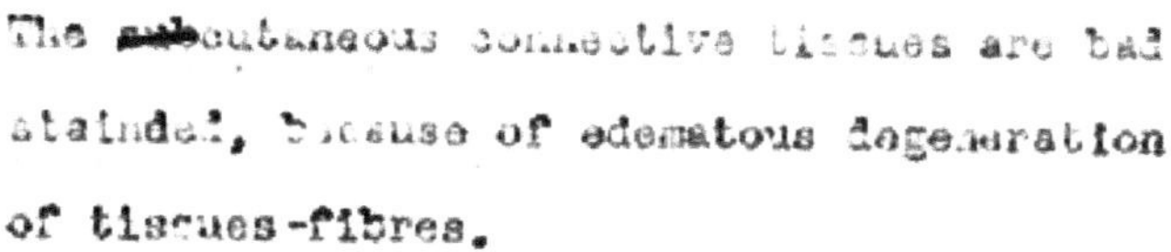

The subcutaneous connective tissues are bad staindel, because of edematous degeneration of tissues-fibres.

N 11

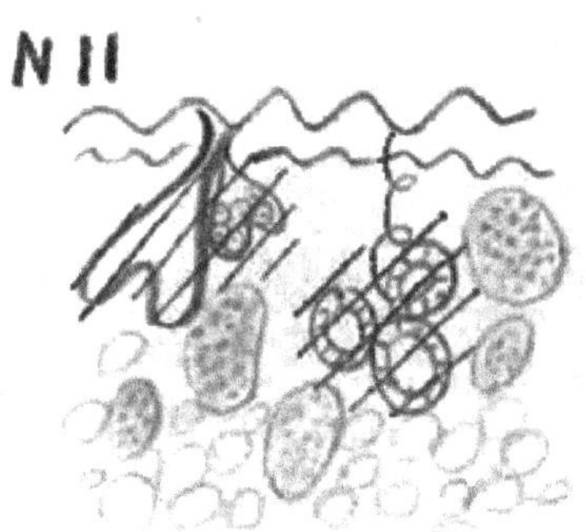

Most parts of epidermis and adnex organs fall into pycnosis and karyorrhexis.

Slight round-cell-infiltration along the blood-vessels and sweat glands.

N. II (skin of scrotum).

Considerable congestion and some serous infiltration in epidermis and cutaneous tissues.

(Accompanied with swelling of pickle cells and roughness of connective tissues).

N.19

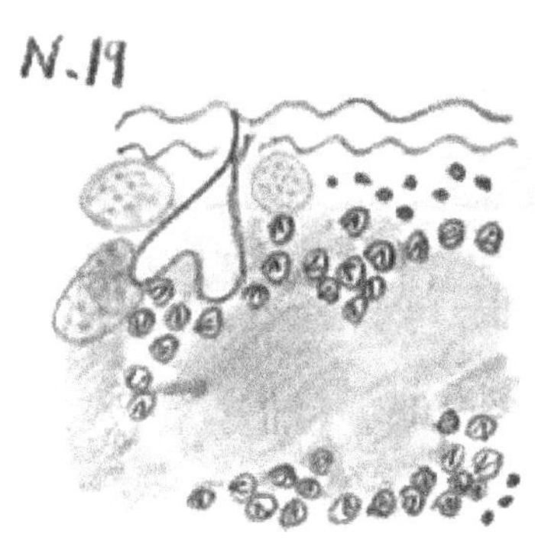

Atrophy of adnex-organs.

N. I9. (skin of r-forearm).

Phlegmon and hemorrhages in subcutaneous tissues, with intense congestion, intense swelling of blood-vessel-walls, fibrinous separation and diffuse hemorrhages.

No. 20. (skin of r-breast).

Phlegmon in subcutaneous tissues, with intense

CONFIDENTIAL 715

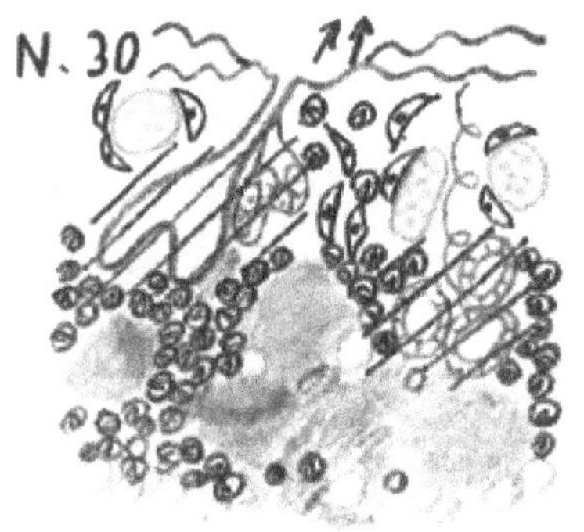

hemorrhages with plenty fibrinous masses, edematous swelling of connective tissues, and diffuse leucocytes (and lymphocytes,- dissemination in subcutaneous tissues.

Some histiocytes around blood-vessels, which fall into somewhat bionecrotic changes.

Degeneration of sweat glands and Folliculi pili.

No. 35. (skin of l-forearm).

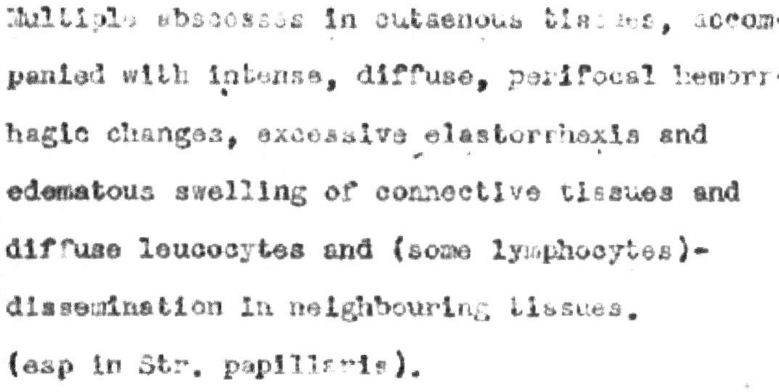

Multiple abscesses in cutaenous tissues, accompanied with intense, diffuse, perifocal hemorrhagic changes, excessive elastorrhexis and edematous swelling of connective tissues and diffuse leucocytes and (some lymphocytes)-dissemination in neighbouring tissues.

(esp in Str. papillaris).

N35

Edematous swelling and atrophia of folliculi.

No. 36. (skin of r-cervical region).

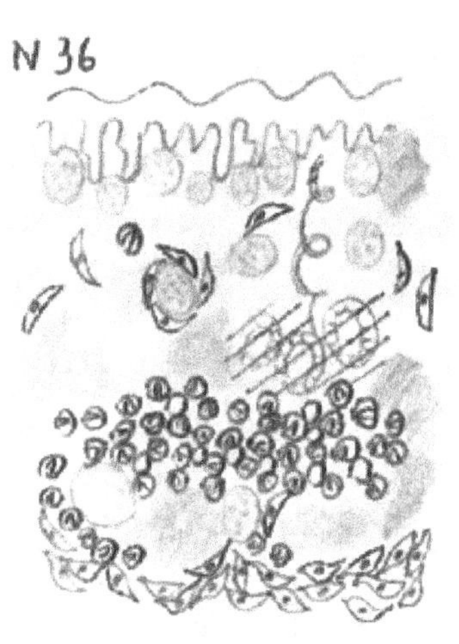

Phlegmonous infiltration in subcutaneous tissues, accompanied with intense congestion and multiple hemorrhages in the neighbouring perifocal tissues. At the other hand, increased some histiocytes, as reparative processes.

In cutaneous tissues, considerable congestion and some histiocytes around the congested blood-vessels.

collapse of sweat-glands.

CONFIDENTIAL 716

N. 36 (b). (skin of r-breast).

Phlegmon in subcutaneous tissues with necrotic focal parts and hemorrhagic perifocal parts (intensely hemorrhagic).

In the neighbouring tissues of these hemorrhagic-necrotic parts, occured some reparative processes (with some increased histiocytes, plasma-cells and some connective tissues).

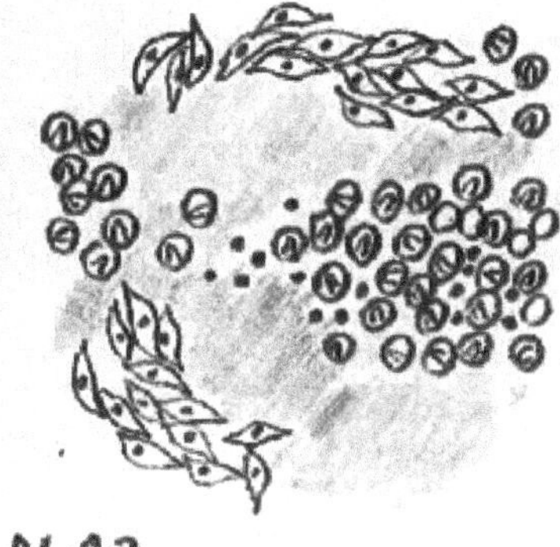

42. (eye-lid).

Intense degenerative changesof cutaneous tisdurd, eiyh hyaline degeneration or elastorrhexis of connective tissues, dilatated blood-vessels (with hyaline degeneration of walls), diffuse hemorrhages and intense edematous swelling.

Accompanied with intense degeneration of adnex-organs and catarrhalic changes of conjunctiva and some subepithelial round-cell-infiltration.

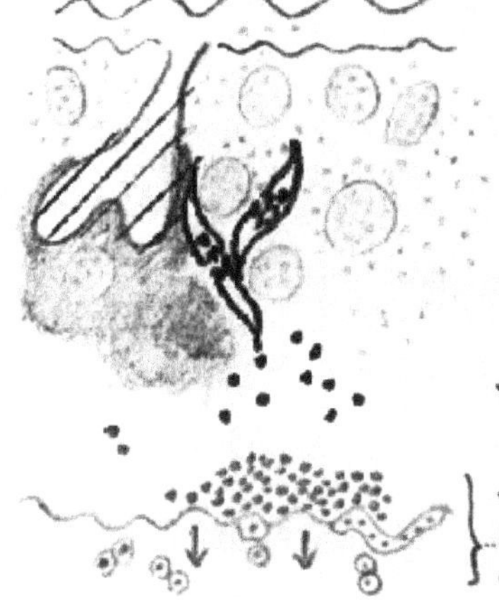

46. (eye-lid).

Considerable degenerative changes of epidermis and cutaneous tissues.

The cells of Rete Malpigigh fall into karyorrhexis and pycnosis.

Swelling of connective tissues and some miliary necrosis in Str. subpapillare.

Edoma of Folliculi pili and collapse of all adnex-organs. Catarrhalic changes of the conjunctiva and some subepithelial round-cell-infiltration. CONFIDENTIAL 7/7

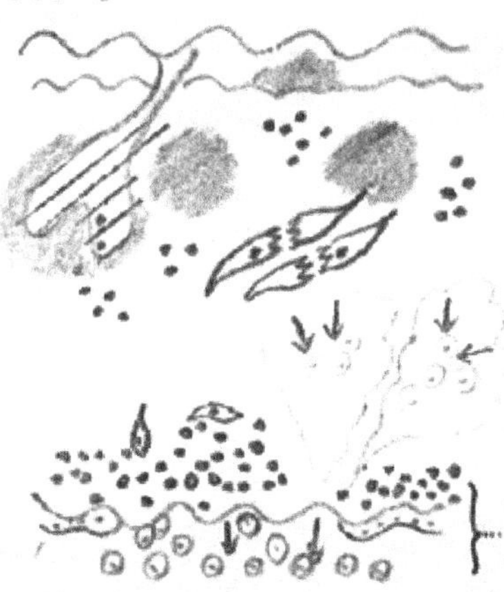

B) S U M M A R Y

(I)

bird's-eye view of all mikroskopically investigation cases.

S-2. (skin of mamma)
Diffuse intense hemorrhges with leukocytes infiltration. Much separated fibrin masses and degenerated adnex organs in this foci.

S-14(a) (Skin of r-forearm)
Intense hemorrhages in subcutaneous tissues with erythrocytes and leukocytes. At the perifokal tissues diffuse phlegmonous leukocytes infiltration. Atrophy of folliculi pili in cutis.

S-14.(b) (Skin of l-forearm)
Diffuse phlegmonous leucocytes infiltration in striated muscle tissues which lie under subcutis, accompanied with some perivascular hemmorrhages. Atrophy of adnex organs.

S-15. (Skin of l-thigh)
Diffuse phlegmonous leucocytes infiltration in all layers, esp. in the muscle tissues which lie under subcutis, with multiple hemorrhages.

S-26. (Skin of abdominal region)
Abscess in cutis and subcutis with multiple hemorrhages.

2. (Skin of forearm-r)
Diffuse phlegmonous infiltration in ~~tissues~~ subcutis.

7. (eye-lid)
Slight round cell infiltration.

11. (Skin of scrotum)
Considerable congestion and edema.

19. (Skin of r-forearm)
Phlegmons and hemorrhages. Much separated fiblin masses.

30. (Skin of breast)
Phlegmon and hemorrhages with much separated fibrin masses in subcutis.

35. (Skin of r-forearm)
Multiple abscess in cutaneouswith perifocal hemorrhages and diffuse leucocytes infiltration.

718

56. (a) (Skin of cervical region)
Phlegmons in subcutis with congestion and hemorrhages. As reparative process, histiocytes accumulation. Collaps of sweat gland.

36. (b) (Skin of r-breast)
Phlegmon in subcutis with periphocal hemorrhages. As reparative processes, histiocytes accumuration.

42. (eye-lid)
Intes congestion and diffuse hemorrhages. Svere catarrhalic changes of conjunctiva.

46. (eye-lid)
Severe degeneration of connective tissues with collapse adnex organs. Catarrhalic changes of conjunctiva.

U

(II)

Phlegmon and abscess formation are recognized in 12 cases (all 16 cases). Accompanied with severe hemorrhages and much separated fibrin masses (which increased bacterial masses). Especially in skin of thigh and forearm (S-14. b. case and S-15. case), phlegmon with hemorrhage extend in the striated muscle tissues which lie under subcutaneous tissues.

Always as tissue reaction, severe congestion and round cell infiltration and esp. in 2 cases as reparative process, histiocytes and plasma cells accumulation in perifocal tissues with new capillary formation According to intensification of phlegmonous inflammation more or less degenerative changes of cutaneous tissue; elastorrhxis, atrophy of rete Malphighii and collaps of adnex organs.

In other 4 cases slighter degenerative changes are recognised.

3 cases in these cases are concerned with eye-lid: diffuse hemorrhages without phlegmon in 1 case and catarrhalic changes of conjunctiva in 2 cases.

719

CONFIDENTIAL

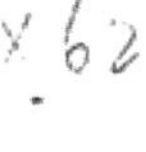

Diffuse hemorrhages in cutis and atrophy of folliculi pili.

x 62

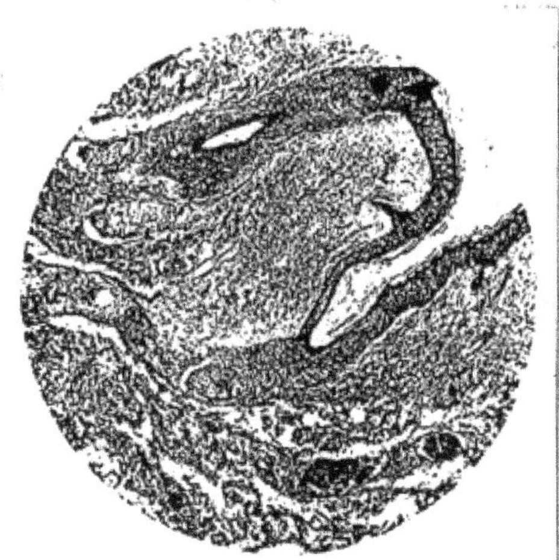

Diffuse hemorrhages in subcutis.

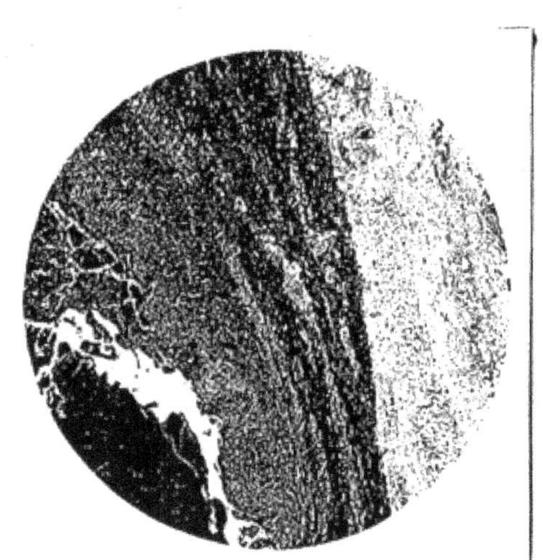

CONFIDENTIAL 720

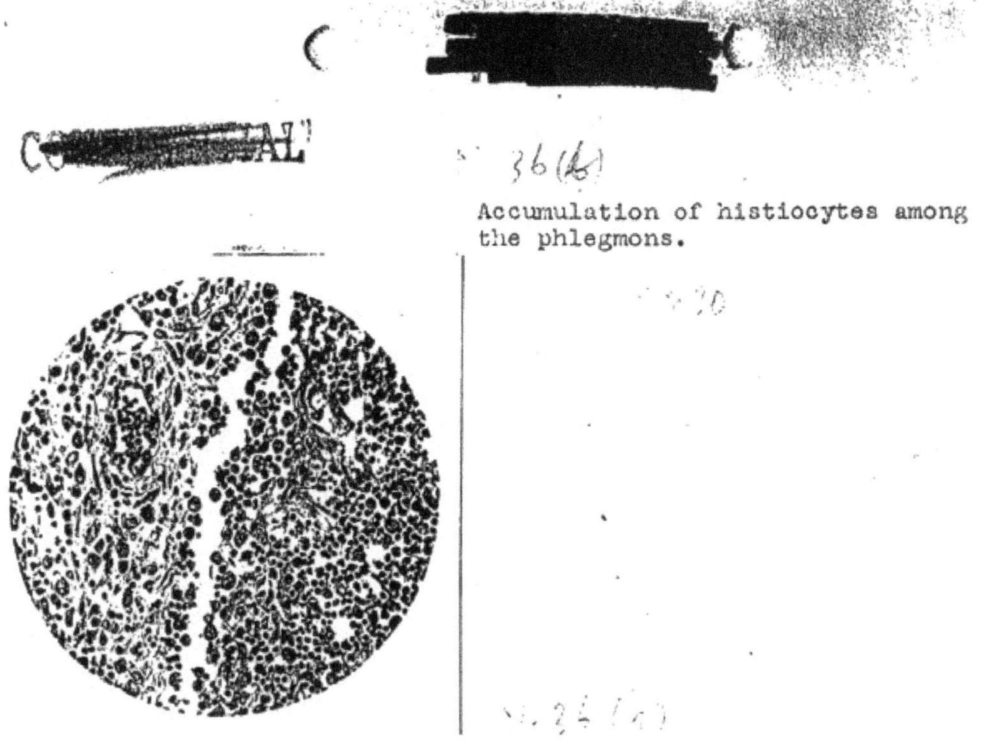

No. 36(b)

Accumulation of histiocytes among the phlegmons.

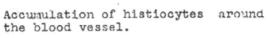

No. 36(a)

Accumulation of histiocytes around the blood vessel.

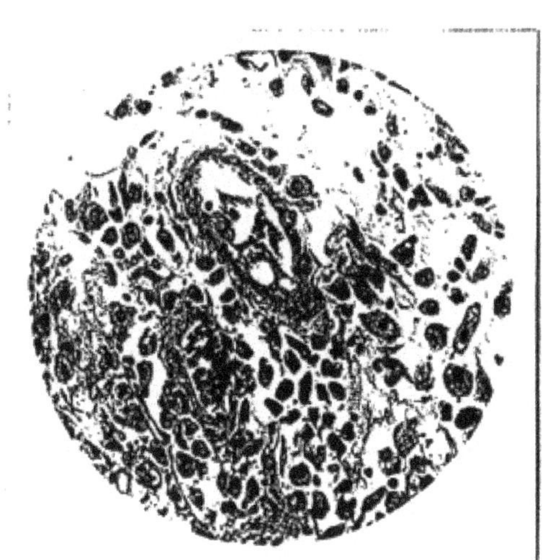

721

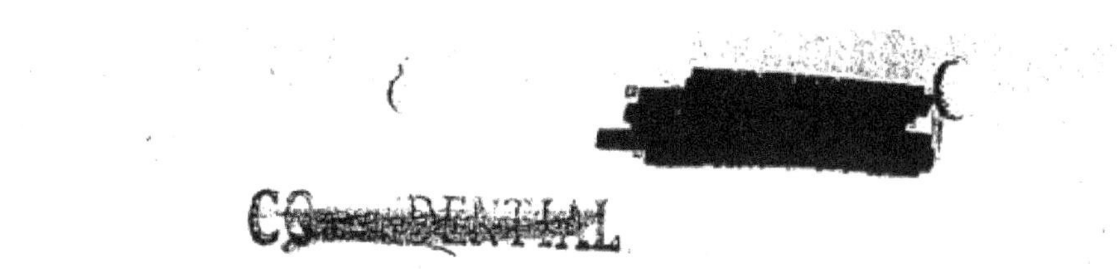

Edema of folliculus pili.

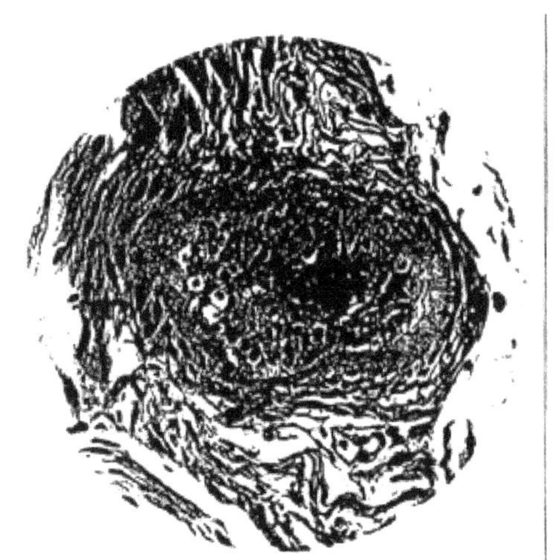

Abscesses and diffuse hemorrhages.

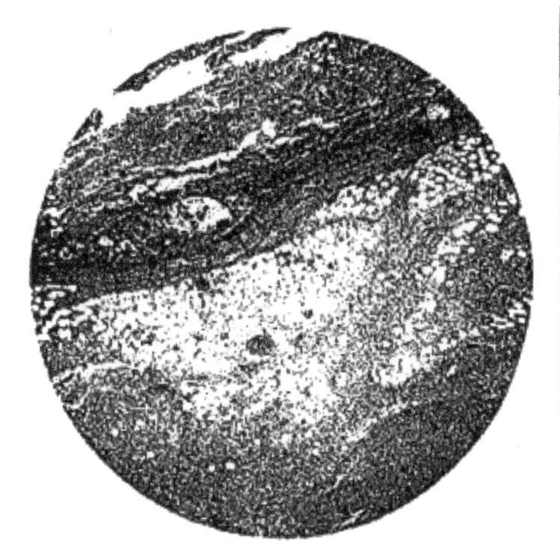

Leucocytic infiltration and diffuse hemorrhages in intermuscular tissues.

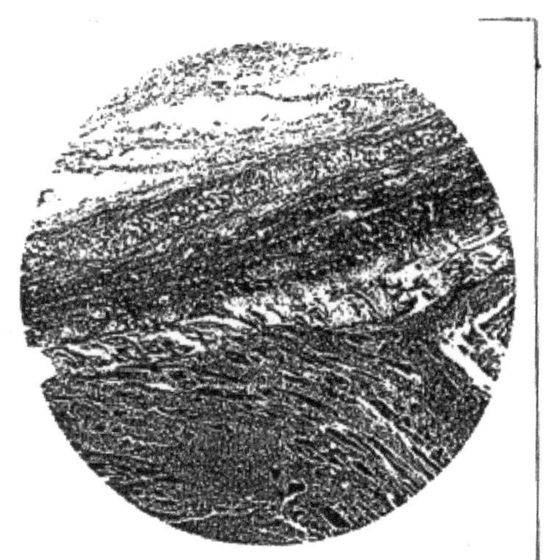

723

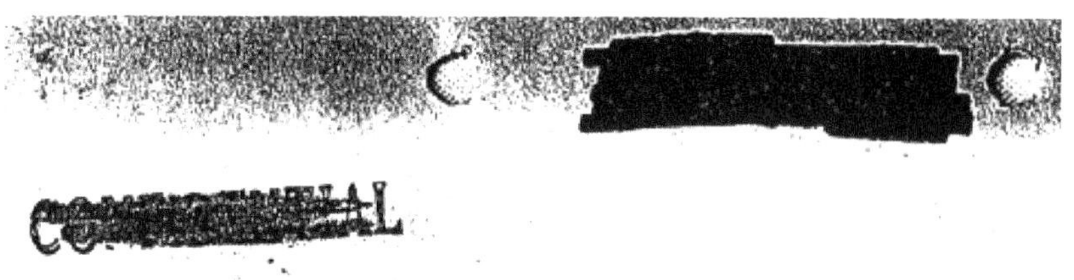

Ovary

O V A R Y.

(A) Micfoscop. Investigation.

S-I. 8 years old.

.Considerable congestion and some fibrinous swelling of blood-vessel-walls.

.Slight edemaous swelling of medullary tissues.

.Considerable chromatolysis or disappearance of nuclei and cloudy swelling of protoplasma of primordial ova.

S-6. 12 years old.

.Considerable congestion and some bacterial masses and leucocytes in blood-vessels (slightly organised).

.Considerable chromatolysis and cloudy degeneration of protoplasma of some primordial ova.

S-22. 3 years old.

.Considerable congestion (with some leucocytes) and some slight hemorrhages in interstitial tissues and some primitive vesicles.

.Chromatolysis and cloudy degneration of protoplasma of primordial ova.

2. 34 years old.

.Slight congestion.

.Most of the primordial ova and some ripe follicles fall into atresia and some remaining bodies show clouoy degneration and desquamation of granulosa-cells.

3. 35 years old.

.Remarkable congestion with some leucocytes and considerable edema (especially in medullary tissues).

.Some degenerative changes of blood-vessels with desquamation of endothe-

CONFIDENTIAL 725

lial cells and some hyalinous swelling of media.

.Disappearance of nuclei and cloudy degeneration of protoplasma of primordial ova.

.Persistence of cystic follicles.

9. I8 years old.

.Intense congestion and serous infiltration (edema) in medullary tissues with intense degenerative changes of blood-vessels-walls (esp. in medullary tissues).

.Corpus luteum menstruationum haemorrhagicum with edematous swelling and dissociation of lutein cells layer.

.Disappearance of nuclei and cloudy degeneration of protoplasma of primordial ova.

IO.

.Remarkable congestion and intense edema in interstitial tissues.

.All follicles fall into atresia.

I2. I2 years old.

.Considerable congestion (with some leucocytes and some bacterial masses as vascular contents).

.Many focus of some localised and some diffuse hemorrhages in interstitia tissues and perhaps also in atretic follicles, accompanied with some leucocytes emigration in interstitial tissues and some desolative changes of rips follicles.

.Disappearance of nuclei and cloudy degneration of primordial ova.

.Many atretie follicles and some ripe follicles and persistence of cystic follicles.

726

I7. 28 years old.

.Intense congestion and some bacterial masses in blood-vessels.

.Existence of some corpus lutein, accompanied with some degenerative changes: cloudy swelling of lutein cells and diffuse hemorrhages in lutein cell layer and T. externa, accompanied with some bacterial accumulation.

.Few primordial ova and some ripe follicles.

20. 32 years old.

.Remarkable congestion and some hyalinous degneration of some arteriole walls.

.Few primordial ova.

29. 3I years old.

.Remarkable congestion and some hyalinous degneration of arteriole walls.

.Remarkable diffuse hemorrhages in corpus fibrosum, as significant pathological changes.

.Few primordial ova and persistence of cystic follicles.

.Edematous swelling of and irregular arrangements of interstitial connective tissues.

30. 6 years old.

.Considerable congestion and some bacterial masses as vascular contents.

.Some edematous swelling of medullary tissues.

.Some slight round cell infiltration around follicles and small bacterial masses in blood-vessel-walls.

3I. 8 years old.

.Some congestion and intense edema at Hilus ovarii.

CONFIDENTIAL

727

.Cloudy degeneration and desquamation of granulosa cells of medium large follicles.

33. 22 years old.

.Intense congestion and some localised or rather diffuse hemorrhages in interstitial tissues and in follicles.

.Existence of corpus folliculare haemorrhagicum, accompanied with extraordiary intense hemorrhages in Tunica externa.

.Intense dageneration of some primordial ova and some ripe follicles, due to some hemorrhagic changes.

.Some of these follicles, which lie in the hemorrhagic focus of cortical tissues, fall into intense degeneration and desolative disappearance.

40. 53 years old.

.Considerable congestion and some roughness of interstitial tissues.

.Disappearance of nuclei and cloudy degneration of protoplasma of primordial ova.

47. 30 years old.

.Intense congestion and some localised hemorrhages and some edematous swelling of interstitial tissues.

.Most of primordial ova and some ripe follicles fall into atresia. Some ~~remarini~~ remaining bodies show some cloudy degeneration and desquamation of granulosa cells.

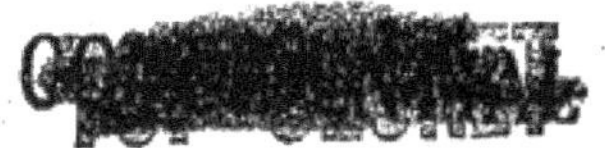

728

CONFIDENTIAL (B) S U M M A R Y

Generally speaking, common changes of all 15 cases are considerable congestion(4 cases in highers grade) and edematous swelling,esp. in medullary tissues(1 case in Hilus ovarii), and remarkable chromatolysis or disappearance of nuclei and cloudy swelling of protoplasma of primordial ova.

Changes of blood-vessel-walls(ex. desquamation of endothelial cells and fibrinous swelling of media cells), and irregular afrangement of connective tissue fibres.Bacterial masses as capillary content or in gland epithelial walls(in 4 cases).

Hemorrhages in 5 cases, not only in stroma, but also especially in atretic follicles(in 1 cases) and in corpus fibrosum(in 1 case) and in corpus luteum.

Bleeding in T. externa of corpus folliculare haemorrhagicum seems to be extraordinary(over physiological bleeding).

Lutein cells of corpus luteum adn grannulosa cells of ripe follicles are fallen into degeneration or desquamation.

In 1 case many primordial ova are fallen into collapse in blood-sea at cortical tissues. Perisistence of atretic cystic follicle is sometimes recognised.

Therefore severe changes of stroma and considerable degenerative changes are recognised.

CONFIDENTIAL 729

OVARY

			N 2	N 3	N 9	N 10	N 12	N 17	N 20	N 29	N 30	N 31	N 33	N 40	N 47	S 1	S 6	S 22
Parenchyma	Primordial Ova	Number	∸	∸	+	|	÷	∸	÷	÷	+	+	+	++	÷	+++	++	+
		Cloudy Degeneration of Ova	+	++	++	|	++	++	+	+	+	+	++	+	+	++	+	++
		Disappearance of Germinal Vesicles	÷	++	÷	|	+	∸	∸	÷	+	+	+	++	÷	+	+	+
		Hemorrhage	−	(÷)	+	|	−	−	−	−	−	−	(++)	−	−	−	−	−
	Ripe Follicles	Degeneration of Granulosa Cells	++	÷	++	|	+	+	÷	÷	÷	++	÷	|	++	÷	+	+
		Desquamation of Granulosa Cells	÷	÷	++	|	+	∸	∸	+	÷	++	÷	|	÷	÷	÷	÷
		Hemorrhage	−	−	(+++)	|	(++)	(+)	−	−	−	−	(+)	|	−	−	−	(÷)
		Emigration of Leucocytes	÷	−	−	|	(+)	−	−	−	∸	∸	(÷)	|	÷	−	−	∸
	Corpus luteum	Hemorrhage	|	|	(++)	|	|	++	−	|	|	|	|	|	|	|	|	|
		Emigration of Leucocytes	|	|	(∸)	|	|	÷	∸	|	|	|	|	|	|	|	|	|
		Emigration of other wandering cells	|	|	(÷)	|	|	÷	÷	|	|	|	|	|	|	|	|	|
	Corpus albicans	Hemorrhage	−	−	|	−	|	−	−	++	|	−	+	|	−	|	|	|
		Cellular Infiltration	∸	∸	|	÷	|	∸	∸	÷	|	∸	÷	|	∸	|	|	|
	Formation of Cysts		∸	++	+	−	÷	∸	÷	++	∸	∸	∸	−	∸	−	∸	+
Stroma	Edema	of Cortex	÷	+	+	∸	÷	÷	∸	÷	∸	∸	÷	÷	÷	∸	∸	∸
		of Medulla	÷	+	++	÷	++	+	+	÷	++	∸	++	|	÷	(++)	(+)	÷
	Contents of Blood vessels	Erythrocytes	÷	++	++	+	÷	++	++	+	+	∸	++	÷	÷	+	+	÷
		Leucocytes	∸	+	÷	÷	(+++)	+	+	∸	÷	−	+	∸	∸	(+)	(+)	(+)
		Lymphocytes	∸	+	÷	÷	÷	÷	÷	∸	÷	÷	÷	∸	÷	÷	∸	∸
	Blood Vessel Walls	Desquamation of Endothelium	÷	+	+	+	+	+	+	+	+	∸	+	÷	÷	∸	∸	÷
		Degeneration of Media	+	+	+	+	+	+	+	÷	+	÷	+	÷	+	÷	÷	÷
		Proliferation of Adventitial Cells	∸	÷	÷	÷	÷	÷	÷	∸	∸	∸	∸	−	∸	÷	÷	÷
	Infiltration	Erythrocytes	−	∸	÷	−	+++	+	+	∸	∸	−	+++	−	−	−	−	−
		Leucocytes	∸	∸	∸	∸	∸	∸	∸	−	∸	∸	+	−	∸	∸	∸	∸
		Lymphocytes	∸	÷	÷	÷	÷	÷	÷	÷	÷	∸	÷	∸	÷	÷	÷	÷
	Proliferation	Histiocytic Cells	∸	∸	÷	∸	÷	÷	÷	∸	∸	∸	∸	∸	∸	÷	÷	∸
		Plasma Cells	∸	−	∸	∸	∸	−	−	−	−	−	∸	−	∸	−	−	−
	Bacterium		−	−	−	−	(÷)	+	+	−	÷	−	−	−	−	−	−	(+)

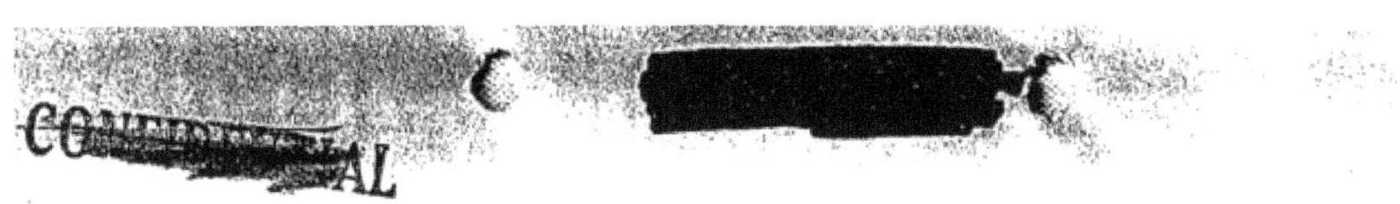

Congestion and some bacterial masses in blood vessel.

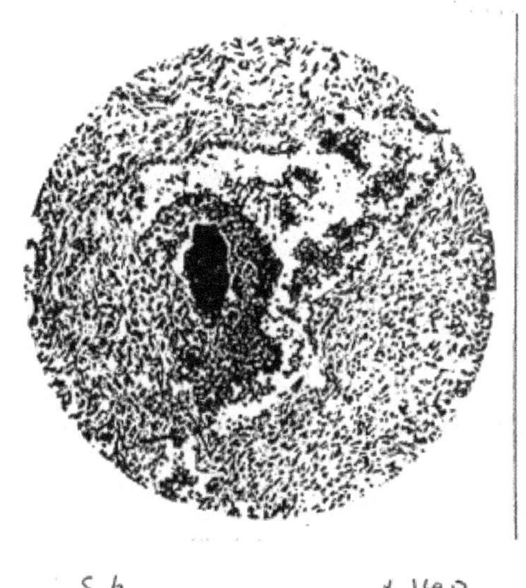

S 6 x 140

Hemorrhages nand some bacterial dissemiantion in cortical tissues.

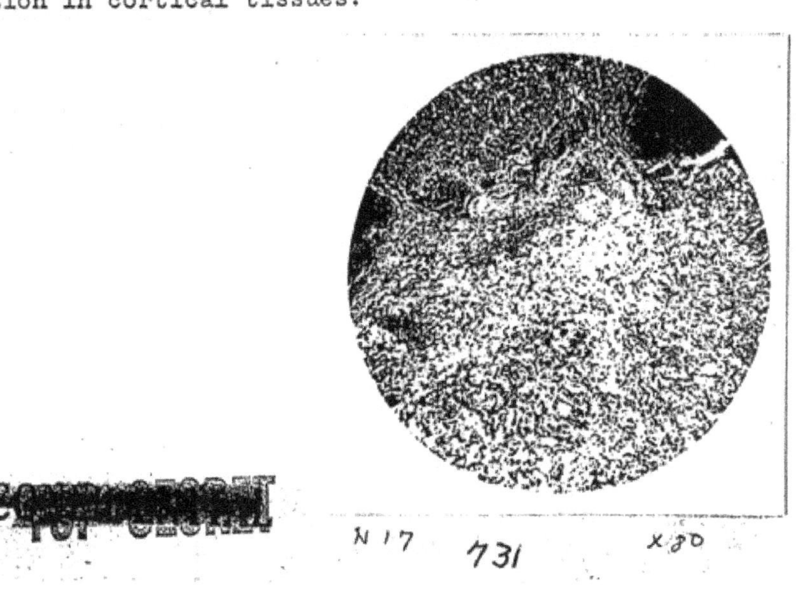

N 17 731 x 80

Hemorrh,ges in cortical tissues.

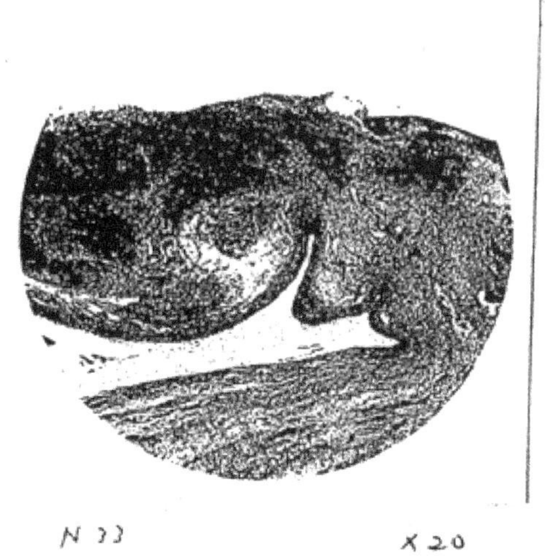

N 33 X 20

Hemorrhgges in corpus fibrosum.

N 29 X 20

CONFIDENTIAL 732

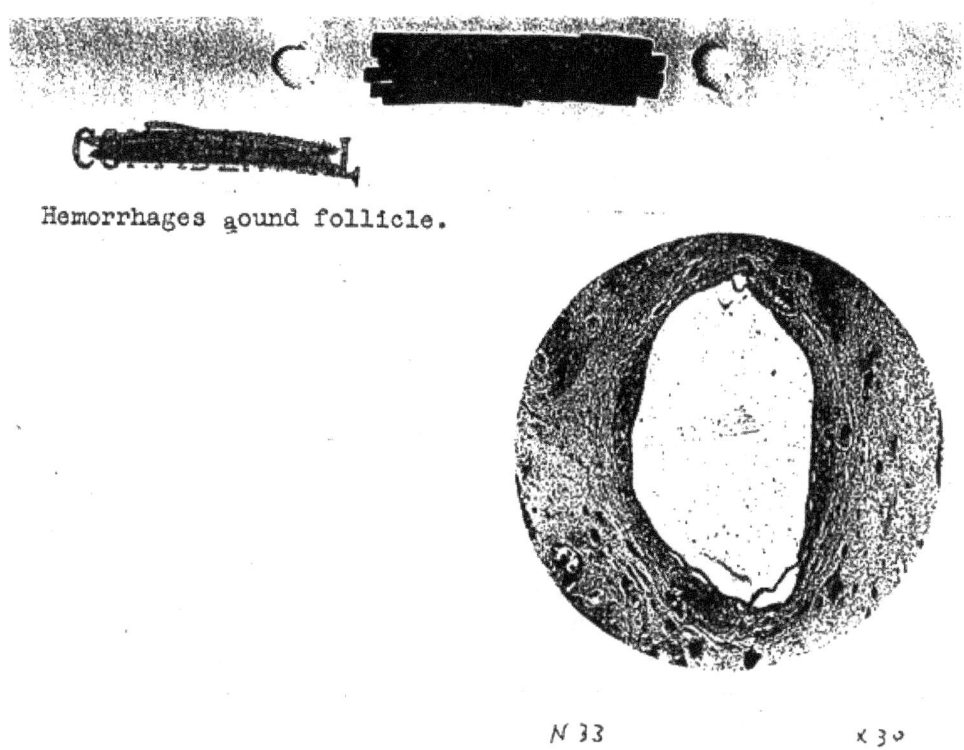

Hemorrhages around follicle.

N 33 x 30

Degeneratiom and desquamation of granulosa cells of ripe follicle.

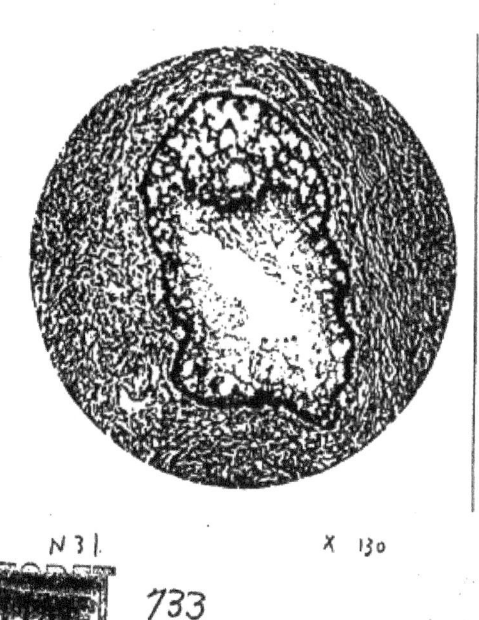

N 31 x 130

733

Other Organs

734

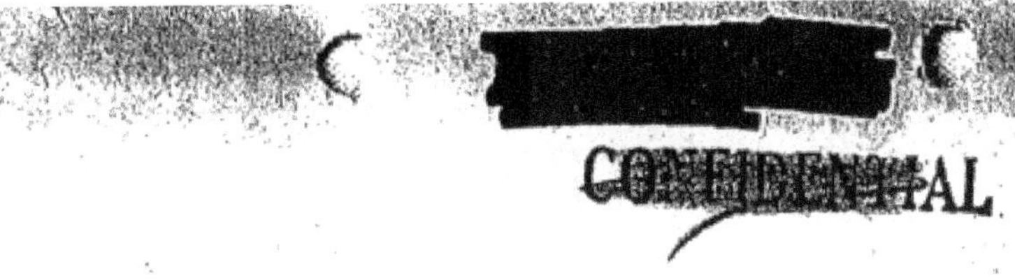

A O R T A.

S-1. Almost normal.

S-2. Almost mormal. slight fongestion of periadventitial tissues.

S-3. Almost normal.

S-4. Almost normal. slight atheromatosis of intima.

S-5. Almost normal.

S-6. Almost normal.

S-7. Almost normal.

S-8. Almost normal.

S-9. Almost normal.

S-10. Almost normal. slight congestion of peri-adventitial tissues.

S-11. Almost normal.

S-12. Almost normal.

S-14. Almost normal.

S-15. Almost normal.

S-19. Remarkable atherosclerosis.

S-22. Almost normal.

S-26. Slight congestion of periadventitial tissues.

S-28. Almost normal.

S-38. Almost normal.

CONFIDENTIAL

UTERUS.

(A) Microscop. Investigation.

N-2. 34 years old.

Type of non-parous.

Considerable congestion, edema and slight hemorrhages in T.muscularis.

Edematous loosening of muscle-fibres.

Slight perivascular round cell-infiltration.

N-3. 35 years old.

Type of multipara.

Considerable congestion and slight edema in subserous and intermuscular tissues.

Slight hyperplaisa of endothelial cells of capillaries.

No remarkable changes else.

N-10. 51 years old.

Type of non-parous.

Remarkable congestion and leucocytes-accumulation in blood-vessels.

Remarkable perivascular round-cell-infiltration(mainly histiocytes).

Some edema in T. muscularis and T. subserosa.

N-15. 30 years old.

Type of multipara.

Considerable congestion and some edema, No remarkable changes else.

N-20. 32 years old.

Type of multipara.

CONFIDENTIAL 736

Considerable congestion, some perivascular round-cell-accumulation and slight hyperplasia of endothelial cells of capillaries.

N-33. 22 years old.

Type of non-parous.

Considerable congestion, some perivascular round-cell-acumulation, slight hyperplasa of capillar endothelial cells and some edema of blood-vessels-walls. No remarkable changes else.

N-36. 48 years old.

Type of multipara. In menstration-pause.

Considerable congestion and some edema with intramural and perivascular round-cell-infiltration.

Desquamation of glandular epithelium.

N-40. 53 years old.

Type of multipara.

Considerable congestion and some edema. No remarkable changes else.

S-19. 58 years old.

Type of multipara. In premenstrual period.

Considerable congestion and edema in intermuscular tissues.

Considerable edematous loosening of blood-vessels-walls.

Desquamation of endothelial cells of blood-vessels.

737

PROSTATA.

N-27.

Considerable congestion and some round-cell-infiltration in interstitium.

With many corpora amylaceae.

(Some places in precancerous state with some irregular cell arrangements --- Carcinoma simplex).

N-42.

Some congestion and some bacterial masses in blood-vessels.

Edematous swelling of interstitium. Swelling and some degeneration of muscular fibres.

With many corpora amylaceae.

N-46.

Considerable degeneration of glandular epithelium.

Some congestion and edema in interstitium.

Edematous swelling and some degeneration of muscular fibres.

With many corpora amylaceae.

S-9.

Some congestion and some edema in interstium, accompanied with considerable round-cell-infilatration at periglandular portions.

S-12.

Some lentilis large places fall into necrotic ruins (tuberculous changes with caseous necrotic changes, accompanied with some miliary calcificated parts and some giant cell formation at perifocal portions).

738

Atrophy and desquamation of glandular epitheliums, considerable hyperplasia of interstitial connective tissues and some round-cell-infiltration.

S-14.

Intensely dilatated glandular spaces, all over the investigated areas, with massive desquamated epitheliums, massive leucocytes and some bacterial colonies.

Remarkable congestion and intense diffuse hemorrhages in interstitiums, accompanied with intense, diffuse leucocytes (and lymphocytes) -dissemination.

Swelling, intense degeneration and some fragmentation of muscular fibres.

S-15.

With the same changes, as in S-14 case described.

More intense diffuse hemorrhages and edema in interstitium.

739

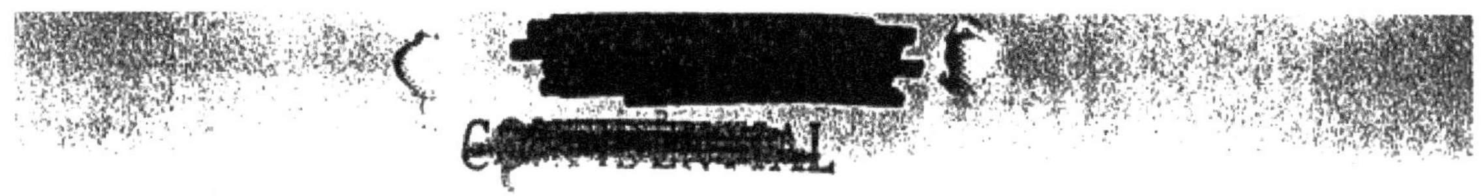

FOLLIAN TUBE.

N-15.

Epitheliums with no remarkable changes.

T. propria with some congestion and some edema.

T. muscularis with considerable congestion, edema and a few round cells infiltration. Some bacterial masses and some leucocytes-accumulation in blood-vessels.

T. subserosa with some congestion and edema.

N-36. Slight catarrh.

Some haemorrhagic-serous masses and some desquamative epithelial cells in tube. Epithelium with no remarkable changes.

T. propria with slight congestion, slight swelling, some erythrocytes-leakages and slight round cell accumulation.

T. muscularis with considerable congestion, edema and some perivascular round cell accumulation.

T. subserosa with considerable congestion and some edema.

740

URINARY BLADDER.

N-19.

Epithelium with no remarkable changes.

T. propria with slight edema, some congestion and some round-cell-infiltration.

Considerable edema of T. submucosa, T. musc laris and T. subserosa.

Considerable hemorrhages in T. subserosa.

Some degeneration of muscle-fibres.

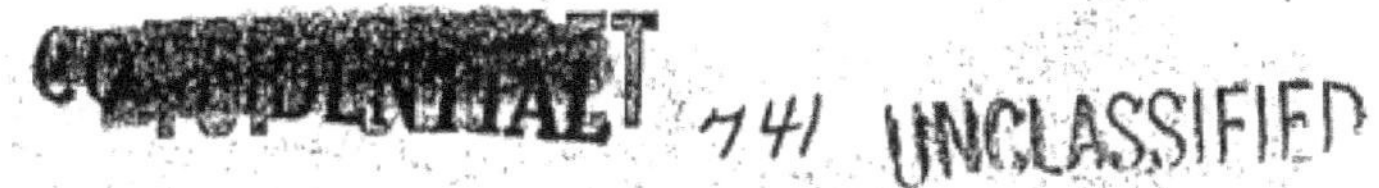

SALIVARY GLAND.

S-6.

Considerable congestion, considerable hemorrhages and edema in interlobular tissues.

Intense dilatation of efferent ducts, filled with massive serous fluids.

Some round-cell-accumulation at periglandular and pericapillary portions.

N-1.

No remarkable changes of glandular epitheliums.

Remarkable congestion, slight hemorrhages and some leucocytes (and lymphocytes) accumulation at perivascular portions. in interlobular tissues.

S-6. Glandula sublingualis.

Considerable congestion, considerable hemorrhages and edema in interlobular tissues.

Intense dilatation of efferent ducts, filled with massive serous fluids.

Some round-cell-accumulation at periglandular and pericapillar portions.

N-1. Glandula submaxillaris.

No remarkable changes of glandular epitheliums.

Remarkable congestion, slight hemorrhages and slight edema in interlobular tissues, accompanied with some round cell (and some leucocytes) -accumulation at perivascular portions.

G A L L - B L A D D E R

N-2. Desquamation of epithelium. Remarkable edema of walls.

N-3. The same as above mentioned.

N-5. The same as above mentioned except infiltration of a few round cells.

N-6. Considerable edema. Infiltration of a few round cells.

N-11. Partial desquamation of epithelium. Degenerative swelling of epithelium. Severe congestion and considerable edema. Considerable small round cell-infiltration. Slight proliferation of histiocytic cells.

N-12. Desquamation of epithelium. Remarkable edema of walls.

N-15. The same as above mentioned except some round cell-infiltration.

N-17. Desquamation of epithelium. Severe congestion and edema.

N-18. Desquamation of epithelium in severe degree. Remarkable congestion and edema. Considerable small round cell-infiltration. and slight proliferation of histiocytic cells. Bacterial masse and leucocytes--accumulation in blood vessels.

N-19. Desquamation of epithelium.Considerable edema of walls.

N-20. Desquamation of epithelium. Severe edema of walls.

N-21. The same as above mentioned.

N-23. Desquamation of epithelium. Severe edema with considerable small round cell-infiltration.

N-26. Desquamation of epithelium. Severe edema of walls and considerable congestion.

N-27. Desquamation of epithelium. Remarkable edema of walls. Considerable congestion and small round cell-infiltration.

N-29. Desquamation of epithelium. Remarkable edema with a few round cell--infilt ation. Some bacterial masse in blood vessels.

N-33. Desquamation of epithelium. Severe edema of walls.

N-46. Desquamation of epithelium. Remarkable edema of walls.

N-47. The same as above mentioned.

S-2. Desquamation of epithlium. Remarkable edema of walls.

S-3. The same as above mentioned.

S-4. Desquamation of epithelium. Severedema.

S-5. Desquamation of epithelium. Remarkable edema and considerable congestion.

S-8. Partial desquamation of epithelium. Considerable edema and congestion. Slight increase of histicytic cells.

S-12. The same as above mentioned.

S-14. Desquamation of epithelium. Remarkable edema of walls.

S-22. Desquamation of epithelium. Remarkable edema of walls. Localised accumulation of histicytic cells with eosinophily.

S-26. Desquamation of epithelium. Remarkable edema and some congestion.